AF529413

Explorations in Anthropology

P. K. Bhowmick and His Collaborative Research Works

Edited by

Swapan Kumar Pramanick

Samita Manna

Explorations in Anthropology

P.K. Bhowmick and His Collaborative Research Works

Edited by
Swapan Kumar Pramanick
Samita Manna

In association with :
The Institute of Social Research and Applied Anthropology West Bengal

SERIALS PUBLICATIONS
New Delhi (India)

Second Edition - 2007

ISBN: 978-818387-100-6

Published by

SERIALS PUBLICATIONS
4830/24, Prahlad Street, Ansari Road
Darya Ganj, New Delhi-110002 (India)
Phone : 23245225 Fax : 91-11-23272135
E-mail: serials@satyam.net.in

Cont

Dedicated

to

Our Tribal Brothers and Sisters

Section II

Religion in Indian Perspective

Section III

Rural Social Institutions and Administration

Section IV

Development Action And Applied Anthropology

Section V

Ethnic Interactions and Their Sequel to Socio-Cultural Transformations

Section VI

Rural and Urban Problems and Related Issues

PART III

Appendices

Appendix I

Appendix II

Appendix III

Appendix IV

1926 – 2003

about Prof P K Bhowmick

Indisputably the greatest doyen of Action Anthropology in West Bengal, remarkable for his critical perceptiveness and constructive judgement, Dr Probodh Kumar Bhowmick (1926-2003) was at once a fine scholar and an able teacher. With his formidable academic credentials, extensive field surveys and searching explorations of diverse disciplines, especially anthropology, sociology, history, folkloristics, archaeology and literature, Dr Bhowmick deserved and won the highest acclaim of distinguished scholars and critics in India and abroad. He started his teaching career at Bangabasi College, Kolkata, in 1952 as Lecturer in Anthropology. Later, in the sixties, he joined the University of Calcutta which he served most sincerely for nearly forty years. He became Professor of Anthropology there and for some time Dean, Faculty of Science. He was Visiting Professor of Anthropology in Sri Venkateswara University of Tirupati in Andhra Pradesh and participated as an honourable invitee in the sessions of the World Congress of Applied Anthropology in Amsterdam and Edinburgh, Italy and West Germany. Coupled with his professional competence was his rare aptitude for research work which earned him a Ph D in 1961 and a D Sc in 1967 from the University of Calcutta. The first doctoral dissertation concentrated on the *Lodhas of West Bengal*–the rites and rituals, religion, magic, prejudices and social mores of an ex-criminal tribal community–while the second one underscored the importance and uniqueness of the socio-cultural specificities of *Frontier Bengal* (including Baleswar and Mayurbhanj of Orissa, Midnapore, Purulia, Bankura and Birbhum of West Bengal and Singbhum and Dhanbad of Bihar). Besides carrying on his own research work, Dr Bhowmick successfully guided the research projects of as many as sixty candidates.

Dr Bhowmik was a prolific writer in both English and Bengali, but not only did he wield a facile pen but also sought to make his writing a medium of objective, detached yet progressivist ethic of human emancipation. He was the author of a number of insightful monographs–*The Lodhas of West Bengal : A Socioeconomic Study* (1963), *Socio-cultural Profile of Frontier Bengal* (1967), *Occultism in Fringe Bengal* (1978), *Some Aspects of Indian Authropology* (1980), *The Chenchus of the*

Forests and Plateaux : A hunting-gathering tribe in transition (1989), among others. His Bengali publications included *Banglar Loka-Utsav* (1968) and *Lokasamaj O Sanskriti* (2003), aside from numerous articles on the continuing heritage and existing condition of the marginalized and down-trodden tribes and castes in India. The man of introspection was one of action, too ; Dr Bhowmick was indeed a man of charismatic personality–alert, agile, active to a fault. So spirited was he in his youth that he participated in the Quit India Movement of 1942 and endured the sentence of rigorous imprisonment inflicted upon him by the British Government for two years and a half. The never-failing source of inspiration for his association with India's freedom struggle was doubtless his father Late Jogendranath Bhowmick.

While doing adequate justice to his teaching assignments, Dr Bhowmick did not refrain from assuming the responsibilities of a dynamic researcher travelling widely in the poverty-stricken, remote villages of India among the Lodhas and Savaras, Santals and Mundas, Chenchus and Kharias. Field study, incidentally, formed an integral part of his academic programme, and he reached a significant milestone in his life in 1955 when he built up the *ashram*-hostel for the neglected Lodha boys and girls in the small village of Daharpur (Fulgeria/Midnapore). Dr Bhomick's dream of the finest flowering of humanity came true with the creation of Bidisa, 'a happy seat of rural view' (to use a Miltonic phrase), in a serene and soothing atmosphere. Considerable patronage and support of Pandit Jawaharlal Nehru and Dr Bidhan Chandra Roy helped him substantially, but the beacon in his spiritual odyssey was provided by his teacher Professor Nirmal Kumar Bose. Two organizations were founded in Bidisa, namely Samaj Sevak Sangha and Institute of Social Research and Applied Action Anthropology with a view to giving a fillip to the work-schedule undertaken by Dr Bhowmick and his disciples.

Tempora mutantur, but the tradition of anthropological/ sociological studies, established by Dr Bhowmick, still continues and will continue for all time to come even after the sad demise of the noble-hearted idealist and social thinker–the dear and affectionate *Jyathababu* of the Lodha community.

Pralay Kumar Deb

Foreword

An anthropologist may be many things : a published scholar, a respected teacher, an advisor to those in power, an activist on behalf of his people, and a research trend setter. As we shall see within the covers of this book, P.K.Bhowmick was all of these. But above all he shared with his American friend Sol Tax what has been called an 'Action Anthropology'. Like Tax, he was unwilling to spend his career in the library or even in the field reflecting on the characteristics of exotic peoples. Bhowmick spent that career acting! In fact, that is how he spent his life. This was an anthropologist (and a person) who would tolerate no abuse, no inaction, no passive ignoring of injustice or suffering among native people. In fact, he began this career at a time when he was considered one of the natives by the British colonial authorities. As a young student he protested their authority and found himself in jail for two years and a half. Sahay refers to him as the messiah of the Lodhas. And he was that but he was also much more. Bhowmick's concern for the oppressed and the ignored is reflected not only in his persistent work on behalf of the Lodha and other Indian tribal peoples but also in the kinds of dissertations he encouraged his students to pursue, in his lectures, in his publications, and in his everyday life.

I cannot imagine Bhowmick without one or more of his students at his side whether he was traveling, lecturing, or simply managing a seminar. What was true of admiring visitors such as myself was also true of his students. Whenever he spoke, he was teaching if one only listened. And if one observed, he also taught with his actions. All of this teaching was an effort to create a heritage, a coterie of young people to carry on his work on behalf of the multitudes of Indian underdogs. The doctoral students he guided and the kinds of work they did are evidence of the success he had in this effort. It is not possible to measure the extent to which peoples of the so called scheduled castes and ex-criminal tribes now live under much improved conditions as a result of the work of P.K. Bhowmick and his students.

Professor Bhowmick's commitment to integrating his teaching and his research with his lifelong concern for human betterment is reflected in the way he identified the areas for research for the students of whom he was the research guide. For the sake of convenience, the dissertations which he guided have been classified under several categories. Even the traditional category of "Ethnography" (containing fourteen dissertations) is rich in problematic research topic with implications for public policy. The other categories are more explicit. The twelve dissertations which have been classified as "Religion in Indian Perspective" are nearly all focused on various aspects of Indian religion related to problems of health and illness among the peoples studied. The four studies classed as "Rural Institutions and Administration" reveal the kinds of problems rural peoples must confront and the manner in which administration does or does not serve them. All of the five pieces of research listed under "Development Action and Applied Anthropology" are, as the category suggests adventures in applied and action anthropology. The set of dissertations which are classified as "Ethnic Interactions and Their Sequal to Socio-cultural Transformations," deal primarily with problems involving inter group relations, migration, and rapid social change. The final, perhaps residual category in which ten dissertations are analysed are called, "Urban and Rural Problems and Related Issues." These studies, like those in the other categories, share in common the fact that they search out problematic social situations, explore their origins and persistence, observe institutional efforts to deal with them and tactfully suggest politically feasible improvements in current policies.

Thus it is that Bhowmick managed to integrate his teaching research, and student supervision into an entity that focused on discovering injustices and deprivations which could be reduced or eliminated. Readers can discover much of this for themselves as they peruse the contents of this book. Note for example how many of these former students found employment, with the aid of Professor Bhowmick, in positions where they could help improve the lives of the people they studied. He had helped to create these very positions by engineering the inclusion of anthropology in the Indian civil service.

His pride and joy the jewel in his crown, if you wish, was his research and action on behalf of the Lodhas. He did, of course, publish traditional ethnographic pieces on these people (see for example, Bhowmick, 1994), but for Bhowmick that was but an introduction to his extensive activities on behalf of the Lodhas. Bose describes him "not only as an anthropologist looking for scientific information, but also as a social worker intensely interested in the uplifting of the tribe through education and economic rehabilitation."(In the Foreword to

Bhowmick, 1994, p. vii) How did he proceed? On the one hand he saw to it that formal education (including adult education) was available to these people and encouraged them to take advantage of it. He also instituted programs to train people in crafts which help earn them a living. On one of my visits to Bidisa, a Lodha cooperative community organized by Bhowmick, a Lodha tailor crafted a beautiful shirt for me as I watched. The most creative activity I witnessed was watching semi-literate tribal people hand setting the English language type for anthropological journals and books. This combined printing-publishing business was most impressive. These were the people who had unjustly been labeled "Criminal Tribes" until 1952. Meanwhile many of the children of these people (both boys and girls) have received a formal education at one of the ashrams which now exist for them.

On the other hand, Bhowmick ensured that the nation and the world become aware of these efforts by creating Bidisa–a small conference centre where scholars and others could meet in private peaceful setting away from the rush of everyday life. Souvenirs were left by visitors not only from other parts of India but from elsewhere in Asia, Europe, and America. His efforts ranged from such global examples to the simple process of nurturing relations with local politicians, civil servants, and officials. I sometimes waited in the car or wandered around a village alone while Bhowmick visited and renewed acquaintances in offices and private homes of police administrators or education officials. His political interventions knew no borders. He introduced the discipline of anthropology into the universities of both Nepal and Bangladesh.

At first glance there appears to be some irony in the apparent parallels between Bhowmick's stance toward the Lodha and imperial British stance toward all Indians. Sahay's description of Bhowmick's efforts to teach these ex-criminal tribesmen "the basic etiquette and manners if they were to be tamed (2003, p. 187), may be misunderstood. Certainly it was not the intent of this anthropologist to focus on the preservation of a quaint culture to create a zoo where they might be peered at by tourists or a theme park where they could peddle their quaint native crafts. He differed from the colonial powers in very important ways. He was not "civilizing' these people so that they could be more easily controlled and exploited. He viewed his mission as helping tribal peoples to free themselves from oppressive conditions. It was his goal for these people to participate on their own as equals in the larger society and economy in which they were immersed.

P.K. Bhowmick took great pride in his two daughters who followed in his footsteps toward careers in anthropology. As a guest in their home, I had the opportunity to witness the strong affection he and his wife had for one another. Together they survived the misery of losing both a daughter and a mentor in one tragic accident. The life and work of this remarkable man and equally remarkable anthropologist stands as a model to be admired and emulated the world over.

Reference

Bhowmick, P.K. 1994 (1st edition 1963). The Lodhas of West Bengal.

Sahay, V.S. 2003 "Messiah of the Lodhas: Professor P.K. Bhowmick (1926 – 2003). The Oriental Anthropologist 3 (2): 184-199.

Endnotes

1. That is the title of the obituary published in The Oriental Anthropologist by V.S. Sahay (2003). I am much indebted to Sahay's article which is an important source of materials in this foreward and supplements impressions from my own contacts with Profeesor Bhowmick.
2. A complete list Bhowmick's publications both in Bengali and English can be found in Sahay (2003, pp.193-99).
3. A well documented history of efforts made by Bhowmick and others on behalf of the Lodha appears in Samita Manna, et.al. "Toward Development" which is Appendix III in Bhowmick, 1994.

Deptt. of Sociology
Akron, USA
21st October, 2004

Irwin Deutscher
Professor Emeritus

Preface

A sudden horrible death snatched him away from this earthly bondage but his valuable works could be kept and remained a part of our national heritage for ever. Professor Prabodh Kumar Bhowmick was a field Anthropologist and an active social worker. This treatise will focus on the versatility of his knowledge specially in the field of Applied Anthropology.

After his death (5th Feb, 2003) it was decided that it would be a nice work as well as a great tribute to his academic imagination if a treatise could be prepared by compilation of the synopses of the theses of his students who got their Ph.D. degree under his guidance. The task is no doubt an arduous one but it would really be an important document reflecting his academic interest, anthropological endeavour and professional zeal. His anthropology had tried to open new horizons dealing with the problems of the ignored and the oppressed. But his concern was not merely academic, his anthropology assumed an active interventionist approach, which was instrumental for opening his Applied and Action Research Institute, at Bidisa, Narayangarh. Along with this, his welfare organisation for the downtrodden, named Samaj Sevak Sangha, was also there.

Prof. Bhowmick obtained his Master's, Ph.D. and D.Sc. Degrees from the University of Calcutta. In his days Anthropology was not so popular like the other social sciences. His anthropological insight was developed when he had the privilege of being supervised by Prof Nirmal Kumar Bose. Prof. Bose's constant guidance, inspiration and training made Prof. Bhowmick a field anthropologist. A part of his anthropology was for the down trodden people. As a teacher he first joined the Bangabasi College in the year 1952. In the year 1960 he got the privilege of teaching assignment from the Calcutta University. He retired from the University in the year 1994, but he remained busy throughout his life as a sincere and untiring researcher for his Action Anthropology, distinguished thoughts and creative writings.

His life since his childhood days was not a bed of roses. When he was only a student of class IX he had to be imprisoned as a freedom fighter for national independence in British India. Being identified as a third class prisoner due to his under age he remained with the criminals in a prison for two years and several months. Very patiently he accepted his imprisonment and appeared for his matriculation examination from there. The sufferings of his life were just started from his school going age. After that in his matured life he had to face many challenges and accepted all those challenges smilingly and put forward his foot steps for future victory. But he rarely did surrender to forces of hostility. He was an uncompromising, optimistic and self-assertive man. He always told "Satatar joy Hobeyee" i.e., victory will come from honesty. He loved the people and made no distinction among their ranks. He was equally at ease from a rustic ruralite to an urban sophisticated man . This important characteristic made him simple, humble and widely acceptable.

This treatise is a tribute to professor Probodh Kumar Bhowmick who was a man who devoted himself whole heartedly for the welfare of the marginalized groups. From the mid fifties of the last century he appeared as a social anthropologist and since then he was actively engaged with different types of field based research works known as Applied and Action Anthropology. Besides his active participation in this field he also encouraged his students and academic and administrative friends to follow his academic path and interest. As a result, he had produced a good number of awardees who got their Ph.D. degree under his guidance. There were as many as sixty persons whose names were in the list of awardees.

Now-a-days in the era of globalization, the interdisciplinary approach for the study of human behavior is very popular. But during his time, his academic endeavour and research would speak about this approach. As a result, many candidates, who did not have anthropology at their post-graduate level, but belonged to different branches of social sciences, had done their works under his guidance. The multifarious aspects of human life and problems were studied by many researchers having different academic backgrounds who got directly their training in his hands.

The present volume is intended to show how Prof. P. K. Bhowmick as an Anthropologist had addressed the contemporary social issues, what were the major areas chosen by him as his research profile, what methods were followed by him–these are the important issues of the present analysis. He had studied man along with his multidimensional cultural activities manifesting both shared traits and uniqueness. Prof. Bhowmick had also studied the behavioural pattern of man in different changing circumstances, within various cultural groups and in different periods of crises. He had studied both primitive man as well as man in contemporary society amidst institutions in different societies. How can anthropology be used for the welfare of human being? What are the rite-de-passages of human beings? All these are vividly studied by him or by his students. So no doubt this book will portrait a transparent vision of P.K. Bhowmick who was a widely recognized Action Anthropologist.

We gratefully acknowledge a good number of persons whose immense contributions helped the publication of this work. Professor Pralay Kr. Deb, the former Dean of Arts & Commerce, Kalyani University, has kindly given his consent to write a valuable brief introduction about the life and works of Prabodh Kr. Bhowmick. As a man of literature his rhythmic and poetic thought have been reflected in his Introduction, which is really immaculate and inimitable.

The foreword of this book is written by Prof. Irwin, Emeritus Professor of Sociology in Akron University, USA. He gladly accepted the request for writing the foreword about the book, containing the work of P. K. Bhowmick, who, according to him, is his "beloved teacher and good friend". So we are really indebted to him for his cooperation in writing this valuable short introduction of this book.

Our sincere thanks are also due to Professor Sachchidananda, former Director of A. N. Sinha Institute, Patna. He is also one of the eminent sociologists in India. Professor Sachchidananda's introductions on two different topics entitled 'Rural Social Institutions and Administration' and 'Development Action and Applied Anthropology' have enriched the quality of the book.

We are really indebted to Prof. Baidyanath Saraswati, senior UNESCO Professor, Indira Gandhi National Centre for Arts, for his irreplaceable article on religion. After our request he expressed a few words, in a letter of communication "If I can be of any help in your work, it will be my greatest joy in life". Such a generous man he is.

Professor M. Afsaruddin, formerly Head of the Department of Sociology, University of Dhaka, is a contemporary sociologist of Bangladesh. His thought provoking article has added a new dimension to the book. Professor Afsaruddin beautifully portrayed the works of P. K. Bhowmick from a different angle. He thinks that P. K. Bhowmick's "dedication to the cause of ethnic groups was so deep that he considers himself as one of them". We are really grateful to him for his valuable contribution.

We are indebted to Professor Harsha N. Mukherjee, Professor of Sociology, Tennessee Tech University, USA, Professor Rebati Mohan Sarkar, retired Professor of Anthropology and Editor, Man in India, Dr. Manis Kumar Raha, former Joint Director of Anthropological Survey of India, Chairman of ISSRA, Bidisa, Professor Vijoy S. Sahay, Professor of Anthropology, Allahabad University, Dr. Amal Kumar

Mallick, former Faculty Member of B.C.K.V. Their enlightened articles have enhanced the value of the book. Their spontaneous cooperation have helped the editors to publish this book as well as their adequate and diversified materials have increased the quality of the work.

We gratefully acknowledge all the scholars who have contributed their articles for this book. In most of the cases the editors have tried to keep it unchanged but in a few cases a little modifications have been made. Without their cooperation the editors could not have prepared the manuscript.

All the synopses have been published in the respective author's names, as the works are of their own. In most of the cases the respective article has been written by the author himself but a few exceptions are also noticed here.* A star mark is used for those articles, which were not written by the authors. We express our sincere gratitude to all of them.

There were many other persons who helped us in planning and organizing the contents of the work. We must mention here with gratitude the help of Dr. Debasish Debnath, who is attached to the Indian Institute of Forest Management, Bhopal. He helped us by providing the original list of the awardees who got their Ph. D. under the guidance of P. K. Bhowmick. Most of the addresses of the Ph.D. awardees were written by Prof. Bhowmick himself in that list. A few years ago Dr. Bhowmick gave this list to him. But as soon as he got the information about the planning for publication of this book, he immediately sent that original list to us which was one of the valuable sources of information for finding the whereabouts of the scholars of Prof. P. K. Bhowmick.

To collect more information about the scholars' present whereabouts we had to take help of many persons who provided us the adequate information about them. We must mention here the name of Late Dr. Manas Kamal Chowdhury, Director, Cultural Research Institute, Dr. Palash Coomer, Deputy Director of Census of India and many other such persons who helped us a lot for this purpose.

Some premature deaths of a few scholars created a problematic situation. In that situation we personally tried to collect the theses and prepared the manuscript for the same. We express our indebtedness to the younger brother of late Tarasis Mukhopadhyay, who resides at Tamluk, Purba Midnapur. We are also very much grateful to Mr. Mitra, husband of the late Krishna Mitra. He did not find the thesis but after our request he kindly prepared a little note and submitted it to us.

We are indebted to the librarian and assistant librarians of Calcutta University. We also express our thanks to Dr. Monaranjan Bhowmick, a teacher of the school of Samaj Sevak Sangha and an active member of the institute. The other members of that institute like Asis Gayan, Srimanta Bhakta, Biswanath Das and many of them are also mentioned for their co-operation by supplying the theses from the Institute.

Our sincere thanks are also due to Biplab Chatterjee, one of the Faculty members of Calcutta University, Debasis Bhattacharyaya, a Faculty member of ISI for their sincere cooperation with us for completion of this work.

The cooperation of the family members of Prof. Bhowmick was spontaneous at every stage of the planning of the work. We mention with gratitude the help of Mrs. Latika Bhowmick, the wife of Prof. Bhowmick, Dr. Pradip Bhowmick and Dr. Pratim Bhowmick, the two sons of Prof. Bhowmick and the helping hand extended by Dr. C. K. Manna and the two daughters of Dr. Samita Manna, one of the editors of this book.

Thanks are also due to Dr. Soumyajit Patra and to Dr. Lopa Mudra Rana who helped us a lot to prepare the manuscript of this book. We express our sincere thanks to our students Karunamayee Paul, Brijendra Kumar Mishra and Sangeeta Pal Lodh.

We are also thankful to Mr. Satyajit Das, Purna Chandra Barik and Swapan Basu who prepared and typed the materials for the book. Last but not the least we express our sincere thanks to the staff of the press for their unceasing cooperation for publishing the book.

Swapan Kumar Pramanick

Samita Manna

List of Contributors

Professor Pralay Kumar Deb
Former Dean of Arts and Commerce
University of Kalyani
Kalyani, West Bengal

Professor Irwin Deutscher
Emeritus Professor
Dept. of Sociology
Akron University
USA

Professor Sachchidananda
Ex-Director of A.N. Sinha Institute.
Patna

Professor Baidyanath Saraswati
Senior UNESCO Professor
Indira Gandhi National Center for the Arts.

Professor M.Afsaruddin
Department of Sociology
University of Dhaka

Professor Harsha N Mukherjee
Professor of Sociology
Tennessee Tech University
USA

Professor Rebati Mohan Sarkar
Retd. Professor
Editor of Man in India
Calcutta

Dr. Manis Kumar Raha
Former Joint Director
Anthropological Survey of India
Calcutta

Professor Vijoy S Sahay
Department of Anthropology
Allahabad University

Professor Amal Kumar Mallick
Ex-Faculty Member of B.C.K.V.
Mohanpur, W. B.

Taniya Sharmeen
Faculty
Department of Anthropology
Dhaka University
Bangladesh

Shyamalkanti. Sengupta
Former Reader in Anthropology
University of Calcutta
Ballygunge Science College
Calcutta, W. B.

Dipali Danda
Retd. Superintending Anthropologist
Anthropological survey of India
Government of India
Calcutta.

A.V.Subba Rao *
Retd. Reader in Anthropology
Vijaywada Government College
Andhra Pradesh

Rajat Kanti Das
Professor of Anthropology
Vidyasagar University
Midnapore, W.B.

T. S. Gangte
Former Director of Education
Govt. of Manipur, Imphal

Bijay Kumar Behera
Retd. Professor of Anthropology
Utkal University
Bhubaneswar, Orissa

Ashoke Kumar Jana
Member of Executive Committee
Social Research and Applied Anthropology
Bidisa, Paschim Medinipur

Niranjan Kumar Ghatak
Joint Director
Minister of Tribal Affairs
Government of India

Madhumala Chattopadhyay
Research Officer (Planning research, Evaluation and Monitoring Division) Ministry of Social Justice and Empowerment;
New Delhi

Late Himangsu Mohan Ray *
Former Head of the Department of Anthropology
Bangabasi Morning College
Calcutta, West Bengal

Swapan Kumar Chakraborty
Lecturer in Anthropology
Calcutta, West Bengal

*Late Professor Kartik Chandra Shasmal**
Former Head of the Department of Anthropology
Bangabasi Evening College
Calcutta, West Bengal

Rishikeshab Regmi *
Retd. Professor of Anthropology
Tribhuban University
Kathmandu, Nepal

Lok Nath Soni
Keeper
Anthropological Survey of India
Calcutta, W.B.

Debashis Debnath
Faculty of Sociology and Social Anthropology
Indian Institute of Forest Management
Bhopal

Pabitra Gupta
Former Vice Chancellor (Actg.) and Registrar
B.C.K.V.
Mohanpur, Nadia.

*Late Tarasish Mukhopadhyay**
Formerly Associated with
Michigan State University, U.S.A.

Asoke Kumar Biswas
Retd. Head Teacher, Calcutta

Prafulla Chakraborty
Former Associate Professor
Sociological Research Unit
ISI, Calcutta.

*Late Vaddi Arjanna**
Former Reader in Anthropology
Government College, Rajamundri
Andhra Pradesh

Mrs. Bela Jana
Reader in Sociology,
Beharilal College of Home Science
University of Calcutta, Kolkata, West Bengal

Sm. Pratima Das Chowdhury
Formerly Associated with the Department of Anthropology
Calcutta University, West Bengal

*Archana Sinha**
Teacher
Midnapur,W.B.

Arun Kr. Chatterjee
Former Keeper,
Indian Museum. Kolkata

Sm. Ratna Mallick
Deputy Director
Cultural Research Institute
Backward Classes Welfare Department
Govt. of West Bengal

Professor Manibrata Bhattacharya
Department of Anthropology
Calcutta University, Kolkata

Satyajiban Chakraborty
Former Reader in Political Science,
Bangabasi College
Kolkata

Chittaranjan Banerjee
Former President
West Bengal Board of Secondary Education
Kolkata

Narayan Chandra Maity
Principal, Mahishadal Girl's College
East Midnapore

Sibnath Banerjee
Former Professor of Political Science
Burdwan University, Burdwan

*Late M.V.Krishna Rao**
Joint Director
Tribal Research Institute
Hyderabad

Sudhir Kumar Biswas
Former Divisional Commissioner
Garhwal, Uttaranchal

*D.R. Pratap**
Former Director
Tribal Research Institute
Hyderabad
Government of Andhra Pradesh

*Lalitha V**
Active Social Worker and Researcher
Andhra Pradesh

Dibakar Basak
Joint Director in National Commission for SC and ST
Lucknow, U.P

Amaranath Pal
Fellow of Asiatic Society
Kolkata, West Bengal

Dilip Chakraborty
Anthropological Survey of India
Dehradun, Uttaranchal

Md. Ahsan Ali
Reader in Anthropology
Dhaka University, Bangladesh

Sujit Som
Former Director National Museum of Man
Govt. of India
Bhopal, Madhya Pradesh

Shyamapada Chakraborty
Member of Indian Information Service
Calcutta, W.B.

Kalipada Malakar
Ex-Deputy Director of School Education
Ex-Lecturer of SCERT
Government of West Bengal

Bidyut Kumar Das
Anthropological Survey of India
Port Blair, Andaman

Kartik Chandra Dalui *
Senior College Teacher
West Bengal

*Kamalesh Guha**
Former Keeper,
Delhi Museum, Delhi

Tilak Bagchi
Assistant Keeper of the Anthropological Survey of India
Government of India
Udaipur, Rajasthan

Kalachand Saha
Former Deputy Director
Cultural Research Institute
Kolkata

Usha Goela
Retd. Researcher and Project Director
New Delhi

Bela Bhattacharya
Reader in Anthropology
University of Calcutta
Kolkata

Swapan Kumar Sinha
NABARD, Calcutta

Subir Bandyopadhyay
Accountant and Social Researcher
Kolkata, W.B

*Late Krishna Mitra**
Former Associate Professor in Social Service Administration
All India Institute of Hygiene and Public Health
Government of India, Kolkata

Subhrendu Maity
Reader in Anthropology, Dinabandhu Mahavidyalaya, Bongaon
North 24 Parganas, W.B

Swaraj Bandopadhyaya
Former Registrar, Tata Institute for Social Sciences
Mumbai, Maharashtra

Mily Dey
Lawyer, Calcutta High Court
Kolkata, W. B.

Sova Rani Chakrabarty
Retd. Teacher, Midnapore
W. B.

Editorial

The most wonder of this wonderful world is humans and still the mystry of human life continues to be unexplored. Anthropology as a separate discipline was developed out of that inquisitiveness to resolve the mystry of human life and behaviour over the last 200 years centering around the problem of man and his culture.

During the 2nd half of the 20th century, P.K. Bhowmick as an oriental Anthropologist tried to establish himself as a field Anthropologist too. He had kept himself busy by doing various researches on the poor, neglected and downtrodden people of our society. Many of his research works were initiated with the tribal studies of which the two authentic ethnographic works were the Lodhas of West Bengal and the Chenchus of Andhra Pradesh.

This treatise is not purely a collection of several articles but has tried to explore the expanding horizons of anthropology of P.K. Bhowmick beginning from the later part of the 20th century. Besides his own works, he conducted a good number of collaborative research works with his students which were hardly practised during his time. The interpretive understanding of all these works would help us to understand the perceptual and analytical mind of P.K. Bhowmick. The contemporary socio-cultural, political and economic factors were equally important to develop his areas of interest and field of study. He did not skip all these factors. On the other hand, these problems created a zeal in his mind to shape his research questions, which he tried to solve through his own personal research and through the research works of his students guided and supervised by him. The present work attempts to identify the second aspect i.e., the areas covered by his research students. It thereby tries to explore how anthropology as a discipline came to be benefited through such explorations.

The entire monograph has been divided into three parts. Part one of this book contains four articles. Each of the authors in his respective article has tried to analyse Prof. P.K. Bhowmick's stand in the discipline of anthropology and has tried to show how anthropology as a subject has been benefited by his endeavours.

Part two of this book includes six parts. The available synopses were categorized thematically into six different sections. Each of the section is introduced by a scholarly article. The first section entitled *Ethnography* consists of fourteen articles (synopses). The introduction is written by Dr. Raha. The introduction of the second section *Religion in Indian Perspective* has been written by Prof. Saraswati and this section contains twelve articles in it. The third section entitled *Rural Social Institutions and Administration* includes four articles. Prof. Sachchidananda, the noted sociologist, has written a scholarly introduction. Section four named as *Development Action and Applied Anthropology* is also forwarded by Prof. Sachchidananda and it contains five articles. The fifth section entitled *Ethnic Interactions and Their Sequel to Socio-Cultural Transformations* is preceded by an introduction written by Prof. Sarkar and this section contains nine articles. Prof. Sahay has written the prologue of the final section entitled *Rural and Urban Problems and Related Issues*. There are ten articles in this section. In this way the available theses supervised by Prof. Bhowmick (fifty four) have been categorically arranged in different sections of this book. This work of categorizing has not been so simple and some times the categorization has been done somewhat arbitrarily. Nevertheless this broad scheme of presentation would help us in understanding the encyclopedic range of interest of Prof. P. K. Bhowmick.

Part three of this work contains appendices. Appendix one incorporates a synopsis written in Bengali entitled *Bartaman Banga Samajer Jadubidya 'O' Lokayat Biswaser Dhara* written by Sova Rani Chakroborty. Appendix two consists of the list of the principal works of P.K. Bhowmick. Appendix three includes the particulars of six synopses of the students of Prof. Bhowmick which could not be collected from the authors. Appendix four consists of the Glossary of the terms 'castes and tribes'.

II

In earlier days generally social anthropologists were engaged in studying the problems of little communities or ethnic groups. After independence, special attention was given to these little communities to explore their problems as marginalized groups. As a result, anthropologists showed their interest in them. How and in which way these communities were surviving or intermingling with the larger culture and society were one of the interesting phenomena to be studied by the anthropologists. So in the earlier works of Prof. Bhowmick many such ethnic groups/small band groups were studied. Major emphasis was given on participant observation and direct face-to-face interview method for pointing out in detail the changing lifestyle of those communities along with their survival strategies.

Section one, *Ethnography*, contains fourteen articles on different marginalized groups. A few of these groups are little known communities. Perhaps in future due to their small number, some of these groups will have to adopt new strategies and in many cases they will have to be merged with other neighbouring groups. Considering their position, the ethnographic accounts of these various groups presents a comprehensive picture of these communities. Different methods of studying these groups, their problems, nature of adaptation, their changing attitude and finally the role of government in initiating development measures for them are all the important subject matters of the theses brought under the title ethnography. Prof. Bhowmick, as an ethnographer, tried to understand the problems of these groups living in various parts of our country.

The main thrust of his ethnographic work was to find out the internal structure and function of the small society of the little communities. As an anthropologist he always tried to understand the human behaviour through a triangular relationship between man, supernatural power and environment. The network of such relationships creates a cosmos i.e., society and culture which are embedded with each other.

The Lodhas of West Bengal (1963) is an ethnographic work where the author directly observed the behaviour pattern i.e., social, political, economic, religious and recreational activities of the members of that community. The vivid description of the events of the life processes of the Lodha community were pin pointed by Bhowmick in this work. Different rituals from birth to death along with the participation of their kin members sharing the feelings of belongingness marked a tribal identity. He also visualized how the life of the Lodhas incorporated the changing environment through the ages. Once they were the hunter-gatherers and now they are the settled agriculturists adopting various element of the regional Hindu culture in their social fabric.

> ... this was the betterment of this downtrodden community and finding adequate means for fitting them into the general social fabric, so that they could share in its progressive life (Bhowmick 1963).

These Lodhas were formerly marked as criminal tribe but after the revocation of the Act in 1952 they were identified as *ex-criminal* tribe.

Any ethnographic work of a little community is ubiquitous in nature. To unearth data on them has a high academic value. Many unknown communities of various groups exist in and around the country without any authentic record and correct figures. So in the field of Social Anthropology such attempt to collect the ethnographic account of these little known communities is a novel idea. It has opened up new horizons in the world of anthropology.

Prof. Bhowmick started his research work amongst the Lodhas as an ethnographer because of the fact that he could travel various remote areas of tribal villages ignoring the risk of his life as the then Lodhas were marked as criminal and many unlawful acts were done by them without any hesitation. He conducted his fieldwork amongst them, studied their life situations and problems. In this way in his later life he himself was identified by them as one of their kin members and very often he was rightly pointed out as *Lodha Bhowmick* by the neighbors. Prof. P.K. Bhowmick has also been referred to as *Messiah of the Lodhas* by Prof. Sahay (2003). In this way whenever and wherever he could get chances to study the ethnographic account of the small community, he tried to look at them.

It is to be noted here that many small groups due to historical upheavals, entered the frontier zone of West Midnapur, which have been taken up for analysis by Bhowmick. He was the pioneer and the master of studying the society and culture of this region. He studied in detail every corner of this area, its geo-physical condition, the variegated nature of population, their interaction pattern etc. During his period the study of caste and tribe were the important dimensions or the major field areas of the anthropologist. Bhowmick kept that tradition through out his life.

Most of the communities which have been studied consist of the downtrodden and marginalized groups either Scheduled Castes or Scheduled Tribes belonging to different parts of the country. Their socio-economic condition in the present scenario is no doubt important when the world is becoming a global village. How are these small communities surviving through the strategies of assimilation and adaptation? What are the roles performed by them in a rapidly changing environment? All these are important facets of the social scientists' field of enquiry.

Actually from the early sixties to the nineties of the last century, Prof. Bhowmick kept himself busy with doing different types of research work. Based on his research endeavour, we get an authentic account of a few relatively unknown communities which are facing identity crises in this present scenario. The *Socio-Cultural Profile of Frontier Bengal* (1976) takes up for analysis a good number of such communities like the Savara: A snake charming community, the Chirmar: A little known community and the Kakmara: A Nomadic Community of West Bengal. He had conducted his ethnographic studies on each of these communities.

The general people maintain social distance from these communities in various aspects of life. The small tribal communities have their distinctive life patterns which can be exhibited in their day to day interaction. Birth, marriage and death are surrounded with rites and rituals. They maintain their uniqueness in these respects. Sometimes they also imitate others following the processes of adaptation. The process of sanskritization also creates its impact on their daily interaction process. These are very natural and spontaneous in village society where they live.

Out of fourteen tribal groups, five groups from the state of West Bengal are studied by his scholars of which the Koras and the Mahalis are the Scheduled Tribes, the Savaras and the Bagals are the marginalized communities and the Bauris are the Scheduled Caste group. Small tribal communities from other states like the Dimasas of Assam, the Marings and the Kukis of Manipur, the Kondhs of Orissa, the Bhoksas of Uttar Pradesh, the Godabas of Andhra Pradesh have been studied by different scholars. All these tribal groups were once very primitive in nature as they previously clinged to shifting cultivation. But with the passage of time and due to various problems they have shifted from their traditional occupation and have accepted agriculture without necessarily having any skilled knowledge about it. The other three communities are the Rauts (clean caste, cattle herders), of Chhattisgarh, the Dhimals (agricultural community) of Nepal and the Nicoborese (Horticulturist) in Nicobar Island. The span of interest and the extent of coverage of such ethnographic work can easily be understood from his work.

Another interesting finding is that except one or two, all these fourteen research scholars have had their disciplinary orientation in Anthropology. Anthropology as a subject with its separate methodology and a distinctive mode of interpretation and understanding enriched the analysis of these ethnographic data.

Since Independence, many attempts have been made by the Government to change the status of these groups. As a result, the ethnographic study of these groups tremendously helped the anthropologists to explore the real socio-economic condition of such groups. Though in many cases the titles of the theses have particular connotation but as they are all about the ethnographic account of various groups, naturally some common outline can be drawn from these studies. In general, the common points which have been covered in all such ethnographic accounts follow the general outline of such discussion and analysis as followed by Prof. P. K. Bhowmick in his own ethnographic research.

These general outlines are the following:

1. to know the culture of the group; (aborigines or marginalized groups who are to some extent neglected);
2. to acquire knowledge about their origin (racial affinity or ethnicity);
3. to collect adequate information about their economy, ecology and socio-cultural life (marriage, kinship and political organization);
4. to collect the detail description of the rites-de-passage, i.e., birth puberty, marriage and death etc.;
5. to know their belief pattern, customs, food habits, art and crafts, religion and magic;
6. to collect the relevant information on changing aspects of their life from primitive life to contemporary life under the various processes;
7. finally to find out the nature of government's help, inclusion of their names in the list and latest position of them in the existing socio-cultural realm.

The study of any ethnographic work has a few dimensions.

Firstly, an elaborate description of the group.

Secondly, to find out the identity of the group in the midst of the other groups.

Thirdly, the nature of social interaction in the form of social distance–pollution-purity.

Fourthly, to find out government's outlook towards them.

Dr. Manis Kr. Raha, in his Introduction to the section on Ethnography, has described very appropriately what is ethnography. He has pointed out the history of the ethnographical works referring the works of a good number of anthropologists whose names could be enlisted as ethnographers for preparing the scientific and rational interpretation and explanation for ethnography. He also explained and analyzed different ethnographical works done by the Indian anthropologists. He interpreted ethnographical work from both diachronic and synchronic points of view. In this way he has tried to mention that in due course the ethnographical work's enclave has tried to reach a greater horizon and the fourteen works have proved this fact.

The Mahalis as basket makers are one of the Scheduled Tribes of Midnapur. Along with their social profile, their economic life is also very significant specially as it is based on their traditional occupation of basketry. Most of their transactions depend on reciprocity, redistribution and limited market exchange which are very interesting giving a unique character to the Mahali tribal economy. The Mahali economy, based on basketry is a special kind of small industry which was developed by them only in that region as their economy was supported by the betel leaf dealers *(Pan Mahajans)* who required big baskets or *Jhuri* for packing the betel leaf and supplying it in different parts of India. Naturally, the Mahalis have to supply *Jhuri* to *Jhuri Mahajan*. But later on some of them have gradually developed their positive inclination towards agriculture due to uncertainty and insecured market condition relating to basketry.

The Godabas, one of the primitive tribes of Andhra Pradesh, are mainly concentrated in Visakapattanam and Srikakulam districts. This ethnographic study reflects a changing status of the Godabas as the British chroniclers first conducted a base line survey on them. For changing perspective, this study was made on a three-tier basis: (i) covering the people living in interior, (ii) at the foot hills and (iii) on the road side. Till now they like to maintain their traditional heritages through performing their rites and rituals in birth, marriage, death etc. They worship various local gods and goddesses having their traditional belief on them. But their changed economy from food gatherers to producers also brings changes in their life. The processes of change including adaptation and absorption with the greater Hindu culture is not uncommon. They claim themselves as Hindu. As a result, Hindu gods and goddesses are also worshipped by them along with other folk deities signifying the presence of their traditional belief pattern.

The Dimasas are one of the Kachari tribes of Assam. They are partially dependent on cash crops (mustard and cotton) maintaining market transaction with others indicating that they are not an isolated group. The Dimasas (a Boro group of Tibeto–Burman family) have double descent both from their father's father and from mother's mother which is a unique social structure. Double clan system i.e., patriclan and matriclan are observed with clan exogamy. Married children are excluded from the original family. They claim themselves as Hindus having the belief in the existence of gods, goddesses, spirits, birth, rebirth and so on.

The study of Maring society in Manipur is another ethnographic work where the main consideration was to bring into light a distinctive 'social form of organization through the concept of social structure'. The Marings do not just constitute another tribe like the Kuki or Naga. They have some peculiar characteristics binded by their collective representations in inter village relationships. They are no doubt the small scale societies and the people maintain the relations between them in an integrated form. *Machi* is one of the biggest Maring villages, where Maring associations are located and studied. Many important structural components of their societies were studied through the analysis of various social groups–territorial and kin groups–like clans, sub-clans, lineage and families, and youth dormitories which represent age grades. On the other hand, their descent, kinship, marriage residence, economic ties, ritual links, political organization are the important functional entity of the Maring society. In their society the structure of authority is based on the succession of generations and the principle of seniority in terms of genealogical strata. Actually the Marings on the hill and the Meities on the plain have been gradually increasing 'symbiotic relationship' between them. Maring society is greatly influenced by Christianity which sometimes helps to fade their tribal identities and in many cases they are considered as a very small part of a category distinct from tribal and peasant types. So they are now in transition.

The Kukis of Manipur in North-East India, a hill tribe of Mongoloid origin, the Tibeto-Chinese family group of language, have also been studied. Once they had their terrible identity as head hunters but in 1919 the British directly controlled the Kuki chiefs. This ethnographic work depicts in detail the social structure of the Kuki tribe. Different social functions, performed through kinship, marriage, religion, festivities etc., are also vividly described. The uniqueness of this study consists in its analysis of the institution of chieftainship, a highest political unit which is the perennial source of their culture, tradition and customs. Now the Kukis are in a changing process. They accept Christianity, on one hand, and on the other, they try to keep their identity by their dress, dance, rituals etc. In this way the Kukis of Manipur as an ethnic group maintain their solidarity and cohesiveness.

The Kondhs, one of the dominant tribes of Orissa, who were once the victims of exploitation by the moneylenders and the local businessmen, are now under the process of changing socio-cultural and economic life. Their traditional lives and values are greatly affected by their changing social and economic life from shifting hill cultivation to agricultural life. The Kondh tribes are famous among the tribals for their human sacrifice which is known as *Meriah*. This detailed ethnographic work depicts that they are greatly influenced by the Hindu ideas, values and practices in their day to day life which are reflected in their various social institutions, cultural beliefs and economic organizations. They worship the Hindu gods and goddesses and are trying to adopt the ways of life of the clean caste leaving the practice of beef eating.

The Koras are a little known Scheduled Tribe in West Bengal. They are mainly distributed in the districts of Burdwan, Midnapur, Bankura and Purulia. Through this ethnographic study it has been shown that this tribal community originally came from the Santal group. All the important lifestyles of them are very much similar with that of the Santals. But due to some internal friction they prefer to identify themselves as a separate group known as Kora denoting small or inferior. At present, this tribal group is not in total isolation. Many changes have already taken place in their socio-economic life like the other tribal groups of West Bengal. This ethnographic account has considerable academic value as it has attempted to highlight the earlier history and culture of the Kora people.

The Bhoksas are another little known tribe in Uttar Pradesh. Once they were engaged in shifting cultivation but now they are known as settled agriculturists. They share some peculiar tribal traits of this region. Many aspects of material culture as well as non-material culture separate them from the mainstream of population. Again on the other side, they are also in the process of absorption and assimilation. This is likely to change their lifestyle and behavioral pattern in near future. Many important primitive traits of their life are continuing amidst the changing traits of modernity. They have many problems amongst which their addiction to liquor along with the exploitation of them by the liquor seller are mentioned in particular. Their continued belief in primitive religion, role of medicinal men and their tribal culture are described in detail highlighting the uniqueness of the Bhoksa tribe.

The ethnographic account of the Nicobarese, who have come from Mongoloid stock of Car Nicober Island, has depicted a typical lifestyle of the Island dwellers. They mainly depend on horticulture and indigenous food, which they consume as one of their principal foods. They call it *pandanus*. Their distinctive social structure and organization has enabled them to sustain their socio-economic life. Majority of them are Christian by religion. Many rituals and prohibitions related to the norms of birth of a child are supposed to be performed by pregnant women. Similarly, other family members also follow many rituals and obligations which are very much similar to the other tribes of mainland India like the Santal, Munda, Mahali of West Bengal who are Australoid in origin.

The Savaras constitute a snake charming community of Midnapur. Primarily they depend on forest produce, fowling and trapping of animals including snakes. They claim themselves as Hindus and live as close neighbours of Hindus. This small community can as well claim the status of either Scheduled Tribe or Scheduled Caste as par the government's specification of backward class. Savara, as a generic term, is identified in some states as a Scheduled Caste or a Scheduled Tribe. But this snake charming Savar till now has not yet been recognized either as SC or as ST. In this way many such types of small, marginalized groups are not listed properly. The ethnographic account of this group vividly describes in detail the society and culture of this group. They are low Hindu castes and try to follow the greater Hindu culture along with their own. As they are poor and their profession carries a very low status, they cannot claim high Hindu status. But the interesting phenomenon of this study is that they have accepted the surnames of Mahisyas like Maity, Jana, Bera, Maji, Khatua, Manna etc. In future they may be assimilated with the Mahisya group if they can improve their status.

As a marginalized group, the ethnographic account of the Bagals, a cattle-herding community of West Bengal, is an important one. Many such small marginalized groups following various occupations for simply maintaining their livelihood are somehow going to be untraceable due to their identity crisis. This Bagal community is not an exceptional one. In the midst of strong neighbouring castes and tribes they are gradually assimilating themselves with those groups and losing their distinctive cultural traits. Their poverty and their poor numerical strength are also weakening their coping strategies and they are now facing the crisis of survival.

The Bauries, the largest Scheduled Caste of West Bengal, are mainly concentrated in the districts of Bankura, Birbhum, Midnapur, Purulia and Hooghly. They mainly depend on agriculture. As a result, many festivals and rituals observed by them are related to their agricultural life and these are very much similar to those of other agricultural castes. They are very much dependent on the other high caste groups of the locality. Gradually through the process of acculturation they are consciously or unconsciously undergoing a process of change.

The Dhimal community of Jhapa district and Damak Panchayat in Nepal was once a small isolated agricultural community. But now they have been accepting changing ways of life due to constant influence of other migrated population. They are not Scheduled Castes or Scheduled Tribes, as in Nepal there is no such provision of identifying people in such a manner. The ethnographic account of the people are described by analyzing the changing demographic and ecological settings of this group. This study is very important as after the land reforms of 1964, some changes took place in the land tenure system as also in the life of the original inhabitants like Dhimal, Mache, Kocha, Rajbanshi, Majhi, Satar, Tharu etc., who live in this Tarai region. The Dhimals constitute an agricultural (peasant) community with patrilocal family patterns. Now they have become more liberal in their attitude towards accepting food, cloth and other easily available consumable goods but they are at the same time very rigid to maintain their ethnic identity i.e., traditional moral and ethical beliefs. This changing lifestyle of the Dhimal community is a very important ethnographic work. It has been shown that the East-West Mahendra High way has opened up new vistas and brought new challenges in their ways of life. Nepal as such has a unique characteristic of its own as it nurtures the tenets of both Hinduism and Buddhism and as it was never under any foreign domination.

The Rauts are a cattle-herder community, a sub-division of Ahir caste of Chhattisgarh. Like Ahir, there are also other cattle herder groups like the Jadav, Goala, Gaoli and so on. They are the clean castes and gradually from pastoral economy they have changed as settled agricultural community. Through this ethnographic work the detailed description of different sub groups of Rauts are known. Like Nai (Barber) and Dhobi (Washer man), the Rauts are the 'Kamin' (locally known as pouni) caste who played various roles in rituals i.e., rites-de passage of the twice born castes. In village society the other castes also serve them. So as a clean caste in the caste hierarchy they have a definite role to play.

III

Religious beliefs, rites, rituals and ceremonies constitute a crucial element of human culture. Religion constitutes a common platform of identity and shapes man's attitude to nature, environment and the supernatural power. It provides a cementing bond and establishes social solidarity in the midst of diversity. Religious values, beliefs and practices are deep rooted in the minds of people. It ensures cultural continuity and does not change so rapidly as it is not volatile. As a result, inspite of modernity, religious beliefs are still prevalent in every society–rural or urban, primitive or modern. All religious groups or ethnic groups have their own sacred world related to the belief in supernatural power i.e., gods and goddesses. Belief in spirit is everywhere, as it is believed that life does not end with the death of physical body. In Hindu religion, for example, birth, rebirth, karma and dharma are inseparable from the idea of the soul. All these belief patterns create heterogeneity of a complex network of religious world. Among the tribal people a simple from of religion is found whereas complex forms of religion are found among non-tribal population.

Considering this crucial importance of religion for understanding human society, numerous research works have been done on the role and significance of religion for human society. Prof. P. K. Bhowmick's research endeavours, of his own and those of his research scholars, have also covered a significant part in this respect. Twelve synopses of the theses on religion, covering its different aspects, have been included in the section on religion.

An illuminating introduction on *Religion in Indian Perspective* has been written by Baidyanath Saraswati. He has very nicely focused on the structural significance of the religious landscape. He has shown that it varies from culture to culture and contains elements of complexity and specificity according to its basic purpose or motive. Various forms of religion–'simple' 'mixed' and 'complex' are prevalent in this universe. The religious world tries to find out man's relation with 'non-empirical world and to the basic contingencies of life (birth, death, illness, evil circumstances)'.

Many important aspects of religion have been analysed by Prof. Saraswati during the time of reviewing of the theses included under this section. The theses have been classified by him into a number of categories considering their scope and ambit. While doing so, Prof. Bhowmick's understanding of religion has also been taken up for analysis. This scholarly introduction will no doubt enrich the subject matter of the book and it will be beneficial for the young scholars of this discipline. As the relevant section will show, many important questions on the religiosity of the people have surfaced and different solutions have been provided for the rational understanding of society in a mystic world.

Bhowmick's work on religion exhibits a micro level religious world in the perspective of a pluralistic Indian society. He has conducted many works on religion. In his anthropological works, man's relation with supernatural power has been vividly analysed. Through these studies, tribal religiousity, which is more primitive in nature, got much more emphasis as it is based on naturalism. He has observed many local festivals which center around various local gods and goddesses or different sacred objects. These local festivals are *Tusu, Bhadu, Charak, Makar, Sitala, Garam, Baram, Manasa* and many others, which take place following local almanac of the year. During the time of these festivals the village deities are worshipped by the village priests. Most of the time they are the local community people. Initially the worship start at the village level through their folk deities, but gradually the villagers of nearby villages–the Hindu and Muslim –come together and join their hands. These are sought to be integrated with the Hindu pantheon and a relational matrix is established. In this way the little tradition and the great tradition merge together incorporating different cultural elements with each other. These festivals establish a double bond between man and man and man and supernatural power. Interaction of different cultural groups gives birth to the process of cultural transmission, providing some common elements on the one hand, and uniqueness and specificity on the other.

Many local rites and rituals are infused with the greater 'Brahmanical *achaar*'. Side by side, various magical practices like witchcraft, black magic, sorcery are performed by the magical practitioners of different tribal groups in their day-to-day life. The villagers are rejuvenated through these festivals and retuals. Monotony, boredom and fatigue come to an end and new fresh light removes the darkness of their mind and body.

Religion in its various forms and manifestations appears in different societies. Cultural systems (like social systems) are relatively 'integrated into coherent wholes'. The religious life of a group is understood by identifying its cultural traits, cultural complexes and cultural patterns which are unique in the perspective of each society. Simple religion with its various belief patterns and practices are still prepondering in different tribal societies. Traditionalism still persists in terms of animism, spiritism and Bongaism among them. Side by side they also share their mind with other dominant culture through cultural transmission. Gradually they have developed a mixed culture consisting of elements of primitive religion and a complex religion developing a system of sacred ecology, sacred specialists and sacred roles and performances. Different magical activities are also practised in the form of black magic, witchcraft, sorcery, evil eyes, omens etc. In this way in the contemporary societies the primitive people are located along various points of a sacred-secular continuum incorporating many Hindu deities like Kali, Durga, Hari and others in their daily life. Now-a-days, some of the major tribes follow Hindusm besides naturalism. In West Bengal the tribes like the Santal, Munda, Kora, Mahali, Lodha, Rabha etc., also follow the same practice in their life. They all are under the process of Hinduization. In the same way through 'out the country the tribes are gradually accepting many Hindu cultural traits and are gradually trying to incorporate many elements of greater Hindu society.

Like tribal society the rural people also exhibit some characteristic features in maintaining the 'rural traits of religiosity'. In general, in village societies, besides the Brahmanical classical tradition, non brahmnical local tradition is followed by people belonging to the low castes. Village societies are generally classified by caste based stratification where the Brahmins hold the superior position. Each village has its own organization i.e., based on vertical and horizontal ties of castes and kinships. Besides, religious rites, rituals, ceremonies and festivals also operate within the broad framework of a regional social structure and civilization. In general the ritually low ranking castes are marked by their deep involvement with the local deities and folk festivals. The majority of them do not necessarily employ a Brahmin priest for solemnizing the annual household worships and the agricultural rituals. But on the other hand, the Brahmins and the Kayasthas are so oriented that any household worship or life-cycle ritual is not considered complete unless it has been solemnized by a Brahmin priest. In this way, the local tradition and the great tradition come in contact through a process of symbiosis. Unity in diversity and diversity among the castes and religious groups thus constitute unique features of the society and religion of India.

The operation of religious complex in metropolitan fringe areas is also another important dimension of the study on religion. In these places, a complex network of sacred activities of the people is associated with performance of traditional rites of passage, visiting of temples and shrines, offering of puja, observing *Manat* (vow), worshipping of images and taking part in *Barwari Puja*. In these ways, they express their faith in Hindu philosophy, theology and other spiritual aspects which show that a large section of people living in a city or metropolitan fringe area also follow the traditional ethos of religious rituals though giving them new forms of expression. Thus religion is still an integral part of Hindu life and continues to be followed by the majority of the people in metropolitan city or urban centers.

India is a land of pilgrimage both big and small. Many pauranic tirthas throughout the country are even today crowded by pilgrims for earning moksha or religious salvation. Different sacred vows are performed by sacred specialists according to the specification of sacred norms of those sacred institutions. Considering these different dimensions, study on the places of pilgrimage is another important field of anthropological research. Many pauranic tirthas have been studied starting from the 1950s of which Gaya, Bhubaneswar, Dwarka, Puri, Tirupati, Kashi, Kalighat are noteworthy. Besides this, many minor places of pilgrimage like Tarakeswar, Bakreswar, Tarapith etc., or different temple cities or district towns also constitute a part of religiousity. These pilgrim centers not only attract people but they also help to make the growth and development of the area as it catters to many needs of the service class providing various services. Business men develop their market network; the flow of pilgrims also develops transport tourism and cottage industry related to the need of that particular sacred complex. In this context we mention the practice of offering holy water to different gods and goddesses and of taking holy bath in it to earn merits on different festive days and ceremonial dates considered as auspicious.

Worship of different natural objects as supernatural beings had started since the very dawn of the formation of human society. Primitive men worshipped nature for getting rid of their evil functions. They could get security amidst insecurity, pleasure amidst pain and joy amidst sorrow. It is continued till today though its morphological structure has changed today. India has its holy enriched cultural tradition from hoary past. Here rivers are personified as deity, as gods and goddesses due to its beneficial functions. As a saver water gives life to the plants and animals. As a result, most of the big rivers of our country are considered to be holy, divine and pure. They are also considered as sacred. Many pilgrim centers i.e., sacred religious institutions are developed on both of its sides. The side of the river is also considered sacred. As a result, performances of cremation rites are done on its side. The holy water of the river, ceremonial dip, worship of the river as a mother deity always take part in every rite-de-passage of our life. Its holiness can never be denied in our every day life. In this perspective the study of sacred complex developing on the side of the important rivers is a very important area of the study on religion.

There is no life without food. Food, as an essential substance stands for the growth and development of plants and animals. In the supernatural realm, food also takes a principal role in establishing a web of social relationships. Prescriptions of different rites, rituals, establishment of totems, taboos, various forms of offering food in the form of *'Naibedya'*, fasting, acceptance and prohibition of food from different religious groups as well as different caste groups are all parts of religion especially in the context of Indian perspective. The two major religious groups–the Hindus and Muslims–are also identified as non beef-eaters and beef-eaters respectively. In this way food like essential substance also creates a diversity in the network of supernatural world both at micro and macro levels. Thus each and every ecological zone has developed its own religious cosmos according to the availability of food as a resource for maintaining life. In course of time, as a superstructure a religious world is automatically established maintaining a dual bond between man with man and man with supernatural power with its regional *'lokachar'* i.e., rites, rituals, ceremonies, sacrifices and restrictions associated with food.

It is even more determined and destined that human body is not free from disease and illness. Irrespective of time, place and advancement of knowledge, people suffer from various diseases. From the point of view of medical sciences, disease does possess a scientific definition. But from the perspective of Indian society–rural or urban, village or city–disease or illness is directly or indirectly associated with some belief patterns. Various factors are believed to be causing diseases like supernatural agencies, evil designs of man and natural agencies. The doctrine of *karma,* the curse of deities or the action of evil spirits or the malevolent action of some planets like Saturn, Rahu, Mars etc.,–all these are believed to be associated with the causation of disease. Socio-cultural factors are also considered important for the occurrence of disease.

As per the practiced cultural norms of a society, different groups show various health seeking behaviour in relation to curative, preventive and promotive aspects. Methods of treatment are also based on the religious belief pattern of rural and urban people. In general the rural folk mainly rely on the spirit-doctors, *gunins* or *ojhas* as they believe in the effects of evil wind, evil eye and evil spirits. In snakebite cases and dental problems the *gunin* as a spirit doctor is accepted by the villagers. In ordinary day to day petty health problems *totka* or domestic treatment is very popular. A few epidemic diseases are caused by the malevolent desire of some gods and goddesses like lord Siva, goddess Kali,Sitala and Manasa. Many community worships are done by the local priests (Brahmin or non Brahmin) to appease the deity. The role of priests or astrologers is important in both rural and urban metropolitan areas. Through their advice, the use of amulets, talisman and stones are very popular even in the contemporary urban areas.

On the other hand most of the tribal societies still cling to their traditional magico-religious belief systems and practices. In spite of a limited modernization process, a large part of these groups continue their traditional faith and belief in supernatural powers till today. They continue to be the strong believers in spirit and soul. The impact of benevolent spirit and malevolent spirit are believed to be evident in their every day life. Magical performances are done by the *shamans* as they believe in the existence of evil spirits which do harm to society. But through these magical performances if the deity is satisfied, the evil spirits leave the place. They also believe in the existence of witch. As a result, witchcraft and sorcery are also wide spread in these societies.

Animal sacrifice, particularly the sacrifice of hen, cock, birds, even buffalo sacrifice are very common in these societies. Besides, many local deities are worshipped by them for the benefit of their community. They also participate now-a-days in different festive occasions of the Hindus or Muslims. But they also go to hospital and bring the children under the programme of modern vaccination and the treatment through modern medicine. These clearly show that primitivism and modernity go hand in hand even in the era of globalization.

Another important practice known as *Guninism* is still in vogue in tribal societies. These *gunins* give medicines, perform different magico-religious practices and are allowed to act as medicinal men irrespective of caste and religious differences. Often they belong to low caste or tribal or *Fakir* community. But the villagers consider them as sacred specialists irrespective of their high or low rank related to socio-economic and political status.

The article written by Sova Rani Chakrabarty in Bengali (see appendix one) has enriched the content or the subject matter in this regard. She has beautifully described the role of *gunins* or magicians and their impact on society. Gunins or magicians may come from any section of society but they could establish their distinctive position in society. No one will raise any question regarding their identity or social position. They are considered as supermen as they can protect society from all sorts of evils. She has also referred to the supernatural world of the contemporary tribal society. Till today the tribals' great faith is on the magico-religious belief system which is performed by the *gunin* or *ojha* or medicine men of their society. Frequently they practise black magic for the welfare of their own group even though doing harm to others. Thus the prevalent norms, values, rituals, restrictions, pollutions, notions of dharma and adharma are all mixed up in a complex fashion with notions of social welfare.

Death is an extreme form of reality of life which no one can escape. As man does not want to believe that every thing ends with physical death, the concept of spirit or soul has developed. Death rites are very essential for transmigration of soul which connects the two worlds–the present and the other world.

The concepts of hell and heaven, birth and rebirth, *karmafal* and *prayschitya* are all associated with religion. The sacred funeral rites specially the 'Sradha' ritual (funeral ceremony) binds the members of the family of the deceased and the dead as the spirit is immortal. Religion helps in performing various rites and rituals and provides a bond between this world and the other world, the body and the soul, man and the supernatural. Death rituals are generally performed through mortuary rites and funeral rites. Through these performances not only the culture of a group is reflected but particular regions with its regional traits become manifest. In this way different sacred funeral rites with its unique characteristics represent the sub-system of religion. Different service classes like the *Brahman, Vaishnaba, Napit, Dhopa; Dom* and *Hari* perform ritual functions and maintain a structural entity. Death ritual has a very significant connotation. Death brings an end to all man-made relations. As a result, through performing the funeral rites, all caste groups from high caste to untouchables find an equal consolation. But though death is a great leveler, even in observing these death rituals, social and status distinctions are maintained. This becomes evident when we find the prevalence of different forms of mortuary rites and different types of rites and rituals associated with different caste and tribal groups in Indian society.

IV

India is a land of villages. Rurality is its core element. Gradually with the advent of time many changes have taken place in rural areas. Joint family, caste system and agrarian social structure are the three major features of rural society. Different social institutions are developed for the smooth functioning of the society. Analysis of the changing pattern of rural society, therefore, will have to take into consideration how the functioning of the rural social institutions are being changed. *Rural Social institutions and Administration* thus constitutes an important area where the social scientists have turned their attention and have tried to find out the nature of their problem. Professor Sachchidananda in his introductory note has nicely analysed the functioning of different rural social institutions and their changing role in the contemporary world. He has also reviewed the four synopses of the thesis included in this section. Prof. Bhowmick through his research work, has also tried to locate the core problems of the rural society. He has shown how the rural people are experiencing the metamorphosis of change and how, the rural administrators as elites, are maintaining there network of relationship promoting and sustaining this process of change. Considering the importance of the rural social institutions, research works done in this area under Prof. Bhowmick's supervision, have been clubbed together and placed in a different section.

Joint family constitutes one such important social institution in rural society. In earlier days joint family was not only important due to its social functions but it was also considered as a sacred institution as the members of the joint family consisted of not only the living individuals, the dead and unborn were also included in it. In this way through this sacred institution, the successive three generations are gradually incorporated in it. But along with changes in other spheres of society, the traditional joint family is also experiencing changes, both in its structure and functions. Now a days, there is no such area where the joint family continues in its traditional pristine form. In some cases, joint families are maintaining their jointness by performing some common obligatory functions. But even within this apparent structural jointness, many changes are taking place in the members' role-behavior. The elders sometimes fail to exert their authority, women members are now more liberated, the male members sometimes involve women in the decision making process. In this way the rural families are in the process of transition. This interest in the study of the family and its changing pattern has given birth to a new sub-discipline known as sociology of family. The changing milieu of socialization as occurring within the family and the problems of the elderly are also considered as important issues for analysis.

Besides the study of the joint family, caste based stratification system, which institutionalizes hierarchy and differentiation among the people, also constitutes an important aspect of the research work of P.K. Bhowmick. He has shown that a symbiotic relationship exists between caste and rural society. The uniqueness of this institution of caste has engaged the attention of sociologists and anthropologists for generations. The principle of superiority or inferiority and the principle of hierarchy and differentiation constitute the main domain of caste system. Though the system has some universal attributes, its contents and connotations are regional, even local. As a result, throughout the country the same pattern is not visible. Consequently, new paradigms have been considered by sociologists and anthropologists at different points of time. P.K. Bhowmick as an anthropologist gave due importance to this field. In his book *'Caste in Bengal Border* (2002)' he tried to endeavor the typical features of caste system as existing in the frontier regions of Bengal. The multidimensional aspects of caste system were studied by him. The situation is somewhat unique in each village with its economic connotations as well as its own associated customs and values. Social distance among various groups are still maintained. Many low caste groups are sanskritized and the little tradition and great tradition are blended with each other. In his article *Caste and Changing Occupation : Study of Belpahari Market* (ibid 2002) he opined that

(1) "...the people tend to disassociate occupation from religion; (2) no one thinks that one should remain chained to one's age old occupation; instead one should go ahead with the time;

(3) they are rather skeptical about the inherent difference among the various castes".

The phenomenon of rural indebtedness and its causes and consequences constitute another dimension of rural society. Poverty and indebtedness are related to each other. Poor farmers or day labourers belonging to low castes or tribal communities become involved in indebtedness for maintaining their livelihood. Particularly during the time of medical treatment, daughter's marriage, death and sometimes for higher education they have to approach on the local money lenders or mahajans. This is the general and common practice even today. Though it is true that through the establishment of village panchayats the general socio-economic condition of these people has improved some what and to some extent the exploitation of money lenders is also reduced, yet the problems of poverty and indebtedness continue to be phenomena worth studying. One such research article has drawn our attention to this problem.

Politics and society are inseparable. For better understanding of rural society and culture, the role of elites as rural administrators should be well understood. Even when the primitive societies are studied by the anthropologists, they have also given importance upon the analysis of the functioning of their political institution. How were different tribal societies controlled by their political elites? What was the source of their power? How is the situation changing now-a-days? And what has been the role of the Panchayets in providing leadership to the whole process of change? These and similar other questions relating to the functioning of political institutions in rural areas, particularly among people belonging to small communities, have drawn the attention of the researchers. In village societies, particularly in West Bengal, the Panchyati Raj bodies have been trying to ensure their democratic character through the process of democratization of both its structure and function. But still there is a gap as our society continues to be basically a caste-ridden society. In the formation of rural self-government the caste sentiment, the caste dominance and affluence of the dominant castes are still major factors shaping and influencing the nature and extent of political power of the masses. Naturally, our collection also includes research done in this area.

V

> An anthropologist does not merely play the part of an observer in a game of chess. He has a greater and deeper commitment, namely, that in India he has to draw a lesson from what he observes, so that he can utilize his knowledge in the attainment of the equalitarian ideal which our nation has set before itself as its goal. ... in which the government or leaders of society are trying to bring about justice where injustice prevails today. And this is where Applied Anthropology has a significant role to play and a heavy responsibility to bear (Bose 1972).

Anthropology is now no more just a matter of curio-study. The horizon of anthropology has been gradually extended through its various branches emphasizing specific issues related to the problems of man. *Development Action and Applied Anthropology* is a special approach focusing on the welfare of the downtrodden people. Through various action researches the anthropologists are trying to find out the root causes of the problems and to develop plans and programmes for their betterment. Even the classical anthropologists like Malinowski (1948), Seligman (1939), Evans-Pritchard (1951), Nadel (1951), Radcliffe-Brown (1952), Forde (1953), Firth (1951) have also mentioned in their works the practical relavance of anthropology. Contemporary anthropologists along with the planners, administrators and other social scientists have also framed and implemented many development programmes for the downtrodden. Tribal Research Institutes in various states play a significant role in this respect. Among the different plan periods, the Fifth Plan period is characterized by the acceptance of the Integrated Tribal Development Programme. Tribal Sub-Plan (TSP) was also introduced during this period at the macro level. Many developmental programmes in education, agriculture, health and hygiene have also been given emphasis in Tenth Plan period. Among the contemporary anthropologists, a few names of Indian anthropologists those who are directly or indirectly associated with Action or Development oriented works particularly for the tribal development may be mentioned here. They are Dube (1958), Sachchidananda (1992), Bose (1972), Vidyarthi (1968), Naik (1972), Bhowmick (1990), Danda (1973) etc.

In the discourses and discussions on Action Anthropology the name of Sol Tax is undeniable as he first coined the term Action Anthropology in 1951.

According to Sol Tax (1968)

> A major characteristic of the Action Anthropologist is that we have adopted what might be called a clinical or experimental method of study. We are anthropologists, interested in anthropological problems, but we pursue them in a context of action. Here the phrase Action Anthropology has become a conventional form.

Since the time of colonial administration anthropology became popular as it involved itself in studying the natives or the aboriginals who live in various remote places. For making their administration easy and communicable the native study was very much important to them. At present also, many contemporary problems–changing socio-economic condition, adaptation, interaction pattern with others, changing status of different ethnic groups and their reactions–all constitute important areas of study in applied anthropology. Besides these, government projects and the impact of the works of the NGOs' are also meaningful as a part of applied anthropology.

Prof. Bhowmick's 'Bidisa' Project is worth mentioning in this connection. The Bidisa experiment is popularly known as an experiment of development for the Lodhas, who were designated as a 'Criminal Tribe' till the revocation of the concerned Act in '1952'. Prof. P.K. Bhowmick started his work among the Lodhas in the early 1950s. In his scheme,

> ...the main thrust was to initiate change and not to depend on

charity, i.e., to generate a self-sufficient economy. The Lodhas have a parasitic mentality; they are basically lethargic and reluctant to work, as they belong to the hunting-gathering group. ... attempts are thus being made to socialize the youths through education and participation and also to develop a 'middle-class norm' through a planned routine, attempts are being made to tackle these psycho-emotional attitudes to broaden their outlook and to gradually assimilate them into the wider society (Bhowmick 1990).

Bidisa is situated in a village named Bagabhera, Narayangarh Police Station of Midnapur District, West Bengal. It is about 20 km to the south of Kharagpur Railway junction of the South-Eastern Railway. This is an ideal complex of the tribals as a good number of tribes like the Lodhas, Koras, Mahalis, Mundas etc., have their original settlements surrounding the complex. It has about 50 acres of land where this complex has been developed and the action oriented research has been started since the early sixties and still now it is continuing. Three ashram hostels have been set-up–one for the Lodha girls and two for the Lodha boys. One primary school and another Junior High School, which will be upgraded into a Secondary level soon, are situated in this complex. Besides these schools, there exists a research Institute named Social Research and Applied Anthropology. The Institute as per its goal and objectives is functioning which is an action oriented research centre. The Bidisa complex has its other facilities for the upbringing of the small tribal children at par with the children of the mainstream population. In this way anthropology as a science of man widens its goal for the service of man.

In the section on *Development Action and Applied Anthropology* there are altogether five synopses which have been collected from those persons who conducted their research works on various problems related to this theme. Scholars who have applied this approach, are otherwise in high bureaucratic posts and were actively involved in the problems of developmental strategies and welfare programmes of the downtrodden. Their actual experience of working with the tribes combined with their empirical and problem solving approach have made these works very much relevant for understanding the micro level problems of designated tribal groups and for the meaningful solutions of their problems which these studies have suggested.

Prof. Sachchidananda has written a critical introduction of this Chapter. He has interpreted, described and reviewed all the five papers systematically with his rational understanding and analysis. With his illuminating discussion, the readers will be guided through a fascinating area of analysis.

In this section, the respective author has tried to highlight the problem after considering the effects of governmental policies on development schemes and projects for the tribals or the downtrodden people. In these five works, the researchers have made some common observations which are really very interesting. As a development anthropologist, each of them has given his specific suggestions in his respective micro level work. All these suggestions are very relevant. In their works all the researchers have found that the target groups are not much benefited as these schemes are not implemented properly. One of the five scholars have pointed out that there is some maladjustment as the non tribal leaders with their vested interests exploit the tribals, though sometimes the 'government was honest in planning the development programmes'. His study was conducted among the Savara, Valmiki, Koya, Konda Reddy, Gond, Kolam and Chenchu tribes in Andra Pradesh covering the entire area from Adilabad district to Srikakulam district. Two other research works were conducted in Garhwal region (Uttar Pradesh) and Adilabad district (Andhra Pradesh). They were officially connected with the implementation of the schemes as they were administrative officers. As development anthropologists they have suggested many new strategies for planning. Along with their own suggestions they have pointed out that without people's participation the development works among the tribes would be in vain. The tribal people have to know their own problems and involve themselves in the process of development.

Another important study was conducted on the Yerukala tribe in Andhra Pradesh. Like the Lodhas of West Bengal, this tribe was also known as 'criminal tribe'. Previously they were also nomadic and due to their territorial displacement they accepted criminality as a means of subsistence. In spite of developmental activities undertaken by government, they are still now suffering the stigma of criminality. Lack of sufficient formal education, and limited job opportunity make the youths among them very vulnerable. Many of them are still continuing their criminal activities. As remedial measures it has been suggested that some small-scale industries can be opened for them. In this way their problems might be tackled as suggested by Lalitha (1989), the action researcher of this group.

The constraints in the development of Scheduled Caste in Uttar Pradesh is another comprehensive study done by the other researcher. He has observed that all Special Component Plans for the target population have mostly failed to achieve its target goal due to several difficulties including lack of proper implementation, selection, distribution, monitoring, co-ordination. Lack of people's involvement in such development programmes has also been noticed. As a researcher, he has given many suggestions for the betterment of the people.

VI

Sumner's (1906) concept of 'we' as the basis of in-group solidarity makes the group different from others, which have been termed as 'they'. The feelings of ethnocentrism, prejudice, ethnic conflict, identity crisis of minority group–all are the resultant effects of this distinction between the 'we' and the 'they'. Today's homogeneous society becomes the heterogeneous society of tomorrow. Particularly if we consider the heterogeneity, India is no exception. Its diversified culture, different religions, ethnic groups, sub groups, regional entities–all these give birth to the complexity of culture.

Culture, society and individuals are interdependent. Without culture there is no human society, no social relationship and no interaction among the individuals, group and community members. Society and group life are both causes and consequences of culture. So culture is an important aspect for studying society. Different social scientists have studied culture as one of the important tools to view and interpret society and to find the nature of social relationships in different historical periods, starting from primitive to modern.

Society can not persist without a culture, nor a culture can exist unless embodied in a society. Anthropologists and sociologists, therefore, even when trying to study culture systems or social systems as independent entities, must always take into account their interdependence. The interaction of men in groups occurs and is defined by aspects of cultural norms, sentiments, beliefs, values and above all languages. In turn, these cultural forms are learned and enacted in social systems. Culture depends upon symbols. It was the exercise of the symbolic faculty, which brought culture into existence and it is the use of symbols that makes the perpetuation of culture possible. Without symbols there would be no culture, and man would be merely an animal, not a human being.

Articulate speech is the most important form of symbolic expression. Without articulate speech we would have no human social organization. Without speech we would have no political, economic, or military organization, no codes of eloquence or ethics, no laws; no science, theory or literature, no games or music except at an ape level

(Bensman and Rosenberg 1975). Ethnic groups are formed and perpetuated on the basis of this symbolic unity. Study of ethnic groups and their interaction constitutes one important field of anthropological study. Social or cultural anthropologists always show their interest in studying this phenomenon. Like many others, Prof. Bhowmick also established himself as a field anthropologist studying a number of ethnic groups in different villages of different regions. Ethnic groups and their interaction with each other in various fields like social, political, economic, cultural or religious life–envisage a picture of a mosaic society. In his introduction to the section on Ethnic Interactions, Prof. Sarkar has analysed the scope and ambit of this area. He has examined different case studies from the works of P.K. Bhowmick and has tried to explore the particular areas from Bhowmick's field study which constitute ethnic study. This introductory analysis of the nature of ethnic interaction and its sequential social transformation will provide an adequate footing to the readers to go through the research articles which are based on this feeling.

The section on Ethnicity contains altogether nine research articles. Different ethnic groups with their domination over others make various types of relationship. Strong emotional relationship is established through co-operation whereas conflict disintegrates them and creates various types of tensions, contradictions and confrontations in social life. Small societies have less conflict and contradiction where as the large societies have more. But unequal distribution of power and influence of different groups is a ubiquitous phenomenon. Throughout the world different ethnic groups are labelled or identified by the power which they possess either by ascription or by achievement.

Generally villages are either multi-ethnic, or multi-religious or both. Even in their day-to-day interaction different ethnic groups share with each other feeling of love and hatred, co-operation and conflict. Through the process of interaction values, beliefs and distinctive ways of life of the groups are communicated to each other. Sometimes due to situational crisis, some groups have to migrate and take shelter in new areas. This again creates another tension in the life of the group. Many such groups are discriminated and identified as minority groups. In rural India, caste is also the basis of discrimination among different groups. In villages, generally the groups, belonging to the low strata, often suffer from the stigma of untouchability or sense of inferiority and this also influences the interaction pattern.

On the other hand, tribal people also interact with the village society constituted by the mainstream community. But discrimation is also there. They have their own community sentiments which make them separate and keep them in isolation. While, due to the increased interaction, they are now sharing many traits in common. Yet they continue to retain their distinctiveness and sense of identity. This gives birth to an interesting configuration of relationship between the tribes and the mainstream community.

Ethnic interaction among different groups on the basis of performance of rites, rituals and festivals is a very common phenomenon of village societies. In many local festivals different ethnic groups take part and do interaction with each other. Tribal people emulate local Hindu cultural traits, low caste groups follow the high caste traits, even sometimes the Brahmin with low economic status accept many of the dominant group's cultural traits.

Villages with multi-religious groups are also in active contact with themselves and may adopt many of the traits of the culture of each other. As neighbors people visit others' houses, and share all sorts of mutual obligations. Again during the time of festive occasions, they come close to each other. But this contact does not obliterate their separate identities. They observe their own rites-de-passage. Intermarriage between groups is not still accepted. Though they pay homage to *Fakir* or *Sadhu* or even accept medicines from them.This is largely done by them while they remain largely within their ethnic boundaries.

The articles in this section show the strategies for their survival and their coping mechanism in different ecological zones. The Dravidian speaking Oraons constitute the third largest tribal group in India. For their survival they live in different ecological zones, adapt to circumstantial exigencies and accept new patterns of livelihood. The Oraons in Chotanagpur, Sundarban and the Dooars live in different areas, practise different types of economy and also adopt various survival mechanisms for smooth functioning. These act as forces of change in their social, cultural and economic organization. But cultural continuity is also there. This interaction between change and continuity offers an interesting spectrum of analysis. As it has been aptly said, socio-cultural phenomena act as intertia allowing a group to a large extent in retaining its traditional identity. Many traits of their culture have been continuing through performing rite-de-passage by which their traditional heritages are continued. In this way they are always in the two opposite processes –'continuity' i.e., showing resistance to accept the new and 'change' i.e., accepting the new for adaptation and survival.

Nowhere in India are the tribal people in isolation. Even the Andaman Nicobar Islands, which is known as the abode of the Indigenous group, is now no more considered as an isolated place.

The Great Andamanese are also adjusting themselves with the changing circumstances as many non-tribal groups are slowly penetrating and in many cases they have to accept some of cultural traits of the others. But inspite of all these, still they are trying to retain there traditional culture. Owing to implementation of different welfares measures of the government, many induced changes are also taking place in their every day life.

In the same way, the Santals are also one of the major tribes of India and Bangladesh. Though in some areas the Santals till cling largely to their traditional culture and society, but in many areas of India and Bangladesh they have changed their socio-economic activities. As they are a large group and are scattered in varied ecological zones naturally according to their situational needs and demands they have adopted the neighbouring culture while maintaining the traditional culture of their own. In one study, in this section, the changing lifestyle of Santals migrated to the Barind tract of the then East Bengal, now in Bangladesh from Rajmahal Hills of India, has been analysed. It has been shown that many changes are taking place in their socio-economic, political and religious life. They are also gradually loosing their traditional linkages and cultural identities due to the stress and strain of their day to day life. Even sometimes due to the enactment of new laws and introduction of new political system, their traditional nature of village organization with the village head man as its chief feature, is no longer functioning. A few of them have accepted Christianity as their religion though majority of them are gradually absorbing the non tribal Hindu culture and being assimilated with them. Many Hindu gods and goddesses have replaced their *Bonga* Pantheon. But it is very interesting to note that at Barind in Bangladesh though Islam is the dominant religion, they prefer Hindu or Christian religion rather than Islam.

Migration has occurred in every stage and phase of human civilization. For better food and comfort, and also for security, people migrate from one place to another. It is also one of the survival mechanisms of the minority group which ensures security. One study included in this section, was based on the Refugees of Bangladesh who got their rehabilitation at Little Andaman. Seven caste groups of various strata have been formed in the studied village named Ramkrishnapur which is a multi-caste one. The immigrant population, coming from different regions, slowly and gradually have created a village organization in the new place. Their new livelihood pattern and the new economy changed their traditional practiced ways of life. They developed a strong adaptability power with the surroundings. In course of time, they began to adjust with the new ecological situation by adapting new techniques for smooth functioning of their society. The non tribal migrant groups have slowly established their relationship with the local tribal groups–the Onges and the Nicobarese. In this way a new network of relationships and interaction patterns has been set-up. In the new place, many of their traditional values, beliefs, and religious practices have been introduced with some modification and, in a similar way, new forms of adaptation with new pattern of livelihood also have emerged for them.

Another interesting study included in this section was conducted on the Sundarban delta region consisting of different multi-ethnic and multi-religious groups. In course of historical process, all these migrants came from different areas and started to settle there. Inspite of their cultural differentiation they have developed a common cultural stream forgetting some of their old values and giving birth to some new cultural traits. This region has developed a new form of allegiance–ethnocentrism in the minds of the people. Rigid caste hierarchy, the notion of Brahmanical superiority, muslim orthodoxy or tribal animism are all in the process of disappearing through continuous accommodation and assimilation of different ethnic group. With this gradual process of adjustment, new ideas and philosophy are being developed. This gives credence to the theory that culture and social organization have spatial specificity.

Study among the religious converts of Midnapore and 24 Parganas throws light on some unique feature of cultural contact. The history of conversion of groups is not a new one in Indian society. It has occurred through centuries. Mostly the low caste groups often convert themselves as Muslims or Christians. But, as it has been found that in spite of their conversion they still maintain elements of Hindu culture by performing rites, rituals and religions practices. They also use their Hindu name or surnames by which it is easily discernable that they are the converts. As a result, another sub culture originates amidst the plurality of culture.

The lifestyle of the pavement dwellers or *footpath basi* provides also another dimension of the study of ethnic interaction. This composite culture has its own distinction. By any stretch of imagination, pavement dwellers do not constitute an ethnic group. They do not share any biological descent, nor do they have any common history or a common language or a sense of shared history. But these people are considered as 'others' by the mainstream society. They also share some common cultural traits. All those who are 'have nots' conglomerate in footpaths for their survival. The common sentiments based on religion, caste, language are not discernible among them. All pavement dwellers, inspite of their origin, belong to this groups of 'have nots'. This common sentiments creates a 'we feeling' among them. Their original culture is replaced by a new culture. Extreme economic deprivation often makes them deviant, make them prone to unlawful acts and promotes sexual promiscuity. Human emotions like love, sympathy and affection have little place in their lives. Kinship ties are loosely developed as they have little or no impression about their kins. Thus the pavement dwellers have developed a new kind of unstructured organization.

Apart from these studies of ethnic groups and the various aspects of their socio-cultural relationships, there are also two other studies of culture of a different nature. One of them is a study on the Bengalees. The process of cultural transformation has played an important role for determining the new status of the Bengalees in contemporary period. Generally the Bengalees are the admixture of different races of which the Dravidian character is more pronounced. But gradually, due to racial admixture, today they cannot claim the purity of the Aryan or Dravidian or any other racial group. In the similar way this process has brought many changes in their socio-economic, political and cultural life. Impact of westernization, industrialization, the impact of pax Britannica all these developed a sense of awakening and a sense of nationalism among the Bengalees. Nationalism unifies them as a larger group merging their separate ethnic identities. But that does not mean that this Bengalee identity is homogeneous or that it does not have contradictory pulls and pressures. In fact, its too much identification with urban, middle class ethos has generated resentment among those who are in the periphery. We are witnessing the resultant tensions today.

The crossbow complex among the cultures of three different tribal groups, viz., the Kadar of Kerala (food gathering and hunting), Negritic-Negroid, the Ahom of Assam (shifting hill cultivation), Mongoloide and Meithei of Manipur (cultivation), Caucasoid is a unique study to know the transformation of culture from one particular period to another, from one specific group to another and from one region to different regions. Many important historical evidences of society and culture are found from studying the material culture analysis (technological objects i.e., crossbow complex) as it is blended with ethnological historical facts. The Portuguese used crossbows against their enemies in the fifteenth and sixteenth centuries. Thus in the historical investigation of the primitive tribes of India, the crossbow complex confronts with the Portuguese history in India. To trace the origin of the crossbow complex in Indian tribal culture, a new domain of Portuguese culture which was very similar to that of those tribal culture was explored. The tribals, who were in different areas, exposed through diffusion with Portuguese culture and adapted crossbow complex culture within themselves. In this way, spread of crossbow in Africa and Asia can also be explained in terms of the Portuguese colonialist expansion in the middle ages.

VII

Various branches of social science have been developed to explore the different and specific problems of man and society. With the evolution of society the problems of man have also been varied in nature. Comte's science of society is a special inquiry for studying man. Comte envisaged Sociology as a science that would be concerned with and would facilitate social progress–and thereby solve social problems (Sullivan et al 1980). Comte's law of three stages, Spencer's theory of evolution from militant to industrial societies, Durkheim's division of labour in society, Weber's concept of rational legal authority–all these studies clearly analyse the evolution of society from simple to complex. Marx was also concerned with the course of evolution of human society. He started from the primitive communistic society which was free from all sorts of exploitation as there was no class differentiation owing to the simple nature of the society and visualized a future form of classless communist society which would have no exploitation.

Like Sociology, in the discipline of Anthropology also, since the mid fifties of the nineteenth century, the anthropologists analysed society in terms of dichotomous segmentation, viz., rural or folk and urban. But this classification is not absolutely perfect and society can not be classified like that in a watertight compartment. Rural society has urban traits and urban society has components of rurality. A complete rural or a complete urban society is not really possible. But a society can be characterized as having a predominantly rural or urban feature. Indian people still basically live in rural societies as agriculture still now predominates over other industries. Each economy has some special traits or characteristics giving birth to a particular type of society. As a result, we see hunting and gathering society having hunting and gathering economy, agricultural society with agriculture economy, industrial society with industrial economy and so on. In the same way rural society has its own problems related to its economy and the urban society is like that, though sometimes many of the problems of each society may overlap.

Anthropologists primarily started enquiring into the primitive or preliterate people mainly the aboriginals. Gradually they extended their areas of analysis and developed various branches of Anthropological science. Primitive people are now in the process of change. They are not in complete isolation. As a result, the anthropologists, in course of their study, got interested in studying folk society. In this way gradually they have extended their scope by studying village societies, peasant societies with special reference to caste, tribe–caste continuum, culture studies etc. Today anthropologists not only restrict themselves in studying these, urban problems also attract them. Many of these problems are overlapping in nature and contemporary anthropologists study the slum culture, different problems arising out from the growth and development of town or metropolitan areas, urban institutions, modern complex form of religion, recent trends of nuclear families, family types, racial problems, cross border activities of the terrorist, etc. Gone are those days when an anthropologist would go to a remote area to study the culture and organization of a primitive, isolated tribal group.

Basically, a social problem exists when there is a sizeable discrepancy between what is and what people think ought to be (Merton and Nisbet 1976). Sociologists focus on the dysfunctions of patterns of behaviour, belief and organization for studying social problems and it generally originates from a changing social structure. When the prevalent values, beliefs and expectations are no more justifiable by the members of the society, who are suffering from the problems then only we think about social problem. For this reason in a particular society, all members are not victims as subjectivism is there. The discrepancy comes from a particular section of population. In the same way from the perspective of time and space, social problems vary. Social problems arise within the context of a particular society

The section on social problem has been preceded by a thought provoking and illuminating introduction by Prof. Sahay of Allahabad University. He has nicely presented the nature of problems related to different societies–rural, urban and rurban or the overlapping problems of each other. All the ten synopses of different scholars are reviewed by his interpretive analysis along with his analytical observations.

Ten synopses have been included in this section. Different types of problems have been studied by the scholars under the guidance of P. K. Bhowmick. Among these ten synopses, two are related to the problems of the tribal people. These two micro studies have revealed a general macro level picture of the tribes in India. Generally in Central India, the main tribes are the Lodhas, Mundas, Mahalis, Koras, Bhumijs, Santals etc. They depend on agriculture. Rice is their staple food but the other required substaintial foods are not available to them in general and women and children in particular. As a result, malnutrion, chronic dysentery, anemia, eye problems–these are all their basic problems. Poor socio-economic status, little or no education, lack of employment, lack of awareness are all the problems of the tribal people of that region.

Another problem that the anthropologists face today is to identify the marginalized tribal groups and to study the endangered population as they are considered as extinct groups. Due to many processes, some historical, some socio-economic, these tribal groups are now on the threshold of human civilization. A day may come when these groups would find there place in the pages of history. The Siyalgir group is like this type of tribal group which lives in Bengal-Orissa border region. They are facing the problem of identity crisis as they are small in number. For their survival they are trying to find out their place in the larger group by loosing some of their cultural traits and adopting the culture of the dominant group (Manna 2002). In this way ultimately, in future, this group may be abolished and in the same way many such marginalized groups may be merged with the large neighbouring groups. Considering this aspect, this particular problem is very relevant in the field of anthropological domain.

Coming back from the problems of marginalized tribes to the problems faced by different categories of people in our fast changing society, we find that the problems faced by women and children occupy a front ranking position. The problem of working women has been taken up in one such dissertation. Some sections of working women like Doctors, Telephone Operators and Nurses have been studied in this dissertation. Living in the patriarchal set-up these women have to compromise with many odd situations both at home and in their work place. The study has analysed the attitude of the working women. How are they adjusting with the situations? What are their coping strategies? What are their suggestions for better coping up? On the other hand, the attitude of the male co-workers and higher authorities shows an attitude of ambivalence influenced both by the norms of patriarchy and the norms of gender equality. They generally accept the working women as their co-partners as women workers are generally more serious and sincere than the male workers.

With the growth of cities or towns and also with the introduction of new industrial centers, a new middle class culture has been developing which is less conservative and more rational. One study analyses how this middle class is responding to the process of change. Krishnanagar is a district town in Nadia district. It had its origin from a village in the early part of 18th century. But, inspite of the traits of modernity, traditionalism still persists there. This micro study was conducted among a few women living in this area to know how they are responding to the forces of modernity. This study shows very clearly that the women are now in transition. The norm of free mixing is prevalent among them. Educated women have shown their positive attitude to select their own partners. But regarding inter-caste marriage still now an orthodox mentality prevails as a good number of women support it. Though a majority of the respondents have provided a theoretical support to the idea of divorce but in reality there is only one incidence of divorce which has taken place there. Thus a changing attitude among women is observed in this study. It has been found that women have been caught in the vortex of tradition and modernity.

The problem of child labour is an extensive problem in Indian society. With the gradual development in the urban sector of a good number of restaurants, hotels, sweet meat shops etc., an increased number of child labour can be seen. They generally come from rural areas and cater to the needs of the shopkeepers. In spite of their degraded status, low salary, unhealthy lifestyle, these child workers flock to these places of work as their parents send them to these places in the face of abject poverty and lack of alternative avenues of work. It seems that push factor, more than the pull factor, acts as a catalytic agency here.

In the same way the study of the life of the cycle rickshaw pullers, which has been taken up in another dissertation, throws some new light on another category of the urban professionals. Rickshaw is very popular means of communication through out the country in general and West Bengal in particular. A sociological inquiry on the life of the rickshaw puller is really an interesting one. It has been found that the cycle–rickshaw pullers migrate from different rural areas to earn their livelihood. Majority of them usually come from Bihar, Uttar Pradesh and Tripura. Many of them had a good ancestral background. But due to increasing alienation from land, poverty and lack of job opportunities and the disintegration of the rural economy, these men are forced to migrate to urban areas and accept this occupation. Lack of sufficient food and being faced with continuous job hazard, they become the victims of diseases like T.B, hydrosil, problems of chest and arms and even some venereal diseases. Children are also the usual sufferers of this process of malnutrition. Though they belong to unorganized sector but through Trade Union they are trying to organize them. Trade Unions play a big role even in fixing fares and in deciding on most of the aspects of their occupation. They are also playing a big role in solving the problems of their family life.

Another uncommon field of inquiry of anthropology is the study of the problems of hospital patients. The doctor-patient relationship and the institutional pattern of hospitals is a special type of problem related to urban society. Hospitals are generally the formal bureaucratic medical institution of a society. Society's development could easily be recognized if we see the number of such type of institutions in a particular society. But the scientific system of treatment that is provided in the hospitals are not easily acceptable to all types of patients belonging to various social strata. The research work on the patients' attitudes to hospital treatment and the types of facilities which they get reveal different types of problems as the infrastructural arrangement are not adequate and there is a differential pattern of access even to these limited opportunities. So hospitals can not be considered as a safe medical institution for all kinds of patients. Considering this particular aspect, patients are not happy. People coming from rural areas and those who belong to the underprivileged sections thereby become victims of the situation. This study has highlighted that infrastructural improvement has to be adequately combined with equality of access and the development of a scientific attitude.

Anthropologists have also shown their interest in the study and analysis of contemporary social unrest and movements. In tribal history a good number of tribal insurrections are found to have taken place. In these movements the tribals have collectively protested against injustice and oppression which they have been subjected to decade after decade. Many such movements like the Santal rebellion of 1855–57 (Dutta 1940), the Birsha Munda movement in Chhotanagpur during 1879–1901 (Singh 1966), the Kol Insurrection of Chhotanagpur during 1831–32 (Jha 1964), the Kuki uprising in Manipur during 1917–1919 (Bhadra 1975) have taken place whereby the tribals have demonstrated their power of collective resistance. They have also revolted against the British (Mathur 1988) and have joined hands with the non-tribals in fighting against British rule. In post independent Bengal, the Naxalite Movement, which quickly spreaded out in areas having considerable tribal concentration, attracted a good number of such tribals. Places like Debra and Gopiballavpur witnessed the intensity of the movement and a large number of tribals participated in it. As the land ownership issue was declared to be an integral part of the movement, that attracted a large number of tribals. But ultimately the movement could not achieve its goal as the tribals were disillusioned and dissociated themselves from the movement. Anthropologists from their point of view have tried to analyse the root causes behind the success and failure of the movement which is very relevant for the contemporary society.

Diagnosing the causes of student unrest in Bengal is another type of analysis of social movement and there is a long list of research materials available in this area. Not only in Bengal but throughout the world students occupy an important place in society. The functioning of educational institutions and the degree of attachment of students with the educational system–these offer some vital clues for understanding the behaviour pattern of students. In-house relationship within these institutions, like the student-teacher relation, student-student relation or the pattern of administration are as much important as the understanding of the role of education in the larger society for the analysis of the nature of student movement in a particular society. Students Unions are formed and many needs are fulfilled and systematized through this organized body. One of the important reasons why the students play a big role either in the sustenance of the present system or in initiating its change is that the students are most sensitive, emotional, full of spirits and fearless. During the time of freedom movement in the thirties and in the post-independence period, during the time of Naxalite Movement in the mid sixties of the twentieth century, students played the most important role. That is the reason why students' activism and participation draw the attention of the masses.

N. B. Sixty scholars had been awarded doctoral degrees under the supervision of Prof. P. K. Bhowmick during the period from 1967 to 1996. Six synopses of the theses have not been included in this book as those articles were not available during the time of publication. The names, titles of the six scholars and their years of award have been given in Appendix III. The original theses of those persons were also not available during the time of writing the manuscript. In a few cases, some of the awardees died or they were not in good health or they could not be contacted due to their changed addresses. But their theses were available. In those cases their synopses have been incorporated in this book in their name but the articles have been written by the editors

References

Bensman, J. and Rosenberg, B. 1975 *Sociology: Introductory Readings in Man, Class and Bureaucracy*. New York : Prager Publishers.

Bhadra, G. 1975 The Kuki Uprising (1917–1919) : Its Causes and Nature. *Man in India*, 55.

Bhowmick, P. K. 1963 *The Lodhas of West Bengal : A Socio-economic study*. Calcutta: Institute of Social Research and Applied Anthropology.

Bhowmick, P. K. 1976 *Socio-Cultural Profile of Frontier Bengal*. Calcutta · Punthi Pustak.

Bhowmick, P.K. 1990 *Applied Action Development Anthropology*. Calcutta: Institute of Social Research and Applied Anthropology.

Bhowmick, P. K. 2002 *Caste in Border Bengal*. Kolkata: R. N. Bhattacharya.

Bose, N. K. 1972 *Anthropology and Some Indian Problems*. Calcutta: Institute of Social Research and Applied Anthropology.

Danda, A.K. 1973 *Development and Change in Basudha*. Hyderabad: National Institute of Community Development.

Dube, S. C. 1958. *India's Changing villages*. London: Roultedge & Kegan Paul.

Dutta, K. K. 1940 *The Santal Insurrection of 1855-57*. Calcutta: University of Calcutta.

Evans-Pritchard, E.E. 1951 *Social Anthropology*. London: Cohen & West.

Firth, R. 1951 *Elements of Social Organisation*. New York: Philosophical Library.

Forde, D. 1953 Applied Anthropology in Government : British Africa. In A. L. Kroeber (ed.) *Anthropology to day*. Chicago : The University of Chicago Press.

Jha, J. C. 1964 *Kol Insurrection in Chhotanagpur*. Calcutta: Calcutta University.

Lalitha, M. 1989 *Tribes in Transition : A Case Study of Kapparallatippa in Nellor District and Sitanagaram in Guntur District*. Unpublished Dissertation.

Malinowski, B. 1948 *Magic, Science and Religion & Other Essays*. Glencoe: Free Press.

Manna, S. 2002 *Crystallization of Caste in Frontier Bengal*. New Delhi: Classical Publishing House.

Mathur, L. P. 1988 *Resistance Movement of Tribal of India*. Udaipur: Himanshu Publication.

Merton, R. K. & Nisbet, R. 1976 *Contemporary Social Problems*. New York: Harcourt Brace Jovanovich, INC.

Nadel, S.F. 1951 *The Foundations of Social Anthropology*. Glencoe: Free Press.

Naik, T.B. 1972 *Applied Anthropology in India: A Trend Report – A Survey of Research in Sociology and Social Anthropology*. Vol–3. New Delhi: ICSSR.

Radcliffe-Brown, A.R. 1952 *Structure and Function in Primitive Society*. Glencoe: Free Press.

Sachchidananda. 1992 Planning and Development and Applied Anthropology in India. In Sachchidananda (ed.) *Tribal India : Past & Present*. Calcutta: ISRAA.

Sahay, V. 2003 Dramatis Personae of Indian Anthropology. *Oriental Anthropologist*, 3 (2).

Seligman, H. J. 1939 *Race Against Man*. New York : Putnam.

Singh, K. S. 1966 *Dust Storm and Changing Mist : Story of Birsha Munda and His Movement in Chhotanagpur*. Calcutta: Firma K. L. Mukhopadhayay .

Sullivan, T. J. 1980 *Social Problems : Divergent Perspectives*. New York: John Wiley and Sons.

Sumner, W. G. 1906 *Folkways*. New York : New American Library.

Tax, S. 1968 Action Anthropology. In L.P. Vidyarthi (ed.) *Applied Anthropology in India*. New Delhi : Kitab Mahal.

Vidyarthi, L. P. 1968 *Applied Anthropology in India*. New Delhi : Kitab Mahal.

Swapan Kumar Pramanick

Samita Manna

PART I

P. K. Bhowmick and His Anthropological Legacy

Professor P. K. Bhowmick–The Field Anthropologist Oriented with Indigenous Vision

Rebati Mohan Sarkar

Anthropology is by tradition and in content and character a field science devoted to explore the multifarious and integrated facets of human way of life. It is with this mode of approach that anthropology has been categorically designated as an ideal field-based science having well-organised methodology to investigate into the patterns and perspectives of the human life situation. But at the very inception of the efforts for studying man the field work sentiment was not at all developed. It was, on the whole, theoretical in its concepts and the concerned scholars were in the habit of collecting information sitting at home in their comfortable arm-chairs. They used to depend on the varied descriptions on human life and thought given by others. The arm-chair tradition in anthropology was thoroughly broken down as a result of new and novel conception developed at the beginning of the twentieth century. It was thought that in studying the diversified domains of human life and behaviour-patterns the data must be procured directly by the researcher and not through the efforts of other people. The anthropologist must feel the situation himself and should present himself personally amongst the people to be studied. Through a continuous scientifically oriented search he must collect the relevant data to avoid inaccuracy and exaggeration. It was taken for granted by all concerned that if the data were devoid of accuracy, the whole endeavour would cut a sorry figure. Thus the arm-chair anthropology was turned down by the field anthropology. In this perspective the name of E. B. Tylor comes first because of the fact that he practically realized the importance and essentiality of direct data collection in the study of anthropology. But that very realization was put to the practical application by Franz Boas and thus he was regarded as the pioneer in that sphere of study. It should be noted, in this connection, that the two famous expeditions named Jessop North Pacific Expedition (1897), organized by Boas, and Cambridge Expedition to Torres Straits (1898–1899), conducted by Haddon, Rivers and Seligman, marked the beginning of the field based anthropological studies in the strict sense of the term. Those celebrated field investigational endeavours were continued and gradually developed with more understandings and precisions by the anthropologists like B. Malinowski, A. R. Radcliffe-Brown, M. J. Herskovits, E. E. Evans-Pritchard etc., who presented the field a status of laboratory for the anthropologists. Unlike the laboratories of physical sciences these laboratories are not bounded by four walls and are cut off from the outside domain for working with full concentration undisturbed by outside influences. Anthropological laboratories are open from all sides and these have free access to all persons as these develop in the midst of human communities. To work in these laboratories demands a specific training specially developed to fit the situation. It needs requisite moulding of mind to be engaged in scientific investigation within these peculiar laboratories where nothing is controlled and favourable. But the anthropologist's endeavour and perseverance as well as love and respect for the people can bring everything under control and unfavourable circumstance become favourable. There is no denying of the fact that the success in working in such a novel laboratory depends solely on the mental adaptability conditioned by the reverential attitude towards the people under study and the region in question.

Professor P. K. Bhowmick was a field anthropologist in the strict sense of the term. He learned anthropology from the field and he had all sorts of qualities essentially required for becoming a successful field worker. His direct entry to the field for anthropological investigation during the early fifties of the last century marked a very befitting beginning because of the fact that he took up a very novel idea in exploring the life and behaviour-patterns of such a tribal community which was a terror to the common people including the neighbouring tribal groups. Prof. Bhowmick from his very boyhood days was effectively attuned with the rhythm of life-philosophy of the downtrodden people in and around his native village which to him was always a source of inspiration. Thus he could make an entry into the inner recess of the peoples' hearts even at the primary phase of his life. The media through which he could reach the sons of the soil were, no doubt, profound love for the regional philosophy and peoples' indigenous world view, and those two factors jointly worked in his mind during the selection of a befitting subject-matter for his research work just after the receipt of the postgraduate degree in anthropology from Calcutta University.

He was attracted by the specific tribal community–the Lodha to conduct anthropological investigations amongst them. Incidentally he was advised and encouraged by some of his mentors of the University to take up such a population group for focusing various anthropological principles and to explore the significant dimensions of a tribal community characterized by a lot of abnormalities. The Lodhas were then identified amongst the general public living in Western Midnapur as a symbol of death because of the fact that their principal activities were centred round merciless killing of the persons traveling through the solitary roads after sunset. They took opportunity of loneliness and used to hide themselves in the roadside bushes. On seeing a person walking along the road a missile was thrown with fierceful force aiming at the person, and when he fell on the ground severely hurt by it or died, the hiding Lodhas ran quickly to that unfortunate person to search out his body for getting money or other valuables supposed to be carried by him. There were many occasions that the Lodhas became totally disappointed as they did not find any money and/or valuables with the person attacked by them. There were a large number of organized gangs of dacoits which regularly made attempts for decoity in the houses of the neighbourhood during the dead hours of night. All of the Lodhas of that time were expert thieves who were in the habit of lifting various materials even from other inner recess of the house with the help of their inborn capacity for stealing silently and nimbly. It was because of those facts the people were entirely terror-striken by the various anti-social activities of the daring Lodhas. All of the people in the neighbourhood of the Lodhas found no other alternative but to surrender their fate to the hands of destiny because, they thought, no worldly method could save them from the evil influence of that danger-oriented human community. Consequently, the very name Lodha became a panic to the people concerned and they felt embarrassed to utter even the name of that community particularly after sunset.

Under such a situational context, Prof. Bhowmick started his work of investigation amongst the problem tribe. It was undoubtedly a unique endeavour in the selection of such a community. Once, I being the student as well as his disciple at the formative stage of his teaching and research career, had an occasion to enquire into the specific reason behind his taking up of such problem oriented community the totalistic life of which was not only packed up with evil activities but also to move amongst them was out and out dangerous and many a time it was highly risky. There were numerous happenings of large scale and depth-oriented criminal activities of the Lodhas who were distributed mainly in the police stations of Jhargram, Kharagpur,

Gopiballavpur and Dantan. Their mischievous activities and hair-raising attacking techniques found conspicuous place in the police records as early as in 1904. The criminal activities of the Lodhas were on the increase in later years and in 1916 the Lodhas were declared a criminal tribe by a special government notification. Then in 1928 the Government became more serious about the Lodhas in consequence of their increased criminal propensity and thereby issued a notification which laid down the fact that a member of the Lodha community on his first conviction under non-bailable offences and under the specific section of the Criminal Procedure Code should be treated as a registered person according to the Criminal Tribes Act. Thus at the time of his selection of the Lodhas as a subject-matter of his research activities the tribe concerned was already declared terrific criminals in addition to the awe-oriented mentality of the general public in respect of the Lodhas.

Despite all those adversities and risky situations, Prof. Bhowmick did not hesitate to make up his mind to go amongst the Lodhas to fulfil his mission. But he was exclusively not inspired by any anthropological significance and its adventurouos dimensions rather his sympathy and fellow feeling attitude for the neighbouring neglected and downtrodden people provided proper impetus for such an endeavouor. Prof. Bhowmick did not like to walk in a smooth and comfortable way. He firmly believed that life was not a bed of roses rather it was full of thorns and to compromise with these one needs proper techniques supported by requisite strength of mind. He always felt embarrassed to follow the pre-arranged routined life and that was why he had to accept various risks in all spheres of life. He was in the habit of presenting himself as a struggling man which gave him a striving mentality to fight with all the adverse situations that he would like to impose on him. It was that very mentality which drew him to look into the condition of life and sufferings of the Lodhas both through the scientific investigation as well as from the view point of humanity which many a time goes beyond the boundaries of science facilitating the proper understanding of boundless human sentiments. Mention may be made that this double-sided approach of studying human events was spontaneous in the mind of Prof. Bhowmick, which was developed and nurtured by him from his early years of life and obviously it belonged to the part and parcel of the basic philosophy of his native village. Prof. Bhowmick always felt proud of recognizing him as a farmer (chasa) anthropologist as because he came from the rural peasant society. In spite of his work and living in the urban sophisticated society, he showed no inclination to so-called sophistication. He was very simple in dress and so also in his general lifestyle. During his visit to the rural areas he used to become more simple which helped him in mixing with the people freely. In his total behaviour pattern he was the man of the common people and in this perspective his mode of approach to the people was perfectly tallied with what Kabiguru Rabindranath said–

"Mor nãm ei boley
Khatya hok
ãmi tomãderi lok"

Let my name be famous in the manner that I exclusively belong to you all.

This particular statement did a great deal in instigating him to think for the suffering humanity. Moreover, Prof. Bhowmick did not like to follow the beaten track–he was always in favour of originality and new dimensional approach. He was out and out influenced by regionalism–he loved his native village, his own district and many a time he did not like to think beyond that regional perspective. Thus a regional sentiment developed in him and it was so strong that he bluntly refuted all sorts of complaints put against him regarding that sectorial nature. He stated all through the time that he went to the Lodhas as their close neighbour and naturally with a free mind together with the deep faith that the terrible human group would be no problem to him because of the regional linkage–a pattern of interaction processed with sympathy and affection as well as awe and avoidance. Prof. Bhowmick always nurtured a curiosity-oriented mind to look into the mysteries and complications working within any system. He was undaunted in that approach.

His regional sentiment was not the result of any sort of narrow mindedness rather it was characterized by deep-based love and respect for the specific territory which, he thought, contributed boundlessly to open his eyes, for looking into the human life-situation and to sharpen his mind for analyzing various human events in their proper perspective. In many of his writings and lectures as well as at the time of simple gossiping he used to pin-point the facts that he had learnt much and thereby enhanced his knowledge directly from his native land and associated people amongst whom he took his birth and came of age. Side by side with his serious types of work he very often engaged himself in writing various events of the society and culture of Midnapur district in lucid Bengali language for the children. Amongst various works of this kind his Medinipur Kahini (The Story of Midnapur) is a case in point. He could write Bengali well and his magic touch of pen made the books suitable for all concerned.

Prof. Bhowmick was, truly speaking, a traveler field worker. He used to move through the places with rapid pace to understand the geo-physical and environmental situations of the region and also to feel the pulse of the people by coming to their close contact. Most of the time he walked through the hills and dales on foot without feeling any difficulty as he thought that without physical association with the whole region of study micro studies in limited areas of the region could not be fruitful. Through an effective tour over the district of Midnapur, which started in the early fifties of the last century and continued till the beginning of the present century, he could develop a concrete idea on the nature and distribution patterns of the variegated human communities in Midnapur district. It was through his untiring tour that he could develop an inquisitiveness to distinguish some significant human communities having peculiar customs, traditions and world view though they were apparently seen to be mixed up with the general people of the region.

In course of his broad-based observations over his favourite region made at the formative stage of his research career he not only identified some indigenous human communities like Chirmar, Kakmara, Savara, Ganju and Siyalgir but also he explored the status and role of these small communities in the broader Hindu social organization. These human communities in spite of their indigenous patterns of life and thinking gradually infiltrated into the broader regional social system through the acceptance of various Hinduized traits. It is to be noted that these aboriginals or semi-aboriginal communities are found to preserve their entity and thus these can be easily identified by dint of their specific cultural traits or the intrinsic composition of the social structure. The very names by which these communities are separately identified have got specific significance. As for example, the Chirmar or bird killer, Savara or snake Charmer, Kakmara or Crow-Killer. Siyalgir or Jackle feeding people illustrate their practical means of existence in their very names. Prof. Bhowmick traced background situation of these peculiar communities and these had been, in all probability, migrated from outside the state. These communities still cling to the traditional pattern of life, though in a limited perspective, of their respective places of origin. A few of them converse amongst themselves in the original tongue–but others have totally lost the ability of speaking in their indigenous language and have accepted the regional language i.e., Bengali as the speaking medium. Sometimes a few non-Bengali words are found to influence the Bengali spoken by them. All these works were conducted by Prof. Bhowmick during the late fifties of the last century and certainly those activities were conditioned by his inquisitive mentality about the land and people of his native region. These small and peculiar communities having alien origin and characterized by the basic traditional elements of their land of emergence have gradually been intermingled with the regional society and culture in question and in course of time those people started shedding off their own cultural traits to accept the indigenous features of the land of their immigration. But in spite of their assimilation to the broader social system they, in many respects, have maintained their isolation. It is because of this fact their identity can still be checked and understood by a serious observer. Prof. Bhowmick had the capacity for such a type of observation and he used to look at various socio-cultural phenomena within the working social system. By dint of that specific quality he could focus the nature and extent of these little known small communities. Perhaps that particular viewpoint gave him requisite impetus to focus discernible light on the formation and workings of the social system of the region which he analysed during later years.

Prof. Bhowmick's entry into the Lodha domain at that time marked the very significant beginning of not only his academic career but also his totalistic life-pattern. As per the traditional tribal studies during that period he started to prepare the descriptive monograph on the Lodhas through the collection of data by the application of participant observation for a long time. Along with the monographic study he put special stress on the criminal propensity of the Lodhas for which they became dreadful to their neighbours, and not only so, the administration at that time was in a precarious condition to put effective resistance to the deep-rooted criminality of the Lodhas. Prof. Bhowmick's The Lodhas of West Bengal (originally The Lodhas of Midnapur) is the labour of his profound love for that ill-fated human community. It was his ultimate challenge to various problematic situations in working amongst the so-called "born criminals." As a monograph 'The Lodhas of West Bengal' is unique in itself and it can be regarded as a model for future workers in that line because it looked into all the spheres of the holistic life of the Lodhas with specific light on their criminal propensity. The Lodhas were known to the people as well as to the administration as the criminals of the first rate but their specific way of life as well as the causes, patterns and perspectives of their criminality were practically in the dark. The general public used to keep themselves away from the Lodhas as far as they could and they did not dare even to peep into the Lodha villages. The then administrative machinery was very rigid to them and the only identity of that unfortunate human group to the administration was the criminal tribe–a brand name given to them as back as in 1916 under a specific government notification. Consequently, the Lodhas had found their prominent places in the Crime Register of the Poloce Department. Here they were put to the severe charges in connection with dacoity, murder, burglary, theft, arson etc. In course of time the Criminal Tribes Act became very rigid to them. It was thought that the criminal activities of the Lodhas could be resisted by the application of the Act with severity and on this issue the concerned administration characteristically became merciless to them.

Prof. Bhowmick did never follow the categorical path of the conventional field methodology. He was always reluctant to follow the theoretically originated methods and techniques for data collection. He used to say that he himself was the method–his methodological principles were conditioned by love and respect for the people and the region together with keen and integrated observations on the daily mode of behaviour of the people concerned from close quarters. In this regard we find in him the reflection of P.J. Pelto's words when he expressed the opinion that the field worker is his own principal research instrument and the various methods of investigation are alternative techniques for objectifying and standardizing the field worker's perception. At the very first instance he used to mix with the people as their part and parcel. When he met the Lodhas for the first time he faced not only a lot of difficulties but also he had to meet with the environment of conspicuous suspicion of the Lodhas as they thought him as an agent of the police and some other investigational organizations. It was quite natural for a human community having criminality as an inevitable means for earning their livelihood and thereby secluded by the neighbouring groups of people to think in that line. They were the people of the underworld and as a natural consequence they tried their level best not to divulge anything to any person coming from outside. Prof. Bhowmick was not an exception to that very sentiment. Thus it took a long course of action to make himself established as a well-wisher and at least not as a hostile person to the criminal Lodhas. It was at that very stage Prof. Bhowmick whole-heartedly utilized his regional sentiment and indigenous perspective of life to make a network of beneficiary groups from all concerned like the local traditional leaders, energetic young men, influential and experienced persons from all the walks of life, administrative personnel, government representatives in various dimensions and lastly, but not the least, from among the Lodhas. He started paying visits and revisits very frequently to the Lodha settlements spread over the western part of the then Midnapur district.

Prof. Bhowmick did not write anything about the specific perspective of the fieldwork conducted by him. He was not interested in focusing the stresses and strains which he had to face during his day to day conduction of field work. But during the relaxing period away from home he used to narrate most of his experiences about fieldwork. At the initial period of his conduction of research work he was in an acute financial stringency together with other familial problems. Despite all the adversities he did not bow down his head to any problem as he always nourished a strong mentality and undaunted attitude of not compromising with any untoward event in life. His work amongst the Lodhas was characterized by many unfortunate happenings. At the very first meeting with the Lodhas he was held by them in suspicion i.e., he might have been, according to them, the informer of the Police who came for collecting information about their criminal activities. In that situation he was practically in a great risk of life and sometimes it so happened. But he could overcome that untoward event by his untiring effort to establish his native features and understanding amongst the Lodhas. His exposure as a man of the region and his association from the boyhood days with the ardent desire for their well-being caused a great deal in establishing himself in the hearts of the so-called criminal people as the man of their own. Once he went to an inaccessible Lodha village for the purpose of study and he worked there all through the day and had to pass the night in a Lodha house. The night stay was not preplanned and hence there was no provision for food. Prof. Bhowmick had to pass the night practically with no food. On the following morning his Lodha host promised him food. But how he did not know. Prof. Bhowmick very often narrated the sincere and peculiar effort made by the particular Lodha individual on that very emergent issue. After haunting for the whole day in search of food for the guest he could catch a pigeon in the evening and on which a "grand feast" was arranged. That particular incidence was practically an eye opener to the fieldworker who could readily apprehend that the criminality could not be the only criterion for the identification of the Lodhas. It might have been the fact that the situational context had imposed criminality on them and it was not supported by their basic philosophy. Once they were habituated in various antisocial activities like dacoity, theft, murder etc., they were practically engulfed by those unfortunate situations and ultimately an environment of criminality started prevailing which entangled younger generations who became the persons of the same fate. The application of the Criminal Tribes Act since 1876 made them established criminals and it so happened that for all sorts of crimes in that region the Lodhas were out and out held responsible. With the increase in the severity of the Act during the pre-Independence period the Lodhas were being harassed indiscriminately on the plea of the commitment of crimes. It was a fact that there were some organized gangs of the Lodhas which actively engaged in dacoity, burglary, pilfering and theft together with murder and that was why the administration of the country became so serious to bring a check over that antisocial situation. But at the same time it should be noted with deep concern that a human being or a community could not be branded as born criminals.

Prof. Bhowmick wrote what he observed. He did not like to follow the footprints of others. Thus his study pattern was always characterized by the indigenous appeal and it became an ideal mode of perception of the socio-cultural interactions in human society. The question was stirring in the mind of Prof. Bhowmick when he came close to the Lodhas in their day to day way of life and thinking pattern. In course of time when he could explore the totalistic way of life, it was seen that their social life was conditioned by normal thoughts and desires like many other tribal communities. His monograph on the Lodha established the facts with concrete evidences that the Lodhas could never be called as abnormal in their lifestyle–they were not the persons with diseased mind. Prof. Bhowmick made intensive study on 31 Lodha villages under 7 Police Stations in Jhargram and Midnapur Sadar Sub-divisions and gave a beautiful and authentic sketch of their social organization, village organization, economic life, magico-religious beliefs, festival cycle as well as recreational life which were the concrete evidences of his long-term fieldwork-based understandings on them. In all the spheres of life one could see the friendly as well as respect-oriented mentality of the Lodhas with the natural world, spirit world and the neighbouring communities. Their amicable relationship was effectually flourished in their attempts to conduct the social system and thus it would be very difficult for anybody to deny the existence of friendly sentiment in the value–attitude system of the Lodhas. Their festival cycle is oriented with the propitiation of various deities seeking well-being for the land and people. The *bandana* or cattle-caressing festival is centered round the heartfelt gratitude to the cattle family. The Lodhas have adopted the *Baramasi* song which narrates the various mental situations and ritualistic activities of the puranic gods and goddesses. Various themes from the *Ramayana* and the *Mahabharata* have been taken up to describe the situation of the country in the twelve months of the year. All these and many other features advocate the fact that the Lodhas have always been in close socio-ceremonial connection with the neighbouring Hinduised communities as their festivals, life cycle rituals as well as recreational life are seen to be crowded with the elements of advanced Hindu groups of people. It suggests their time-long interactions with the healthy social system of the surrounding communities, and until and unless there has been a good and friendly understanding, interchange of thoughts and ideas cannot be so extensive and effectual.

Prof. Bhowmick had shown the working patterns of four indigenous temples while highlighting the instance of close integration of Lodha Life with the broad religious spectrum of the people. In that temple organization along with other advanced caste groups the Lodhas also find a conspicuous position in the religious domain of the rural surroundings. The priest of the *Jaichandi* temple of Pitalkathi in Jhargram Sub-division belongs to the Lodha tribe. From time immemorial the Lodha priest and his descendants had been conducting the ritualistic activities as per Brahminical tradition and the members of all the advanced caste group did not hesitate for a moment to send their offerings to the goddess through the medium of the Lodha priest. In that particular context, the Lodhas, no doubt, had been getting a prominent place in the sacred complex of the region in question. It was observed that after the concrete process of Brahminisation, which came late in the region, Brahmin priest had been appointed by the organisers of the temple. But it could not dissociate the Lodha priest from his position. Both the Brahmin and the Lodha priest started working together. The total receipts in kind and cash from the local devotees were equally shared by the Brahmin and the tribal priest. The temple of Pitalkathi, according to Prof. Bhowmick, is the dumb witness of the Lodhas' social acceptance in the region concerned from the time immemorial. On that ground it can easily be said that the Lodhas were always parts and parcel of the regional communities but their criminality made them a secluded group of humanity. The circumstances arising out of the specific changing situation in the ownership pattern of forest–the abode of the Lodhas who used to hunt and gather various constituents of life there for their total subsistence.

Actually speaking, the Lodhas were originally hunting-gathering tribe who did not know anything about food production. Their complete dependence on nature mould their life in a particular philosophical setting. Their life-philosophy was oriented with nature–on which, according to them, their fundamental rights of using rotated smoothly. Their old pattern of living, according to Prof.Bhowmick, was seriously affected as they were uprooted from their basic economy centering round forest, and that very situation upset the equilibrium of the whole society. It was necessarily followed by the practice of various antisocial activities. At the very first instance those were practised individually and later on there developed a group habit which turned them into the criminal tribal group. On the basis of their transformance from the hunter-gatherer tribe into the criminal tribe Prof. Bhowmick observed that the loss of livelihood caused loss of self-confidence. Due to their lack of any professional specialisation they failed to adjust themselves with the greater economic structure. They ultimately suffered from the lowering down of their social status because of the stigma of criminality. Being faced by chronic poverty together with the police oppression, punishment and torture they lost their enthusiasm in life and thereby developed an apathy in staying at home. All those factors made the lodhas a socially isolated tribal group. Despite living side by side with the other neighbouring communities, the Lodhas had been segregated from the other people only because of their criminal offences for which they were not responsible.

Criminality cannot be a regular profession of any human community and Prof. Bhowmick has asserted that the Lodhas are completely devoid of any linkage of criminal sentiment with their criminal activities. Had criminality been their traditional profession, then there should have been psycho-social and ritualistic attachment with that very professional practice in their daily routine of activities. Occupation with which the people are concerned is always respected by the human group and in all stages of cultural development it is generally seen that various ceremonial performances are observed for the betterment of the occupation patterns and also to solve various problems relating to these. The Lodhas observe a large number of ritualistic performances–they have numerous folk songs and folk dances which are performed throughout the year but none of these reflect anything about their criminal propensity which has become, in course of time, their principal identifying character amongst the people of other communities.

After reaching such a conclusion by the conduction of field based investigations, Prof. Bhowmick became highly instigated to focus the very fact that the criminality of the Lodhas was the direct result of their economic displacement. Finding no other means to save themselves from starvation, the bewildered Lodhas were compelled to bow to the domain of anti-social activities knowing fully well that their social status would be heavily affected. Thus the unfortunate Lodhas survived at the cost of their good name. But their effort for survival very naturally deeply condemned by the administration which became very rigid in giving severe punishment for their crimes. The ill-fated tribal group failed to get any sort of consideration either from the administration or from the general public, and due to which the Lodhas had lost their morality and gradually sank down to more and more criminal acts. A vicious atmosphere had been created in the Lodha settlement which exerted evil influence to the children also who in course of time became automatically associated with the criminal activities.

The Lodhas of Midnapur was not only to be considered as the subject matter of Prof. Bhowmick's research which brought him D.Phil. degree in the mid-fifties of the last century but they played as eye opener in looking into the human distress in their helpless condition with humanitarian sentiment. Prof. Bhowmick's humanitarian appeal for understanding the actual cause of the unfortunate situation was always processed with the principles of human science. Therefore, his inquisitiveness to search out the nature and extent of Lodha way of life was not ended with the completion of work for the D.Phil. degree rather it continued with a tremendous speed and multisided approaches to suggest measures and find out the ways to bring back the Lodhas to their so far lost traditional healthy life. Prof. Bhowmick's sentimental attachment to the region and his deep love and respect-oriented outlook for its people enhanced his enthusiasm for doing something concrete for the ill-fated community which in spite of its simple and amicable nature had to accept the stigma of criminality.

Prof. Bhowmick got requisite inspiration from his mentor Prof. N.K. Bose regarding his direct involvement with the well-being of the criminal Lodhas though the work was not so easy. But he readily made up his mind to work for the rehabilitation of the Lodhas under the sponsorship of the government. At the very first step a voluntary organization named Samaj Sevak Sangha was established to take up the work of rehabilitation of the disorganized Lodhas through the adoption of systematic procedure. The work was taken up during the early phase of the sixties of the last century and as per development programme of the Central as well as State governments. In 1952, the Lodhas along with other Criminal tribes of India were relieved of their age-old stigma of criminality and became known as Denotified tribe. While working for the rehabilitation among the Lodhas Prof. Bhowmick put discernible light on the two basic issues–(1) chronic economic difficulties and (2) social neglect for centuries. In order to look into those two basic factors Prof. Bhowmick arranged the total perspective of the Samaj Sevak Sangha for the purpose of economic as well as social rehabilitation of the so long neglected Lodhas. At the very outset, Prof. Bhowmick started the troublesome work of making the Lodhas economically supportive through the acceptance of settled cultivation as well as their permanent settlement in a particular place of habitation with great hesitation in respect of its fate. It so happened that the preliminary efforts for approaching Lodhas for the uplift was vehemently opposed by those people and many a time they became furious and showed their hostility against the workers of the Sangha. But Prof. Bhowmick with his scientific trend of mind as well as his profound sympathy for the Lodhas so long detached from their advanced neighbours could cope with the situation. He understood the fact that until and unless the mental situation of the Lodhas was changed by making the social atmosphere around them favorable and they were allowed to mix freely with the non-Lodhas, their disgusting attitude could not be brought under control. On that very particular concept he started work of rehabilitation of the Lodhas at Daharpur and Dhansola villages. The centres for rehabilitational activities were started in two dilapidated mud-built huts at far off places. It was the very simple and sincere beginning of the work for Lodha rehabilitation. After a long turmoil and continuous trial and error, Prof. Bhowmick could win success. It was, no doubt, a continuous process and during which Prof. Bhowmick had to face so many confrontation with the government officials attached with tribal development activities, the local influential people, the Lodhas as well other voluntary organizations working side by side with him. But Prof. Bhowmick, by virtue of his scientific appeal, firmness of approach, undaunted mentality and the specific capacity for doing hard labour could surpass all those hazards and thereby could develop an effectual and ideal centre for the well-being of the downtrodden community which ultimately became a model in the sphere of rehabilitation of the ill-fated humanity.

The rehabilitation work of the Lodhas was specifically characterized by a two-way process. It provided the uprooted Lodhas with a solid footing–the ill-fated people could secure blessings for their honest and prestigious life in course of time. On the other hand, the Lodhas made Prof. Bhowmick an efficient applied anthropologist who also got a solid footing to apply his hard earned anthropological knowledge for human benefit. Prof. Bhowmick did not like to change the social and economic settings of the Lodhas only through the development of their materialistic life but he suggested measures for their change in life by the critical analysis of their specific pattern of need oriented philosophy and psycho-social surroundings in which they had been living for long time. It was for that reason he felt urgently to get the advice and suggestions of the efficient social workers, experienced government officials working in the domain of tribal welfare as well as the devoted social researchers investigating into the diversified nature of social problems in the different phases of his activities to ameliorate the condition of the Lodhas. Thus from a mere centre for economic rehabilitation of some limited Lodha families Daharpur became the focal point in organisaing the change and development of the Lodhas as whole. Daharpur ultimately took a new name–Bidisa. It is not a new name, a mere nomenclature but a new understanding, a new philosophy and a unique set up to attract all the lovers, workers and thinkers on the suffering humanities. It was Prof. Bhowmick's expectation the Bidisa would diffuse light of knowledge and consciousness to all concerned and in course of time it became true to the totalistic context. The novelty of Bidisa is centred round its humanitarian appeal for conducting development work which must be processed by scientific research. Bidisa is characterized by its own approach in respect of the development of the down-trodden community with unhygienic mentality which have been devised after long and effective discussions amongst the specialists. Bidisa was established with the pledge to fulfill three dimensional perspectives for tribal development–firstly, to work on humanitarian grounds for bringing Lodhas back to the accepted course of life characterized by new identity; secondly, to bring a change in the outlook and the method of evaluation of the administration concerned together with the neighbouring people; and thirdly, for the conduction of experiment. Here lies the difference between the various other voluntary organizations and Bidisa in the line of tribal development. Prof. Bhowmick as practical anthropologist (the term used by Malinowski) could understand the practicability of academic outlook in the development programme and it was for that reason he started an exclusively academic organization named Institute of Social Research and Applied Anthropology , in 1974, which was meant for the academic instruction to be given to the Samaj Sevak Sangha in its different types of developmental work. Through the effective initiative and earnest appeal for human development Prof. Bhowmick could construct a model academic platform of Bidisa and under the auspices of the Institute of Social Research and Applied Anthropology different types of national and international seminars and symposia were started which animated and activated the various working efforts for development. A biannual journal named *Man and Life* was started to communicate the results of various discussions of the scholars in the conferences, the nature, problems, prospects and constraints in the sphere of work and the exchange of ideas in relation to the successes and failures. Thus Bidisa, the dream child of Prof. Bhowmick, took the active role of employing the science of man into the service of man to establish prosperity, security, self-reliance and mutual dependence in the day to day life of the human communities especially of the Lodhas.

Bidisa, it is to be noted with great concern, has been identified as the lone model organization for applied anthropology in India, and for giving it a particular shape in the line of global perspective of Applied and Action Anthropology. Prof. Bhowmick kept no stone unturned to provide it a prestigious and academic stand. But he had to fight continuously with the adverse situations–he came in serious confrontations with the local self-interested influential persons, neighbouring tribal groups other than the Lodhas and even the government officials who were most often and sometimes completely ignorant of the tribal sentiments and philosophy. Thus he always claimed that any sort of tribal development work must be done after close-set discussions amongst the social scientists, social workers, government officials and the tribal representatives concerned. He felt seriously that the want of coordination amongst the workers of different dimensions was the root cause of failures in many endeavours for development of human communities despite spending of money as well as energy. Thus during his conduction of the work of rehabilitation amongst the Lodhas he felt the urgent necessity of creating healthy and attractive platform where the administrate personnel, academicians, social workers and the representatives of the peoples concerned would sit together to engage themselves in the discussions on many-sided points to avoid pitfalls. Bidisa was pledged to perform that specific task which was designed and activated by the undaunted personality like Prof. Bhowmick, and of course, also through the close coordination of his associates. Bidisa experiment has become a successful achievement in the life of Prof. Bhowmick and there is no hesitation in saying that he will ever be remembered in the domain of applied social science not only in India but also in the world for the planning, execution, and running of such a novel institution which has been pledged to arrange for a close marriage between the academic sphere and the administrative domain–a highly desirable requirement in working with human groups.

Prof. Bhowmick's specific attention to the diversified communities with tradition-bound life-situation which was activated during the fifties of the last century, ultimately gave vent to the exposition of a different understanding which he preferred to call socio-cultural interactions in the frontier region. In this sphere it is seen that Prof.

Bhowmick has attempted to make the micro-study of conflict and cohesion of the diversified ethnic groups having different life-way and thought-ways. His principal aim of study is to depict the totalistic socio-cultural setting of the region forming the western border of the then Greater Bengal. The specific area which he has selected for his work is the western boundary of Midnapur district that is contiguous with the districts of Balasore and Mayurbhanj in Orissa and having its spread northwards along the districts of Singhbhum and Dhanbad in Bihar (now Jharkhand). This particular tract is also associated with Purulia, Bankura, and Birbhum districts of West Bengal both in geographical as well as in social settings. Prof. Bhowmick has observed with great concern that this particular landmass criss-crossed various political boundaries is an integrated landmass having a distinctive cultural background of its own. This specific geo-physical domain had been under the influence of changing political situations for a long time conditioned by the arrivals and departures of various kings and rulers as well as other groups of political dignitaries but no one could bring any devastating effect on the local cultural traditions because of its integrity and spirituality. It was Prof. Bhowmick's specific observation in course of his tours through the region at the earlier periods of his academic career, and in later course it became his determination to analyse the situational context underlying the long time conflict and cohesion, accommodation and dissension, as well as assimilation and isolation amongst the varied ethnic groups in the territory in question. He prefers to call this territory as frontier region because of the fact that this specific tract is like a buffer region which is characterized by many socio-historical and culture specific events exemplified by migrations, aggressions and conquests. While analyzing the historical perspective of this region he has shown that this part of the country is specifically influenced by the colonial endeavours made by the Portuguese, the French and the British. These influences are still found to be reflected in the rural life of the region concerned. The coming of the Pathans and the Mughals and their political activities were deep-rooted in this territory. From the very remote past the area had been and are still being influenced by the life-ways of the primitive people constituting many tribal groups like the Santal, Munda., Lodhas,Kheria, Mahali, Kora and along with them various small and isolated communities like Chirmar, Savar, Kakmara etc., were included. Besides this the territory under study is the meeting point of two streams of the *Orissan* and the *Radh Bengali* cultures forming a synthesis of cultural features which are characterized by the development of a specific philosophy of life and tradition orientation. But Prof. Bhowmick strongly believes that the basic substratum of the traditional culture of the region is characterized by the tribal life and thought. That specific tribal orientation pattern of life was so strong and took firm shelter on the soil of the region that it could not be displaced even by the infiltration of powerful Brahmininical tradition. How the traditional tribal-based indigenous culture reacted with the different dimensions of Brahminic thoughts and ideas influenced by the concrete refinement of thinking became the main points of discussion in the study of the frontier region as taken up by Prof. Bhowmick.

It is to be noted that in the throwing of discernible light on the question of cultural interactions and integrations together with its isolation or segregation Prof. Bhowmick did not walk in a conventional way, rather he tried to devise a different path designed from his own conception of the circumstances. It was not an hurried survey, but a time-long micro-study. He studied the population patterns, rural social system, religious centres and various festivals related to diversified folk life from close quarters and along with those he tried to dissociate the culture traits for analysing those separately to understand their specific significance. The social system of the rural territory is characterized by multifarious interactions of various thoughts and ideas and in order to get the close and clear view of those Prof. Bhowmick tried his level best to make an entry into the inner recess of the working and thinking patterns of the various smaller and larger communities within the villages, households and temple organizations. He traversed through the different fairs and festivals observed on the village levels and community levels, and put insider's view on the interacting patterns of diversified traits which gave him ample opportunities to examine the integration as well as isolation of various infiltrated caste groups oriented cultural traits. His analysis of the various facts puts forward the truth that in this frontier region the systematic behaviour patterns of different groups have been fused together and it is nothing but a concerted appeal to meet the challenges of adversities in socio-political ways of life. In this frontier region the conflict and composition in the configuration of socio-cultural life are, according to him, highly illustrative and from which he has highlighted various theoretical orientations working within this broad-based and age-old frontier society.

When the wave of *Aryanisation* inundated the indigenous custom and tradition oriented landmass chiefly dominated by the primitive communities, it could inflict some influence, no doubt, but it failed to make an entry into the very root of the local cultural traditions. That was why the impact of Brahminism could not spread its supremacy on the traditional way of life conditioned by the thoughts and behaviours of the indigenous society. Thus it seems that the so-called great tradition failed to become highly effective in repressing the little tradition as in other parts of the country. Non-Brahmin concepts and non-Brahmin domination put limitations on the Brahmin oriented, caste-based economic and political spheres unlike many other places. It is the characteristic feature of this frontier region. There were many a time organized social movements amongst the indigenous non-Brahminic castes and communities which indicated categorically the united efforts of the lower caste and community groups to lodge protest against the Brahminic tradition-oriented customs and beliefs. In the domain of folk religion, the domination of the non-Brahmin priest was at the highest level and which is also continuing to a large extent during the present period. Thus it is proved that in this frontier tract the non-Brahminic little tradition-based population groups could not be brought under subjugation by the Brahminic great tradition through the general process of sanskritization. Here Prof. Bhowmick has observed a different dimension which has been in action through time and space. As per his opinion, the non-Brahminic traditions i.e., non-sanskritic characters are so powerful in this tract that amongst the population group here has developed a trend of extremism which he has preferred to call radicalism–a specific frontier trait. In order to support his observation Prof. Bhowmick has given a picturesque description on the reciprocal interactions between Brahminic and non-Brahminic as well as shastric and non-shastric way of life and philosophy. In this domain of study he has been able to show that the Brahminical supremacy failed to exert influence on the people as a whole and it is to be regarded as their utter failure in infusing in the indigenous population rigid conservatism or traditional Puritanism. The historical perspectives as opened by Prof. Bhowmick through his inquisitive analysis of the social system bring to light the specific pattern of supremacy of the non-Brahmins here in the spheres of socio-political as well as ritualistic performances especially that are related to the folk stratum.

The much discussed important socio-cultural events in sociology and anthropology like *Sanskritisation* (Srinivas) and *Brahminisation* (Bose) were not functional rather it was abortive in this frontier tract. Because of the fact that the working of the economic organization based on caste group oriented agriculture was controlled by the Brahminic tradition and it provided economic security to the people, there was always a tendency of the general public to come under the influence of such economic set-up and thereby to submit to the Brahminic dominance. But the breaking down of the occupational linking of the caste group together with the deterioration of social legislation of the caste based society owing to changing socio-political affairs of the country the economic stability of the caste groups could not be maintained. Moreover, after the attainment of independence the Government of India promised substantial help and cooperation to the lower castes as well as the tribal group. As a result of this during recent period the society has taken the reverse course in its movement. A particular caste group in the lowest stratum of the Brahminical hierarchical system is seen to be eager in going back to its original tribal status from which it once made an entry into the caste order maintained by the great tradition. The situation of socio-political events has given the people of that sanskritised caste group an opportunity to think it is convenient rather rewarding to embrace the social status from which they originally emerged. It is regarded a kind of security as well as an effort for making an end of the age-long exploitation.

It is the conspicuous phenomenon of retribalisation which Prof. Bhowmick has detected occurring for a long time in this tract specifically dominated by various transformed low castes and tribal groups. By putting reference to the concept of *Santalisation* as adopted by Gautom (1973) where an all-rounded effort has been identified in which the traditional Santali behaviour and local ethnic traditions have been given special importance for revival of the past honour and prestige of the tribe. Prof. Bhowmick in course of his study has put forward the fact that the Santals living in the regions along the borders of Midnapur and Bankura districts provide an example of the pattern of change of mentality. The Bengali Hindu peasants of the region are highly influenced by the Vaishnava sect. On the other hand, the Santals and other tribal groups came under the influence of Christian missionaries and became converted to Christianity. The converted tribals received economic benefits and also they got the opportunity for education themselves. These situations attracted other tribals and backward communities, and they became inspired in course of time to embrace Christianity.

Side by side with these, Prof. Bhowmick noted the change and development of tribal mentality which resulted amongst the Santals of Midnapur and Bankura locality in a sort of insurrection in the field of their traditional beliefs and practices. In order to put resistance on the tremendous influence of Hindu religion in the one hand, and the special effort taken up by the missionaries for Christianisation on the other, the Santals here tried to strengthen the tribal mentality and indigenous values by establishing the new religious belief know as *Saridharam.* According to Prof. Bhowmick, *Saridharam* could be equated with the Kherwar movement in Chotanagpur. This process of reinforcement of the traditional pattern of thinking and varied cultural traits is getting more and more conspicuous during the present time. Prof. Bhowmick became very much enthusiastic in presenting such a regional study completely based on continuous field observation but he always felt that it was a positive effort to open up the broad horizon of studying regional anthropology and which can be elaborated with the additions of more and more works in the different regions of India. But, at the same time, he was of opinion that the work on regional anthropology needed such a kind of researchers who should not only be well-acquainted with the basic social situation of the region of study for a long time but also they must have got the basic quality of love and respect for the region and the people concerned. He reiterated that the regional anthropological survey and research could never be made authentic and animated by hurried superficial working procedure.

Supernaturalism is a universal phenomenon amongst the tribal people, and not only so, that rural people especially those who belong to the lower section of the society having indigenous way of life are the patrons of supernaturalism. The tribal and the rural folk very often take the help of supernatural methods to solve their varied problems of life. In short, supernaturalism is found to be interwoven with the life and philosophy of these people in such a way that without putting requisite stress on these issues the holistic life of these people can never be explored. While working among the variegated societies in the rural settings Prof. Bhowmick came across many instances of supernatural ways and means for the solution of the problems, like to get recovery from diseases, to resist the attack of epidemics, to keep the villages free from evil influences, to protect the crops in the field from destruction, and many others. It instigated him to conduct a specific work on supernaturalism to find out its complex influences on the people and their social system. The tribal and the rural folk try to express themselves in occult ways when they do not find any wordly explanation to analyse a specific situation or it may be the fact that the worldly affairs are out of their reach. In this situation there have developed a number of secret institutions for cultivating occultism. The sphere of occultism is nurtured and conducted by some specialists known by the different names like *gunin, ojha, deonara, janguru* etc. These persons are believed to have possessed some supernatural powers and due to which they can fight with the adversities caused by the evil spirits or by any unnatural phenomenon. Prof. Bhowmick in his study on occultism could open up the inner recess of the secret cults related to occultism and he had shown how occultism had taken a dominant role in the working of the rural/ tribal societies. He also went to the extent of showing the parallel phenomena of occultism in the shastric literatures of India and how those were found to be integrated with the life of the people. The phenomena of deep penetration of the various occultism-oriented belief-patterns cut across castes, classes as well as political and religious differentiation, and that was the central theme of the study as conducted by Prof. Bhowmick. It showed how the occult practices help certain individuals to get prominent status in caste hierarchy despite their low social position. The study also examined how and when the people from the upper rungs of the society approached the practitioners of occultism, having inferior social position, neglecting the barriers raised by purity-pollution concept of the Brahminical tradition.

Prof. Bhowmick's devotion to anthropological investigation is characterized by love and esteem for the people especially the down-trodden communities on whose life and philosophy the different facets of this human science are formulated. Prof. Bhowmick's profound respect as well as inquisitiveness for the patterns and perspective of the life situation of the people of the region, where he was born and brought up, made him a field anthropologist in the long run. His field-based investigation was not time-bound. Thus what he wrote and thought were the results of his life-long continuous fieldwork. His work and thinking on the Lodhas did not, therefore, end with the preparation of the detailed and substantial monograph on them, rather it continued till his departure from this mortal world. He firmly believed that the study on a particular community knew no permanent stoppage, there might be some temporary halts, and so an anthropologist must spend his time and energy to examine how his former data were in the process of change through time and space. He should learn from his own work. Side by side with the continuous fieldwork, Prof. Bhowmick allthrough the time applied his vision to look at various social phenomena and to analyse their working patterns from close quarters. He was always reluctant to import various concepts of anthropological studies from outside. He was all through the time in the regular habit of highlighting various social phenomena in the background of localised and native thought patterns and was prompted to christen those in the indigenous way. Therefore, field orientation having its continuity through time together with the specific view-points influenced by indigenous appeal were the novel twin approaches through which Prof. Bhowmick could have done a miracle in the sphere of the theoretical and practical applications of the knowledge gathered from the domain of human science.

Research Methods in Cultural Anthropology and the University of Calcutta

Harsha N. Mookherjee

Basically, the primary objectives of Anthropology are "to explore the nature of man as an evolving, culture-bond creature, living in organized societies–each different from every other and yet similar in many ways" (Hoebel 1972 : 5). Hence, Anthropology, the scientific study of man, is comprised of four sub-fields, such as, the physical/biological, cultural, archaeological, and linguistic anthropology. Each of these branches has its own separate method of study in understanding man, his environment and natural resources.

It can be argued that Cultural Anthropology started to separate distinctly from Sociology around the turn of the 20th Century with the works of Emile Durkheim (cf. Kottak 2004). Durkheim drew his theory on organization of simple and complex societies on his works of the religions of native Australians (Durkheim 1912/1915), as well as consideration of mass phenomena, such as suicide rates in modern nations (Durkheim 1897/1951). We have noted that Anthropology mostly concentrated in the study of less known isolated groups or societies of remote areas, where as sociological studies were mostly devoted among the people of so called modern societies and their immediate patterns of living and problems. However, we cannot ignore the works of Comte, Spencer, Marx, and others, where most of their contributions were ideological and less related to direct fieldworks.

For example, Comte regarded the study of sociological phenomena as having two pragmatically justified aspects, the static and dynamics. An approach through the static aspect leads to "the investigation of the laws of action and reaction of the different parts of the social system–apart, for the occasion, from the fundamental movement which is always gradually modifying them" (Comte 1839-42, IV: 324). Social dynamics, on the other hand, are concerned with conceiving each of the "consecutive social states as the necessary result of the preceding ..... and the object of science is to discover the laws which govern this continuity and the aggregate of which determines the course of human development" (Comte 1839-42, IV: 365-366). It is interesting to note that Comte saw specialization as a subversive threat to orderly progress, but Durkheim showed that the division of labour leads to an increase in a new and higher form of social cohesion (cf. Durkheim 1893/1933: 226). Many cultural anthropologists have proposed that the distinctive feature of the anthropological approach is its holistic framework. Comte quite properly discussed this subject in the context of the organismic analogy (cf. Comte 1839-42, IV: 355).

Herbert Spencer (1866), on the other hand, introduced the "survival of the fittest," following Charles Darwin's concepts to the interpretation of the nature and functioning of society. He consciously attempted to prove that human nature was an evolutionary product. He insisted that human nature is modifiable, and it has undergone and will continue to undergo drastic changes in conformity with a universal law of development (cf. Spencer 1883: 45-46). He believed that bio-evolution and cultural evolution are intimately connected. Similarly, modern anthropological opinion also supports Spencer's belief that in the transition from hominoid to hominid status mutually reinforcing biological and socio-cultural changes took place. However, according to Sol Tax (1955) the historical evolutionary school played an important role in the development of Cultural Anthropology in the eighteenth century.

Marx and Engels' formulation of the principles of cultural evolution is considered as a contribution to the explanation of cultural differences and similarities with respect to all cultural types. In addition, Engels' later works (1954) relate to Marxism and the development of Cultural Anthropology. In explaining institutions, Marx (1904) considered different varieties of institutions. He split the non-ideological aspects of socio-cultural life into two parts: the economic structure ("the real foundation") and the "legal and political superstructure." He then distinguished three major socio-cultural segments: (1) the economic base, (2) the legal-political arrangements or social organization, and (3) "social consciousness" or ideology. Marx and Engels then proclaimed that the explanation for both parts of the superstructure -social organization and ideology–were dependent on the economic base.

It is important to note that both Spencer and Marx expected the triumph of the individual over society in the long run as the society changes from rural, simple type to the industrial phase. For example, the similarity can be seen in Spencer's ultimate industrial phase and Marx's stateless and classless utopia at the proletarian victory in his conflict arena. For both Marx and Spencer, "the withering away of the state was a withering away not only of the political apparatus but of the entire supra-individual, socio-cultural nexus of restraint" (Harris 1968: 468). Durkheim, on the other hand, saw the transition, the division of labour, as a strength of social organism over the individual. Durkheim explained the situation as an intensification of the mutual dependence of individual and social group (cf. Durkheim 1933: 407). He then argued in favour of the necessity of the discipline concerning "social", as distinct from individual, and "functional". In his influential contribution of The Rules of the Sociological Method (1938, orig. 1895), Durkheim first narrated the methodological principles of such a discipline. In the process, he reaffirmed his superorganic position, which is in many respect different from Spencer's organismic model and Marxist tradition. However, Durkheim's ideas are deep rooted in Kroeber's exposition of the autonomy of the cultural level, and also of Leslie White's "culturology", and in French Anthropology (cf. Harris 1968: 468-513; Kroeber 1944; White 1959).

Research Methods in Anthropology

Traditionally, Anthropology specialized in narrating the socio-cultural life of the less known societies of the world. For example, early scholars worked among the Native American Indians, Native Australians, Native African communities, the Tribes of Indian Sub-Continent, and others. These scholars traveled to distant lands to study small groups of nomads, foragers, and cultivators, and gathered first hand knowledge. This knowledge gathering process, known as ethnography, became a required field experience and information gathering technique for the Cultural Anthropologists. Thus, early Ethnographers /Cultural Anthropologists lived in small-scale, relatively isolated societies with simple technologies and economies.

Ethnography thus became a primary research strategy for the Cultural Anthropologists in studying societies of greater cultural uniformity and less social differentiation than the societies of large, modern industrial nations. Traditionally, Cultural Anthropologists tried to understand the "whole" living pattern of a particular culture. In the process, the Cultural Anthropologists adopted a free-ranging strategy for gathering information. Therefore, they moved from "setting to setting, place to place, and subject to subject" to discover the totality and inter-connections of social life (cf. Kottak 2004).

Cultural Anthropologists, in general, focus on ethnographic field research and employ varieties of field techniques to gather information and put together a picture of the total lifestyles of the unknown or less-known society under study. The varieties of field techniques being used by the Cultural Anthropologists are as follows: (1) direct, first hand observation of daily behaviour, "participant observation"; (2) conversation with varying degrees of formality, maintaining rapport, "interviews"; (3) gathering information and tracing the "family trees" and the degrees of relationship, "the genealogical method"; (4) in depth interviewing leading to the collection of "life histories"; (5) discovering local beliefs and perceptions; and others.

The method of ethnography, thus, "provides a foundation for generalizations about human behaviour and social life" (Kottak 2004: 324). Cultural Anthropologists also use the ethnographic fieldreports of different societies "to identify, compare, and explain cultural differences and similarities, and build a theory about how social and cultural systems work". This type of research method is known as "ethnology". Therefore, the Cultural Anthropologists, who use the ethnological research method, may not do any field research at all, just study the available ethnographic reports and data to develop their own conclusions.

During 1860s and the earlier decades of the nineteenth century scores of ethnographic reports of different societies appeared as contributions of many poorly qualified travelers and missionaries. Edward Tylor (1865) estimated the quality and quantity of the ethnographic materials available at the beginning of the period 1860-1890, and raised the question of general evolutionary directions and the origin of language, writing, naming, tools, marriage, fire, and myths.

All theorists of the latter half of the nineteenth century developed their propositions primarily by means of the "comparative method". The basis for this method was the belief that socio-cultural systems bear differential degrees of resemblance to extinct cultures. To apply the comparative method, it is important to use the essential logical, deductive operation. The assumption is that the older forms are the simpler ones, but in practice many different kinds of logical assumptions are involved. This process leads to ethnological studies, and the works of Lowie (1937), Morgan (1870), Murdock (1963), Tylor (1889), and others are examples of such studies.

Anthropology in the United States

However, during the first half of the twentieth century, the basic research strategy in the United States was mainly formulated by Franz Boas (1948). Boas's primary strategy was in ethnographic field research, where the researchers would pursue their varied interests "mindful of data, free of prejudice, and distrustful of all schemes" (Harris 1968: 250). Boas's ideas and procedures are labeled by some scholars as the "historical particularism", but his students denied of any "Boasian School of thought". Boas and his students built "professional, university-based anthropology particularly from the ground up" (Harris 1968:251). To Boas there was up limitation of one single research method–according to the need, psychological, sociological, diffusionist, functional, or cultural-circles–whatever it took to be highly critical objectivity. Boas emphasized both the particularist and generalist approaches. He encouraged speculative conclusions as much as could be supported by empirical findings. In other words, the researchers should have an interest in focus, and they should collect information as needed to support their ideas, no matter whatever the research method(s) needed to apply. Boas was faithful to his inductive principles, and always presented the evidence of ethnographic findings from which he arrived at his conclusions. Boas was the 'Anthropology in the United States' and his prominent students were Alfred Kroeber, Robert Lowie, Fay-Cooper Cole, Edwin Sapir, Melville Herskovits, E. Adamson Hoebel, Ruth Benedict, Margaret Mead, M.F.Ashley Montagu, Frank Speck, and others.

British Anthropology

Almost at the same time, similar to Franz Boas, W.H.R. Rivers (1911; 1914) at the Cambridge University in England developed the "diffusionism", the British School in Anthropology. Rivers with his ethnographic studies among Melanesian and Polynesian cultures confined his historical reconstructions to Oceania. Rivers ideas of "explaining cultural differences and similarities by appealing to convenient combinations of migrations, additions, losses, and mixings of trait complexes was applied on a worldwide scale" by G. Elliot Smith and W.J. Perry (Harris 1968:380). Perry (1923) and Smith (1928) reconstructed their "diffusinoists" ideas of world culture through their extensive fieldwork among the inhabitants of the Nile Valley, Egypt. Thus, Rivers, Perry, and Smith paralleled many members of the Boasian School in the British Diffusionist ideas.

On the other hand, another group of scholars basing on their intensive fieldstudies among a small group of aboriginal societies, and intensive analysis of the data developed the "functionalist" framework of the "British Social Anthropology".

A.R. Radcliffe-Brown (1952), following Durkheim's ideas of "social solidarity" and "function" developed the "systemic formulation of the concept applying to the strictly scientific study of society" (1952: 178). With the inspiration of Durkheim's emphasis of social solidarity and function, Radcliffe-Brown combined the concepts of : social structure" and "function" to develop his "structural-functional" ideological theme. He gave more emphasis to "social structure", and considered "function" as a contributing factors to the maintenance of social structure (cf. Radcliffe-Brown 1949). Therefore, this theory of "structural-functionalism" totally agrees with Durkheim's approach to socio-cultural phenomena to maintain the conditions of social cohesiveness.

However, Bronislaw Malinowski and others placed greater emphasis upon "functions" by associating the biopsychological needs of the individuals in the society. Malinowski's Trobriand Island monographs (Malinowski 1922; 1935) consitute the greatest ethnographic description ever known, and his concepts of functions are well developed. Malinowski and Radcliffe-Brown denied the value of speculative reconstruction of history, they both emphasized the need to study the existing social institutions, conceived of cultures as a whole, and both developed a concept of function in terms of the social effect of institution (cf. Kaberry 1957). The influence of Malinowski's work on sex and the family earned for him a substantial reputation outside of Anthropology (Malinowski 1927). Malinowski's ideas rested mostly on individual needs and he especially emphasized that "functionalism" should include the "emotional as well as intellectual side of mental processes", and the individual should be considered as a full biological reality for the analysis of culture. "The bodily needs and environmental influences, and the cultural relations to them, have thus to be studied side by side" (Malinowski 1939: 939).

Anthropology at the University of Calcutta, India

In summary, it is found that all of the above theory buildings in Anthropology have been developed using two primary research methods, Ethnography and Ethnology. India being one of the colonies of the British Empire until 1947, formal training in Anthropology at the university level did not start before 1917. Anthropology was introduced first in India at the University of Calcutta in 1917 as the "study of social institution" in the curriculum of Political Science, Economics and Political Philosophy and then in 1918 as a subsidiary subject to Ancient Indian History and Culture. However, several ethnographic studies were conducted in India before 1917 and later by some administrators and scholars, like Dalton, Ibbetson, Hutton,

Nesfield, Risley, Thurston, and others. The Department of Anthropology was established at the University of Calcutta under the leadership of R. Chanda in 1920. Chanda contributed to all branches of Anthropology, while L.K.A. Iyer studied the pioneering ethnography of the Tribes and Castes of Cochin (1939), and The Anthropology of the Syrian Christians (1926); S.C. Mitra concentrated on folklore of North Bihar; and B.C. Majumdar conducted research in aboriginal areas in Central India. At a later date, a student of W.H.R. Rivers, trained at the University of Cambridge, England, K.P. Chattopadhyay took the leadership of the Department of Anthropology at the University of Calcutta, India. Professor Chattopadhyay introduced Professor Rivers' "British Diffusionism" in Indian Anthropology. Among his theoretical contributions, the analytical premises and conditions for the growth of exogamy and endogamy was highly remarkable (Chattopadhyay 1931; 1994). At the same time, T.C. Das, being influenced by Malinowski's functionalism, got involved in empirical ethnographic analysis. He introduced fieldworks in the academic curriculum and in practical training process. He imbibed his students in finding functional meaning of all observable facts and focused the practical aspects of anthropological knowledge in handling life problems of ethnic groups. His Purums (1945) and Bengal Famine (1943) had earned him international reputation (cf. Basu 1974).

The stalwart anthropologist, N.K. Bose revived the Cultural Anthropology in the Department of Anthropology at the University of Calcutta as well as in Indian Anthropology. Inspired at Franz Boas' inductive natural history approach, he got interested in analyzing the roots of Indian society, especially in the caste system of India. His consistent concern had been the "nature of unity in diversity in the structure of Indian civilization and the problem in transforming an old civilization into a revitalized new nation" (Sinha 1972: 6). He developed his theoretical model on a greater scale conducting a survey of selected cultural traits all over India. He showed that the regions or states of India could be seen separated by differences of languages, but these differences are "eventually replaced by a unity of beliefs and aspirations which gives to Indian civilization a character of its own" (Bose 1961: Introduction). He further supported his ideas by indicating that Indian civilization developed a pattern of cultural pluralism. He added, "Indian civilization encouraged diversity of cultures, while in its economic organization, it tried to weave all communities into a network of interdependent, but distinct, entities" (Bose 1971).

From methodological point of view, Bose (1949) emphasized that anthropological study, like Indian civilization, should involve a combination of aspects, such as, the analysis of social history, administrative records, studies of villages, the caste associations, and the wider social networks of the kinship systems, fairs, and others. In other words, study should include ethnography, analysis of cultural elements in festivals, use of classical texts, use of medieval literature, pilgrim centers, fairs and markets, analyses of land revenue records, and economic history of regions (cf. Sinha 1972).

In addition, Bose's participation in Gandhi's Non-Cooperation Movement during the Indian Independence Movement, and the influence of Gandhian ideology and Marxist socialism directed his intellectual involvement into the Applied and Action Anthropology. He took a consistent position against a communal basis for administrative categorization of backwardness of the scheduled castes and scheduled tribes of India. He suggested "modern India should set her primary task as dispersal of political power to the toilers, irrespective of castes and communities" (Bose 1952; 1954). Bose inspired his students, a group of young scholars, his colleagues, and friends.

At the inspiration of N.K. Bose, one of his students, P.K. Bhowmick, later became a Professor and Head of the Department of Anthropology at the University of Calcutta, India, built the residential complex at Bidisa, West Bengal, India. This residential complex became the Field Camp and Research Center of the Institute of Social Research and Applied Anthropology. Bhowmick took the responsibility of improving the living conditions of the Lodhas, designated as a criminal tribe in West Bengal, India, and changed the habit of the Lodhas at the above Research Center. Bhowmick completed an extensive ethnographic study of the Lodhas of West Bengal (Bhowmick 1963), where he found that the Lodha life was mostly entangled with crime and jail, and the children of the jailed parents were left to their fate and essentially ended into their parents' occupations of criminality. He was convinced that "the Lodhas were the victims of a colonial policy of administration and the crime among them was the result of an organic response to a changed socio-economic situation" (Bhattacharyya 1978: 21). He conceived the idea that crime could be checked if the children could be dissociated from their criminal parents and be raised in a more congenial environment. So Bhowmick's attempt of Lodha rehabilitation experiment became a pioneering model of Applied and Action Anthropology in West Bengal, India. At present, this Applied Anthropology Research Center provides the rehabilitation facilities for the Lodhas, Mundas, Oraons, Santals, and other scheduled castes as well as other poor communities in the area with the cultivating lands, seeds, equipments, programmes for re-socialization, necessary trainings along with food and shelter for the adults and education for the children, with an aim to integrate them with the mainstream of the larger society, without sacrificing their cultural identity.

Bhowmick's participation in the Indian Independence Movement and his revolutionary mind brought him close to the understanding and sharing the lives of many suffering tribes and scheduled castes of West Bengal. He fought for the sufferers individually and in groups, in the political arena. In his academic life, being inspired with N.K. Bose's explanation and study patterns of Indian civilization, Bhowmick (1976) narrated the distinctive characteristics, social, religious, ritual, economic as well as the political milieu of a region of West Bengal from the holistic point of view. He showed how historical accounts could be of enormous help in the analysis of the social phenomena. He tried to explain the "conflicting orientations of people in a frontier region living amidst frequent and drastic social and cultural changes", which are important to understand the differences between the core and the fringe of a national culture. The idea is to show that "the core is represented by status quo, stability and conservative syndrome, while the fringe is represented by constant flux, accommodation and radicalism" (Sachchidananda 1977).

Reference

Basu, M.N.	1974	"Fifty Years of the Department of Anthropology, Calcutta University." pp. 5-15, In Indian Anthropology Today ed. by Dharani Sen. Calcutta: Department of Anthropology.
Bhowmick, P.K.	1963	Lodhas of West Bengal. Calcutta: ISRAA.
Bhowmick, P.K.	1976	Socio-Cultural Profile of Frontier Bengal. Calcutta : Punthi Pustak.
Bhattacharyya, S.	1978	"Institute of Social Research Applied Anthropology", Post Plenary Congress on Applied and Action Anthropology. Xth. International Congress of Anthropology and Ethnological Sciences, Souvenir, pp.21-24.

Boas, F. 1948 Race, Language and Culture. New York: Macmillan.

Bose, N.K. 1949 Hindu Samajer Gadan (in Bengali language). Calcutta.

Bose, N.K. 1952 "Democracy and Social Change in India," The Modern Review, April.

Bose, N.K. 1954 "Who are the backward classes?", Man in India 34 (2):

Bose, N.K. 1961 "Introduction", Peasant Life in India, Memoir No 8. Calcutta: Anthropological Survey of India Publication.

Bose, N.K. 1971 "An Anthropological View of Indian Civilization", Acharya Jagadish Chandra Bose Memorial Lecture (unpublished).

Chattopadhyay, K.P. 1931 "Contact of peoples as affecting marriage rules." Presidential Address, Anthropology Section, Eighteenth Indian Science Congress. Nagpur, India.

Chattopadhyay, K.P. 1994 Essays in Social Anthropology. Kolkata: K.P. Bagchi & Co.

Comte, A. 1830-1842 Cours de Philosophie Positive. Paris: Bachelier.

Durkheim, E. 1915 (1912 orig.) The Elementary Form of the Religious Life. J. W. Swain (trans.), London: Allen & Unwin.

Durkheim, E. 1933 (1893 orig.) Division of Labor in Society. G. Simpson (trans.), New York: Macmillan.

Durkheim, E. 1938 (1895 orig.) The Rules of the Sociological Method. S. Solovay and J. Mueller (trans.), New York : Free Press.

Durkheim, E. 1951 (1897 orig.) Suicide. J. Spaulding and G. Simpson (trans.), New York: Free Press.

Engels, F. 1954 (1884 orig.) Origin of the Family, Private Property, and the State. Ernest Untermann (trans.), Moscow: Foreign Languages Publishing House.

Harris, M. 1968 The Rise of Anthropological Theory. New York: Thomas Y. Crowell.

Hoebel, E.A. 1972 Anthropology: The Study of Man. New York: McGraw-Hill.

Kaberry, P.	1957	"Malinowski's Contribution to Fieldwork Methods and the Writing of Ethnography." Pp. 71-91, In Man and Culture: An Evaluation of the Work of Bronislaw Malinowski ed. by R. Firth. London: Routledge & Kegan Paul.
Kottak, P.C.	2004	Anthropology: The Exploration of Human Diversity. New York : McGraw-Hill.
Kroeber, A.	1944	Configurations of Culture Growth. Berkeley: University of California Press.
Lowie, R.	1937	History of Ethnological Theory. New York: Farrar & Rinehart.
Malinowski, B.	1922	Argonauts of the Western Pacific. New York : Dutton.
Malinowski, B.	1927	Sex and Repression in Savage Society. London: Routledge & Kegan Paul.
Malinowski, B.	1935	Coral Gardens and Their Magic. London: Allen & Unwin.
Malinowski, B.	1939	"The Group and the Individual in Functional Analysis." American Journal of Sociology 44: 938-964.
Marx, K.	1904 (1859 orig.)	The Critique of Political Economy. I.N. Stone (trans.) Chicago: International Library Publication Co.
Morgan, L.H.	1870	Systems of Consanguinity and Affinity of the Human Family. Washington, DC: Smithsonian Institution.
Murdock, G.P.	1963	Outline of World Cultures. New Haven: Human Relations Area Files.
Perry, W.S.	1923	The Children of the Sun. London: Methuen.
Radcliffe-Brown, A.	1949	"Functional: A Protest." American Anthropologist 51: 320-323.
Radcliffe-Brown, A.	1952	Structure and Function in Primitive Society. London: Oxford University Press.
Rivers, W.H.R.	1911	"The Ethnological Analyses of Culture." Presidential Address, Report of the British Association for the Advancement of Science 81:490-499.
Rivers, W.H.R.	1914	The History of Melanesian Society. Cambridge: Cambridge University Press.

Sachchidananda.	1977	"Book Review, Socio-Cultural Profile of Frontier Bengal." Man and Life 3(1 & 2): 129-130.
Sinha, S.C.	1972	"Anthropology of Nirmal Kumar Bose." Pp. 1-22, In Aspects of Indian Culture and Society edt. by S.C. Sinha. Calcutta: The Indian Anthropo-logical Society Publication.
Smith, G.E.	1928	In the Beginning: The Origin of Civilization. New York: Morrow.
Tax, S.	1955	"From Lafitau to Radcliffe-Brown: A Short History of the Study of Social Organization." Pp. 445-481, In Social Anthropology of North American Tribes ed. by F. Eggan. Chicago: University of Chicago Press.
Spencer, H.	1866 (orig. 1864)	Principles of Biology. New York : Appleton.
Spencer, H.	1883 (orig. 1850)	Social Statics. New York: Appleton.
Tylor, E.B.	1865	Researches into the Early History of Mankind and the Development of Civilization. London: J. Murray.
Tylor, E.B.	1889	"On a Method of Investigating the Development of Institutions: Applied to Laws of Marriage and Descent." Journal of the Royal Anthropological Institute 18: 245-269.
White, L.	1959	The Evolution of Culture. New York: McGraw-Hill.

Methodological Approaches in Studying Anthropological Problems

Amal Kumar Mallick

The Anthropologists' interest to make the discipline useful for the benefit of the society gave birth to many concepts leading to the development of different branches of Anthropology. Radcliffe-Brown used the term "Applied Anthropology", and Malinowski "Practical Anthropology." Terminological confusions or controversies as well as debates on the issue of academic theoretical anthropology vs applied anthropology notwithstanding, there is an absolute unanimity about the fact that the field work constitutes the basic hallmark of anthropological studies and there is practically no alternative to this.

The logic behind this approach is that every part of the social life of man, individually or collectively is likely to mirror its cultural history in entirety. Traditional as well as modern ideas and practices find their ways in social behaviour. So what better way of knowing the people in the social context can be devised than the field work among such people in the live situation which is essentially a natural one unadulterated by extraneous variables?

Reliance on experiential field work as the primary context in which anthropological researches are conducted is the distinctive feature of the twentieth century Cultural Anthropology. Primary data are collected by them through living with the people being studied, asking them questions about various aspects of their life, observing their everyday behaviour and interacting with them in the natural setting in their own environment. First hand information thus collected form the basis of modern theories.

The picture was different in the nineteenth century. Morgan's classic work Ancient Society of 1877 was based on the second hand data collected by missionaries, explorers etc., who per chance got glimpses of different cultures. It was Franz Boas who turned the tide in the next century. With the passage of time importance was gradually placed on the discussion of field techniques and field work experience itself. Methodological issues involved in designing a field work study, collecting the data, analyzing the data and drawing conclusions there from are being described in detail to render any ethnographic study dependable.

There are many commonalities regarding problems and issues in all field works. Two field work situations are necessarily different even for a single researcher for the same cultural group, not to speak of the variations with respect to different researchers as well as variations with respect to a particular researcher at different points of time. This is the reason why it is possible to think of methodology regarding field research in Anthropology.

Observation of person(s) in the local setting gives the first hand personal knowledge and it is known as Ethnographic Study. Malinowski, considered as the Father of Ethnography, defined the ethnographer's objective as "to grasp the natives' point of view, *his* relation to life, to realize *his* vision of *his* world". This led to two approaches of Anthropology which are inter-related.

(1) *Emic* : actor-oriented, i.e., 'how natives think' and
(2) *Etic* : observer-oriented, i.e., 'what the observer thinks about the natives' thinking'.

It is only the field study which is capable of giving the correct picture of the people and society.

The field techniques of ethnographers include (1) Participant observation, (2) Interview with interview schedules, (3) Genealogical method, (4) Work with well-informed informants, (5) Life-history collection, (6) *Emic* (actor-oriented) as well as *Etic* (observer-oriented) approaches and (7) Longitudinal studies. Each of them obviously has many advantages and disadvantages which have been described in details in many earlier and contemporary text books on social sciences, specially Anthropology. Depending upon field situations one or more techniques, can be employed, of course subject to the expertise of the researcher.

In earlier times *qualitative methodology* dominated the scene because observations yielded only qualitative data. With the passage of time due to the advancement of methodological knowledge qualitative data are now quantified for statistical treatment. *Quantitative* research techniques like structured interviews and surveys are also being used. Combination of *qualitative* and *quantitative* methods (Bryman, 1988), which complement one another, gives comparatively more reliable picture of the situation. In-depth or intensive study is the characteristic of anthropological research; there is no doubt the need for extensive study, that again in not-too-a long-period. Modern techniques of Rapid Rural Appraisal (RRA), Rapid Assessment Procedures (RAP), Focused Ethnographic Study (FES) etc., are some of the modern techniques widely used in anthropological research.

Broadly speaking, observation and interview (both of various types) are mostly preferred by the field researchers. The techniques used by a researcher vary according to training and interests (not excluding biases) of the researcher concerned, the problem under investigation and the people, *'sine qua non'* of the research.

Since most of field research is done through living among the people, talking with them, observing them and writing down whatever is considered to be significant ; various mechanical aids viz, camera, tape-recorder and many modern gadgets-electronic or otherwise-facilitate these tasks. Those too have many disadvantages. Rowe (1953) has discussed about the aids of earlier times and Beins (2001) enlisted sources about the modern aids to make observational research comparatively more objective.

Besides observation, genealogical method, (Rivers, 1910) Life-history collection (Dollard, 1936), Census Analysis (Richards, 1938), Psychological tests, specially Projective Techniques (Henry & Spiro, 1953) and Folklore-collection (Fischer, 1963) are some of the approaches to field study of the formative period of anthropological research.

Since the days of Radcliffe Brown's (1923) proposition that there are two methods of study of culture or civilization (which according to Tylor is "that complex whole which includes knowledge, belief, art, morals, law, custom and any other capabilities and habits acquired by man as a member of society") viz, "local method" and "inductive method", anthropology has progressed at rapid speed. Many new methods as well as variations of old ones have appeared in the scene. Yet the classic approach of observation and interview still dominate the scene. The cause is not far to seek. The former one is the primary method of data collection in any branch of knowledge, be it in the field of natural science or social science, humanities or law, art or industry. It is primary even in the sense that the new born babe is first acquainted with the world, which seems to be a 'big booming buzzing confusion' to it, through collection of information with the help of all the five sense organs, specially eyes. The observation necessarily includes both connotative and denotative meaning.

Similarly, since communication and interaction are the only means of knowing each other, interview method is also considered as an important method in social sciences and behavioral sciences that is wherever human beings are involved.

So primary anthropological data are to be collected either by observation method or interview method of various types and variations or modifications. Secondary anthropological data, which constitute the rest, may be collected by other methods or in combinations.

In the context of field work Srinivas has talked about three stages that ethnographers have to pass in the process of this field work. A field worker is 'once-born' when he first goes to the field, he is 'twice-born' when he lives among his target population for data collection and he is 'thrice-born' when he returns from the field and prepares his field report.

There are sixty (60) such 'thrice-born' field workers who completed their Doctoral Dissertations under Calcutta University by the guidance of Prof. P. K. Bhowmick.

From the survey of the research work conducted under Prof. P.K. Bhowmick, it is evident that ethnographic work is most preferred branch of anthropology among the researchers. The next preferred topics are related to religion which is another important dimension of anthropological work. Besides, the researchers also have shown their interest in culture and society and contemporary rural and urban problems which are now-a-days the important area of the anthropological research. A few researchers had Masters' Degree in Political Science ; as a result, a special field Rural Institutions and Administrations got place in the anthropological studies. Another important branch, i.e., Applied and Action Anthropology also attracted a good number of students. The unique methodological approaches in the anthropological research studies under the guidance of Prof. Bhowmick have been well represented in the researches conducted. All the works having different anthropological dimensions have clearly revealed the uniqueness of methodological approaches in Anthropology.

References

Atkinson, R. 1998 *The Life History Interview*. Thousand Oaks. California : Sage.

Bailey, K. D. 1987 *Methods of Sociel Research; 3rd Edn.* N.Y : Free Press.

Beins, B. C. 2001 Observational Research. *In* Michie, J. *Encyclopedia of Social Sciences, Vol. 3*. London : Fitzroy Dearborn.

Bryman, A. 1988 *Quantity and Quality in Social Research*. London & Boston : Unwin Hyman.

Cannell, C.
Kahn, R. L. 1968 Interviewing. *In* Lindzey, Garner and Aronson, (Eds.) *Handbook of Social Psychology. 2nd Edn. Vol. 7*, New Delhi Amerind.

Dollard, J. 1936 *Criteria for Life-history*. New Haven : Yale University Press.

Fischer, J. L. 1963 Socio-psychological analysis of folktales. *Current Anthropology*, 4, 235–295.

Gilbert, N. (ed.) 1993 *Researching Social life*. London : Sage

Henry, W. E. &
Spiro M. E. 1953 Psychological Techniques : Projective Tests in Field Work. *In* A.L. Kroeber (ed.) Anthropology Today. Chicago : University of Chicago Press.

Radcliffe-Brown, A. R. 1923 The Methods of Ethnology and Social Anthropology. *South African Journal of Science*, *20*, 124 -147.

Richards, A. I. 1938 The Village Census in the Study of Culture Contact. *In* B. Malimonski (Ed.) Methods of Study of Culture Content in Africa. New York : Oxford University Press.

River, W. H. R. 1910 The genealogical method of anthropological enquiry. *Sociological Review* , 3, 1-12.

Rowes, J. H. 1953 Technical Aids in Anthropology : a Historical Survey. *In* Krober, A. L. (Ed.) *Anthropology Today*. Chicago : University of Chicago Press.

Weick, K. E. 1968 Systematic Observational Methods. *In* Lindzey, Gardner & Aronson, Elliot. *The Handbook of Social Psychology. 2nd Edn.* Vol. 7. New Delhi, Amerindm.

A New Mentality–Professor P.K. Bhowmick

A New Mentality is Even More Important than the New Science and New Technology'–A. W. Whitehead

M. Afsaruddin
Taniya Sharmeen

Prabodh Kumar Bhowmick–not just a name in the list of successful Indian Anthropologist of all time–it is the name that actually symbolizes humanity, integrity, honesty, truthfulness and a great representative of compassion for the oppressed ethnic communities. I remember him, as renowned anthropologist Sol Tax portrayed him 'India's finest intellectual in recognition of his contribution to the advancement of social anthropology in practical'. To me and, I think, to all of us who are engaged and interested in the study of ethnic groups, he had been a great source of inspiration and encouragement. He possessed a surrealistic, extraordinary personality that was totally devoted and dedicated to the well-being of underprivileged ethnic groups of India in general and West Bengal in particular. He studied Anthropology as a holistic human science and by practising that he entered into the inner soul of the underprivileged and deprived communities.

Born in the British colonial era, in a small village called Amdabad situated in the district of Medinipore in West Bengal, P.K. Bhowmick was very much attracted by the 'Quit India' movement and 'Swadeshi' movement. He started his education in a national school when the "Non cooperation Movement" was at its peak. These national schools were very much influenced by the philosophy of Deshbandhu Chittaranjan and Deshpran Birendranath[1] and other prominent patriots. In early days of his academic career, he was swayed by nationalist thinking from his teachers. The strength of nationalist thought was so profound in his mind that in the year 1942 he actively participated in the "Quit India" movement and eventually was sent to prison for two and a half year by the British Raj[2]. This was a crucial part and time in P.K. Bhowmick's life because he carried out this patriotic romanticism of dedicating and devoting one's life for the well-being of the country throughout his entire life. In this period of his life he was indoctrinated with 'peoples' philosophy' and their worldview that shaped up his academic interest and motivated his research works.

After passing the matriculation examination in 1945 he took Anthropology[3] as a major for the intermediate examination. The approach of this unique discipline fascinated him so much that he did his graduation and post graduation in the same subject. The methodologies, research techniques and its approaches toward studying humankind resonated with him to a great extent. Anthropology to him, if I could remember precisely, was the most down to earth discipline if we could understand its depth, and ensure its best use for humanity.

However, in my opinion, labeling P.K. Bhowmick only as an Anthropologist would be very unfair judging his excellence, brilliance and intelligence. As I saw him at work in the Institute of Social Research and Applied Anthropology, working for the Lodhas, Chenchus and other tribes, he was a true social scientist who excelled profoundly in the areas of Sociology, Applied Anthropology, Social and Cultural anthropology and also as an inquisitive linguist. Taking a closer look into his academic writing will help us understand the depth and range of his talent. I would like to mention some of his writings that have profound impact on the study of ethnic communities, to different areas of social, cultural and anthropology of religion as well as practising anthropology at the grass root level. These are:

- The Lodhas of West Bengal–A Socio-Economic Study, (1963)
- Occupational Mobility and Caste Structure in Bengal, (1969)
- Socio-Cultural Profile of Frontier Bengal, (1976)
- Occultism in Fringe Bengal, (1978)
- Some Aspects of Indian Anthropology, (1980)
- Applied Action Development Anthropology, (1989)
- The Chenchus of the Forest and the Plateau–A gathering-hunting Tribe in Transition, (1989)
- Primitive Tribal Groups in Eastern India: Welfare and Evaluation, (1994)
- Rethinking Tribal Culture in India, (2001)
- Caste in Bengal Border, (2002)

Apart from these books in English, P.K. Bhowmick also wrote six books in Bengali and near about 200 academic papers in different renowned journals[4]. His first book The Lodhas of West Bengal–A Socio-Economic Study, helped him to earn the prestigious Ph D degree (then D Sc) from Calcutta University. In his own opinion, this book was one of the best works of his academic career as it changed the course of his and others' life.

After graduating in Anthropology, P. K. Bhowmick decided to devote himself into research but was not sure where to start. At that time, two of his teachers Professor Tarak Chandra Das and Professor Meenen Basu[5] inspired and advised him to do a research on the Lodha Community. When P.K. Bhowmick started his fieldwork in 1952 among the Lodhas many of his colleagues and well-wishers tried to discourage him. Because at that time, 'Lodha' and 'Crime' these two words were synonymous. The Lodha belonging to primitive tribal group of West Bengal are found to be distributed in the Western part of Midnapur, especially in Jhargram, Nayagram, Gopballavpur, Sabang, Binpur and adjacent district of Orissa[6].

Presently, Lodhas are found to be at the fringe area of the forest and most of them are landless labourers. So either they are seen working in agricultural fields or, as non agricultural labours working, say on railway tracks, roads etc. They mainly survive on the collection of forest produces and fuel wood, cotton, roots & tubers and hunting games and fishes, which they continue throughout the year. As they are familiar with the variety of snakes, so they catch snakes and earn money by snake charming and selling the skins of the snakes. They struggle hard for their survival. During lean period, they eke out their existence on collection of mollusk or water lily.

During British regime they were declared as one of the 'criminal tribes', and hunting and gathering was their main economic pursuit. As the British East India Company enforced a novel land use system for maximizing revenue extraction and the zemindars, created by the Permanent Settlement Act of 1793, brought all "unproductive" woodlands under cultivation in order to maximize yield of land revenue. The oppression by zemindars and moneylenders forced the forest tribal of the western districts of Bengal to migrate en masse to neighbouring districts. Permanent Settlement thus marked a watershed in the ecological history of eastern U.P., Bengal, Orissa and Bihar, which sealed the fate of the pristine forest tracts including sacred groves. The Zemindars converted many forestlands into arable lands making the forest dwellers, such as the Lodhas, homeless.

After making the forest dwellers (in this case the Lodhas) homeless, the Zeminders, patronized by the British East India Company brought some neighbouring agrarian communities from the Chotanagpur plateau and Santal Parganas to these lands. These agrarian communities converted these lands and controlled the ownership and production in consequence. After loosing the stakes of their survival and livelihood, the Lodhas did not find any way other than resorting to dacoity, pilferage, and burglary to survive. This criminality made stigma on them and they became oppressed, exploited and neglected by others even after attainment of India's Independence. However, with the efforts of progressive anthropologists like N.K.Bose, P.K. Bhowmick they were first declared as de-notified community in 1951, and, then, came into the list of Scheduled Tribe. Finally, they became Primitive Tribal Group in consequence of the declaration Fifth Plan.

When P.K. Bhowmick decided to do his research among the Lodhas in Midnapore, they (Lodhas) were still tagged by the title British Raj gave them i.e., 'the born criminals'. They were very much oppressed by the local people and were not at all friendly to the strangers. At the beginning of his fieldwork in 1952, P.K. Bhowmick encountered several threats from the community and later he had to seek assistance from the local police station for the time being. For this police connection the Lodhas suspected P. K. Bhowmick as an informer of Police. But with utter patience and tolerance P. K. Bhowmick established rapport with the Lodha community during his fieldwork following the method of participant observation. He thoroughly surveyed 31 Lodha villages in 1952 and collected information regarding their social organization, economic organization, reasons behind criminal activities, and religion with other socio-cultural and economic profile[7] . One of the unique and exceptional features of his study was that he studied the Lodhas from both emic and etic perspectives[8] .

He felt that if the Lodha community is studied from an anthropological perspective using insiders point of view, it will not tell us the both side of the story because the Lodhas were considered to be the 'born criminal tribe' at that time. P.K. Bhowmick, from the very beginning, was a strong believer that there was no such thing as born criminals and always opposed this concept stoutly. To him, it was the ambience, the surrounding environment and unavoidable circumstances that pushed the Lodhas to criminal acts for mere survival. He felt that it was necessary to recognize that all tribal communities are not alike, that they are products of different historical and social conditions and that they belong to four different language families and several different racial stocks and animistic moulds. Some of them belong to the primitive stock with a continuous cultural history, others have been pushed out of the mainstream and have been "drop-outs" of our main history, yet others are created by various legal and economic interventions in society.

P.K. Bhowmick always believed that history has indeed been

extremely unkind to the tribal characteristics of the people. The entire burden of the logic and the rhetoric of modernization have sought to "detribalise" the vast range of these communities. Besides, those communities that are now marked as "tribal" have not been viewed with any degree of respect by the surrounding alienated middle classes and intellectuals. He always emphasized the fact that there is so much in the tribal way of life that the country needs to emulate. Tribals are not known for raping their women, beating and abusing their children, exploiting nature beyond satisfying the minimum human needs, burning widows, and above all things segregating and stratifying labour in terms of caste.

While working among the Lodhas, P.K. Bhowmick realized that a century and a half of deeply flawed education, which has taught us to imitate the West in every respect, has also taught us to leave the tribals out as the apes of the great Indian society to some extent. In addition, all that we have so far doled out in the name of tribal policy is but an attempt at extermination of tribal identity so that they remain without a voice and make space for our progress, become our low-grade clones and provide us with cheap labour. In the process, we have forgotten that much that is valuable in society, culture and heritage is of tribal origin, that in fact the tribal still has so much with him, which we stand to benefit by learning. He carried out these realizations throughout his entire life. After completing his survey and fieldwork among the Lodhas for almost eight years, he submitted his PhD thesis to the University of Calcutta and eventually was awarded the prestigious doctorate degree in 1960. In 1963, he published his book *The Lodhas of west Bengal–A Socio-Economic Study*[9]. Regarding this highly acclaimed publication Legendary social scientist Professor Nirmal Kumar Basu remarked, "In many respects Dr. P. K. Bhowmick's account of the Lodhas is of great value to anthropologists"[10]. However, throughout his fieldwork he published several academic articles in different well-known journals like *Eastern Anthropology, Folklore and Man in India*, etc.

During this prolonged period from 1951 to 1963, he never lost contact with the Lodhas and earnestly was trying to do something for them. Whilst working there he planned to start the process of "Retribalization" initially among the children of Lodha community. He planned to give education to the young Lodhas and considered to detach them from the transgression prone ambience without hampering their cultural identity. At that point, he was encouraged by Professor Sol Tax's famous "Fox Project" that was taken to rehabilitate the Fox Indians in Kansas, America. Inspired by that P.K.

Bhowmick launched his dream project, his brainchild "Bidisa" in 1955 where "Institute of Social Research and Applied Anthropology" was established to practice applied anthropological research[11]. His plan for retribalization became successful in the year 1964 when he started giving general education to the young Lodhas in his ashram known as Bidisa. His aim was to prove that there is no such thing as genetic criminality. He also aimed to educate young Lodhas, prepared them for the wider socio-cultural and economic arena with their identity. His aim was to gain respect, hold identity and at the same time prepared to take part in the larger community and society to re-establish their pride and honor. He never ever aimed to "civilize" them in strong western connotation. He gave his entire life, his total labour for the development of Lodha community. Later he started working for the other communities too realizing the strong urge for developing and formulating a comprehensive tribal policy, which will help both the nation and the tribal people. This dragged him to work among the Chenchus in Andhra Pardesh. His highly acclaimed publication *'The Chenchus of the Forest and the Plateau–a Hunting Gathering Tribe in Transition'* vividly illustrated the changing pattern and the transition of the Chenchu community. It was an important publication that documented the change in their social, economic, cultural and religious organization also shedding light on the factors and confounders responsible for change.

It would be very unfair if we forget about his D Sc Thesis *The Socio-Cultural Profile of Frontier Bengal* which is to me (personally) one of his most outstanding works. He considered eight districts of three provinces that are in the border of West Bengal as a specific zone. In this book, he sketched the socio-cultural outline as well as the change in traditional livelihood. He also discussed about the geo-political and cultural history of this area and gave us a detailed account on the rural profile, reorientation of religion, status and rank mobility, reinforcement of social relations and assimilation and isolation of the frontier Bengal. After this magnum opus, he wrote *Occultism in Fringe Bengal* which discussed elaborately the rites-rituals, magic and the *mantra-tantra* (black and white magic) used in the districts of frontier Bengal and their influence in daily life.

The above discussion gives only a glimpse of this eminent man's academic accomplishments. His other writing on Applied and Development anthropology are also considered as the pioneer writings in Anthropology of South Asia. His writing on the primitive tribal groups in Eastern India where he discussed about the welfare and evaluation process and another book titled *Rethinking Tribal Culture in India* are the most referred to books in all writings on Indian as well as Asian tribal studies. Since his work with the Lodhas and Chenchus, he started advocating his thoughts regarding the necessity of understanding the cultural, social and political systems of ethnic community from their perspective. He felt that it is necessary to recognize that the tribal polity is more closely regulated by the aesthetic pulse rather than ethical drives, and, therefore, the implementation of the tribal self-governance provisions will have to go hand in hand with a special programme for encouraging tribal arts, oral traditions and their unique skills in crafts. If we fail to recognize this difference, which is vital to the social organization of tribal communities, and fail to respect it, we will end up creating bands of forced nomads who will multiply the urban chaos already overburdened with problems. His dream project Bidisa was actually established for promoting these ideas and disseminate various education, art and aesthetic programmes for the local Lodha community.

While inviting scholars from Europe, North America and other countries of the world for various purposes like pure academic activities, seminars and workshops at Bidisa (in the Institute of Social Research and Applied Anthropology), Prabodh Kumar Bhowmick always wanted to spread his dream among his friends, colleagues and disciples. Working for the oppressed, unprivileged ethnic communities was his motto. Institute of Social Research and Applied Anthropology at Bidisa is an embodiment of his spirit. He was also explicitly interested in expanding horizon of Action and Applied Anthropology and application of Anthropological knowledge for solving practical problems of life and society. Bidisa also provided a breeding ground and a springboard for many young anthropologists at home and abroad.

In addition to P.K. Bhowmick's academic accomplishments, he was a great teacher and an immense source of inspiration and encouragement to all his students. He was the most admired faculty among the students of Calcutta University. His exceptional record of supervising 60 successful Ph D students all over the subcontinent illustrates how great a soul he was. Outside India, many of his Ph D students have become professors in different universities in Bangladesh. I remember him taking several viva voce examinations as an expert, and chairing the Ph D Exam Committee in Department of Sociology, University of Dhaka as well as other Universities in Bangladesh.

I remember P.K. Bhowmick as an ultimate source of motivation to all of us particularly who are engaged in the study of ethnic groups as well as practising action anthropology. In my personal experience, he was such a devoted and dedicated person for the well-being of tribal community that he actually considered himself as one of them. He was the "Uncle or Jyatha" to the Lodha children. He dedicated all his life for the development of these under privileged groups and, sometimes in his own words "even neglected" his personal household and family priorities. Although accomplishing so many achievements and excellences, he was the most down to earth person that I have ever seen. Always wearing *khaddar kurta* and *pajama* he never thought about self-interest. He lived a very simple life with high thinking. He always stayed at Bidisa, away from the comforts of his home at Kolkata. His only mission was to live and work for the under privileged ethnic communities for whom he spent many valuable years of his life even sometimes neglecting the duties and responsibilities towards his family. It was possible in my opinion, only due to his better half Shreemati Latika Bhowmick.

It is said that behind every successful man there is a woman, this was very true in P. K. Bhowmick's life. His wife, my respected Latika *Boudi,* is an amazing and outstanding person who supported not only emotionally but also economically this unassuming extra ordinary person. While I was in Calcutta for my medical check up, I stayed at their house and I recollect three of us chatted for long hours about ups and downs of our life. P. K. Bhowmick was praising Boudi and telling me how she gave away all of her jewelries and valuable belongings to fulfill P. K. Bhowmick's dream project at Bidisa or to help poor students. I recall P. K. Bhowmick telling me about the emotional downfalls of his life at the loss of their daughter, the controversial case on him by the university authority, and a person forged his signature and made false documents. I was amazed by the strength of his personality, his integrity, his patience and by his honesty how he fought at the court and made the University to return his degree with utmost honour.

His contribution to the field of Social Science was so vast that it can hardly be matched. His sincerity towards the well-being and development of the ethnic communities was so immense that subcontinent had lost not only an extraordinary anthropologist or social scientist but also an eminent policy thinker and an astonishing human being who but come once in every hundred years. I will never forget his cordiality, kindliness and warmth for his family, friends, disciples, students or to his subordinates. Lastly, I would like to conclude this obituary reference by quoting a line from the condolence letter that I sent to Samita Manna, Professor of Sociology in the University of Kalyani, daughter of Professor P. K. Bhowmick, "We may have professors of erudition but not with the human qualities your father had cultivated for the under privileged ethnic groups". May his soul rest in peace forever.

References

1. Ray, Pranab 2004 Adhyapok Prabodh Kumar Bhowmick : Karma-o- Jiban-Darshan. Calcutta p. 4.
2. Ibid., p. 5.
3. Ibid., p. 5.
4. Ibid., p. 269-281
5. Ibid., p. 5.
6. Debnath, Debashis 2002 Hunter-gatherers in India: A study on hunting gathering activities as economic pursuits as well as rituals among the tribals in Eastern part of India, Edinburgh Conference on hunting and gathering societies, Edinburgh, UK
7. Ray, Pranab. 2004 Adhyapok Prabodh Kumar Bhowmick : Karma-o- Jiban-Darshan. Calcutta p. 181
8. These two concepts first used by Kenneth Pike.
9. Ray, Pranab. 2004 Adhyapok Prabodh Kumar Bhowmick : Karma-o- Jiban-Darshan. Calcutta p. 191
10. Ibid.
11. Ibid., p. 186.

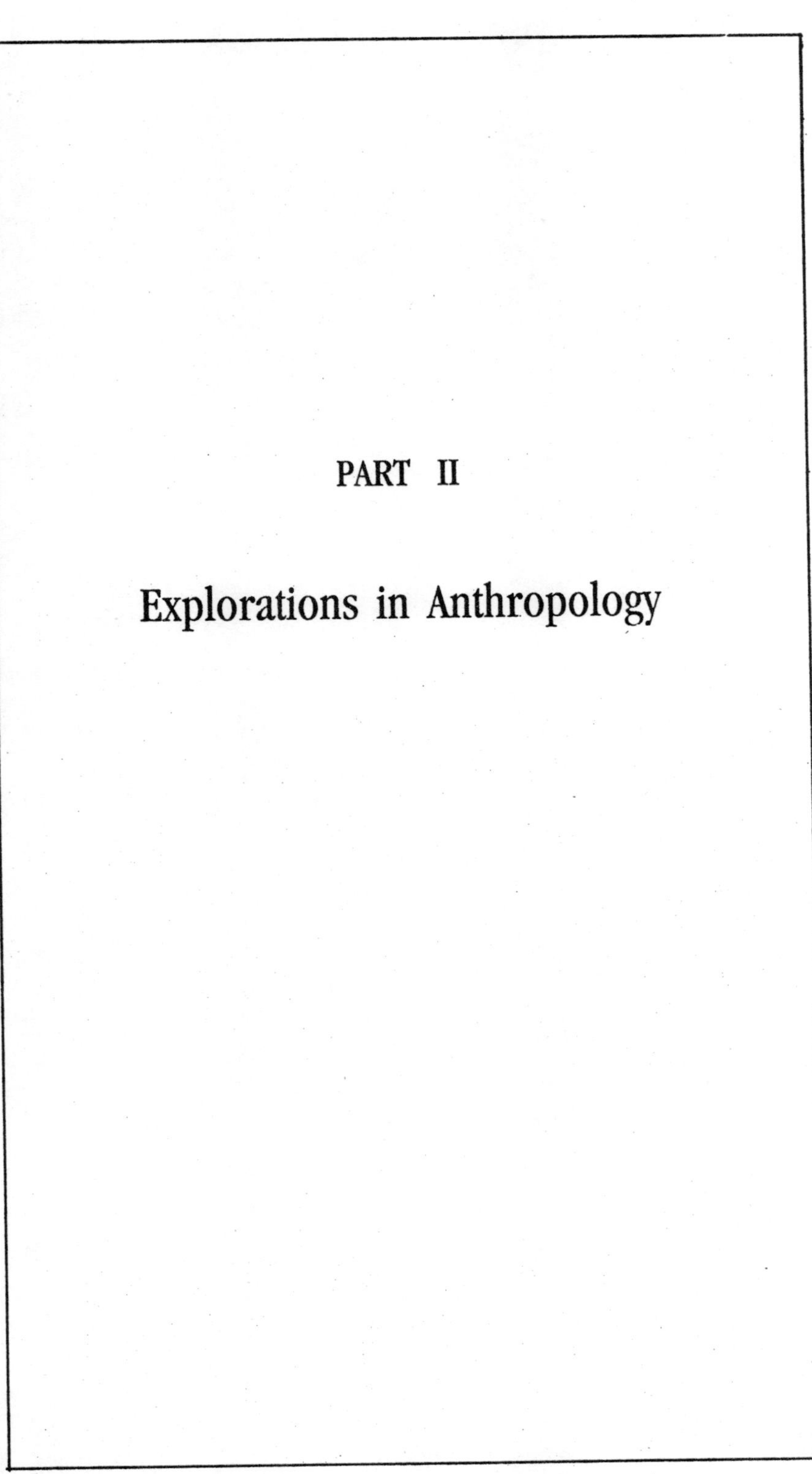

PART II

Explorations in Anthropology

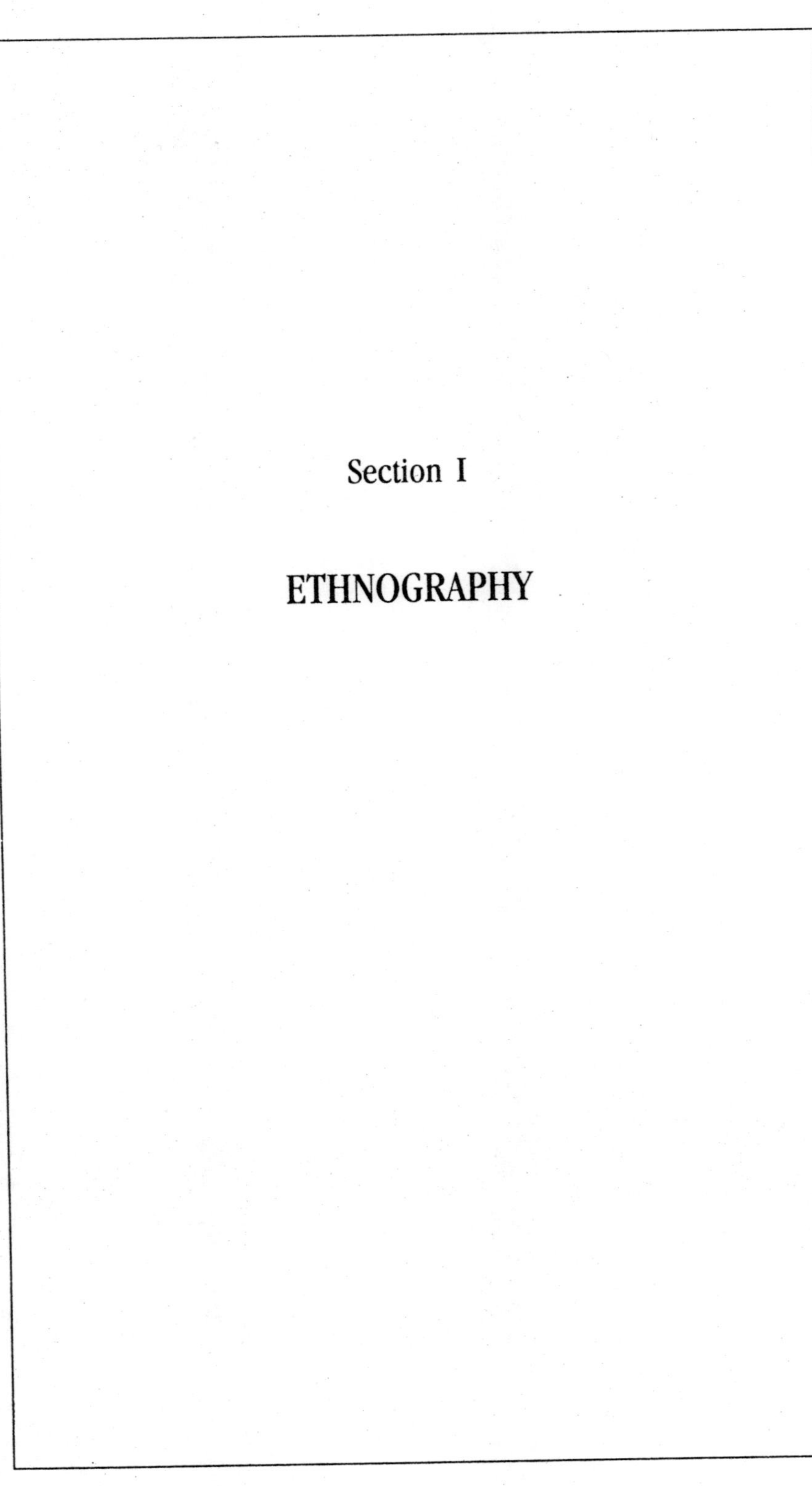

Section I

ETHNOGRAPHY

Introduction

Manis Kumar Raha

Ethnography as defined by Lowie "is the science which deals with the 'Cultures' of human group" (1937 :3). Here by 'culture' Lowie meant "the sum total of what an individual acquires from his society– those beliefs, customs, artistic norms, food habits, and crafts which come to him not by his creative activity but as a legacy from the past, conveyed by formal or informal education (ibid)".

According to Radin "Ethnology should be one of the easiest subjects in the world to define. It is manifestly the study of the culture of aboriginal peoples, more specifically these aborigines with whom the Europeans have come into contact since the fifteenth century" (1966:3). Radin made this definition to realize that today it has come to mean both more or less than such a definition would seem to imply (ibid).

As regards the origin of Ethnology, Radin thinks that "Ethnology in the narrower sense of the terms owes its origin to those studies of customs and beliefs of mankind that began in the seventeenth century and received their clear expression in eighteenth....Ethnological theory was cultivated long before it ever dawned upon students that each primitive group had a specific culture and a very specific history" (1966 : 253).

While considering the relation of ethnography with the sister disciplines, Lowie is of opinion that ethnography is that part of anthropology "which is not primarily concerned with races as biological division of Homo Sapiens, and does not interest itself in the psychology of individuals except in so far as it reflects or influences society" (1937 : 3).

Meiners on the other hand did not accept the fact that ethnography covered total culture of human being or a group of human being. While analyzing Meiners' works, Lowie found that Meiners "treated man's bodily diversity along with his social characteristics, but what was far worse–he arbitrarily selected for discussion certain phases of social tradition to the exclusion of others" (cf Lowie 1937 : 10). For example, Meiners eliminated religion from ethnological studies for mere convenience sake. He also less defensibly disregarded all "but a few of the most remarkable customs–for to describe and explain all the practices of all people" (ibid : 11). Gustav Klemm according to Lowie was "clearer in his formulation and a more potent influence on research". Klemm collected information about different aspects of culture of human being. But Klemm was prone to accept uncritically the psychological judgments of travelers and is equally naïve in connecting mentality with geography–(cf Lowie 1937 : 15). Waltz on the other hand, was very cogent in comparing civilized and uncivilized conditions. In his studies he had stressed that the "the degree of culture is ... far less an index of innate endowment than the vicissitudes of history" (cf. Lowie 1937 : 17).

However, in connection with ethnology Lowie has reacted that "ethnology implies an orderly arrangement of date, the verifiability of its findings, a logical basis of its conclusions. But in conforming to the canons of all sciences it must not adopt the particular techniques of physics, or geology except where the cultural data as such demand such course" (1937 : 280).

But ethnology "is bound to rank co-ordinate with other sciences insofar as it continues to investigate objectively and intensively that segment of reality which falls to its province" (ibid : 291). It clearly indicates that Lowie is against the induction of techniques from other pure and biological sciences. In connection with the prospect of ethnology, Lowie feels that "our science as a whole can neglect no aspect of social life as intrinsically inferior to the 'rest' and 'its hope lies in maintaining the universalist and objective approach....' " (ibid : 290).

Another important purpose of ethnology, but a secondary function, "is of examining the validity of the theories of the evolutionary school' and this secondary function led to the stressing of a number of problems that were clearly by-products". (1966 :4).

The ethnographic study which was a part of Anthropology as the Indian Anthropologists think, entered India through the colonial rulers. In fact the ethnological studies started sometimes after the British established their supremacy in India. The British Government felt that in order to tighten the control on the people and run the administration smoothly and efficiently their administrators should have considerable knowledge about the culture and language of different groups of people of India. The British government advised their administrators to acquire knowledge about different groups of people of India having different racial affinity, different ethnicity, different language and culture in different areas with variable ecological condition and so on and also the area they inhabit. Being inspired and instructed by the British Government some of the British civil servants took up the project of studying the people, their language and culture and also their habitat. Some other civil servants of their own, got interested of the Indian culture, and studied them and their land. In order to assist the administration, some scholarly oriented British administrators posted in different parts of India, were assigned to undertake specific studies (Vidyarthi 1974 : 5–6). This decision of the colonial administration prompted those scholar administrators to study different ethnic groups in almost all parts of India and ethnographic glossaries from north, east, south, west and central parts of India were published.

These studies mainly began sometimes early eighteenth century and continued till early twentieth century.

The establishment of the Asiatic Society in India in 1774 by Sir William Jones helped a large number of the civil servants and others to publish their findings on many groups of people, their languages and culture and also on the land they lived. "Particularly due to the influence of the Asiatic Society, a series of such studies were initiated during the second half of the eighteenth century" (Danda 1996 : 5-6).

The establishment of Royal Asiatic Society in Bengal (at present the Asiatic Society) brought a new dimension in the anthropo-ethnological studies in India. It undoubtedly played a very "dynamic role in furnishing knowledge about man, nature and culture through its researches and publications. The pioneering activities of the Society stimulated the British administrators, scholars, missionaries, travelers, etc. to undertake surveys and investigations amongst the tribes and castes in different parts of India (Das 1997 : 9).

It is not that all these ethnographic studies were undertaken by the civil servants and others, but some anthropologists also showed keen interest on the people of India. They also studied specific groups of people along with the non-anthropologists. These anthropologists were mainly the non-Indians. The Indian anthropologists started their work during much later period as anthropology as a discipline began functioning only in 1920 in the University of Calcutta. Therefore ethnographical works began much earlier than the anthropology entered India.

Though the ethnographic study as a scientific study started in India with the British occupation in India, but a number of ancient Indian literatures give good account of the life and activities of different groups of people. "India's traditional literature such as *Manava Dharmasastra* (1350 B.C. literarily Sacred Science of Man), *Kaulilya's Arthashastra* (1320 B.C.), *Charaksamhita* (1st/2nd Century AD),

Susrutasamhita (around 4th Century AD), *Vatsayans' Kamasutra* have important anthropological bearings. These literatures provide important information on socio-cultural and physical anthropology as well applied and medical anthropology (Danda 1995 :24 :38), Das 2000 : 106). Sketchy accounts on the socio-cultural life of the some Indian people in the diaries of Buddhists monks, travelers, missionaries, and such other persons are also available. Even the employees of the then East India Company wrote down many things about Indian life and culture in their diaries. The accounts of the British officials also give us a better picture about the economy, ecology, socio-cultural life, religious beliefs and practices, political activities etc. of the people (Das 1997 : 5-13).

In addition, journals like *Indian Antiquary, Asiatic researches, Journal of Bihar and Orissa Research Society, Man in India* and such other journals also published many good ethnographic/anthropological works.

Even before the beginning of the Anthropology as a discipline, a good number of ethnographic studies on both tribal and non-tribal people were undertaken. While some of these are quite lengthy, some others are small and sketchy. These accounts have been published in reports, accounts, census reports, and even in book forms such as survey and settlement reports, statistical accounts etc. Most of the authors of these ethnographic notes, reports and books have been written mostly by non-anthropologists and partly by foreign anthropologists.

But with the introduction of anthropology in Indian Universities, gradually Indian anthropologists came to the field. They primarily undertook ethnographic study and selected mainly the tribal groups as their subject. Therefore after anthropology was introduced as a discipline in Indian Universities, a good number of ethnographic studies were published in book form. A large number of ethnographic notes were also published in different journals and periodicals.

A survey of the ethnographic literature on tribes that appeared between 1979 and 1988 in book form, or articles in journals was published some years ago (Danda 1996). This survey was undertaken in order to assess the emerging trends of the tribal studies in India. Danda could spell out six broad aspects after analyzing the available information.

1. General Ethnographic study of tribes.
2. Social aspects of life of the people incorporating information on family, marriage, kinship, political organization, structure of the society and such others.

3. Cultural Aspects, highlighting beliefs, rituals, customs, values, worldview and such others.
4. Economic Aspects primarily depicting livelihood pattern.
5. Development particularly highlighting what has been the outcome of various induced programmes introduced by the Government. This includes improved methods of agriculture, animal husbandry, land development, irrigation, establishment of schools, health canters, promotion of crafts and industries, and such others. Evaluation reports on various development schemes have also been included in this category.
6. Trends of change incorporating information on the processes involved like modernization, industrialization, urbanization, Sankskritization, Hinduization and so on.

Further, it is also seen that since the beginning of anthropological studies in India till the present era, whatever works have been produced in our country, majority are tribal ethnography. Danda has also confirmed this. He writes, "Any account of the history of anthropology both as a body of knowledge as well as an academic discipline, evidently demonstrate its major preoccupation with tribal ethnography" (1996 :14). The Indian Anthropologists had and still have an inherent desire to study tribal people and their culture. This trend continued till late fifties. During sixties Anthropologists took a small turn from this trend. They continued to study tribal people and their culture ethnographically, but they started to focus on certain specific problem–faced by the tribal people. Say for example changes in their culture due to some external and/or internal factors, economic crises, impact of industrialization and urbanization, processes of Sanskritization and so on". For obvious reasons, with the passage of time, particularly in the context of the developing nations, trends of change in the life of the tribal people and their cultures became an important area of enquiry if not the most important one. As a result, despite continued interest in ethnographic exercises instead of tribal ethnography as such, the tribal studies including tribal ethnography, emerged as the most important sub-discipline of anthropology (Danda 1996 : 14-15). No doubt so many very valuable ethnographic works have been done and no doubt till date many scholars and students of Anthropology are still interested in the ethnographic studies, especially tribal ethnography, even then with the progress, advancement and diversification of Anthropology, particularly when academicians have been bent towards specific problems of the humanity, ethnography could not make much headway for different reasons. Danda has also felt that "tribal ethnography during the decade not only suffered in terms of extent of coverage, the same seems to lack both precision and depth" *(1996 :15).*

While analyzing the available ethnographic materials from different tribes of different areas of India, Danda has marked some variation of tribal studies done in different states and Union Territories. He has also noticed some gaps both region-wise and tribe-wise. But more important gap which the author has noticed, is the thematic gaps in these studies (1996 : 31-34).It is expected that these gaps should be taken care of by the future anthropologists and ethnologists/ ethnographers and a 'total' study will be produced.

In this section of the book the editors have included abstracts/ summary of some Ph.D. dissertations. These dissertations were prepared by scholars under the able guidance of Late Prof. P.K. Bhowmick and subsequently they were awarded the Ph.D. degree. Most of these are ethnographic studies. Below I briefly describe the works done by the scholars.

The first work was on the Bauri, a Scheduled Caste of West Bengal. Late K. C. Shasmal did this work in 1967. The title of the dissertation was *The Bauris of West Bengal.* The study shows the life and activities of these Bauris of Hooghly district of West Bengal. Their contact with high caste Hindus brought many changes in their culture and in this way their status in the society have been up-graded.

The next dissertation was *Culture and Society of the Gadabas of Andhra Pradesh* written by A.V. Subba Rao. All through this dissertation the author discussed culture and society of the Gadabas, a primitive tribe of Andhra Pradesh. He studied this tribe in Visakhapatnam and Srikakulam districts. The culture and society of the Gadabas are in the process of modernization.

S. K. Sengupta in his dissertation on *Society and Economy of the Mahalis of Midnapur* undertook the study in 25 villages inhabited by the Mahalis. The traditional occupation of the Mahalis was basket making. But with the change of situation they have to depend on other sources of income like share-cropping, labour, etc. The change of occupation has also brought changes in their socio-cultural life.

The next dissertation was by Dipali Ghosh (Danda) who worked, on the Dimasa Culture entitled *Life in Kachari village : Dimasa Life way.* The unique social structure is the unique feature of the Dimasa Society. Among them descent is traced through both father's father and mother's father. Their contact with alien culture, exposure to market economy, introduction of the district council and acceptance of a large number of Hindu cultural traits have brought enough changes in their culture.

Late Himangsu Mohan Ray submitted his dissertation on *The Savara–A snake charming community of West Bengal* in 1978. The Savara are a semi-nomadic group and they mainly earn their livelihood through snake-charming. Through his study the author made emphasis on ecological adaptation. Their traditional occupation was snake-charming but deforestation and wild life rules forced them to move for some other occupations. They have also adopted many Hindu traits.

In 1979 Loknath Soni submitted his dissertation on the Rauts, a nomadic cattle-harder group inhabiting Chhattisgarh. They have now accepted agriculture along with cattle-herding. So a shift from pastoral economy to an agro-based economy is noticed among them.

The Dhimal is a community in Estern Nepal with agriculture as their main source of economy. Dr. Rishikeshab Regmi in 1984 submitted his dissertation on *Society and Economy of the Dhimal.*

Rajat Kanti Das in 1986 submitted his dissertation on *An Analytical Study of the Maring Society of Manipur.* They claim that they do not belong either to the Naga or the Kuki group of tribes. The Maring are guided by strong in-group feeling. The authority based sucession and principle of seniority are basic guiding principles of their social structure.

A study on the *Socio-Cultural Life of the Kuki of Manipur* was undertaken by T.S. Gangte in 1990. He studied this tribal group on historical perspective. He examined the operating forces which played important role in their day-to-day living. With the introduction of modern education, spread of Christianity, impact of development programmes and many other factors brought marked changes in their life and activities.

Bijay Kumar Behera undertook a study on the *Socio-Cultural change among the Kondh.* The study highlights the nature and processes of change in the socio-cultural life of the Kondh of Baliguda area of Phulbani District, Orissa.

An Ethnohistory of the Koras of West Bengal was studied by A. K. Jana. The Kora have much resemblance with the Santals. The author studied this group in great details and covered their way of life, social institutions, rite-de-passage, magico-religious life etc.

The next study was undertaken by Madhumala Chattopadhyay. She studied the *Child and Maternal Health among the Nicobarese of Car Nicobar Island.* The study highlighted that the health of the Nicobarese mothers and children (0-6 years) of interior village is better than that of the Nicobarese mothers and children (0–6 years) of the exposed villages.

Niranjan Ghatak undertook a study on *the Bhoksa–A Little Known Tribe of Uttar Pradesh.* These people are agriculturist and also have some expertise on handicraft. The study highlighted different aspects of their life and activities and also changes in their culture due to different external and/or internal forces.

References

Danda, A. K. 1995 *Foundation of Anthropology in India*. New Delhi : Inter India.

Danda, A. K. 1996 *Tribal Ethnography. Research in Sociology and Social Anthropology : Third Survey.* New Delhi : ICSSR.

Das, A. K. 1997 *Tribal Research and Training : Trends of Activities through decades in West Bengal,* 39(1).

Das, A. K. 2000 Development Needs of the Tribal people and Applied Research through Plan periods. *Man and Life,* 26(1& 2).

Lowie, R. H. 1937 *The History of Ethnological Theory*. New York: Rinehart and Co.

Radin, P. 1966 *The Method and Theory of Ethnology*. New York : Basic Books.

Vidyarthi, L.P. 1974 The Rise of Anthropology in India and Tribal Ethonography. *Bulletin of C.R.I.,* 10 (1 & 2).

Society and Economy of the Mahalis of Midnapur, West Bengal

Syamalkanti Sengupta

This study on the Mahali and their economy is an outcome of research done from an empirical point of view. The frame of reference of this work was *Society and Economy of the Mahalis of Midnapur: The Earning Patterns of Tribal Basket Makers.* This work was done from the perspective of *Economic Anthropology*. The economy of the Mahalis as basket makers was that of small scale in nature. Their products of basketry were mainly for three categories of consumers: the *Kisan* (peasants), *Jhuri Mahajan* (basket traders) and *Pan Mahajan* (betel leaf dealers). This research was the outcome of the painstaking field work in 25 villages in Midnapur, West Bengal. The work was shaped to unveil the embeddedness of economy in the Mahali society. The spatial distribution of the Mahali population in 25 villages was considered to compare the small-scale economy of the basket makers of different ecological requirements in a given point of time. Thus synchronic appraisal was analysed empirically. Maximization of income was reflected through consumers' interests on the products of the Mahali. Three categories of consumers appeared at the very outset in the choice of the products : the peasant, the betel leaf dealers and the basket traders. Pricing was determined on demand as per market principles of three types: the peasant market, the betel leaf growers or betel leaf dealers' market and basket traders' market. To the Mahali they were known respectively as *Kisan haat, Paan chasi* or *Pan mahajan haat* and *Jhuri mahajan haat*.

This research comprised of two major areas : the impact on the economy of the tribe concerned and their social profiles. In the former area, the theoretical assessment of the separate tools and concepts and their needs for understanding small-scale economies where mode of transaction depended on reciprocity, redistribution and limited market exchange, were considered. In the later area, embeddedness of small-scale economies in social structural predisposition were looked into and analysed.

The economy of the Mahali was delineated through their

attachment with the twin occupations of basketry and agriculture. The nature and extent of basketry and its place in Mahali economy was explained through types of production and its maximization within the enclave of the basket makers, basket traders and the betel leaf dealers. As the author has shown their inclination towards agriculture became unavoidable due to the fall of steady income from their traditional occupation.

The social profiles on the other hand, exhibited the size and composition of families, kinship terminologies and behaviour, concept and treatment of diseases with ethno-medicine by the Mahali herbalists and spirit finders, role of witchcraft in controlling over-exploitation of resources for basketry products. The researcher also analysed the concepts of sacred and profane and the role of rituals, festivals in the life of the community as a whole.

The issue of comparison between the society and economy of the Mahali of Midnapur and the Mahali of West Dinajpur was also considered by the researcher. But though both the districts are situated in West Bengal and in reality West Dinajpur had the highest Mahali population but the economic opportunities in those two districts were different. The West Dinajpur Mahali seldom found any scope to sell their baskets to the betel leaf dealers because the status of betel leaf growers in that area was very weak. Thus basket traders as a separate category of Mahali basket consumer were non-existent. The Mahali there, purely prepared baskets to meet the peasants' requirements. This situation dictated the Mahali to produce profuse number of baskets for sustained living for the peasant market but this market was not conditioned for bulk supply. Besides, the raw materials or green bamboo with which Mahali did their basketry works were not adequate. The bamboo groves available in the villages could bear the load of 15-20 families of Mahali inadequately for three months. Therefore, the sustenance for other nine months depended on agricultural production as *bhagh-chasi* (share cropper) or *kisan* (owner cultivators) of small parcel of lands or *munish* (agricultural labourer) on daily wage basis. These conditions reflected the notion of the dependence of the Mahali on twin occupations like that of Midnapur only with the difference that in West Dinajpur the Mahali dominantly depend on agriculture where as in Midnapur they were predominantly dependent on basketry having cash income from the *Jhuri Mahajan* and *Pan Mahajan* successively. The Midnapur Mahali always tried to do over exploitation of the bamboo groves of the village which only allowed limited number of Mahali families usually eight to ten families per village. Thus the small-scale economy of the Mahali became different in two districts as they were operating in two different ecological settings. Therefore the economy of the Mahali in Midnapur offered a kind of demand-supply scheme of pricing of the baskets based on the maximization of the production whereas the Mahali basketry in West Dinajpur hardly followed the maximization principle because of the paucity of raw materials and limited demand of the products by the peasants. Therefore, this work on the earning patterns of the Mahali of Midnapur revealed the small-scale economy of the tribe in question and presented a separate economic pattern than that of the Mahali of West Dinajpur.

In explaining the situation of research on Mahali the numerical position of the Mahali was taken into account. From different census report it was indicated that the West Dinajpur comprised of highest Mahali population and Midnapur was just after it. Midnapur drew the attention of the present researcher because of the uniqueness of the location of the Mahali within an ecological situation.

Accordingly the present researcher prepared the frame of reference in grasping the small-scale economy of the Mahali and how their economy was embedded in society. In doing research on the Mahali and their production of basketry, the researcher came across a situation which were influenced by the betel leaf cultivation in the area of his study. Centering round this cultivation there emerged two categories of people: the betel leaf dealers popularly known as *Pan Mahajan* and the basket traders known as *Jhuri Mahajan*. The betel leaf dealers urgently required big baskets or *Jhuri* for the packing of betel leaf for supply in different places of India. This market situation attracted the basket traders to purchase and accumulate baskets from the Mahali to supply them to the betel leaf dealers. The Mahali found no chance to visit the betel leaf dealers directly but to sell their baskets to the basket traders. Thus the sizes of the baskets, the quantity of the baskets and the time of supplying the baskets were controlled by the *Jhuri Mahajan*. Naturally the *Jhuri Mahajan* as intermediary influenced the pricing and volume of manufacture of the baskets. The principles of maximization were only operative on the demand of the baskets by the *Pan Mahajan*. The basket traders sometimes created artificial dearth of baskets to exercise control over the *Pan Mahajan* to procure baskets at higher rate. Similarly the production of baskets by the Mahali was controlled by the basket traders which sometimes put economic pressure on the Mahali by releasing artificial pressure on the demand when both the supply and the production of the baskets by the Mahali decreased. This situation directed the Mahali to seek income from the other sources like share cropping, agricultural day labouring and other job of labourers under the contractor in different construction works.

The Mahali economy was of a special kind. Professor Bhowmick my research guide, by virtue of his acquaintance with the rural problems and the economy of the Midnapur understood the dependence of the Mahali on twin occupations. His insistence on empiricism drove me to collect data from 25 villages in different areas of undivided Midnapur. He seldom made any compromise even though it was a time consuming, painstaking fieldwork over a spatially distributed Mahali at a given point of time. For making a synchronic study he insisted on me to compare economy of the Mahali resided in different police stations. His empiricism was reflected through his research guidance and his wide range of personal publications.

Life in Kachari Village–
Dimasa Lifeway : An Ethnographic Study

Dipali Danda

The study of Dimasa culture was undertaken by me under the guidance of Prof. N. K. Bose and Prof. P. K. Bhowmick. Initially the idea was to write on a particular aspect of their life; that is, being relatively isolated and located in interior forests how do they react to the advent of cash economy. As my initial contact with these people was through market, this aspect of their life preoccupied my thoughts. After some field exposure specially with Prof. Bose my attention fell on their descent systems which is unique in global context. But as my intimacy grew the emphasis on harmony in Dimasa culture fascinated me more. Finally I decided to make a holistic study of the Dimasa life and culture with special emphasis on their social structure. This was how the study of *Life in Kachari Village–Dimasa (Kachari) Lifeway : An Ethnographic Study* was undertaken by me.

The Dimasa constitute one of the Kachari tribes of Assam. The literal meaning of the word Dimasa is river folk. 'Di' means Water and 'Sa' means son, that is, the people who are the 'sons of water'. In actual practice they prefer to live by the side of rivers. Linguistically, the Dimasa belong to the Boro group of Tibeto-Burman family. The exact place from where they migrated to the valley of Assam is yet a matter of speculation. No available historical record gives detail of their place of origin and route of migration. The other branches of Kachari tribes, i.e., the Boro Kachari and the Sonowall Kachari are concentrated in the Goalpara and Sibsagar district, respectively. The Dimasa are concentrated in the district of the united Miker and North Cachar Hills. (of late, Miker Hills has been cut out from the United Miker and North Cachar Hills to form a separate District Karbi Ablong).

Until 1961, the Dimasa had been treated as a sub-tribe of the Kachari tribes. In the 1961 census, they were classified as a separate tribe and the total population of the Dimasa of United Miker and North Cachar Hills was 210, 705, the males and females being 110,313 and 110,392 respectively (Census of India 1961).

During 1964-65 I conducted field investigation among the Dimasa in United Miker and North Cachar Hills districts of Assam. In 1966 I visited them again to supplement the data already collected during the first phase of fieldwork. On one occasion I stayed with the people continuously for six months. Staying elsewhere it was not easy to visit the village everyday as they are situated in the interior forest surrounded by hills far away from the semi-urban centre. Another major difficulty was to get a house in a Dimasa village as they usually do not allow a non-Dimasa to get into their house. The situation had become more difficult as I was a woman. But when I had earned their confidence my identity as a woman researcher contributed a lot to discover many finer naunces of Dimasa culture through women informants. I had access everywhere and was allowed to observe and participate in different socio-religious functions. I was specially invited to attend all ceremonies, feasts and festivals that took place during my stay in the village. In certain cases the Dimasa women were forbidden to attend some of the ceremonies. But they became so liberal to me that at one stage nothing could happen in the village without my presence or knowledge.

All the villages are homogenous, i.e., inhabited by the Dimasa people only. It is commonly observed that their villages are located in a particular tract where their concentration is more. It is almost axiomatic that there must be a river flowing near the village, which proves the myth that the Dimasa people love rivers. In North Cachar Hills most of the Dimasa villages and towns are named after the names of rivers flowing nearly (for eg., Haflong, Maibang, Maher etc.). The neighbouring people of the Dimasa are Kuki and Zemi naga.

Agriculture is the mainstay of the Dimasa economic life. For their subsistence, they mainly depend on shifting cultivation locally known as *Jhum.* The land of the Dimasa village can be divided into three types. These are the *jhum* land, dry land and wet land. The *jhum* lands are those where slash and burn methods of cultivation are practised. Mixed cropping is done in the *jhum* field. The dry fields are used primarily for the cultivation of mustard seeds. This land can be cultivated for consecutive years. Naturally, the ownership of this type of land is more or less permanent. The dry lands are usually situated on the plains whereas the *jhum* lands are situated on small hills. The wet lands are used for the cultivation of paddy. The ownership of such land is also permanent. The wet lands are taxable, the *jhum* and the dry lands are tax free.

The economy of a Dimasa village is not self-sufficient. Because of their partial dependence on cash crops (mustard and cotton) they are rather compelled to establish economic relationship with other communities through mostly market transactions. A market, apart from its economic aspect, is an essential institution to the Dimasa. It is the main outlet and the information centre to them.

The uniqueness of Dimasa social structure lies in their descent system. They present a case of double descent. Double descent is found in six widely scattered cultural areas, viz., West Africa, Bantu speaking South Africa, India, Australia, Melanesia and Polynesia. Everywhere it shows some local variation in terms of residence and social organization as per the socio-cultural adaptation of the group practising it. In India it is so far represented by the Dimasa tribe of Assam.

The Dimasa trace their descent both from their father's father and from mother's mother ignoring father's mother and mother's father. Double descent among them shows some sort of gender-bias. A man primarily reckons his descent from paternal grand father and concurrently from maternal grand mother. A woman primarily reckons her descent through her maternal grand mother and then from paternal grand father. The Ego is affiliated with both of his/her paternal and maternal ancestors with one speciality, that the importance and intensity of affiliation vary according to the sex of the Ego. A kind of sexual dimorphism is thus observed in this respect. In brief, the characteristics of double descent of the Dimasa may be enumerated as follows.

1. It is reckoned through both paternal grand father and maternal grand mother.
2. Gender bias is very much conspicuous in determining one's descent group.
3. Coexistence of double clan system is manifested through primary and secondary affiliation.
4. Primary affiliation perpetuates for generations in vertical line and secondary affiliation transmits in zigzag fashion in alternate generation.

Owing to double descent an individual has to operate between two descent groups which ultimately locates double clan system in the society in the form of patriclan and matriclan. Both the classes are exogamous in nature. The marriage rules are as follows

1. It prohibits marriage between the members of same patriclan and matriclan and thus double clan exogamy is strictly observed.
2. It prohibits union between consanguines.

3. Cross-cousin marriage is allowed as it does not violate the rule of clan-exogamy.
4. Sororate and levirate are permitted.

The people are strictly monogamous. Married children are excluded from family due to structural reason, hence family is mostly nuclear composed of husband, wife and their unmarried children.

The Dimasa consider themselves to be Hindu, though they have only a faint idea about Hinduism. They have their own gods and goddesses. Now-a-days some of their traditional deities are identified with the deities of Hindu pantheon. They have elaborate worship of area god and clan god. But they cannot think of any image of the deities and spirits whatsoever. Earthen mounds are raised on the occasion of worship and sometime the emblem of certain gods are placed there. Though the Dimasa gods and spirits do not have any anthropomorphic shape, they belong to either of the sexes, and some of them have spouses too.

The Dimasa believe in reincarnation. It is a general belief that according to one's earthly deeds, one is destined to have better or worse life in the next birth. In order to have birth in human form one should lead an honest life–a person should take care of his/her old parents, should be loyal to one's spouse, should not violate rules of incest, nor indulge in adultry or black magic, or practise any unlawful activity of theft or murder. An evil doer will be reborn as a hateful animal or it may be so that he/she would not be reborn and will wonder in the air like a spirit which, according to Dimasa concept is a severe punishment to a human soul. Thus the concept of good and evil, honesty and dishonesty are reflected in the idea of rebirth.

Changes are quite perceptible in certain spheres of Dimasa culture. Due to their conservative outlook these could not touch the core of their culture. Three main factors are mainly responsible for bringing change in Dimasa life. These are contact with alien cultures, exposure to market economy and the introduction of the district council office. All these factors collectively have contributed to a better integration of the Dimasa with the national life.

Culture and Society of the Gadabas of Andhra Pradesh–An Ethnographic Profile

A. V. Subba Rao

The Gadabas are a little-known community in Andhra Pradesh. So far, there were no exhaustive ethnographic reports on the Gadabas in Andhra Pradesh, except scanty references in Census Reports. Some sketchy references are also available from some Governmental agencies.

J. C. Molony, Superintendent of Census Report, Madras (1911), depicts three main sub-divisions, Bonda Paroja, Gutub or Boda Gadaba and Parengi Gadaba among the Gadabas.

A. Aiyappan, in his report, *the. Socio-Economic Conditions of the Aboriginal Tribes of Madras (1948),* mentions six sub-divisions namely, (a) Boda or Gutub, (b) Alluru, (c) Parengi, (d) Kollyi, (e) Kapu, and (f) Kathera Godabas. According to B. S. Guha, the Gadabas belong to Proto-Austroloid group.

Some scholars have tried to find out the origin of the name of Gadabas, but there is no unanimity in their opinion. In a Savara dialect, the word 'go' denotes greatness and 'da' signifies water. Hence, the euphonic combination of the word 'Goda' would be great water, meaning the river Godavari. But Aiyappan does not agree with the suggestion that the word Gadaba is connected with the river Godavari, because the Gadabas had never been anywhere near that river. Contradicting the views, he tried to put his own opinion that the word Gadaba has originated from the word 'Kadava' in Tamil, because of their prominent ear-rings (Kadu in Tamil means ear). He also says that it may be more proper to derive it from the Sanskrit word 'Gutwara', which in Oriya will be 'Gatbara', and may become 'Godbara' or 'Godaba'. Gatbara means locomotive and it coincides with their one-time profession of bearing the palanquins, i.e., moving from one place to another.

As there is no account of any nature so far on the ways of life of this aboriginal group of people, the present writer preferred to study the culture of Gadabas and its change under the local culture impact.

As long as they were under the direct touch with the kings, the Gadabas were well-off, since all their difficulties were looked after by their lords. The process of change started only after the Estate abolition, when the kings began to take away the privileges so long enjoyed, in view of their own natural limitations. With the enforcement of the Law of Estate Abolition, the Gadabas, in the compelling situation, were left only with the paltry pieces of land that were given to them by the kings, but were deprived of the benefits of the forests and the hills, since these were no more under the control of the kings. These unforeseen circumstances made them territorially and economically displaced, and clamped them within the small limits of the gifted lands.

Following the 1961 Census of India, the population figures of Gadabas in Andhra Pradesh are mentioned in Table 1.

Table 1

Population in the State (1961 Census)

No.	District	Male	Female	Total
1.	Visakhapatanam	6517	6212	12729
2.	Srikakulam	4322	4536	8858
	Total	10839	10748	21587

Out of 21587 total population of the Gadabas in Andhra Pradesh, 1442 people were taken up for study as a representative sample. This sampling was made keeping in view to cover all the three sub-divisions of Gadabas in Andhra Pradesh to bring out a comparative analysis. The people studied came from 350 families, and out of this population 943 were from Kathera Gadabas, 312 from Gutub Gadabas and the remaining 187 were from Parengi Gadabas.

Altogether six villages were selected for this study. These were selected at random with a coverage of the area concerned. Out of six villages, three were chosen from hinterland, less affected by Development Projects, and three other from roadside areas. This was done with a view to compare the ways of life of the Gadabas–their culture in general analysed from acculturation point. Selection of villages distributed in three sub-divisions signifies regional variations in culture, on the basis of ecology. To find out the occupational variations based on regional conditions, one more village in Andhra area (Srikakulam) was also covered in addition to the above six villages.

To collect data, a preliminary census was undertaken. Major data were collected through participant observation as most of the life activities of the Gadabas were the focal point of this study. Data on religious and festival cycle were collected not only from observation, but also from the persons who were involved in the rites and ceremonies and knew them in details. To substantialte the facts, specialists like, medicine-men, headmen and other elderly persons were interviewed to describe their roles and nature of participation.

To speak of the sub-division, the Gutub Gadabas live near Makkuva of Salur Taluk, and around Madugula of Chodavaram Taluk. The Kathera Gadabas were mainly living near Salur Town in Salur Taluk and near Krishmadevipet in Narasipatnam Taluk. The Kathera Gadabas inhabited around Kurpam of Srikakulam district (Parvathipuram Taluk) and the Parengi Gadabas are mainly living around Madugula in Chodavaram Taluk and near Andhra in Pachipenta Development Block in Srikakulam district.

The Kathera Gadabas used to cut a lock of hair specially at the time of their marriage so that, they are called Kathera Gadabas (*Kathera* is a Telugu word which means *scissors*). The Boda or Gutub Gadabas mostly stay in the roadside villages. The word Boda denotes big and though the name indicates their higher position, the Kathera Gadabas in Andhra Pradesh are larger in number and consider themselves superior when they compare themselves with the other two sub-divisions. On the other hand, the Parengi Gadabas will have to fix up a Parengi Branch at the marriage booth, as one of the preliminary rituals at the time of their marriage ceremony and that identifies them as Parengi Gadabas. Parengi is the name of a tree in Telugu, which is generally found in the forest.

Visakhapatnam and Srikakulam districts lie on the east coast of the erstwhile composite Madras State. Srikakulam was previously a part of Visakhapatnam district, but later it was formed into a separate district, including some part from Visakhapatnam and some from the old Ganjam area. The Gadabas in Andhra Pradesh are concentrated only in Visakhapatnam and Srikakulam districts. It is noted that the Gadabas are mainly concentrated in Chodavaram Taluk or Visakhapatnam and Salur Taluk of Srikakulam district.

Out of six villages, three are from the forest area, and the rest from the areas where some of the welfare programmes were undertaken by the government for the uplift of the tribal communities in this state.These have been studied to understand the impact of induced change.

Generally, the Gadaba villages are homogenous in nature, though also a few Valmiki families live separately on one or the other side of the village.

Altogether six villages have been taken for study, as mentioned earlier, for a comparative analysis. Among all the three endogamous division, the Kathera Gadabas are both numerically and socially dominant. As they form the majority of the tribal population, a detailed study has been made of them in 4 villages with a view to note their speciality, and the remaining two villages have been studied for ecological and socio-economic study of Gutub and Parengı Gadabas.

Table 2

Particulars of the Villages

District	Community Block	Village	Sub-division
Visakhapatnam	Madugula (Chodavaram Taluk)	Kasipuram	Parengi Gadabas
		Gutub Gadabapet	Gutub Gadabas
		Jallampalli Gadabapalam	
	Koyyur (Chintapalli Taluk)	Peda Gadabapalem	Kathera Gadabas
		Nimmagadda Gadabapalum	
Srikakulam	Salur (Salur Taluk)	Manchadavalsa	

Regarding the plain's castes, *Kapus*, *Sondhis* and *Sowcars* are the neighbouring groups of the Gadabas in almost all the areas of both the districts. The *Sowcars* (bania) have no village of their own, but they run business in all the tribal villages. On the other hand, the *Kapus* are living in their villages as the immediate neighbours of the Gadabas. The constant touch in their daily routine with the *Kapus* brought about a considerable change in the social and economic life of the Gadabas in Andhra Pradesh.

The settlement patterns of Gadabas in Visakhapatnam differ from that of Srikakulam district. The Gadabas of Visakhapatnam have round-shaped huts constructed as a separate unit, and there is no link or connection between one hut and the other. But in Srikakulam the villages are constructed in rows, and all the huts are connected to each other, having just a partition of mud-wall in between. The repair of the roof is done generally every alternate year, or once in every three years. So, the expenditure on housing among the Gadabas cannot be considered as a constant drag on their annual budget.

The present study is an attempt to show the changes that have occurred beyond the baseline i.e. the British Chroniclers made a baseline survey of the culture of the Gadaba as they are an ancient tribe with their primitiveness.

This study manifests a clear-cut divergence in some of their manners, custom, as well as, economic condition and activities. The variations are mainly due to geological setting and the potentialities of occupational sources. Besides that, the impact of the ways of life of the neighbouring castes and tribes have had also considerable influence on the ways of life of this tribe. The study was made on a three-tier basis : covering the people living in the interior; at the foot-hills; and on the roadside areas.

The influence of the neighbouring plain's castes like, *Kapus* and *Sowcar* (Banias) on the ways of life of the Gadabas, has gone a long way, sometimes helping them to change their attitude of sticking to their traditions, and the circumstances also sometimes forced them to imitate the plain's castes, cutting across the traditional barriers, so as to catch up with the new approaches, which they thought would eventually result in their own uplift or betterment.

Sometimes, the changing economic condition forced them to compromise with their established modes of culture, replacing them with some modified alterations, so as to meet the present social needs, but not by totally abandoning the traditional patterns, which might undermine their cultural values. Some of these customs like marriage, religious festivals, and death ceremonies, are mainly dependent on the economic position of the group concerned. The economic life of them can not be generallised, taking the tribe as a complex whole, but can only be analysed by taking the sample of the group living in different areas, under various circumstances. For example, the people living in the roadside villages are having better chances, not only to sell firewood, but in taking up new occupations like, agency business, work of domestic servants, basketry, and other seasonal occupations like serving as agricultural labour, working in quarry, etc. But this opportunity is very much less, or sometimes totally denied in the case of the people living in the interior, as the sources are very limited for them, even if they are keen to get themselves changed, by taking up new ways of life.

Though their economic condition is not sound, the Gadabas are not in favour of violating their traditional strings, because of their inherent affinity towards their age-old customs. But as they are generally poor, when they have to perform a major ritual or social function involving a good deal of expenditure, they do not totally bypass their age-old customs, but instead, cut short the ceremonies, making a compromise with their traditions and prompted by the changing demands of the time.

The Gadabas are partly food-gatherers, and partly food-producers. Besides agriculture they are also seen engaged in food gathering in the hills. As the wet lands are scanty, some of them also depend on daily labour and their secondary occupation is basketry, they not only collect forest produce for their food purpose, but also for marketing. Apart from edible items, money-making products they get from the forest are timber, rose-wood, ginger-leaves and bamboos. Now-a-days age old barter system is declining by giving place to cash transactions.

The prevalence of monogamous system, the high incidence of nuclear families, and the increasing number of cases of marriage by elopement to avoid payment of bride-price, which is obligatory in the case of marriage by purchase, are all attempts to cut short the traditional marriage procedures, and points to the gradual acceptance of circumstantial changes.

The incidence of polygyny among them is very low. Another noteworthy thing is that they are preferring to marry either the girls of their own village, or the nearby villages, sometimes even deviating from the norms of their traditional life, because love-making and courtship are more convenient among those who live in the same village, or in nearby villages. Of such cases, marrying one's own sister's daughters, and the replacement of the clan system by the surname system in marriage alliances, can be taken as clear example of deviation. This makes it possible for them to select their life-partner easily without much ado. To marry ones own sister's daughter which was once prohibited, has been more or less acceptable now, due to the impact of plain's customs, where marrying one's own sister's daughter is a common practice.

As the ages role on the Gadabas are forgetting their own clan names, and it is very surprising to note that there are very few people who can say their clan names. The Gadabas are not following strictly the clan exogamy but marrying on the basis of surnames. They generally prefer to marry cross-cousin. Among them marriage by negotiation is socially prescribed and recognised form of marriage but this type of marriage is a costly affair to them as both the parties have to offer some formal fees and celebration. As a result, marriage by elopement, marriage by capture, marriage by exchange and marriage by service are popular to them. But among all these four types the incidence of marriage by elopement is very high among them. Divorce is permissible in their societies and the village panchayat is very much competent body to permit it.

They have tribal or village council. The traditional tribal council in their areas has the village council consisting of four members namely–

1) *Pettamdar,* who is the head man of the village and holds the supreme authority for controlling the villagers,
2) *Kulapedda,* who is also considered as a powerful person in setting all matters concerning the village,
3) *Pujari,* who is the expert in all matters related to rituals.
4) A wealthy man of the village.

The Kathera Gadabas practise witchcraft and sorcery. They perform even expensive religious ceremonies. They worship trees and stones in the name of gods. In addition they also worship Hindu gods like *Rama*. In Visakhapatnam district temples are found in the name of *Rama* in almost all the tribal villages (in the area of my field study), that shows their eagerness to cope up with the Hindus. The important religious functionaries in this society are marriage priests *(Disari), Pujari, Pujarini, Janni* and medicine men. The Gadabas are very particular about keeping out the Christians as untouchables. Even the Christian school teachers who are posted in those villages are not allowed either to sit on their cots or to enter into their houses. They are not even allowed to stay with them in the main village. Of late, some minor concessions are given to them, just as taking water from the common well of the village. It is regarded as a special privilege given to the teachers. But they never allow any *Valmiki* in the village to take water from their common well. In view of the fact the area is subjected to the plans of community development, the impact of which is found though at present in a limited scale, it is hoped that considerable amount of development would take place in the years to come.

The above statement can well be justified by presenting the fact of some modifications, not only in the traditional marriage ceremony, by cutting it short to avoid payment of bride-price and number of feasts that have to be usually offered which involves a financial burden. In some areas, the Gadabas are now burying the dead, instead of cremation, because cremation would cost them some hundreds of rupees, if they had to strictly observe the advice of the specialist, who spells out the actual number of animals that have to be sacrificed during the performance of death ceremony, to satisfy the dead ancestors.

With the inception of the panchayat system or the local self-government in the tribal areas, a considerable change has occurred in the composition of the Tribal Councils. Almost all the villages are represented by an elected member in the Board, and the same panchayat member is invited to take part even in the Council discussions. So the Panchayat member or a President is playing a dual role in village affairs. Sometimes, it happens that the *Pettemdar* and the panchayat board member is one and the same person.

So the tribal Council of any village along with the panchayat president not only acts as the custodian of the social customs, and as tribunal for solving the disputes, but also as guardians to look after the interests of the village. The Gadabas in these areas are found to be loyal to the persons but not to the parties.

An Analytical Study of the Maring Society of Manipur

Rajat Kanti Das

The bulk of the data for the thesis were collected during trips undertaken to Maring village in course of a research project sponsored and financed by the Indian Council of Social Science Research, New Delhi. These were further developed and critically analysed during the researcher's attachment to the Department of Anthropology, University of Calcutta as a U.G.C. Research Fellow from 1980–1984.

The study focused on the Maring social structure prompted by the notion that societies could be regarded as original wholes. Obviously, the main consideration was to bring into light a distinctively 'social form of organization through the concept of social structure'. The initial understanding of the Maring society was that of a social body with an 'anatomy' of the social relations and 'physiology' of functional connections. Even some time back, the Maring, as a tribe of Manipur, stood out as a distinct group in more than one sense. They just did not fit in the old scheme of classifying into Naga and Kuki group of tribes. They were regarded as 'independent' tribe in the sense that they did reveal some distinctive features in the social realm. They were distributed in a defined territory in the form of well demarcated villages, which had functional links in between them at one level or the other and which could be regarded as forming a part of the larger structural whole represented by the tribe itself. Inter-village relationship was in essence 'collective representations'. From this point of view, there could be a simplistic formulation of a social structure based on the particular complex of collective relationships and collective representations. This study strove at identifying the structural units or social groups in the Maring society and the structural factors or institutional principles that had gone with them. Such an analysis has to start with the stand that the system that marks the total structural pattern has a stability of its own. Social structure in the form of a social system may be apprehended 'as a unity made up of parts and process that are linked to one another by a limited number of principles of wide validity in homogeneous and relatively stable societies'.

The question is how stable and homogeneous the Maring society is? Probably, no analysis of social structure can present the 'whole' society, what is more, no society today can be said to form a coherent whole. It is difficult to find an 'integral community' in the real sense of the term. The Maring are also no exception to this. But this realisation had come towards the end of the study in the form of an important finding. The study itself was more an attempt to examine the Maring social system as an 'analytical system'. Following Nadel (1957), this could be expressed in a limited series of proposition about the way in which the social groups are established and about the relations between them and between their members.

Edmund Leach's approach to the study of Kachins of Burma (now Myanmar) could be useful in understanding the Maring situation today. More important perhaps is his emphasis on seeing social structure in a state of flux. It has to be admitted that later developments in the Maring society could be attributed to a process of change, which has rattled even the structural viability of the Maring society. One only realizes the true importance of 'political system' in shaping the rubric of the society.

At the structural level, one cannot but follow an 'idealised model' representing general consensus of the participants with regard to the best mode of performance. Side by side it becomes necessary to take into account the actual performance with variations. Society as a manifestation of social system, which is one way of describing 'a model of the social reality', and social structure as a structure of social groups based on collective relations are sufficient indicators of an explanatory model. Very broadly speaking structure provides the actors with social space to perform. For a long time the Maring gave an impression of being structurally self-contained. Admittedly, institutional structure alone may not be sufficient to analyse change and conflict that have made such a powerful impact on the Maring society today. But it is doubtful whether these developments could be totally delinked from structure.

Leaving aside the question of mathematical precision, which is hard to achieve in a study like this, one must see that the unit of general survey and the unit of personal observation tend to coincide (Raymond Firth, 1951). In other words, there should not be a wide gap between the unit of general survey and the unit of personal observation. It should be the endeavor of the researcher to make sure that the unit he or she selects for intensive study is sufficiently representative so that the generalizations made could be applicable to the larger community. For this research work, the unit of actual study was the unit of personal observation. The selection of villages for actual study was done with an eye to their representative character. In this task due consideration was given to their demographic character. Not to speak of demographic factors, 'mere size tends to govern the quality as well as the quantity of social relations' (Raymond Firth, 1951). This aspect revealed itself at the time of general survey. For example, almost all the important Maring associations were located at 'Machi', one of the biggest Maring villages. Machi also represented a parental village of the Black Maring group. Incidentally, the Marings may broadly be classified into three sections on the basis of the colour of the border of the cloth they wear. These are as follows :

(a) those who wear red-bordered clothes;
(b) those who wear black-bordered clothes;
(c) those wearing red and black–bordered clothes.

The last–named one was a later addition, which was done with the intention of projecting the central village of this group as the traditional Maring centre.

If anything, this type of classification only reflects affinity and link between some villages. Obviously, the establishment of a new type of link is possible only after the separation of lineal ties, which is but natural in a basically segmentary type of society. Clearly, it has a structural dimension. This type of differentiation also exists in some of the Burmese tribes, as in the case with the Karens (Red Karens, Black Karens and White Karens).

The Maring villages may be grouped under two categories:

(1) Parental villages;
(2) Satellite villages formed out of parental villages.

A parental village gives rise to new villages, which at the beginning are of temporary in nature. Ultimately, some of these temporary settlements may take the form of a new village. There has been a growing tendency on the part of big Maring villages falling in the category of permanent or parental village to function as more or less self-contained units. This is also reflected in the social organization. Many of the villages were supposed to have originated from a common village in the past. Besides Machi, the study of other parental villages like Khudei Khullen (Red Maring), Khunbi (Black Maring), also provided an important insight into the working of the Maring society. Data from Kharou Khunou (Black and Red Maring), a village on the Myanmar border, and Sandangsenba (Red Maring), a village at a short distance from Imphal, were collected with a view to see the range of variation. For the same purpose, Khoibu, representing a different dialect group, though accommodated in the Black Maring section, was studied in details. No doubt, the study of a village was a unit of study involves a degree of an 'analytical isolation', but it is unlikely to create a methodological problem of an altogether new dimension as long as the village forms a part of a wider system of social relations. The present situation, of course, indicate to that.

Social groups in the form of territorial groups, kin group and age–grades form the core of Maring social structure. Accordingly, villages representing territorial groups, clans, sub clans, lineages and families representing kin groups, and youth dormitories representing age grades were made the focus of structural analysis of Maring society. Once the 'most relevant' social groups were identified and their nature examined, it became necessary to find out the principles of social grouping. This was to explore the 'social reality' of the groups affecting the interactions of persons. In view of this, factors, which not only controlled the behaviour of social persons but also had a bearing on the social structure, were identified and examined in their proper context? The determining factors were, (a) descent, (b) kinship, (c) marriage, (d) residence, (e) economic ties, (f) ritual link, (g) new associational ties. The whole research design was chalked out with a view to contributing to their functional growth.

It has been made abundantly clear that the analysis of the Maring society was done in relation to the 'ideal model' representing an 'absolute whole system'. And such an ideal system was found to be more unstable than a really stable one. Probably Leach is right when he says,

"What one must do is first analyse out the ethnographic facts by reference to abstract whole systems conceived of as existing in unstable equilibrium, and then postulate that the confusion of reality arises from the interpretation of these unstable ideal systems."

Still, the application of a structural model to Maring society has its advantages too. In a society like the Maring, which is guided by a strong in-group feeling, the people develop a conception of how their society is organized and this is the type of 'model' Leach (1954) had spoken of. A model may be a 'stereotype', but application to actual communities is 'decidedly flexible'. To the investigator it appeared that till that time whatever changes had taken place could not affect much the basic character of the Maring social system based on the principles of lineality, segmentation, seniority and age-sex differentiation. These still got expressed in social relations. In other words, it may be said that Maring social relations could exist by virtue of the norms or rules that people used to apply in their actions.

From the structural point of view, the Maring society could be identified as an amalgam of a structure of authority based on the succession of generation and the principle of seniority defined by an individual's position in terms of genealogical strata.

Beyond the intra-tribal behaviour and relationship pattern it was the inter-community relationship which had started assuming much importance in case of Maring. Indeed, their reliance on the Meiteis of the plains in the economic field has been definitely on the increase. Actually, it is the 'symbiotic relationship' between hill and valley peoples which has been emphasized by the Maring-Meitei relationship. Leach (1961 a) has amply demonstrated how this type of 'symbiotic relationship' occurs almost throughout the entire Indo-Burman region. Probably, the Maring and their relationship with the Meiteis should not be seen in isolation. In a cultural sense, the Maring could be spoken of as a tribe, but they may also be considered as very small part of 'a category distinct from tribal and peasant types' (Lehman, 1963). Accordingly, to Lehman, this category comprises a whole series of mountain–dwelling people in a region stretching from 'Assam (and the neighbouring states of Nagaland, Mizoram and Tripura) across all of mainland South-east Asia and into tribal areas of Southeast China'.

Their contact with the Thadou Kukis and Tangkhul Nagas sometimes developed into conflicting situations. But conflicting situations had also started developing from within the tribe. Different dialect groups with single village representations were loosely attached to the Maring society. Other than dialectical differences, they revealed some distinctive features in kin organization pattern and ritual forms. At least in one case the people not only demonstrated their differences, they also took the extreme step of seceding from the Maring society. This was, of course, a later development.The rapid spread of Christianity was in no way less responsible for creating another conflicting situation between people of older generation and those of younger generation. This has structural implications as well because the principal of seniority, one cornerstone of the Maring social structure, got affected by it. Of course, Christianity to some extent was successful in lessening the economic burdens of animist ritual requirements of the people. It was Christianity again which was responsible for generating a new type of allegiance, sometimes going beyond the consideration of one's own tribal identity. In the case of Maring, their own tribal identity was the first consideration. Identity here was structurally ingrained rather than the simple expression of mind. Or the knowledge that underpins the institutionally organized structure probably gets crystallized in the minds of individuals.

The utility of a study like the present one may be put to question. Taken separately, it may be of limited academic interest. But its value would be considerably increased if is not considered in isolation. The total network of inter-group relations, at every level of scale, throughout the whole area, should form the background to understand the process of social formation. No less important is to analyse the social life of mountain–dwelling people, who need not necessarily be seen as operating exclusively from within its confines. The question of social and cultural dynamics is involved with it. The study of social structure makes sense in as much as it holds the key to understanding the nature of a tribe set in the classical mould of anthropological tradition. This is the way the concept of social structure used to find expression in anthropology, built around empirical knowledge of 'small scale' societies.

Even in the changing situation of inter-tribal conflicts, the members of each tribe have been oscillating between the compulsive or obligatory behaviour patterns at the social structural level on the one hand and opportunities for accepting greater social and political roles on the other, which are not limited to the confines of a socially bounded tribal system. This particularly applies to the Marings revealing structural qualities to a significant extent.

References

Das, R. K. (1988) *Tribal Structure.* New Delhi : Inter-India Publication.

Firth, R. (1951) *Elements of Social Organisation.* London

Leach, E. R. (1954) *Political System of Highland Burma.* London : G. Bell and Sons Ltd.

Lehman, F. (1963) *The Structure of Chin Society.* USA : Illinois University Press.

Lopez, J. and Scott, J. (2002) *Social Structure.* New Delhi : Viva Books Pvt. Ltd.

Socio-Cultural Life of the Kukis of Manipur– A Historical Analysis

T. S. Gangte

The purpose of the present work is to focus on the unexplored wealth of Anthropological and Sociological potentials that are available, which have not yet been given proper empirical studies to the extent modern scientific knowledge would have achieved.

This work tries to project that every walk of life of the Kukis, be it social, economic, political, religion, etc., is a manifestation of their social structure based on cultural heritage. Changes have been brought about in their social matrix by modernism, western education, Christianity, etc. Notwithstanding, some aspects of their social institutions withstand the onslaught of such changes, of course, not without conflict between traditionalism and modernity.

The North-Eastern territory of India comprising of Assam, Manipur, Meghalaya, Mizoram, Nagaland, Tripura and Arunachal Pradesh was curved out gradually from the original Province of Assam of British India except the Princely States of Tripura and Manipur. It had been termed as the 'Land of Seven Sisters'. The region covers an area of approximately 2,55,000 square kilometers with a population of 2,65,13,685 as per Census of India, 1981. Out of these, Manipur has an area of 22,346 square kilometers and a population of 14, 33,681.

The entire North-East India is populated by variegated groups of people. Migration of people from Burma to these areas was very common and, as such, we find people of Mongoloid origin in respect of their physical features, cultures, tradition, language, etc. The autochthones who settled in the hill tracts were subsequently identified and differentiated one from the other, based on various historical processes of stress and strains. Communication difficulties, to a great degree, had contributed to their being in isolation for a number of generations. These adjustmental processes, in course of time, differentiated some groups from the bigger ones, while other groups found themselves in aligned conditions with some groups to compose a large social identity or aggregate. Such alienation and alignment of different groups came to bear various ethnic appellations identifying themselves as distinct tribes. This is a common feature in many places, but this is a very significant to this tract of land.

It is true that there are not a permanent crystal–line structure in the stage of historical and social development and, all the time, due to interaction and adjustments, these groups of people are found to accommodate themselves in different degrees in varied situations. It is also expected that their society has less and less of hierarchy and less and less of economic specialization.

In order to be eligible for constitutional benefits which have been declared after independence, these groups have been identified as 'weaker sections' and listed separately as 'Scheduled'. In this part of India, there are altogether 131 Scheduled Tribes with identifiable characteristics and traits, distributed in different areas of this region. Likewise, there are 179 languages and 544 dialects in the region, according to the Linguistic Survey of India. Out of this, there are 29 tribes in Manipur with as many dialects as there are tribes, if not more, belonging to the Tibeto-Chinese family group of language.

It is true that the enchanting land known as the North-East region of India attracted waves of diverse racial groups through ages. It has come to stay as the confluence of the most colourful mosaic of ethnic, linguistic and cultural diversity. The culture and tradition of the people often overlap the man-made political units of the region. Political loyalty mostly transcends the boundary of each political unit. The Kukis living in Nagaland, Assam, Tripura and Manipur have closer cultural traditional and ethnic affinity with the people of Mizoram, Chittagong Hills of Bangaladesh and the 'Chins' of Chin Hills of Burma, than with their immediate neighbours. They yearn to remain under a single political unit. Sometime ago movements with this end in view were started in Chin Hills of Burma under the leadership of Vumkhohau on the eve of independence of Burma under the yoke of the British rule and for the unification of *Zomi* under the banner of Zomi Revolutionary Army covering the areas now inhabited by the Kukis and Mizos in Manipur, Assam, Tripura, Nagaland and Mizoram.

The same holds good with the Nagas. Despite conspicuous nature at the height of diversity in ethnicity, culture, tradition, language, etc., their peculiar emotional upsurge to integrate themselves, burying their hatchet, age-old war of attrition, under the nomenclature of 'Naga' and a language called 'Nagamese', which is pidgin Assamese, is indeed examplary. This is solely due to the belief in the myth that all the Nagas have a common origin. The differences are superficial and are secondary and of temporary nature. Their unity and solidarity is more basic and fundamental. This encouraged them to demand for a separate state for Nagas which was eventually materialised.

These groups of people came to the region at different points of history. Some of them came in the pre-historic days and others came at different points of time of history. Thus, even though some of them belong to the same ethnic group, time-gap in the waves of migration between different groups contributed greatly to their present wide-range of divergence and multiplicity.

One spectacular glaring factor is that of the most contrasting nature between the Nagas on the one hand and the Kukis on the other. Despite the fact that the Nagas have extreme diversity in language their sense of unity and solidarity in the name of 'Naga' is spectacular and admirable. As against it, though they have far more advantageous nature in culture, tradition, language, etc., the Kukis cannot maintain unity and a common political platform.

Introduction of research hypotheses by way of field work paved the way to in-depth study of some selected villages. A door-to-door study of the said selected villages by 'participant observance' covered 236 families. In doing so, some case history was taken up that substantiated with the revelation of various lifestyle of the Kukis. Some of the genealogies clearly showed as to how have they adhered to the traditional system, and as also, in many ways, deviated from them. The lifestyle of the Kukis has been examined with a view to grasping the operating forces playing in their day-to-day living, with special reference to the Kukis of Manipur. Their institutions, such as, political, economic, religious and social, in the face of changing pattern of life with the introduction of modern education system, spread of Christainity and the onslaught of various agencies of change brought about by the developmental programmes of the Government, present significant materials for study.

The Kukis had been the dominant tribes spreading their authority over a wide range of hill areas surrounding the valley of Imphal during hey-day of the Maharajah of Manipur and subsequently during the British period. Thus, the hill areas of Manipur were the domain and the head-hunting ground of the Kukis till they were subjugated and controlled by the British in 1917-1919 Anglo-Kuki war. The most permanent and lasting effect of this war was not only the suppression of Kukis, but creation of permanent boundaries of Manipur that exists till date. The Maharajahs of Manipur were contented with periodical massacres, collection of spoilts thereof and temporary extension of influence for specific purpose. The Kuki Chiefs were their allies. After 1919, however, the British assumed direct administration over the hill tribes in general and on the Kuki Chiefs, in particular. Consequent upon this, decentralisation of administration by opening of sub-divisional Headquarters at Tamgnelong, Churachandpur and Ukhrul became imperative solely with a view to checkmating the Kuki Chiefs in order to avoid recurrance of hostile activities of the latter. Despite this, the British were shrewd enough that they did not loose sight of the effective administrative mechanism of Kuki chieftainship system. The British rulers made use of the Chiefs and their office of Council of Ministers called *Semang-upa*. This helped the kuki chiefs to maintain their authority and hold over the people, thereby, unifying the clans that composed the Kuki tribes called Kukis, and expressed their identity as such. Authority of the Chiefs also greatly enhanced the strength of their customary laws which were the perennial sources of Kuki custom, tradition, culture, language, etc.

In contrast, with the introduction of western education through the Christian Missionaries, spreading from the Lushai Hills, awareness of having been dominated by the chiefs and being identified as Kuki were more consciously made manifest among the commoners by the newly emerged public leaders from amongst the commoners creating false propaganda that the meaning of Kuki and derivation of the *Kuki* was foreign in origin that conveyed derogatious or derisive meaning. The authority and leaderships of the Kuki chiefs thus begun gradually to erode. Ultimately, with the dawn of independence in India, the idea of chieftainship being thrown out of power was supplanted by a new set-up of administration known as 'democracy' which in a resurgent India was spontaneously accepted by the leaders of so-called public leaders and the commoners. Besides this, the term Kuki was rejected mainly in the previously known Lushai Hills and Manipur. Recognition of tribes as listed in the 'Scheduled Tribes' in various states hastened the process of disintegration among the Kukis, for the new Constitution of India accorded special privileges to such recognised tribes. Along with this, tension, enmity, conflict, factionalism between and among the erstwhile Kukis became the common feature of their life. The people became crazy for being recognised as Scheduled Tribes so as to be able to enjoy the fruits of the Constitutional privileges. Indeed the immediate adverse affect of all this was telling heavily on the unity and solidarity of the Kukis.The seeds of disintegration thus burgeoned among them. Therefore, in a system of administration where counting of heads and majority rule prevails, the Kukis were the worst sufferers. They are now in minority wherever they live, because they have become very badly divided and too widely scattered in different administrative units in the entire North-East region of India.

The empirical study of such people would no doubt open a new vista leading to the store-house of knowledge for the social anthropologists and sociologists. Many aspects of life of the Kukis which could not be easily uncovered or appreciated with a superficial knowledge of their social system would have misled an outsider. An in-depth study of their life would not only enrich knowledge but also help the people concerned understand them in a better way.

The villages under study were inhabited by the Chongloi, the Gangte, the Kipgen, the Sitlhou, the Haokip, the Singson and the Lhungdim clans. They provide both similarities and diversities and reflect ethnic relationship or otherwise. The areas covered in the selected villages are mainly in the Churachandpur district and the Sadar Hills sub-division of the Senapati district of Manipur. Locations of the villages afford accessibility from the national and state highways. Those are not, however, within the areas that can be considered as urbanized or at the outskirts of the growing towns of different districts. Nevertheless, the villages are not absolutely without the touch of modernity, albeit modern amenities and avenues of modern employment etc., are scarcely available. Though urbanization is a part of inevitable result of civilization and planned development requiring bringing in of all facilities of up-to-date living at the door-step of rural population, and despite changes in the matter of administration with the introduction of Village Authority Act, 1956 coupled with negation of authority of the Kuki Chiefs, the traditional system of village administration continues to hold stage.

Having briefly highlighted the broad perspectives of the research work and what would be its impact, chapterisation and processing of the data and information collected have been taken up as given below.

1. Chapter one deals with facts and fables, dealing with historicity of the people concerned beginning from origin, migration, conversion into christianity so as to analyse between the conflict and conformity of the traditional and indigeneous religion and christianity, i.e., traditionalism and modernity.

2. Chapter two deals with the setting of the research work, such as, country of the Kukis, where they live, geo-physical distribution, changing political boundaries, till date, Manipur, showing a historical and political overview, nature of economic involvement with geo-political setting including their interactions with other ethnic groups of tribal and non-tribals who were neighbouring groups of people.

3. Chapter three deals with Institutions and Formalities of the people so as to manifest their social, economic, religious and political relationship in their day-to-day social intercourse.
4. Chapter Four deals with life-cycle ceremonies beginning from birth to death including many rites and rituals associated with the performance of such social functionaries.
5. Chapter Five deals with Political Organisation, such as, the Chieftainship and its associated institutions that are its functionaries. Chieftainship being the highest political unit among the Kukis is the perennial source of culture, tradition, customs, etc., and is indispensable for proper understanding of Kuki society;
6. Chapter Six deals with Social Ceremonies. It is mainly through these institutions which are made manifest in the form of ceremonies in more than a thousand ways of expression of inter and intra personal relation.
7. Chapater Seven deals with supernaturals; rituals and ceremonies. Human societies whether primitive or advanced communities believe in certain form of supernatural-being which govern their welbeing or otherwise.

With all this background, a good number of people are now thinking over a new dimension. Changes are inevitable when science, technology, modern education and new job opportunities have brought all the people together to a greater world wherein ethnic identity should not be over emphasised. Besides, Christianity has cut a deep gorge into their lifestyle and the people have no other alternative but to roll down in it by embracing Christianity. At the same time, Indian democracy in constitutional form has opened up many opportunities and, as such, people are not simply confined to its narrow cell; but many think that the good elements of cultures which have so long been sustaining the group together, affiliated them with the nature and established friendships with many through rites, rituals and celebrations, should not be discarded. Rather, these will take them to a glorious history of the past, which all the time favoured them with cultural touches and re-touches in order to shape the profile of the group. India is a land of many groups having diverse origin and identity. It is an epitome of *Mahabharata*, i.e., Pan-India where Naga, Kuki, Kirata, Asura and other groups mingled among themselves to form a confluence of eternal unity in diversity. The traditional dance and festivals of Manipur are such examples which continue even today in the life of the people for their identifications so that these may be allowed to vibrate in the symphony of Indian culture. Unity in diversity with a feeling of nationalism, which is the only binding force for group identity, may be allowed to imbue the life and culture of these colourful people of ancient India.

Socio-Cultural Change among the Kondh

Bijay Kumar Behera

By and large, the tribal societies in India particularly till the attainment of Independence have remained relatively isolated from the mainstream of national life. The tribal areas are characterized by their aloofness and lower level of economic activity and a somewhat closed social structure. They maintain an uninterrupted long tradition of cohesive social structure and value system. The British Government advocated a policy of complete isolation followed by a policy of exclusion of the tribal areas. They thought the task of administration in interior and mountainous tribal areas was difficult and without any gain. So they followed an approach of *leave them alone* towards the tribal communities. They also had the belief that the tribals were better and happier in their own society and environment and there was no need to interfere in their lifestyle. But, after India became independent, the Government of Orissa took special measures for the upliftment of the tribal communities. In the process of economic modernization and introduction of welfare and development measures of the Government and through non-government agencies, many changes in social, economic, religious and political life of the tribes of Orissa have taken place.

The present study has been undertaken among the Kondhs of Baliguda area of Phulbani district of Orissa. Numerically, the Kondh is the largest tribe out of the 62 tribal communities of Orissa. The Kondh constitute 4 percent of Orissa's total population and 17.15 percent of State's tribal population. The total Kondh population of the district Phulbani constitutes 38.08 percent of the total population. The Kondhs are well known in anthropological and historical literature for the pernicious practice of human sacrifice, which is known as *Meriah*. To get a correct and comprehensive knowledge of Kondh life in the changing situation, extensive empirical study has been undertaken in three phases in 1966, 1980 and 1988. Investigation of the different agents of change, such as caste Hindu neighbours, Christian missionaries, weekly market, private agencies, improved transportation, education and mass communication have been undertaken. At the same time, the impact of the implementation of the Government schemes and programmes has been evaluated. The study provides insight into the nature and processes of change affecting the life and culture of the Kondh in particular and those of the Orissa tribal communities in general.

The main objectives of the study are as follows:

1. To investigate the different agents of change such as caste Hindu neighbours, Christian missionaries, weekly tribal market, private agencies, education, improved transportation and mass communication and their impact on the Kondh tribe.
2. To investigate developmental schemes of the government implemented on the tribe Kondh, their acceptance by the Kondh and the merits and demerits of the schemes.
   (a) To assess the functioning of the Block Development programmes and benefits accruing to the Kondhs .
   (b) To assess the impact of Large-size Agricultural Multipurpose Cooperative Societies (LAMPS) and to find out to what extent the cooperative movements in the area is one of the chief instruments for the economic development of the tribe.
   (c) To find the extent of response to Ashram School education among the Kondhs.
3. To investigate into the techno-economic changes brought about due to the impact of different agents of change.
4. To study the occupational diversification and mobility among the Kondh.
5. To identify, classify and analyse the changing technology and economic pursuits adopted by the Kondhs and to assess their acceptance in the society.
6. To study and analyse institutional change (such as changing Kondh family, changing marriage system, changing dormitory life) taking place among the tribe due to impact of different agents of change in operation in the area.
7. To investigate and discuss the nature and extent of transformation from Muthadari system of political organisation to the modern political system.
8. To evaluate the impact of Christianity as well as the caste Hindu neighbours on the religious beliefs and practices of the Kondh.
9. To finally assess and evaluate the trend of development and change occurring among the Kondh due to the impact.

In the advent of change and development in the area of study the Kondh social institutions, cultural beliefs, economic organisations and politico-religious structures have undergone transformations. The most peculiar character of change and transformation noticed among the Kondh is largely due to the dominant influence of the Hindu neighbours, although in accelerating the process of change, the influence of Christianity, the impact of industrialization, spread of communication network and above all education cannot be ignored. Emulation of Hindu ideals, values and practices in the day to day life of the Kondh, often in some cases to the extent of dispensing with their own traditional norms and values, has consciously or unconsciously affected and enthused the Kondh.

The joint and extended forms of families are breaking down to nuclear forms. Nuclear families follow hard rules of ownership right. With the widening of generation gap and growth of differentiation between the old and traditional and the young and educated, estrangement in the family has appeared, thus affecting the traditional organization of Kondh family. The internal harmony of the institution of family nourished by parsimony of family economy, decisive decision making of the family members and status based social relationship among the members of the family has been torn down allowing uneconomic family budget, dissension among family members and disapproval of family status positions.

Traditional types of acquiring mates through captive, elopement and abduction are being considered degrading and such practices are being eschewed. Preference is given, more and more to negotiated forms of marriage and dowry transactions are increasingly being adopted leaving behind bride-price. Child marriage has been largely stopped. Acquisition of multiple women and the propensity of heading a large size family are under decline.

The Kondhs have been fascinated by the Oriya kinship terms and have adopted them and the younger generations hardly know their own terms for some of their kinsmen. The cooperative character of their clans and descent groups no longer is emphasized. The most interesting trend of development observed among the Kondhs is their taking recourse to ritual friendship and ritual kinship. Thus they are extending the social relationship beyond the boundary of their own ethnic group. They espouse ritual kinship terms and are happy establishing such ritual ties more with members from outside their own community than with members from within their community.

In the sphere of economic life there has been a shift from shifting cultivation to wet-land paddy cultivation and most of the Kondhs have developed a taste for taking rice as a staple diet. Traditional barter system has been replaced by monetary system of transaction and monetization and market orientation have largely filled the life of the Kondhs now. Due to generation of employment opportunities in the nearby towns and industrial complexes, there has been a great deal of occupational mobility among the Kondh. However, the Kondh youths now-a-days clamour more and more for white-collar jobs than blue-collar ones.

Marked changes have been noticed among the Kondh in respect of choosing new house patterns with multi-room accommodation and cross ventilation inside the rooms. In the recent years they have been successful in acquiring new iron implements and a variety of agricultural implements more suitable for paddy cultivation and other cash crops. In their dress patterns, there is a marked change now. The Kondh youths are enthusiastic about wearing coloured lungis and do not like to remain bare-bodied, rather they love to wear shirts. They have developed a strong sense of well-clad gentlemanship. Of late, people in more and more numbers are taking tea and milk and have learnt to prepare food items in the south Indian type. They have developed consciousness of good physique and hygiene and are using detergents and toilet soaps and have developed new sense of aesthetics including personal decoration by making the living rooms clean and decorative. The erstwhile traditional practice of tattooing the limbs of the body is declining steadily, and sometimes it is becoming difficult to discern a Kondh (if well dressed) from that of another Oriya neighbour.

The Kondhs have shown great interest in participating and observing great Hindu festivals and fairs at the village level and are worshipping Hindu gods and goddesses and following the ritual practices of the clean caste groups of the neighbourhood and trying to raise their ritual status by leaving beef eating etc.

In the wake of politicization and prevalent electoral party politics, the Kondh villages have become faction-ridden and vested interest groups have emerged in the community. Some of the unpleasant incidents and intra-community and other communal conflicts which occur sporadically here and there are often fanned by the local political agents who used to have a stake in the socio-political life of the Kondh.

Beyond the sphere of worldly life and living, some of the Kondh families have espoused new religious cults and practices for purgation of life following the higher Hindu ideals. Some of the individual Kondhs have joined *Nadia Kirtan* parties and have turned devotees of the *Chaitanya Mahaprabhu*.

The most astounding socio-cultural change in the study area, which deserves special mention here, is that new social groups have emerged under the titles of *Kondh-Gauda, Kondh Lohar* and *Kondh Kumbhars.* The formation of these new social group owe to their living as co-villagers of the Kondhs from generation together. Mostly these menial Hindu caste groups used to render services to the Kondhs in the capacity of their respective occupational orientation. The *Gauda* (Cow-herd) used to herd the cattle of the Kondhs; the *Lohars* (Blacksmith) used to prepare and repair iron implements and the *Kumbhars* (potters) used to supply the earthenware vessels to the Kondhs. These artisan groups were brought to these areas and were settled in different Kondh villages in individual households by the *Muthadars* and *Mutha Mallikes* (the traditional highest Kondh functionary) in the *Muthadari* system. Since the *Muthadars* are hailed from among the caste Hindu communities and as many of their relations were brought and settled in the area to take up settled agriculture, the services of these artisans' menial caste groups were required. For rendering services these artisan castes were getting patronage of the *Muthadars.* In the process some of these individual families served the Kondh and gradually crept into the Kondh village community structure. They picked up 'Kui' as their language, observed many of the Kondh rituals, tattooed their girls in the Kondh way. Their intimate association with the Kondhs differentiated them from their caste Hindu counterpart. The *Muthadars* and other caste Hindus accorded a label with the pre-fix of Kondh to their respective caste names. Now, they are called as *Kondh-Gauda, Kondh-Lohar* and *Kondh-Kumbhar* by one and all in the locality.

These groups stand separate from their Oriya counterparts. They marry within their own group following the basic principle of caste endogamy. In the ritual hierarchy they occupy a lower status, lower than that of the Kondh in general and the *Gauda, Lohar* and *Kumbhar* caste groups of the locality.

It is evident that centuries of contact with the Hindu neighbours have influenced the Kondh culture and ideology to a remarkable degree. Exclusion of the Kondh community has long been dismantled in the historical process of intimate interaction with the Hindu rulers (Muthadars and Mutha Mallick) of the area. These rulers have been instrumental in bringing about certain changes in the day to day life of the Kondh. New forms of organizations and ritual practices were introduced in the Kondh community which the latter did not resist. Reconciliatory methods were being adopted by the regional administration, for bringing about such changes in the lifestyle of the people. The major thrust of the regional administration was to integrate the Kondhs into the regional caste Hindu fold through adoption of Hindu rituals and a variety of Hindu religious nuances. It was appealing to the Kondhs at the same time and the Kondh leaders were positively responding to the stimuli and in turn, influencing their fellowmen for a change in ideology. Paradoxically enough, on certain occasions the heads of the regional administration were utilizing the Kondh priests in observing rituals for the welfare of the farmers' family members and others. Thus the Kondh priests were highly esteemed by the Hindu neighbours for they entertained the belief that the Kondh priest could control the uncontrollable and appease the unruly forest deity more skillfully than the Hindu priest. This mutual interaction in the field of ritual was fostering, rapprochement between the caste Hindu neighbours and the Kondhs, and the Kondhs thereby were easily influenced by the Hindu religion.

The impact of the Christian missionaries as compared to the impact of the Hindu religion is negligible although the Christian missionaries have been working in the area quite vigorously since 1901. However, Christianity has tremendous impact on the *Panas*, the Scheduled Caste neighbours of the Kondh. The *Panas* in fact were the first group of Christian converts. Although the missionary activities through a variety of aids and incentives have attracted most of the *Panas*, the Kondhs have been reluctant to adopt except in a very few cases. The Kondhs are poor but proud of their cultural heritage and cultural status the same way as that of the neighbouring caste Hindus. The general feeling circulates among the Kondhs and the Hindu caste members that adopting Christianity amounts to degrading one's social ritual status which is considered more important than acquisition of wealth or material gains. The Kondhs do not want to degrade their social status positions as compared to the other ethnic groups in the regional hierarchy. The Kondhs used to refrain from doing the acts which is usually done by their *Pana* neighbours. The social and ritual opposition between the Kondh and the *Pana* enters the sphere of economic pursuits: the Kondhs pursue cultivation as owners of land; the *Pana* are petty businessman and act as middlemen and are landless. Thus, the Kondh ideology as against the *Pana* ideology refrains the Kondhs from mass scale conversion to Christianity.

Multiple development schemes under a variety of welfare, employment and poverty alleviation programmes of the Government are being implemented in the Kondh area by various State Government departments. The development institutions and agencies of the

Government like, the District Welfare Office, the Block Development Office, Integrated Rural Development Projects, LAMPs etc., are taking up the development activities at the same time. The Kondhs remain ignorant of which agency does what work and they do not estimate these agencies to be different wings of the Government and rate them as the same. Often they approach the agencies on their own for getting the benefit, but they get confused in the formal bureaucratic process. The very compartmentalization of development work creates confusion. On the one hand, the development personnel who are to implement the programme are very casual in their work and display indifference towards the poor Kondhs and on the other the Kondhs have realized the Government officials misappropriate the money in the name of development work and even if somebody has got some benefit either he is rich or influential. The little benefit whatsoever can never filter down to the Kondh in the street. Welfare and development activities, instead of serving the people for betterment of their life, have generated chaos and confusion and of late, the Kondhs in particular have grown aversion towards any such welfare and development programme of the Government.

It is distressing to note that, in the recent decades, operation of development schemes in the Kondhs hills and plains has attracted small business class people and contractors who infiltrate into the area to play their business quite lucratively and in course of their stay exploit the innocent Kondhs unabated. Presently, these outside infiltrators in collusion with the local officials and the Pana middlemen indulge in anti-Kondh and anti-social activities and create disturbances in the area affecting peace and harmony. Often problems are being created for the Kondh to realize political ends. The simple living Kondhs suffer from suffocation in the changing socio-political scenario.

To the advantage of the Kondh, Ashram Schools have been established in the Kondh villages. Ashram School education serves the dual purpose of imparting teaching to the Kondh children in the classes and to acquaint them with the school curricula, and to inculcate educational socialism among the Kondhs, who for generations were deprived of getting formal schooling. Residential provisions of the school serves as a great incentive to the Kondh children. Besides, all the expenses of lodging, boarding, reading and writing materials including dresses for the Kondh children in the school are borne by the government. Thus, education is made freely available to the Kondh children. In the last few decades, one can say that education through Ashram School has been a great success. The Ashram School educated

Kondh youths today have been capable to understand the day tc day happening in their area and in the country and have developed self-awareness and confidence to face the challenging situation. Educational modernization has in certain socio-cultural spheres upset the traditional institutions nevertheless it has liberated the Kondh youths from traditional moorings and anchorage. The ascriptive status orientation and the decision-making process by the elders have undergone tremendous transformation and the educated youths have started making allout efforts to participate in decision making processes in their society.

LAMPs are in operation in the study area specially meant for the Kondhs. This cooperative institution normally provides credit facilities to the Kondh members, undertakes marketing of the produce of the Kondh and supplies consumer goods to the Kondh villagers. Ideally this is supposed to be one of the noble institutions for the betterment of the Kondhs. But in practice, LAMPs have been operating in the area in a hostile manner. The irony is that even with the knowledge of the LAMP officials, credits are given to non-tribals, especially to the *Panas,* the Scheduled Caste neighbours, in the name of the poor Kondhs. The Pana gets the benefit from the LAMPs whereas the needy Kondh is deprived. The whole process of distribution of credits is so complex and handled bureaucratically in so vary complicated way that only people having influence at the level of the LAMPs office get the benefits and the majority of the poor Kondhs do not get access to the LAMPs for credit. Kondhs prefer to take loans from the Banks than from the LAMPs, although in the latter case terms of repayment are not very stringent. People do not wish to incur loans from the LAMPs in fear of getting exploited and cheated by the LAMPs officials and the Scheduled Caste brokers. Only a few of them dare to transact with the LAMPs.

Essential commodities, like salt, kerosene, narcotics and cheap garments and clothes are usually being sold in the cooperative shops. These shops are meant for the Kondh tribals. But many non-Kondhs and even the petty businessmen of the locality buy these commodities from them and ply their business. At the time of need the Kondh does not get his requirements from the shops and stop coming to these shops and starts buying them from the local shops and other vendors. The local vendors and shopkeepers take advantage of the situation and sell the commodities at a higher rate. In some seasons, the marketing officers of the LAMPs procure the produce of the Kondhs and in some seasons do not. Normally, procurement of the produce of the Kondh tribals is made by LAMPs with a view to checking exploitation of the moneylenders and the local businessmen. But due to the negligence of the LAMPs officials and irregular and unrewarding procurement devices, the Kondhs become the victims of the local moneylenders and traders. They are doubly exploited thereby. Unless and otherwise operation of LAMPs is revamped in the interest of the Kondhs, it will continue to negatively affect the people.

The overall change in the socio-cultural, economic, political and religious arenas of the Kondh community can be attributed to a powerful acculturating process overtly operative in the area of study largely but substantively nourished by the caste Hindu neighbours. This long drawn-out process has historical relevance which holds good for tribal situation in Orissa in general. With the onset of welfare and development activities of the Government, in the recent decades, and with the opening of the tribal areas to the people of the outside communities, and with the introduction of bureaucratic state administration and control, the scenario of the Kondh culture and community is in the ferment of change and development, treading the path at the same rate, encountered in the backward areas of India in general.

Ethnohistory of the Koras of West Bengal

Ashoke Kumar Jana

Ethnohistory' is the history of peoples normally studied by the anthropologists. Anthropologists defining ethnohistory tend to specify that it relies on written documents but where written records are lacking or scanty it supplements through the collection of oral history and analysis of their ethos and ways of life.

From the pre-historic period to the present day, the entire structure of many societies has undergone sea-change in different degrees and there were migration of many ethnic groups due to various causes some of which are mentioned below.

1. Scarcity of food and employment for their survival.
2. Changing political canvas and varied degrees of exploitation.
3. Ravages from natural calamities, etc.

In consequence, man had to face certain abrupt and seemingly insurmountable difficulties, which compelled them to itinerate for their survival by adjustments. Then the Aryans came to the Indian scene, and later the Muslims, who occupied their pride of place in Indian history. All these people might have blended to depict different ethnopolitic picture reflected on the Indian population of the time. Sometimes, powerful invaders in circumstantial exigencies compelled the others to take shelter in solitude. But pre dominating neighbouring groups exercise tremendous impact on them and these might have accelerated the process of interaction and assimilation. The Aryan theory has, however been discarded as myth.

Thus we find historical factors of stress and strain and surrendering of some groups to the powerful ones, might be responsible for bringing about a change, in different degrees and helped many autochthonous groups to acquire new habits of the material lifestyle and social organizations. Thus, the worship of alien gods and goddesses in India was studied in certain regions. This process of interaction produced the constellation in different distinctive identities with the passage of time. And in course of time many of the autochthonous groups imitated the culture and tradition of the dominating groups who later identified themselves with new names. This process has been described by various authors as the process of Hinduization, acculturation or sanskritization.

Of course, the peculiar features of caste with its hierarchical ladder, connected with notions of purity and pollution and typical occupational grades–are somewhat unique to Indian history and civilization. The Brahmins were at the top of the society but there existed fringe communities at the peripheral levels, who were identified as *Asura, Rakshasa, Anarya* i.e., non-Aryans or *Savara, Kirata* and so on. These communities exist even today and they are now considered as 'buffer or fringe communities' of the dominant cultural groups. The Koras constitute one such group.

The Koras are a little known Scheduled Tribe in West Bengal. They have concentrations in the adjoining states of Bihar and Orissa. The Koras speak an Austro-Asiatic language of the Mundari group and, thus, have some resemblance to the big 'Hor' or the Santal group, indicating an inherent relationship with the Santal. A few clan names have Santal affinity. It might be that once the big 'Hor' race was split up into many segments due to certain circumstantial exigencies, either due to growth of population or competition in the economic fields in narrow environs. May be, one or many of these factors were responsible for the splitting up of the big 'Hor' community into more than one.

An attempt has been made by the researcher to describe, in detail, their ways of life, social institutions, rite-de-passage, magico-religious beliefs, including their world view, in order to have a systematic ethnographic account of them. The other Austric speaking people, including the Santal, the Mahali and the Munda, who live more or less, in the same ecology and environment have been considered to some extent to understand these people.

The following remarks of Risley (1891) will support this. As he has said, the Koras of Bengal are more or less Hinduised...their priests are Brahmans,...But lay as...who are members of the same caste in Bengal...many Koras are cultivators, others live by tank digging, road making etc. According to Risley (1891), they are allied to the Mundas. Roy (1915) suggested that they are of Oraon origin, practising different types of occupation, specially related to earth work such as raising embankment etc.

There has hardly been, as yet, any systematic study on the Koras. In fact no full length monograph is available and, as such, a thorough study of people is considered important along with other related groups, just to examine the nature of detachment from the original 'Hor' groups, i.e., the Santal.

The aims and objectives of the present study are as follow :

1. to get a socio-cultural profile of the community;
2. to trace the extent of affinity, i.e., the ethnohistory of the people;

3. to highlight the process of change since the last published account of the community;
4. to reflect the attitude of the community towards development and its impact, and
5. to bridge the gap of information about the community.

The Koras are one of the Scheduled Tribes of West Bengal. They are widely distributed in the districts of Burdwan, Midnapore, Bankura and Purulia of West Bengal. Some of them are also found in the plantation areas of Jalpaiguri district. They are bilingual and can speak and understand regional Bengali language also.

The present work on the Koras is not only a scrutiny or re-examination of the old surveys made, but a fresh attempt to include all those aspects with a wider approach. It covers four important districts of West Bengal where the Kora concentration is high. Altogether ten villages were surveyed in depth, namely, Shitli, Ranbania, Dudhebude, Jharia, Birkham, Labdapara, Raghunathpur, Gobindapur, Sanka and Barsul. Apart from these villages, some other villages of these four districts were also visited by the present rersearcher for collection, collation and corroboration of all the data and verification of the information collected during the present study.

The standard anthropological methods and techniques have been used in this field study. The participant observation method has often been considered as the opportunity to know the people intimately in their own environment. This has been supplemented by other appropriate methods relevant for investigation. In the researcher's bid to reconstruct the history of a people from the oral sources, he has followed also the sampling method. As it was not possible to talk to every one or to some hand picked persons. Stratified random sampling was made in order to collect data from a limited number of informants who were chosen on the basis of some criteria deemed critical for the research, viz., age, sex, education, experience, reputation for reliability or the period of their residence in a particular locality. And, as such, a good number of villages in different areas of West Bengal have been studied to get a clear picture of the people living in different geo-physical and ethnic set-up.

The initial difficulty of the researcher was removed due to co-operation of the local people with their endemic knowledge in the language and dialect, as he received help from them in eliciting correct information from the respondents and from the field. Thereby, their conditions of living could be seen from a close range, and suggestions could be made for improving their material condition of living so as to enable them to compete with other advanced sections of people.

With regard to the history and culture of the Koras, it is presumed that among the tribals many names have been attributed to them by the stronger neighbouring communities, e.g., the appellation of 'Santal' might have been derived from the nomenclature Simantapal or 'border guard'. The term 'Kora' might have also been derived from Santali word Kora, which means small or little. Possibly, the Santals or the 'Hor' group in the historical past considered a section of the big 'Hor' group to be their inferior, as they might have mostly depended on earthwork, being landless. As such they began to consider them small or inferior, i.e., the 'Kora'. And thus, occupation-bound caste system had a definite role to play while ascribing them the term 'Kora', denoting 'small' and/or 'inferior'. In case of the Mahalis, similarly, it indicates that they are mainly bamboo workers. In Santali language 'Mah' means bamboo. Therefore, those who depended on bamboo for a living, in later period, and accepted or depended on bamboo work have been regarded as the' Mahali'. Thus, the caste-bound neighbouring groups could split up the community and reconstitute the Kora or the Mahali.

It is a fact that the Koras have migrated from Chotonagpur plateau. In West Bengal, their number is now about 96,835, of which 48,960 are males and 47,875 are females (1981 Census). Racially, the Kora belong to Australoid tribe. Although Grierson (2000) views that the language of the Kora is derived from Mundari, the Kora language *(Thare)* varies from region to region. They are the descendants of a 'forsaken' child. There is a myth to the effect that once upon a time a Mundari couple went to the jungles for hunting and gathering. Suddenly, they found a newborn baby crying. There was no man to be seen near about. The Munda couple picked up the baby and reared him up, as they were childless. As the Koras are the descendants of a *kuriey paoa chhele or kurano chhele* (a boy who had been picked up), he was called a 'Kora' boy. There is another story in this regard. They are known as Koras because they speak in *karah* dialect, which is not easily understood by the neighbouring caste and communities. So they are known as *karah bhasar lok* or those who speak in a harsh language or are known as Koras.

The present study covers 10(ten) sample villages in the districts of Midnapur, Burdwan, Bankura and Purulia. Some of the villages have a multi-ethnic population in which other caste people and those of other communities live side by side with the Koras, while the other villages are entirely inhabited by the Koras. In Midnapur district, three villages are chosen among which village Shitli is a multi-ethnic village. The remaining two are located by the road-side and are inhabited by the Koras i.e., they are homogenous villages.

These villages are selected at random, and the total Kora households covered by these villages are 255, consisting of a population of 590 males (50.99%) and 567 (49%) females. As per survey data, 209 (35.42%) of the males and 229 (40.38%) of the females belong to the age group of 0-14 years. This agrees with the general pattern of the country, as this age group constituted something around 40%.

The Kora families have been categorized on the basis of the number of members as 'small', 'medium', 'large', and 'very large'. Some small sized families have been found in almost all the villages where widows and widowers live either with their minor children or alone. Out of the 255 families, 83 (32.54%) have three members each or less. The medium sized families are predominant numbering 127 (49.80%) in all the Kora villages. Such a family consists of parents and their unmarried and married children. The number of large sized families is 44(17.25%). In village Sanka, no family of this size has been found, whereas in the other villages such large sized families are in existence. This type of family consists of parents, their married sons and unmarried children. The Koras have been classified into four distinct groups, according to their marital status. These are unmarried, married, widowed and divorced. Out of the 590 male persons and 567 females, 313 (53.05%) males and 248 (43.73%) females are unmarried. The number of married males is 260 (44.06%) and that of married females is 262 (46.20%). In village Ranbania, the married females have outnumbered their male counterparts by two, which appears to be due to some persons' having more than one wife. During the field survey, 114 (2.37%) males and 50 (8.81 %) females are found to be widowers and widows, respectively. These persons are found to be living with their unmarried children. Some young widows are found living with their children without taking resort to a second marriage. The cases of divorce are generally settled at the traditional community council level, which is known as *Jati-Sabha*. The total number of divorced males is 3 (0.5%) and the corresponding figures for females is 7 (1.23%).

Among the Kora individuals, those who are just able to read and write a little or can sign their names, are considered literates. Out of a total population of 1157 in the 10 villages, 238 (20.57%) persons are literate by this standard.

Non-labour/labour working force of the Koras in the selected villages has been estimated by the survey. It is significant to note that the working force of the tribe is higher than the labour force (in 15-60 years age-group). Out of the 590 males, the number of labour force is 373 (63.22%) and that of labour force among the females is 328

(57.84%) out of 567 females, whereas the working force of males is 433(73.72%) and that of the female working force is 370 (65.25%).

Speaking about their settlement pattern, their huts are generally rectangular shaped with mud walls, four sloppy roofs with straw thatches and supported by bamboo poles. The houses are located on both sides of the roads across the village and facing towards south. The *Ote* (floor) is made of beaten earth. The courtyard is always kept clean and sometimes plastered with cowdung paste. The small shades for goats and fowls (*Simora*) and cowshed (*Urigora*) are kept attached to the hut. The kitchen garden (*Bagri*) is characterized as a household necessity where vegetables are grown.

Agriculture is the principal subsistence pursuit of the Koras. About 68.62% of the families have their own land and most of them work in those lands as well as in other's on share-cropper basis. Some of them also work as agricultural day labourers on other's fields. Both the males and the females participate almost equally in the agricultural activities. Paddy is the principal crop cultivated by the Kora community and they follow both the methods of broadcasting and transplanting. Fishing is generally carried on in the water-logged paddy fields and in the nearby water bodies. It is operated both by the males and the females.

Once in every year, the Kora people go out on hunting by way of recreation which is carried on exclusively by the males. This is known as *Birshendra,* which takes place either on the 7th or the 14th or the 21st day of *Baisakh* (March-April). Agriculture is another important avocation of the Koras living by the side of other castes and communities. All of them learn agricultural operations from the Hindu caste farmers residing in the nearby villages.

As regards the social organization of the Koras, it is a net work of relations existing among individuals and groups in their society. Four sub-groups of the Koras have been identified, viz., *Modi Kora, Kurmi Kora, Nagbansi Murale Kora* and *Dhanger* or *Orang Kora*. These sub-groups are strictly endogamous and follow clan exogamy. In the villages under study, we find 24 clans, namely, *Tundu, Hansda, Barda, Tirki, Kisku, Hembram* etc., which have close affiliations with the Santals.

Family is the basic social unit among the Koras and it influences the individual in every sphere of life. Out of the 255 families, the number of nuclear families is 127 (43.80%), nascent/conjugal families is 26 (10.96%) and broken families is 29 (11.37%). The total number of polygynous type of families is 2 (.78%). The Kora society is patriarchal and patrilineal. They practise both patrilocal and neolocal residence. Monogamy is the most prevalent form of marriage among them.

Polygamy is also practised, but the cases are rare. Out of the 255 families, only 2 persons are having two wives each. Generally the first wife is taken with the consent of the elders after going through elaborate marriage ceremonies, whereas the second wife is acquired by mutual consent or elopement.

The culture traits are transmitted to their offspring through the process of enculturation and acculturation which comes by virtue of their association in both domestic spheres. In this phase, the parents provide frame work of those values and norms which they define as appropriate. The individual tends to develop a type of personality which is in harmony with the cultural pattern and tradition of the Kora community.

Kinship terms of the Koras show that they have both classificatory as well descriptive kinship terms. Only a few of their traditional terms (*son-Hatingya : grandson-Joy Kora, grand daughter-Joy kori*) are still lingering among them. Behaviour pattern among the primary relatives of the Kora is quite similar as found among the neighbouring caste and communities. The Koras have classificatory system of relationship and have eight terms of primary relatives and thirty-three distinct kinds of secondary relatives. Among these there are also 151 tertiary relatives. Each term has anthropological notation, term of address and term of reference. Changes are noticed in the use of kinship terms (Bengali language). Teknonymy have been involved in many kins. Both joking and avoidance relationship have importance in the understanding of structural situation particularly from the point of view of consanguinity and affinity.

Politically, the Koras have their own traditional community council, known as *Jati-Sabha*. The head of the *Jati-Sabha* is called *Manjhi* and the assistant as *Kotal*. In Burdwan district, the head of the Council is known as *Morol* and the assistant as *Chharidar*. In Bankura also the Koras have a community council, known as *Namahal* and it comprises of nine villages. The supreme authority of *Namahal* is known as *Raja* and his assistant is known as *Mantri*. These posts are non-hereditary, except that of the *Morol*. The *Raja* and *Mantri* are elected from among the members of *Morol* and *Kotal* respectively by voice-vote. The main duty of the *Jati-Sabha* is to solve the social problems. If anybody is found guilty of theft, he is punished physically and a fine is imposed, to boot. They deal with the cases of elopement, quarrels due to suspicion of fidelity and mutual distrust, divorce, violation of community endogamy etc. The power of the traditional council has been minimized now and it is gradually being passed over to the statutory Gram Panchayat.

The ethnographic profile of the Koras and their cross-cultural comparison show that they possess certain degree of similarities in their socio-cultural milieu, which is due to their supposed origin from the Santals, or the big 'Hor' race of Mundari speaking people. This is also due to their close association at the level of regional culture and common mode of adaptation with identical ecology and environment. At the same time, each community shows its distinctiveness in certain ethno-cultural marks.

Religion is an integral part of culture of human society and it plays a vital role in the Kora socio-economic life. The researcher studied 255 households. Only 25 (9.80%) families have been converted into Christianity in village Dudhebude of Midnapore district. The rest 230 families (90.19%) declare that all of them profess Hinduism. A sacred specialist is called in for propitiating their deities from the neighbouring Brahmin caste people who worship Lord *Shiva* and goddesses like *Kali, Durga, Manasa* and *Shitala*. There are two *Thans* (sacred seat of god/goddess), known as *Mahadeo Than* and *Garam Than*. The Kora devotees attend the *Than* for various purposes. These are related to their actual life situations, in which they find no other alternative but to depend on their deities, who are considered by them to be the chief controllers of human destiny. Thus, religious beliefs are concerned with the blessings of gods in adverse circumstances in life. This is done by the supposed operation of sacred power through propitiation, i.e., offerings, prayers and sacrifices. Offerings to the deities are of varied nature and these are very traditional in the Kora society. For each deity, a specific type of offering has to be made and then the worship is performed by the sacred specialist. The Koras observe a ritual in connection with agriculture, which is known as *Muth* for getting a bumper crop. Another ritual performed by them is connected with agriculture, which is known as *Jantal*. *Pukurbiha* is yet another ceremony performed for use of water from the newly dug tank, which is an important ritual in connection with the digging of a new tank by the Koras.

Totemism is a common feature among the Koras and most of them believe in their mysterious relation with some animals or plants. They consider that the totemic plants or animals have helped or protected their respective ancestors of the clan concerned and show reverence to these. They do not destroy the totem objects. The Koras also refrain from eating their fruits or flowers. The dead totemic plants or animals are given full honour and are attended to in their last hour accordingly. Taboo is another sacred belief, which has a rather negative value in any belief. The exclusion of the Kora women from certain religious festivals and ritualistic observances during their periodical menstruation are practised as taboos. Even the Kora women or girls in such conditions do not prepare and supply food to their elders and respected persons.

The Koras celebrate various fairs and festivals throughout the year. They observe *Bandhana Parab, Enga Parab, Holibonga, Gram Bandh Puja* and *Chhatu Sendra* etc. During these festive occasions, they participate in various types of dances and songs, e.g., *Dong-nach, Nangre-nach, Jhumur-nach, Karam Nach, Danr nach* and *Pata nach*. These are participated both by males and females. *Kathi nach* and *Tusu* nach are performed separately by males and females.

The Koras believe in supernatural powers. Their belief in supernaturalism is reinforced by their illiteracy and poverty. These may be one of the important reasons for the unsanitary conditions of living and unhygienic practices among them. Their food habits are invariably affected by their unhealthy practices. The belief system regarding health and illness among the Koras varies from person to person. According to some informants, there are certain types of diseases which are physically caused, viz., measles, cholera, dysentery, diarrhoea, hysteria, fever, rickets etc., which they believe, may be cured by magic spells and sorcery. There are other kinds of diseases also which are physically caused, viz., wounds, burns etc., which may be cured by physical application of medicines. The Koras also believe that the etiologies of internal diseases are caused due to the wrath of the deities and evil spirits and these can be cured only by magical practices. They believe in the powers of forest deities, family gods and goddesses and supernatural agencies. Therefore, different kinds of offerings or sacrifices are made to each of the respective spirits and deities. According to a number of tribal elders and medicinemen, the most popular techniques of curing a disease are chanting of the appropriate *mantras*. This is often prescribed for curing various ailments, like epidemic, snake bite and also for getting rid of an evil spirit.

In conclusion, it may be stated that this big Mundari tribe, distributed in different parts of the region, with varying ecology, had to move from one place to another due to various pulls and pushes. These enabled the group to be alienated from the main stock and this alienation (Bhowmick 1989) took place as per Hindu caste rule, i.e., mainly on the basis of their occupation, as happened in many cases. Of course, further research on the physical features of all these groups may throw more light in the process of alienation, which took place long time ago. As a detailed ethnographic account of the tribe is lacking, the humble report of the researcher may fill up the gap to some extent that has been continuing to exist for long. Again, due to rapid industrialization and urbanization in different parts of the country, bringing some kind of uniformity in the lifestyle of the people, the hiatus between the Koras and other mainstream population increased, which, if not attempted to bridge now, may go beyond repairs in the near future. For this purpose, social scientists may be approached by the administration to do their precious bit in this regard.

This ethnographic monograph attempts to highlight the earlier history and culture of the Kora people, which is not available as yet in a coherent and systematic way.

In course of detailed description, comparison has been made with some of the neighbouring tribal groups viz., the Santal, Munda and Mahali and all these practically indicate some basic resemblance with some variation caused by change of ecology or other interacting ethnic forces. Of course, change is a continuous process in all the cases though it varies in degree. Besides, after independence some facilities have been extended to the tribal people in general as they are considered to be 'Weaker Section' of our total population. And this assistance or the facilities are provided for them in the Indian Constitution. So welfare measures undoubtedly brought some changes in respect of the economic life, education and health and hygiene of these people but these are not up to our expectation. But communication facilities, exposure of the people in different socio-political situations brought all these groups of people to the bigger societies and thus a slow change of world view is noticeable. All these together in course of time will change the socio-cultural life of the people and under such circumstances this short ethnographic account will serve as a base-line survey to note the various changes in time and space dimension. India is a country where we find variegated groups of people who are found to show transformations and blending due to historical upheavals and interactions. Under such historical processes the entire community may be transformed to some extent and this base-line ethnographic account will show the background of the people on the basis of which some assessment can be done.

References

Bhowmick, P. K. 1989 *The Chemhkus of the Forests and Plateaux : A Hunting-gathering tribe in transition.* Calcutta : Insititute of Social Research And Applied Anthroplolgy.

Grierson, G. A. 2000 *Languages of North-Eastern India : A Survey.* New Delhi : Gyan Publishing House.

Risley, H. H. 1891 *Tribes and Castes of Bengal.* Bengal : Secretariat Press.

Roy, S. C. 1915 *The Oraons of Chotanagpur.* Ranchi : Man in India Office.

The Bhoksa–A Little Known Tribe of Uttar Pradesh

Niranjan Kumar Ghatak

The Bhoksas are one of the five Scheduled Tribes of Uttar Pradesh. They have acquired the said status since 1967. Before 1967, the Bhoksas or Buksas were treated in the category of Scheduled Caste in Uttar Pradesh.

The origin and the base of the community is very difficult to trace. But a few stories about the same may be mentioned here. One is a comparatively simple story which fixes them as Rajput from Delhi, who either settled in this region voluntarily or were exiled to the Tarai, during the Mughal period. The other story afloat is to the effect that certain Rajputs, being about to rebel against the Mughal ruler, sent their wives with their maidservants as escorts of Kahars to safety, through this wild track. The rebellion failed. Their husbands were all killed and the Bhoksas were supposedly the offsprings of the union of Rajput women and their Kahar servants. Crooke (1896) has however stated that the Bhoskas came from Dakhin while others have specifically mentioned that they migrated from Delhi.

The Dehradun Bhoksas say that after defeat of their king in a battle with a Muslim warrior, it was not possible for them to live in their household, because their life and the chastity of the women folk were at stake. The Muslim warriors not only damaged their property, but also were eager to get the girls in their possessions, so, they fled into the jungle to save their life and chastity and also to protect their community from the danger of total annihilation. They now do not remember the name of the Hindu king and the land of their original habitat. The Nainital Bhoksas also told the same story. They tell that after the death of king Jagat Deo, Daranagar was attacked by the Muslims who were once defeated by Jagat Deo with the blessing of goddess 'Chandi'. Jagat Deo had two sons–Jagga and Gulgulia. Both of them were ready for a fight, but they hesitated to do so thinking that the defeat might lead to the end of the community at the hands of the Muslims who were previously repulsed by their father. As a precautionary measure, the king ordered the women and children should be sent to a safe place along with their servants. Only the warriors should be in Daranagar for a final showdown. If they won the battle, the women and the children would be escorted to their families from the forest hide out and, if they lost, at least their sons would remain alive in the world. This was the history of their migration into Tarai.

The Bhoksas identify themselves as 'Thakur' claiming their origin in the line of Rajput descent. They are patriarchal and these rules govern both inheritance of property and residence after marriage. They follow patrilineal descent and patrilocal residence. Although Bhoksa society is an admixture of some social groups and these groups are also segmented into a number of sub-groups, yet their interactional pattern does not suggest any kind of social hierarchy existing among them. The sub group names among them have perhaps been derived from their different place names of original settlement, in the remote past.

Every Bhoksas *(Khera)* habitation consists of several clusters of conical huts arranged in lineal pattern (in Nainital district) in such a manner that a portion of the shed or roof of the hut is inter-linked with the other huts. But in Dehradun the arrangement is in a topsy-turvy manner, and in sprawling areas. Sometimes, we find that the distance between one hut and another is more than even 50 yards. The arrangement of huts is invariably based on kinship basis. Close kinsmen, like brothers, brothers-in-law build their huts very close to each other. Bhoksas prefer to live in isolation among their people only, but some of the settlements have a mixed population in which other caste and community people also live along with the Bhoksas. Thus it is very clear that the Bhoksas are gradually increasing in number and this has compelled them not only to readjust themselves with their environment, but also with the technology introduced and with the new groups of people elsewhere for their essential needs of life. In the traditional forest setting, there were some other groups who lived along with the Bhoksas. These groups were the Muslims, Punjabi-Sikhs and others belonging to lower castes and also higher castes. Thus, the village inhabited by the Bhoksas may be grouped broadly into three categories as mentioned below.

1. The village exclusively inhabited by the Bhoksas.
2. The village inhabited by multi ethnic population where they are found to live not only amongst various castes, high and low, but also with the Muslims and

3. The village where the Bhoksas live with other groups but where the Bhoksas are the dominant group.

The Bhoksa houses are generally rectangular in shape. Most of the houses consist of one bed-room and a kitchen under the same roof. The Bhoksas are non-vegetarian and they take mutton, pork, fish-and egg. Their staple food is rice with 'dal' (pulse). Generally, the Bhoksas eat what they grow. In the past they were growing only paddy and many varieties of food grains. So their food is enriched by a number of items of their own field products. Now they not only eat rice but also take wheat, maize etc. along with it.

The hairstyle of the Bhoksa women deserves special mention. The hair of the Nainital Bhoksa women is typical; they tie their hair in the shape of a bulging ball at the middle of their head. The women seem to take pains to arrange their hair in this fashion. The hairstyle suits them and they look graceful in it, especially when the head is covered with 'Orhni' (scarf). But nowadays many of the young women are discarding this style and adopting a simple type of hair dressing with 'Jura' (hair ball) at the back of the head. The Bhoksas love to decorate themselves, and their women are found of wearing ornaments, even a small girl wears a few items of ornament.

Tatooing, i.e., 'Godna' is found prevalent among the Bhoksas. It is frequently found among the women, some men also do the tattooing, specially their names on the forearms. Some of the women make 'Gundi' marks on their forehead by tattooing. Though tattooing is found prevalent yet it has not been given social importance and gradually it is going to fade out.

At present, the Bhoksas are settled agriculturists. But, traditionally, they were slash and burn cultivators and gatherers. Their economy has been developed in very unfavourable condition. For this on the one hand, the Muslim invaders were responsible and, on the other, the stagnant condition of agricultural pursuits were also responsible. The ecology of the land and their unhygienic habitations in uncongenial region are perhaps the most important factors that stood in their way to development.

Table 1

Particulars of the Villages Surveyed

Village	Households	Population		Total
		Male	Female	
Nainital				
Beria	32	107	79	186
Birpur	9	27	23	50
Pipal Sanna	30	105	113	218
Rajpur	24	96	93	189
Thari	36	102	102	204
Bhuri	44	197	180	377
Khumbari	57	180	179	359
Sinhali	28	86	83	169
Vikampuri	19	58	57	115
Dehradun				
Tiparpur	158	506	402	908
Midnapur & Badripur	40	130	102	232
Mehuwala Khalsa	43	109	101	210
Total	520	1703	1514	3217

Table 1 depicts details of the villages surveyed along with their population structure (Bhoksas) in which males and females have been distributed on an age-group basis. In the Nainital district, nine settlement camps have been set up among which Khum Bari and the people of village Sanna are multi-ethnic-groups. These are developed villages in comparison with the other roadside villages. Though the villages of these areas are near the forest enclaves, yet the above two villages have been getting more exposures to the outsiders than others, i.e., villages Beria, Birpur, Thari, Bhuri, Sinhali, Vikampuri etc.

Three villages have been selected from Dehradun district for study. All these villages are multi-ethnic in nature and are located near the forest area. The people of both the villages are settled agriculturists, where the Bhoksa also have taken to agriculture as their primary occupation. These settlements have been selected at random and the total number of Bhoksa households covered in the study are 520 out of a population 0f 3,217 of which 1,703 are males and 1,514 are females. The villages have no definite lay out plan, whether they be of a mixed population or are inhabited exclusively by the Bhoksas. It is rarely found that non-Bhoksa families are living in the midst of the settlement of other groups. The Bhoksa settlement is generally based near the forest, having an approachable kutcha road towards the villages. The main source of their water supply these days is usually the tube-wells. In addition to tube-well, there may be natural springs or rivers around the villages. In every Bhoksa village, it is observed that their tribal deity 'Bhum Sen', is represented by the elevation of a mud-mound, which is situated in front of *Pradhan* (traditional head of the village) house. And the *Chomtra Than*, the place of a goddess is generally situated near a stream, and also under a big tree in the vicinity of the village.

Attendance of the Bhoksa students in the school is extremely poor, and that in the months of July and August (the agricultural season) is comparatively even lesser than in other seasons. Bhoksas generally send their children to the school in their later age.

According to the existing system, the school-going children take part actively in the execution of agricultural activities in different phases of the process. In the past, they lived in the forest as a forest dwelling community. They made their living by food gathering, pasturing cattle and a little hunting that they could do. They were accustomed with the forest life.

The forest provides them all the required materials for the settlement and also provides fruits, roots, barks etc., for their subsistence and is the source of grazing ground for their cattle or domestic animals. After independence, the situation of the Bhoksa community has changed. Forest is now not free to them, as in the past when they practised sudden cultivation. Further encroachment in the forest is not possible. But due to their living in the proximity of the forest, they get some special privileges from the forest department, e.g.

1. They are allowed to collect dry wood from the forest for their personal use.
2. They are permitted to get the wooden poles from the forest, free or at concessional rates from the forest after having the permission of the forest department.
3. They are allowed to graze their domestic animals in the forest.

Above all, forest provides ground for pasturing their cattle. Rearing of cattle is treated as a source of income to them. This is not the only consideration of keeping cattle as an unavoidable part of their plough cultivation. For plough cultivation, cattle however are required too.

On the whole, it may be said that in the past forest provided food and shelter for them. But at present, forest still supplies them with one essential material for their daily life, namely, shelter, and helps them economically by supplying forest products. Thus, forest may be treated as a source of their secondary income.

The traditional *Takat Panchayat* is very active in its role. In social factors or in some inter-village conflicts the disputes are still being resolved in the *Takat Panchayat*.

In the past all the Bhoksa inhabited villages were uni-ethnic in nature. No other caste groups preferred to live in settlement along with the Bhoksas. In some sporadic cases it was found that some others groups make their settlement at the outskirts of the Bhoksas. But at present it is found that other castes groups as well as the Muslims are living side by side with the Bhoksas in Dehradun district. Similar trend is also found in the Bhoksa inhabited villages of Nainital district but this is not as prominent as in the Dehradun district.

The Bhoksas are gradually attuned with the belief of Hindu mode of life and accept the Hindu god and goddesses in their dav to day life. They worship *Siva, Laxmi, Chandi, Ammbamali, Hanumanji, Ram* and *Sita* in both the districts. The influence of Hindu deities is found more in Dehradun district, though Nainital Bhoksas are also accepting the same along with their traditional belief. They visit the worshipping place of Hindu, attend puja and prayed to the God for giving them prosperity and health in the material life. Similarly, they also show their faith in the Muslim religion and Sikhism. They visit Masjid or Gurudwara with a prayer for their material benefit. They also visited Muslim *pir* or *fakir* for some treatment when their local *Bharara* fail to cure the diseases of the patient.

Most of the Bhoksas are addicted to liquor, even their women folk drink and create a taste for it among the children. Among most of them, liquor is a necessary accompaniment of almost all social and religious functions which requires fulfilment of tribal obligations regarding hospitality and entertainment.

Magical practices are applied to agriculture, disease and other crises relating to birth and marriage ceremonies. Magical methods are also employed in driving away the evil spirits, in warding off the influence of the evil eye and in curing diseases caused by the mother goddess and other supernatural agencies. The educated or conscious people consult doctor in the case of ailment and other diseases. But the majority still have faith in the Bhoksas *Bharara* whose magical spells and amulets are believed to be most effective in any crisis of difficulty of the Bhoksas.

Bhoksas do not start any work without consulting a *Bharara*. *Bharara* is their advisor in the case of any mishappening or illness or forwarding off any danger of evil eye. Their belief in the *Bharara* and super-natural world is so high that they can not come out of it. At present Bhoksa people have become more conscious and consult local doctors or sometimes visit hospital for some diseases. It is also stated that at present *Bharara* themselves advise the local people to consult the doctors if they fail to cure any patient by their local treatment.

The common practice of the liquor sellers who are outsiders mostly exploit the innocence and simplicity of the Bhoksas by selling liquor to them on credit and they charge exorbitant rate of interest which goes on accumulating to enormous amounts in course of a few years. Many Bhoksas have been totally ruined on account of their drinking habit and due to the exploitation by liquor sellers.

The Bhoksas–a little known tribe in Uttar Pradesh–was once found to inhabit in the unhealthy, swampy, malaria infected areas of Tarai region and hence, had experienced physical and cultural isolation to some extent. But at present many changes are taking place in their ways of life social, economic, political, religion and recreational life. But their condition of poverty is still continuing. Educational level among them is also very low, but due to their continuous contact with the other caste people the Bhoksas are now gradually becoming more interested in education of their children. This is likely to change their lifestyle and behavioural pattern in near future.

Reference

Crooke, W. 1996 *The Tribes and Castes of the North-Western India.* Calcutta: Government Printing Press.

A Study on Anthropological (Bio-Social) Aspects of Child and Maternal Health among the Nicobarese of Car Nicobar Island

Madhumala Chattopadhyay

The Nicobar Islands are situated in the South East of the Bay of Bengal between 6° to 10° 'N' latitude and between 92° to 94° 'E' longitude. Twenty two small islands constitute about 262.32 Km. of the long chain of Nicobar island of which only 12 are habituated. Car Nicobar is the northern most island of the Nicobar group, about 75 miles off the little Andaman and separated by 10° N latitude channel from Andaman group of island. Harmender bay, the new settlement of Car Nicobarese, is located in the little Andaman, the southern most island of the Archipelago. About 150 Car Nicobar families were resettled here. The car Nicobar was originally habitated by the tribals. But in course of trade and voyages in the long past some outsiders, particularly Muslim traders from West Coast of India intermarried the tribal women and settled at Car Nicobar along with the original settlers. After independence, Car Nicobar acquired great importance on account of its trading facilities, especially in copra and betelnut. Car Nicobar is a declared tribal area and outsiders in general are not allowed to visit the island any time without the permission of the concerned authority.

In the past, several studies on various aspect of Nicobars were although made successfully, the study on mother-child health and their nutritional status did not receive as much attention as it deserves. So in the present study the researcher has shown her intention to highlight the mother and child of the selected villages of Car Nicobar. Secondly, Car Nicobar represents majority population (about two third) of the Nicobars and so the study on Car Nicobar may cover the major population to show an over all picture. Thirdly, from the hoary past, external trade developed between Nicobars and the outside world. The island of Car Nicobar being situated on traders route, it had an advantage of coming in contact with the outsiders. Naturally, it was an exposed island since long past. There was also an unexposed population in the interior part of Car Nicobar. In the interior villages of Car Nicobar traditional food habit is in vogue there, where as 'introduced' food is more liked by the people in exposed villages. On the basis of their food habits, the present study has been conducted to observe and compare their nutritional status. Lastly, at present, 150 tribal families of Car Nicobar have been rehabilitated (1973) in Little Andaman (Harmender Bay) where they do not have all the items of their traditional food. The study includes resettled families in order to compare their nutritional status with Car Nicobarese.

The objects of the study on nutrition were to evolve various programmes aiming at good health of mother and child by reducing the rate of child mortality, morbidity, health hazards throughout length and breadth of the country as have been embarked upon by Govt. of India in collaboration with the benevolent international institutions. In partial fulfillment of the noble mission of the Govt. the present work has been taken up.

This investigation has been concerned with the following aspects.

1. Assessment of the nutritional status of the Car Nicobarese–mother and children (0–6 years) living in Car Nicobar, as also Car Nicobarese rehabilitated at Little Andaman (Harmender Bay).
2. A study of the Nutritional Anthropometry of the mother and children so as to assess the prevalence of Protein Energy Malnutrition in them.
3. A study of the prevalence of certain communicable diseases, viz., diarrhoea, amoebiais, measles, malaria of Car Nicobarese mother and children–by cross sectional study.

The people of Car Nicobar mainly depend on their traditional product of *pandanus* as principal food. From *pandanus* a pulp is prepared by some indigenous process and called 'Kuen'. *Kuen* and some coconut kernel with milk of nut make a good meal for the inhabitants there. But this *pandanus* is a seasonal fruit, being available from September to March. The period of field study was so fixed that their principal food *pandanus* would be available and its nutritional effect on the tribal health could be properly measured. (fieldwork was conducted in different phases from 1989 to 1992).

In Car Nicobar, there are 5 interior and 10 exposed villages. Among those, 3 interior and 5 exposed villages were chosen which are tribal dominated. Villages were chosen in such a way that the proportion of population of the chosen exposed villages among the total population of the exposed villages was equal to the proportion of population of chosen interior villages among the total population of interior villages. Harmender Bay was taken to compare the migrated population from Car Nicobar with the population who are living still in Car Nicobar. Great care was taken to select each mother-child unit at random sampling to ensure that parents of both of them were Car Nicobarese. Mothers were chosen through the method of random sampling. Those mothers were chosen who had children below 6 years of age. The chosen age ranged for children was 0–6 years. The sample size of each selected village is chosen to be proportional to the population size of that village. Anthropometric measurement (stature, weight, sitting-height, circumference of head, chest, mid-upper-arm) were taken on 492. Car Nicobarese mother (Car Nicobar 441, Harmender Bay 51) and 760 children(Car Nicobar 691, and Hermender Bay 69), pignet, pelidisi and Korperfulla indices for mother and pignet, pelidisi, weight/height and mid upper-arm circumference/hear circumference indices for children have been calculated. These indices show the nutritional status. Hemoglobin level of mother was estimated. Quantitative diet survey (consecutive 7 days) was undertaken in 2 interior (Kakana & Kimios) and 2 exposed (Mus & Chukchucha) villages in Car Nicobar and in Harmender Bay by weighing raw food of each individual. Information on socio-economic condition of the family, health care of children etc. were collected.

Car Nicobarese mothers strictly observed some food restriction in antenatal and postnatal stages. Would be mothers take fish during pregnancy but not octopus, which may, as believed by them, lead to the birth of an albino baby. There is also a bar for pregnant lady of taking meat of bat as it may lead to the birth of a baby covered with fur coat. During pregnancy, Nicobarese women do not take lemon, may be in apprehension of acidity and subsequent illness.

Car Nicobarese pregnant women also observe some restriction in hard work. In their belief hard work namely, washing of clothes, weaving mats, collecting wild fruits, stitching of clothes etc., have a possibility of birth of physically handicapped baby.

Among Car Nicobarese the whole process of birth is regarded as unclean. There is a trained *Dai* (mid-wife) in every village who attends the normal delivery cases of that village. For birth one delivery house *(pati-yong nyio)* is built away from the village, near sea beach. When labour-pain starts the pregnant mother is shifted to the delivery house where the trained *Dai* attends the expected mother. *Dai* cuts umbilical cord with the help of sterilized scissors. After birth of the baby, coming out of the placenta from mother's womb is awaited. When the placenta comes out and the baby sounds its first cry then only the umbilical cord is cut off.

After delivery, the umbilical cord and placenta are buried in (the kinval) an isolated place of the graveyard. In case of complication only, pregnants are shifted to hospital. But now-a-days due to easy hospital facilities sometimes some pregnant mothers use to attain hospital.

After delivery Car Nicobarese mothers remain unclean for at least three months. She does not use her fingers for eating. She eats food with a spoon. During this unclean period mother has to remain confined within the house near the delivery house. After 3 to 6 months stay in that house mother and baby are shifted to another residential home, specially built for bringing up the child, within the village area and located at least 500 yards away from the communal kitchen. Mother and child may stay there upto two years. All these measures are adopted by Nicobarese to avoid pollution. This custom, has a good effect both on mother and child allowing them rest, proper nursing and care to the child and keeping off any infectious diseases. During lactation period the infant is given bath with warm water both in the morning and evening. After every bath the baby is massaged with coconut oil. During isolation period mother has to take great care of herself too. She has to drink luke warm water, take bath in warm water. As a matter of convention, mothers do not take fish for about a year until the baby can walk. But they take chicken or pork soup during this period.

Long back, when people had innumerable superstitions, Nicobarese used to kill the second baby of the twin which was the symbol of an evil spirit that would harm the family and so the second baby was killed. Presently, mother keeps the 1st baby of her twin with herself and gives the second to her relative to look after or for adoption.

Breast feeding of Nicobarese Children ranges a wider period from two to three years. If any mother does not have sufficient breast milk after delivery, the baby is breast-fed by some other lactating mother of that house or locality. Now-a-days they start breast feeding just after birth of the child as per doctor's advice. This Yellowish breast milk, secreating just after delivery, contains high protein and colostrums, useful aids to a new-born.

Car Nicobarese is of Mongoloid stock. Majority of them are Christian. Their main occupation is horticulture. Diet survey shows that per day calorie intake per Car Nicobarese pregnant mother and per day protein intake per children (1–6 years) exceeds the amount recommended by the ICMR. Because of high fat consumption 29.13% mothers from interior villages 15.92% from exposed villages and 27.45% mother from Harmender Bay are obese according to pelidisi index. Their fat consumption is high and is obtained mainly from coconut and pig fat. Although a few children are malnourished but acute malnourished children could not be found. Infections are common in children (above 2 years). Diarrhoea, boils, scabis, malaria, tuberculosis are widely prevalent. Mothers take special care of the children up to two years of age because of their social system. Immunisation coverage of children shoots high to 99.00% mother accept undergoing tubactomy operation after having 3 to 4 children. Most of the Nicobarese mother still now prefer their age old practices as the modern method of sterilization causes physical strain, special pain etc.

From the nutritional studies it is evident that health of mother and children (0–6 years) of interior villages and Harmender Bay are better than those from exposed villages although average income of the people of interior villages and Harmender Bay are less than people of exposed villages. In this connection it should be mentioned that every family has its own land for horticulture. The traditional food (*Pandanus*, Yam, banana, coconut etc) habit is still continued by interior villagers and Car Nicobarese from Harmender bay which has been given up to a broad extent by many of the people of exposed villages (except Mus village) which directly attributes to the reason of such variation in health within the same ecological set-up.

The Savaras : A Snake Charming Community of West Bengal

Himangsu Mohan Ray

The Savara of West Bengal are considered to be a semi-nomadic community, mainly earning their livelihood by snake-charming. These snake-charmer Savaras are found in the district of Midnapur in West Bengal. The word 'Savara' or its phonetic variation includes a larger generic group–as many primitive communities were regarded as 'Savara' by the dominant caste Hindu neighbours. The term therefore has a wider connotation which includes primitive forest–dwelling communities as well.

Originally the Savaras were dependent on forest produce and fowling and trapping of animals including snakes. But after gradual deforestation at later stages they lost their original habitations and began to migrate to different villages.

This study is an ethnographic account of the Savara–a snake charmer community, who are now no more in isolation; different aspects of their lifestyle are interlaced with bigger societies living around them.

In this study, not only their ethnographic profile has been portrayed but also emphasis has been laid on their social ecology and nature of adjustments with different groups. How this group of people in the midst of caste hierarchy make their living by snake charming? This aspect of economic symbiosis has been pin-pointed with gradual adjustment phases in the changed ecology as well as articulation into the social and economic system.

Most of the Savaras are expert as *Gunin* or spirit doctor or medicine man. They believe in the unseen presence of soul in all their activities and actions to help or deter them, who practice divination when a serious disease or epidemic breaks out. The appointment of these occult practitioners also depends on the nature of the disease and the nature of the spirit. The *Gunin* or medicine-men are those whose function is to cure disease with the help of medicinal plants. When required they apply magical spells to cure the diseases. They give amulets or charms to cure a person or to save him from the attack of evil spirit. Occasionally they act as sorcerer. They utter long-winding incantations to drive away spirit or ghost. When a pregnant woman suffer from labour pain, they are called to provide her relief by occult mentods. In case of snake-bite the Gunins counteract or extract the poisons by means of incantation and medical herbs and shrubs.

The Savaras described by the author in this monograph are a group of people who are experts in snake catching or snake charming. Monkey dancing is another form of their professions. A section of the Savara people embraced Islam in course of historical processes of stresses and strains.

II

As a sample, 10 villages of Savara have been selected from the district of Midnapur, West Bengal. These villages are shown in Table I. The total number of families of these ten villages are 151, consisting of a population of 812, of whom 409 are males and 403 are females.

Table 1
Location of Village

District	Subdivision	Police Station	Villages
			Dakshmin Damodarpur
		Mahisadal	Peada
	Tamluk		Nilkuntha
			Kuthigora
Midnapur		Nandigram	Damodarpur
			Burunda
	Contai	Bhagabanpur	Paschim Masuria
		Khejuri	Haludbari
			Paniksha
			Shyampur

The socio-cultural life of the Savaras reveals some unique features. They generally live in villages with a few families forming a close kin-group having consanguinal or affinal relationships, with a common clan organisation. Generally their villages are set-up by the side of a pond or a canal. A Savara village is formed by a cluster of huts. These huts are very small, ill-ventilated and unhygienic. Their houses are mud-built and thatched with straw in a rectangular shape sometimes with two, four or eight slopes and have a small door and a small window. These huts are constructed apart from each other and generally surrounded by a small kitchen garden. There is an open courtyard which forms an open space in front of every Savara hut where a *Tulsi than,* a pyramidal earthen mound with a Tulsi *(Vecimum Sanctum)* plant is constructed there for family worship. It is worshipped as god *Hari*. By the side of the mound, a *Manasa (Opunta Cactus)* plant is also planted and worshipped as goddess *Manasa* (goddess of Snake).

49.00 percent of the Savara family live in medium sized (4–6 members) families. Very large families (10 or more) are 8.50 percent only. The Savaras are mostly illiterate. Out of the 10 villages, only one was found to be a teacher of a junior high school and another a Government service holder. Recently, however, they are taking an interest in education and sending their boys to school. Out of 10 villages only 42 and 4 of them were found to have secondary school and collegiate education respectively among the population of 812.

Majority of the Savara still practise their traditional occupation i.e., snake-catching and snake charming. For snake catching, the Savaras form a small group with six to ten members. For the collection of snakes the Savaras go to the forest area or the riverside or to the paddy fields where the snakes are generally found in plenty. The best season of snake catching is Autumn, just after the rainy season and before the advent of winter. The big snakes are usually taken out for show and exhibition and are kept in *Piris* (bamboo-strip containers). In the villages, they move from door to door playing the snakes in groups of 2 to 5 or 6 members and also display these in the market places. Another problem faced by them is the risk of snake–bite. At the time of catching or playing the snakes they are often bitten by these. As hospital services or modern method of treatment are not easily available to them, they have to depend on medicinal herbs or roots and extraction of poison by spells which cause death in many cases. Economically they are very backward because they have no permanent or stable source of earning. So they continued the occupations like, snake-catching and snake charming, and took monkey dancing which is another means of livelihood of the Savara of Midnapur. They purchase young monkeys from Orissa or from Kolkata. After that they train the young monkeys and use them for their earning sourse of income. Angling of rods, mat making, bidi binders, rickshaw pullers, gardeners and in some cases begging etc., which are as alternatives to them and feed the regional economy without creating any maladjustment into the system. Not only that they play the snakes for money and food, but also sell these, at times, to the laboratories, where these are used for research purposes. To please goddess *Manasa,* the different songs are sung by the snake charmers assuming that the goddess *Manasa* will protect them from snake bites as She is thought to be the deity of snakes. Apart from this, they practise agriculture, but as they are not big cultivators, so mainly they work as day labourers. Only a few are engaged in professional job.

III

The Savara live with the Hindu castes as neighbours. But their social status is not recognised by these castes, though they are getting Brahmanical assistance. At present they are demanding equal status with these Hindu castes and try to maintain a high standard of ceremonial purity. They would not take cooked food from some lower castes. They always try to establish marital bonds with the other caste people and try to establish ceremonial relationship with caste Hindu people. But the establishment of these types of relationships is not always possible due to their awkward occupation and nasty livelihood. They observe some religious festivals, but they are not accepted as co-neighbours in the village and are not allowed to enjoy the same status. Thus the hiatus still remains unbridged due to unequal social status.

The Savara society is patriarchal and the decent and inheritance are patrilineal. After marriage the girl is identified with her husband's clan and she observes the customary rituals of her husband's family.

The Savaras have some affiliations to specific legendary heroes like *Basu, Angada, Kalketu* and *Jara* but in reality their society is not hierarchically arranged like the caste group. Though they have *gotra* or clan but in the selection of spouse these *gotros* or clan don't perform any role to play. The Savaras are the endogamous group and the clan is patrilineal.

The clan names or *gotra* names of the Savaras are like the local Hindu *gotra* names following the names of *Risi* and *Sage*. The Savaras have very close association with the Hindu caste hierarchical model and as a result the slow process of absorption is going on and they are gradually becoming a part of greater Hindu society.

Considering their surnames one interesting phenomenon has been observed. It is found that in all villages of the Savaras the Mahisyas are the dominating caste. The surnames of the Savaras are like the Mahisyas eg., *Maity, Jana, Das, Bera, Maji, Khatua, Manna, Patra* etc., which clearly indicate that the Savaras in the past lost their original surnames owing to interaction and communication with the other Hindu communities. In future they will be assimilated into the Hindu fold by adopting the surnames of the Hindu castes. Inter-caste marriage with Mahisya and Jalia Kaibarta also take place among them.

The wives are not only the partners but partners in economic life too. A son is generally preferred by them as per the doctrine of Hindu Shastra. Divorce is permissible in their society. The families of the Savara are monogamous.

In Savara society the artificial or ceremonial relationships are common. In rural societies this type of relationships like 'Dharam'– friends, father, son, daughter, mother, father in law, mother-in-law etc., are preceded by the word *dharam* which implies a socially sanctified relationship.

No distinctive differences can be observed among the life-cycle of the Savara. Like the other socio-economically poor caste group they also maintain their birth, marriage and death ritual. No special performances are observed in their day to day life. In course of their day to day interaction they gradually accept the Hindu mode of life and with the slow process of absorption and assimilation, they generally observe the Hindu rites and rituals in their lifestyles. Premarital sex relation or extra marital sex relation is also very common. From the field survey it is observed that the age of marriage of girl and the age of marriage of boy are reported to be between 10–16 years and that of the boys between 16 years-22 years respectively. In most of the cases the girl is younger than the boy.

Like all other caste groups barrenness is considered a matter of misfortune. Paradoxically pregnant woman as well as the birth of a new child is a blessing for them. For safe delivery and normal birth of a child some rituals are made in their day to day life. For a pregnant woman, in the fifth month, a *Sadh Bhakshan* ceremony is to be held and it is called as *Sadh*. Midwife, barber and Brahmin priest perform different rituals and do various activities from the five months, when the baby is in the mother's womb, to the rice giving ceremony where the baby is given the first rice food for his growth and development. Their marriage is celebrated in the fixed months of the calendar year. The priest takes the major role to negotiate the marriage. According to the rules of patriarchy, the bride leaves her father's house and stay permanently in the in-law's house. Now-a- days, bride price has been changed and in its place dowry has been introduced. Many rites and rituals take place in both the houses concerning the marriage ceremony. Many guests and friends come and join in the feasts for their enjoyment, pleasure and also for strengthening the group solidarity.

The Savaras allow the widow, the divorced or separated man or woman to remarry. Such type of marriage is called 'Sanga marriage'. Only in the presence of village headman or any aged person this type of marriage takes place. No Brahmin, barber and washerman takes part in it. This is a simple type of marriage.

Death is also normal and natural to all. Generally, the Savara cremate the dead bodies but sometimes they bury specially in case of infants and children. In their community the death pollution period is continued for ten days and on the day of eleventh the *Sradh* ceremony takes place.

The disposal of the dead and funeral ceremonies which are performed by the Savaras have become more Hinduised now. The customs in the cremation ground, the rituals of death pollution period, and the purificatory ceremonies observed by the Savaras bear many distinct Hindu traits. It is also observed that the washerman and the barber serve in the death ceremony, as they do in case of other caste Hindu groups. Thus the funeral customs correlate with those of the local Hindu castes showing gradual assimilation into the Hindu fold.

Savaras have their own village organisation apart from the village Panchayat. *Malik* or *Mukhia* is the headman of the village. In all ceremonial functions the decision of *Mukhia* is the final decision. At present the power of the headman has been lessened to some extent. Next important position is occupied in their society by the messenger or *Bailiff-Dakua*. He as a messenger asks the villagers to attend the Panchayat meeting when it is held. The post of *Dakua* is not hereditary. He is selected by the villagers. But now a day the Savaras have come under the present democratic Panchayat system. Naturally, the major decisions are not taken by them but only the local community problems are solved by them.

Ancestor worship is also one of the most important rites of the Savaras. On the day of *Shyama Puja* i.e., worship of goddess *Kali,* they observe this ceremony. They believe in the existence of ancestors and their interest and intervention in the worldly affairs.

The Savaras observe festive days in different seasons of the year. These festivals may be classed into three categōries according to the nature of the activities associated with these. These are economic, social and religious.

Goddess *Manasa* i.e., the deity of snakes, is one of the most important deities of the Savaras. Goddess *Manasa* is a household deity but She is worshipped outside the home. Any Tuesday or Saturday is fixed for this worship for the protection of family members from any danger. Goddesss *Kali* is also worshipped by them not in the month of *Kartik* (Oct–Nov) but as a family deity when they are attacked with any disease they worship Her at midnight. No image is made for this worship.

They also worship goddess *Lakshmi* as She is the symbol of wealth and prosperity. Except this they worship god *Satyanarayana*, god *Hari* and participate in many festive days of the Hindu when they engage themselves in worshipping various gods and goddesses. Many important festive days are also remembered by them of which the *Makar* festival, on the last day of the month of *Paus* (Dec–Jan) and *Charak* festival on the last day of the month of *Chaitra* (March–April) are important also. They also worship lord *Shiva*.

IV

A good number of other groups of people also claim themselves as 'Savara'. For instance, the Lodhas of West Bengal as an ex-criminal tribe, also sometimes assert themselves as 'Savara'' and the descendants of King Biswabasu of Orissa. There is also another group of people who are called 'Paniabhanga Savaras' or 'Jossa Savaras'. They make 'Panias', that is comb from horns". (Bhowmick 1976). This ex-criminal Lodhas are scattered throughout the western jungle-covered tract of Midnapur in West Bengal and also in parts of Orissa and Singhbhum. They are very distinct from the snake charming Savaras. In the western part of Midnapur and the border region of Bengal and Orissa the Siyalgir community are also claiming themselves as Savaras to get entry into the larger society or in order to overcome their identity crisis (Manna 2003).

Another little-known community, the 'Chirmars', also identify themselves as 'Savara'. They are now mainly concentrated at Chirmasai, small sector of the town of Midnapur. These people are known as 'Shikaris' or fowlers whose traditional occupation is 'trapping and hunting'. Some of the 'Chirmars' assert that they are an old branch of the 'Savara' or 'Kirata' group who have been often mentioned in the Epic Literatures like *Ramayana* and *Mahabharata*. The 'Chirmars' or the 'Shikaris' of Midnapur claim that they are the descendants of *Kalketu*, the mythical *Vyadha* or trapper. This group of people also assert themselves as Savara though they have no relation with the snake charming Savaras.

The Hill Kharias of Mayurbhanj also identify themselves as Savara. The Savaras of Hill Kharia appear to have proceeded along the valley of the Mahanadi and hence entered what are now known as Ganjam and Visakhapatnam districts.

The 'Bendkars' of Keonjhar in Orissa also assert themselves as 'Savara'. The Hill 'Bendkar' cultivate *Kangui, Kheri, Khodo, Gangoi, Makai* or *Maize* etc. They have no relation with the snake charming Savaras. The 'Kolian Santals' are also called 'Savaras' by the Mal-Paharias because they also catch poisonous snakes though they are not professional snake charmers. The 'Khandesh Bhils' were referred in the famous 'Ain-i-Akbari' by Abul Fazal, who also assert themselves as 'Savara' The 'Gadabas' of Orissa and Andhra Pradesh also identify themselves as 'Savara'.

The above facts clearly indicate that a good number of community groups identify and assert themselves as 'Savara'. So the term 'Savara' is apparently a generic term, possibly attributed by the settled agriculture affluents to the local non-agriculture forest dwelling communities. Thus in course of time they found their place in the local Hindu social system. Specially in Epic literatures, all these groups of people have been mentioned as Savaras. The people thus found an easy access to the hierarchical Hindu society through assimilation and regional Hinduisation. In fact it is very difficult to identify who among all these groups are the real 'Savara'. The author's field study has revealed that the Savaras are such a community who are professionally snake charmers. So the above-mentioned communities and tribes though they identify themselves as 'Savara', the nature of their profession do not support their claim as such, because they have no relation with snake charming.

This ethnographic account of the Savara, a small community, deserves an attention from the social scientists. The varied condition of their existence is an example of social inequality. As Savara is a generic term, the identification as well as the placement of the group is not uniform throughout the country. Different types of occupational association have defined their relationship in relation to other caste group in the caste hierarchy where caste not only acts as 'dynamic and resilient social formation' amidst class and power

The Savaras have now been notified as a Scheduled Tribe in the states of Andhra Pradesh, Madhya Pradesh, Orissa and West Bengal. They have also been notified as Scheduled Castes in Tripura. But until now the snake charming Savaras of West Bengal are not treated as a Scheduled Tribe. Through these findings the Government can immediately declare them as a Scheduled Tribe or a Scheduled Caste so that they could receive special attention and as a backward community special benefits may be extended to them. This will inspire them with human values and make them active participants both in the programmes of their own development and progress of the country as a whole.

References

Bhowmick, P. K. 1976 *Socio-Cultural Profile of Frontier Bengal.* Calcutta : Punthi Pustak.

Manna, S. 2003 *Crystallisation of Caste in Frontier Bengal.* New Delhi : Classical Publishing.

The Bagals of Border Bengal–A Cattle-Herding Community in Search of Identity

Swapan Kumar Chakraborty

Bagals of Border Bengal–A Cattle-herding Community in Search of Identity is a fact finding study on a group of people which till date were deprived of many facilities. They have repeatedly attempted to the authority concerned for the inclusion in a list of schedule and to get recognized as a Scheduled Caste group. My attempt here is to narrate an ethnography and to verify how far their mode of life and details of cultural pattern are related to some extent to the other groups who are recognized as scheduled castes.

In the present study, chapters have been arranged as per the following schedules. Chapter one, i.e., 'Introduction', covers ethno-historical situations of some tribe and caste groups in the Indian scene, cultural characteristics of Border Bengal, scheduling of some groups after independence, a brief note on identity problems, objectives and methodology of this work. Chapter two, entitled 'The Setting', shows geo-physical situations within which the Bagals live along with other tribes and castes. Chapter three, 'The People', analyses the myths of origin and migration of the people, population structure, food habits, literacy, languages for communications of the Bagals of the villages selected for study. Chapter four, 'Material Culture', focuses on the different materials and equipment made and used by the Bagals to satisfy their day-to-day needs. Chapter five, 'Economic Life', illustrates the occupational structure of the Bagals with an emphasis on their different modes of food production, collection of forest and other resources available in the locality, division of labour, land-holding pattern, economic interaction in the neighbouring ethnic groups and the weekly markets etc. Chapter six, 'Social Organisation', delineates the basic structural principles by which the individuals and the group behave and organise to achieve the goal. In this regard different unit of social organisation, viz., clan, lineage, family, kinship and their interrelationships and functions have been described. Chapter seven, 'Political Organisation', deals with the mechanism of social control of the Bagals when their peace and harmony is disturbed due to various factors, local disputes, violation of societal norms etc. Chapter eight, 'Life Cycle', enlightens different important phases of life, viz., birth, puberty, marriage and death, and also how the different rites and rituals are observed by the Bagals, in connection with these life cycle rites, are noted carefully. In Chapter nine, 'Religion', an emphasis has been given to understand their different deities, spirits or ghosts and their mode of propitiation, their different rituals, beliefs and practices; and also their involvement and participation in different communities and local festivals.

In course of this ethnographic study of the Bagals, cross-cultural comparisons have also been made with some other tribes, viz., the Santals, the Mundas, and the Lodhas with a view to examine the similarity or distinctiveness of the cultural traits between them. Similarly, emphasis has also been put to co-relate the linkages of the cultural traits with the local Hindu castes. In Chapter ten, 'Conclusion', an attempt has been made by the researcher to discuss the cultural identity of the Bagals in the regional social order.

The Bauris of West Bengal : A Socio Economic Study

Kartik Chandra Shasmal

The Bauris, one of the largest Scheduled Castes of West Bengal, are mainly concentrated in the districts of Bankura, Birbhum, Burdwan, Midnapur, Purulia and Hooghly. They are considered as a lower group of people having no Brahminical assistance in their ceremonial, religious and social performances. Although, they are recognized as Scheduled Caste in this state, yet the sub-caste appellations of the Bauris indicate their migration mainly from Manbhum, Mallabhum and Dhalbhum in Bihar. Such migration, in course of time, brought about remarkable changes in their mode of living and compelled them to adapt dominant and superior traits of the regional Hindu culture in which they were absorbed through a pretty long time.

The present research is based on an ethnographic study of these people in their present social setting who live in the district of Hooghly.

The investigator is mainly concerned with the Bauris of eight villages located in the district of Hooghly viz.,1.Khejurdah, 2. Bhabanipur, 3. Melki, 4. Derala in Dhaniakhali Police station and 5. Sarkhola 6. Kamrai, 7. Haringere and 8. Amrah in Polba Police station, in the sub-division of Hooghly Sadar for the purpose of collection of data.

The investigator undertook extensive survey in these villages from 1962 to 1965. During this period he had to stay, from time to time, in these villages with the Bauris for days together, to observe different aspects of their economic, socio-religious, political and recreational life. These are all neighbouring villages, which form almost a uniform and a compact region.

The Bauris of West Bengal live in villages which in most cases, are multi-ethnic and in a few cases mono-ethnic. In the multi-ethnic village, they live along with the Hindu castes and communities, Muslims and other tribal groups .

Table 1 shows the details of Bauri population in each such studied village.

Table 1

Distribution of Bauri Families with Population of Each Village

Name of Police Station	Name of the Village	No. of families	No. of males	No. of females	Total
Dhaniakhali	Khejurdah	24	58	64	122
	Bhabanipur	39	95	96	191
	Melki	34	83	58	141
	Derala	21	61	65	126
	Sarkhola	15	39	44	83
Polba	Kamrai	22	70	54	124
	Haringere	16	47	39	86
	Amrah	76	204	193	397
Total		247	657	613	1270

Among the Bauris 4–6 membered family is very popular. Due to economic hardship very large sized families are rarely found (only 8 families out of 247). They are very poorly educated. Only 7.16% individuals are literate. But gradually they have developed a positive awareness towards education and the guardians are gradually getting interest to send their wards to school.

Generally, agriculture is the main occupation of the Bauris of this area but as they have no agricultural land of their own, they have to work as agricultural labourers or day labourers. But regarding their traditional occupation, Risley (1891) pointed out that they were earlier engaged as agricultural labourers and palanquin bearers. But the Bauris were a basket-making caste in lower Orissa. Though agriculture is their primary occupation but this type of occupation could hardly meet their bare necessities. For this reason they have to accept different secondary occupations as and when available from their society. These are generally fishing and fish-selling, work as village watch man, profession of *ojha* and medicine men, domestic servant etc.

The Bauris have a distinctive position in the village society. They live with different castes like the *Brahman, Kayastha, Mahisya, Sadgop, Goala, Tanti, Napit, Muchi, Dom* and *Hari* etc. In the village caste hierarchies the Bauris hold the low status but their position is high as compared to their low castes like the *Dom, Hari* and *Muchi*. They do not accept food from them but sometimes water is accepted. They have no fixed barber or Brahmin to do their socio-religious activities due to their low social status. But on the other hand the Bauri women often act as midwives and all the higher caste people used to take their help during the time of their delivery.

The Bauris are strictly an endogamous group. Marriage is strictly restricted among their own group. They have four major sub-castes. These are : 1) Meno, 2) Dhulo, 3) Sikari and 4) Mulo. Besides there are other sub-castes also. All these sub-castes are arranged hierarchically. But in their daily interactional level these divisions do not create any significant hindrances for maintaining their social solidarity. Only according to them the Mulo Bauris are the lowest in the ladder as they carry palanquins, rare domestic pigs and take pork as their food.

Only one *gotra,* called Kashyap is found to exist among them. All though they have secured a place in the Hindu social system yet traces of totemism still survive amongst them. They pay respect to red-beaked herons. They do not kill a heron and never touch its carcass. Even when a dog dies, they do not dispose of the corpse. For this a *Dom* (Scavenger) is employed.

The Bauris are a patrilineal and patrilocal people. Majority of them live in neuclear families. Joint or extended families are very few due to their poor economic status. Ceremonial friendship like *Phul* (flower), *Gangamati* (clay of the Ganga), *Makar* (capricornus) etc., is very popular among them.

Generally each and every village council is controlled by rich influential members of the upper castes and the Bauris have very little say in its conduct. The Bauris of different villages take part with other caste members in the meetings of formal or informal council of the village and observe the general social customs.

Except this formal village council they (Bauris) had once their traditional caste council (Jati Sabha), but at present these *jati* councils do hardly exist. However, such a council has five definite officials. The headman of the council is known as *Deshmaji*. The following are the main officials of the caste council–

1. *Deshmaji* : Headman of the Council
2. *Dewan* : Assistant of the Deshmaji who also acts as tax collector
3. *Pathar* : He assists Deshmaji in socio-religious ceremonies

4. *Paramanik* : Cooks for ceremonial feasts
5. *Deko* : Messenger or Bailiff of the Deshmaji.

All these posts are hereditary. The caste council imposes fines, orders for arranging primitive fees, ostracises a man from the community. The Bauris of this locality are mostly illiterate and very poor. As they spend most of their time in different agricultural activities and in procuring the prime necessities of their day-to-day life, they find no time to take part in active politics. But in the Panchayat and general election, they work for different political parties with a zeal. They do not understand the election manifesto but want to know which group will give them more facilities, in return. The local influential members, who belong to different political parties, influence them by holding out hopes of providing more facilities to them.

Like all other caste groups the whole life of the Bauris is full of different phases of cycles with ceremonies and festivities. No exception is found except their low socio-economic position in the caste hierarchy. As a result, some sort of restrictions are found in the matter of rituals and ceremonies. Close caste–knit organization plays an important role for maintaining their own solidarity. The life starts from the very birth of the individual in a family where the female member (girl/women) bears the important task in it. Through menstruation a girl understands her feminine role and different rituals also make her to understand that she is gradually approaching to take the burden of her motherhood. Generally, there is no special puberty rites and rituals among the Bauris. Only the girl is supposed to be unclean during that period (3–4 days).

Pregnant women are generally welcomed by their family and society. The pregnant women have to observe certain restrictions for the well being of the would be born child. On the seventh month of pregnancy an auspicious day is fixed up for the *Sadh* ceremony. On this day the pregnant woman is celebrated with new clothes, wooden bead necklace, a red cord for the waist and some items of food and seven kinds of sweets and a good number of guests and relatives are also invited to take part in it. Gradually time rolls on and the date of delivery appears and as usual an aged woman of the community acts as a midwife to make the delivery smooth. Due to their poor socio-economic condition no separate room is allotted for this. The birth takes place generally in the varandah or the adjoining place near their room. Male members are not allowed to enter the place of delivery. Different caste rituals are performed of which the changing of earthen vessels is an important one. All the members of the same lineage observe pollution for nine days and also perform the *Hanri Barano* rite. Only dry food, as parched or flattened rice, is given to the mother of the child to eat, and some tepid water to drink. The baby is fed with the milk of a goat or a cow after delivery.

On the 4th day the mother is given rice, a quantity of pulse with poppy seeds (Papa ever somnifurum), and a curry with chili to eat on this day. This curry must be given to the new mother as a treat and food. This meal continues till the 8th day. On the ninth day the *Natta* (Narta) ceremony takes place. This ceremony is arranged only for the declaration of the end of the pollution period. After the *Natta* the members of their family, except parents, can join in any social and religious celebration and the mother can also participate in the domestic work as usual. No barber generally serves in the house of any Bauri. As a result, one person among them is selected to perform the role of that of a barber.

In the same way similar types of ceremony is arranged on the 21st day of the child birth. A ceremonial bath takes place, where mother and child take part in it. A few villagers also attend it. Thus the child grows up and the first day rice feeding ceremony (*Mukhebhat*) comes. It is one of the auspicious days coloured with feasts and rituals, Barber and Brahmin (degraded) also find their place in it. The nature of celebration depends on the economic condition of the family. No name giving ceremony is performed among the Bauris but a name is selected for the newborn by their family members.

The Bauris are endogamous in nature. The bride and bride groom are selected from their own group either from their own village or from the neighbouring villages not too far from their own village. The role of a go-between *(Ghatak)* is an important one for this occasion. Like other caste groups the marriage ceremony takes place in the house of the bride. As per the norms of patriarchal society, the newly married couple leaves the bride's paternal house and goes permanently to live in groom's house on the very next day of the marriage .

Series of rituals and marriage-related functions accompanied by kin groups and friends are observed and performed in both the families. Remarriage between a widower or divorced man and widow or divorced woman is very common among the Bauris. Divorce in their society is very frequent, as there is no hard and fast rule or custom to be observed in this connection. The father of the bride does not demand any compensation, because he will get a higher bride-price in *Sanga* marriage of daughter. The bridegroom's father and other members of his family want to have a grown-up girl, who can help the family by participating in many agricultural activities, if required. The wife of *Sanga* or *Nika* marriage is known as *Sangali* or *Nikali* bau i.e., wife by *Sanga* or *Nika*. The *Gharjamai* (resident son-in-law) practice is rarely prevalent in their society.

Among the Bauris, disposal of the dead and the funeral ceremonies are associated with a number of elaborate rituals. There are two ways of disposal of dead bodies : 1. cremation and 2. burial. Death pollution related rituals are strictly performed by them as the concept of the spirit of the dead is directly associated in it. They observe some restrictions during this pollution period only to show their respect to the departed soul. Generally, the members of the family of the deceased do not use oil, and eat fish etc., during the unclean period of eleven days. The members of the lineage or *bangsha* observe this restriction. Every day after taking bath the eldest son or the person who performs the last rites has to offer some parched rice and water to the soul of the dead, at a particular place near the bank of the pond, where a *Bena* plant (*Andropogon squarrosus*) was planted after the cremation, and the place was cleaned with cow dung solution.

On the 3rd day - *Tita Bhat* (bitter rice) was offered to the dead.
On the 5th day - *Pindi was offered to the dead.
On the 7th day - *Pindi was offered to the dead.
On the 9th day - *Pindi was offered to the dead.
On the 10th day - *Ghat* or *Kaman* (bathing and saving ceremony) ceremony was observed.
On the 11th day - *Sraddha* ceremony was observed.
On the 12th day - *Alap-*pindi* was given to the dead.
(**Pindi* ball of boiled rice without *neem* leaves (Margo leaves)).

In case of some abnormal death like the death of a pregnant woman, any accidental death due to snake bite, death of a young child and death due to drowning, burial takes place.

The religious beliefs and practices of the Bauris do not differ much from those of the neighbouring Hindus. They believe in mysterious powers possessed by certain objects and persons. These powers may either be beneficent or maleficent. Not only that they have deep faith in various deities but also they recognize the existence of various powerful spirits. The deities are known as *Debatas* and the spirits as *Bhuts* or ghosts. These spirits are, according to their activities, classified by different names. The deities are worshipped by the Bauris in different months of the year for the welfare of an individual, as well as, of the whole community. On the other hand, the spirits are appeased or in many cases, driven away through counter action by magician or sorcerers. To combat the influence of the spirits, there are spirit-doctors, locally known as *Gunins.* Besides these, the Bauris in their day-to-day life, take precautions from a class of persons,who are believed to possess evil eyes. They think that these persons could do harm to anyone at whom they may look with greedy eyes. This type of look is generally called *Najar laga* or *Dain Khaoa.*

It is a popular belief among the Bauris that supernatural spirits are invisible but they might become visible when they wished. These spirits have feelings, emotions and desires like any human being but they do not seem to be subservient to moral laws. The deities such as, *Bhagaban* (the Supreme God), *Basumata* (Mother Earth) etc., may be benevolent who generally do not do any harm to people; or they may be malevolent such as, *Sitala, Manasa, Chandi, Kali,* etc., these deities are looked upon with awe and reverence.

The Bauris, men and women, children and adults, believe in the existence of a mysterious spirit-world and are of firm opinion that evil spirits can do harm when they are dissatisfied for any reason. So the Bauris are very cautious not to offend them. They believe in a large number of spirits and ghosts who are believed to reside in the burial or cremation grounds and in many deserted dwelling houses. Some of these evil spirits may be benevolent to some individuals when they are harboured and regularly fed with the blood of animals and other tit-bits they like. All these vicious spirits are souls of men or women who died by accident or had unnatural deaths like suicide; death from snakebite or death caused by animals. The souls of women who die at the time of or after delivery, become very dangerous spirits. These spirits prefer to live a little away from the locality or by the side of a village road in a large tree or desolate huts. There are well-trained spirit-doctors in the Bauri community who can combat against the activities of these evils. These evil spirits are classified and termed according to their modes of mischief-making which are as follows.

1. *Bhut,* a) *Pencho,* b) *Dain,* 2. *Bramhadaitya,* 3. *Shakchunni,* 4. *Petni or Chirkun,* 5. *Kudro,* a) *Kal Kudro,* b) *Dhan Kudro,* c) *Besai Kudro.*

Almost in every season, the Bauris engage themselves by participating in different religious ceremonies and festivals to secure blessings of the deities and to break the monotony of their life. Thus a large number of festivals are found to be in vogue among the Bauris of this locality. Most of their festivals are regional in nature, in which the Hindus largely participate. They worship the goddess *Durga,* goddess *Saraswati,* celebrate *Dol* (festival of colours), *Jhulan* (Swinging festivals), *Ratha Jatra* (Sacred Chariot drawing ceremony) etc., along with the upper caste members of these villages.

Worship of goddess *Manasa* (goddess of snake) is performed with great pomp by the Bauris in the month of *Ashar* and *Shraban* (mid June–mid July, mid July–mid August). In the month of *Bhadra* (mid-August–mid September) the Bauris worship the idol of *Vadu* for the whole month. The chief participants are the barren women. There is no prescribed incantation or formula for the worship.

The *Tusu* festival is mainly associated with great rejoicing, in which all members of the community take part. This is generally observed throughout the month of *Pous* (December–January) but the period of observance may be shortened according to the economic conditions of the celebrants. Though it is exclusively a festival of the females yet males too are seen taking part in it. At present, this is not held communally but observed by individual family members, in which other female members of this community generally take part. Mainly the last three days of *Pous* (December–January) are selected for this celebration.

In this celebration, an image of *Tusu* is purchased from a *Poto* family (idol-makers). It is a female deity seated on a Lotus with two hands, one bearing a receptacle of collyrium and the other bearing a flower.

At the time of offering the food, the assembled members sing *Tusu* song. The *Tusu* songs are mainly jocular songs. These songs are sung by women, while male members play *Madal* and *Dhol* (drum) in accompaniment.

Except these festivals cattle caressing festival or *Goparvan, Bhut parvan* or ancestor worship in the month of *Kartik* (October-November), *Poush Parvan* (December-January) etc., are performed by them for their satisfaction and enjoyment.

This type of ethnographic work specially on a particular community like Bauri is very much important for recording the ethnographic accounts of a marginalized group who are identified as a Scheduled Caste community. Some of the important traits of their lifestyle easily indicate that once they had some traits of aboriginals but due to the gradual process of acculturation and admixture with the high caste groups (process of Sanscritizaton) they are gradually able to upgrade their position. In this way the little tradition and the great tradition are merged together unveiling a new horizon.

Reference

Risley, H. H. (1891) *Tribes and Castes of Bengal.* Bengal : Secretariat Press.

Society and Economy of the Dhimal—An Agricultural Community of Eastern Nepal

Rishikeshab Regmi

Damak is a multi-caste Panchayat in the Jhapa district where a very old agricultural community called 'Dhimal' inhabits since a long time past. They are supposed to be the first settlers of this Panchayat and are 2783 in number. This society was completely isolated from the rest of the country till 1970 when the East-West High way was constructed, which connects western Nepal with Eastern Nepal near Naxalbari, West Bengal.

Since the beginning of the sixties, Nepal has been witnessing a great deal of changes in the field of politics, economics and means of transport and communications. Because of these changes and development, the society at large has been showing significant interaction between the various ethnic groups, resulting in total and partial socio-cultural changes in all spheres of their life. These aspects of changes in culture have not been well-studied by any native scholar, as yet.

Due to the opening of the new highway, many ethnic groups from the mountains of the north have migrated to Jhapa district, as also to this Panchayat. Thus Damak became the most mobile place and a centre for education, small industries and trade and commerce. The result has been a total social, cultural and political transformation of this agricultural community.

Every society has a value system, which helps it to maintain its cultural consistency and continuity. The members of the society having their own cultural pattern react emotionally with their value system for maintaining stability of their culture. Traditions, institutions and values of a consistent cultural pattern have an inherent force which strives to maintain the socio-cultural identity of a particular group of people. Damak as the area of study was selected, because it is the biggest Panchayat of Jhapa district in Eastern Nepal, where the first Land Reforms Act was introduced by his Majesty's Government of Nepal about fifteen years ago. Here the Panchayat Land Revenue Act has also been introduced.

Moreover, this is an area where we can clearly observe the fast socio-economic, ecological and cultural changes that are taking place. Because of these factors, the small and isolated Dhimal community is under constant pressure of other migrated people.

According to many social scientists, social systems possess a tendency to re-establish some form of balance when confronted with changes or pressures that are systematically disruptive. This homeostasis has been variously termed as 'stationary equilibruim process' (by Kurt Lewin), 'structural-functional equilibrium' (by Talcott Persons), and 'steady state' (by Gregory Bateson).

In this study an attempt has been made to determine how certain demographic, ecological and social changes are interacting with the traditional settings in Jhapa and Damak Panchayat in particular.

It is very important to see the patterns of social change and the underlying process of economic development. The main questions or points that arise in this connection are:

(1) To what extent do the traditional social institutions of the Dhimal community are undergoing changes; (2) how far they have been able to retain their traditional culture in the prevailing changing conditions due to contact with different people in different situations; and (3) are the traditional social institutions really disintegrating or just adapting themselves to the changing values and social-organisational needs of modern time?

The method of systematic developmental approach with a structural one has been adopted, by which relationships between the family systems and external ones could be established. Emphasis has been given to the relevance of economy and occupational variables and their influence on family structure and formation.

A simple questionnaire form was used for taking interview followed by observation and discussion, as is generally used in anthropological fieldwork. In all, 126 complete interviews were recorded with the help of informants in different settlements, who were selected for the purpose for having expert knowledge of their community.

The techniques of formal and informal interviews, group-discussions, genealogy, observation, participant observation, case study have been used as tools for the purpose of this study. Schedules and questionnaires, available documents and other relevant statistics have been used in order to have a total picture of the Dhimal society and its economy and development.

Jhapa, the area selected for this study, is the biggest district of Nepal tarai, where land reforms in Nepal were first introduced 1964, thereby bringing revolutionary changes in the land tenure system, as also in the life of the original inhabitants like the Dhimal, Meche, Kocha, Rajbanshi, Majhi, Satar, Tharu, etc., who live in this Tarai.

A large number of hill people migrate regularly into the plains every year for want of land for cultivation in their own habitations. Recently this trend has reached its peak. The opening of East-West Mahendra Highway has further brought about remarkable changes in the social, economic and political life of this population, due to frequent outside contact and gradual development of this area.

Jhapa has 44 village Panchayats, of which Damak is the largest and more densely populated and developed area. This is also the richest Panchayat, where considerable urbanisation and industrialisation has been noticed. Gradual introduction of modern technology, associated with economic development and political consciousness of the people have generated a process of change in the social and political institutions of the societies living in this area.

It is to be mentioned here that in Nepal, there is no such scheduling of the communities as in India. In India we find Scheduled Castes and Scheduled Tribes enjoying constitutional benefits. In Nepal, all communities are treated as caste like groups within a social stratification system. The truth or otherwise of this argument can be ascertained only after intensive sociological and anthropological studies of the various communities living in the tarai.

The traditional picture of Dhimal society is that of an agricultural (peasant) community, with patrilocal family-patterns, where males control all the social institutions and affairs outside the domestic limits. Land was tradionally held in three ways:

(i) by relatively big local landlords(land-owners);

(ii) by middle and small classes of tenants as peasant and

(iii) by a few owners who do not reside in the Dhimal village, but participate as share-croppers and agricultural labourers.

To this general composition, a further element has been added in the form of hill-people who have migrated into their villages. They have made a strong impact on their economic system and are forcing them by force and other temptations like offering high prices, to sell their lands, on which their livelihood depends. Thus they are being converted into a landless class of labourers.

Large–scale migration of the local population from the hill areas of the tarai to get lands here has aggravated the problem further. Encroachment of forest lands was made as a natural corollary of population increase over the years due to rush of these migrants. As a result, soil erosion is occurring and is having most adverse effect on agriculture. Availability of new cultivable lands in this area is very limited and the grazing lands for animal husbandry, which is a vital need for agricultural operations and domestic subsistence, have become rare.

Land fragmentation is inherent in the social system of the Dhimals as well and when a property is divided among the sons in each passing generation, the amount of land thus owned generally becomes very small in size and unfit for cultivation. The exploiting system of land tenure causes rampant rural indebtedness and they are ultimately compelled to sell out their lands for debt. These two socio-economic factors coupled with an overall shortage of land, for many years, have driven quite a number of people into the state of 'near destitution' in the village of Demak Panchayat.

Changes initiated from outside are gradually taking place here, and these are found to have made quite an impact on the traditional structural patterns of this society.. Most of the transformations have been occuring due to outside contact. This influence is likely to continue in the coming years. Land which is the backbone of their economy is on decline now. The farmers of these villages solely depend on land to maintain themselves. It is closely related to the patrilocal character of these families. Any further change in this important economic factor of ownership would have a great impact on family patterns leading to their disintegration. If they lose their lands in this manner, their social position would be very insecure in future.

In regard to the directions in which changes are taking place, the present study points to the following:

In the first place, family patterns are slowly changing in a direction where more formal and equitable status for women is being given. Women are gradually beginning to abandon their traditional role of being confined only within the domestic sphere. The channels being used to transcend the domestic roles are education and small-typed business (selling of liquor and other items and/improvement in handlooms as small-scale cottage industry). This will probably affect the distribution of authority within the traditional households in future. Thus patrilocality will begin to change in the direction of a more 'democratic' family structure.

There is another sphere in which changes take place.Interaction models based on kinship and village *Choumajhi* connections are being transformed and community and kin-relationships are becoming more individualised in nature. The joint family is becoming smaller and is breaking away from the system of traditional relationships. Relationships outside the family system follow other channels. This trend is already seen in religious spheres and festivals. Traditional festivals and worships are becoming shorter and more formalised. They are influenced by the Hindu migrants and accepting some of the features of their religion, as their own.

Thus the traditional integration of several structures (patrilocal family structure, economy based on the use of land, kinship system of relation, a relatively monolithic closed animistic type of religion) into a coherent whole at the village level, is being gradually broken and substituted by a more mobile system.

The horizon of marital contact is widening with the increase in inter-caste/community marriages. The younger generation is trying to assume bigger roles of political leadership at a wider level. One of the village youth has already secured a seat in the National Assembly of Rastriya Panchayat (Parliament).

These trends are likely to continue and likely to transform the society's whole fabric of culture and social relations, moving more towards caste hierarchy and social stratification.

But, whatever changes–economic, social, religious and political–have taken place, they have not undermined the traditional pattern of social structure of the Dhimal society and the village net-work. The changes that have occurred due to outside contact in the Dhimal society, have been gradually absorbed so as to fit with their own patterns, without breaking up the traditional social patterns completely. All these counter-acting forces under the impact of the Hindu culture and other political, social and religious factors, have been so operating, that there is gradual absorption of these new values in the social system of the Dhimals without causing any conflict or disintegration.

Though they have become more liberal now in their attitude towards food and cloth by being exposed to the new and challenging and superior cultures, they have at the same time, strictly retained some of their traditional moral and ethical beliefs.

As a matter of fact, the East-West Mahendra Highway has opened up new vistas and brought new challenges to the mode of living and culture of the Dhimal society.

These people are now awakening from the slumber of centuries and the time is not far off when they will be at par with other Nepali people in all spheres of life and activities, contributing their share as a united people to all-out national development. For this, however, the Government has to assist them to make a quicker progress, educationally and economically, to make them more effective, as well as, a developed community.

They should not be kept apart as a backward ethnic group. There is no special provision for scheduled tribes and castes in the Constitution. The present Constitution of Nepal aims at creating a society free from exploitation, through class-co-ordination and decentralization of powers. The country has diverse geographical variations. As a consequence, all different groups of communities are not equally developed. The policy of His Majesty's Government of Nepal has been to give facilities and economic aid to the people of the remote areas which are really under backwardness and physical isolation. Tremendous consciousness and development among all the communities of Nepal, after 1950's revolution has been attained in the field of education. Then gradually the means of transport and communication system was improved, not of course in many hilly regions of Nepal. As in the case of Damak due to the opening of East-West (Mahendra) Highway in 1970, its outlook has been totally changing. Political consciousness, community interest have swept their heart pertaining to their existence as a separate identity. The practice of democratic norms and its understanding, impact of land reform, education policy, civil code and other programme have brought changes in their economic and social life.

National integration is the sole aim of His Majesty's Government of Nepal. It does not like to give tribal identity constitutionally to its various dozens of ethnic groups although they have a lot of tribal characters in their elements of socio-cultural life. It has been felt that a separate tribal identity may give birth to isolationism which will endanger national integration and development process. They are treated as backward communities and they are found in most parts of Nepal. They are aspiring to achieve social economic and political goal pursuing various strategies. They are actively participating in Panchayats which has a partyless character. The process started in 1960 and contains many democratic norms.

The collective goals of various communities are achieved through the medium of village, district and national panchayats in Nepal. The village groups, whatever their caste or community affiliation, must maintain their cohesiveness for all round development of their villages. In this process then the active democratic participation of the people of various caste groups is very essential.

In Nepal, there are various population groups maintaining their own identity in a set of ecosystem interacting at different levels of adjustment, thereby giving rise to a degree of differentiation in the process of socio-cultural articulation. Again, this level of differentiation has given birth to a number of strata in their respective population structures in terms of ethnicity. One such stratum of population is Dhimal. Like Dhimal, many other ethnic groups and their population at different socio-economic and technological levels are living in a traditional set up in various demographic shapes and size at different geographical zones of the kingdom. Their exposure to various levels of country's projections are not proportional. Thereby a sort of disparity in most of the country's developmental programme has become evident. Of late some provisions are being made not only by the Government but also public agencies and social institutions by adopting some need based target oriented schemes for their all round development, so that they can be tuned up along with the country's mainstream. For this, the concept of regional planning has been introduced in Nepal since 1972.

Nepal can be regarded as an extension of some of the elements of the cultural core of an Indian subcontinent. Both these neighbouring and friendly countries have witnessed similar forms of art, culture, religion and philosophy. Nepal's culture is a blending of the cultural tracts of Aryan and Mongoloid groups of people. The most distinctive feature of such culture is religious syncretism based on the tenets of Hinduism and Buddhism. This culture has been able to preserve its unique character because never in its history has Nepal been subjected to any foreign domination.

The Dhimal society may slowly lose its distinct identity and get mixed with the mainstream culture like many other underdeveloped communities. Socialization and social interaction of the Dhimal people with Hindu society is moulding them into a large society.

Some provisions for reservation for different jobs and seats for them may be ascertained in His Majesty's Government service and educational institution, but our attention should be fully concentrated on the integration of Dhimal people as an identified community with the mainstream of national culture. Eventually we can hope that H.M.G. of Nepal would make a full fledged planning and projects only after the thorough identification of such backward society in Nepal, and their real psychological and socio-cultural problem, if they are to be really uplifted as contributors to the unfication of Nepal.

Social Anthropological Study of Cattle-Herders in Chhattisgarh

Lok Nath Soni

The Rauts, a cattle-herder community, are spread over the whole of Chhattisgarh with their distinctive name and specialised occupations. Previously, they had no permanent settlement and led a semi-nomadic life along with the herds of cattle. Occupationally, they were cattle-herders, cattle-breeders and graziers. Most of their time was spent in jungle, tending the cattle. But, at present, they are living in the villages and towns with other caste people and have become an indispensable part of village life and Hindu society.

The fieldwork was conducted from March, 1973 to August, 1974 by short and long trips to the field. Due to working on a caste, which is divided into twelve endogamous sections, the author selected the villages for study separately for different sections of the Raut in different areas of Chhattisgarh, where they live in viable number. At the time of selection of the villages, it was borne in mind that there should be elderly persons who can give full information about their own caste and customs. The population size of the village was not the only measuring factor of this study, but greater stress was laid on the fact that the village should be a multi-caste village and well represented by any of the sub-groups of this caste. Apart from this, it has also been felt that the villages inhabited by the different sections of the Raut should be chosen for study irrespective of their distance and size. In all, the study has been conducted in eleven villages of the region. For the methodological approach, I prepared a guideline and interviewed most of the respondents belonging to different sections of the Raut caste. I stayed with them in their houses and keenly observed their behavioural patterns and other things related to their culture during various field trips to different areas of Chhattisgarh.

The name 'Ahir' is derived from 'Abhira', a tribe mentioned in archaeological inscription and Hindu inscript. "The Abhira appear to have been one of the immigrant tribes from Central Asia who entered India shortly before or about the commencement of the Christian era" (Russell and Hiralal 1975). Though the Ahir, as has been said by many ethnographers, take their name from 'Abhira', they do not appear to be fully representative descendants of the Abhira. 'Ahir' is an occupational caste comprising many indigenous groups, and has developed around the original tribe of Abhiras. The Ahir constitute about one-tenth of the total population of India. The Ahir are known as 'Raut' (also pronounced as 'Rawat') in Chhattisgarh. Rao (1979) writes about the Yadav and says that it is a category consisting of several allied castes. Yadav is a synonym of Ahir.

The Raut is a sub-division of the Ahir caste. They show some cultural and occupational identity with the other cattle-herder groups of India, such as the *Ahir*, the *Yadav*, the *Goala*, the *Gaoli* and so on. They pursue the same occupation of cattle-rearing, cattle-grazing, as also the sale of milk. The Rauts are unevenly spread in different parts of Chhattisgarh. They are spread across scores of villages. It is not possible for them to maintain marital relations with all of them. The same is possible only with a small part of the total. This part has been called one's 'effective jati' comprising those with whom a Raut actually maintains such relations (Mayer 1960; Klass 1966). Here, the ecological factor plays a vital role. For example, the 'Jheria Raut' of Bilaspur district have no marital relations with the Rauts of Raigarh district and Phuljhar area of Raipur district in Chhattisgarh because of various socio-ecological factors, poor economic condition and other social hazards which did not allow them to extend their relations with those groups of people. In the same way, it occurs with some other sections of the Rauts too. So Mayer's conception of 'effective jati' is very right in gratification of the caste relations and limitation of further interaction in socio-religious matters.

The Rauts live with the other castes as a part of the Hindu peasantry of Chhattisgarh. They follow the Hindu ethics of religion and worship the village and home deities. Over a long period of time, there have been regular socio-economic contacts between the Rauts and other local peasant communities in the area. They generally keep a sacred tuft of hair (*choti*), wear an amulet and carry a *lathi* (wood stick of 4'–5' long). Their caste role is so important in this area that other caste people often seek jobs assuming the title 'Raut'. Generally such impersonation largely happens in the fairs, where these persons try to get employment by claiming themselves to be the Rauts. When the author enquired about this matter, he was told that in the fairs of Sheorinarayan, Peethampur, etc., in the Bilaspur district, the persons belonging to lower caste groups sought their employment in the hotels by introducing themselves to be the Rauts. The Raut is a clean caste, so the people like to be served by them.

Traditionally, the Rauts were cattle-herders, but at present, they have adopted a variety of occupations as their caste vocations. They graze the village cattle and are employed as village and private graziers. Along with grazing of cattle, they also guard the standing crops in the village and in return of their services, they are paid in kind or on a share-basis. They also supply drinking water to the houses of the farmers and work as water-carriers. They bring water from tank, wells and rivers depending upon the local resources of water. Ritually, they are considered to be a clean caste and people take food cooked by them. Even, the *Brahmans* accept water from their hands. They can enter the kitchen of the high caste Hindus. Their role as ritual specialist during birth, marriage and death rites is also very important. The Raut caste is also known as a principal *Kamin* caste in Chhattisgarh and in some of the rituals their presence is essential, viz., marriage, death, etc. The Rauts sale milk and milk-products. They cultivate land and grow food crops. Their average landholding, however, is small in Chhattisgarh.

The Raut caste of Chhattisgarh is divided into twelve endogamous sections, and they have got their ethnic links in different parts of Chhattisgarh. For example, we see that the *Jheria* and the *Thhethhewar* Rauts are spread over a wide area of Chhattisgarh. The *Bandaiya, Bhorathiya* and *Darhoal* sections of the Rauts are small in number and their population is further declining now. The *Bandaiya* and the *Darhoal* Rauts are found in Bilaspur division, while the *Bhorathiya* Rauts are found in Raipur division. Other sections of the Raut caste i.e. the *Kanaujia*, the *Deshaha, Menav, Athhoriya, Magadha, Kawarai* and the *Kosariya* are concentrated in fairly large number in certain parts of Chhattisgarh. Out of these, the *Kanaujia, Deshaha, Menav, Athoriya* and the *Kawarai* Rauts live in the Bilaspur division, while the *Magadha* and the *Kosariya* Rauts live in the Raipur division.

All these groups are endogamous in nature. They are patrilocal and patrilineal. All sections of the Raut regulate their group by different norms. Some sections engage Brahmins to officiate in marriage and other rites of life cycle while some others only consult the priest to fix the date of marriage. Some of the sections sanction the use of palanquin in marriage, and some of the sections do not allow it to be used. In the same way, death-rite is observed by many sections by cremation and burial, while the others practise only burial. It was, however, marked that all sections of the Raut caste are attempting to upgrade their position and changing their customs to conform to the upper caste norms. The Rauts claim to belong to the rank of *Kshatriya*. So they identify themselves as followers of *Sri Krishna* by placing themselves in the rank of the *Kshatriya*.

Thus, the Rauts who were nomadic cattle-herders in the incipient stage of their civilization, have now settled down in Chhattisgarh villages, and have combined agriculture with their traditional occupation of cattle-herding, which shows their shift from pastoral economy to agricultural economy, involving them in the process of pastoral-agriculture continuum. Vidyarthi (1974) has nicely dealt with the cases of *Garerias* and *Ahirs* of Bihar by placing them in the pattern of pastoral agricultural continuum. These two castes of *Garerias* and the *Ahirs* have combined agriculture with the traditional occupation of sheep rearing and cattle-rearing, respectively. This combination of agriculture and pastoralism gave rise to a new type of socio-economic life. It has been aptly marked in the Chhattisgarh villages that by agriculture, the Rauts get fodder for their cattle and money for their own livelihood, which constitute a two-fold economy and make the Rauts a part of the peasant economy and culture.

The interaction-pattern of the peasant Chhattisgarh is vital due to the distinct occupations of the different ethnic groups in Chhattisgarh villages. They are inter-dependent on each other and contribute to the needs of others in day-to-day life. The Brahmans do the priestly work in birth, marriage, death and other religious functions, and they are locally known as *purohit*. The Raut, *Nai* (barber) and the *Dhobi* (washerman) are the principal *Kamin* (locally known as 'pouni') castes, who work as ritual agents in rites-de-passage of the twice-born castes. The other *Kamin* castes are Kumhar (potter) who supply earthen pots on different occasions; the *Chamar* make the shoes and the women of this caste traditionally serve as nurse during child birth and are locally known as 'Suin'; and the *Mahara* and the *Ghasia* castes people work as palanquin bearer during marriages of the twice-born castes.

The interactive relation which has been shown by describing the role and function of different castes is not only limited to serve the twice-born castes, but it applies on them too. In their own concern, they are served by the other castes. In case of the Raut, we see that some sections of them employ the *Brahman* priests to complete the marriage, and other ceremonies and rites. They are also served by other *Kamin* castes which have been described in earlier lines. So we find that the Raut are not only a *Kamin* caste, but they are also served by other castes of the local peasantry.

The other castes of the regional peasantry were linked with their caste occupations. To some extent, they cultivate land and grow food crops. The *Goldsmiths* (*sonar*) prepare gold and silver ornaments. We know that ornaments are symbolically attached to the Hindu caste people since ages for customary use. Ornaments are essentially to be worn in some parts of the body and they are gifted by the parents to their daughters at the time of wedding. The *Baniyas* are the grocers and merchants; the *Thakur* till the land and do some other jobs; and the *Dhemur, Kahara* and the *Kewat* have got the same occupation of fishing. The *Koshtas* weave clothes, but in Udaipur area of the Raigarh district, the *Panika* and the *Ganda* caste people do weaving. The *Telis* press oil. Some other ethnic groups have adopted carpentry as their occupation such as the *Gond*, the *Kanwar* and the *Penika* in the local peasantry. The *Chamar, Mahettar* and the *Dewar* are the untouchables. The Mahettars are the sweepers and the scavangers. The Chamars are the shoe-makers. The *Dewars* are semi-nomad and pig-herders. The *Agharia* and the *Kurmi* are good cultivators in this region.

The vocational specialisation of different castes which is more or less hereditary makes them interact to fulfil the needs of each other. In one aspect of its function, it is socially approved economic behaviour, which highlights the social obligations observed by such communities. In case of the Raut caste in Chhattisgarh, they graze the village cattle, and sale milk and milk-products. In the same way, other castes of the peasantry have got their own occupations. In this way, they have been trained in different skills of production and transaction is made, whenever necessary, is cash or kind, to get the things they need. Such occupational pursuits have brought many a caste people into a cooperative guild, for providing the need of others under the cohesive system of caste, which still persists in the Indian society. Thus, the caste system plays an important role to regulate the behaviour of an individual, and impels the whole caste to pursue the same pattern of occupation, but the intensity has not remained the same at present due to a number of reasons pertaining to social, economic and political constraints. This is the main base of interaction among the castes relating to exchange of goods and services to get the commodities of their need and fulfil other obligations.

References

Klass, M. 1966 Marriage rules in Bengal. *American Anthropologist*, 68-70.

Mayer, A. C. 1960 *Caste and Kinship in Central India : A Village and its Region.* Barkeley and Los Angeles : University of California Press

Rao, M.S.A. 1979 *Social Movements and Social Transformation : A Study of two Backward Classes Mosvements in India.* New Delhi : Mac Millan.

Russell, R. V. & Hiralal, R.B. 1975 *The Tribes and Castes of the Central Hiralal Rai Bahadur Provinces of India.* Vol. II. Delhi : Cosmo Publications.

Vidyarthi, L. P. 1974 Pastoral Communities in India. *Review of Ethnology*, 4(10 & 11).

Section II

Religion in Indian Perspective

Introduction

Baidyanath Saraswati

Religion, like culture, is brought into social and philosophical perspective. The English word *religion* comes from re-legare i.e.to gather' or 'collect'. Philosophically, it tends towards re-legare i.e. what unites, links up man to his divinity. In its numerous classical usage, the word *religion* always indicates a bond, a decision, an obligation, a reversal (when it is not a scruple), a superstition, etc. The Sanskrit word dharma (Pali, dharma) is far more comprehensive than the English word religion. Derived from dhri (which means to hold, keep, maintain), it reflects in no less than ten different contexst : (1) attribute of mind, (2) function of the sense organs, (3) duty, (4) nature of attributes, (5) deeds according to occupation, (6) specialty or peculiarity of man in different places, (7) attributes of an object, (8) difference in human conduct according to time, (9) certain objects in total perspective, and (10) in special sense Hindu dharma, Buddha dharma, Christian dharma, Islam dharma, and others.

There are many ways of trying typology of religion. Religious landscape has some structure. Hence, data on religion can be classified within a suitable geographical framework. Historians have considered the origin and growth of religious institutions. Philosophers have focused on the structure of the ultimate concerns. Theologians have produced theories about man's relationship with God. Anthropologists have taken into account the nature and organization of beliefs and practices at various levels of culture. For others, the key concern is creative experience. Even if each of these classifications is made for specific purpose, none is so easily labeled.

The basic form of religion may broadly be classified into 'simple' 'complex' and 'mixed'. Most anthropologists deal with the 'simple', form of religion whose characteristic features are : (a) belief in the divinity-given form of life, existing since the beginning of the world, (b) ahistorical, unfounded, unformulated, (c) beliefs and practices transmitted orally from one generation to the next, and (d) essentially descriptive, that is without explanation.

Among anthropologist, Professor P. K. Bhowmick was concerned with social philosophy as well as social work, portraying the inner consistency of integral life and culture. His study of the *Ramayana* and the *Mahabharata* (1982) shows theoretical possibilities of constructing a form of cultural consciousness, imagining the integration of tribe and caste, through India's great epics, a stabilizing factor in the maturation of human psyche. He trained his daughter Sarita (1981,1984,1987) in search for presentation of value-carrying symbols, integrating folk and classical with a sound argument for its truth. His first daughter Samita has taken a position that anthropology and sociology, in realistic terms, are dependent upon one another. Bhowmick kept road open for his students to revolve around the question of validity of religious beliefs, searched for evidence of things seen. Here are some of his students who laid emphasis on faith as method.

Tarasish Mukhopadhyaya : Religion and Society

The perception of man's religion is both simple and complex. The characteristic features of the simple form of religion are: (a) belief in the divinity-given form of life, existence since the beginning of the world, and thus a-historical, un-founded, un-formulated; (b) belief and practices transmitted orally from one generation to the next; (c) religious experience, interwoven with aesthetic experience, shared collectively in such performances as ritual dance and festivity; and (d) essentially descriptive.

Mukhopadhyay's study of *religion and society in eight villages of Eastern Midnapur in West Bengal*, brings into perspective the importance of the weekly or bi-weekly market, festivals, and other recreations which help establish bond of integration among the village deities, no matter a Hindu or a Muslim. It was observed that the *Brahmans* and *Kayastha* are so oriented that any household worship, even life-cycle ritual, is not considered perfect unless it had been solemmized by a Brahmin priest. This gesture helps to establish an autonomous cultural system having the local 'little tradition', and the regional 'great tradition', coming into close contact. This process of symbiosis necessarily manifests the channels of cultural transmission, helping unity in diversity.

Ashoke Kumar Biswas : Religious Complex

The complex form of religion has the following characteristics: (a) faith organized around the personality of a divinity (God); (b) emphasis on textual knowledge, sacred performances organized around the body of scripture; (c) rituals conducted by Sanskrit pandits (specialist). Highlighting the aspects of metropolitan fringe, the study makes use of both oral and textual tradition.

Biswas studied Hinduism in urban fringe of the metropolis of Calcutta, highlighting how deep its roots are. Though traditional forms of ritual are gradually withering away, the core belief is somehow inescapable. For example, three-fourth of the families studied openly expressed preference for a proper ritual at the time of marriage, while others preferred registered civil marriage or celebrating the occasion in the temple of Goddess *Kali* at Kalighat. So is the case of the sacred-thread ceremony observed by the Brahmins. The non-Brahmins also have a firm belief in the existence of divinity, practising both magic and herbal medicine.

Prafulla Chakraborty : Tarkeswar Pilgrimage

Pilgrimage research has in recent years gained academic popularity. Anthropological studies of pilgrimage are based on the activity of the pilgrims (performance of rituals), and the organization of the sacred specialists. Among the other aspects of pilgrimage, which must be taken into account, are communication process, cosmological aspect associated with performance, and ultimately the purity of body and mind.

Chakraborty had studied various processes of pilgrimage operating in Tarkeswar, a regional, or a relatively minor place, highlighting its relevance and justification and famous for the temple of *Taraknath,* situated in a commercial area. The importance of this study lies in so far as it reflects the secular aspect of a religious institution. For instance, here the priesthood is no longer considered a religious way of life, but a business where religious faith turns to tourism. For the frustrated, alienated, unsecured, and unemployed youths, pilgrimage to Tarkeswar is an escape from aimless everyday life.

Vaddi Arjanna : Sacred Complex

The perception of water as a sacred element is widely spread in all parts of India. All rivers are sacred, pure and holy, hence important *tirtha* (sacred place, water) where people bathe to earn merits, especially on the occasion of certain specific constellations appearing, when purification rites are performed, a movement into and out of water. The pilgrims behaviour is representative of the physical body transcending over spiritual gravitation (purity).

Arjanna's study of religious behaviour is a demonstration of the proposition, or a form of argument for the experience of a non-being (river, mountain, trees and plants), independent of our acts. The theory of sacred complex and propositions known as *lokachar* and *sastrachar*, or the little tradition and great tradition, form a theory, the essential core of religion. The operation of religious act (ritual) through time is the rule that has to be followed strictly. World-views are formed on the basis of religious experience.

Devasis Devnath : Tribal Religiosity

Tribal religion has a particular social dimension emphasizing: (a) man has relationship with the world of nature (all creatures); (b) all existence, living, non-living and ethereal are placated; and (c) the soul exists even after death. Christian missionaries as also Hindu interactions have contributed new thoughts into tribal psychic zones. Assimilation (content of foreign religion) has in fact helped developed tribal thought. The tribal world, sharing a common ecological setting with the rest of human population, assumes a new form, unique in itself.

Theories of the nature of 'primitive religion' have moved between two poles: (a) intellectualistic and rational, and (b) psychological and irrational. Indian civilization embodies the thoughts and customs of *Brahmanical culture* on an ordered scheme of life, known as *varnashrama dharma*. Another section of people, whose culture is controlled and determined by surrounding ecology, forest and ocean, seem to be in isolation. This study focuses on the interrelationship between Eco-system and rituals of the tribal people. Some tribal groups do reflect strong sense of ethnocentrism. Nevertheless it has been found that traditionalism, syncretism, Brahmanization and secularization come in subsequent stages like cultural waves in a continuum.

Arun Kumar Chatterjee : Religion, Magic and Witchcraft

Religion may be defined as an overall system of beliefs and symbolic actions that orient the individuals within the society towards the higher supernatural forces. Magic is man's attempt to manipulate, to propitiate or communicate with the supernatural forces with specific ends in view. Witchcraft is necessary evil, designed to take revenge (on enemies).

Kondhs of Orissa, who were once shifting cultivators as also hunters and fishers, required supernatural aid, an essential or intrinsic relationship between man and nature, an aspect of religion. As they moved from shifting cultivation to settled cultivation their lifestyle changed, but the magico-religious performances have somehow continued. This is an important point in itself. Naturalism provides a real, existential dependence.There is an essential or intrinsic relationship between man and nature.

Bela Hait : Food and Ritual

Food helps sustain life. At a higher level of understanding food is *brahmana* (the highest reality that expands). Without food, there is no life. There are various types of food. Rituals sanctify food. Also there are food-taboos. The ascetics live on charity, accept broken fruits. The Brahmins are supposed to take food only after having fed the Gods. Food is an essential item in the performance of Hindu rituals. All forms of divinities accept food offered by human beings. There are food taboos which people must follow for their own good.

Food is the basic need of life, an aspect of God. Production of food and food habits of the people (from the Stone Age to the Age of Science) depend on the truth of premises that ritual is necessary. Ritual, a source of creative energy, means performance of an act, in conformity with tradition, moulding the behavioural pattern of the individuals and groups. Different kinds of food are offered to the deities, and different rituals are followed in doing so. Totems and taboos, rituals and fasting mark the occasion. Specific beliefs and practices are followed among different communities, families and individuals, exploring the immanent value of the created order.

Archana Sinha : Health and Illness

Of the things not to be avoided in life is illness. Health has direct reference to the healthful physical condition produced by bodily exercise, rightly practised under the guidance of a teacher who has mastered it.

Diseases prevailing in both rural and urban areas have been studied in different contexts. Behaviour pattern associated with disease, shows that a sick person approaches a healer or a medicine-man, depending on the nature of disease. Gods and Goddesses possess power to punish or cure a sick person. Patterns of belief and behaviour may vary, to some extent, in tribal, rural and urban contexts. Difference lies on the ground of being ones sinful act, or effects of the wind, evil-eye, evil-spirits and energy field of *Gunins* and *Ojhas*. The cases of snake-bite are treated by *Ojha* or *Muslim Fakir*. The general understanding of the people is that disease is not only the physical, chemical, or biological processes but it is also due to a number of socially and spiritually determined factors.

Pratima Chowdhury : Disease and Treatment

There are two sources of disease: (a) physical, that is, lack of harmony in the functioning of the nervous system, in the flow of bile and in the circulation of the phlegm or 'airs' (which are the vital forces); (b) external stimuli emanating from astrological influences, witchcraft and evil spirits. Both produce sharp pains, and both are curable.

Disease, prevails everywhere, at all times. Human groups, primitive to modern, have tried to diagnose the cause of disease, and prescribed ways of remedy or cure. Various factors are considered responsible for causing disease such as super natural agencies, human agencies, and natural agencies. There are three main groups of diseases: natural, supernatural and human agency with a few sub-groups. Natural concepts for the occurrence of disease are predominant among the people. On the theoretical side of religion, the causation of disease is associated with the doctrine of karma. Blindness, paralyses etc. are considered as punishment for sinful acts in previous or existing life. Belief in 'evil spirit' is also found among the people. Disease occurs also due to malevolent action of some planets like Saturn, Rahu, Mars etc. Many people apprehend that ear pain, injury, paralysis, eczema, vomiting, rickets, etc., occur due to some magical action performed by sorcerers and witches.

Ratna Gupta : Death as Viewed in Society

For Hindus, death is a deep sleep. At death, speech enters into mind (manas) and mind into the divinity of fire (tejas). A renewed death may await man in the other world. Man may escape renewed death. He who knows it remains immortal. At another level, life and death form a cycle. This cycle continues through ritual. Hence the importance of death ritual.

Here the concept of death is viewed in scriptural perspective, representing traditional texts such as Upanishads, as also tribal belief. However, rituals vary from Brahmin to non-Brahmin castes. Death has been an object of innumerable arguments propounded by philosophers and scientists of the world. Physical scientists have described it to be a simple biological phenomenon, that is, cessation of life and activities. For social scientists death has a deeper meaning. Concepts and rituals observed by different caste groups have common features. Ancestor worship continues from one generation to the next. Rituals of death reveal the true features of Hinduism, centered on the institution of caste. The concept of soul, the idea of purity and pollution and the idea of rebirth are related to it. Death, viewed at micro level, throws some light on Hindu social order. It may be concluded that attitude to death and the mode of observance of death rituals reveal social structure, and pattern traditional culture of every human group.

References

Bhowmick, P. K.	1982	Varna-Jati and Indianization of Indigenous Ethnic Groups in the Mahabharata. *Man and Life,* 8 (1-2).
Bhowmick, P. K.	1982	Ethnocultural Contacts, Conflicts and Co-operation in the Ramayan : A Sociological Overview. *Journal of Social and Economic Studies,* 10 (1-2).
Bhowmick, S.	1981	Study of the Festivals of Kisan and Birghias of Netarhat. *Folklore,* 22 (9).
Bhowmick, S.	1984	Brahmanization in Border Bengal : A Case Study in Western Midnapur. *Man in India,* 64 (1).
Bhowmick, S.	1987	Folk Belief Behind a Festival : A Case Study in Midnapur. *Folklore,* 19 (1).
Sarswati, B. N	2000	*Sociology of Religion, Third Survey of Research in Sociology and Social Anthropology* Vol. 2. New Delhi : Indian Council of Social Science Research.

Anthropology of Tribal Religiosity : A Micro-Study in a Common Ecological Setting

Debashis Debnath

From the inception of human civilization, man continues interacting, adjusting and adapting to his surrounding environment, both physical and social, to meet the need for his survival and livelihood. At the same time he is facing some puzzling and enigmatic situations, which are explained by him as due to existence of supernatural entities. Thus religion is an essential part of the socio-cultural system of which the primitive religion is the religious beliefs and practices of those traditional societies, which are known as so-called 'primitive small-scale' or 'pre-literate peoples'.

Theories of the nature of primitive religion have moved between two poles: one intellectual and rational, the other psychological and irrational. The main proponents of psychological theories are Edward Tylor, Herbert Spencer, Robert Marett, Bronislaw Malinowski, Lucien Levy-Bruhl, Sigmaund Freud and a few others. Tylor and Frazer, both of whom said primitive religion is characterized pre-eminently by a belief in magic and unseen forces or powers, represent the intellectual-rationalist position. On the other hand Emile Durkheim, who saw religion as the deification of society and its structures, exemplifies another intellectual-rationalist approach to primitive religion.

India is a vast country having varied cultures and ethnic diversities. Her culture and civilization stemmed mainly from Hindu culture, which is synonymous with religion. Gosling (2001) described 'Hinduism' as a family of culturally similar traditions, a unity-in-diversity. It is polycentric and can not be reduced to any simple formula or essence. Broadly speaking, the great tradition of the Indian civilization embodies the thoughts, values, customs and the world view of some privileged class based on *Brahminical culture* and ritualistic traditions that depend on an ordered scheme of life, known as *Varnashrama Dharma.* But a section of people whose culture is controlled and determined by their surrounding ecology and environment, seem to be in isolation from the great traditions of the

Indian culture.They are the so-called primitives or autochthones (tribals). of India. The yardstick of civilization in terms of their isolation from the network of social relations and cultural communications with the centres of civilization has adjudged their positions. In the matter of development or assimilation of other cultures, the economic backwardness and apparent social injustice have thwarted them. Even today, they maintain a fair degree of their cultural distinctiveness of their own. They are intending to perpetuate their old pristine customs, habits and behaviours even in the new location by 'cultural inertia' (Boas 1911, Sahlins 1964, 1977). They are now under the process of transformation which is somewhat natural, slow, but patent due to limited acculturative, assimilative or absorbing factors in and around them. In India there is no ready made difinition for studying a tribe but to collect the relevant information of the tribe the antecendents of that group through elaborate study of their myths, migration etc., are required (Beteille 1977).

The tribal religion in India is the result of the interactions and adjustments to the surrounding physical environment while they undergo anxieties and uncertainties in facing some situations unintelligible to them. These are attributed by them to be presence of spirits or supernatural agencies, which are either controlled and subordinated by some occult and esoteric practices and propitiated or placated with offerings, sacrifices and prayers. Thus, their religious life can be described as the combination of magic and religion interlaced inextricably as the complex phenomena of supernatural beings, sacred geography, sacred specialists, sacred performances, tinged with ceremonials.

This study focuses on the inter-relationship between eco-system and rituals, of the different tribal groups who are in the same or common ecological setting, in course of their adjustment and survival both physical and social. The objectives of the study are given below.

1. To study the livelihood pattern and resource use by the tribal groups under study.
2. To study the belief system among the tribes under study.
3. To study various sacred spots and sacred centres in the various parts of the ecosystem and to reveal the inter-relationship among sacred ecology, performer and social system.
4. To study the magical practices among the tribes under study.
5. To study the structure of rituals and the changing scenario in the ritual activities, showing the collective activities and individual attitudes among the tribals living in similar or common ecological setting.

The study is based on an elaborative and intensive fieldwork with observation, interviews and case history method which are mainly followed for data collection.

The present study was conducted in a common or similar ecological setting, i.e., in the western part of border Bengal known as west Midnapore which has been described by Bhowmick as 'Frontier Bengal'. The region has always remained a centre of different religio-cultural and socio-economic activities. The autochthones with their cultural identities weathered many ravages of time and manifested radical changes in the ecological system and convolutions in the social structure. In this region, several anti-Brahminical movements took place in the past and the southern part is the confluence of non-Brahminical and Brahminical cultural streams (Bhowmick 1976).

In the present research, the tribal groups have been selected on the basis of their traditional economic pursuits and different cultural as well as historical background. They migrated from the western side due to pressure of population or for a better livelihood. The selected tribes of this region, the Lodha, the Kora, the Mahali, the Munda and the Santal, are living in close proximity. Linguistically they belong to the Austro-asiatic subsection of Austric language family. They became fragmented on the basis of economic pursuits in the form of so-called occupation during the bygone historical phases. Though they originated from the Austric speaking stock, they have different myths or tales, with varied measures of affinity. Among them, the Santals, the Mundas and the Mahalis show their closeness in respect of myths of origin, contrary to those of the Koras and the Lodhas. These patrilineal, patrilocal and patriarchal tribal groups have well-knit social organization with totemistic clan systems, which regulate the marriage alliances by following exogamous nature. Almost identical clan-names reveal their genesis from the common stock. The traditional political system for maintaining racial or ritual purity or the settlement of the disputes in the village is still working. But the new statutory Panchayat body has been introduced in the villages. It envisages decentralized planning through democratic process in local level government.

These tribes under study are living in different villages of this region, which are sporadically distributed either on the sides of scrub-jungle or the arable land areas, mainly centering a pond or a pool. Even, some villages are considered now as caste villages. Present setting of some villages still presents a forest ecology and environment which has gradually been transformed into deforested tract due to indiscriminate and marathon axing of the forest land, who reclaimed the land for agriculture which gave them security and assertive power.

The study was conducted among 507 families belonging to five tribal groups living in 14 villages. The total population covered in this study is 2434. As regards their marital status the number of widower is comparatively less than widow because men practise remarriage. But divorced women are not allowed to marry generally. In the analysis of working force the women's participation is less in economy among the agrarian communities than the pre-agrarian communities. Due to their poor socio-economic condition, majority of the tribal families in all communities live in small nuclear families.

In this region agriculture is the only pursuit preferred by the local people. The original agrarian economy of the Santals and the Mundas started with the cleaning up of jungles through long historical processes and demanding situations. They depended on cultivation and daily labour both agricultural and non-agricultural, because of their varied land holding pattern. A good number of Lodhas are landless and marginal agriculturists and they depend on manual labour, collection of forest produces from scrub jungles and molusca, water lily etc., from the near-by water resources. The Koras are also engaged in different types of agricultural activities. All these tribal groups have very little or no education. But nowadays they are showing their increasing interest towards their children's education.

The traditional pattern of religious life or simply the traditionalism still persists in terms of 'animism', 'spiritism', 'Bongaism' etc., in their religious sphere. But gradually there have developed a complex of spiritual beings, sacred ecology, religious personnel, festivals or worships with associated rituals or sacred performances followed by their concerted involvement in communal or group activities. Different magical activities reflected in terms of black magic or witchcraft, sorcery, evil eyes, omens along with various taboos or negative magic are practised in their real life.

Their beliefs in spiritual beings can be divided into benevolent and malevolent. The benevolent spirits constitute various classes of world of divinities: (i) the supreme deity, (ii) the village tutelary deities, (iii) sub-clan spirits, (iv) ancestral spirits, (v) household deities, and (vi) regional Hindu deities and folk deities of border Bengal. All the deities or gods are placed at the holy spots in the inner-sacral zone. Each village is dotted with such sacred centres where they are propitiated in the usual manner. The malevolent spirits like *Kalpurush, Jonka* or *Jankhia, Gomuabhut, Kundras* etc., are supposed to reside at the outskirts of the village or on the boundary of village, which is classified by them as the outer-sacral zone.

The sacred centres or places are believed to be set apart from the natural part of the surrounding ecosystem by means of several normative meanings and symbolic markings, guided by their myths, values, knowledge etc. These are hierarchically categorized. The major festivals are celebrated in place of sacred groves associated with clusters of *Sal (Shorea robusta)* trees and *Mahul (Bassia latifolia)*. These sacred groves are more visible now in this changing ecology. Instead, one or two uncut big trees in the middle of the village are considered as the village shrines, known as *Baram than* or *Jahera*. These trees are of usually common types in this locality such as banyan, pipul, margosa, wood-apple etc. The Santals, the Mahalis, the Koras assert the various village shrines as their traditional *Jahera*. With the rise of status, the nature of worship and the ritual pattern done by the sacred specialists differ from one to another. The religious functionaries are named as *Dehiri* among the Mundas, the Lodhas and the Koras, and *Naeka* among the Santals, who propitiate the village gods along with other associates. They are believed to maintain contact between the supernatural powers and the community. Generally the worships or the magical practices are performed at (i) individual level, (ii) household level, (iii) family level and (iv) village level.

At the individual level, the magical and occult practices are being done to counteract the actions of the malevolent spirits. Many cautions are being taken as suggested by the *ojha* or sorcerer. There is a systematic training of secret occult art and it is generally started on *Thapan Sankranti* (last day of *Jaistha;* May-June) and continued to *Dak Sankranti* (*last day of Aswin:* Sept-Oct), when systematic training to the youth section is imparted to hold their tradition. Besides the area is full of snakes and scorpions. The sorcerers also arrange the worship of the goddess *Manasa,* the persiding deity of snake. The concept of disease and method of treatment are based on some deep rooted beliefs and curative measures through some techniques as employed by the sorcerers. This consists of oil divination, magical spells, sanctification of nails, application of herbal medicines, etc.

The household worships are held at the north east corner inside the main room or at the stone kept before the domestic hearth. The heads of the households perform the rituals to appease the ancestral spirits on various occasions as commemoration in connection with major festivals.

The family worships are held at the courtyard or at a patch of land within the house boundary or in the open field at the side of the white ant hills to propitiate the sub-clan spirits or the family deities.

These are done in an elaborative manner under the supervision of the eldest member of an extended family or lineage. Sometimes the Santals, the Koras and the Mundas worship the *Karam tree (Adina cordifolia)* in the same place in a jubilant manner in connection with the germinating ceremony or to get rid of the mischevious spirits. In the family worships, the rituals are shortened as in the household worships, excepting the *Karam* festival among the Mundas and the *Kundam Dangri Bonga* among the Koras. The rituals are associated with extra-ritualistic activities like songs, dances etc.

The village worships are the annual cycle of festivals in the villages, held in an organized manner in association with agricultural operations and rhythmic climatic change throughout the year. Thus relationship with supernatural world is being maintained through various rituals which they perform through some orderly ritualistic activities. The village festivals are always associated with communal feast, drinking, dancing and singing. The community or village festivals are associated with the propitiation of presiding deities of village and protecting deities of cattle in response to seasonal changes and the economic pursuits. Thus we find that the festivals are organized either as thanks-giving ceremony after the cultivation or prayer before the harvests. Most of the village festivals are performed in the traditional manner with an adoption of various religious traits as adjustment with the surrounding culture. The festivals are the recesses in between hard life in economic activities. The Santals perform *Baha* and the Mundas *Ba* or *Sahrul* for offering fruits or leaves to the village tutelary deities. In this setting the agrarian tribes perform the *Sohrai* or *Got, Bah* or *Baha, Sahrul, Ulikanther,* which are traditional festival of their original habitation, following the Hindu almanac.

After migration to this setting, the tribes under study have been interacting and adjusting themselves with the ecosystem and also with the surrounding wider society. They have been incorporating cultural traits borrowed from the regional brahminical culture into their own. Hence, a change in their religious sphere has occurred, and is still occurring. They perform the rituals and organise the festivals or worships mainly in connection with *Akhan, Sar* and *Bani, Khamar Puja* or worship of the courtyard, *Nal Sankranti* and *Bandana,* all of which centre round the act of domestication of cattle and pursuit of cultivation. *Akhan* is the first day of *Magh* (Jan.- Feb.) and is observed as the New Year's day in the agricultural calendar of the local Hindu peasants. Prior to this, the Lodhas are seen to worship *Bani* and *Sar,* the Mundas and Mahalis are found to propitiate the Goddess *Luxmi* in the month of *Agrahyana* (Nov-Dec.). All the tribes, excepting the

Santals, are seen to arrange the *Khamar Puja* on the day of *PousSankranti* or the last day of *Pous* (Dec-Jan.) as a token of completion of and to venerate the presiding deity of crops, the cultivation activities. Again, the Lodhas and the Mahalis observe *Nal-Sankranti,* a celebration in the pre-harvest period on the belief that paddy plants should be ceremonially fed on the particular day, like the pregnant women folks, to have a bumper crop. Thus, the pre-agricultural Lodhas and the basket-making Mahalis observe the other magico-religious rites concerning agriculture, borrowing it from the neighbouring people, who belong to the Hindu peasant caste, as their reference groups.

Even all the tribal groups have traditionalised the worships of *Dharam, Sitala* and *Manasa* keeping the balance with local situation or to overcome the anxieties or uncertainties of unforeseen calamity in this new set-up. They hold the respective functions for the welfare of the village through good crops, assuring good health, protection of the villagers from epidemic diseases, the welfare of the family through increase of wealth and peace. The regional Hindu gods and goddesses and the folk deities have been incorporated in their pantheon for the prosperity of the village and well being of the family. Thus, the puritan values of religious sense are under the process of addition and alteration, with the incorporation of religious traits. This has developed a new idea of syncretism.

The author has discussed comprehensively the nature of brahminical rituals. The Lodhas and the Mundas are responding much to these brahminical ritual patterns than the Mahalis and the Koras. The Santals have lesser affinity with this. Their attitudes towards the brahminical rituals are seen only in the worship of goddess *Manasa,* done by a sorcerer. So among some tribes this incorporation is made at the individual family level, depending upon the capability.

In life-cycle ceremonies, traditional rites are generally performed, but in a few cases Brahminical or Vaishnavistic rituals have been incorporated. Mundas are seen often to invite the Brhamin for the supervision in their marriage or death rites and the Lodhas also invite the Vaishnava mendicants in their rites of passage. The Koras are seen to observe some Brahminical rituals in their rites of passage even though the surrounding Brahminical supremacy. The Santals and the Mahalis are next to the Koras in observing their traditional customs.

Such religious attitudes bring changes in the peripheral area incorporating cultural traits. This process of change can be defined as Brahminization (Bhowmick 1985).

The secular aspects of their religious life provide an entertainment and diversion to them through non-religious rituals. They are very close to religious rituals. Sometimes these are inter-mingled. Community feast, drinking, dancing and singing together form a social environment in which social euphoria and sentiments are very much expressed. In a few feasts and festivities, like *Sohare, Karam* and *Dassae* this part is well vibrated in a rhythmic manner. These are not confined within these festivals. They come out of the village boundaries, while they are participating in the worship of the goddess *Kali* of the adjoining villages or at the pandals of *Durga* images or participating in the *Charak* festival. Thus, there is general trend of change towards secularization in the process of inclination towards secularistic activities.

From the above discussion it will be clear that the tribal groups under survey have common linguistic origin and cultural entities which are now in the process of rapid transformation, adapting with the surrounding ecology and environment, both physical and social. This has been reflected in every aspect of their life, but in the religious behaviour this is more apparent. Like many other tribes, they have conventional system of magico-religious beliefs and practices, but the continuity sometimes loses its spontaneity due to accommodation of new traits. Their performance in respect of worships of traditional deities of the village shrines or in the household, express the old values. But these old traits or set of beliefs are in the process of change when their religious pantheon or the rites and ceremonies are examined. Thus we find *Dharam, Sitala* and *Manasa* have been included along with the details of worship pattern. The degree of addition and incorporation of new values, beliefs and customs to old value are buttressing the cultural traits harmoniously and ultimately reflecting the admixture in the new set-up.

In this sacred-secular continuum, the tribes under study are in different positions depending on the adjustment and adaptation with the surrounding situations after coming to this new location due to various reasons. Thus, it can be observed that traditionalism is in the core of their culture and simultaneously the changes at the peripheral parts of their cultural system are palpable. In this scenario the Santals reflect reluctance to this system due to their strong ethnocentrism or group cohesiveness. They express contra Brahminical feelings through songs and lore. The Mundas are seen closer to Catholicism or elasticity to absorb many regional traits into its core structure. The attitudes of the Koras towards the religious sphere show the gap to remain in this continuum due to their missing link in the contact with the existing techno-economic system. The Mahalis though act as an occupationally specialized satellite communityto the dominant Hindu society the poor economic condition do not allow to them to hold sway on Brahminism which rests on affluency. Their linguistic affinity and historical forces pull them toward their pristine values and customs. On the other hand, the Lodhas have affinity with Vaishnavites in the forest tracts of this region. To conclude, in this study it has been found that traditionalism, syncretism, brahminization and secularization come in subsequent stages like cultural waves in a continuum.

References

Beteille, A. 1977 *Definition of a Tribe in Tribe, Caste and Religion.* (ed.) Delhi : Ramesh Tahapar.

Bhowmick, P.K. 1976 *Socio-cultural Profile of Frontier Bengal.* Calcutta: Puthi Pustak.

Bhowmick, P.K. 1985 Tribal Situation in West Bengal. *Indian Anthropologist,* 15(1).

Boas, F. 1911 *The Mind of Primitive Man.* New York: Macmillan.

Gosling, D. 2001 *Religion and Ecology in India and South-East Asia.* London and New York.

Sahlins, M.D 1977 Culture and Environment. The Study of Cultural Ecology. *In Horizon of Anthropology.* (ed.) Sol Tax and Leslie G. Freeman. Chicago: Aldine Publishing.

Sahlins, M.D. 1964 *Tribesman.* Englewood Cliffs. N.J. : The Prentice Hall.

Stratification and Religion in the Rabha Society of Tufanganj

Pabitra Kumar Gupta

The Rabhas of Tufanganj, a sub division of Cooch Behar district of West Bengal, are changing their style of living. Matriliny is gradually disappearing. Patriliny is taking its place. The Rabhas are a little-known community in West Bengal. The Rabhas living in the districts of Cooch Behar and Jalpaiguri belong to the 'Koch' section. They are divided into a number of Husuk-exogamous clan. Some of such clans are also totemisitic in nature. The present dissertation is an attempt to study the social structure and religion of the Rabhas in particular and to analyse the social, economic, cultural and political life of the Rabhas of West Bengal, in general.

The Rabhas of Tufanganj live side by side with the Rajbansis, a Scheduled Caste, for generations altogether. As a result of intimate contact, they have started to borrow some cultural traits from the Rajbansis. A process of Hinduisation has resulted in distinct changes in their attitude and style of living. From matriliny they are moving towards patriliny. They are advancing towards Hinduism from animism. They are becoming a caste from a tribe. The present day Rabha culture differs very little from that of the Rajbansis of the region.

The Rabhas are Mongoloid. They have similarities in appearance with other Mongoloid people of North Bengal, Assam, Meghalaya, Arunachal and Tripura. Linguistically, the Rabha dialect forms a part of the Bodo language. Bodo Language belongs to Assam–Barmese, branch of Tibeto-Burman language. In Tufanganj and other parts of Western Dooars, the Rabhas speak the local Bengali dialect (Rajbansi dialect).

The Rabhas of Tufanganj along with their breathren living in Jalpaiguri district are educationally backward. Most of them are still illiterate. The total percentage of illiteracy is 91.61%. Agriculture is the main occupation of the Rabhas like Rajbansi and other Hindu caste. In the past when the entire locality was covered with dense forest, *Jhum* cultivation was practised. The Rabhas call the system as shifting cultivation (Tanjia).

As agriculture is the main occupation of the Rabhas, cattle and buffalo play a very important role in their life. Ducks, pigeons, pigs and fowls are also kept by them. Handloom weaving is one of the most important cultural traits of the Rabhas. But now due to contact with the outside world this has undergone a change. Recently, the tribal welfare department, Government of West Bengal has started an Eri Centre at Nararthali near Kamakhyaguri under Kumargram Police Station. Rabha and Mech girls are recruited there as trainee-cum-worker.

II

Seven settlements have been selected by the present author and all of them are within the Tufanganj Police Station and Tufanganj Block Development office.

Table I

Sex-wise Distribution of the Rabha Population in the Settlement Studied

Name of the village	Male	Female	Total
Rasikbil	188	173	361
Baroshalbari	399	387	786
Haripur	79	69	148
Bharea	154	142	296
Mughabhog	40	33	73
Bhandijilas	35	32	67
Bansraja	71	65	130
Total	966	901	1867

Various aspect of the socio-cultural and religious life of the Rabhas of Tufanganj sub division of Cooch Behar district of West Bengal are studied and discussed in the dissertation. At the very outset of the study, it was stated that the process of Hinduization had resulted in distinct changes in the attitude and style of living of the Rabhas of Tufanganj.

From the study it is found that in the sub division of Tufanganj, there live the forest Rabhas and the village Rabhas in two ecological sections. The Rabhas living in the forest are culturally isolated from their brethren living in the villages who have close relation to the Rajbansi and others. After 1947, a large number ofrefugees hailing from East Pakistan (now Bangladesh) had come to Tufanganj and they have settled in the villages inhabited by the Rabhas. These refugee immigrants belong to different Hindu castes. The Rabhas of Tufanganj and different Hindu castes of the locality owing to their intimate contact with the Rajbansis for a long time, have borrowed the Rajbansi elements in their culture.

As Tufanganj is the only sub division of the district having Rabha people, so the investigator selected the Rabha society as his sample and conducted the work in the year 1973-1976.

Tufanganj is both a border sub division and frontier sub division. It is between Jalpaiguri district of W. B. (Alipurduar subdivision) and Goalpara district (Dhubri and Kokrajhar sub division) of Assam. The Indo-Bangaldesh frontier lies on its eastern part. Rangpur is the district of Bangladesh on the other side of the front. Some Rabhas of the sub division live in the reserved forest as forest labourers. Their style of living is even today traditional to a great extent.

The Rabha society of Tufanganj sub division clearly shows a combination of two different types of culture–traditional and modern and both matriliny and patriliny.

The investigator adopted the geneological method, interview, case history, and participant observation method. As regards ethnic environment, it may be stated that the forest Rabhas, at Rasikbil live with the Oraons as their neighbours. The village of Barashalbari, Haripur, Bharea, Mughabhog, and Bansraja are multi-ethnic in composition while the forest Bastis are fully composed of Scheduled Tribes people, the villages exhibit mixed population of Scheduled Castes and Scheduled Tribes.

III

Analysis of the social structure and stratification of the Rabhas shows that the Rabhas of Tufanganj have been changing their social structure with their change in the lifestyle since the second World War. Their aspiration to become Hindu has considerably changed their traditional social stratification system.

The Rabha society of Tufanganj is divided into a number of clans known as *Husuks*. It has been noted that the *Husuks* are exogamous. Some of them are also totemistic. The Rabhas' marriage system is controlled by *Husuks*. In the past *Husuk*-exogamy was strictly followed. But after becoming Hindu by religion and Sudra by caste, the village Rabhas do not follow the rigidity of *Husuk*-exogamy. Previously, a Rabha could marry a girl belonging to his father's *Husuk*. But now they are following the marriage rituals of their Hindu neighbours.

Marriage in the father's clan is becoming prohibited among the Rabhas in addition to prohibition of marriage in mother's clan. It has also been observed that prohibitions relating to the totemic objects are now not seriously observed by the Rabhas living in the villages. Contact with the Hindu castes of the area is probably responsible for the same.

A Hindu *gotra* (clan) has now became the main *Husuk* of the Rabhas. It is the Kashyap *gotra*. When a tribe becomes a caste it is given the Kashyap *gotra* status. After conversion to Hinduism the Rabhas of North Bengal are identified as Kashyap *gotra* like their Rajbansi neighbours.

Rabhas have medium sized households. They live in nuclear families. In the past, the households were matri-kin oriented. But the recent trend is towards patri-kin-orientation. They have come close to the Rajbansis and other patrilineal neighbours. It has also been noticed that now Rabha parents live with their married sons with or without son's wife. The Rabhas like to marry within their own community. The Rabhas living in forest *bustees* are very strict in this matter. Marriage with the Rajbansis, Saha, Garoa, etc., are held among the village Rabhas. Marriage with a Rajbansi or a Saha or a Goala (Milkman) or any other Hindu caste is considered to be a matter of social prestige among the Hinduised Rabhas.

Monogamy has become the normal practice among the Rabhas. Following the Hindu castes of the locality, the Rabhas avoid the cross-cousin marriage. The rules of inheritance and succession have also undergone radical change. The Rabhas were in the past matrilineal and matriarchal. The property was owned by the females. The rules of inheritance followed the female line. It passed from mother to daughter preferably the youngest daughter. Now only the non-Hindu sections living in the forest *bustees* practise it. But after becoming Hindu they follow the Hindu rites. Property is owned by the males. The rules of inheritance follow the male line from father to son.

The traditional village council of the elders does no longer exercise authority. It has lost its power. Dispute relating to the social and religious affairs which were previously settled by the village council are now referred to the village Panchayat. The introduction of the Panchayat Raj is responsible for the decay of the traditional village council system of the Rabhas.

As far as the socio-religious rites and ceremonies of the Rabhas are concerned, significant changes have occurred. In birth, name giving and other allied ceremonies the Rabhas of Tufanganj today follow the customs of the local Hindus (mainly the Rajbansis). The traditional rites are only followed by the forest Rabhas. Like the Rajbansis, the village Rabhas observe pollution for 30 days. They now follow the local Hindu method in their marriage ceremony. A Brahmin conducts the ceremony as per the *Shastras*. All Rajbansi rituals and rites are observed by the Rabhas.

In death ceremonies some of their traditional rites (*mai-le-san*) have been retained along with the following of the local Hindu pattern of life. The dead body is burnt by the side of a stream (*Chika Hasmi*). There is no fixed burning ghat. A chicken is hanged upon the poles just over the earth. The Rabhas believe that the soul of the dead is alone so the chicken will accompany the soul of the dead. A similar rite is also observed by the Garos. Mourning is observed for three days, on the third day every member of the house takes purificatory bath. There is also a system of shaving. On the fourth day another rite is performed. It is called *Tau Leng Chai*. This rite is performed by the female members. The Rabhas believe that if the departed soul goes to heaven, foot prints of the bird, especially of *Sankhachil* (a kind of Kite) will be visible on the covered rice-dust. It may be noted that the Lepchas of Darjeeling and Sikkim believe in the contrary footprint which reveals that one spirit has possessed the soul.

Some changes are now found among the Hinduised Rabhas of Tufanganj. The death ceremonies of the Hinduised Rabhas are similar to those of Rajbansis of Cooch Behar and Jalpaiguri districts. The Asamese Brahmin or the Rajbansi Adhikari presides over the ceremony.

IV

In ceremonies connected with agriculture, hunting etc., the Rabhas follow the traditional as well as the system observed by the local Rajbansis.

They worship spirits and objects living in rivers, forests and hills. At the same time the village Rabhas worship different Hindu deities. The Rabhas of Tufanganj have embraced the *Vaishnavite* form of Hinduism. They have of course not fully discarded the *Sakta* form. Their leaning towards *Vaishnavism* is very prominent. Thus in the village inhabited by the Rabhas we find *Hari Bari* (temple of Hari).

Discussion on the *Gita*, the Bhagavat, the *Ramayana*, the *Mahabharata*, the *Chaitanya Lila* etc., are held regularly in the *Haribari*. Generally elderly folk, both male and female participate in it. They are now observing the religious ceremonies and feasts like the local Rajbansis.

The *Saktas* worship *Prakiti* (female) in one or the other forms of the consort of *Siva-Durga, Kali or Parvati*. Animism is associated with blood worship and libidinous rites. The Rabhas were in reality pure animists and the forest Rabhas are still animists. They worship various spirits and objects of nature. Spirits of rivers and springs, forests and hills and wild animals etc., are the objects of worship to a forest Rabha. On the other hand both animism and Hinduism are to be found among the Rabhas living in the villages. The Rabhas are till now following their traditional belief pattern connected with the worshipping of various deities living in rivers, forests and hills. The existence of different spirits and their influence on their life is tremendous. Some of the important deities are mentioned here.

Runtuk and *Bashek* are the household deities of the Rabhas. They are the two daughters of the *Rishi*. There is no image. Rabhas call them *Dhana Lakshmi*, the goddess of wealth. Upon the bamboo platform a reddish earthen pot full of rice is placed. All religious festivals take place after worshipping the *Runtuk*.

Mahakal–In the month of Vaishak or Asar, pigs and hens are sacrificed for that deity. Meat is cooked and a priest performs the function. Women are forbidden to be involved in it.

Gang Raja–The worship is held for good crop and to protect the crops from insects. A duck is sacrificed and then the sacrificed duck is cooked and offered with boiled rice to the *Gang Raja*.

Nur Bai–She is worshipped for the well being of the child and the expectant mother. After the child birth *Maitani* is invoked for their beliefe and satisfaction.

Michik Bais–She is also a female deity worshipped for the welfare of the community. Cooked meat with home made liquor are offered to the deity.

There are also some communal deities for the welfare of the community as a whole. Such as *Bisah Hari, Raj Daktar* and *Raj Mantar*. *Lakhi Jung*, a stone as a symbol of God is worshipped by them. A duck is also sacrificed to show their reverence to the god.

Mahamaya is another deity worshipped by them. Liquor and cooked pigeon are offered to the deity.

Gancha Pani, a stone regarded as a deity is also worshipped by them for their well being. Besides they also believe the impact of evil spirits in their day to day life. A few of them are worth mentioning. Such as *Bulua Rai, Dekal, Jaura* (Soul of the dead man) and *Pertani*. They have no images. Only their spirits are worshipped as deities by offering different items of food like boiled rice, curry, meat etc., by throwing out these sacrificed food from their house to the out skirts to show their honour to those spirits.

V

It has been shown that the Rabhas have been promoted from a tribe to a caste. They are now considered as Sudra. But it is interesting to note that the Rajbansis, who were also converted from a tribe (Koch) to a caste were assigned a superior position in the Hindu caste hierarchy. They had become Kshatriyas. The local Brahmanical and Vaishnavite traditions are being followed today by the Rabhas. The concept of *Siva, Hari,* purity and impurity, birth and salvation have influenced their socio-religious behaviours.

The Hindu looks upon the Rabha as a Jati which lives in a different way, eats pigs and fowls and lies at the bottom of the scale of the caste system. But at present, the Rabhas have accepted different Hindu deities like *Siva, Kali, SatyaNarayana, Balaram, Kamkshya* and also worship them.

The absorption of the Rabha culture within the fold of Hinduism has undoubtedly enriched both the Hindus and the Rabha. It has infused a spirit of broadness among the Rabhas and expansion among the Hindus. This will surely help develop the spirit of love and co-operation among them. Thus the spirit of fraternity and integrity of the Hindu religion is still functioning as a binding force for the society.

Religion and Society in Eight Villages of Eastern Midnapur, West Bengal

Tarasish Mukhopadhayay

In this dissertation, our initial concern is to approximate a somewhat arbitrary 'natural unit' of rural society called Kelomal or Kalua Mahal (a cluster of eight contiguous villages), which by virtue of its entity within the revenue-boundary of the former zemindars of Tamluk Parganah is considered hypothetically to share a sense of historical, social and regional unity in common. Side by side, the cluster of eight villages has been taken for granted as if they are occupying an intermediate position between any of its co-villages on the one hand and the domain of the former zemindars of Tamluk Parganah on the other. To start with, the structural canvas of Kelomal, having the scope of maintaining an interplay of social, economic, political, religious and other systems, intertwined with a tier of reciprocity and interdependence, is expected to offer more meaningfully convincible precise principles of social and religious activities in a regional setting than considering any one of the village of Kelomal, as a unit of study.

The proposed research is an understanding of the religion and society in a cluster of eight contiguous villages in deltaic eastern Midnapore, West Bengal. These villages, in common parlance called Kelomal or Kalua Mahal (a zemindary estate), are located in the domain (Pargannah) of the former zemindars of Taluk, and as such share a sense of historical, social and regional unity in common. Side by side, the eight contiguous villages occupy an intermediary position between a single village on the one hand and the Parganah on the other. In accordance with our objective, attention will be focussed on finding how far this village cluster serves as a viable unit in determining the extension of religious and social activities in a field–which is wider than any single village. Approximating a somewhat arbitrary 'natural unit' or rural society–linked together by economic, political, religious and other social ties, these villages are likely to offer more exclusive features of 'social network' than any single village, selected at random.

Revealing the diversity in caste composition and social position of different castes, the impact of their traditional occupations or religious practices can be discerned. The function of several village-based and co-operatively organised institutions, within the village cluster of Kelomal, and how they help to perpetuate a clear-cut sense of membership either in a single village or as residents of Kelomal on different occasions are to be examined. The orientation of worship, with reference to social and ideological structure of rituals, and the diversities in both doctrine and practices between caste groups living in Kelomal are to be elucidated. Finally, the role of religious-ritual and celebrations as a mechanism for identity and integration are to be observed. The purpose of the study is also to examine how the concept of 'tradition' as continuity, contributes towards the integration mechanism of society, between different families and caste groups in Kelomal.

From the information at hand it appears that some of the oldest families in Kelomal have been residing here for about 300 years. Incidentally, the numerically dominant *Mahishyas* are not only the early settlers, but also instrumental in settling a number of castes residing in Kelomal.

The present population in Kelomal includes a total of 20 castes and a section of Muslim-Weavers. They are distributed in 629 households. It is noticeable that except the numerically dominant *Mahishyas,* other castes, including the Muslim-Weavers, are by and large segregated from their village neighbours. On the other hand, the members of five Scheduled Castes viz., the *Muchi, Dom, Rajbanshi, Dhopa,* and *Karengas* encompass the line of an impure, under-privileged and disavowed section of the local society in Kelomal.

This affinity is well-marked among the practitioners of an occupation in a market situation, where they usually identify themselves or else are identified by their regular customers, as the resident of Kelomal. Here, within the village cluster we find striking differences in caste composition, village gods and goddesses, religious festivals, local norms and tradition–although their inner motivations intertwine themselves through conformity to certain local rules and cultural norms called *Deshachar.*

But this generalization is not distinctly valid for the different groups of immigrant *Brahmans* and the *Dakshin Rarhi Kayasthas*–who are considered by their co-villagers as the followers of an altogether different 'tradition'. However, in view of maintaining a network of Jajmani, which is specifically religious and ritual in orientation, the members of different castes are obliged to follow a sort of systematized relationship with the functional, artisan and other servicing castes although in some cases these ritual specialists may live outside the village cluster.

The religious orientation of folk-deities mostly celebrated through the initiative of the *Mahishya* village headman, during the village festivals, differ characteristically from the upper castes household festivals and other rituals–in connection with the worship of the different forms of Mother goddess, called *Sakti Puja* in general.

We find that the implicit significance of an upper caste oriented village or a neighbourhood, involving the effects of caste stratification and differences in religious orientation, hardly interrupt the non-elite ritual communion. On the contrary, at times they are linked together by some common beliefs, values and religious practices and this process objectively intertwines the members of different 'traditions' in shaping the history of the locality. Although the immigrant upper castes (the Babu) are more involved with the Sakta religious rituals of the 'Great Tradition', and the rest of the castes (the Gariblok) with the local level folk rituals of the 'Little Tradition', there is a free communion between the two cultural traditions. This process helps bridging members belonging to *Babu* and *Gariblok.*

It has been observed that for maintaining a 'common identity' the members of a particular caste share mostly the same traditional occupation and persistently obey the values of co-operation and cordiality in support of their own interest. Side by side, they are also dedicated to their caste-based religious practices and share the stigma of purity and pollution together with their own caste men. This process enhances a feeling of solidarity and cohesive identity not only among the members of a particular caste 'vertically' in Kelomal, but also those who are distributed 'horizontally' outside the jurisdictional entity of the village cluster.

After reviewing the 'primary occupations' of all the 21 castes (including the *Jola Tanti*), it is noticeable that only a total of 10 castes viz., the *Vyasoktasreni Brahman, Napit, Malakar, Karmakar, Swarnakar, Dom, Rajbanshi, Karenga, Muchi* and *Jola Tanti* depend exclusively on their specialized traditional occupation. The institutional role of the village headman in all the eight villages of Kelomal has been examined to follow up the historically achieved authority of the village headman, in support of other elders, and especially the way they pertain some of the traditional 'secular' and 'sacred' institutions not only within the functionally 'minimal area' of a village, but also embracing at times a number of culturally interdependent villages within and outside the cluster of eight villages also.

The traditional authority of the village headman is significant in connection with a confederated decision making and local administration–although the validity of these arrangements have no legal basis at present. The village headman also acts as an important pivot in matters of enforcing the traditional village rules and the *Parganah-oriented* custom. As such, any case of violation is considered a punishable offence.

In spite of that, we notice a distinctive functional drawback in the role of the village headman today. They have no control and authority over the immigrant upper castes. Equally they never interfere with the Muslim-weavers, because of their identity as a distnict religious group. This distinction to some extent divorce the numerically dominant *Mahishyas,* artisans and other service castes from most of the immigrant upper castes. Because of this, in the composition of the society in Kelomai it is possible to identify two culturally distinct halves, involving the fervent patrons of the two 'traditions' altogether.

Whatsoever, out of a total of eight villages, the *Mahishyas* have been found to be responsible for maintaining the 'secular' and the 'sacred' institutions in five villages. The three other villages viz., Bhubankalua, Dubkalua and Balikalua are jointly administered and taken care of by *Mahishya* and *Uriya Sristi Karans.*

In eastern Midnapore and especially around Kelomal, ecology plays a very important role in determining the formation of weekly and bi-weekly market. For attending these markets, the sellers and the customers come from a radius of about five-miles. One can avail of the facilities of a weekly or bi-weekly market on different week-days. Yearly Pujas, festivals and other recreations are also arranged in these markets, for the regular participants of the market concerned.

After analysing the worship of Goddess *Chokra Kali,* we find that the local *Mahishyas* who are mostly dedicated to the worship of *Lord Siva, Lord Hari* and other prophylactic village deities such as : goddess *Sitala, Manasa* etc., are virtually indifferent to the worship of goddess *Kali, a Sakta deity,* that demands the ritual of blood-scarifies. But, here it may be a coincidence that the *Mahishya* youngsters (Chokra) of the neighbourhood has possibly been inspired to start the worship of goddess *Chokra Kali,* being guided by their direct knowledge of *Sakta* worship, prevalent among the *Madhyasreni Brahman* and the *Dakshin Rarhi Kayasthas* of the village.

In the village festival of goddess *Sitala,* it is customary to worship a number of village deities as well. This custom helps in establishing a bond of integration among the village deities–no matter a Hindu or a Muslim in origin. But it may be important to note that the villagers never extend the list of deities, existing beyond the physical entity of its own. This orientation on the other hand, justifies the symbolic reference of an individual or a group of villagers' common identity and village consciousness–in way of discriminating between the village gods and goddesses, distributed in adjacent villages. As for example in connection with the village festival at Dubkalua, we cannot undermine the positive role of the folk-singers of goddess *Sitala* and *Alabibi*. For instance, during the concluding part of the folk-drama, called *Sitala Mangal*, centering the supernatural activities of goddess *Sitala*, the phantasm of *Sitala* (a mahishya) go around the theatre to bless the audience–touching the fly-whisk on their heads. At that point, the villagers' enthusiasm to get blessings from Sitala is so convincing that as if the goddess in person is present before them. This *emic* view of the average villagers of Dubkalua, reflects their religious belief and practices, in a more meaningful way.

After reviewing the ethnographic content of intra-village and inter-village dimensions of the aforesaid religious-rituals it is found that these are controlled primarily by the elders in a neighbourhood and the respective village headman–especially where the festival is arranged. Furthermore, as these occasions intertwine a number of hierarchically stratified caste groups through certain firmly persuaded local belief and religious doctrination, they help at least momentarily to override the existing unreserved feelings of casteism, economic rivalry and social prejudice–normally which are so phenomenal not only in Kelomal, but also in villages surrounding this locality. But it is significant that the immigrant upper castes in Kelomal do not indulge themselves too much either in the village festival of the folk goddess *Sitala* or the *Gajan festival* of *Lord Siva* and other ritual-clienteles castes, following the locally established principles of the Jajmani system.

Incidentally, in course of this study we have observed that the religious life of the different sections of *Brahmans* and the Dakshin *Rarhi Kayasthas* is so oriented that any household worship even a life-cycle ritual is not considered perfect or satisfactory, unless it had been solemnized by a Brahmin priest. Along with this ideology, the priest use a prescribed scriptural text, to make the worship more convincing and ritually meaningful to their clients. This gesture helps establishing an autonomous *cultural system* for the effective functioning of a style of life among the upper castes, in contrast to the intermediate castes and other inferior Sudras in matter of domestic rituals and festivals.

It is notable that the people belonging to the ritually inferior castes, are marked by their deep involvement with the local folk-deities and folk-festivals. The ratio of household worship are few and far between. Also the majority of them do not necessarily employ a Brahmin priest for solemnizing all the annual household worships and especially agricultural rituals. Furthermore, here the religious worship are more often a caste or community affair, observed conventionally under the authoritative control of the caste man and other village elders, for the general welfare of caste men, a particular village or a neighbourhood. This remarkable correspondence between the nature of involvement and participation in religious rituals, out line the religious life of different castes living in the village cluster of Kelomal. From these findings, presumably, an economist might venture to explain this situation in an altogether different way, taking the agrarian modes of production and the distribution of power in an ecological setting, as the key variable for the very nature of social inequality–expressed through the realms of differential prestige, ritual rank, and even involvement in a *textual cultural tradition*. But we are convinced that the issue is not just a question of expanding the local economy or productivity, as an excuse for the very ritual-orientation of the inferior castes in Kelomal.

However, after analysing the principal modes of ritual diversity between the followers of two distinct *traditions*, we wonder, exactly how the religious life of the lower-ranking Sudras was historically oriented around the mechanism of *oral tradition*, leaving aside the reliance in and the authority of the elaborate rules, laid down in the *Sastric* texts. But in spite of that, there exists some form of cultural homogeneity, at the ideational level, between the members of hierarchically arranged castes, which is expressed categorically through pilgrimage, for spiritual attainment, and the patronage of certain locally recognized awe-inspiring folk-deities and folk-festivals, in view of ignominy and local sentiment. Another point which deserves attention is that, for a better understanding of the society in terms of the dramatic expressions involving identity and interaction, in varying social and ritual contexts, our concern had been to discover the relative continuity of varied 'social system' in the explicit reality of its immediate regional setting.

Our findings on the religion and society in a cluster of eight villages demonstrate the overall significance of the village cluster in the context of ecology, *Parganah*-oriented territorial entity, and the concomitant features of regional social structure and especially the social organization of religion presumably which is appropriate to and necessary for the historically achieved identity and cultural distinctiveness between the members of different 'traditions', expressed through the channels of 'social networks' and the overall manifestation of the village level 'sacred' and 'secular' institutions.

In spite of the fact that the village cluster of Kelomal is a part and percel of the former revenue-boundary of the zemindars of Tamluk *Parganah,* we may consider it hypothetically as a cross-section of the rural society in eastern Midnapore as well. However, within the village cluster, we notice a somewhat distinctive ramification in the lifestyle of the members of different hierarchically segmented population, pivoting the regionally recognized system of 'social status' and 'class status' in support of their individual identity in a relative way. This broad frame of reference outlines the degree of cultural homogeneity vis-à-vis diversity between the members of different 'traditions' those are often expressed objectively through the realms of 'vertical' and 'horizontal' ties of caste, kinship, economics and religion, broadly within the framework of a regional social structure and civilization.

In this dissertation we have illustrated how far the different caste groups, within the premises of a typical village life in Kelomal, contribute to maintain the 'transmissive channels' of network not only within its co-villages, but also with other surrounding villages and *Parganahs,* including the exigencies of extension with distant urban centres and even states located beyond the administrative jurisdiction of West Bengal.

Next, when we go beyond a single village, but objectively within the historically derived village cluster of Kelomal, a different picture comes into view. Here the village cluster serves more the function of a 'minimal area', where the de facto carriers of the local 'Little Tradition' and the *de jure* counterpart of the regional 'Great Tradition' come into contact. This process of symbiosis, in an order of succession, manifests the channels of cultural transmission among the members of different 'traditions', within the limitations of the regionally-recognized concept of 'social status' and 'class status' which we have experienced not only in Kelomal, but also in course of our overall concern with an 'approachable region'–beyond the juxtaposition of eight villages.

Religious Complex in a Metropolitan Fringe

Asoke Kumar Biswas

Hindu religion is one of the most ancient and enduring religions of the world. There are other ancient and widely professed religions too. So it naturally poses the problem, as to what components of a religion have to be taken into consideration, for studying the religious complex of a social set-up, particularly of an urban fringe of any metropolitan city, which forms an admixture of different faiths.

The conceptual framework of the present study includes, however, a careful treatment of some basic doctrines and principles of the Hindu religion.This has been done by the application of social-anthropological methods, by collecting relevant field data.

The author has chosen his subject 'Religious Complex', as religion is the sheet-anchor of Indian culture, and he thinks that through the anthropological approach the study of religion will help him to explore and understand different aspects of religious behaviour of the group of people under his study, i.e., the Hindus, residing in the area.

The author has tried to ascertain how far the religion of Hinduism is practised, as yet, in an urban fringe of the metropolis of Calcutta. As a matter of fact, he has tried to study how far a fringe area of the metropolis carries forward or helps the spread of Hindu religious tradition, under modern urban phenomena, or in other words, a new form of enquiry has been undertaken by him in the field of social anthropology in order to survey a complex society of a metropolitan fringe.

In this research, however, the author has limited himself to a set of problems connected with the study of religious complex, for which he has adequately described the religious activities of his informants under investigation.

This research is mainly concerned with four major sets of problems.

1. How is this northern fringe of the metropolis upholding its religious eminence by accommodating various influences of modern developments of the metropolis of Calcutta?
2. What is the nature and degree of responsiveness to various types of religious activities of the different castes in this area?

3. What are the trends of diversity in conception of religiousness present among them?
4. Are there any significant changes which seem at present to be overtaking the traditional forms of beliefs and practices?

The present study, based on religion in all its complexes, provides an appropriate area for the understanding of the diversity of conception of religiousness of the people who live there. Here the problem has been chosen by the author for the study to indicate different aspects of religion. Different types of religious performance are generally observed by different caste groups. These are on the whole, combination of several individual religious acts, connected with widely believed concepts of Hinduism. Several such religious acts and concepts of belief might be knit together into a still wider complex, constituting the religious complex.

But the structure of religion in an urban fringe is so broad-based and has become so complex by gradual accommodation of various pressures of modern developments of the city, that to deal with his present problem, the author has selected a smaller unit or field for this investigation.

First, the author has selected the Wards 3 (Paikpara) and 5 (Belgachia) of Calcutta Corporation, comprising as a small area on the northern fringe of the metropolis, for convenience of his field study.

Secondly, since the Hindus constitute the vast majority of the total population of these two Wards (3 and 5), and especially the Bengali-speaking Hindus are the dominant force of the area, the author has confined his interest to the study of the religiosity of the Hindus. So the author wants to limit his references and investigations to Hindu religion only, keeping out Islam, Jainism and Sikhism from the ken of his study, although there are a few people of these religious groups there.

The subject of enquiry is limited only to religious practices and beliefs of the Hindus. But the information on castes, occupations, education, family composition, housing condition, marital status, migration, etc., have also been obtained to get himself acquainted with their social conditions, and their impact on religious beliefs and practices of the community involved.

The author has also collected information on other relevant topics as best as he can. These were thoroughly observed, and interviews and discussions were held and local records were collected, wherever available. The author has tried to reach as many families as possible, in these two Wards (3 and 5). He did not depend on random sampling.

426 Hindu families were contacted and information was collected from them. There were six non-Bengali Hindus among the total number of families under investigation.

Extensively and intensively, the author used observation and interview techniques. During the fieldwork the author had to use all necessary field techniques, e.g., using schedules, supplementing these by case-histories, and personal observations.

Photography is also an important technique, which he used widely during his fieldwork. The field investigation was done by the author from December 1969 to January , 1973.

Background information collected from the informants of this area revealed the historical process of gradual structural growth in this area in its earlier rural and present urban setting. The Belgachia and Paikpara, among the 38 villages taken as base by the East India Company in early Eighteenth Century still retain their old names. The major portion of this area was previously a village known as Panchannagram in the district of 24-Parganas, in the province of the then Bengal–now West Bengal.

This area thus witnessed a relatively late process of urban growth starting from early twenties and gaining momentum after the partition of India, when the homogenous character and the old *Paras* (Sonnies) began to change, as an increasingly large number of people belonging to high, middle and low income groups began to settle in this area. But the older structural substratum based on caste-hierarchical pattern remained intact, which is found even now in *Paras* such as *Dompara* in Anath Nath Deb Lane of Belgachia, which happens to be the main throughfare of this area linking the older settlement of Paikpara.

The principal aim of this study was to explore how far the people of this area were upholding their religious affinity and eminence by accommodating various influence of radical developments of a city of modern times like Calcutta, the nature and degree of responsiveness to religious activities, the trends of diversity in conception of religiousness and the significant changes, if there were any, which had moulded and reshaped the traditional forms of beliefs and practices of different castes of Hindu families living in this area.

In course of such contacts, 35 different castes were identified, and in accordance with their opinion a caste ranking in the line of Varna-Jati Model i.e., *Brahman, Kshatriya, Vaishya, Sudra* and *Scheduled Caste* was made out of these families, 265 were members of caste groups belonging to the upper Varna classification, 124 belonged to *Sudra* classification, and 37 belonged to the lowest rank i.e. Scheduled Caste. The total number of population of these 426 families is 1999, including 1097 males and 902 females. The percentage of literacy was quite high (85%) in comparison to the literacy level of West Bengal (30.50%).

The lifestyle ritual were classified for the present study into the following groups, viz., (i) conception or pregnancy, (ii) birth and *Annaprasana* (first rice giving ceremony), (iii) *Upanayana* (Secred thread), (iv) marriage, and (v) death and post-death rituals.

Regarding ritual observance during the pregnancy it was found that 188 (44%) families observe the same types of rituals in the 5th month of pregnancy. The number is also the same in the 7th month, while it increases to 260 performed by 29 different castes during the 9th month. But 50 families do not observe any rituals during pregnancy.

According to data, delivery in case of 276 families surveyed took place either in hospitals or nursing homes. As the first ritual act of the life-cycle used to take place at the time of birth at home, it could not, therefore, be performed in these cases. Thus an important ritual of the life-cycle had to be abandoned in these cases, and the ritual value of birth was lost. In case of birth in the house, this ritual is however observed.

Generally the mother and the new-born child remain under the state of pollution for a number of days. According to data collected, the period of pollution has been fixed from 3 to 30 days. Different caste groups observe them for different periods. It varies from family to family and caste to caste and even within the same caste. It was again found that 132 (30.90%) families after the child birth did not observe the days of pollution at all, while 294 families observed it for different periods as mentioned above.

As the child grows older, a ceremony of first feeding rice to the child is held, which is called *Annaprasana.* The different caste groups among the 426 families observed *Annaprasana* or feeding of first rice in the 6th month after the male child was born, and in case of a female child the ceremony was held generally in an odd month, according to convenience. 79 families, i.e., 18.50% did not observe this ritual, while 347 families 0f 81.50% observed the ritual.

Initiation of the young male of the *Brahman* caste into full male religious status within the group through sacred thread *Upanayana* ceremony is an important phase of Hindu rite of passage. It was observed by all the 75 *Brahman* families studied, but in some cases, it was performed even without a Prayaschitta *(penance)* in case of transgression of prescribed age limit. Again the rituals were observed in one day, instead of four, in the majority of the castes, which is the normal religious mandate and practice.

Nearly three-fourth (73%) of the families expressed a preference for a religious ritual at the time of marriage, while the remainder preferred civil marriage by registration, or to celebrate it at the temple of Goddess *Kali* at Kalighat.

Though some important traditional forms of rituals are gradually withering away, but the system of taking dowry, either in cash or kind, is still maintained and supported by the majority of the families. Regarding the marriage rituals, some striking variations were also noticed in the families of different castes, depending on their socio-economic condition, social status and cultural taste.

The families studied performed the death ceremonies in the traditional religious manner. Among the informants 73 out of 426 could state that either they actually performed these rituals, or they knew their family tradition. The death rites are performed by the families of different caste groups by cremation. Practice of burial was not found in this area. There are four categories of *Sraddha* performance, e.g., it is held just after the death, annual worship after completion of one year's mourning, annual ritual worship of ancestors on the day of Mahalaya, and sacred *Sraddha* Jajna at Gaya.

All Bengali-speaking non-*Brahman* castes have to observe the period of mourning at least for 30 days. The *Sraddha* ceremony has been also modified in accordance with the economic status of the families, as well as, the present mode of living in this area.

When the data on domestic worship of the families were collected, it was found that 343 (80.50%) families spent at least sometime daily in pursuit of religion, while 83 (19.50%) of the families reported that they never performed any such *Puja* (worship) in their houses. There was no time fixed for daily worship or any caste difference could be ascertained in this connection. 346 (81.20%) families reported that they had a habit of keeping images of deities, along with the picture and models of national Heroes, spiritual leaders, religious preceptors and parents in different corners of the houses, or in the temple within the premises of the households. 80 (18.50%) families had no images or any pictures whom they considered worthy for worship.

In general, the informants expressed their personal devotion to the religious preceptors through performance of *Puja, Jap-Tap* (prayer and penance) and chanting incantations. Again, a new feature was noticed among the different families that they desired to become disciples of the great and reputed *Gurus* (religious preceptors like *Sain-Baba, Mahesh Jogi, Balak Brahmachari* and many others). After being disciples, they wanted to follow the life and ideals of their *Gurus*, and in all only 37.00% of the total number of families studied could select their *Gurus* and follow their instructions.

Again, personal reading of Sacred Books was considered by some informants as one of their religious duties. Of the sacred books, the *Gita* was read by the highest number of literate persons. *Brata Katha* and *Panchalis* (the sacred tales of religious practices) were also read by a good number of informants.

But 72 families out of 426 had the regular habit of reading of these Sacred Books. On the other hand, 172 families spent at least some time for such reading, which might be considered as occasional reading of religious books.

The festivals were observed in four different ways : viz., (a) on the day of festivals, flowers, sweets, fruits, etc., were sent to the local temples in the name of the deity who was worshipped ritually, (b) observance of the festival and worship were done by the members of the household in their premises, (c) the *Puja* were performed by the family priest at the premises of the family concerned, and (d) the *Puja* was offered on communal basis.

According to Hindu calendar, 52 festivals were observed by the different caste groups living in this fringe area. The Hindu families were aware that the central feature of Hinduism was the wide-spread custom of pilgrimage to important regional or India-wide temples or shrines.

On the other hand, 110 families of different caste groups including twice-born caste men did not visit any of the pilgrimage centres during the said period. 25.20% families wanted to visit the pilgrimage centres for tourism, festive, recreational and other reasons, while 51.40% families went for visiting the temples and shrines; to fulfill a vow previously made by them; or to have *Punya* (religious merit); or for observance of specific rituals.

Another interesting feature relevant to the present study was the participation of some of the informants in devotional rites through different religious organisations, specially in *Kirtan* or *Sankirtan* (devotional songs), reading and recitation from the Epics or *Puranas*, social service and discussion on the topics of religion, Five such organisations, viz., *Bhagavat Sabha, Hari Sabha, Ram Krishna Mission, Bharat Sevasram Sangha* and local *religious Adda* (assembly) organise such devotional performance. But only 21.00% of the families took part in such activities for the said purpose.

It was also noticed that they often used to visit important shrines and temples, after making *Manat* (vows to deities). Excluding 6 castes, viz., *Kamar, Kumar, Rajak, Ugrakshatriya, Muchi* and *Oriya Kayastha,* the families represented by 29 other caste groups were found to have made such *Manat* for cure of diseases, getting employment, passing of examination or obtaining promotion, success in service, earn profit in business, or to win a case. These were mainly for the fulfillment of secular desires. Fulfillment of these *Manats* were performed by offering the hair of the child to the deity at the shrine, offering of fruits, sweets, clothes, ornaments, human blood, metallic-articles, coins, images and sacrifice of he-goats. All these articles however had some value to the temple establishment.

It is interesting to note that like other rural people the informants of this metropolitan fringe also believe in magical power. A good number of families still believe that there are some diseases which are caused by supernatural powers, and their cure also require something more than ordinary mode of treatment. This is done by wearing talisman and by taking magically potentiated herbs or medicines, or by applications of magically potentiated mustard-oil or water.

To cure diseases and overcome difficulties, the informants like their rural counterparts, often take the help of the *Ojhas* (witch doctors), who give them amulet or talisman to wear or water to drink, uttering some *Mantras* (incantation). Oil consecrated by *Mantras* are also used for this purpose. It was found that magic or spirit, directly or indirectly, had influenced some of the informants of different caste groups..

Similarly, trees, plants and animals were considered as sacred by them and worshipped in some cases. The informants offered *Puja* to the *Tulsi* (Basil plants), the *Aswatha* (an Indian fig tree), the *Pipal (fichus religious),* and the Banana Plant on different occasions. The cow was also the most sacred animal to them. They considered the cow as most sacred.

Certain taboos were also observed by the informants, specially in regard to food. A large proportion of the informants constituting 302 70.90% families could mention the nature of taboos. The remainder 124 families of different caste groups could not mention them.

Barwari or *Sarvajanin* (Sarva–all; Janin–People) *puja* or community worship–new type of worship is now being organised by the people of this area. The number of such *Durga Puja* was 14. Goddess *Durga, Kali, Saraswaty, Jagadhatri, Annapurna* and Lord *Shiva* and *Kartick* were worshipped in the *Barwari Puja*. The folk-deities like *Sitala* and *Manasa* were also worshipped in the *Barwari Puja.* Besides these, specially during the *Saraswati Puja* there sprang up numerous mushroom *Barwari Puja* organisations.

In the attempt to know the general impression of the informants about the Hindu concepts of religious beliefs, they were asked to give their opinion of *Swarga-Narak* (Heaven–Hell), *Pap-Punya* (Sin-Spiritual merit), *Ihalok-Paralok* (present world–world after death), *Punar-janma* (rebirth), *Atma* (Soul) and *karmafal* (the result of what is done). It was found that though about half of them were aware of these terms, most of them could not give their exact meaning or definition. Only the number of those who gave satisfactory answers had been recorded.

Mention may be made here that while answering about one concept of term in the negative, an informant gave affirmative answer for others and vice versa.

It was found that 194 (45.50%) families had faith in *Swarga-Narak* and also nearly 52 percent of the families believed in *Pap-Punya.* In connection with *Karma,* a basic distinction must be made according to Hindu conception between *Karma* that trail from one life to another, i.e., from one existence to later existence. The informants wanted to make this distinction clear, with 206 (48.40%) believed in both types of *Karma,* while the remainder did not believe that its effect were carried over from one life to the next. They were also asked whether they believed in *Atma.* 51.90% answered in the affirmative.

When asked whether they believed in the concept of *Punar-janma,* which means a link between a chain of births, beginning from the very first to unlimited regeneration, only 92 informants said that they believed in *Punar-janma.* 155 (36.40%) informants expressed their views on *Ihalok-Paralok.*

All these answers revealed their belief in the concepts of Hinduism. A good number of the informants answered these questions negatively, which indicated that they did not understand the meaning of the concepts.

Thus we find that the people of this area have an interest in Hinduism and follow its norms and modulations. This trend manifests itself in the compass of social homogeneity and coherence found among the people of this area. A Hindu family of a modern metropolitan fringe has to participate in various kinds of religious activities. The social set-up of an urban fringe, however do not restrain them to worship, or to attend religious festivals, or to participate in the ceremonies held within or outside their household.

Firstly, the Hindu community of this fringe area is divided into several caste groups, the *Brahmans,* the *Kayasthas,* the *Vaishyas,* the *Sudras* and the Scheduled Castes (untouchable) constituting the principal caste groups. None of these caste groups, however, is categorically related to any of the particular religious activities of the area.

The development of this fringe area is now well-marked, but in spite of its growth and development, it has developed a kind of rural character or village atmosphere, due to its close contact with and migration of the people from the surrounding villages and hinterland to this place, as it happens to be an important trade centre of the state.

The level of education, economic and caste status do not, however, hold back the families from participating at different levels of religious activities within or outside the household, on prestigious considerations.

Secondly, it was found that modern urban development and social, political and economic situation of recent years in the metropolitan city of Calcutta and its fringe area have, more or less, changed the conception of old traditional values and religious relationships. But this does not mean that the average Hindu families of this area have been uprooted from their religious faith, or religious institutions or performances do not attract them.

At present, there is no visible or factual evidence that the families living in this fringe area want a complete break-off with their religion, or that they don't like to be involved in matters related to religion.

Apart from the variations in rituals, one still notices enough differences in their mode of life and behavioural pattern among the various caste groups, each tends to split into economically and/or culturally distinguishable class; yet they do not cross the boundaries of their castes. It is equally applicable to the poor, as well as the rich families.

The large majority of families, in one fashion or another, have expressed their belief in the principal ideas of the concept of Hinduism (Shastric conception of Karma-Dharma). Yet, it must be mentioned that this religious belief is more in the nature of unconsciously accepted principles of Hindu philosophy and theology than a fully understood and developed intellectual affirmation.

In the midst of undergoing considerable secularization, the Hindus of this fringe area of Calcutta metropolis are found to perform traditional rites of passage, visit temples and shrines, offer *Puja*, observe *Manat* (vow), worship images, take part in *Barwari Puja*, have faith in Hindu philosophy, theology and other scriptural mandates, in general, this secular atmosphere has introduced signified performance of the rituals and associated activities. A complex network of sacred activities of the people is associated with and react upon the dominant trends of changes in the society, but the belief in religious norms and formalities is ingrained in the mind of a large section of informants, which do not allow them to completely break away from the patterns of traditional observances of religious rituals. Yet, everything has not remained the same as before. Indeed the existing pattern is incorporated with many new forms. Accommodation and acceptance of these new forms and patterns is now essential for the preservation of modern Hindu ways of life in this area.

In some cases it was found that no relationship has been established between religion and their daily life. The participants do not find life enriched by religious behaviour and sacred acts; though the number of such families is small. Thus religion is still an integral part of Hindu life. It still influences the behaviour of the people in this country.

The Hindu families of this northern fringe of the metropolis of Calcutta still remain the faithful pursuers and protagonists, although in a somewhat modified from, of the great Indian religion, Hinduism. They do not reject major features of Hindu religion; even they do not reject spirit-belief, and with all these, they have accepted renovations and have abandoned orthodoxy. It is an ethical adjustment based on inherited traditions and popular understanding of the basic features of Hindu religion.

Tarakeswar–
Study of a Hindu Place of Pilgrimage in West Bengal

Prafulla Chakrabarti

Every religion prescribes certain places as sacred which men of faith visit periodically or cherish to visit at least once in their life. Monks, sages, wayfarers, and even kings, merchants and ordinary householders have been drawn towards such centers with a sense of inner compulsion. Through their patronage such centers have grown up and flourished to become places of pilgrimage sanctified by tradition.

Unlike other religions, Hinduism is remarkably free from compulsion and coercion in tenets and directions to its followers. It does not lay down any concrete prescriptions to its followers to visit the holy places. Nevertheless, pilgrimage to holy places like Amarnath, Badrinath, or Pashupatinath Vaishno Devi in the Himalayan region; Somnath on the Arabian sea; Puri on the Bay of Bengal; Rameswaram or Kanyakumari on the Indian ocean; Jwalamukhi in the Punjab Hills; Hardwar and Beneras on the Ganges; or Kamrup Kamakhya in Assam and many others are of inestimable value to the devout Hindu.

From the very beginning places of pilgrimage have been variously conceived by different scholars. A great deal of attention has been paid to the institution of pilgrimage and to the different aspects of this tradition. While these works provide one with valuable information about the utility of the institution, it was not until the mid-50s of the last century that systematic studies on pilgrim centers were initiated by the anthropologists .For example, Redfield (1955) pointed out that in order to study the complexities of Indian civilization and of social organization of tradition, study of traditional sacred centers could provide valuable information. The concept of ontogenetic transformation of cities provided by Redfield and Singer (1954) served as a useful tool for the study of a pilgrim centre. One finds the concept of network and centres of integration of Indian civilization particularly relevant from the viewpoint of the Indian tradition. The conception of place of pilgrimage as a dimension of Indian civilization and its analysis of structure in terms of three analytical tools: the 'sacred geography', the 'sacred performances' and the 'sacred specialists' used first by Vidharthi (1961) in his study of Gaya,which was followed by many scholars later in the study of many Hindu sacred complexes like, for instance, Bhubaneswar, Deoghar, Dwarka, Janakpur, Pashupatinath, Puri, Rameswaram and Tirupati, Kashi, Kalighat, Nathdwara and so on.

II

The present study seeks to examine the various processes operating in this minor regional centre of pilgrimage. It would also throw light on the social function of religion, particularly how does religion help the existence of society as an ordered and continuing system of relationships. More specifically the idea behind this intensive study of Tarakeswar is to make a comprehensive understanding of the variety, complexity, and richness of the culture of this religious complex, to examine the structure and function of this relatively recent and non-puranic place of pilgrimage and to see how it reflects the characteristics of the Indian civilization. Besides the analysis of history of origin and development, socio-economic condition, sacred complex, pilgrims and pilgrimage, its diverse impacts on local, regional and extra-regional populations would also be examined. While discussing the functional aspects of the pilgrim town, the persistence of traditional values and the emergence of newer ones, if any, will also be examined.

It is hoped that the present study will fill up some of the gaps noticed in the past studies of Indian civilization. This study is an attempt to provide some missing links to the works done by other workers earlier.

III

We note that earlier works on the places of pilgrimage are centered on such places which have a more or less old history of origin and development and are regarded as *puranic tirthas*. The regional or relatively minor places of pilgimage generally escaped attention of workers. Consequently, it is not known whether the patterns observed in major places of pilgrimage, namely well developed sacred geography having defined boundary, multiple segments, clusters and centres of varying degrees of religious importance, diverse sacred performances showing the sanskritic and folk elements, and sacred specialists of deferent cultural levels, also occur at the regional sacred complexes.

The earlier works further reveal that not much attention has been given to the local social milieu in maintaining the sacred character of the town, that the different groups of people living at a place of pilgrimage have different commitments and behaviour system of the town, seem to have received very little attention. Another limitation of the earlier studies of the pilgrim centre is a somewhat casual treatment of the pilgrims, who are actually the 'consumers of the sacred'. Even when they have received some attention by earlier scholars, they have hardly been considered in relation to their demographic, socio-cultural, economic, psychological characteristics so that the relevance of pilgrims vis-a-vis pilgrim centre could be properly assessed. Consequently, questions like who consumes what, whether all categories of Hindu population do participate in the pilgrimage, to what extent the behaviour of pilgrims gets influenced; whether the purposes of pilgrimage vary in relation to social background and so on, remained unanswered. Such a trend encouraged this scholar to take up the present study of Tarakeswar.

Tarakeswar, a famous place of Hindu pilgrimage in eastern India, has more than a century and a half, attracted many pilgrims form far and near. Its importance and development, are mainly due to the temple patronage of *Taraknath*. The town of Tarakaswar minus *Taraknath* leaves nothing. An attempt has been made here to study the dynamics of this pilgrim centre.

IV

This study is based on multiple research design. Its approach is deductive posivistic but nevertheless, it does not exclude inductive – inferential approach. It used both textual and contextual data. The textual materials include published and unpublished data from the Census, municipal records, temple office, district court records, and private documents (registers, letters, diaries, manuscripts of scholars). The scholar depended upon a number of field methods for the collection of data. These were (a) observation, (b) household enumeration, (c) case history, (d) genealogy, and(e) interview. Participation observation was adopted while undertaking a number of pilgrim tours to Tarakeswar. A large number of people were interviewed on aspects relevant to the purpose of the study. Field investigation was carried out between 1975 and 1977 covering a total period of about eighteen months. It was conducted among the priests first. After making a census to ascertain their number, lineage, domicile and length of priesthood, the genealogical method was used to collect data like age, migration, occupational mobility land–holding etc. The next set of informants was the pilgrim–guides locally known as *pradarsaks* which was followed by the barbers, potters, sacred water sellers, owners of *saraimaliks* rest houses, temple and estate employees.

Simple random sampling without replacement was adopted to study the socio-economic condition of the Tarakeswar town. The census household list, duly updated, served as the sample frame from which a 20 per cent sample of households was drawn. In all, 470 heads of households were surveyed from the pilgrim town.

The third stage of field work was conducted among pilgrims. For operational convenience, it was decided to interview 450 pilgrims. In order to get an appropriate coverage, the survey was spread over a period of two years noting three different occasions within each of them (i) the period of maximum attendance of pilgrims, (ii) that of minimum attendance and (iii) the period in between. While the socio –economic, religious, and other related information of the sample pilgrims were collected by interview, the data relating to their act of pilgrimage were gathered either through direct participation in the event or by systematic observation of the pilgrim behaviour.

From the key informants like the head of the monastery, local political leaders, teachers, leaders of the organization of the priests, of the *sarai-malik* sangha and of the *pradarsak* sangha etc., information were collected by depth interview, sometimes using a tape recorder. For capturing the glimpses of important ritual and festive moment photographic technique was used.

V

Tarakeswar is a growing town in a rural setting of West Bengal. Since the establishment of the temple of Lord *Taraknath* in early eighteenth century by an immigrant Kshatriya king and a Dashanami monastery later by a *Saiva* monk belonging to the Giri order, it has passed through several developmental phases. The emergence of the deity, however, is associated with a folk legend having some historical basis which describes the interaction of many uncanny events with a host of factors, e.g., dream, supernaturalism, plants, animals, and humans, like in most legends from medieval Bengal. The main motive behind the establishment of the *Siva* temple by the non-Bengali king, Bishnudas, was possibly because he wanted to maintain his status and dignity among the peasants and artisans who constituted the majority in this area as also to subscribe to the religious sentiments of the local to subscribe to the local people. For, he might have felt that there were the famous religious centers of the *Saktas* in Kalighat and Tarapith, and of the *Vashnavites* in Nabadwip located nearby but no *Saiva* centre of similar importance around, although the area was inhabited by the low caste *saivites* mostly. In order to fill up the vacuum the king possibly brought the image, which is made of reddish black stone available generally in Northern India and not in the alluvial plains of Bengal and established it here.

Eventually Tarakeswar grew into a famous place of Hindu pilgrimage in Eastern India and people from various regions of West Bengal and surrounding areas began to visit this place throughout the year for paying obeisance to Lord *Taraknath*. The flow of pilgrims, however, vary greatly depending on the nature of ritual and festive occasions. Since the last few decades there has been a continuous increase in the number of pilgrims averaging three to four thousand persons a day. This increasing trend of visits has largely been due to the natural increase in population, improved transport facilities, influence of mass media like films and folk–dramas produced to glorify the miracles of the cult, radio and newspapers and the propagation of the gospel of Lord *Taraknath* by the sacred specialists and the local residents. As a result, during the *Sravani* (July–August), *Sivaratri* (March), *Chaitra-Sankranti* (April) festivals some two to three lakhs of people are reported to congregate here.

Besides being a religious seat, Tarakeswar has become an important centre for commerce and a nodal point for linking the three adjacent districts of Burdwan, Midnapur and Bankura with Calcutta. Thus it seems to have a two fold importance : (a) holy aspect centered on the temple of *Taraknath* and other sacred spots in the precincts to which the pilgrims are solemnly enjoined to pay their worship, and (b) a secular aspect confined to there commercial area of Chaulpatti, Manoharpatti and the Bus Stand complex which the people of surrounding region use for exporting rice and vegetables, and importing seeds, manures etc.

The religious complex of *Taraknath* finds its expression through three principal components : the 'sacred geography', the 'sacred performances' and the 'sacred specialists', conforming thus to the basic pattern of many puranic places of pilgrimage (Vidyarthi 1961). For example, the existence of a well-demarcated boundary isolating the sacred locally known as *Siva-kshetra* or *Bahar garh* from the secular zone, large number of sacred centres of different sectarian relevance which are scattered either singly or in clusters or segments with varying degrees of importance : local, regional or national, point to the similar structural alignment as to other notable places of Hindu pilgrimage. The sacred performances include a large variety of rituals like *darshan* (auspicious view of the deity), *snan* (holy bath), *mundan* (tonsure), *puja* (worship), *dharna* (Surrender) and so on. The practice of offering of the holy water of the Ganges over Lord *Taraknath* after carrying it from a long distance with yolk-poles reminds one of the similar practice in Deoghar (Bihar) or Aiyappan temple in Andhra Pradesh. But the most popular rituals here appear to be the *dharna* and the *dandi*. As for the other dimension of a sacred complex i.e., sacred specialists,we may note that excepting the *mohant*,the other groups of specialists, by and large, do not follow the same as reported by the author elsewhere. The priests resemble, in respect of their cultural and social behaviour, more closely to the general population of the town.

Secular aspect of the religious complex is clearly manifest in its economic sphere. The religious estate earns from various sources, e.g., regular payment of annuities by the state government, gifts and donations from pilgrims, rent and tax from the house and establishments, interest from the bank against fixed deposits, lease-outs through auctioneering of fishing-ponds, tonsuring centre, sites for stalls, etc., the investment of fund in the bank for interest, keeping buildings and other establishments for rent, and leasing out of various sources of income show the secular aspect of this religious institution.

But it should, however, be borne in mind that this religious estate is different from a formal economic institution in so far as it is an institution without the usual profit orientation of an enterprise. For instance, the income which it receives from different sources is spent mostly for the daily worships, benefit to the devotees, enhancing the religious image of the place, and spending on charitable and relief purposes. A portion of the income is spent on salaries of the employees also who are responsible for the various services of the estate and the temple.

In an indirect way, the religious institution of Tarakeswar has provided economic opportunities to a good number of professional castes who cater to the needs of the pilgrims by providing their caste occupational services. The pundits, priests, barbers, potters and various other caste-occupations of the town and surrounding areas have been deriving considerable benefit out of the temple by a process of ritual re-inforcement, thereby retarding the professionalisation of occupations to a certain extent. People living far way from Tarakeswar also derive economic benefit indirectly from the temple. The places from where the pilgrims initiate their journey or take rest on their way to Tarakeswar attract various groups of people who earn their living by selling rituals and snack articles to them. Some such places are Kalighat, Bally, Sheoraphuli, Singur, Hamargachi, Lokenath and so on. The pilgrimage of Tarakeswar has helped to develop a number of cottage industries like manufacture of pottery, yoke-poles (*bank*), reticulated sling (*sika*), incense sticks, pintings on glass, handloom etc., in the neighbor-hood. All these bear the testimony that apart from its religious influence, the economic net-work of the religious complex of Tarakeswar has also spread into its hinterland benefiting thousands of people of different vocations. And day by day,along with the continuous increase in the religious importance of Tarakeswar, there has been a simultaneous increase in its socio-cultural and economic importance.

The *mohunt* was and still is supposed to look after the affairs of the temple. He being the principle *sevayat* (priest) of Lord *Taraknath* and the *tithe* guru (supreme religious head), enjoys the right to offer worship to the deity first. He has some intimate relation with the deity which are both mythical and ritualistic.

There has, however, been a change in his power since 1940 because of the change in the administrative control of the temple-estate. For a secular administration has been set-up to look after the estate. The *mohunt* is now advised by a committee consisting of members from both secular and religious organizations. He no longer patronizes only the holy scriptures and confines himself to his residence but also attends to the literary, cultural and religious meetings, invites external agencies for the development of the town in general and encourages modern education.

VI

Every research undertaking must have two objectives in view. First, it should contribute fresh input into the already existing knowledge and thus helps advancement of knowledge of a particular discipline. Second, it should have an applied aspect dealing with the welfare of man and environment. The present study of Tarakeswar has covered both the aspects. Although basically it is a product of anthropological work nevertheless, it transcends its boundary to reach into the arena of sociology of religion. For, the study intends to drive home what actually is being done in the name of religion rather than being offered well-known platitudes about what the texts tell us, for what is being done has social consequences and implications.

As the world intellectual community becomes ever more secularized, it becomes increasingly difficult for intellectuals to understand the motivation behind, and the organization of a major activity of human kind–the practice of religion. Yet, given the degree to which religion apparently permeated social life in the past, and perhaps still does even to day in at least in some countries, an understanding of religious activity would seem crucial for our understanding of society.

That historically people in most societies have exhibited a high degree of religiosity seems to be a general assumption of many historians and social analysts. Thus, for instance, the history of many societies has been written, at least in part, in terms of the rise of new mass religions, the rendering of their hegemony by challenging counter-religion and sects and the attempts of the initial religions to maintain their dominance.

For the present day, matters are somewhat more complicated. Data indicate, for instance, that the church attendance has dropped off precipitously in many western countries, and in Canada. There is a world-wide trend toward secularization, so that religion is now relatively unimportant in most people's lives whatever may have been the case in the past. On the other hand, in the United States, religious participation seems to have remained quite high. It appears to be undergoing a powerful revival in the Middle East. And in India, many millions of people continue to participate in religious festivals and make pilgrimage to religions centers. India seems to be dwindling between sacredness and secularism because of the contemporary political issues.

The present study of Tarakeswar while reveals the structural dynamics of this Great Tradition also shows the unconscious acceptance of prevailing rites and practices. To many a priest, priesthood is not a way of life but merely a *byabasa* (business) rather than *britti*. To some pilgrimage is getting changed from an act of religious faith to tourism and search of amusement and pleasure. It takes place largely because of 'H' (*huzuk*) factor. But the long trek with its necessary paraphernalia ; including the slogan *Bhole Baba Par Karega* poses some basic questions concerning the socio-economic situations of the contemporary society and cannot be treated as a passing phenomenon or efflux of errant enthusiasm. For instance, the increase of tension and frustration in life, the more loss of faith and self-reliance might occur. To the frustrated, alienated, lonely, unsecured, unemployed youth, pilgrimage to Tarakeswar is more a temporary escape from aimless everyday life. Tarakeswar remains, and may continue to remain, like most other places of pilgrimage, a refuge to the helpless but the manner in which it soothes the weary souls may change in tune with changing times.

References

Redfield, R. 1955 *The social organisations of Tradition. Eastern Quarterly*, 15 (1).

Redfied, R. & Singer, M. 1954 The Cultural Role of cities. *Economic Development and Cultural Changes*, 3.

Vidyarthy, L.P. 1961 *Sacred Complex in Hindu Gaya*. Bombay : Asia Publishing House.

Sacred Complex in Holy Godavari (Rajahmundry) in Andhra Pradesh : An Anthropological Study of Religious Behaviour

Vaddi Arjanna

In India since hoary past, rivers, mountains, trees and plants were considered as symbols of holiness. These were sometimes personified as deity, gods and goddesses. In effect, man's association with nature in emotional plains developed this idea of *naturism* as the origin of religion, as propounded by Muller.

The river as sacred goddess always supplies water perennially to make the fields fertile and develop a green scenery of crops and also provide them with fish. The flowing rivers, again, remove the impurities through their currents. This makes communication network easy by boats, steamers and ships. With all these potentialities and direct benefits to mankind, the rivers are considered holy and as such in most cases divinities are attributed to them. Thus, most of the famous rivers of our country are regarded as sacred. A ceremonial dip, immersion of ashes of cremated bodies on performing cremation on their banks are considered to be holy. As a result, from time immemorial, most of the rivers have become sacred. This enabled them tc develop other institutions and complexes as per exigencies of the situation to fulfill the need of the pilgrims visiting the places from time to time. The inner significance of such pilgrim spots of the rivers at specific junctions of confluence have been treated as very important. This becomes a part of Indian civilization and this helps to create a mentality of Indianism through contest, interaction and assemblage of the pilgrim from time to time and else at specific time in groups or batches accelerating the idea of integration.

Hinduism is a flexible religion which differs in some places through regional or localized cultures, characterized as *Loukik* (Saraswati: 1970 : 47) and these are associated with the common masses essentially through verbal testimonies or the collective memories and these *Lokachars* (folk behavioural patterns) were gradually accommodated with it.

II

The significance of the river Godavari, specially in Hindu religion, has been emphasized corroborating many myths and mythologies. However, this particular site near Rajahmundry has been considered a holy or sacred site and pilgrims have begun to buzz in for a ceremonial dip in order to earn merit or *Punya* by taking a bath and even offering worship to the goddess through Brahmanical assistance of the priest or *Pujaris.* Again sometimes dead bodies are cremated here or the ashes from the cremation ground of distant places are immersed and the *Sradh* or purificatory ceremony is held with the help and assistance of the Brahmin or *Pujari,* since he is the only authorized person to perform this rite. Myths and mythologies narrate these, and ultimately the river Godavari has become one of the *Puranic Tirthas* (i.e., a holy place mentioned in the scriptures). Besides, after twelve years, *Pushkara* sets in, when it attracts many pilgrim, Sadhus, Sannyasis (both holy men or hermit) and many people of varied nature who not only emphasize its sacredness but also increased commerce and trade potentialities contribute in different ways in increasing the importance of the river in the cultural and economic life of the country.

In course of discussion the origin of the river has been mentioned. It starts from Triambakam in the district of Nasik in Maharastra and its different tributaries fall on it. Ultimately, they all mingling together join the Bay of Bengal. In course of time, changes have taken place in its route, either through natural or man-made causes. Many projects and barrages have been constructed from time to time to give water supply to certain areas on its banks.

From the legendary past, the Godavari has been personified. It has been described how the beloved consort of Lord *Shiva,* the Godavari slowly rolled down to earth, specially to the Deccan (Dakhinapath). The importance and significance of the river have been reiterated time and again. Hundreds and thousands of pilgrims who nestled on the temples on its bank have gradually made the river popular and has contributed in building up its sacred character.

Historical background has been emphasized through legends and documented history. Various kings from time to time reorganized Rajahmundry and gradually it changed its geophysical contours according to the importance. Muslim and British administrators added more complexities from time to time with the establishment of railway station etc. Thus, the present day Rajahmundry is of a different nature with many facilities and comforts, and has sprung up as one of the important commercial trade centres of Andhra Pradesh.

III

The sacred complexes of the holy Godavari have been studied with a view to understand the :

1. development and transformation of Rajahmundry, the important places on the bank of the river where many sacred centres or holy spots for the Hindus have sprung up with historical background. As per mythological suggestion, the Godavari is considered to be holy or sacred only at this place;
2. the details of the temples, which are dotted at different areas of Rajahmundry, specific purposes of worship and festivals, celebrations to have not only the living symphony but also to record the gradual historical superimposition of one culture on the other :
3. behavioural pattern of the devotees along with the action-pattern of the priestly specialists ; and
4. the character of the devotees, their purpose and details of involvement in celebrations and ritual.

All the above points taken together reflect a particular type of system operating in the cult, and these are nothing but the tips of an ice-berg of the greater Hindu tradition which signifies Indian civilization and its continuity and changes.

In the present study almost all the sacred centres of the city, namely the temples and shrines (49), mosques (8) and Churches (14), total 71, have been discussed. Again, to study the nature of religiosity of the pilgrims or the devotees, four shrines have been studied in-depth. These are:

1. Uma Markendeswara Aalayam, dedicated to Lord *Shiva;*
2. Uma Ramalingeswara Swamy Aalayam, dedicated to Lord *Shiva;*
3. Kotilingeswara Kshetram, dedicated to Lord *Shiva;* and
4. Sri Venu Gopal Swamy Aalayam, dedicated to Lord *Vishnu.*

History, legend, iconography, nature of worship, sources of income, nature of worship of deity, along with the sacred specialists who take part in ceremonial affairs have been dealt with in details. The nature of offering of worships by the devotees, the organization of the temples and the Brahmanical dominance in the management of temples have also been noted. There are a few festive occasions when special worships are done and the devotees assemble in large numbers from far and near. Again, some aspects of the pilgrims who offer worships in these four temples after taking holy dips in the river, along with the distances they cover, purposes for which they offer the worships and the nature of offerings made to the deities have been recorded carefully. In this way, the psychological orientations of people have been projected and their relation with great tradition through scriptures and Brahmanical assistance have been verified. The Pan-Indian situation and the Great Traditional complex have become evident whenever the regional barriers have been removed. The commercial potentialities of the place have increased due to the involvement of the people through religious rites and rituals. The ceremonies of obligations and mutual dependence and the invocation of the supernaturals through such religious rites have also made the place a centre of religious attraction and economic importance.

IV

All ceremonies and celebrations require sacred specialists, known as priests, *Pujaris*, *Purohits* or *Archakas*. Their formal affiliation, nature of duties and obligations and other formalities have been recorded carefully to describe the Hindu method of worships and celebrations associated with the sacred complexes of the holy Godavari. The holy Godavari in course of its sacredness gradually accommodated many shrines and people in and around the region. The people here are acquainted with the *Sashtriya* rituals and celebrations that take place throughout the year. Under such circumstances, attempt has been made to discuss various rituals and celebrations of the Hindus which take place in the locality. Celebrations and festivals are also associated with a sense of holiness and as such, the river Godavari and the temples on its bank also observe all such festivals promising happiness and joy to people when a dip in the holy Godavari is taken. Of course, during the festive occasions some temporary shelters or sheds are constructed in many temples and a festive atmosphere prevails all around the place. This condition practically attracts many friends, relatives and pilgrims to attend the festival and as a result, a social milieu of ties is made among the groups of the attending people. A detailed account of such festivals, month wise, with the main deities along with the special features of the occasions have been given (Table 1). It can be said that all these worships and celebrations are made according to the scriptural guidance which have been composed by the Brahmanical scholars. The Brahmins prescribe and lead such matters all the time during the occasions.

Table 1
CALENDAR OF MAJOR FESTIVALS

Name of Festival	Date & Month of	Corresponding	Main deity worshipped	Special features
1. Samvatsaradi or Ugadi	First day of *Chaitra*	March	*Gramadevathalu* (village & local deities)	Worshipping artefacts of professions, eating pickles of fresh neem flower.
2. Sriramanavami	9th day of *Chaitra*	March - April	Sri *Rama* & *Seetha* along with *Lakshmana* and *Hanuman*	Marriage celebrated for the images of *Rama* and Seetha
3. Vinayakachaviti	4th day of *Sravana*	August	*Vigneswara* or *Viyayaka* or *Ganapathi* along with *Siva* and *Parvati*	Offering stress boiled rice flour-balls Vundrallu, for Lord *Ganesh* and worshipping books and other articles of learning.
4. Dasara or Vijaya Dasami	10th day of *Aswaijin*	September-October	*Devi* or *Durga* or *Parvati* or *Adi-Sakthi*	Weapons and other articles are worshiped as a symbol of success.
5. Deepavali	30th day of *Aswaijin*	October-November	Celebrating the death of *Bakshasha* king *Narakasuru*.	Lines of lamps in the house, fire works in the evening and worshipping *Dhanalaxmi* Goddess of wealth
6. Sankranthi	3 days i.e. 15th, 16th, 17th day of *pusya*.	January	Happy occasions of harvesting of crops. All local deities worshipped	Varieties of sweets and other dishes prepared and distributed among relatives.
7. Mahasivaratri	20th day of *Magam*	February	Lord *Siva*.	Fasting the whole day and walking through the night along with worshipping Lord *Siva* or Holy Dip in River or Sea.

Generally, it is expected that by participating in these occasions people should earn merit or *Punya* which will ultimately give *Moksha* salvation from the cycle of birth. All the sacred centres of the Hindu India have such attributes which satisfy the material needs, fulfillment of vows to bring overall satisfaction to the individuals and to their families. It also contributes peace and happiness in the mind of the people.

The present study undoubtedly constitutes an ethnography of the sacred Godavari which, from legendary, Puranic and historical times, attracted the attention of the Hindus. Among them, as it has been pointed out, there are diversities and differences in the caste-ridden Hindu society. We find not only the poor and the rich but also caste groups having both low and high status. In such a system, where economic sufficiency, affluence and material prosperity are considered as cherished goals, religion, must provide some ways of achieving it. As such, rituals are observed and worships are made to change the material life to a higher and better stage which can automatically bring about a prosperous life as it is understood. However, the sacred complexes, which have grown slowly but steadily through the origin of myths and mythologies, connected with the place have made it a pilgrimage. After every twelve years, through *Pushkaram*, it assumes an all India character when the sacred character of the place reaches its peak. But the shrines and the temples around the bank and the holy dips for *prayaschitta* or expiation, all the time attract individuals to this place and thus we find vibrations of Hindu way of life all throughout the year. Rites, ceremonies, celebrations are observed to combat the unwanted situations of the material life. It is a fact that this holiness has been maintained and continued by a group of sacred specialists, the *Archakas*, the Brahmin priests or the *Pujaries* all the time through a series of involvement on varied occasions. Thus, the *Sashtric* or Brahmanic doctrines of the Hindu philosophy is continued, perpetuated and handed down to the posterity. As per Vidyarthi (1979 :14).

> It is a great tradition oriented in the sense that it represents the higher form of Hinduism as reflected in the predominance of Sanscritic sacred centres, in the significance of the sacred performance of the Shradha, as well as in the all pervading influence of the Brahmanical priesthood and sacred intelligent.

We accept this while we go through the cycle of manifestations, which take place in the Godavari, the sacred zone at Rajahmundry.

But, we cannot also deny that the presence of varied groups of people, high and low, rich and poor, respected and despised–all come and attend it. The family oriented men with material or worldly outlook, as well as ascetics and hermits–all congregate here and interact to give a mosaic pattern of Hindu India. They form an unseen bondage and ties of obligation through which groups of diverse ethnic and cultural groups are interlaced with the tinge of religiosity. The notion of folk tradition undoubtedly reflects Redfield's 'little tradition', but it is of a different nature in the Indian situation. Through a collective reflection, a new dimension of Hindu India is being reflected with:

> .... distinctiveness which is apparent to the outside observers and expressed in the group consciousness of the people (Redfield 1960 : 4).

It is an undeniable fact that–

> The number of Hindu sanctuaries in India is so large and the practice of pilgrimage so ubiquitous that the whole of India can be regarded as vast sacred *Kshetras* organised into a system of pilgrimage centres of varied importance (Jha 1979:155).

Though Lord Vishnu temple (19), Siva temple (7), Anjaneya or monkey god or Hanuman temple (7), Ganesh temple (5), Durga or Parvati temple (3), regional (Local or Miscellaneous) temples or shrines (3 plus 6) are all situated on the bank of the river, their first attraction is not the deities, but a holy dip in the river at a particular point. After the holy dip, worships are taken up. In this connection, Ostor remarks.

> They live in myths of the past and in the idle talk...they are powerful majestic deities who rule the heavens... .They are timeless, capable of taking any form and yet they appear at the annual festivals (Ostor 1979 : 1).

Thus, gods and goddesses appear to have worships from the pilgrims while taking bath in the river for earning merit. All these have been blended and inextricably woven into each other in such a way that differentiation is hardly possible. Through the action patterns of the priests, worship of the pilgrims and scriptural directions and rituals, people are bound in an integrated manner. Thus a discernable mind will find a mystic combination of all these mental and material phenomena as reflected in the symphony of life of Hindu India. It reminds us the eternal truth about India, i.e., Unity in Diversity. As Bhowmick (1980 : 196) remarked :

> Hinduism as a major religious faith in India has a wide variation in its concepts and rituals from region to region as is observed amongst the different castes and communities inhabiting the country. ...But the process of transmutation and assimilation can be well delineated by a critical analysis of the prevailing practices and religious rites and beliefs of the people of a certain area. And in assuming, we find that 'unity in diversity' is the dominating spirit of Hinduism.

The spirit has been reverberated again and again by many saints and *Avatars* (God-incarnates) from time to time when they bring all important rivers of India in a *Sloka* (Sanskrit couplets) for all sorts of domestic rites, rituals and ceremonies. We find the name of the sacred river Godavari along with some other holy rivers of India which are considered to be sacred. It is interesting to note here that the emphasis is all the time on the basis of sacredness along with a spirit of integration to note when all people of India stand for one-India and Hinduism. The particular Sloke is as follows :-

> Ganga cha Jamune Chaiba,
> Godavari Saraswati,
> Narmade, Sindhu, Kaveri,
> Jalesmi Sannidhing Kuru.

After chanting the above *Sloke* or Sanskritic formula all rites start and the water for worshiping is treated as water of all the sacred rivers with which any ceremony should commence.

Thus, the river Godavari which is believed to have been brought down by Sage *Gautama* from the matted hair of Lord *Siva* is sacred and holy and this has been continuing as a place for purification in the Hindu social system.

However, the sacred or holy site of the Godavari is the bathing-ghat for the pilgrims who, by taking holy dip purify themselves. Even necessary *Praysachitta* or purificatory rites are performed, specially after the death of a person and by immersing the ashes or calcinated bones to the river. The soul of the departed persons thus gets salvation, or the soul of the dead person is believed to have a permanent haven in the heaven. A few years ago, an image of the mother goddess Godavari has been installed on its bank where pilgrims offer worship or *Puja* through the *Brahman* priests, popularly known as *Pujaris, Pundits* or *Acharya*. In this way they interpret the Brahminical traditions through rites and ceremonies, through worships and thus they get gifts from the persons by offering worships or doing purificatory ceremonies. In this way, the traditional Brahmanical code of conduct is being transmitted to the ordinary people. As a continuous process it started in ancient times and is being extended today. It binds and attracts the people to the core of Hinduism leading to integration through self-satisfaction. This brings security and oneness among the diverse groups at least for the time being. This is the force of 'Indianisation' or the process of Hinduism which is evinced through visiting sacred or holy places located all over the country. Thus, the pilgrims move throughout the year. Especially on festive occasions they not only visit the holy places for bathing in the sacred river, but also visiting on other sacred centers like the temples and the shrines. Again on material aspects the process initiates other types of interactions, accentuates commerce, trade, tourism, transport facilities and, above all, helps distribute the local cultural traits to its outer zones.

So the holy Godavari with its sacred complex and geography reflects Hindu India which always enshrines the notion of 'unity in diversity' re-establishing Brahmanical order in the caste-ridden hierarchical Indian society.

References

Bhowmick, P. K. 1980 *Some Aspects of Indian Anthropology.* Calcutta : Subarnarekha.

Jha, M. 1979 *Dimensions of Indian Civilisation.* New Delhi : Classical Publications.

Ostor, A. 1980 *The Play of the Gods.* USA : University of Chicago Press.

Redfield, R. 1960 *The Little Community Peasant Society and Culture.* USA : University of Chicago Press.

Saraswati, B. N. 1970 Contributions to the understanding of Indian civilization. Dharwar : Karnatak University.

Vidyarthi, L. P., Saraswati, B. N. & Jha, M. 1979 *The Sacred Complex of Kashi–A Microcosm of Indian Civilization.* Delhi : Concept Publishing Company.

Food and Rituals–A Study of Their Interrelationship in Fringe Bengal

Bela Jana

Food is one of the most important basic needs of human beings without which it could not continue to live in its present form. All the activities, services and ideas of culture of mankind are directly or indirectly associated with food and food habits. From the old days, the production process of food and food habits of the people of different societies are mostly related with variety of rituals. Due to non-availability of historical records of early period, no systematic information on the details of rituals and their association with the food can be properly obtained. However from the period of Indus valley civilization and more particularly, from the Vedic age, we get an idea of food habit and food production activities among the people.

Now with the advent of time and gradual change of climate, technology and culture, the production process of crops or the agriculture and the food habits have also undergone changes. With this change in production process rites, rituals-ceremonies/festivals etc., began to be performed with emphasis on the idea of more production. To this end, sometimes taboos and prohibitions have also been observed. Thus, rites and rituals relating to food occupy a prominent place in human culture.

We know that from the early Stone Age, people had encountered their surrounding and struggled to make food stuff available from it. Gradually with the change of climate, changing technology, there was a change in culture. Agriculture appeared in the scene and slowly it came to its modern form, of course, with variations in its change pattern from place to place.

In our country people give much more importance to various food items. From the old age most of them used to offer prayers to god/supernatural powers before they take their principal meal. Much emphasis was laid upon hospitality as well as the purity of food. From the very early Vedic age Indians are very much attached to the great importance of food and since then it was given so importance that people did not accept new corn without offering it to fire or god/deity.

It is understood that various crops and fruits etc., grown in favourable geographical conditions form the food habits of the population. And they give favourite food stuffs to their god/super natural powers as offerings. Thus, in following religious rites during worshipping deities, life-cycle ceremonies etc., the offering of food play a very important role.

Rituals mean the performance of certain religious rites in conformity with tradition, manners and customs etc., of a society. Here the rituals play an important role in moulding the behavioural pattern of the individuals and groups. There is no doubt about it that the nature of rituals may vary in degree in different socio-economic, religious and related cultural situations. This variation may be pronounced even within a particular group/community of the same region depending upon the related socio-religious and other status of the community.

Many of the ancestral traditions and customs practised from hundreds of years ago are still followed by the vast majority of the people whether they relate to life-cycle events like birth, death and marriage or to any other community worship, festivals or so. The food habit of the people, offering of food to the deity and the following of related rites and rituals create much impact on the overall social behaviour of the people in the society.

People in rural areas maintain their livelihood depending on the natural environment through a significant process of regular interaction.

As food item is considered to be the most important aspect of livelihood, some of the favoured food items, which are generally consumed for survival, are offered to the deities (god/goddess). Here a meaningful correlation is found between the food production and tribute aspects of rural people. In different societies, offering and taking of food for oneself is indicative of great reverence and devotion and respect for super natural powers. *Naibedya* is such kind of offering in the family ceremonies and calendar festivals through out the year. Some times totems and taboos are connected with the offer too. Of course, variations in the nature of worships and offerings are found in the same communities and individuals and kin-groups due to ecological differences and some times on priestly directives and cultural modifications. Different kinds of produced food are offered to the deities and different rituals are followed in doing so.

Thus, it is nothing but a process of balancing the mode of living with nature where the rites, rituals and other related cultural activities and festivals are shaped accordingly. Along with this, the ceremonies, festivals etc., are powerful and potent factor in uniting people either as active participant or observer.

Social cohesion and solidarity are thus strengthened by such ceremonialism. India in general and West Bengal in particular have congenial climatic change with fertile land, fresh and rich vegetation of different crops and suitable combination of ecological and soil conditions. So West Bengal has been selected for the field research in understanding the food-ritual interrelationship in our rural social scenario. With this end in view our study intends to find the interrelationship of food, food habits and rituals at various ecological zones of contemporary Bengal. To have a thorough knowledge on the aspect, observations were made on the types of food availability, food habits and their ritualistic characters as found in the rural ecological conditions.

Under the circumstances, most of the people in the Bengali society all over West Bengal are very much serious in following their traditional norms but they also accept change and in the process, they adjust with the environmental conditions to which they belong.

As ecology has much impact over food production, cultural traits are expected to be in tune with the ecology and environment where the groups of people are involved in it. So at the beginning, the study was made to ascertain the geography and ecological conditions that influence food production. The composition of the ethnic groups along with their culture and the rites and rituals, which they follow during worshipping of various gods and goddesses and festivals at their homes or in temples–have all been taken into consideration while making this study.

Food continues to play an important role in the religious life of man through which man relates himself with the supernatural entities for protection, prosperity and happiness. Religion has developed numerous symbolic ways and forms of using foods. All these have deeper meaning to the people concerned. Thus, food is not only for substance but it has also a cultural value.

Thus on the basis of theoretical ideas and observations, an attempt has been made to understand empirically how ecology, food and food habit mould the cultural/behavioral pattern to some extent with the advancement of technology and science.

It has already been stated that the main objective of the study is to find out the influence of food as offered to the deity during rituals and the change in the food habit of the people at different ecological zones in the contemporary rural society of West Bengal.

On the basis of considerations as discussed, the researcher

conducted her study on the rural society. Six randomly sampled villages from three different ecological zones in fringe areas of West Bengal were chosen for the purpose of field study and detailed analyses were made on the basis of data obtained from these villages.

The selection of eco-zones was done as per the availability of reference in authoritative books and journals. In the selection of villages, purposive random sampling was followed. The object was to find out the growth and availability of varied food crops, the change in food habits and the related ritualistic behaviour of the people, in a region. And, thus an attempt was made to understand the interrelationship of food, food habits and the rituals in the rural social ecological conditions.

Fieldwork was undertaken in the concerned villages at different ecological zones of the selected districts of the state of West Bengal namely Purulia, Midnapore and 24 Parganas. The main objectives of the study were to find out

i) the geographical conditions of the particular locality–the village;
ii) the sources and the availability of foodstuff in the locality;
iii) food patterns and the food habits followed by the people;
iv) the ritual differences among the caste groups; and
v) the nature of festivals, rituals, rites and food patterns for understanding the culture, economic and social aspects of the groups or communities.

Table I

Nature of sample surveyed villages

Eco-Zone (s)	Village (s)	Police Station	District
I	1. Keshargarh	Hura	Purulia
	2. Golkunra	Purulia Muffasil	Purulia
Laterite	3. Mymensingh colony	Jhargram	Midnapore
II	1. Thakurnagar	Khejuri	Midnapore
Alluvial Plain	2. Dihi Madan Malla	Baruipur	24 Parganas (South)
III Island in Delta	1. Pathan Khali	Gosaba	24 Parganas (South)

Depending upon the ecological variations in the districts, the villages under the purview were grouped together into three zones.

Zone I included Keshargarh, Golkunra and Mymensingh areas while Zone II comprised of Thakurnagar and Dihi Madan Malla and Zone III involved Pathankhali village in deltaic region of Southern part of Bengal.

Data were collected on the contemporary situation involving items of information like village settings, population characteristics, caste, family structure, literacy level, labour force and their living conditions (including of income, debt, savings etc.,) which have direct bearing with the growth of food in the area. Information on characteristics of fairs and festivals, worships, rites and rituals life-cycle events and related ceremonies and *bratas* were also obtained. The field study was based on the methods of participant observation, interview techniques with open-ended as well as structured-questionnaires. Data were collected from each household in the concerned villages.

A set of questions were prepared and administered on the village people with particular emphasis on native cultivation, production and availability of food stuff, food habits and changes due to modern technology, offerings in worship, lifecycle event, fairs and festivals including *bratas* etc.

The basic units of study were the families from various castes and communities in rural areas. They included Hindu castes, Muslims and a few from tribal people.

The survey set itself to the task of what might be called a record of material culture with customary traits and rituals (type of foods and drink), worship of deities, festivals, fairs etc., along with cultural, social and occupational mobility.

All these were followed up by two specimen schedules–one for each household and the other for the village as a whole.

Moreover, group questions were also made in order to understand changes in the attitude and behavioar of the entire group as food and related food habits, influences of rites and rituals in the life and living condition along with other information on the social and cultural activity and traits, community worships, fairs and festivals etc.

Keeping all these in view, a thorough analysis of the field data was made by using the anthropological vis-à-vis statistical techniques and a comparison was made with the first hand knowledge that based on census data and documentary evidences based on journals and books.

The three ecological zones which were taken up showed different characters though in some cases their conditions were closer to each other. The Eco-Zone I where the natural condition is rocky and undulating, the rainfall is scanty, irrigation is poor or nil, there exists food scarcity and the variety of production of food is very little. The quality and as well as quantity of food stuffs are affected as a result of that. Further, people in villages which were in the proximity of town have no agricultural support base. Therefore they meet their food and other requirements from the town markets and thereby they have some urban touch in their cultures.

The villages that fall in Eco-Zone II enjoy better irrigation facility though the soil condition is a bit saline. Food production in these areas is no doubt favourable. And, most of the households produce all kinds of foodstuff including vegetables, fruits, roots, tubers etc. as there are many orchards.

The last Eco-Zone III is situated on the reclaimed land of estuarine being at the extreme areas of South Bengal. This zone is having good quality production of foodstuff. Nature has also helped the area through atmospheric condition and ample vegetation in quality and quantity. Anyway, in this zone people are comparatively happier than in the other two zones.

But the inhabitants in all the zones have their own cultural values relating to their social and customary lives as well as their food habits. Though there is much publicity regarding food recepies and protein contents and nutritional values, these people have food habits linked with their cultural heritage, which they rarely attempt to change. Further, people in different zones follow some restrictions on some food items and food habits. This has been found to be particularly true with respect to the high class educated people like Brahmins and others.

Under the circumstances the communities shape their food habits, cultural heritage, worshipping of deities, observance of family and community ceremonies, fairs and festivals etc., on the basis of the natural environmental influence. These are also being changed today due to the impact of modernization. Specific religious beliefs, tradition etc., also influence the different ethnic groups differently. To this context, totems and taboos, worship and bratas etc., act very definitely among these communities as well as among different families and individuals.

Concept of Disease and Methods of Treatment (Medical and Non-Medical) in West Bengal

Pratima Chowdhury

Disease prevailed everywhere at all times and climates. Human groups, primitive to modern have tried to diagnose the causes of diseases and prescribe systematic procedures for their remedy and cure. Various factors are considered responsible for causing diseases, like supernatural agencies, human agencies, and natural causes. To combat against such disease causing agencies, people of different ecological settings have taken different measures. They cannot think of any alternative measures of treatment except their embedded traditional beliefs. Thus the people in most of the cases offer unconscious resistance to many modern types of medical treatments or avoid these altogether. Therefore, in order to understand the culture of a particular period, it is necessary to find out what people do when they face illness and what are the medical concepts, practices and behaviour of that period.

This problem has been studied from different points of views as below:

1. Some villages from the district of Midnapore and along with this, a few cases were studied in different zonal pockets of Calcutta. Most of the cases were related to villages, as the villages are the central cores of Indian traditions. Urban cases are studied to find out the existence of traditional belief patterns and its changes with the access of modern education and communication with other cultural groups.
2. Diseases prevailing both in urban and rural areas include epidemic and endemic diseases. References in the Purana had been studied to find out the references of these diseases with their puranic names. This has helped to study the emergence of new types of diseases at subsequent periods.
3. Study of concept of diseases has revealed the idea of the people regarding causation of various diseases from which they suffer, some based on traditions and others on modern medical theories.
4. Methods of treatment have been studied from different angles. Treatment patterns are mostly associated with the concepts of

diseases, because a man seeks the advice of a doctor according to his notions of the causation of a disease. For example, during pox, the person who strongly believes in disease-goddess *Shitala*, the deity responsible for causing this disease, takes advice and medicines from the priest of the *Shitala* temple and makes vow to Her instead of taking advice from a physician. Methods of treatment have been studied from economic and educational points of view also, to find out the effect of education and economy on treatment.

5. Influence of various gods and goddesses who are considered as disease gods and goddesses, have been taken into account, because these deities play an important part in the daily life of these people.
6. Information had been taken from the people who belong to different caste groups, to ascertain the notion of causes of various diseases and to assess whether these vary with the caste hierarchy or not.

For the collection of data, a schedule was prepared with a number of questions on different aspects of concepts and treatments.

Information on types of diseases and concepts of diseases were collected by case history method. Data in a large number of cases were collected by personal interviews.

Generally three cases in each family were studied to find out the occurrence of family diseases if any.

Information on a few types of treatments, such as treatment through religious rituals, magical ways of treatments etc., were collected by means of narrative method and by observation method.

The author collected data on treatments of spirit intrusion, evil eye, evil wind, *mayer daya* (pox caused by mother Goddess), by participant observation method.

For analyzing the collected data, the standard statistical methods were applied to find out the frequency and percentage distribution of diseases among the caste groups studied.

Regarding the selection of informants, the author took information from two-three persons of each family who were then suffering or have suffered from different types of diseases within last three years. The author made a sample survey, with a view to make it as far representative as possible. In a village among the dominating caste, the sample family was taken as nth and as the strength of a caste decreased the number of sample family taken in these cases also proportionately decreased in the ratio of 3:1, 2:1, 1:1 etc.

In Calcutta data were collected from some zonal pockets like

Kalighat, Bhowanipur, Shyambazar, Ballygunge, Baghajatin Colony, Garia, Tollygunge, etc. From these regions information was collected only from those families who were interested in such social surveys. 282 families from different caste groups were studied of whom 213 were from rural areas and 69 families were from city Calcutta.

From the finding the types of diseases recorded are 62 in number. These various types of diseases have been again categorized into 16 groups. Such as infectious, cardiac, skin, eye, etc., for the convenience of analytical study. From the data it was found that most of the people were not aware of their health status, until it becomes serious like skin diseases, intestinal worms, rickets etc. Therefore it can be said that definition and classification of the diseases are nothing but a cultural expression.

Different types of concept of diseases causation have been grouped into three main groups such as Natural, Supernatural and Human agency with few sub-groups. Natural concepts for the occurrence of diseases are predominant among the people of rural and partly of the urban areas. Belief regarding the causation of diseases is associated with the doctrine of 'Karma'. From the data it has been found that blindness, paralyses etc., are considered by some people as punishment for sinful acts of previous or existing life.

Belief in evil spirit of different types is also found among all the people. *Bhut, petni, shakchunni* are thought to be responsible for epilepsy, diarrhoea, etc. Diseases also occur due to the malevolent action of some planets like Saturn, Rahu, Mars etc. One more popular concept found from this investigation is human agency. People believe that ear pain, injury, paralysis, eczema, vomiting, rickets etc., occur due to some magical action performed by *Gunin,* (Sorcerer) and *Dains* or witches.

Regarding the procedure of treatment it is found that there exists mainly two types of treatments :

1. Folk medicine which includes :
   a. Religious (rituals and ceremonies)
   b. Magical (with some performances in occult way)
   c. Totka or domestic treatment
2. Scientific treatment includes:
   d. Allopathic
   e. Homeopathy
   f. Ayurvedic

From the data it is found that for some diseases like typhoid, heart diseases etc they consulted allopathic physician, take vows to goddess *kali,* etc., But for pox, they only take vow to goddess *Shitala* and take measure suggested by the priest of that temple.

Led by a belief in itemes having occult qualities, people take amulets, talisman, stones etc., from the temple of the respected deities or from the priests who worship them.

For curing some specific diseases they consult *fakir, ojha, gunin* for snakebite, ear pain, dental problem etc.

Besides these types of treatment homeopathic and ayurvedic treatments are also popular among the people of rural and urban areas.

Therefore from the above discussion it has been found that the rates of occurence of disease depend upon the adaptation and mal adaptation of the human groups in an environment. Cultural activities are also important in this regard. Unhygenic conditions of living are also involved in the sense that the studied agricultural people cultivate the land, which is always mixed up with night soil. This in turn causes different types of skin diseases and hookworm.

Occurrence of the coronary diseases is mainly found among the urban people. Data show that in rural areas where people laid a comparatively peaceful life they do not suffer from the disease of heart. But the urban people are suffering from different types of heart diseases as they lead a hectic life full of stress and strain.

Study of the concepts of diseases also can focus on the particular culture of a society. It is found from the data that concepts of supernaturalism plays a very important role and the concept that disease caused due to violation of some moral laws is highly effective in maintaining social norms.

Regarding the methods of treatment it has been found that those who have relatively high socio-economic status, education, etc., take allopathic and homeopathic medicines. But in Calcutta, here people of lower income groups do more allopathic treatments as they get medicines from charitable hospitals or health centres.

Caste system also plays a key role in the notion of the causation of disease. In villages, the low caste groups are still suppressed by the upper caste groups both in the field of education and economy. Hence, diseases caused due to malnutrition and lack of knowledge of hygiene are mostly found among them.

Absence of health centers in the rural areas is another important factor for the spread of diseases.

In Calcutta the existence of traditional belief patterns and other non-medical methods of treatment indicate that people living amongst modern medical equipments are encircled by traditional beliefs and ideas, which have not yet been possible for them to distangle from their daily life.

Religious supustition plays an important role in the spread of disease. Some people still are afraid of taking vaccines as goddess *Shitala,* the deity of pox might get angry at them and may cause this disease.

Therefore it can be said that concepts of disease and methods of treatments (medical and non medical) depend on the cultural set-up. Beliefs are mostly influenced by religions. The multi-causal concept of disease is prevalent among the people, and during the critical moment the barrier of caste or class is temporarily eliminated. To overcome the crisis period it was found that a *Brahman* takes medicine prepared by a *hadi* (sweeper) or an amulet from a *Fakir* (Muslim priest) without any hesitation.

This problem has its various applied aspects. Social anthropologists are the best persons who can freely mix with them and spread among them some ideas about health, hygiene and prevention of diseases.

The problem has also a pragmatic value for the society. It is often found that nowadays in many hospitals and medical clinics, the views of social anthropologists regarding psychological treatment of diseases are highly appreciated by the doctors, as it is found that many patients refuse to take modern medicines, or respond to such treatments due to their embedded concepts regarding the causes of different diseases which are entirely different from the modern medical system, as also their lack of knowledge and superstitions. They mostly attribute the causes of diseases to disease gods and goddesses or supernatural spirits, and take treatment according to their local conventions. Sometimes, they are fortuitously cured but mostly they suffer from prolonged and preventable diseases for their folly. Therefore it is necessary to find out the cause of mental confusion of such patients. Social scientists, who are aware of the traditional concepts of diseases prevailing among the people of particular castes and localities can easily find out the problems of such patients and help the doctors by affording suggestions. This type of investigation also throws light on the darker side of the various social prejudices among the people, for which they suffer from different types of preventable and epidemic diseases which can be removed by making them health conscious by spreading knowledge of basic hygienists among them.

Knowledge of the concepts of diseases prevailing in a particular society helps the doctor and the social worker to treat the patients psychologically, by which the people can recoup their health rapidly by taking proper medicines.

Therefore to find out the actual problems of health among the village or urban people this type of study is very helpful for the society itself.

Concept of Illness and Health Seeking Behaviour in West Bengal : A Micro Study

Archana Sinha

Usually, health is part of a bi-polar conceptualization and is juxtaposed to illness at the other end. It is more appropriate to think it as the polar opposite to 'illness in contradistinction to health'.

In the living world, diseases prevailed everywhere, at all times and climates among the human groups. From the primitive to modern times, man has tried to diagnose the cause of these illness and prescribe systematic procedures for prophylactive and curative measures.

Health and illness are continuous processes and are inter linked with each other in inverse proportions, moulding the behavioural pattern of the community. In the present study, a few rural and urban centres were taken as the field of study. To be precise, this study is not at all a comparative one. All the cases relate to the villages of Midnapore district, as the villages are the central core of Indian tradition. Along with this, a few cases were specially studied in different zones of Tamluk town to find out the existence of traditional belief pattern and subsequent changes that have occurred among these people having access to variegated modern equipment, education and communication with the other cultural groups, due to the urban impact.

This investigation into the *concept of illness and health seeking behaviour* in rural areas of the district of Midnapore, West Bengal is undoubtedly a micro study. It indicates some ways to the determining of relationship between the concept of illness and health seeking behaviour, i.e., the reactions of the people towards diseases, sickness as well as the nature of combating the same in various families of different caste groups with a view to note the caste-wise variation of the occurrence of disease in groups, their concept and treatment patterns.

Diseases prevailing among the people and the groupings of these diseases in both urban and rural areas including endemic and epidemic diseases have been taken into account.

This study also revealed the concept and causation of various diseases according to the views of traditional society and also how they are changing in modern times

Health seeking behaviours have been studied from different angles. Behavioural patterns are mostly associated with the concept of diseases, because a man seeks the advice of a healer (both medical and non-medical man), according to his notions of the causation of a disease.

The health seeking behaviour has been discussed in relation to curative, preventive and promotive aspects. Methods of treatment have been studied from various angles such as economic status, educational background and rural urban differences.

Influence of various gods and goddesses who are considered to be in possession of evil powers have also been taken into account, because those gods and goddesses are playing an important role in the day-to-day lives of these people. Information have been taken from the people belonging to different caste-groups and tribal groups.

The data were collected through interview method. Schedules were framed taking into consideration the objectives of research and these schedules were filled in by the researcher at different places fixed up by her for the study. Observation and case history methods were also considered as and when required. The field work continued from 1984 to 1988. The researcher made a sample survey for selecting her informants. Regarding data collection the researcher took information from two or three persons of each family who were then suffering or have suffered or have experience in different diseases within a period of last ten years. Where the information was concerned with persons below the age group of eighteen years, the data were collected from their parents or guardians who had narrated the facts.

The villages and urban areas under study for the purpose of asserting the health, disease and behavioural pattern of the people of West Bengal with particular reference to some areas of Midnapore district, are twelve in number. As has been mentioned, they all belong to Midnapore district

Table 1

Name of the Places, Caste and Communities in Sample

Sl. No.	Name of Places	Type	Caste/Communities
1.	Saiyadpur, Khandagram, Payrachali, Radhaballavpur, Astara, Nakibasan, Payratungi, Mathuri, Khanchi, Narandighi	Rural	Brahman, Kayastha, Mahishya, Subarnabanik, Sadgop, Kansabanik, Malakar, Tili, Kamar, Goyala, Napit, Majhi, Tanti, Dule, Dhopa, Hadi, Vaishnab
2.	Fulgaria	Tribal	Santal, LodhaMunda
3.	Parbotipur	Urban	Brahman, Kayastha, Mahishya, Subarnabanik, Sadgop, Kansabanik, Malakar, Tili, Kamar, Goyala, Napit, Majhi, Tanti, Dule, Dhopa, Hadi, Vaishnab

The concept that disease is caused by the malevolent desire of some gods and goddesses, such as, Lord *Siva*, goddess *Kali, Sitala, Manasa* etc., is also very much predominant among the people of the rural areas. The Hindus believe in *karma* (consequence of deeds). They believe that some diseases occur due to sinful deeds of a person done in previous life. The evil spirits, like *Bhut, Petni, Shakini, Jakabhut* etc., are believed to be responsible for some illness. The human agency or mystical powers like an evil eye, evil mouth and evil touch or witchcraft (*Dain*) play an important role in the matter or causation of various illness.

Regarding health seeking behaviour, two types of treatment are found in rural areas–a) by traditional means and b) by scientific medicines.

(a) The traditional means include :

1. Religious
2. Magical
3. Planetary action
4. *Totka* or pseudo magical treatment

(b) The Scientific medicines include :
1. Allopathic
2. Homeopathic
3. Ayurvedic, and 4. Unani.

The religious explanation of treatment has also been observed in the diseases, which are thought to occur due to sinful acts of the patient. In these cases, they perform *Candrayana* and *Prayaschitta.* To cure oneself from the effects of evil wind, evil eye and evil-spirits, they only consult the spirit-doctor or the *Gunin* or *Ojha.* It is further found from the data that there is a belief that due to sinister influence of hostile planets, fatal diseases, accidents etc., occur and in these cases they consult astrologers and take amulets from them, so that one can get rid of the effects of such sinister influences.

Snake bite cases are treated by an *Ojha* or a *Muslim Fakir.* Dental pain is treated by *Ojha* or *Gunin. Totka* or domestic treatment is very popular and common in the rural areas of Bengal. Disease gods and goddesses are very important and popular in the rural setting and they have much significant role to play in curing diseases.

In the rural areas, high caste groups try to suppress the low caste group people, both in education and economy. Malnutrition is found mostly among the low caste people. Absence of improved health care centres in rural areas contribute to the spreading of diseases. Religious misconceptions also play an important role in the spread of diseases.

To overcome the crisis of illness, it has been found that a *Brahman* may even take medicines prepared by a *sudra* (very low caste), without any hesitation. It was also observed during this study that the native method of treatment is gradually being replaced by modern method with the spread of education. When the rural areas had a relatively isolated existence, the native way of treatment was widespread and it was being practised simultaneously with magico-religious practices. Under the impact of modernization in some areas, the indigenous system is rather getting less widespread, though the magico-religious system is still persisting in most of the areas. It has also been seen that the modern system of medicine, when available, was accepted and the magico-religious system did not come in conflict with the western system.

In conclusion, it may be said that it has been realized that diseases are not only the result of physical, chemical or biological processes but also due to a number of socially and culturally determined factors. This realization of multifactorial causation of disease process has brought the social and medical scientists close together to fight against this common enemy viz., human disease.

Religion, Magic and Witchcraft among the Kondh of Bataguda Area of Phulbani District of Orissa

Arun Kumar Chatterjee

Religion, magic and witchcraft are very important institution of any community at the level of folk culture. These institutions have great influence in almost every sphere of tribal life with their simple subsistence economy. Even their socio-political life is not excluded from the range of their magico-religious belief and practices.

In earlier days, the Kondh of Bataguda area were engaged in shifting cultivation but at present they are forced to leave their age old practices and adopt settled agriculture for maintaining their livelihood. Kondhs are primarily cultivators. They also depend upon hunting, fishing and gathering for subsistence. In all the sphere of the socio-economic life the Kondh magico-religious performance have got a very important role.

When Kondhs were only shifting cultivators, their magico-religious practices were also mainly connected with the protection of crop and for saving them from the wild animals. The magical practices relating to hunting and fishing are no longer operative due to the change of their livelihood from shifting cultivation to settled cultivation. With the change of economic pursuits the functions of those magico-religious rituals are also going to affect to a considerable extent the economic life of the Kondh. At the same time some new rituals are also coming up. The *Kutagatanju's* (Shaman) performances to satisfy *Buru Penu* (Bhumi God) sacrificing fowl with some spells in the agricultural field to have bumper crops etc., are examples of a later addition in the Kondh magico-religious rituals list.

The present study is an exploratory study conducted for a period of eight years (1980-81 to 1987-88) among Kondh villages of Bataguda in the Phulbani district of Orissa. This study focuses that religion and social structure are inter dependent. Keeping this in view, the present study tries to understand the different issues of crisis of the Kondh in their day to day life. And at the same time, the study tries to explore their dependency on the performance of different magico-religious belief patterns.

The Kondh religion is remarkable by their fear of the unknown and the adverse impact of the malevolent forces of nature. The Kondhs are spirit worshippers. Their annual cycle is full of ritual performances in synchronization with the change of seasons and economic activities. The religious functionaries of this area is called *Tlamba* who is the priest. It is he who conducts and regulates the rituals of the village in association with the *Patra,· Mutha Head* of this area. *Kutagatanju*, a class of specialist (Shaman) among them, who are the diviners of repute, enjoy a respectable position among them. He defines the causes of diseases, distresses or any other such event and suggests remedies thereof. He detects various social offences. The ritual mechanism is occasionally associated with esoteric and cruel practices.

Kondh people are strong believers in spirit and soul. They believe in the existence of double soul. In every sphere of life they invoke *Pedaric,* the spirit of the dead ancestor, who, they believe, are very often the main cause of their sorrow and distress. So to make the *Pedaric* satisfy they offer different types of offerings to them by the Shamans. Before *shradh* ceremony, the spirit of the dead man is known as *Duma* and again the same *Duma* becomes the *Pedaric* after the ceremony. The changing nature of soul is very common. It may take any shape like that of a tiger or snake for sometime and with the help of the Shamans, the villagers can understand the effect of soul and can make the society free from his evil impact.

The Kondh people used to perform different magical practices for community gain. These are generally done during the time of fishing, hunting or for making their land fertile, for sowing, for rain making and also for protection of crops as well as for clearing the forest for shifting cultivation. In their day to day life, they practise different magico-religious performances for the well being of the community. In their society, the roles of Shamans and sorcerers are immense. Generally, the Shamans hold prestigious position and perform dominant role in the Kondh society. In their *Kui* language the male Shamans are called *Kutagatanju* and the female Shamans are called *Kutagatalies.* In every sphere of the life of the Kondh tribe the role of *Kutagatanju* and *Kutagatalies* is very important. If some one is suffering from fever or stomach trouble or from any other diseases they call *Kutagatanju* and accept his prescription. They are also called witch doctors. In every case they try to detect the cause of such diseases and prescribe to perform some magico-religious performances to cure the patient. Sometimes they think that their old ancestors *(Pedarics)* are dissatisfied with them and these diseases are caused by their curse. Shamans are benevolent all the times. Usually they do not make any harm to others. Their work is beneficial for the community.

The Kondh even now follow all sorts of magical performance through *Kutagatanju* (Shamans) to derive certain benefit in economic activities, in law and justices and also sometimes to take revenge against their enemies. It is socially approved when it is beneficial to the society and it is disapproved by the society when it is harmful.

The magical benefits and practice of the Kondhs are very common in those areas. In magic no appeal is made to the spirit. The *Kutagatanju* (Shamans) generally worships a particular deity who seems to send evil spirits to do harm to the society. The Shaman through his dreams can understand everything and acts accordingly. As a result of his magical performances, the deity is satisfied and the evil spirit leaves that place.

Usually the following types of spirit gods are worshipped by Shamans through various magico-religious practices.

Table 1

Types of Diseases

Name of the Diseases	Name of the Deity
Epidemic	Tribapenu
Blood Vomiting	Rakhaspenu
For good fishing	Asipenu (Deity of Fish)
For Hunting	Stone (symbolises hunting)
For Fertility of Land	Buru Penu (Bhumi God)
At the time of sowing	Buru Peñu (Delsa land)
Protection of Crops	Buru Penu (Delsa land)
Magic for Protection of Crops	Buru Penu (Delsa land)
Clearing the Forest	Sarupenu

The Kondh tribe is too much superstitious and show their conservative attitude towards their primitive religion where the Shamans and sorcerers prove their indispensability. In general, sorcerers observe different taboos and omens prevalent in their societies before going to do some magical performances. They follow these blindly to achieve success. As for example, if a hen crows that is bad indication for a magician to start his journey for magical performance and in their language it is known as *Sirutapiki Mangari Dari*.

Before going to any magico-religious work, sorcerers remember their dead parents and also the souls of the great magicians whom they consider their *guru* (teacher).

If a person dies then *Kutagatanju* will go and see the dead body and perform some magical rituals to ascertain whether he has been killed by sorcerers or had a natural death. When a person dies, he is carried to the cremation ground and if all the bones of his body are not burnt then they will think that the person is killed by a sorcerer otherwise all bones of the body would have been burnt.

In the Kondh society the evil eyed female is called *Dayali* and evil eyed male is called *Dyanju* and witch (female) is called *Shilongudi.*

Sorcerers are called *Penumlimba Punenju.* They perform the magico-religious activities for doing harm to others. In the Kondh Society these sorcerers have also a great role, as because people get their help for satisfying their personal enmity or personal clash. The sorcerers' activities are often detected by the Shamans *(Kutagatanju)* and then those sorcerers face a lot of problems. Normally the 'Kondh' people are taking their help in disguise not openly as they are going to *Kutagatanju* for any purpose, even for detecting the social offenders of their community. Sometimes through a contiguous magic they can kill a person. The Kondh believe such power of the sorcerer and use it if they dislike the person in an extreme form.

Witches are called *Shilongudi* (in *Kui*) in the Kondh society. They are strong believers in the existence of *Shilongudi.* It is their staunch believe that a lady can become a *Shilongudi* at the time of delivery. She may not come back in the same form as she was before delivery. At that time the people of their community will kill her otherwise she will survive as witch.

In the Kondh society the number of Shamans are numerous · almost in every village there exist one or more male or female Shamans. Usually these Shamans are not full time professional workers. In exchange of their work they take some form of remuneration either in cash or in kind. Normally they wear artificial dresses and decorate their bodies to execute power and to make influence on their client who sit with awe and submission. Sometimes these Shamans play the roles of teacher, doctor and priest of their community. But generally they are restricted to the following activities.

1. Curing of diseases
2. Propitiation to the supernatural power controlling the evil spirit
3. Protecting immunity by use of charms
4. Averting dangers through 'White Art' and 'Black Art'

5. Controlling weather for good crops.

Buffalo sacrifice *(Kedujatra)* involves a major magico-religious rituals which has been practised by the Kondh people. They worship *Tadapenu* (goddess of Earth) by sacrificing buffalo for good agricultural production and to make their land fertile. In earlier days they used to practise human sacrifice for the said reason. Monkey sacrifice *(Makdakedu)* is also prevalent in their society.

The sacrifice of animal and their torturing before sacrifice is an expression of their faith in such magico-religious practice. In the past, the Kondhs of this area used to practise human sacrifice also with a view to increasing the fecundity of their land as well as to ensure a good and quality crop of turmeric grown in their land. Since the prohibition of human sacrifice they have started to buffalo and monkey sacrifice. Witchcraft and sorcery continue to be the common practice in the Kondh society even now.

Hinduism or Christianity could not influence the Kondh religion very much. In that case their magico-religious performances would have been changed remarkably. The Kondh people are worshippers of spirit of their dead ancestor. Some time they get their advice and try to satisfy those spirit through the Shaman *(Kutagatanju)* which indicates that these people are providing respect to their past and the dead ancestors. They sacrifice buffalo to their mother goddess *Tadapenu* to show their regards to Her. They believe that this type of sentiment towards their own religion make their society stronger and united.

The influence of magico-religious rituals is prominent in the Kondh socio-political life also. The Kondh is an endogamous tribe along with a number of subgroups and those subgroups are divided into a number of exogamous clans. The clans are the regulative bodies in their social interaction and as agencies for regulating their social activities. The clan organization of the Kondh people of this area also functions as an administrative unit which is known as *Mutha.* Each *Mutha* has its Mutha Head or *Mutha Mallik* who functions as landlord, administrator and Head of the magico-religious performance. Before performing *Kedujatra* (buffalo sacrifice) Kondh villagers of the concerned *Mutha* will go to *Mutha* Head to have his consent for the religious performance. He will deside the venue, date and time of the said ritual. This buffalo sacrifice is the largest magico-religious practice where all the people of the *Mutha* along with people belonging to other *Muthas* will participate. They will act as observer and will not participate in any ritual. The inter-relation between the *Mutha* organization and its magico-religious practices show the deep rooted origin of these practices.

In spite of the apathy of the tribals towards modern amenities, the state and the central government and some other social service agencies are making efforts to ameliorate the condition of the people by bringing this tribal belt under the comprehensive area development scheme. Efforts are being made to introduce plough cultivation among the Kondhs in place of their age old shifting cultivation.

Whatever may be the effort of the Government and the social service agencies for bringing socio-economic change among the Kondh people, it can be said from close observation that the Kondh of Bataguda area are not suffering from their cultural decay, rather they have strong belief and respect to their culture and magico-religious performances.

We may look down upon their *buffalo sacrifice (Kedujatra)* and other magico-religious rituals but they have got their own justification for those. They have also their closely integrated system of magico-religious rituals associated with every sphere of their life.

Through those magico-religious rituals the Kondh are making good efforts for the manipulation of the mystical power in order to cope up with their socio-economic situation.

Death as viewed in Society among the Castes

Ratna Gupta (nee Mallik)

Inspite of the magnificent emergence of an age of Science and Technology, the discriminatory outlook on the basis of caste still characterize the Indian society and the study on Indian caste system is one of the widespread and controversial topics among the social scientists since the long past.

Indian social order is governed by caste laws and every Indian will agree that he is born in a caste, for the caste and his whole life is guided by caste relations.

As for the origin of caste, it is held that the Indo-Aryans during their invasion to India introduced four 'Varnas' like *Brahmana, Kshatriya, Vaisya* and *Sudra,* wherein lay the seeds of the caste system, which became widespread during the *Rig Vedic* era.

In the subsequent periods various sub-caste groups having their peculiar features as in the case of castes have originated.

In the present thesis entitled *Death as Viewed in Society among the Castes,* the hypothesis have been formed centering the strongest inevitable incidence called 'death' and attempts have been made to study how the society has viewed death from different angles of vision. Attempts have been made to investigate the various concepts of death and how far these concepts vary in the hierarchical strata among the different castes of Bengal.

It is an acceptable fact that "We are indeed in the process of dying as soon as we are born" and so in every society various concepts and elaborate funeral rites exist encircling death. These concepts and rituals vary from caste to caste though they are all derived from the core of traditional beliefs of Hinduism. The study covered the variation of the concepts and rituals and the ways they have deviated from the traditional norms, ideas and behaviour. As in Hindu social system, caste has formed an essential part and surrounding this, the rites and rituals have grown over the death and funeral of a person, so the 'caste' has been taken here as the basic unit.

Attempts have also been made to view death in historical

perspective i.e., the view point on death as represented in the traditional Hindu religious scriptures like *Upanishads* and *Gita*.

Study of tribal beliefs of death and rituals have also been taken into account to establish the continuity of past in relation to the present. Then the concept of death and how people face death and what concepts have grown and how it varies among the different caste groups of Bengal have also been covered. The belief in life after death, the concept of transmigration of soul, rebirth, *karmafal* (reward and retribution of the deeds of the earth), ghosts and spirits which are associated with the concept of death have also been observed.

Another important feature which is associated with death and mourning is the concept of purity and pollution which has also been covered in the present study.

Various rituals have grown up around beliefs regarding death. The researcher has gathered information regarding these rituals from different castes, which will show that these rituals vary from Brahmin to non-Brahmin Castes. A significant point to be noted here is how far the caste at the top of the hierarchical ladder follow the minute elaborate details of the funeral rituals and on the other hand, how and why the castes at the lower levels are less particular about observing these minor details of rituals.

Death has been an object of innumerable arguments propounded by the philosophers and scientists of the world. Physical scientists have described it to be a simple biological cessation of life and activities, but to the social scientists death has a deeper meaning. They do not accept it as a simple and isolated phenomenon. Almost every culture has provided some answer to the meaning of death which is the final rite de-passage and like birth and marriage is universally regarded as a significant social event overshadowed with rituals. Though apparently a man severs all human bondages with society yet he continues to play an eternal and important role even after his death. In every human society death is a painful event so it is the duty of the social researcher to study death meaningfully in the social background.

In this background attempts have been made in the present study to study the concepts of death and associated rituals prevailing among the various Hindu castes in relation to their greater traditions as traditional values and norms are revealed during the major crises of life which are not generally present in the routine behaviour of everyday life.

For the purpose of research work, the present writer had undertaken extensive fieldwork among ten selected castes viz.,

Brahman, Kayastha, Mahishya, Sadgop, Gandhabanik, Malakar, Napit, Dhopa, Tanti and *Hadi* living in the districts of Midnapore, Birbhum and certain parts of Kolkata. These castes have been classified into upper, middle and lower groups and the lowest group *Hadi* has also been considered as they have the status of untouchables.

For collection of data, field investigations were carried out in 13 villages of the two districts of Midnapore and Birbhum and some parts of proper Kolkata. Information was collected through a structured schedule. Case history, narrative and participant observation method were also followed. A total of 200 cases were studied from the different caste groups starting from *Brahmans* to the lowest group of *Hadis*. Investigations were conducted at different times during the year from 1971 to 1973.

During the course of the research studies it has been observed that there is a relation of rituals with caste and religion, which form the foundation of Hinduism. The values of sentiments of the caste oriented Hindu society centering the concepts and rituals of death were explored with a concentrated focus on caste. Views on death, concept of soul, immortality among the Hindu society revealed that the traditional concept of transmigration of soul, karmafal (consequence of one's action), associated with the concept of Hell and Heaven was prevalent from antiquity down to the modern time underlining the rational modern concepts.

It has been observed that there is a relation between the concepts and ritual observances of different caste groups and the major rituals have some common features. The form of ancestor worship which continue from one generation to the next bridges the gap between the two generations. It binds the different castes linking up the different periods of civilization reflecting the uniqueness of the Indian society. The rituals of death revealed the features of Hinduism which are centered around the institution of caste. The concept of soul, idea of purity and pollution and the theological ideas of rebirth are all related with it. So the study of the concept of death at micro level among the selected Hindu castes will automatically throw some light on the Hindu social order (at macro level) as a whole along with the theological ideas of Hinduism.

Rituals are derived from the core of belief relating to death. We find very little variation in scriptures in case of death rites as people have the ingrained fear of harmful spirits of the dead.

But a marked difference was observed between the Brahmin and non-Brahmin castes. Occupying the superior and higher status, Brahmins were well versed in scriptures and as they conduct the death rituals they are quite aware of all the values, and purpose of the rituals in details. This is not found among other lower castes as they follow the rituals as per the directives of the Brahmins. Not only there is absolute lack of this consciousness but also the lower castes generally omit the minor details and elaborateness of the rituals and the elaborateness decreases in case of castes belonging to lower hierarchical order. This phenomenon leads us to the conclusion that the social hierarchy coincides with the ritual hierarchy.

The degree of the effect of 'Brahmanization' is greater among the upper and lesser among the lower castes. The sacred funeral rites, specially the *Sraddha* (funeral ceremony) rites performed to bind together the living and the dead, lead the members of family to think more about their spiritual unity.

They consider the family as a ritual unit, a part of which had passed into the other world and a part of which has not yet been born.

This study has also analyzed the process of change regarding the observance of death rituals along with their causes. In case of death people are very particular in following their traditional ancestral norms, so for assessing the extent of social change, the death rituals and practices play an important role.

Moreover rites and rituals represent the traditional mode of behaviour by reflecting implicit and explicit beliefs, ideas, attitudes and sentiments.

From the point of social integration the study of rites and rituals occupy an important place, as these rituals are associated with beliefs interlaced with traditions and act as a natural unifying factor.

The study of concepts of death with its associated elaborate ritual system offers primary channel for the study of values and life orientation also, it clarifies and reinforces relationships among the living and the dead.

So it may be concluded that attitude to death and mode of observance of death rituals reveal the social structure and traditional cultural pattern of every human group.

Though apparently a man severs all human bondage with the society with his death and though death is a painful social event yet death gives life its weight, its importance and dignity and the deceased plays an important role in the society.

Rituals in Tradition and Modernity

A Socio-Ethnographic Study of Funeral Rituals among the Hindus of the Kangsabati Valley of West Bengal

Manibrata Bhattacharya

The present study is concerned with the people belonging to Hindu religion of the rural region of the Kangsabati Valley of South West Bengal. The study was undertaken with a view to see and evaluate a few current conceptions about Indian society. The study also intends to see how far the mortuary rites could be viewed as an isolable unit of culture in a well defined situation, funeral situation, when rituals are practised as a set of symbols as an organized pattern of a sub-system of religion.

The present study has been undertaken on account of the following factors:

The area is one of the remotest areas where the backward sections of the state reside with acculturated tribal people.

The process of sanskritization has influenced less the autochthonous people as the area is lying far away from the centres of the Hindu Sanskritic culture.

The entire river valley shows diverse geomorphic features with different ethnic groups clustered in different sub-regions along the river valley.

The present work is entirely based on fieldwork which was carried out at different spells during 1968–71. At first a number of case histories were collected through pilot survey in three selected villages. Extended case history and situational analysis had also been used to collect data from a large number of ethnic units distributed in a wide area. As it was not feasible to cover all the villages of the Kangsabati Valley, systematic sample survey was done and accordingly, the villages became the study unit. There were twenty five study units where fifty from sub-units i.e., social groups, jatis, were found. Besides participant observation genealogical methods were also used as per requirement of the project.*

II

A descriptive analysis of ritual and social structure reveals the role of different ritual specialists and kin groups. With a review of the historical development of the study of funeral, in general, attention is shifted to the particular case of the sequence of funeral rituals in South West Bengal.

Rationalistic positivists of the nineteenth century concentrated their studies upon ancestor worship as an archetype of primitive religion and its evolution. French empirical schools later criticized this notion and developed a different scheme for the study of religion, as collective symbolism which maintains social solidarity. Psychologists have been interested in studying individual behaviour at this liminal stage, and Freud (1952), for one, made substantial contributions to the understanding of the ambivalent attitude of the personality towards death. Later anthropologists have been more interested in approaching the funeral rituals and have taken up the problem where it was laid down by the rationalistic positivists, structuralisits and psychoanalysts. As early as in 1867 Tylor (1866) noticed the association between "other world beliefs" and "body-soul" dichotomy; this association led him to regard ancestor worship as the archetypal form of primitive religion. Influenced by Tylor's concept of ancestor worship as an archetypal form, Spencer formulated different stages in the evolution of religion, from belief in the soul to the worship of deities (1896). Frazer (1911, 1913, 1935) also following Tylor, postulated three stages of unilineal evolution from Ages of Magic, Religion to Science; he compiled details of customs and beliefs associated with death from a number of primitive and archaic societies, demonstrating that a man is thought to be more hostile to his descendents, after death, than while living. Tylor was criticized by Jevons (1902) and Durkheim (1947) for placing emphasis upon ancestor worship as an archetypal religion. Although Durkheim maintained that ancestor worship is not widely distributed, this notion was disproved by Crooke's demonstration (1908) that it is actually widespread throughout India, Africa, Polynesia, Melanesia and Malayasia and also by Warner's study in Australia, in which he

* The project was initially registered under the supervision of Professor P. K. Bhowmick, formerly Dean of Science, Calcutta University, but the work was carried out and submitted independently for the award of the Doctorate Degree.

found that the ancestor spirit is closely associated with the totemic well and with cult objects. Later anthropologists did not give much attention to the evolutionary development of religion or to the reconstruction of the elementary form of religious life, due to the lack of conclusive evidence. Despite Durkheim's criticism, the study of ancestor worship has attracted a number of students, who have shifted away from the evolutionary approach. The idea that ancestor cult is associated with unilateral descent group, lineage or clan, has inspired the British social anthropologists, Radcliffe-Brown (1952 a, 1952 b) and Fortes (1945). Robertson (1927) pointed out that the deity is conceived as 'father', having authority, claiming to be honoured and served by his son. Eliade (1958) thinks that in the historical development of religious thought, 'supreme god' and 'sky gods' are replaced by other 'religious forces' e.g. ancestor worship. spirit worship. The Anne Sociologique school has further analysed the funeral ceremony as a social fact (Hertz 1960), funerals as another manifestation of ancestor cult. Hertz holds that death raises a severe problem to the maintenance of the ongoing social system, a problem which must be solved socially, not psychologically or physically. Therefore, there is a belief in the existence of the 'other world' and the rites of initiation and marriage. Each of these institutions entails the ending of previous status, followed by a new integration, that is –rebirth. Especially indebted to the Anne Socioloique school were later anthropologists, such as Radcliffe-Brown who in his study of Andamanese (1948), suggested that mortuary rituals promote social solidarity. Malinowski (1927) was also influenced by this approach. He held that the function of public ceremony is to maintain the cohesion of the group but he went further in his analysis of the personality system, following, Frazer's notion that deep emotional revelations and the instinct for self-preservation are the sources of funeral ceremonies and beliefs in immortality. Gluckman (1937) criticized Malinowski's explanation of mortuary institutions as a "response of the individual to death" because loved and unloved parents were buried in the same manner with more or less the same emotion. Gluckman (1937) followed the Anne Sociological school in his study of Southeast Bantu and Warner (1937, 1959) and Wilson (1954, 1957) also follow the same approach. Geertz (1973) also demonstrates how the problem of social change can be studied through the analysis of death rituals.

Another aspect of funeral ceremony which attracts both psychologists and anthropologists is the ambivalent attitude of the living towards the dead. Freud's (1952) study of the ambivalent attitude places emphasis upon biologically 'given' conditions; he attributes the hostility of the sons to jealousy of their father's sexual rights, maintaining, however, the idea that primitive man (as compared to modern man) has a greater amount of ambivalence because of his characteristic following of physical impulses. Psychological concerns in the study of funeral customs of primitive people can be marked in Malinowski (1927). Although Malinowski followed Frazer, particularly in his assertion that the reaction of the living to the dead is instinctive horror, he felt that the emotion aroused is a combination of love and fear of the dead. He explained that love is associated with positive feeling for the living, and fear with negative feeling for the corpse. It is against the fear of the dead body, he sees, that man has developed funeral customs and beliefs in after life. The conclusion of Malinowski was challenged by Radcliffe-Brown in his study of the Andamanese in which he pointed out the sociological side of fear associated with collective feelings and collective consciousness and hostility existing between the world of the living and the world of the dead. Physiological aspects of fear and attitudes towards death have been studied by Anthony (1940). This study supports the conclusion that a person's attitude towards death appears to be learned rather than instinctive. Opler's study of Apache group demonstrated that factors which are associated with ambivalence are of relations of social interdependence. A similar study was made by Fortes (1949, 1959) on Talensi. Gough (1958) suggested that the socialization process and kinship relations are related to differential distributions of hostile and friendly attitudes.

In the present study, the ambivalent attitude to the dead is an important one. Attitudes here are restrained by social usages and the bereaved are constrained by cultural patterns to act in a certain specific fashion. The culturally prescribed behaviour involves ritual specialists and kinsmen in the process by which family members survive the death of a near relative, and return to their original condition with a new set of roles and relationships.

III

Among the Hindu communities of South-West Bengal when a man comes to the end of his life a series of rituals have to be performed elaborately by the bereaved. The ritual performance begins immediately before the death of an individual and it is continued for a number of days after death. The funeral ceremony comprises of all the rituals which are observed and practised in connection with the death. The most vital period of the funeral ceremony begins from the day of the death and extends upto the day of ceremonial rice ball *(pinda)* offering to the deceased and converting his status from *atibahika* (body less form) or *pret* (spirit) to *pitri* (ancestor). This ritual of rice offering with some other form of acts concerning the elevation of the status of the deceased is known as *sraddh*.

Sets of ritual performed immediately before death

A few hours before death (natural) the ritual of expiation or purification of the body–*angaprayaschittya* is performed on behalf of the dying person. In this ritual a Brahmin priest is appointed to guide the participants and to supervise the supernatural acts done by the family concerned. The eldest son or, in his absence, the youngest son, acts as the chief performer. He also becomes the chief mourner after the death of the person and must perform all the important acts in connection with funeral rituals. The role of the eldest son reveals his relative status in the family. Just before death, reading of selected passages from the texts and the uttering of sacred names of the gods like Hari, Ram, or Krishna and others is done by an elderly member of the family or lineage at the ear of the dying person. The underlying motif of this "hearing of sacred name" implies that with the spell of the sacred name the person can smoothly and successfully cross the way "between this world–and other world". Another ritual named *pather sambal* i.e., "means of the way" is performed just at the time of death. It includes pouring down water (sacred or simple drinking water), milk, fruit, sweet etc., in the mouth of the dying man. It is a common belief that the dying person takes this food as the means by which he will be in a position to satisfy his hunger on the way to other world.

Sets of ritual performed after death

As soon as the dying person has breathed his last, the members of the family express grief and burst into tears. Within a short period however the elderly persons become busy, to arranging requirements for the disposal of the corpse. The preparation of the corpse takes place in a room or, rarely, in the courtyard. This ritual includes smearing of clarified butter *(ghee)* or mustard oil *(sanchi or sarsertel)* with or without turmeric paste *(halud)* and covering of the body with a cloth upto the shoulder of the corpse. Then the body is placed in front of the altar of basil plant (Ocimum sanctum)–locally known as *tulsitala* or *tulsi-mancha* where sacred water sprinkled on the corpse by the eldest or youngest son of the deceased. The face of the deceased is marked with dots of sandlewood paste and the body is garlanded by the family members or lineage members or affinal relatives. Meanwhile, all the articles required for cremation are collected by the bereaved members. A female member hammers a nail into the spot where the person breathed his last. When the preparations for the final disposal of the corpse are completed, the kinsmen who are younger than the deceased salute (pranam) by touching the feet of the deceased. At this time near relatives, again, show their grief with lamenting cries. In this situation sons or brothers or, in their absence, distant relatives or neighbors of the same caste, carry the bier on their shoulders and set out for the cremation ground. Generally female members do not accompany the funeral procession. At the time of departure, the eldest female of the family, or son's wife, follows the procession upto a little distance from the house, sprinkling a cow-dung solution in order to purify the house, and its surroundings. Upon the death of someone in the household, earthen cooking waters, cooked food and drinking water kept in the house are considered to be polluted and all these vessels are generally thrown away at a selected place, which particular place is considered to be unholy one.

On the way to the cremation ground, the funeral procession must halt at a traditionally selected spot known as *bisramsthan* i.e., 'halting spot'. It is a popular belief that ancestors come to meet the deceased at this spot and it seems to the pallbearers that the weight of the corpse increase.

The cremation ground is generally located at the outskirt of the village on the river bank. Though there is no apparent line of demarcation of different cremation spots for different castes, the people can easily recognize the proper spots where they should cremate.

Upon arrival at the cremation ground, the bereaved perform a number of rituals. The upper caste people generally engage a Brahmin priest at this time. The important rituals at this stage are the erection of the pyre, the bathing and anointing of the deceased with ghee (clarified butter) or oil or paste of oil and turmeric, the deceased is dressed in new clothing, marks of sacred symbols (i.e., *tilak*) are placed upon the forehead, the bridge of the nose and the upper arm with earth from basil plant alter or with sandal paste. An offering of food– known as pinda is made to the deceased, with the recitation of sanskritic mantras (among the upper castes) by the chief mourner after bathing. Then *mukhagni* ritual is performed, in which fire is put into the mouth of the deceased. This ritual must be performed by the chief mourner, usually the eldest son, or in his absence any other son of the deceased. Thereafter, the relatives or other kinsman who accompanied the procession set fire to the four corners of the pyre. After the burning of the corpse, the chief mourner, having bathed, prepares rice and pulse in a new earthen bowl, either on the flame of the pyre, or in a separate place near the pyre. This cooked food is offered to the deceased.

After the corpse has been consumed by the flames, the chief mourner pours water from an earthen pitcher onto the pyre and the others follow him. Thereafter, the chief mourner collects charred bone-fragments which will be ceremonially immersed in the holy Ganges; those who cannot afford the expenses of this ritual do not gather the bones; instead, they throw away the unburnt portion of the body in the nearest river or stream. A figure representing the deceased is drawn on the burning spot after the cremation courie shells, copper coins and turmeric pieces are placed on eight different parts of the figure. An earthen pitcher filled with water and a small basil plant (Ocimum sanctum) are placed on the head of the figure. Before departing from the cremation ground, the chief mourner, in order to crack the pitcher, strikes a blow on it, looking behind. In the cremation ground, the chief mourner wears a strip of white cloth which is fastened either by a Brahmin, or by any relative around his neck.

On the way back to the village the survivors place thorn, pricks and stone at the junction of the two roads in order to make a barrier and follow the mourners. Then they take bath in a tank or in the river (as the case might) and embrace a sacred banyan tree *jor-gachh*, in order to cleanse themselves of the impurity which defiled them as a result of carrying and burning the corpse. Further purification is achieved by touching fire and the altar of basil plant and eating *gangamati* i.e., (sacred clay collected from the river Ganges). This ritual of purification is performed by funeral attendants coming into the house of the deceased. Meanwhile, the female members of the family make the house clean by cow dung paste and after the arrival of the funeral attendants, the women go out to bathe.

There is a proverb in Bengal that all are the same in the cremation ground and so there is no separate cremation ground for different castes. But in many villages I have noticed that different castes have different areas or spots in a cremation ground.

The adult members of the family do not take food during this day. If they are unable to observe the fast then only soaked *gram* and pulse-grains (Psoralia corylifolia) locally known as *kalai* can be taken; cooking in the house and eating food will be forbidden to the bereaved until the first meal-taking ritual *(titavat)* is observed. From this day the chief mourner observes a number of restrictions. A complete social isolation of the mourner's family can be marked at this time.

Sets of ritual performed during mourning periods

The mourning period begins from the day of the death and lasts till the completion of purification locally termed as ghat or *kheuri*. The duration of the mourning period varies from caste to caste. It also varies among the relatives according to the nature of relationship with the deceased. During this period the chief mourner undergoes rigorous experiences which are manifested in the performance of mourning rituals and obligatory restrictions. Mainly, the eldest son is obliged to act as the chief performer of all the rituals. Mourning rites and obligations also vary according to the kin relationship, rules of descent and sex. During this time the bereaved cannot put oil on their heads, shavings, cutting of hair and use of soap at the time of bath are strictly forbidden. Meat, fish and egg i.e. non-vegetarian items of meal along with onion, brinjal, green leaves salt and oil, etc. are strictly forbidden. Cohabitation with the wife is not allowed. Movements are restricted. The chief mourner must use a straw-mat or a piece of woolen blanket for sitting or lying purposes. It has been stated previously that the mourning period varies from caste to caste. Five or six years ago, Moira, Kumor, Malakar, Subarnabanik, Keot and others had to observe thirty (30) days as mourning period. But recently they have reduced the duration of mourning period to fifteen days. This reduction of mourning period has been made after a convention held separately by respective castes.

The most important rituals performed during this period are the receiving of fried rice (khai) and sweets from the relatives on second days. On the third or second day, at noon or in late morning, a ritual named *bena gachh pota*–fixing of bena plant (Aeligops indica) is performed. At this time, a Brahmin priest is employed. This ritual includes the offering of water,milk, fried rice *(khai)*, sweet, tobacco (if the deceased was a habitual smoker of hubble bubble) and betel-leaf and a twig of neem tree (Melia azardictar) for a tooth brush in front of the bena plant (Aeligops indica). These are offered in the name of the deceased. On the same day, or after one day, at night, occurs the ritual of taking the first cooked food, a ritual which is locally named *titabhat* or bitter rice. From the day, the family can take cooked food with the restrictions that the chief mourner can take rice only once in a day. During the mourning period, rice-balls (i.e., *pindas*) are offered to the deceased by the chief mourner, with the help of the Brahmin priest. At this time a 'sacred meal' locally termed *habish,* should be taken by chief mourner at least for the last three days. Then comes the day of purification-ghat or *kheuri* which is performed on the last day of the mourning period. On that day, the house is thoroughly cleaned and purified with a cow-dung solution; clothes are either given to the washerman or washed by the female members of the family, and the cleaning of metallic utensils and the disposal of earthen vessels, used during mourning period, should be completed before a purificatory bath; at noon a barber is asked to shave the heads and faces and to pare off the nails of all the male bereaved.

The chief mourner, before shaving, offers rice-balls (*ghat-pinda*) under the direction of the Brahmin priest. He bathes and receives a gift of cloth from the *kutum,* affinal kinsmen.

In the evening, another receiving ritual *loukikata* i.e. formality is observed as relatives, caste fellows, friends and villagers participate in the ritual of giving money to the bereaved. This collected money is taken into the house by the chief mourner where another ritual called *kuberpuja* is performed. The mourning ritual is ended with the commencement of a ritual feast *khur hadibhat* rice cooked in a new earthen pot from where all the consanguinal relatives except the chief mourner, take food.

Sets of rituals performed on the final day.

The next day, another elaborate ritual–the worship of and offering of food to the deceased, as ancestor, is performed. The set of acts observed this day are termed *Sraddh;* the gift making and entertaining of the Brahmins and other relatives in a communion feast, and the final purification of the house are the important rituals on this occasion. The following day, after *Sraddh,* another set of rituals offering *pinda* i.e., riceballs, entertaining of the relatives and the Brahmins is performed. In short, these are the rituals–a set of culturally prescribed ways which should be followed in order to deal with the changing situation. Each ritual, and the ceremony, as a whole has provisions in which variations may occur, according to the choice and prevailing socio-economic condition of the persons involved.

The observances of the ceremony are confined to four places; (i) the house, (ii) the way leading to the cremation ground and to a place under a sacred tree, (iii) the cremation ground and (iv) the tank. Another important feature of these rituals is the use of cooked rice which recurs at every stage. A third factor is repeated engagement of the Brahmin, especially among the upper castes. Gift taking and offerings in various forms are also other important social and cultural aspects of the ceremony.

IV

Ritual specialists involved in mortuary rites

Brahmin priests are engaged at different stages in the funeral ceremonies. The appointment is more prevalent amongst the upper castes, in comparison with the outlyings. The latter engage degraded Brahmin priests. The degraded Brahmins are also appointed by the upper castes in different rituals. The Brahmins who perform the act of putting fire into the mouth of the deceased are locally termed as *mughpora bamun* or *deshpurohit*. Their status is decidedly inferior to the other Brahmins in the society. The Brahmins who receive the first gifts in *sraddh* are known as *agradani bamun*. The Brahmins who conduct the ritual acts and recite the sacred texts are supposed to be of superior status and are locally known as *tantradharak* or the holder of the sacred texts. The outlyings appoint degraded Brahmins in purification and in *sraddh* and, if it is possible, on the next day of the *sraddh*. These people sometimes observe all these performances in a single day, that is, on the last day of pollution. Some outlyings who intend to be more Hinduized, or want to raise their status in the caste hierarchy, or those who are much high than other castes, appoint a degraded Brahmin priest during the mourning period, at the time of *pinda* offering, and to perform–*sraddh*, *basi sraddh* and purification separately, like the upper castes.

The Vaishnabas are appointed at the time of cremation, in the final purification, *sraddh* and on the next day of *sraddh* i.e. *basisradh*. The Vaishnabas offer their services in two ways: as professional singers of the sacred names and as conductors of the sacred acts and rituals. In the funeral procession, and on the day of purification, they are appointed as professional singers to sing the sacred names. On the occasion of *sraddh* although rarely, the Vishnabas are appointed for the same purpose. Besides, on the day of purification, the Vaishnabas put sacred marks on the forehead of the mourners; on the same day they assist the mourners in the ritual of walking round the basil plant (Ocimum sanctum) altar. The next day, before or after *sraddh,* he is appointed to perform a ritual called *dadhikado* i.e., rolling on the curd and rubbing it on the body addressing the deceased with lamenting voice. On the occasion of sacred feast, on the day of the *sraddh,* the Vaishnabas are often invited to take part in the communion meal. The upper castes appoint Vaishnabas mainly for devotional songs, to perform *dadhikado* and in sacred feast. The low caste Hindus and some outlyings appoint them in the ritual of waling round the basil plant alter, in addition to the above. The appointment of the Vaishnabas for ceremonial singing, however, is practised only by these who can meet the expense. Except in a few cases the tribals do not appoint the Vaishnabas in funeral ceremony. Some outlyings engage them as a substitute of the Brahmin priest. They also appoint the Vaishnabas as Guru or preceptor.

A barber (Napit) is appointed on the day of final purification by most of the *jatis,* irrespective of status. His service is to crop the hair and to cut the nails of the mourners (both family and lineage members). The upper caste Hindus, especially the Brahmins, appoint them in connection with the fixing of the bena plant. After a purificatory bath, the barber spreads new cloths, upon which the chief mourner and his wife walk as they return to the house. These barbers who are engaged by the upper castes, generally, do not offer their ritual service to the outlying jatis. But this is now not so rigidly followed. The outlyings have no barber and, among them, one caste fellow acts as a barber. Recently, though, these people have begun to appoint a degraded barber who is known in the western region as *Maghaya napit.* Sometimes the outlyings go to urban areas for a hair cut and clean shave. The appointment of the washerman is practised more by the upper castes and less by the outlyings. The people belonging to the upper castes believe that purification cannot be done unless the clothes are cleaned by a washerman. A few *jatis* belonging to low castes, but who now have achieved some higher position, practise this ritual as a mark of the achievement.

The Doms (Scavengers) are appointed occasionally by the upper castes and rich people of better social position among the outlyings, such as the Mahatos, the Suris and others, in funeral procession and on the day of purification on the way of return from the tank to the house. The Doms play musical instruments with the funeral procession, in the event that a married woman died, leaving her husband behind. They play typical music which is locally termed *Ay-o-dang-ra.* This has its own peculiar beat and rhythm. The villagers are so familiar with the music that, when they hear it, they can understand immediately that a woman has died, leaving her husband. This is supposed to be very auspicious, according to Hindu beliefs.

The *Hadis* (untouchable castes) are engaged to do menial work and they are regarded as very low. They are usually engaged by the upper castes to clean the house, particularly after the communion meal. Besides the *Hadis*, the *Bauris* and the *Ghasis* are also employed for the same type of work. This service is defiling, hence, untouchable castes are employed.

The people of two distinct social groups, the *Vats* and the *Patkars*, are connected with funeral ceremony. They are not at all concerned with funeral ceremonies. They come uninvited. As soon as they get the news of the *sraddh* ceremony they arrive in the house and demand payment. Coming near the house, a *Vat Brahmin* produces a peculiar sound by striking a bellmetal container with a stick and makes a loud noise with irrelevant works. If the bereaved family members deny payment, the *Vat* then exerts sentimental pressure of creating chaos in various ways in a befitting manner (which he thinks suitable for the situation). To avoid unnecessary troubles the bereaved bargain with the *Vat* and finally pay him either in cash or in kind.

The *Patkars* are low caste. On receiving the information of a death, they visit the house and claim money, utensils or other articles which had been used by the deceased when he was alive. A *Patkar* tells the mourners that he comes at the direction of the deceased who he met in a dream after his death. In the way of communication the deceased told him about his inconveniences due to lack of utensils in the other world. The Patkar says that he is directed by the deceased to bring these things from the relatives. The *Patkar* shows a sketch of the deceased to convince the relatives of the communication with the deceased.

V

Role of relatives in mortuary rites

Throughout the funeral rituals, the agnatic and cognatic relatives of the deceased have their respective roles and performances. The non-affinal relatives are termed *Bhayad* i.e., 'brothers' (consanguinal kin) and the affinal, *Kulum*. The *Bhayads* observe, in most cases, similar restrictions, though less stringent. Those who fall within three or four generations are less polluted and have fewer restrictions, than do the immediate cognates. They observe restriction for a short period, three days. While they may and observe the pollution and consequent restrictions, they may as a token, perform some acts such as bathing, paring the nails, etc. The lineage members participate in cremation if they are present. They also participate in the ritual of the "parched paddy offering", "planting a bena plant" and "offering parched, paddy and water". They also attend the "first meal taking" ritual. On the third or fourth day, they smear mustard oil on their heads and bodies. On the final day of purification they have their hair cut, nails pared and faces shaved, and take a purificatory bath in the tank. On the same day, in the evening, and on the next day, i.e., the day of *sraddh* they participate in a communion feast. In many *jatis,* the ritually offered cake of rice powder, is taken by the lineage members. On the next day of the *sraddh,* they attend the rituals and the communion feast.

The kins who are related by marriage, or affinal ones, first participate in the "parched paddy offering" ritual on the second day, by offering a gift of parched paddy to the bereaved. Their role is most important on the final day of purification, when they offer clothes, garland, etc. to the bereaved. In some *jatis,* the relatives, i.e. the *kulums,* draw the bereaved by their hands from the water after the purificatory bath. It signifies the social reincorporation of the bereaved into the society from which they were segregated during the pollution period. The *Bauris* and the *Ghasis* practise a typical ritual, in which, after bathing, the chief mourner climbs on the shoulder of his wife's brother, and is carried up to the house. On the same day, arriving in the house, the affinal relatives who take their wives from the bereaved, ritually offer money to the bereaved. Among the caste Hindus particularly among the *Gandhabanic* of Kanlradara, the amount which is given by the relatives should return, with or without, some extra amount. On the day of *sraddh,* the bereaved should formally seek permission from the affinal relatives and other elderly persons of the village before holding the *sraddh* and communion feast. Among the caste Hindus and the outlyings it is a custom to offer special entertainment (providing food) to the relatives in the next day of the *sraddh.* The relatives offer help, in kind, to the bereaved, in connection with the communion feast, held on the occasion of *sraddh.*

VI

It has been observed that in the practices of upper castes, local traits which are non-textual are always present. This feature of the ritual pattern reveals the influence and incorporation of indigenous practices on the rationalized, standardized and developed ritual behaviour of the upper castes. This behaviour pattern also demonstrates the influence of Vaishnab ritual in the Brahminic tradition, and a place of Vaishnab ritual specialists vis-à-vis Brahmin priests. The combination of these different ritual behaviour into a complex whole is unique among the people of the South West Bengal.

References

Anthony, S. 1940 *The Child's Discovery of Death*. London.

Crooke, W. 1908 Ancestor Worship and the Cult of the Dead. In *Encyclopedia of Religion and Ethics*. New York.

Durkheim, E. 1947 *The Elementary Forms of the Religious Life*. Glencoe.

Eliade, M. 1958 *Patterns in Comparative Religion*. New York.

Fortes, M. 1945 *The Dynamics of Clanship Among the Tellensi*. London.

— 1949 *The Web of Kinship Among the Tallensi*. London.

— 1959 *Oedipus and Job in West African Religion*. Cambridge.

Frazer, G. 1911 *Taboo and the Perils of the Soul : The Golden Bough*. 3d. London.

— 1913 *The Belief in Immortality and the Worship of the Dead*. London.

— 1935 *The Golden Bough.* Voll. II. New York.

Freud, S. 1952 *Totem and Taboo.* New York.

Geertz, C. 1973 Rituals and Social Change. In *Interpretation of Culture*. New York.

Gluckman, M. 1937 *Mortuary Customs and the Belief in Survival After Death Among the South-Eastern Bantu.* Bantu Studies.

Gough, E.K. 1958 Cults of the Dead Among the Nayars. *J. Amer. Folklore,* 71.

Heriz, R. 1960 *Death and the Right Hand.* Glencoe.

Jevons, F.B. 1902 *An Introduction to the History of Religion.* London.

Malinowski, B. 1927 *Sex and Repression in Savage Society.* London.

Radcliffe-Brown, A.R. 1948 *The Andaman Islanders.* Glencoe.

— 1952 Taboo, in *Structure and Function in Primitive Society*. Glencoe.

— 1952 Religion and Society, in *Structure and Function in Primitive Society.* London.

Robertson S.W. 1927 *Lectures on the Religion of the Semitcs*. London.

Spencer, H. 1896 *The Principles of Religion.* New York.

Tylor, E.B. 1866 The Religion of Savages. *Fortnightly Review,* 4.

Warner, W.L. 1937 *A Black Civilization.* New York.

— 1959 *The Living and the Dead : A Study of the Symbolic Life of Americans.* New Haven.

Wilson, M. 1954 Nyakyusa Ṛitual and Symbolism. *American Anthropologist,* 56.

— 1957 *Rituals of Kinship Among the Nyakyusa.* London.

Section III

Rural Social Institutions and Administration

Introduction

Sachchidananda

Institutions refer to established codes of conduct for carrying out group activities. They refer to a set of rules and procedures which provide guidelines for human activities. In fact they are blueprints for human action. In every social organization there are certain usages, rules and procedures.These forms and procedures are called institutions. They are recognized and accepted by society and regulate relations between individuals and groups. If the rules and procedures form institutions, individuals belong to associations. The latter refers to the human component. In every society there are institutions of various kinds, such as social, economic, political, religious and educational.

Sociologists have studied a large number of institutions which exist in Indian society. Most of them have concentrated on family and kinship. In recent times scholars have made perceptive and analytical studies of important economic and political institutions. Some of them have disappeared and new institutions have emerged. Some of the old institutions have also undergone transformation. They have changed both in form and content. Some of them have changed in structure. Some others have lost their own functions and assumed new ones. Many institutions have withered away and have been replaced by new institutions formed under the inspiration of western ideas to meet new social challenges. The role of caste panchayat and their interaction with statutory panchayats have also been examined. The functioning of commercial and rural banks in providing credit to farmers has also received attention of scholars. It has been found that they have not been able to replace the existing old credit institutions of money lending even though the latter are highly exploitative in nature.

The advent of Panchayati Raj in its present form, after the promulgation of the 73rd amendment of the Constitution, has also engaged the attention of sociologists. They wish to explore as to how far Mahatma Gandhi's ideal of reaching power to the people has been realized in the different parts of the country. If the wishes of the Father of the Nation have not been fulfilled and the move towards self rule is only half way through, its reasons have to be identified so that remedial action could be taken.

The decadence of the Joint Family

The Universality of nuclear family does not mean that the family structure is every where the same. Kingsley Davis has listed some of its major forms. The independent nuclear family is a characteristic of modern urban-industrial societies. In non-industrial societies different types of extended family are still found. In India, the joint family has existed from ancient times. It was in the past a corporate body with property held in common, worship of the family deity and authority exercised by the head of the family usually the eldest male in the eldest male line. The family property was not strictly impartible but partition was infrequent. In such families three or four generations used to live, work and eat together. Religion was the most important cementing force in the joint families since it included ancestors and unborn children along with the living members. The living members were, infact, the trustees of the house. The central idea was that the family is a temple of sacred traditions. Irawati Karve has made a detailed study of joint family and its characteristics. M.N. Srinivas has described the working of the joint family (Okka) among the Coorg in Karnataka. He holds that Coorg Okka is a very much stronger institution than its counterparts among the higher castes of South India. But even there the joint family is said to be weakening.

The report on the 1951 Census of India contains some information on the state of the joint family. On the basis of classification of households by the number of members it has been held that families do not continue to be joint and have the habit of breaking away from it and setting up separate households is quite strong. I.P. Desai, on the basis of his research, holds that the former characteristics of the joint family such as co-residence, commonsality, worship and even property are becoming less important as criteria of jointness. The joint family does not vanish with the residential separation. What is lacking is the detailed study of how the contemporary joint family functions and the extent to which the intra-familial relations have altered. In one of the studies reported later in this chapter some of these changes have been described in detail. Some people in rural areas have stuck to the joint family as they find it convenient and useful to meet their current needs.

Caste Councils

The Indian caste system is a unique system of social stratification. It is evidently connected with economic differentiation. Caste determined a person's activity throughout his life from cradle to grave. Each caste had an occupation assigned to it. Caste provided the basis for division of labour in sociely. It is intimately connected to religion also. Each caste has distinctive rituals. Caste determined one's relationship and interaction with other persons in society. Castes functioned with an unwritten code of behaviour. This code operated through caste councils or panchayats. Any breach of caste norms attracted punishment. The caste panchayat was constituted by caste elders living in the village. The punishments differed with the gravity of the offence. For minor offences fines were levied. For offenses of a more serious nature, excommunication, temporary or permanent, could be ordained.

It is seen that caste councils function variously among the lower castes than among the higher castes. These caste councils were different from caste associations which grew up towards the end of 19th century and began asserting the identity of castes and tried to protect and promote their interests in society. They also worked for social reform and education among its members. Some of the lower caste associations tried to claim higher status for themselves by inventing a myth of their origin and also by sanskritising their way of life by adopting vegetarianism, observing fasts and banning window remarriage.

There have been some studies of caste councils and the origin and growth of caste association. But none of these had shed any light on the relationship between these organizations and the statutory panchayats established by the government in various states as an exercise in self rule. A couple of studies reported in this chapter later, attempt to describe the changes in the functioning of caste council of some Scheduled Castes in some villages of 24 Parganas District of West Bengal. The author discusses the interface between the caste councils and the statutory panchyats and shows how they have suffered on this account.

Rural Credit Institutions

One of the important aspects of rural economy in the present day India is the provision of credit for the peasantry. Rural society has to be dealt with at two levels. Most of the peasants are subsistence cultivators. Only 30% cultivate for profit from the sale of the surplus produce. These comprise rich peasants, middle range peasants and money lenders. They provide credit to the poor peasants who comprise small farmers, share croppers and landless labourers. They take loans to meet both their productive and non-productive needs.The productive needs included finance for inputs for agriculture in the form of seeds., fertilisers, insecticides and small agricultural appliances. The unproductive needs arise from their chronically deficit budget. They take loans to meet their expenditure for purchase of food grains in times of crop failure, purchase of seeds, repair of houses, meeting social obligations at the time of birth, marriage and death, health and medicine and servicing old debts. Since most of the credit requirements are immediate and recurrent they approach the local moneylenders for loans. As the moneylenders know the debtors from close quarters, they make the loan available immediately without much procedural formalities. The loans advanced are at high rates of interest. But the loanees do not mind it as their needs are met timely and loan is available both for productive and unproductive purposes. The alternative lending agencies created for meeting the credit needs of the people in the form of Co-operative societies, Rural banks and Commercial banks have a protracted and complex time taking procedure for the grant of the loan. The poor uneducated peasant finds it difficult to go through this long process. He is not competent to negotiate the loan. His travails are accentuated by the corruption prevailing at the lower levels of the bureaucracy.

In these circumstances it has been found difficult to eliminate the moneylenders who continue to exploit the peasantry. As one of the studies reported in this chapter reveals that most of the rural families are in debt and some of them have taken multiple debts. Rural indebtedness is an endemic phenomenon all over the country. In recent years the inability to meet debt obligation has led to suicide by peasants in Andhra Pradesh and Haryana. This situation calls for urgent remedial action. This can be done by taking two pronged initiative for curbing private moneylending through strict legislation and simplifying loan procedures of the alternative rural credit agencies. As of now, the poor peasantry is born in debt, lives in debt and dies in debt. Earlier this situation led to the system of bonded labour. Although bonded labour has been abolished by law, the system is continuing in a latent form in many areas of the country. Urgent steps have to be taken to streamline the rural credit system as it has important social implications. It is the rural poor who suffer on account of the vicious circle of poverty and debt. It is an important plank of poverty alleviation.

Panchayati Raj

In recent years Panchayati Raj has gripped the minds of both political scientists and sociologists. Form ancient times Panchayats had an important role in managing the affairs in villages. Through it people had full opportunity for self rule. However, with the rise cf the colonial administration, the activities of panchayat were circumscribed. On Gandhiji's insistence panchayats were included under Article 46 of the Constitution. In the late fifies legislation was enacted for democratic decentralization. Since then Panchayati Raj as an instrument of self rule was on the State's agenda. However, Panchyati Raj was not a part of the Constitution and its pattern was dependent on the powers delegated to it by the state government. However, it was only in 1993 that through the 73rd amendment that the adequate powers were given to the Panchayati Raj institutions. In these elections people could vote for their own candidates at different levels. It is seen that the Panchyati Raj elections are a replication of elections at the state and central levels. The voting behaviour is influenced by caste, money and muscle power. People have note yet forgotten their age old values. Although, legally, political parties do not set up candidates, their hidden influence is there. The rural elite are able to reinforce their influence and position by being elected through the democratic process. In most of the cases power has not reached the people at large and the rural poor do not have full participation in making decisions for managing village affaris. The political structure of the country is deeply entrenched in its old social order. It bears the legacy of the past. The mindset of the people will take time to change. The balance of power politics has not been altered to any substantial extent. One study reported in this chapter discusses the factors of this continuity of pattern of rural administration in West Bengal.

II

Dr. Satyajiban Chakraborty conducted his doctoral research on the joint family in District of 24 paragans, West Bengal. Family is one of the basic social institutions in all human societies. In India, for a very long time the extended or the joint family survived through the ages. In recent times, however, it is fast disappearing from both rural and urban areas. The author has made a deep sociological study of the evidence and the process of the disintegration of the joint family in nine villages of the 24 Parganas district.

The Hindu way of life has been to a large extent responsible for the origin and growth of the joint family system. The Hindus do not consider life on this earth as an end of human existence. The deep belief in the phenomenon of rebirth and the constant interaction with ancestors during worship and festivals, has helped the survival of the joint family system. In addition to the religious sanction behind the joint family, the notion of property in land provided additional strength to it. The owner of the landed property or the *Karta* (manager) of the joint family made it a strong socio-economic unit. In course of time, religious norms gradually developed along this concept and these helped to keep the family in tact. In this way the joint family supported the existing property system. The advent of industrialization altered the whole situation. The agrarian economic relationships were eroded. Instead of group there was emphasis on individual. Collective ownership of property was replaced by individual ownership and the family pattern changed from joint to nuclear.

The area studied experienced cultural inroads from a number of western powers like the English, the Dutch and the Protugese. From the beginning of 19th century, these foreign cultures began to exert great influence on the social life of the people even in rural areas. The nine villages chosen for the field study represented various shades of impact. The author intended to study the nature, structure and functioning pattern of the existing family system and also to examine the causes of disintegration of the joint family. The universe comprised 7088 households of which only 258 were reported to be joint families. The entire process of change has been assessed with reference to the *Dharma Shasatras* in which related norms have been prescribed. Earlier the personal relationship, collective living, acceptance of the authority of the head of the family and leader were extremely important. The author has also dealt with the division of labour in the joint family. The strengths and weaknesses of joint family has also been brought out. One of the chapters deals with the factors for the break-up of the joint family both in action as well as in spirit. Industrialization and urbanization have hastened the process. Though India is still largely an agricultural country, the commercialization of agriculture and the impact of industrialization coming through neighboring towns has played havoc with the institution of the joint family. In an agro-bassed society the property relationship made possible by the concentration of economic power in the hand of the joint family, no longer exists. Power is shared by the adult working members of the joint family. The older and the younger generation observe religious rites particularly the mortuary rituals as a matter of custom not out of deep conviction in the concept of continuity of life through rebirth. The changes in the role of the head of the family and the erosion of concept of *Karmaphal* are largely responsible for the loosening of the bond that maintain togetherness in the joint family.

It has been noted that the status of family changes from nuclearity to jointness or from jointness to nuclearty with the passage of time. Now no joint family has members belonging to more than three generations.

The strains and stresses in the joint family are so varied and strong that they lead to its break-up. The notion of unbreakability of marriage no longer holds good. The author has noted some cases of divorce but the percentage is very small. This is due to the fact the women are completely dependent on men economically. Some of them are compelled to live an unhappy life on this account. The nature of inter-personal relationship in the existing joint families is no longer the same as it was in the traditional joint family. The authority and control of the head of the family are no longer absolute. The father-son relationship is one of adjustment and accommodation rather than that of domination or subordination. The parent-daughter relationship has also changed. The same is the case with husband–wife relationship. It is now more based on a spirit of cooperation and accommodation. The daughter-in-law is no longer helpless victim of the tyranny of mother-in-law.

The division of labour in the joint family has undergone transformation. Both men and women are involved in work within and outside the home.

In joint families that still exist the members appreciate its advantages and that is why they still continue in that system. The change from jointness to nuclearity is however, very pronounced as only 3.6% of the families under observation still continued to be joint.

Caste is a unique feature of the Indian social system. It is characterized by a hierachical social order in which life and activities of members are governed by rules and regulations framed by the caste council or Panchayat. Dr. Narayan Chandra Maiti has made a study of the traditional caste panchayat of three Scheduled Caste communities in the district of Midnapur, West Bengal. Attempts have been made in his thesis to highlight the pattern of changes in the mechanism of social control from pre-independence days to the rule of Left Front government in West Bengal.

The caste panchayats perform both sacred and secular functions aimed at the maintenance of social harmony and the caste structure. It is an organ for promoting solidarity of caste and for preserving discipline among its members. Any breach of caste rules invites punishment by the panchayat. The panchayat has been functioning for several centuries. A number of persons are vested with certain ritual activities, local administrative power and political authority. The panchayat has a code of conduct and functions principally on the basis of traditional and local custom. It has the authority of imposing fine and punishment including ex-communication on wrong doers. All the social and religious activities of the members of different castes depend upon the leaders of the panchayat. The offences calling for punishment of ex-communication are killing of a Brahmin, killing of a cow, beef eating, sharing meals or smoking hooka with a member of a caste lower that his own. Other offences of less serious nature such as accepting food from a person of lower caste. Crossing the seas could be atoned through purificatiory measures. Other offences dealt with the caste panchayat are keeping a woman of other caste as a concubine, seduction or adultery with a married woman, refusal to fulfill the promise of marriage, refusal to send a wife to her husband after attainment of puberty, refusing to maintain a wife, non-payment of debt, petty assault, insulting a Brahmin etc. The punishments awarded by the panchayat were excommunication, fines, feast to be given to caste men, corporal punishment and ritual expiation for ignoring some caste rules.

Besides studying the working of the panchayat, the author has tried to asses the nature of social mobility or social movement of the people of the region. The changes are being manifested through action patterns initiating higher caste groups or by adopting more urban or sophisticated way of life. The study was made in six villages with reference to Paundra Khastriya, Namasudra and Rajbansi communities. The relationship between caste panchayats and statutory panchayats has also been brought out. The data on the nature and function on traditional and statutory panchayats has been collected through case history method. The informants were interviewed with reference to the working of the Panchayats in the pre-independence, the post independence period and the left front period. They were put into three groups. Old people in the age group of 60 years and above, middle aged between 40 to 60 years and the young age people in the age group of 20 to 40 years were interviewed to get a picture of changes taking place over several decades.

It appears from the study that the caste panchayat is still powerful and plays a decisive role in village affairs. The members of the caste panchayat are generally selected from well to do persons who are capable of taking charge of village administration in tune with the higher caste in the population. It was also obligatory to obey the decision of the village head-man and caste panchayat in general.

During the entire period covered by the study a number of social movements had created an impact on the life and activities of the Schedule Caste people. Steps were taken to provide safeguard for them. Other changes on the socio-economic and political front have dealt a serious blow to the caste hierarchy and promoted an egalitarian democratic base for the regional caste structure. Many persons among the SCs sanskritized their lifestyle and have tried to improve their ritual status.They have been able to compete for positions of power. They have also entered the administrative machinery. The hierarchically arranged caste system and caste organizations have gradually been transformed into class conscious village organization through the statutory panchayats. The Scheduled Caste people have been encouraged to walk on the road to development through self reliance, initiative and a sense of security. The study reveals that the caste councils have suffered in importance. Caste rigidity is becoming weaker day by day and new democratic norms are gaining momentum. New technology, new employment opportunities and the spread of education have weakened the caste system and the caste panchayats now have to play the role of vanguard in this respect and see that the interest both economic and political of their caste men are protected and promoted.

Dr. Chittranjan Banerjee made a study of the sociological implication of rural indebtedness in five villages of 24 Pargana district in West Bengal. It has been observed by many authorities that the Indian peasant is heavily in debt. In fact, he is born in debt, lives in debt and dies in debt. Recent improvement in the economic condition of the peasant has not made a dent in this matter since the vicious circle of poverty and debt continues its strong grip on the peasantry.

The author has made a detailed survey of five villages and found that 428 families live in debt. The average debt of a family is about Rs.1100/. About 84% of the cultivator families are indebted. The total debt includes ancestral debt and personal debts. The majority of indebted families is in the debt range of Rs. 251/-to 700/.

Debts are incurred for a variety of needs. Peasants borrow for both productive and non-productive purposes. The non-productive debt are on account of chronically deficit economy arising from consumption, religious and social ceremonies like marriage and death and for repayments of old debts. The unproductive debts exceed productive debts. In fact, unproductive debts account for 75% of the total debts.

There are two resources of credit–institutional and non-institutional. The latter agencies supply the bulk of rural credit. The institutional agencies only supply 18% of the total volume of debt. Money lenders or Mahajans are the chief creditors who give loans without much hassle. The procedure for the sanction of loans from banks and cooperative society is complex and irritating for the peasant. Such loans are given against the mortgage of land. The money lenders charge exorbitant rates of interest. The rate varies from 11% to 15% per month. The moneylender advances loan before the sowing season on condition that the debtor would sell the entire produce to him at a price dictated by him. Thus, the peasant is exploited twice in the bargain. He has to pay high rate of interest and he has to sell his produce at a price which is lower than the market rate. Inspite of this peasant goes to the Mahajan because the loan is available immediately. Repayment of the loan is slow but the moneylender is satisfied with only the interest. In his way the peasant continues to be in debt. The moneylender trusts the debtor. If the latter does not pay up he would not get any further loan. The unproductive loan is disastrous for the family. It leads to agricultural inefficiency and creates family problems. The moneylender wields great influence on the debtors during the local and funeral elections. Thus, besides economic power he also gains political power, with the result that he captures important positions in the panchayat and cooperative society. It is seen that in this process of exploitation caste or community ties do not stand in the way. Well-to-do Scheduled Caste cultivators exploit their brethren as money-lenders. Similarly Muslim moneylenders have no hesitation in exploiting poor Muslim cultivators.

The benefit of technological changes has not been utilised by poor cultivators. The rich peasants who are also moneylenders corner all the development schemes as they are aware of the procedural formalities and also have good deal of influence in the administration. They take the land from the poor peasantry as share croppers. With the help of institutional finance they are able to take two crops from the same plot of land.

The small peasants are not able to do this because of financial constraints. The result is that the rich peasants are getting richer and the poor peasants are becoming destitute. The well-to-do peasants are able to send their children to schools and colleges and have better chances to improve their quality of life. While the debt is a bridge between the debtor and creditor, it widens the gap, social and economic, between the two.

Poverty leads to debt and debt leads to further poverty. With the spread of education and the operation of democratic politics a sense of deprivation and a feeling of injustice has been generated in the minds of poor peasantry. This situation contains within itself the germs of violent agrarian unrest. The culture of silence is giving way to culture of protest. Political parties with the ultra left ideology have been able to mobilise the peasantry in their favour. Perpetual rural indebtedness in short, leads to diverse socio-economic problems and contains the seeds of violent agrarian conflict.

Immediate steps are necessary to break the vicious circle of poverty and debt by providing viable assets to the poor peasantry. This would reduce the need to borrow. Institutional finance should be made available quickly by simplifying the procedure.

In any society political institutions are extremely important. They are the instruments through which the administration functions. Shibnath Banerjee made a perceptive and analytical study of patterns of rural administration in West Bengal. He traced the continuity of certain trends creating impact on governance in villages. These trends are continuing from before and are influencing the working of the administrative institutions even after the advent of democracy. Soon after independence, democratic decentralization was put into practice in the shape of Panchayati Raj institutions. Democracy implies self rule and self rule means the participation of mass of the people. But this is impossible unless the local governing institutions are themselves democratized. Carl G. Taylor held that so long as local self government institutions are not conceived as parts of the same organic constitutional and administrative framework, the structure of democratic government will remain incomplete. In course of time the Panchayat system was introduced to give rural people the chance of having a share in the local administration.

Researchers have felt that mere laws are not enough. Since direct democracy is not possible, representative democracy has been put in operation. It was seen that free choice of one's representative is not there even at the Panchayat election level. This is because the political structure of a country is not autonomous. It is closely interwoven with the socio-economic set-up.

Caste factor is uppermost in the minds of the people. Candidates belonging to the numerically dominant caste win most of the seats. Dominance depends upon a number of factors such as numerical strength, control over land and also education. Caste at the political level is quite relaxed in respect of endogamy. Castes form coalitions to contest election. Usually leaders of the locally dominant caste are elected to Panchayat. Those elections are not contested with symbols of political parties but they do influence the election result. However, it will be a gross oversimplification to say that village politics can be explained entirely with reference to caste. Economic considerations are another important determinant of voting behaviour. The bulk of the peasants is extremely poor. The peasants are threatened with reprisals and withdrawal of money lending facilities, if they vote against the wishes of landlords or money lenders. Thus the rural elite are able to influence the election. In recent times literacy has become the third important factor. Those who are completely illiterate do not know the value of franchise and do not turn up for voting. At the local level introduction of adult franchise has become a mockery because most of the vote rs do not have the basic minimum education.The writer concludes that illiteracy is responsible for failing to give the people the proper yard stick of choosing their representatives. The author holds that the political structure of the area is deeply entrenched in its social order. The legacy of the past weighs heavily on the present. The mindset of the people will take time to change.

Joint Family in the District of 24 Parganas, West Bengal : A Sociological Study

Satyajiban Chakraborty

Of many Hindus Social Institutions, the one that has survived through ages but is now fast disappearing both from rural and urban societies, is the extended or joint family as it is known in India. As in other parts of India, joint family has been a living institution in Bengal from by–gone days and as usual, it is disintegrating to such an extent that hardly any traditional type of joint family either in the villages or in industrial centres may be traced. Though many studies on joint family and the nature and character of this age-old institution in Bengal and the factors leading to changes in its nature have been made, yet considering the importance of the area, there is always a scope for analyzing it afresh in specific situational contexts. A sociological study of joint family in West Bengal is indeed a desideratum.

Family is the basic primary social unit in which an individual is born, brought up, socialised and ultimately end his life. MacIver and Page (1962) rightly observed:

> Of all the organisations large or small, which the society unfolds, none transcends the family in the intensity of its sociological significance.

The importance of family in social life can hardly be minimised. A baby's first contact is in the family which offers him readymade ways of doing things. Goode (1965) rightly observed:

> The family is the fundamental instrumental foundation of the larger social structure in that all other institutions depend on its contributions. The role behaviour that is learned within the family becomes the model or prototype for the role behaviour required in other segments of the society. The content of the socialisation process is the cultural traditions of the society, by passing them on to the next generation, the family acts as a conduct or transmission belt by which the culture is kept alive.

The family structure is not the same everywhere. Though in industrialized society nuclear family based on companionship is the prevalent form yet the composite forms of family is not completely absent. In most primitive societies joint families were the dominant form and they are also found in non-industrial societies of to-day. The Indian society is now in a transitional phase, passing from an agrarian society to an industrial society. Naturally the family structure is also undergoing serious changes.

The members of the joint family live, converse and dine together and in course of their daily routine, they come across through various prescriptions of do's and dont's. These prescriptions not only regulate their behaviour pattern, but also shape the basic character of individual members. The inter dependence of the members of joint family and their dependence on the family itself wields its members into a homogeneous and compact unit. The common way of life strengthens emotional solidarity and cooperation among them.

Hindu view of life is, to a large extent, responsible for the growth of joint family system. The Hindus do not consider this life on earth as an end in itself–it is rather a temporary stage in the continuous evolution of the soul which always moves towards perfection. In this process of evolution, they are guided, assisted and protected by their ancestor. "The living members of the family are, so to speak, trustees of the House which belongs to the 'pitris', the ancestors, in the interests of the 'putras', future members of the family." This notion of family had given birth to the growth of joint family system. *Mahavagavad Gita* too echoes the same notion of the birth of family.

But the foundation of joint family appears to be not religion but property system. In rural society, as the ancient India essentially was, land was the main source of living. Obviously the owner of landed property became the manager of family in such a society and other members felt obliged to stay with him as separation from him would bring uncertainty in life. Religious norms and institutions were gradually developed presumably to keep the family intact so that the existing property system may be preserved.

Had it not been so, the advent of industrialization could not have disintegrated the joint family system. Industrialization required reorientation of the old economic relationship as the agrarian economic relationship cannot meet the demands of industrial society. Industrialization put emphasis on individual, rather than collective ownership and in the process, family structure changes from joint to nuclear pattern.

It may be noted that no comprehensive study has been made on joint family of West Bengal which once played dominant role on conditioning individual and group life. Our interests, attitudes, aspiration and demands are initially articulated in family environment. These have a far reaching effect on the society at large what one learns in his infancy may be modified at a later stage of life with new experiences gained from outside contacts but the basic foundation of an individuals personality remains almost in tact. This personality is largely the product of the process of socialisation carried throughout the life-cycle within the family environment.

A comprehensive study of the extant joint families in West Bengal would be meaningful and representative if a social investigator selects an area which comprises both rural and urban population. In this context 24 Parganas of West Bengal appears to be the ideal district. There are some villages which are not linked up with the rest of the district through transport system; there are others connected with the metropolis through a network of railways and roadways. The district also contains important industrial centres like Bongaon, Barasat, Baranagar, DumDum, BudgeBudge, Titagarh and Ichhapur with Calcutta as the heart of the communication network. It is a district, which contains the characteristics both of rural and urban ways of life. Its existence from the hoary past is testified to by its references in the Epic, Puranas and ancient literatures.

The district of 24 Paraganas experienced the onslaughts of various foreign powers–the English, the Dutch and the Portuguese. It became, therefore, the centre of cross culture exerting great influence in bringing about an unprecedented change in the socio-economic profile of the district.

At present, the district of 24 Paraganas has been bifurcated into North 24 Parganas and South 24 Parganas. We know that the emergence of joint family system is a characteristic feature of agro-based society and industrial society encourages the formation of nuclear or conjugal family. Both these symptoms are evidenced in the district under investigation.

After first round visit to several villages the author consulted his guide, related his experiences to him and finally selected, with the concurrance of the guide, the following nine villages/towns of the district for his field study, with an idea that these villages represent the entire district 1) Batanagar of Mahestala Police Station, 2) Rudrapur of Habra Police Station, 3) Bhalenda of Rajarhat Police Station, 4) Phulsara of Gaighata Police Station 5) Kulia of Bagdah Police Station 6) Mohanpur of Deganga Police Station 7) Teghari of Khardah Police Station 8) Birinchibari of Basanti and 9) Joygopalpur Police Station.

The purpose of the author is to study the nature, structure and functional pattern of the existing joint families in the district and also to examine the causes of disintegration of joint family. The author has also taken into consideration of the rural-urban setting of the field area. Printed schedules and questionnaire were used in the field study. The schedule contained 28 broad questions with about 70 sub-questions.

The field areas contain 7088 households, of which 6830 households are nuclear units and 258 are joint families. The field study covers all the joint families in the area and the author has interviewed 1186 persons, both married and unmarried.

The whole thesis has been divided into seven chapters :

Chapter one deals with the purpose and intent of the author to study joint family. This chapter also deals with the methods adopted in the study. There is no documentary record from which we can have a precise knowledge of the structure of joint family in ancient time, but we can guess the nature of traditional joint family from the Hindu view of life as depicted in *Dharma Shastras, Epics* and other *ancient literatures*. An analysis of the data collected from the field area will give an idea of the nature and structure of the existing joint families and it can be observed whether there has been any change in the nature and composition of joint family. This has been dealt with in Chapter Two.

Chapter Three attempts to find out whether any change has been brought in within the existing joint families. To get an idea of the nature of joint family, the study of inter-personal relationship is important. Collective living requires leadership. This leadership was provided by the Head in the joint family. If any change occurs in the role of the Head, or if leadership becomes plural or shared, collective living is bound to be affected with a consequent change in the inter-personal relationship among the members of the family. This change has been dealt with in this chapter.

Chapter Four deals with division of labour within the family. Dichotomy of functions among the members reveals the character of a social organisation. It will also give us an idea of what services the joint family renders to its members and to the society as a whole.

Chapter Five deals with the strength and weakness of the joint family. The joint family is a century-old social organisation. In the evolution of human development, many organisations and institutions have sprung up and disappeared, but the joint family is still surviving. It is, therefore, imperative to study its strength and weakness in order to guess the possible future of this social organization.

Chapter Six deals with the question of disintegration of joint family. It is suggested by many that the joint family has disintegrated in

India or is in the process of disintegration. Industrialization and urbanisation demand a life-pattern which is considered not conducive to common living in a joint family. Industrialization definitely affects our interest, attitudes and mode of life. But India is not yet an industrialized society; through after commercialization of agriculture and introduction of the programme of industrialization, she can no longer be treated as purely an agro-based society. Hence, it is necessary to analyze whether joint family can adjust itself with the changed situations or its disintegration is a fait accompli.

Chapter Seven is the conclusion made on the basis of observed facts and findings. In an agro-based society, the property relationship that once made possible the concentration of economic power at the hands of the Head, no longer exists and this power is shared to-day by the adult working members of joint family. Moreover, both the older and younger generation observe rites, such as, *asoucha* and *Sradha* ceremony; as a matter of custom and tradition and not out of any deep conviction in the concept of spiritual continuity. This changes in the role of the Head and the shakened belief in the concept of *karmaphala,* it may be concluded, are responsible for the loosing of the bond that binds the members together in joint family.

In the district of 24 Parganas, there is a strong tendency of almost all the families to pass from nuclearity to jointness or from jointness to nuclearity. The age of marriage for male in the district varies from 24 to 27 years and for female from 18 to 22 years. If, therefore the first issue is born at the age of 25 or 26 or 28 years, a grandson is likely to be born at the age of 52 to 55 years. Most of the people live up to this age. But a great grandson may be born at the age of 77 to 80 years and in a very few cases a man lives up to this age. This accounts for the rarity of four-generational joint family in the district of 24 Parganas.

There are strains and stresses in family life; the notion of unbreakability of marriage does no longer hold good. Yet the rate of divorce is very low in the district. The author is inclined to observe that the economic dependence of women on men is the real reason for low rate of divorce.

It may be concluded that the nature of inter-personal relationship among the members of an existing joint family is no longer the same as it was in traditional joint family. The following trends are observed :

1. The authority and control of the Head over the members of the family are no longer absolute;
2. father-son relationship is one of adjustment and accommodation instead of domination and subordination;

3. a new dimension has entered into parent-daughter relationship;
4. husband-wife relationship has become one of cooperation and accommodation;
5. daughter-in-law is no longer a helpless victim of the domination of the mother-in-law.

As regards division of work between sexes, it is observed that men predominantly work outside the home, while women activities are confined to domestic duties. But today both men and women are involved in work both within and outside home. This has changed the complexion of joint family. In a traditional joint family, it could not be conceived that a male member would do the job of household or a female member would go outside the family for work. As the traditional family structure was based on this type of division of labour, a change in this situation has affected the entire male-female relationship within the family.

The joint families still exist because they have certain advantages which nuclear family cannot ensure. But the members of joint families (258) in the area under study in proportion to the total households (7088) is so insignificant (only 3.6%) that one can safely conclude that the disadvantages of joint family to-day are more pronounced than its advantages.

Industrialization and urbanization not only open up job opportunities available on the basis of individual talent, education and skill, but also develop a new system of social values not consistent with the common living in a joint family. Industrialization and urbanization, therefore, have a direct bearing on the dissolution of joint family.

Industrialization and urbanization have created social conditions in which joint family appears to be anachronistic, yet it still exists to-day, however small its number be. But the existing joint family is different from its traditional type in many respects in structure, function and inter-personal relationships. This change in one of the oldest social organizations has a tremendous impact on the social structure itself.

References

MacIver, R. M. and Page, C. H. 1962 *Society : An Introductory Analysis.* London : Macmillan and Co.

Goode, W. J. 1965 *The Family.* New Delhi : Prentice-Hall of India.

A Study of Sociological Import of Rural Indebtedness in the District of 24 Parganas, West Bengal

Chittaranjan Banerjee

The study based on the field survey reveals that the peasant families sank ever deeper into debt, losing incentive and efficiency, neglecting improvement to their lands. Of the total 508 cultivating families of the five villages studied, 428 families live in debt. The average debt per family comes to about Rs. 1093.00. On an average, about 84.30% of the total cultivating families are indebted. The total debt includes both the ancestral and personal debts. The majority of the indebted families are within the debt range of Rs. 251–Rs. 700. Of the total 428 indebted families, 187 are within this range.

The study highlights that the cultivators borrow for a variety of needs. They borrow for both productive and unproductive purposes. But unproductive purpose like the domestic consumption, religious and ceremonial functions and repayment of old debt, far exceeds the loan for productive purpose. The unproductive expenditure amounts to 75.60% of the total, as against 24.40% of the productive expenditure. So the finding is that the bulk of the borrowed money is spent mostly for unproductive purpose, and very little is left for augmenting production.

The field survey reveals that, of the two sources of credit–1) institutional and 2) non-institutional–the non institutional agencies play the most dominating role in the supply of rural credit. Against the Institutional Agencies, share of 17.75 percent in the total loan market, non-institutional agencies share of the total loan is 82.25 percent.

The study also reveals that the money lenders or the Mahajans occupy the top position in the list of creditors. From them loans are easily available. The mode and manner of sanctioning loan by the institutional agencies like Bank, Co-operative societies and the Government is complicated and sometimes irritating to the peasants. Such loans are given against the mortgaging of land. They supply loan for agricultural development, but this is not the only requirement of the farmers.

The exorbitant rates of interest charged by the Mahajans reveal their exploitative nature. The rate, as the present survey revealed, varies from 15.10% to 11.71% per annum.

The Mahajans also follow various operational strategies to exploit the average innocent and illiterate cultivators. They maintain fake accounts. The practice of using blank paper with thumb-impression of the debtors is also prevalent. The trader-cum-money-lender advances loan before sowing seasons, on the pledge from his debtor that his entire produce will be sold to him. The Mahajan therefore, exploits in two ways. On the one hand he charges a high rate of interest, and on the other, offers a lower market price to the cultivator for his crops.

It is further revealed that the cultivators are aware of the exploitative nature of the Mahajan loan yet, for various socio-economic reasons, they have to fall back upon the money lenders.

They also know that non-repayment of a loan will block the way of fresh loan, and debt if accumulated, will lead to forfeiture of their property–both movable and immovable, by the Mahajans.

The unproductive loan is disastrous. It ruins the peasantry. It leads to agricultural inefficiency. It creates family troubles. Poverty stricken villagers sometimes migrate to the city and face a hazardous life. This, in turn, adds problems to city life.

The cultivators are held down in poverty and apathy. By virtue of their advantageous monopoly position, the money lenders exert covert influence on their clients during local and general elections. The money power of the money lenders enables them to enjoy the socio-political power. They capture the Panchayets and control the co-operative societies, they also maintain closer link with the men of administration to reap the benefit of the development programmes of the Government. In the domain of loan, caste and community constitute no barrier–high caste people make loan from the lower caste, and vice-versa. The loan, therefore loosens the caste system and brings different castes together in the economic frontier. It is not true that only the high caste oppresses the lower one. For the lower caste people are also being oppressed by the money lenders of their own caste.

The two villages viz., Badebarasi and Uttar–Jyotishpur, are mainly dominated by the Scheduled Caste population. The big jotedars of these villages also belong to that caste. Yet the poor villagers are not spared.

The village Baragachhia also reveals that the Muslim Mahajans do exploit the Muslim cultivators. Therefore, neither caste nor religion may be considered as factors responsible for the perpetuation of economic exploitation of the rural people.

In fact, the problems of indebtedness is so deep rooted that it requires a multi-pronged attack for its solution. Alternative institutional agencies for supplying loan, when needed should also be set-up.

The benefit of technological changes have not been utilized by the average cultivators. These have gone to the big jotedars who know the procedural formalities and have influences on the administration. But now with the control over technological development due to their financial viability and power of large investments, the big jotedars are taking the role of share-croppers. An average cultivator, due to his meagre financial capacity, is unable to introduce double cropping. He does only the normal *amon* during the monsoon cultivation. *Boro* or the high-yielding variety during the winter seasons of paddy cultivation is beyond his reach. Some big jotedars are taking lease of the lands of the small farmers during the *Boro* seasons. These jotedars have thereby not only enriched their economic position, but also competing with the statutory financial institutions in the loan market. As a result, the poor becomes poorer and the rich becomes more rich.

The study highlights that within the same agrarian economy two economic classes are living side by side. One is the debtor class, who are poor, and the other is the class of creditors who are economically viable. The latter's economy enables them to send their children to schools, colleges and university, and their wards can acquire new values and ideas. But the other groups are the subjugated section of the society without getting any benefit. There are, therefore, two values for these two economic classes of people of the same rural economy. Loan acts as a bridge between the debtor and the creditor, but it widens the gap, social and economic, between the two.

No real development of the Indian agriculture, and therefore no real progress of the country, in its rural sector, could be expected unless the problem of rural credit is solved. Poverty makes the people indebted, and indebtedness creates further poverty. The farmer is unable to come out of his sub-human level of living. But the spread of education, liberal ideas, democratic experiment, have created in his mind a sense of deprivation and a feeling of injustice. Instead of fatalist submission to his lot, he expects a better reward of his labour and good living. When this expectation is belied, a sense of discontent, and even resentment, brews up in his mind. This psychological factor in a depressed economic atmosphere contains within itself the germ of violent agrarian unrest. In fact, the abject poverty of the peasants may push them to the desperate situation of expressing their pent-up feeling of injustice in the most violent way, with organised provocation or scope. The tradition bound, peace-loving and God fearing people of rural India may become the source of violent agrarian movement, if political parties pledged to ultra–left ideology, are able to mobilize, utilize and electrify the peasantry.

Perpetual rural indebtedness, therefore, not only creates adverse socio-economic import and hinder development of agriculture, but also contains the seeds of violent agrarian conflict in the future, unless this problem is effectively handled. Socio-economic and political fall outs blasted by the rural indebtedness should be deterred at any cost, for making the rural life worth living, and for preserving, promoting and sustaining the peace and prosperity of the country, primarily agricultural and yet, wedded to the principle of democracy and socialism.

The tremendous influence which indebtedness exerts in shaping the control of our rural society especially its effect on the peasant life, has induced the author to undertake the present study. This area of research has remained until now relatively neglected and unexplored, though it is of crucial importance to the social and economic life of the village people, particularly in India, which is mostly an agricultural country. It is true that from time to time, some of the sociologists have studied the Indian villages with growing awareness of rural dimension of India. But none of them so far has studied in depth the problems connected with rural indebtedness or could evolve or suggest any effective measures to tackle them.

The present author has taken up the study of sociological import of rural indebtedness in the district of 24 Parganas, as he happens to be a resident of this district for long and knows the agrarian society intimately. The study was undertaken in Nov, 1971, and completed in July, 1976. Attempt has been made in this study to discover the depth, magnitude and the sociological import of the rural indebtedness, by making an intensive survey in the five villages of the district of 24 Parganas in West Bengal. The study has, however, been restricted only to the cultivator families of the villages concerned. A cultivating family is defined as a family engaged in the cultivation of any piece of land, owned or leased.

Total 1

The Total Number of Cultivator Families (village wise)

Name of the Villages	Number of Cultivator Families
Baneswarpur	42
Bargachhia	168
Harinavi	40
Badebarasi	93
Uttar-Jyotishpur	165
Total	508

Total 2

Cultivator Families and indebtedness

Name of the Villages	Number of families having Land and Free from Loan	Number of families having land but involved in loan
Baneswarpur	Nil	42
Bargachhia	38	130
Harinavi	Nil	40
Badebarasi	15	78
Uttar-Jyotishpur	27	138
Total	80	428

In course of the field study, printed schedules and questionnaires were used. Case history method has also been adopted for this study.

The five villages, taken together, had a fairly representative character. Uttar-Jyotishpur and Badebarasi are located in the Southern part of the district and inhabited by people mostly belonging to the Scheduled Tribes. The village is totally lacking modern means of communication. Harinavi is very near to the metropolitan city of Calcutta enjoying the impact and benefit of industrialization and has aco-operative society and a nationalised Commercial Bank. The village Baragachhia though situated very close to Calcutta is, however, deprived of the facilities of modern means of communication. It is a typical traditional West Bengal village predominantly inhabited by the Muslim cultivators. The last village Baneswarpur, situated in the extreme northern part of the district is distinctive for its proximity of Bangladesh border. The great majority of its inhabitants today are refugees from former East Pakistan.

The author made door to door census for obtaining demographic figures of the villages. The procedure adopted for collecting the data was largely informal and non-directive.

The huge volume of indebtedness is a disturbing feature of the Indian rural society and the dominant feature of the problem of rural indebtedness in India arises from the activities of the money lenders who earn mainly by capitalizing on the perpetual poverty of the peasants. Poverty is the prime factor behind indebtedness of the cultivating class. The agriculturists have to incur debt because they are poor and they remain poor because they borrow, for a part of their earnings goes into the pocket of the money lenders in the form of repayment of principal with interest, leaving very little even to meet their bare needs. These rural indebtedness and rural poverty form a vicious circle as one leads to the other land *infinitum*. This is the bare truth of rural India, eating into the vitals of the people and affecting their socio-economic life.

Traditional Caste Panchayat and Aspects of Social Movement : A Micro Study in Eastern Midnapore, West Bengal

Narayan Chandra Maiti

The study is based on the traditional caste-ridden hierarchical social order in which the life and activities of caste members are governed by caste rules and regulations framed by the governing body of the caste, known as Caste Panchayat. But with the passage of time, many changes have taken place in the social milieu through modernism, introduction of western education, industrialization, urbanization etc. Constitutional and legislative measures as well as various social movements also influenced the people, particularly the lower castes in a great way to change their earlier attitudes, beliefs and faiths. In consequence, the structure of the society as well as mechanism of social control has also undergone a change to a considerable extent. Notwithstanding the fact that some aspects of their social institutions withstood the onslaughts of such changes, of course not without conflict between traditionalism and modernism, they still somehow exist.

Attempts have been made in the present study to highlight the pattern of changes in the mechanism of social control governing the life and activities of the people of Eastern Midnapore from pre-independence period to till date.

India is highly diversified, socially and culturally. This diversification in respect of its physical features, ecology and environment has had tremendous impact on the population which inhabit her.

The caste system is a unique feature of the Indian Society. This is one of the oldest institutions in our country. Caste and civilisation have always been of great interest of study not only to the foreign scholars, but also to the Indian scholars. The study of the caste system and the village communities of India has been a subject of considerable interest to many Anthropologists or Social Scientists. Over and above, the scholars are of opinion that the role of caste, though it varies in content from village to village or region to region, is primarily embodied in the structure of the village society, as a whole. In reality for any understanding of the patterns of the social organisation, the important role of caste is undeniable. Caste is the main basis of the Hindu society and nobody can properly understand the Hindu Law and social institution without the good knowledge of the system of caste and the rules concerning it.

The traditional caste system is a type of social stratification in which the individual's social status, that is, his or her prestige and honour in the society, is determined by his or her birth into a particular caste. Moreover, this status is directly linked to the position of his or her caste group within the hierarchy of caste. In other words, a person's status is determined by the status of the group to which he or she belongs. In India, in spite of disparities and differences among caste groups, we find almost all of them faithfully adhere to the traditional norms which have been handed down to the posterity. However, some members of the caste enjoy more privileges and benefits, whereas others get comparatively less. Each caste has a distinctive status and rank in the regional caste ladder. Hence, in a regional setting some castes are considered high, some in the middle rank, some in the low status and some others are in the very low rank of the regional hierarchy.

In this system of stratification, a person's social status is determined not so much by the caste to which he or she belongs but by the occupation he or she takes up, the income derived from it, and, generally, by the person's new lifestyle.

The most important feature in the caste system is its mechanism of social control and control over the power enjoyed by the rural Panchayat system. Almost every caste has a traditional caste Panchayat. The caste Panchayat, in general, performs both sacred and secular functions and also helps to maintain social harmony within the caste structure. A caste Panchayat is an organ for promoting solidarity of the caste and for preserving discipline among its members in the trial of an offence-against the caste rules. Evidently, Panchayat was an ancient Hindu institution comprising a number of persons vested with certain rituals, local administrative power and political authority. The term 'Panchayat' signifies an assembly of five. However, in practice, this number has not always been adhered to strictly.

The caste Panchayat had, however, no written code of conduct and functions principally on the basis of traditional and local customs. The caste Panchayat has the authority of imposing fine and certain other punishments, including ex-communication of the members of their castes in the case of commission of serious offences. Evidently, almost all the social and religious activities of a Hindu depended entirely on his association among the members of his own caste or sub-caste. One could not even imagine to exist after being ex-communicated from the caste he belonged. The offences calling for the stringent punishment of ex-communication from the caste may be enumerated as killing a Brahmin (termed as Brahmahatya, signifying killing of the divine), cow-killing, beef eating, sharing meals or smoking Hooka (nargile) with a member of a caste lower than his own. Other offences of less serious nature, e.g., accepting food touched or cooked by a person of a lower caste, Sea voyage etc., were however, atonable through various purificatory measures, for examples, bath in the holy river Ganga. Some other offences dealt with the caste Panchayat are : (a) Keeping a concubine of another caste, (b) Seduction or adultery with a married woman; (c) breaking of incest taboos; (d) refusal to fulfil a promise of marriage; (e) refusing to send a wife to her husband on her attainment of puberty age; (f) refusing to maintain a wife; (g) non-payment of debt; (h) petty assaults; (I) breaches of the customs of trade peculiar to the caste; (j) killing a cow or any other sacred animal; (k) insulting Brahmin and (l) defying the custom which is a taboo to the caste, regarding feasts etc., during marriage and other ceremonies.

The punishments that these Panchayats impose on individuals are as mentioned below.

1. Out casting, either temporarily or permanently
2. Fines
3. Feasts to be given to the caste men
4. Corporal punishment and
5. Sometimes religious expiation

The present study intends to highlight the following objectives.

1. To study the composition and functions of the three selected caste Panchayats, viz., (a) Paundra Kshatriya (Pod), (b) Namasudra (Chandal), and (c) Rajbanshi (Fisherman) in six villages of Eastern Midnapore, West Bengal. The communities under study are taken, as they belonged to the backward scheduled castes and live in an agricultural set up. Hence they are a traditional community. Thus, in the present work, attempts have been made to delineate the degree of change among the tradition bound backward communities.
2. To study the changes in traditional caste system due to modernization, industrialization, development of communication, growth of new ideology as well as introduction

of various legislative acts corroborated with the statutory Panchayat system.

3. To study the structure and functions of modern Panchayat system operating in six villages of Eastern Midnapore comprising Tamluk and Haldia sub-divisions.
4. To study the social movements of the three studied caste communities in this region.
5. To study various new organisations and meetings participating in distinctive activities for elevating the social status.
6. To study the above mentioned three communities, all of whom have constitutional status as scheduled castes and for this they are getting more benefits after independence particularly with the introduction of the new Panchayat system in accordance with the Panchayat Act of 1973.
7. Moreover, this area (Tamluk & Haldia) again, has the advantage of proximity to Haldia Port and as such, urbanization has begun to make an inroad in and around the area, i.e. , in its hinterland, and enhances the facilities of inflow and outflow of the surrounding areas. Naturally, after independence not only constitutional benefits are accrued to them but the area also has undergone sea changes which have brought about an over-all developmental picture. These changes, which are operating in different directions, may enable these caste groups to adjust themselves, accordingly.
8. With this background, the researcher has tried to assess the nature of social mobility or social movement of the people of the region under study. The changes are being manifested through various action patterns, imitating the higher groups or castes of the locality, or by accepting more urban or sophisticated way of life. But internal organization in which caste played a dominant role have tilted to the changes which practically ensure their social mobility. It might be due to the acceptance of new traits, new rules and procedures that dominated among the so called higher caste people.

The data collected for this research work were through fieldwork method. The fieldwork was conducted in the six villages of Eastern Midnapore between January, 1989 and February, 1992. The selected villages are of two types : (i) three mono-caste and (ii) three multi caste. The villages are situated within a radius of 40 k.m. from Tamluk sub-divisional town. These villages have been selected on purpose with a view to gather the variegated response of the Scheduled Castes communities and the process of social change and changing scenario of traditional vis- a-vis statutory councils. Table 1 depicts the list of villages under study.

Table : 1

List of Villages under Study

Sl. No	Name of the village hamlet	Mouza	Police Station	Jl. No.	Area of Village	Studied communities in acres
1.	Gopalpur	Gopalpur	Sutahata	30	252.56	Paundra Kshatriya
2.	Ataphala	Ataphala	Sutahata	112	159.72	Namasudra
3. a)	Rajnagar	Rajnagar	Tamluk	160	71.13	Rajbanshi
b)	Rajnagar Baharjola	Rajnagar	Tamluk	161	155.01	Rajbanshi
4.	Joynagar	Joynagar	Durgachak	123	494.63	Namasudra Paundra Kshatriya
5.	Madhabpur	Madhabpur	Durgachak	111	132.42	Namasudra Paundra Kshatriya
6.	Bargoda	Bargoda	Nandakumar	6	538.15	Namasudra Rajbanshi

Source : Census of India 1981

The studied area of Rajnagar (JL No. 160) and Rajnagar BaharJala (JL No. 161) is shown as one and single unit for study. The reason behind selecting one mono-caste and one multi-caste village from each of the caste community, villages under study lies in the fact that the nature of social control, vis-a-vis mechanism of caste control, is expected to vary in mono-caste mosaic and pluri cultural multi-caste setting. The demographic aspects of the caste composition of each village have been collected through census survey. No stereotyped questionnaire were used at any stage of this field investigation. On the contrary, according to the availability of adult informants (the household heads or their representatives) of all the families in six villages were interviewed. Side by side, the anthropological technique of participant observation was followed whenever possible. The researcher participated in the daily life of the villagers and tried to attend their important events of festivals, ceremonies, conflicts etc. Beside the data collected through census in some case studies of individuals and events of disputes were recorded, which were of specific interest. The aspects covered were land holdings, litigation feuds and developmental work. Information through some secondary sources were also collected. These sources include village Hand Books, Panchayat Samity Records and Census Reports.

Data on the nature and functions of traditional and modern Panchayat system has been collected by case history method. For this purpose, three sets of informants have been selected to record their views in different periods of time viz., (i) Pre-Independence Period (up to 14th August, 1947), (ii) Post-Independence Period and pre Left Front Period (1947-1977). (iii) Left Front Period (1977-February,1992).

The set of informants has been categorized into three groups, viz., I) old persons in the age group of 60 years and above who have their experience about pre-Independence scenario that has provided the basis of information regarding the socio-political status of the contemporary people. ii) middle aged men with the age group of 40-60 years, who have their practical experience regarding the socio-political situation of the post-Independence era, through the slow changing processes. iii) Persons in the age group of 20-40 years who are practically very modern and who have the opportunity to see the varied types of changes operating in this country. The sets of informations have been verified and corroborated with the existing published materials.1040 families belonging to different communities have been closely studied. The sizes of the families are as follows : a) Small sized families having 3(three) or four members. b) Medium sized families, having 4-6 members, c) Large sized families having 7-9 members. d) Very large sized families having at least 10 members.

It appears from the investigation and study that Indian society is a tradition-bound, caste-ridden society and caste plays a decisive role in the management of village affairs through its governing body, which is most commonly known as caste Panchayat. Caste Panchayats regulate and control the behaviour of the members of a particular caste and maintains unity and solidarity among its members. The members of the caste Panchayat are generally selected from among the well to do and affluent persons of the locality. They by virtue of their economic position, wisdom and numerical strength are capable of taking charge of village administration and caste formalities in tune with the so-called higher section of the population. It was also obligatory to obey the verdict of the village Headman in particular and caste Panchayat in general. The socio-economic and political activities are vested in the hands of these bodies. In one sense they are regarded as the guardian of the village. But things have started changing.

Various social movements like *Arya Samaj Movements* started in

1875 at Bombay under the leadership of Swami Dayanand, *Bhakti Movement* of Mahaprabhu Sri Chaitanya Deva in early sixteenth century, *Ramkrishna movement,* Indian's struggle for *freedom movement* and subsequent *Quit India Movement* in 1942 under the leadership of Mahatma Gandhi. Post-Independence agrarian movements like *Bhoodan movements* led by Acharya Vinoba Bhave, *Tebhaga movement, Operation Barga, political movement,* like that of *Naxalite movement* and other *Communist movements* made an impact in the direction of making egalitarian social structure and awakening of class consciousness among the Backward Classes. Moreover, the statutory Panchatati-Raj system with universal adult franchaise and various constitutional measures and legislative enactments for the safeguards of the Backward Classes introduced during the post-Independence era, specifically during left front era, have dealt a serious blow to the caste hierarchy and formed an egalitarian and democratic base of society. The Scheduled Castes and Backward Communities *Sanskritised* some aspects of their style of life and thus tried to improve their ritual status. They were numerically significant and politically ambitious. They have been able to compete for positions of power. They are now being represented in different stages of administrative machinery. Thus the hierarchically arranged caste system of traditional society and its consequent caste organisations have gradually been transformed into class conscious village organization through statutory Panchayat. There is no doubt about the fact that the Panchayati Raj Institutions have encouraged the development of self-reliance, initiative and social sense of security by placing the ultimate responsibility of self-governance on the citizens themselves. It makes authority a trust and ensures equal consideration for all. This picture was quite absent in the traditional caste ridden society which was dominated by the economically and socially affluent persons of society. It is quite clear from this study that caste Panchayat or councils began to wane and a democratic outlook and strong political ambience became stronger during the Left Front Ministry regime. Thus we find that caste rigidity is becoming weaker day by day and a new democratic or rather political affiliation is gaining momentum. Above all, new technology, new employment opportunities and spread of education are on the strides to weaken the cancer of casteism. The authority and jurisdiction of caste Panchayats are thereby being curtailed. Democratic bodies, political parties and voluntary organizations are increasingly taking the place of traditional caste Panchayats as agencies of local authority structure.

Pattern and Continuity of Rural Administration in West Bengal

Shibnath Banerjee

The present work entiled *Pattern and Continuity of Rural Administration in West Bengal (with special reference to some Districts)* is a theoretical-cum-empirical study. The writer believes that theory and practice are mutually helpful towards the achievement of truth– a real scientific vision. Fieldwork is a basis of the practical approach to the theoretical conception. The wide perception in the practical field helps to enlighten the theoretical conception. The writer relied not only upon available literature but also upon his personal field experience in his study of rural administration in West Bengal. The writer is deeply conscious of the fact that the field is the centre of his work. To no other source he is more indebted than to those of the field- friends who gave him honest and correct information.

II

While considering the content of the thesis and the methodology followed in its preparation, the writer opines that the Panchayeti Raj institution that has been introduced in West Bengal is in accordance with the principle of democratic decentralization advocated by the framers of independent India. Democracy, to them, implies self-rule; and self-rule, in practice, means the participation of the mass of the people in the administration of the country. But this is well-nigh impossible unless the local-governing institutions are democratized. For a national or even a provincial government elected at periodical intervals fails to inculcate among the people a sense of belonging to the administrative set-up of the country. The duties of the electorate in modern representative government generally end after the choice of their representatives. Neither can they share in the day-to day administration of their country nor can they hold the representatives responsible to them always. That is why John Stuart Mill (1927:365) in his plea for local self-government observes: "Reading newspapers, and perhaps writing to them, public meetings, and solicitations of different sorts addressed to the political authorities, are the extent of the participation of the private citizens in general politics, during one parliamentary election and another". In other words, there is a big gap between the electorate and the government in modern democracy. And this gap can be filled up if there is a local self-government which will act as a link between the democratic government and the people at large. The introduction of the local self-government gives the people the opportunity of conducting their local affairs and of having a real taste of self-government.

Thus the real meaning of self-government is that it must not be confined merely to the national or state level but should be extended to the district and village levels. It would be a half-way journey towards self-rule if a democratic government ceases to operate beyond the national or state level. Carl G Taylor and others who have made a fervent plea for the democratization of local-governing institutions in India quoted the First Five Year Plan to support their contention (1966:331): "The constitution has provided for democratic institutions at the Centre and in the States, but so long as local self-governing institutions are not conceived as parts of the same organic constitutional and administrative framework, the structure of democratic government will remain incomplete". It is this thought that has inspired the framers of Independent India to advocate for the establishment of the Panchayat system which is deemed to give the rural folk the chance of having a share in the local administration. Accordingly, various laws and resolutions were passed for the introduction of the Panchayat system in different parts of India.

But mere laws and resolutions are not enough. Rather they are worse than useless as they may lead the people to believe that they are really living in democracy while, in fact, they are not. Since direct democracy is not possible today so indirect or representative democracy is to be accepted. And the main tenet of indirect democracy is free choice, i.e., choice of the representatives on his or her merit. This is as true of national or state administration as it is of the local administration. It should be remembered that this study was made in the sixties of the last century and it was found from empirical investigations that free choice, the core of democracy, was virtually non-existent in the Panchayati administration of the then West Bengal. The writer is of the opinion that the political structure of a country does not stand by itself. It is closely interwoven with socio-economic conditions of the village people.

The writer observed during interviews that, among the socio-economic factors influencing rural life, the consideration of caste seems to be the uppermost in the minds of village people in choosing their representatives for the Panchayat. A Kayastha (scribe) or a Brahmin (priest) would like to vote for Kayastha or a Brahmin candidate in preference to the candidates belonging to other castes in spite of the fact that the latter are regarded as more efficient than the former. Generally it is found that the candidates belonging to the numerically dominant caste have come out successful in the Panchayat election. The question that may be asked here is: what is meant by caste dominance? Prof Srinivas (1966:10) observes: "For a caste to be dominant, it should own a sizable amount of the arable land locally available, have strength of numbers, and occupy a high place in the local hierarchy". Thus a caste to be dominant may be either large in number or exercise economic power by virtue of the large amount of property at its disposal. Again it may acquire such dominance because it wields political power or inherits a literary tradition. But with the coming of franchise, numerical strength has become more important than the other factors of caste dominance. Sometimes, of course, numerical strength, good economic condition and traditional ritualistic status combine together to enable a particular caste to dominate in village politics.

Again for the purpose of sociological analysis, a distinction is to be made between caste at the political level and caste at the social and ritual level. From the social and ritualistic point of view, caste is an endogamous group differentiating itself from similar other groups from the standpoint of endogamy. From the political point of view, on the other hand, such endogamy is found to be relaxed and different castes enter into alliance with each other to form bigger entities for winning the Panchayat election against their rival caste-groups. And by caste dominance, the writer has meant the dominance not only of a particular caste but also of the caste-groups. In short, the writer endeavoured to show that in elections to the local self-governing bodies in the villages of West Bengal, caste considerations are very important and usually the leaders of the locally dominant castes are elected to the Panchayats. Though the political parties were not allowed to contest in the Panchayat election with party symbols, yet they did penetrate into the village politics by exploiting this caste sentiment of the people.

The same picture emerges in the case of the Panchayat peopled by two different major communities, namely, the Hindus and the Muslims. Thus in those wards of the Gram Sabha or in the Gram Sabha itself where the Muslims are numerically dominant they were found to monopolise the seats of the Panchayat. Similar is the situation in the case of the Hindus dominating a particular Gram Sabha or in its different wards. Again where the Hindus and the Muslims were proportionately equal, they shared the seats of the Panchayat among themselves equally. From all these evidences, the writer tried to develop his thesis that the consideration of caste or community obscures the free choice of the voters in the election of their rural self-governing institution.

It would, however, be a gross oversimplification to state that village politics can be explained entirely by reference to caste or community. The consideration of caste or community is, indeed, a very important factor, but not the only factor to be taken into account in the analysis of the structure of the village Panchayat. Economic condition is another important determinant of the voting behaviour of the people. The villages of West Bengal, nay the whole of India, are agricultural and poverty-stricken. As the villagers are extremely poor, it is impossible for them to vote without any fear or favour. Threats of reprisals and of the withdrawal of money-lending compel the village folks to vote for the economically influential men of the village. Moreover, the writer observed that the agricultural base of the village society provides for less social mobility and, as such, the village people still cling to their old standards of value-judgement, like attachment to caste or community.

Literacy, according to the writer, is the third important factor influencing the voting behaviour of the people. The ordinary villagers plunged in illiteracy lack the power to discern talent, to comprehend the nature of the work the Panchayat is called upon to do. Even a casual glance at the election of the then Panchayat would lead one to conclude that the people were more interested in just taking part in an election than in seeing whether the candidate had been suited to the task he was called upon to perform. Not only this, in most cases, a large percentage of voters would not turn up at the polling booth for voting. In justification of his observation, the writer quoted the Seventh Evaluation Report on Community Development which remarked that in many cases there was a virtual lack of interest in the election of the Panchayat members. The writer is of the opinion that the introduction of the adult franchise will be a mockery unless the people have the basic minimum education required for its effective exercise. This is as true of the election to the Panchayat as it is of the election of the Parliament or the State Legislature. The writer is aware that literacy is not a full-proof test of the political maturity of the people, but all the same a democracy afflicted by illiteracy and entrenched in an environment of casteism and communalism is a weakness in itself. Summing up, the writer concluded that illiteracy is also responsible for failing to give the people the proper yardstick of choosing their representatives and thus compelling them to fall back upon caste or communal representation.

The writer did not fail to mention that the political structure of a country which is deeply entrenched in its social order is not an overnight growth. It bears the legacy of the past. With this idea in mind, the writer at the outset of his thesis discussed how the rural bodies at the base level were caste-ridden and non-democratically (i.e., hereditarily) formed in the pre-independence period and how it had left its impact on the rural bodies of West Bengal in the post-independence period at the initial stage.

III

Going beyond the ken of the discussion contained in his thesis, the writer likes to give a rider that the Panchayeti Raj bodies of West Bengal, nay of India as a whole, have traversed a long way towards democratization, both in structure and function. But have they been able to ensure free choice of the electorates and their spontaneous participation in the deliberations?

True, the Gram Samsad, the lowest rung of the Panchayeti Raj bodies, has been created for the poorest of the poor and the lowest of the low to give vent to their opinion without any fear or favour. The writer has supervised four scholars who worked on Panchayat and almost all of their findings confirm that though a democratic penumbra is set up for the democratic functioning of the Panchayats, the common people are still not very close to the Panchayats. They have not yet forsaken their age-old values. The caste feeling is on the wane, but it has not died down completely. Curiously enough, the political parties who have been given the legally recognised role for the democratic functioning of the Panchayats are not very much active in replacing this age-old mentality of the rural folks. Perhaps they are afraid of disturbing the balance of rural power politics.

The methodology followed in the preparation of this thesis was the case history method. The writer consulted different historical records relating to the pattern of rural administration of Bengal from the Hindu period down to the British days and carried out empirical investigations of the present administrative set-up of rural West Bengal in order to find out continuity, if any, between the past and the present. In the selection of the Gram Sabhas, the writer consulted the District Census Handbook and finally, with the help of random sampling method, picked up only those villages where there was a constellation of several castes and communities in order to make his study broadly representative in character. Investigations were done on the basis of a questionnaire, both structured and unstructured. In all, the writer tried utmost to make his study full-proof, though he is fully conscious that this is well-nigh impossible.

References

Mill, J. S. **1927** ***Representative Government,*** **Oxford.**

Taylor, C. G. **1966** **et. al. *India's Roots of Democracy,* London.**

Srnivas, M. N. **1962** ***Caste in Modern India and Other Essays,*** **Bombay.**

Section IV

Development Action and Applied Anthropology

Introduction

Sachchidananda

The Scheduled Tribes constitute about 8% of the population in India. They are largely concentrated in middle India right from Gujrat to Tripura. In this area they live interspersed with non-tribal people. In the north-east, however, they constitute the bulk of the population. The Indian Constitution makes a distinction between tribals living in middle India with sprinklings in the Cis-Himalyan region and in the south and those living in the north-east by making separate provisions for their administration as well as development action. In the former area they constitute between1% to 40% of the population of different States. They are administered under the Fifth Schedule. The other area constituting the tribal majority States have been put under the Sixth Schedule.

In the colonial period there were three different approaches to the tribal problem. The first was the policy of isolation or 'leave them alone'. It is not that there were no interventions in tribal affairs by the colonial administration. From time to time there was unrest and even violent rebellions in different areas. After they were crushed with a heavy hand, some reforms in the administrative system in regard to land, forest usurious practices, etc, were taken up, but these were no more than a humanitarian exercise. The spirit of national reconstruction was absent. The second approach was that speedy steps should be taken for their assimilation into the dominant Hindu society since the tribals were only backward Hindus who had been pushed into the hills and forest by the pressure of non-tribal peasantry. The third approach was that of integration of the tribal population with the regional society at political, economic and social levels. This would not eclipse their identity while at the same time giving them full opportunities for development. However, this is a long drawn out process.

After independence it was realized that the isolationist policy was neither possible nor desirable. As citizens of a free country, the doors of development and modernization could not be closed for the tribals. The Indian constitution broadly aimed at protecting them from exploitation and activating effective steps for their socio-economic and educational progress. To speed up this process protective discrimination was provided for them through reservations in legislature, educational institutions and in government services.

Pandit Jawaharlal Nehru the first Prime Minster of India was deeply impressed by the views of Dr.Verrier Elwin and initiated the five point approach to tribal development through what is popularly known as the 'Tribal Panchsheel'. The five points of this policy were as follow:

1. The tribal should be allowed to develop in their own genius.
2. Tribal rights in land and forest should be protected.
3. Development as far as possible should be channelised through their own institutions by promoting local leadership.
4. Tribal areas should not be overwhelmed by developmental schemes. In fact government should 'hasten slowly'.
5. The results achieved should not judged merely by statistics of expenditure but by the quality of human character evolved.

Although national leaders espoused this policy and approach its implementation was half hearted and its spirit was lost. The bureaucracy administering the tribal areas did not make a distinction between tribals and others. In fact the review of the functioning of the Special Multi-purpose Tribal Blocks in 1959 revealed the virtual absence of the tribal touch.

To make amend for this, when the Fifth Plan was on the anvil the expert committee headed by S.C. Dube to formulate new strategy for tribal development, recommended that social and economic development of the tribal people should be through time bound area development programmes suiting the genius of the people, progressive elimination of all forces of exploitation ensuring a move towards the goal of equality and justice. The focus was on integrated approach of tribal development with a view to improve the quality of life of the people. This was to be conceived through the Tribal Sub-plan. Compact areas where the percentage of tribal population is 50% or more were brought under the Tribal Sub-plan. As the basic unit of planning and execution, integrated tribal development blocks were created to cover the entire Sub-plan area. Resources for the sub-plan were pooled together by earmarking an amount from divisible State Plan outlay, special central assistance from the Home Ministry, grants from the central ministries and institutional finance. However, it was realized that the tribal Sub-plan idea had some inherent shortcomings with the result that the expected outcomes were not forthcoming.

By the end of eighties of the last century it was realized that economic betterment may be part of overall development process but it could not be treated as a sufficient condition for overall tribal development. Belshaw holds that development is an organized activity aimed at satisfying certain basic needs and to orient the tribals mentally to adopt new skills, attitude and lifestyle. This is necessary for building up the inner strength with appropriate social and cultural infrastructure to meet the challenges of fast changing times. In other words, development is a multi dimensional process for interrogated upgrading of social cultural, economic and human conditions of the people necessary for a balanced growth of society. The disquiet visible in certain tribal areas reveals the big psychological gap between tribals and non-tribals implementing development schemes.

In the implementation of planned change through development action either by government of voluntary agency it is necessary to understand the crucial role of the development personnel. In many areas it was discovered that they lacked faith in the programme and were half hearted to implement them. The block staff at the lower level is bogged down under heavy paper work, attending meetings, preparing statistics, receiving visitors and auditors. All these leave little time to devote to implementation of the programme and it is not able to live up to its role as a catalyst agent for change. At the level of implementation, most development programmes became exercises in execution of tasks. Development staff utilize people for achieving the targets only and their participation on development effort has remained generally a slogan. In many mixed areas it was seen that the beneficiaries of development schemes were the non-tribals who succeeded in monopolizing the fruits of development. It was also realized that by and large the cultural values, practice and habits of the tribals were not taken into account.

While providing for stoppage of exploitation of the tribals by non-tribal landholders and moneylenders, the development personnel did not take into the account the exploitation from within. It was discovered that members of certain primitive tribes were subject to exploitation by more advanced tribes, such as Birhor by the Oraon and Paharia by the Santal. They were exploited by their own headman who grabbed most of the development schemes. A class of tribal middle-men emerged ostensibly to help the ignorant tribals get benefit from government schemes. These people got a cut from the grant of subsidy meet the tribals in general.

During this period, many large scale developmental activities took place in tribal areas through the putting up of large dams, mining activities and industrial establishment. This led to displacement of tribals from their hearth and home entailing large scale misery. The displaced population was relocated in areas with which the people were not acquainted. It was a great psychological shock. The compensation was swindled by cheats and the tribal was left resourceless and friendless. These development induced projects forced the tribals to sacrifice their interest for the good of the nation as a whole. In most of these cases development led to destitution.

Besides development action through government agencies many voluntary organization and some social activists took up the task of tribal development in diverse ways. However, their zeal and interest was not matched by a deep knowledge of the tribal mores and ethos. They were also not able to assess the actual needs of the tribals in different areas and tried their own strategies for the improvement of their quality of life. In most of their efforts they were not able elicit the co-operation and participation of the tribals in developmental work.

In 1993 through the 73rd amendment in the Constitution it was decided to take democracy to the grass roots by giving power to the people through the Panchayats. An elaborated model was set up for the introduction of Panchayati Raj at three level, viz., Gram Panchayats, Panchayat Samitis and District Panchayats. For the first time, the Panchayats were made part of the Constitution of the country and powers were given to the people to act through the Panchayat bodies as measure for self rule. After some time it was realized that the Acts passed by the State legislatures constituting the panchayats and their functioning did not meet the requirements and aspiration of the local people in tribal areas and needed some amendments so that they can produce better results and allow greater freedom to the tribals to look after their local affairs and to speed up development in their own areas. In pursuance of this objective a Committee was appointed under the Chairmanship of Shri D.S. Bhuria, M.P. ,in June 1994 to examine all related issues and make recommendation on the salient features of law on extending the provisions of 73rd amendment in Scheduled Areas. The Committee submitted its report in January 1995 in which important recommendations were made. It was on the basis of these recommendation that the Parliament passed the Extension of Panchayat Act in Scheduled Areas in 1996. The rational for extending is explained in Part IX of the Constitution.

(i) These were to provide self rule for the tribal population.
(ii) Village governance with grass root participation of tribal people.

(iii) Suitable administrative frame work with traditional management practices.
(iv) To safeguard and preserve tradition and custom of tribals.

The PESA Act enjoins that any legislation on Panchayat for tribal areas shall be in consonance with customary law, social and religious practices and traditional management practices of community resources. Under this Act, village is defined as a group of habitations forming a community managing its own affairs according to tradition and custom.

The Act lays stress on the establishment of Gram Sabha. The aim is to safeguard tradition, customs, identity, community resources and settling disputes in the customary mode. The Gram Sabha approved plans, programmes and projects for social and economic development. It has to identify the beneficiaries and furnish utilization certificate for the funds used.The acquisition of land for development projects or rehabilitation of displaced persons has to be decided either by the Gram Sabha or at the Panchayat level. Planning and management of minor water bodies and the license for water use, lease for minor minerals has to be made on the recommendation of the Gram Sabha. It has to function as an institution of self government. Mandatory power has to be given to Gram Sabha. The Gram Sabha has to regulate or restrict the sale and consumption of liquor act as the owner of minor forest produce, prevent alienation of land, manage village market, control money lending and exercise control over local plan and resources including Tribal Sub-plans.

Reservation of seats in every tier of Panchayati Raj has been provided for the Scheduled Tribes to the extent of half the number of seats. Reservation has also been made for other communities in proportion to their population. The post of chairperson is reserved for ST. It has to be ensured that higher level Panchayats do not assume power or exercise authority of lower level Panchayats or Gram Sabhas.

There are several shortcomings in the Act such as it does not cover all tribal population. The expected role or the linkage with the Tribal Advisory Council has not been defined. Customary laws and social and religious practices of most tribal communities have not been codified. Defining village as a habitation of a community is difficult. The extended act impinges on various existing laws related to tribal governance. The spirit of PESA is to ensure participatory democracy as the basic unit of governance–Gram Sabha, but the State acts have empowered the Panchayats and not the Gram Sabha. The level of awareness of tribal people particularly elected members and officials about Panchayats is not up to the mark. It is therefore necessary that a comprehensive traning programme should be drawn for elected Panchayat representatives, officials and for awareness and capacity building of people in the Schedule V areas.

Soon after independence the government established one after the other Tribal Research Institutes in those States where tribals were found in large pockets. These institutes were meant to conduct researches in applied anthropology. An effort was made to utilize anthropological insights to facilitate tribal welfate activities. The research work was focused on problems of land and forest, health, education and in economic activities, such as agriculture, animal husbandry, cottage and household industry and cooperation. This knowledge could be used by the planners and administrators in the formulation of schemes as well as in their implementation. The research staff was also involved in the evaluation of welfare schemes, such as forest labour cooperative societies, Ashram schools, educational activities, etc. In many institutes, training programmes for developmental workers were also organized. Short course were devised for school teachers, Welfare Inspectors and even for Police Officers to orient them in tribal culture. However, the vast data put at the disposal of State governments was not much used and their research output and books adorned the shelves in libraries and educational institutions. The institutes were not entirely free in the choice of the topic of research. These were either dictated by the Welfare Department at the State level or the research projects had to be approved by the government. The result was that by the end of the century the tribal research institutes have lost their lusture and were existing only by inertia.

Besides the research done at the Tribal Research Institute a number of scholars produced doctoral theses on different aspects of Applied Anthropology. Some of these were conducted under the guidance of Professor P.K. Bhowmick. A short account of five such studies which have been included in this section, is given below.

II

Dr. Sudhir Kumar Biswas conducted a study of the ecology and cultural perspective of Garhwal region on Uttar Pradesh. Its thrust was on the exploration of development strategies pursued in that region. The strategies were examined from the perspective of beneficiaries. The study begins with a historical review of development work in the Garhwal Himalyas. The author holds that the planners failed to appreciate the informal constraints in the development process. The study attempted to identify the inadequacies in development design. Since development anthropology is directly related to the study of social change and culture contacts, anthropologists believed that the primary requisite of socio-economic development of any area should be an appropriate climate in which the will to develop springs from the minds and hearts of the people and it is not impassed from outside. In Garhwal the administrators blamed the people for the lack in initiative while the people held the Government responsible for the low pace of development. The perception of the problem of the hill men and women were not taken into account and as such the active participation of the people was not available.

At the end of the study, the author makes a number of suggestions to remedy the situation. He makes a strong plea for region specific development and emphasizes the micro approach, so that the maximum number of people among the poorest of the poor could be raised about the poverty line. He advocated continuous growth of wealth with an effective redistribution mechanism. He has also recommended full integration of backward, forward and horizontal linkages for the framers. According to the author, the biggest draw-back in the implementation of hill development is the absence of regular evaluation and monitoring of the field activities. He also makes suggestion for new action schemes including soil conservation, horticulture, animal husbandry, tourism, integrated watershed management and the development of alternative source of energy. The role of hill women in the productive economic system is to be fully recognized and their participation in the development process should be facilitated. Effort should be made to promote participation of the people. Serious effort should be made to create the climate for change.

Dr. D. R. Pratap is mainly concerned with the structural functional aspects of changing plan strategies with a historical perspective in respect of the tribal areas of the Adilabad district. The study begins with a description of the tribal situation prevailing in the area in the early forties of the last century when interventions were made for the welfare of tribes and backward classes by Professor Hamiendrof who was at that time the tribal Advisor to the Nizam Government. He has discussed the strategies of the protective cover provided and its implementation. Later he compares the developmental strategies in the pre-independence and post-independence period. He also brings out the socio-cultural constraints in the various development strategies.

Towards the end of this study he has tried to give a development model for the tribal areas in the Adilabad district.

He has divided the planning exercise in three phases. The first phase he calls the 'primary activity' includes the area group identification for preparing a resource inventory. After this data have to be collected on lifestyle and other indicators of economic development. This phase also includes identification of cultural barriers and promoters of the development process.

The secondary planning activity is an analysis of prevailing development situation and formulation of micro strategies on the basis of resource endowment, cultural and economic condition and mobilization of finance. The inter-sectoral linkages have also to be identified and administrative structure for the implementation of programme should be devised. The next stage is the promotion of suitable tribal leadership to ensure people's participation. In this stage necessary infrastructure for the development programme has to be built up. Rural industrialization based largely on forest and mineral resources will go a long way in reducing the dependence of people on outside agencies. Spread of education will facilitate the development process. In the fifth and last stage, the self generating state of the plan will be attained through community resource mobilization, programme formulation and execution. The politico-regional implication of the traditional power structure and the social structure of the Gond region demonstrate the need for keeping in view socio-power factor in delineating the centres of development.

Dr. V. Lalitha studied the lifestyle of Yerukala, a criminal tribe in Andhra Pradesh and suggests different strategies of change. The community acquired its criminal character on account of economic and territorial displacement. Their lack of assets and the general famine conditions of the Madras presidency compelled them to take up criminal activities for subsistence.

The Yerukala were originally a nomadic community in the districts of Gountur, Kurnool, Kudapa, Anantpur and Nellore in Andhra Pradesh. They were made to spy over the activities of the enemies of the then rulers. When the British occupied the territory, these people lost their former occupation. Some of them settled down in agriculture, or take up trade such as rope carpet and basket making. Some of them became village watchman. The rest took to crime for their livelihood. They committed highway robberies and theft in nearby villages. Lack of education, land skills condemned them to a life below the poverty line.

The study describes their social structure, educational facilities and the nomadic habits of their ancestors to have an insight into their present living condition. An effort was also made to find out their condition in the new settlement. The study also describes the modus operendl of their crime. Case histories were collected with the help of an interview schedule. After the repeal of the Criminal Tribe Act, some of these ex-criminal tribes settlement were converted into free colonies and its inhabitants took up different jobs in neighboring areas. The author feels that the aim of reforming them by keeping them in separate settlements failed. The government concentrated more on the prevention of crime than on reformation of criminals. Sometimes innocent people were also regarded as criminals because of living in the criminal settlement. The stigma of criminality is still sticking to them, some of them are still without jobs. They are keen to have land patta conferring ownership right, irrigation facilities and cottage industries. It has been found that most of the people are easy going and not a hard working lot so they need some employment which will given them immediate gains.

Inspite of development activities undertaken by government an atmosphere of discontent prevails in these settlement colonies. Houses have been constructed for them but the young men, both educated and uneducated, want jobs. The unemployed youth engage in anti-social activities, such as pick pocketing, snatching and similar activities which gives them an easy income. It is necessary to put some small scale industries near the settlements. The reformatory measures should not be stopped and should be carried on. They are also put into difficulty due to the stigma of criminality and unless this is wiped they do not wish to come out of their shells to prove their integrity.

Dr. M. V. Krishna Rao made a study of social development and maladjustment in some areas of Andhra Pradesh. He has also described the situation of maladjustment among the tribes of State at various point of time and has tried to analyses the causes of such mal-adjustment. He has also tried to assess the direction of social development among various tribal groups and to identify the factors hindering the diffusion of innovations. He has brought out the socio-cultural implication of development and suggested remedial action for the removal of the bottle neck so that tribal unrest is contained.

The study area covers the entire territory from Adilabad district to Srikakulam district. This area is divided into seven regions based on economic and cultural homogeneity of the tribes in that area. The tribes taken up for the the study are the Sabar, the Valimiki, the Koya, the KondaReddy, the Gond, the Kolam, the Chenchu, etc. The chronological sequence of maladjustment followed by the enactment of protective measures and introduction of development programmes spread over the period of 200 years has also been discussed with special reference to Andhra Pradesh. Tribal unrest in the region has been viewed as a manifestation of tribal maladjustment. The most important feature of this phenomenon has been the loss of hold on land and forest exploitation by greedy money lenders and deceitful merchants, erosion of traditional means of livelihood in the wake of private and government managed hydro projects based on local water forest and mineral resources. The author holds that the government was honest and sincere in planning the development programmes. However, with the progress of implementation process non-tribals started manipulative polices with the connivance or tacit approval of the local tribal or non-tribal leaders who concerned the benefits for themselves and denying the tribal beneficiaries his due share. In course of time, the government or the establishment starts playing to the tune of powerful non-tribal vested interests. All these resulted in distrust and suspicion by the tribals of the real intentions of the government.

The author differentiates between the nature of tribal movements of pre-independence period and post independence period. While the former was the product of the evil mechanisms of the local feudal landlords and outside exploiters supported by the then colonial administration, in the latter case, the same elements of exploitation operated but with active connivance of the establishment whose declared objective is to dispense social justice to the weaker section of the population. They rose against the colonial rule whose sole aim was to drain out the vital resources of the country to the detriment of the local population. In the latter case, the unrest was caused by the attitude of the deceptive establishment which says one thing and practices just the opposite. It is therefore, necessary to reorient the administration, so that it implements the development schemes with a human face only then the maladjustment can be removed and social justice will prevail.

Dr. Dibakar Basak has made a comprehensive study of the constraints in the development of Scheduled Castes in Uttar Pradesh in an anthropological perspective. He has identified major difficulties in the implementation of Special Component Plan. The allotment of funds and physical targets at the state level appeared to be notional as the disaggregation of the targets was not effectively carried out. At the district level there was no clear picture of what was to be done under the Special Component Plan. The targets were so ambitious that they could not be achieved. The number of programmes in the Special Component Plan was nearly 188. The difficulties in the implementation in the programme lies in the nature of administrative mechanism at the organizational level and of the co-ordination. The selection of Scheduled Caste families under various trade and small business was not done on the basis of choice, capacity and availability of raw materials. The extent of assistance made available to Scheduled Caste beneficiaries was quite inadequate and the input did not result in generating income to take these families above the poverty line. The Harijan Kalyan Development Officer posted in the district for the implementation of the programme was not given adequate administrative and financial powers. Back-up services such as link with various programmes like marketing etc., were lacking. Proper training was not given to the staff for implementing the programme.

The allotment of ceiling surplus land to S C person was not implemented in the right spirit. The S C were given no priority in the allotment of land although the guidelines provided that 50% of such surplus land should be allotted to landless S C persons. The size of the holding allotted to beneficiaries was uneconomic. It was not cultivable. The problems in proper utilization of land were lack of irrigation facility and finance difficulty of land leveling, poor quality of soil and lack of skills.

In the programme of rehabilitation of S C bonded labours, there is no provision of financial help, food, etc., immediately after the release of a person from bondage. The financial assistance of Rs. 4000.00 was found to be inadequate for the rehabilitation of the released bonded labourer. Schemes were distributed to the beneficiaries without their choice or capacity for performing a particular activity. On account of this, the rehabilitation programme was more or less a failure. No attempts were made to integrate the programme with other poverty alleviation programme. The administration failed to keep a watch on bonded labourers resulting in many beneficiaries going back to bondage.

Provision was made to give incentive to the S C students at the pre-matric stage. The Programme did not cover large number of students at the elementary level. Many students were denied the facilities of mid-day meals, uniform and text book grants. The rate of scholarship were also inadequate. Malpractices were also discovered in the disbursement of scholarship. There was inordinate dealy in reaching scholarship to the students. The time taken was sometime six to eight months. The monitoring of the entire programme was poor.

There is provision for reservation of services for Scheduled Castes. The representation of Scheduled Caste in services was not found upto the mark. The shortfall was quite high in Group A and B posts. Only in Group D the percentage of reservation was satisfactory. Due care was not taken in maintaining proper rosters and at times wrong model rosters were followed resulting in maladjustment of vacancies received for SC. Reserved vacancies were allowed to lapse on the pretext of non-availability of Schedule Caste candidates.

The U.P. Government has introduced certain precautionary, preventive and punitive measures for victims of atrocities. The present system of collection of records is weak. The investigation reports of the police was sketchy. The police failed to provide adequate protection to SC victims with the result that they fail to present their case in the Court. The high rate of acquittals even in serious cases calls for framing suitable measures for booking the offenders. The delay in the disposal of cases undermines the confidence of SC in the judiciary. It helps the accused to get bail and intimating the prosecution witnesses. The police deals with atrocity cases just as a breach of law. The various socio-economic maladies responsible for the atrocities are not taken into account.

Besides the government, many voluntary agencies are working for the development of Scheduled Castes. Most of this programmes relate to education. All the programmes are being conducted by field workers who lack professional commitment. The continuity of the personnel could not be ensured due to poor salary and other facilities. Community participation in various programmes was extremely poor.

The author makes a plea for the development programmes to be composite and integrated. All the linkages from plan formulation to delivery should be taken into active consideration. Efforts must be made for people's participation. This can only be done when the local programmes are drawn up by the people themselves. Monitoring, follow up and evaluation is extremely important. Due assistance may be given to efficient voluntary agencies by assuring the flow of funds and by building up their capacity for development action in their areas.

Social Development and Maladjustment : A Case Study in the Tribal Areas of Andhra Pradesh

M. V. Krishna Rao

The introduction of technological change in tribal societies, as part of the national strategy of development through directed change, is considered as a symbol of hope for tribal people in their struggle for modernization. Many tribal societies, for centuries, have lived close to hunger, chronic illness and perpetual ignorance. It is to fight these three fears that the dynamics of systematic development has been set in motion to bring hope in place of fear, prosperity in place of poverty and knowledge in place of ignorance. But past experience shows that this prosperity and knowledge are confined to a small section of the group due to uneven percolation of development effort leaving a large section of tribal society unevenly developed. But the expected development, though inadequate, gave taste of what it could actually provide. Consequently hopes soared high and people's needs multiplied without a corresponding step up in development effort. This gap between rising aspirations and real benefit acquired by the tribal resulted in disillusionment of the tribal with the development institutions and the consequent maladjustment. This situation of social maladjustment or social disorganisation is amply illustrated by surfacing the discontent, unrest and constant occurrence of violent incidents in tribal societies.

The introduction of innovative technologies in tribal societies is intended to make them active partners in the modernisation process sweeping through the country so as to integrate them as equal partners in the larger society. But the dynamics of development not only set in motion growth impulses but also gave rise to situations of social maladjustment as exemplified by the persistent unrest for the last two decades or more.

Social maladjustment is the product of accumulated social problems, and it occurs in a dynamic social situation. The causative factors of social change can be classified into biological, physical, psychological, technological and cultural as proposed by different social scientists.

The tribal societies in India especially those in Andhra Pradesh provide many situations of social maladjustment in the wake of development. The innumerable programmes of tribal welfare introduced during the various plan periods have unleashed a series of reactions which are both positive and negative in their impact. While the positive impact gave rise to sustained growth, the negative one resulted in maladjustment and the consequent disharmony as expressed in group imbalance, Naxalism, minor uprisings or other disruptive activities against the established system. The Tribal uprising of 1968-70 in the tribal areas of Srikakulam district, the persistent erruption of violence from time to time in the tribal areas of Adilabad, Karimnagar, Warangal, Khammam, East and West Godavari, Visakhapatnam and Vijayanagaram districts i.e., throughout the length and breadth of tribal areas in Andhra Pradesh bear ample testimony to the prevailing situation of social maladjustment in tribal areas.

This situation of maladjustment may be the product of several factors. Two factors, viz., incapability of intended constitutional and legislative measures to provide necessary shield from exploitative forces from outside and the destructive impact of directed changes on the beneficiary society which resulted in interplaying of complex and contra indicative factors like disrupted customary life and loss of effective social control system, disturbed social structure, decreasing hold of magico-religious practices and uneven economic growth. The ultimate consequence is snow balling of these disturbing factors into extremist movements under varied brand names. Due to the development strategy and the consequent sequence of development programmes various situations of tension and turmoil emerged. The ultimate consequence was the emergence of a paradoxical situation of development in which both prosperity and parasitism coexist, resulting in the emergence of a backward section among traditionally advanced groups. It is the remnant 'no changer' section of both the advantaged and disadvantaged groups that suffered most as tradition became outmoded and modernity eluded them, the result being maladjustment.

II

The present work is mainly addressed to the task of studying the on going process of development and the prevailing situations of maladjustment among the tribal societies of Andhra Pradesh.

The main aim is to identify the situations of maladjustment among tribes of Andhra Pradesh as a consequence of erratic and uneven percolation of development effort and to suggest remedial measures.

The main objectives of the present study are as follows :

1. To present a brief history of Andhra Pradesh, its geomorphological canvas and its tribal profile.
2. To study the strategies and approaches to tribal development with a historical perspective.
3. To describe situations of maladjustment among the tribes of Andhra Pradesh at various points of time and undertake the causative factor analysis.
4. To assess the direction and extent of percolation of social development among various groups and identify factors hindering the diffusion of innovations.
5. To study the socio-cultural implications of development with special reference to tribal societies, and to suggest remedial measures for the removal of bottlenecked development and for solving the recurring phenomena of tribal unrest.

The main tool of the study is case study. Besides content analysis of various research studies, news paper reports, articles and journals are also taken into consideration to supplement case studies. The researcher's extensive field knowledge spread over a period of 20 years is synthesized to bring out the situations of maladjustment and shortcomings of the development programmes.

The study area extends from the tribal areas of Adilabad district to the tribal areas of Srikakulam district covering about six districts in between the two. The tribal area is divided into the following seven regions based on the economic and cultural homogeneity of the tribes inhabiting the areas.

1. The Savara-Jatapu areas of Srikakulam and Vijayanagaram districts.
2. The Bagats-Valmiki areas of Visakhapatnam district.
3. The Koya-Kondareddy areas of East and West Godavari districts.
4. Koya-Banjara areas of Khammam and Warangal districts.
5. The Gond-Kolam areas of Adilabad district
6. The Chenchu pocket of Mahabubnagar and Kurnool districts.
7. The Yerukalu-Yanadi region of Andhra and Rayalaseema districts.

The disturbances caused to physical, human and cultural ecology can only be understood in the background of development of infrastructure introduced in the tribal areas.

This includes the various types of educational institutions introduced, roads laid, electric lines constructed etc., along with varied and many new concepts and strategies which were also introduced. The introduction of three tier Panchayat Raj system i.e., Village panchayat, Panchayat Samiti/Mandal Praja Parishad at Block/Mandal level and Zilla Parishad/Zilla Praja Parishad at district level as instrumental for dynamics of development is discussed in detail to show its impact on traditional leadership pattern and existing social control institutions. To prevent dilution of political power, administrative authority and development effort various protection, concession and privileges have been provided in the Constitution of India and through special enactment of Central and State legislatures for the benefit of Scheduled Tribes.

The chronological sequence of maladjustment followed by the enactment of protective measures and introduction of development programmes spread over a period of 200 years have also been discussed with special reference to Andhra Pradesh in this study.

III

Though Andhra Pradesh is a pioneer in enacting the most full proof protective regulations especially the Land Transfer Regulation, still tribal land, the most important source of tribal livelihood continues to pass into the hands of non-tribals. It is therefore essential to create awareness amongst the tribals of the (a) consequences and (b) severity of situation so as to make them realize that mere enactment alone will not help the tribal to retain their lands. It is essential to implement the provisions of the protective regulations with political commitment coupled with executive action by way of posting honest and committed officers so as to ensure their effective implementation. Further it is necessary to devise methods to help needy tribals to raise the money required to meet their requirements because of which they sell their land.

The emerging statutory tribal leadership could neither provide the necessary progressive leadership nor project itself as the real champion of the tribal cause as evidenced by the hold of extremists on tribal masses especially the tribal youth. The statutory tribal leadership has become a carbon copy of the leadership of the larger state and national political parties.

It is neither feasible nor desirable to stop the on going political process as part of the larger national and state political systems. For this purpose, it is imperative to provide statutory status and powers to the traditional leaders of tribal councils in programme, planning and amending the existing Acts and Rules related to the governing District Mandal and Village Level statutory bodies.

Besides, both the elected and traditional leaders are to be given comprehensive training by evolving special courses and organising forums for discussion in order to impart them knowledge of relevant statutory laws, techniques of programme planning, execution and decision making activities.

All these indicate the need for a new pattern of development that ensures promotion of 'economic activities and lifestyles based on the concept of man in nature rather than man in confrontation with nature'. It is therefore essential to formulate forest and ecological rejuvenation programmes with the tribal man as the key factor for its success. His interest and participation can be ensured only when he becomes the real partner in the afforestation and allied strategies intended to arrest ecological decay.

But the cry to involve the local tribal in any afforestation activity is meeting with stiff resistance from Forest Department. A point in illustration of the antagonistic attitude of the Forest Department is clearly brought out in the case of implementation of a Government Order issued by Government in Forest Department itself. As per the G.O. each family of the landless labourers belonging to the weaker sections have to be assigned one or two hectares of degraded forest lands specially identified for the purpose of raising tree species as per the stipulation of Forest Department. The Forest Department is to provide all the needed inputs like seeds, saplings, fertilisers, manures, etc., to the tribal family. Subsistence wage is also to be paid to the tribal beneficiaries during the gestation period of the plantation. While the tribal enjoys the *usufruct right* only, the Forest Department will get royalty, as per a fixed rate with the starting of economic returns from the plantation. It is really a comprehensive and very realistic Government Order for involving the poor local tribal in such needed afforestation of the degraded forest areas.

But when the Secretary of Tribal Welfare called for a meeting with the highest Forest officials to work out the modalities of implementing the G.O, they pleaded their inability to implement the G.O. as there was no degraded forest land in Andhra Pradesh. They also said that even though the tribal was given only *usufruct* right i.e., Tree patta only without any right over land, the tribal would alienate his land to the non-tribal similar to his agricultural land. But the Principal Secretary, Forest Department took a more realistic view and said that when the G.O, is issued by Forest Department, the responsibility for its implementation squarely lies on the Forest department. It is therefore necessary to bring about a change in the attitude of the programmers. Unless this hostile executive mind is mended it is difficult to execute programmes for the benefit of both forest and tribal.

It is essential to take an integrated view of causes for the very low literacy rate of tribal and chalk out a programme that helps in rapid spread of adult literacy, formal education and technical and professional education.

Medium of instruction can be the state official language. However, from Primary level onwards the medium of instruction should be in regional language. With a little training, say for a period of 3 to 4 months, a semi educated tribal youth i.e., a dropout from 10th class or under graduate or even graduate level will be more preferable to teach in pre-primary and adult literacy classes with a little monetary incentive for teaching the latter.

Supervision and inspection should be more meaningful and purposeful rather than a routine matter. It should be useful for the realistic assessment of teaching capacity of the teacher and learning level of the taught besides suggesting corrective action for improving the quality of education.

Politicisation of the teacher associations which has been an on going process as part of larger union activities at the State level should be kept at the barest minimum and the teacher's unions should be made to realize that they have a major responsibility for the promotion of tribal literacy and education.

It is therefore imperative to protect tribal interests in land and forest besides promotion of education. Ultimately, it may be concluded that to contain maladjustment and promote tribal welfare, it is essential to protect him from outside exploitation, prevent ecological decay, and promote his educational advancement.

The history of tribal maladjustment in India spread over nearly 200 years manifesting itself as resistant movements or violent tribal uprising show a common repeated chain of movements, movement after movement, the latest being the Indervelli massacre and the aftermath of continued turbulence.

Over the years the various tribal movements have essentially been emanating from similar cause i.e. the loss of hold on vital life-sustaining forest produce and cultivable lands, exploitation by greedy money lenders and deceitful merchants, denudation and destruction of traditional means of livelihood in the wake of private and government organised hydro-electric, irrigation and industrial projects based on local water, forest and mineral resources etc.

But it must be admitted that while planning and at the beginning of implementing development programmes, Government has always been very honest and sincere. As the implementation process progressed, the non-tribals who are in sizeable numbers usually wake up to the reality and start manipulative politics with the connivance or tacit approval of the local statutory tribal or non-tribal leader with the avowed objective of garnering the benefits for themselves denying the tribal beneficiary his due share. Government or the establishment also starts playing second fiddle to the mechanism of the powerful non-tribal vested interests for obvious reasons. This resulted in distrust and suspicion by the tribal of the real intentions of the government.

Lastly, one vital difference is to be noticed between the tribal movements, (the manifestations of prevailing situations of maladjustment) of pre-independence period and post independence period, that is, while the former was due to evil machinations of local feudal landlords and outside exploiters aided and abetted by the then colonial establishment, in the latter case the same elements of exploitation operated but with the active connivance of there whose avowed objective is to dispense social justice to the weaker sections. The tribal rose against the colonial establishment whose sole aim was to drain out the vital resources of the country to the detriment of local population especially the tribal whereas in the latter case he has been rising against a deceptive establishment whose practice is to systematically violate what it preaches. The product of the problem is to positively motivate the existing establishment to make it practice what it preaches. Then only growing social justice becomes a reality and the recurrence of maladjustment ceases.

IV

Throughout the country the tribals are backward. Their socio-economic condition is poor. For the allround development of the society, after independence, special measures have been taken for their uplift. But in most of the cases, majority of the projects were failure. This is not the case only of the tribes of Andhra Pradesh, but majority of the states prove these findings. For this reason, the study relating to the nature and intensity of maladjustment is essential and needful. It will help to make a new strategy for social development of the tribal population. Different solutions of the problems of maladjustment should be devised, so that the tribal people will be benefited at last.

A Study in Development Anthropology in the Ecological and Cultural Perspective of Garhwal

Sudhir Kumar Biswas

With the dawn of independence a revolution of rising expectations overtook the people of our country. Therefore, it became the pious duty of our Government to launch a war on poverty, sickness, squalor and unemployment and to uplift the masses of the country from the nightmare of ignorance, low standard of living, low level of national income, inequality of opportunity and ensure social justice.

The goal of achieving these objectives was no less important than the political objective of independence of the country. This led our leaders to espouse a strategy of socio-economic development as embodied in the national planning. But owing to many factors adversely operating in the economy, the goal has been receeding too far. That the National Planning has not delivered the goods to the desired extent and much less in the hill region of Garhwal of the then U.P. is a fact difficult to be refuted. The Planning which we have been nourishing and unfolding with motherly care largely failed because of a lack of correct perspective and of a dispassionate appreciation of the perception of the people from below for their benefit. The need is to identify the areas of weakness resulting in faulty implementation of the planning process. It is here that the services of researchers in development Anthropology assume paramount importance.

The logic of the present work lies in the fact that having sojourned in the hill region of Garhwal for about three years, the present researcher has seen the sad spectacle of failure of planning from close quarters. He had a first hand information from the local populace about how they take various plans and policy measures which chiefly intend to ensure their welfare. On the basis of this knowledge the present researcher was encouraged to study the problems of planning in the Garhwal region in their correct perspective and tender, in all humility, suggestions that, if applied, may prove to be an effective therapeutic treatment of the whole malaise. Broadly speaking, the present study is a critique of the planning strategy as pursued in the Garhwal Himalaya. It is a historical-cum-economic and chiefly anthropological study, a threefold analysis of what the Government did, what it failed to do, and what it should do in future. It aims at a study of the socio-economic development against the anthropological backdrop.

Indeed, it will be unsustainable to claim that all the possible literature and available material on the subject has been explored and all possible viewpoints have been taken into account while analysing the situation and forming judgment and giving suggestions. However, it can still be claimed in all humility that my best endeavour to do the maximum possible within the limitations imposed on a private venture of this kind. Again much less sustainable will be the claim that mine will be the last word on the subject.

The term development means different things to different people. In its basic meaning it refers to a process and in contemporary context the process is a movement towards a condition that some of the worlds nations are supposed to have attained. The goal of development as recognised now is to bring about an important change in the quality of life of all the people in a country. It aims at the eradication of poverty and removal of ignorance, want and disease which are the lot of many nations. India is also suffering from the malaise of under development. To fight these problems of under development, she adopted a strategy of development as enshrined in her Five Year Plans. The plans, however had their own loopholes. By the time the first and the Second Five Year Plans had been implemented, the phenomenon of regional imbalances in the socio-economic levels was increasingly realised. Therefore with the beginning of the Third Five Year Plan the concept of regional planning was evolved and for development purposes U.P. State was divided in five economic regions. One of these regions was the hill region consisting of the Garhwal and Kumaon division.

During the Fourth Five year Plan period, a hill development Board with Chief Minister as its Chairman was constituted at Lucknow for accelerating the pace of development in U. P. Hills. A separate Hill Development Department, under a senior IAS officer of the rank of secretary, was created. The work of this department was to formulate and implement plan for all the Hill Districts of U. P.

Even with this arrangement problems of development continued in Hill areas. In fact Hill Development had a number of constraints.

1. One of the necessary requisites of socio-economic development of any area is that it should have an appropriate climate that the will to develop springs from within the minds and hearts of the people themselves inhabiting that area and that it is not

imposed from outside. But in the case of hill areas like Garhwal such a will to develop is not so much evident in the minds of the people. The youth population largely remained uncommitted and non-involved and there was a heavy outmigration on their part.

2. Mere will of the people to develop is not sufficient. It should be backed with financial resources to develop so that the private sector may play a significant role in the mighty task of development.
3. Ever increasing population growth is one of the major constraints to hill development. In fact, the pressure of population on arable land has been increasing year after year. "Cultivable land is limited and alternative job opportunities have not been created sufficiently." (Sixth Five Year Plan, hill region, U. P.)
4. The major portion of the terrain is undulating and rugged which puts a great constraint in the way of developing agriculture, transport and communication system and of other socio-economic overheads needed for the overall development of the region.
5. Landslide and erosion are special problems of the area.
6. Inadequate facilities of irrigation is another constraint operating in the hills. The topography of the area is such that terrace cultivation is the only option open for the farmers in most of the cases.
7. The altitudinal variations in climate, culture and mode of living are again another constraint.
8 Ignorance, superstition, traditionalism, old customs, timeworn practices and fatalism all form an impenetrable wall against modernity. The difficult problem of transition from tradition to modernity has not been achieved in most of the cases in the hill areas.
9. Intensive and adequate research on various aspects of hill life is not being done. The work of researchers that seek to improve hill life needs co-ordination with the work of the administrative personnel who are responsible to implement various plan targets and implement development projects.

This study has a thrust to explore development strategy as pursued in Garhwal. It aims at exploring the operation of development policies not from above, through the eyes of the policy makers, but from below, through those of the supposed beneficiaries. Hence it has to seek cooperation of the people in a large measure as also of those who implement the various policies and programmes in the region.

The period of study has been divided into two well marked parts viz., 1) pre 1962 period and 2) post 1962 period.

With the aim to support the study with relevant data following techniques have been adopted.

1. Content analysis of various treatises, books, brochures, research publications pertaining to the two periods has been made with a view to studying the evolution of development strategies and their various impacts.
2. Thorough study of the government reports, plan documents, official records, gazetteers and secondary data provided by the government agencies has been made in order to find out the various socio-economic changes that have an important bearing on anthropological development in their ecological and cultural perspectives.
3. Systematic study of the cultural, social and economic conditions of the hill societies as also of the anthropological and ecological changes that are taking place in the hills of Garhwal has been undertaken and survey research techniques have been judiciously used to support conclusions. Case studies have also been undertaken to supplement the findings.
4. In addition to the above, an intensive study has been carried out in five villages from five districts of Garhwal division. These villages have been selected one from each district on a random sample basis. Opinions have been collected from the head of the each sampled family. Their response to the questions on the possible reasons for their backwardness and prospect of development programmes have been analysed and corrected with other available data.

The whole work is divided into three major parts. Part I is subdivided into three chapters a) Introduction of development anthropology; b) Setting of the region; and c) Ethnographic profile of the region. Part II has been subdivided into three Chapters. The fourth chapter attempts to make a historical review of development strategy in the Garhwal Himalayas. Chapter five covers aspects of development. The seamy side of development strategy in the context of cultural and ecological perspective appears in Chapter six. Part III comprises only one chapter which provides a summary and conclusion so as to evolve a useful model of development in the context of hill region of Garhwal.

A study in Development Anthropology in ecological and cultural perspective of Garhwal stimulates several pertinent issues both at conceptual and functional levels. In the present study those issues have been analysed and discussed with the objective to ascertain and evaluate the type of reasoning that has gone into the formulation of Garhwal development plan. It is with the same analytical spirit, that the socio-cultural and ecological endowments of Garhwal have been discussed. The objective has been to reach an understanding based on the perception of aims and constraints, for the formulation of the new action schemes. These new schemes are expected to motivate the planners, policy makers and the administrators to implement these objectives and strategies of development in this hill area. The present study is, therefore, designed as a theme of development anthropology devoted to search and identify the socio-cultural and environmental approaches to development planning which might be made useful at the operational level for the management of the activities which make up the development process.

A development plan, as an operating document, which need not be always identical with a plan model, should contain some basic qualities. To judge a development plan, one must, therefore take into account the socio-economic landscape, as well as the informal constraints which the planners had to respect. When the U. P. Hill development Plan is examined from this stand point, it appears that the planners had failed to appreciate this fundamental principle. The present study is, therefore, directed to identify the adequacies of design in development strategy as an effort to streamline the economic growth and to stabilise the society.

Socio-economic growth presupposes a condition in which material and human resources are transformed into a source of high creative activity. This is the foundation of development strategy. The foundation in the case of hill development is essentially made by the factors like availability of capital, capacity of the people to save, condition to convert the savings into productive investment, skilled man-power to handle productive technologies and the latest advanced knowledge for production and management in the fields of agriculture, horticulture, social forestry, development of pasture land, animal husbandry and small scale and cottage industries.

Development anthropology is "directly related to study of social changes and culture contacts". An anthropologist believes that the primary requisite of socio-economic development of any area, should be an appropriate climate in which the "will to develop springs from within the minds and hearts of the people themselves inhabiting that area and that it is not imposed from outside.

In Garhwal, policy makers have blamed the people that they lack initiative in development. The people on the other hand treated the government responsible for the slow processes of development. In order to find out the correct answers, five villages, one from each district of Garhwal division, were selected for intensive study. These villages are situated at different altitudes and in different valleys like Nayar, Pindar, Bhilangaru and Tons. The villages have mixed population of Brahmin, Rajput, Scheduled Caste and Scheduled Tribes. There were 206 families in five villages and opinions were collected from one person from each of these families. The resultant information are that 169 of the 206 families believe that the biggest problem of Garhwal is economic backwardness and the present development effort is very slow to produce any tangible result. 146 families, namely, 70% households are ready to participate heartily in the development activities but they feel that unless government changes the development strategy, their participation will be futile.

Social justice and environmentally sound development are complex subjects. The principal aspects of the notion of social justice are 1) eradication of poverty, 2) an equitable distribution of income, consumption and wealth, and 3) popular participation in work and decision making. This social justice must be realised for various groups of people like the Brahmin, Rajputs, Scheduled Castes, Scheduled Tribes etc.

The study emphasizes upon the fact that the problems of Garhwal have to be assessed and appreciated keeping in view the perception of the problem by the hill men and women and also that an active participation of the people has to be sought at every level. In order to reach the above objectives a number of suggestions have been given in the present study.

1. Region Specific Development Plan : Islands of Development

It would be more appropriate to think in terms of region specific development plan, rather than overall development plan for the Uttaranchal Sector, for Garhwal region. Region specific development plan means plans prepared for a specific group of people living in a specific area in identical environments. It is a planning with micro approach towards socio-cultural and environmental endowments. Region specific development process has to be integrated and intensive. This is a grass root approach and the process will not be complete until the poorest of the poor of the area rises above poverty line.

2. New Strategy of Development

Growth and development have not resulted in increasing the quality of life of the people substantially in Garhwal. The hill folk of this region are to be made richer, happier and more equal by integration into the developing national economy. A step in this direction calls for a new strategy of development. There should be continuous real growth with redistribution through mass programmes. This will imply massive soil conservation work, intensive and diversified crop production, horticulture, animal husbandry and small and cottage industry with strong market infrastructure.

3. Integrative Mechanisms for Development

The main objectives of hill development are increasing the lot of the marginal primary producers and landless agriculture labourers through greater productivity of their resources and ensuring employment opportunities for the youths for an improved quality of life of the society. The real progress may not be a practical proposition unless the persistent poverty is attacked from all sides. It has to be done by an integrative mechanism of programme, projects and organisations at household level. In case of agriculture, horticulture and social forestry and allied sectors like dairy, poultry and sheep rearing and the like. These various functions have to be integrated. There should be full integration of backward, forward and horizontal linkages for the farmer.

4. New Technique of Implementations

The biggest drawback in the implementation of hill programme is the absence of regular appraisal and micro monitoring of field activities. There should be quarterly appraisal of the plan programme, so that things could be rectified without losing time and resources. An action technique for micro monitoring of the fieldwork is advocated. This technique may function in the following ways : A. Classification B. Accountability C. Monitoring D. Incentives E. Disincentives F. Follow up Checking and Verification G. Publicity and H. Development Camp.

5. Core Programme : New Action Schemes

The study directs a shift towards a more viable package programme for development. These include soil conservation, horticulture, forestry, animal husbandry, pasture development, tourism, integrated watershed management and the development of alternative source of energy. These new action schemes are expected to introduce qualitative changes in the process of development.

6. Women and Development

The ethnographic profile of Garhwal shows that the hill women play a crucial role in the productive economic system. The main features of socio-economic framework of this area are agriculture and animal husbandry in the lower and middle altitudes and sheep husbandry, limited agriculture and profession of wool spinning and weaving in the high altitudes. Men of Garhwal, whether a pahari Hindu or a Bhotia do only ploughing and repairing of tools. The remaining jobs like carrying compost manures, sowing, weeding, harvesting etc., are done by women. Therefore there is need to involve hill women in the design and implementation of development programmes in the hills so as to make them more active and effective participants in the economic well being of their own families at the micro level as well as at the macro level.

7. Inadequacies : Education and Bureaucracy

Inadequate economic growth and inequality of income, poverty and malnutrition, illiteracy and explosion in the numbers of the landless and tiny agricultural holdings that cannot support a farming family and the continued losing battle against unemployment are some of the realities and challenges of the Garhwal region. The present study unequivocally advocates the fact that no amount of development effort can remove these serious draw backs without having some changes in the inadequacies of educational curriculum of the university and the bureaucratic set-up of Garhwal Himalayas.

a) Research and Educational Curriculum :

The present day university educational curriculum is not responsive to and adequately suited for the challenges of hill area development. The Government has to soon initiate a process of creating a net-work of new branches of knowledge like appropriate technology for hill development, environment, organisational sciences, resource planning, service oriented to delivery system and location problem specific research.

b) Bureaucracy :

Bureaucracy plays a crucial role in the successful implementation of developmental policies. They face in the process of implementation of the realities, challenges and the inadequacies of socio-economic, socio-cultural and ecological environment. These problems could be successfully met only by creating an appropriate ethics among the bureaucrats and are normally allured to take a short term view of their decisions. The bureaucrats of Garhwal hills have to take a long term perspective.

8. Development and Social Changes : mass Participation Culture & Ecology

Economic changes may not always produce social changes which are envisaged in this process of economic growth. The green revolution has benefited mostly the bigger farmers and education and prosperity have not led to the eradication of social evils. The number of people below the poverty line had not decreased substantially in spite of the best efforts of the planners. There is increase of dropouts from the schools. Most of the bonded labourers are yet to cross the poverty line even after their emancipation from bondage.

Harmonious socio-economic development is possible when people participate heartily in the process of development. The participation does not come unless people are conscious and serious about it. The people of Garhwal are intelligent and fully aware of their problems. The culture had given them an adaptive character which is an all time asset for development. The women are very hardy and committed to progress. The "will to develop" is there but there is not yet the atmosphere of change. The climate of change must precede the "change" itself and the government can ensure this by twin action, namely, by providing adequate funds, training, new technology and infrastructural requirements of hill programmes and by encouraging the people to participate in the development process right from the preparation of the plan to the implementation of the schemes.

The society of Garhwal is heterogeneous in character, yet it displays a remarkable quality of unity of understanding. The people call themselves Garhwali, and they feel proud of this. They want economic progress and at the same time to preserve their own culture and group values which they believe, will bring quality of lives for them. This is a remarkable trait in the character of the Garhwalis.

Garhwal is the land of gods. People from all parts of India visit Badrinath, Kedarnath, Gangotri and Yamunotri, every year. They carry love and affection and the Garhwalis reciprocate them with equal tenderness. The spirit of Garhwal mingles into that of India. Alakananda, Bhagirathi and Yamuna all roll into the mighty Ganga, the symbol of life and prosperity of India. Garhwal has to reach that height of national prosperity–the economic growth, social stability and cultural heritage. The present study writes this theme of hope and aspiration, progress and fulfillment.

Anthropology in Action in the Tribal Areas of Adilabad District, Andhra Pradesh : A Study in Changing Plan Strategies

D. R. Pratap

Anthropology in action in the changing plan strategies in the tribal areas of Adilabad district has been selected as the topic of the present thesis. For two and a half decades the present author has been intimately associated with the welfare administration and planned development of tribes of Adilabad in various capacities as a welfare executive responsible for implementing welfare programmes (of the previous social services Department of the Nizam's Dominions which was conceived and nurtured by Prof. Haimendorf and I was also a project executive officer of the Utnoor multipurpose project which was a product of national policies. Since then, I have been actively engaged in conducting and guiding empirical studies on tribal life, culture and development as Head of the Tribal Culture Research and Training Institute, Hydrabad.

It is this long experience both as a research worker and as developmental functionary among the tribals of the state in general and the tribals of Adilabad district in particular that prompted me to take up the strudy.

The study mainly concerns the structural functional aspects of changing plan strategies with a historical perspective as exemplified in the tribal areas of Adilabad district since 1940's till date. Accordingly the following objectives have been framed.

1. To discuss the tribal situation of 1940's and the state policy and development strategies adopted by Prof. Haimendorf for the welfare of Tribes and Backward castes.
2. To examine critically plan programme and action administration evolved by Prof. Haimendrof.
3. To describe the strategy of protective cover afforded and the modus operandi of evolving and implementing it.
4. To compare and contrast the pre-independence and post independence development strategies vis-à-vis the prevailing life of the tribals.
5. To discus the socio-cultural carriers and barriers of native life

in the context of the various development strategies adopted.

6. To critically examine the changing structural-functional aspect of development administration in the context of programmes to be implemented and the human development situation to be tackled.
7. To evolve a development model for the tribal areas of Adilabad.

For the purpose of the study the time span is broadly divided into two periods of development :

1. The decades ending by 1952 during which the tribals of Hydrabad derived the benefits of development programmes and protective measures.
2. More than two decades of planned development undertaken since the inception of Five year plans.

For the collection of data pertaining to the said two periods the following techniques were adopted.

1. Scanning through the relevant old official records of Board of Revenue, State Archives, Revenue Secretariat, Concerned District Social Welfare Office and Tribal Development Block Office, Administration Reports, various commission and committee reports for collecting qualitative and quantitative data.
2. Content analysis of various history books, reports and research publications pertaining to two periods of study for the evolution of Protective and Developmental measures and Action administration during the two periods.
3 Construction of case studies illustrative of the factors that hindered or helped the programme implementation process from personal experience and knowledge of the two periods.
4. Collection of case histories of knowledgeable tribals who derived benefits during the two periods.
5. Systematic recording and observation of the cultural, social, economic and political condition of the tribal societies of the two periods and survey research techniques are liberally employed whenever necessary.

Pre-independence approach to tribal development was ameliorative in the sense that, the various programmes and legislations that were implemented and enacted during this period were meant to mitigate tribals' sufferings and prevent exploitation from outside, without attempting to strengthen his economic base or promoting his economic status with systematic development approach.

The years preceeding the planning era witnessed the beginning of the welfare approach with programmes of development sporadically implemented in the absence of systematic and comprehensive programme of development both at state and national levels. The phrases 'welfare approach' and 'welfare administration' indicate the policy evolved and machinery established to implement the policy by the welfare state.

Since India attained independence in 1947 it became a welfare state guaranteeing equal opportunities to all its citizens and took special steps to alleviate the suffering of the weaker sections besides promoting their wellbeing through the opening of a number of educational, health and other institutional and the whole approach became a welfare approach. The welfare approach was systematised and the constructive and systematic stage of this welfare approach began with the initiation of Community Development Programmes in 1952.

However in the tribal areas of Hydrabad especially Adilabad district the approach initiated in 1944 by Prof. Haimendrof for the amelioration of exploitation and suffering of tribals with a positive development oriented programme of action which was also continued between 1948 and 1952.

Among the districts of Andhra Pradesh, Adilabad is the biggest district in this area.The river in South India, i.e.,Godavari and its tributaries ikePenganga,Kadam andPedavagu pass through the district.

Adilabad has a high chunk of population belonging to weaker sections like Scheduled Castes and Scheduled Tribes and the percentage of Scheduled Tribe population in the district is 13.14 which again is another indicator of the backwardness of the people of the district.

Table I

Distribution Population

Name of the Tribe	Y e a r (1961)	Y e a r (1971)
	Population	Population
Gond (including Naik Pond)	93334	117478
Kolam	16459	26277
Pardhan	9334	10385
Andh	1468	2404
Thoti	429	1131
Tambada	As the Tambadas of Telangana region were included in Scheduled Tribes list only from July, 1976 by Presidential order, their population figures (1971) were not readily available.	

Gonds are the most dominant tribe of the area popularly known as Raj Gonds meaning princely Gonds.

Tribal Development which had its roots in the British ameliorative and welfare oriented isolationist policy of the first half of the 19th century took comprehensive shape with the initiation of the 5th plan in the latter half of the 20th century when a growth oriented approach was initiated.

In India the first attempt to develop tribals and other weaker sections with the help of an action plan was introduced during the Nizam's dominions. Development of settled cultivation along with the provision of plough-bullocks under hire purchase system was introduced along with the organisation of a network of co-operative credit societies, promotion of education, health and hygiene.

The Gond Education Scheme was introduced with a view to prevent the exploitation of tribals from land alienation by outsiders. Protective measures were initiated by declaring the predominantly tribal areas as notified areas in Adilabad district in 1943 and creating a 'Chenchu Reserve' of about 75000 acres in Amarabad plateau in 1942 besides appointing a special tribes officer in 1944 to look after the interests of tribals of Adilabad in land and forests.

It has been found that as a result of this policy, none of the tribal people lost their land to non-tribals (except in one case who alienated only two acres of land even though all of them are holders of sizeable chunks of land).

As part of their learning and job training they were also taught improved agricultural practices in the training centre.

In general it can be safely concluded that the initial development could fruitfully throw out a band of tribal elite. But its impact on larger masses of tribals may not be far reaching and sizeable as it was initiated on a small scale and that too on an experimental basis.

Development in the Post Independence era

For the first time in the world history democratic planning was adopted as instrument for rooting out rural poverty and ushering in progressive transformation of villages in which an Indian lives based on the cardinal principles of people's participation and self help.

Comparative Study of the Development Strategies and Situations in the Two Periods

The present study is intended to be a discussion and comparison of the different strategies and achievement of the periods between

1942–1951 and after i.e. between Prof. Haimendorf's experiment of the erstwhile Hydrabad state and the planing era of the post independence period.

The Adilabad experiment of Prof. Haimendorf was introduced at a time when the whole society was riddled with feudalism and bureaucratic administration to whom spending money for amelioration of the suffering of the weaker sections was unpalatable and welfare approach was unknown. The fatalistic philosophy or Karma Sidhanta was reigning supreme in the minds of both rulers and the ruled. Prof. Haimendorf had to undertake studies on some of the primitive tribes like Chenclus, Konda Reddies and Raj Gonds. He was also entrusted with the responsibility of evolving and implementing welfare programmes for these and similar groups in view of his anthropological expertise and knowledge about the living conditions of these groups.

On the other hand, developments since independence were aimed at the diffusion of sophisticated technology and every plan has been striving to modernise the livelihood patterns besides introducing them to new avenues of employment. However, the process has been slow and not of the expected pace as both the area and the people are not completely prepared to reap the full benefits of development due to inherent cultural barriers which could not be properly identified and programmes so oriented as to overcome them.

In the first stage, the problems of tribals were tackled with a holistic approach involving assignment of lands, preparing a tribal elite for assuming leadership at village levels through training and instilling among the tribals a sense of co-operation so as to provide the necessary support for future economic activities.

The next stage was the community development era during which the Block, as the base unit of development, was empowered with a schematic budget and sectoral planning as per the uniformity of all India model. Planning became highly centralised without ever trying to study the tribal social system as a distinct entity with contours of its own interacting within the limits of its own local ecology.

The third stage was the integrated and the Sub-Plan approach period into which much intellectual thinking and methodological importation was given. Planning from below at the Block level and Integrated Tribal Development Project Area and identified areas of tribal concentration in the state as micro, meso and macro level units of planning respectively was expected to result on accelerated tribal development. Christellers Growth Centre concept was imported as the nucleous of micro level planning.

In spite of the limitations of the concept, the idea of growth centre can be a useful tool in gauging the people's requirements in terms of services and for systematising the level of these services, the areas of their operation and their financial aspects.

With these study results, the following three phased planning activities may be undertaken.

1. Primary Planning Activity

i) Area group identification preparing resource inventory
ii) Collection of data on :
  a) Cultural standards of living
  b) Indicators of economic development
iii) Studying cultural barriers to and carriers of the development process

2. Secondary Planning Activity

iv) Prevailing development situation analysed
v) Structuring macro strategy on the basis of–
  a) Resources endowment
  b) Cultural and economic contours
  c) Mobilization of finance
vi) Identification of inter-sectoral linkages
vii) Sectoral projections with inter-sectoral linkages
viii) Framing the administrative structure

3. Tertiary Planning Activity

ix) Formulation of action Programmes
x) Implementation

The next stage has three distinct actions.

1. Organising the necessary administrative infrastructure;
2. promoting suitable leadership to ensure the people's participation;
3. laying of the necessary infrastructure so that the infrastructure serves as a spring board for the productive activity planned for the next stage.

The tribal areas of Adilabad are placed in a paradoxical situation. The agro-forest and mineral resources are located in the tribal areas and even today a few industries based on these raw materials are either located in the fringe or in the heart of the tribal areas. Thus modern industrialization process has started in the tribal areas.

With this stabilizing action tribal society has become self reliant with minimal dependence upon outside agencies. Extensive education will at this level help the tribals to reap full advantage of the situation.

The fifth stage is the ideal self generating stage when plan formulation, financing and executive action all generate from within the society. The society through community action becomes self reliant in skills, knowledge, resources, mobilization, programme formulation and execution.

Lastly it is increasingly realised that human behaviour is conditioned by territorial consideration and that human perception, expression etc. all have an integrative relationship with the ecology.

Area bound human behaviour expresses itself in social control institutions, social unit distribution and a ritual performance zone. The politico-regional implication of the traditional power structure and the social structure of the Gond region of Adilabad District as already discussed demonstrate the need for keeping in view the socio-political factor in delineating the area of development. This could be further strengthened and rationalised by adding the rituals component so that it becomes a comprehensive politico-socio-religion unit of development.

Tribes in Transition : A Case Study of Kapparallatippa in Nellore District and Sitanagaram in Guntur District

V. Lalitha

There are some groups of people in India whose criminal propensities are well known and hence are marked as 'Criminal Tribes' by the administrators. These tribes are kept under a vigilant watch both by the people and the government. The study of 'criminal tribes' should no longer be a vague and obscure one. It concerns us very vitally because these 'Criminal Tribes' form a part of society and hence they should not be degraded. They are poor, devoid of formal education and oppressed by fears which arise out of lack of modern knowledge.

The Yerukalas (including the Katheras and Dongadasari–sections of Yerukalas) of Kapparallatippa (Nellore district) and Sitanagaram (Guntur district) are two examples of such ex-criminal tribes of Andhra Pradesh. A survey undertaken by the author in these two villages revealed that though these people constitute a minority in both of these districts, they are sometimes the cause of real threat to the neighbouring places. These Yerukalas are commonly stigmatized as dacoits, burglars, pilferers, thieves and railway wagon breakers.

It has been ascertained that Yerukalas were previously a nomadic horde to be found chiefly in the districts of Guntur, Kurnool, Cuddapah, Anantapur and Nellore of Andhra Pradesh. These Yerukalas used to act as 'Charus' or espionage staff who used to collect secret information from the enemy territory and pass it over to the rulers who employed them. When the British occupied the country, these people lost their former jobs of, charus i.e., the intelligence staff. Some of them settled down in agriculture, in petty trades, in handy-crafts like rope making, mat and basket making etc. A few of them also took up the job of village watchmen. A small number of these retrenched people took to crime to keep their body and soul together. They were, mostly, living in forests and hills and had been committing mainly highway robberies and petty thefts in nearby villages. Thus, the loss of livelihood, due to the various measures taken by the British authorities had put their organized life in complete disarray which resulted in the increase of crime.

Lack of education, paucity of skill on arts and crafts, getting Pattas for their lands with inadequate irrigation facilities, having no fixed income through employment, compelled them to lead a life below the poverty line. Wherever necessity arose they had no other alternative except to take to any antisocial activity, including crime, for their subsistence.

The study shows how the Yerukalas had acquired criminal tendency because of the pressure of economic and territorial displacement. This displacement seriously affected their old pattern of life leaving them to maladjustment in their society. The general famine conditions of the Madras Presidency and the non-availability of any legitimate means of subsistence compelled them to take up criminal activity for subsistence. Their behavioral pattern i.e., the easy going ways of life gave them scope to pursue criminal activities. In addition to all these factors, the so called zemindars and landlords, who were the investors of crime, encouraged them to take up crime for their own selfish ends.

The present study is a comparative one which describes a coherent picture of the life style of the Yerukala criminals at Kapparallatippa and Sitanagaram ex-settlements and suggests different ways and means to bring about a change in them.

Attempts have also been made to study the demographic aspects, family organization, educational facilities and birth place and the migratory aspects of their ancestors to have an insight into their lives.

Another important aspect of this study is to know whether or not they want to continue to live in their new settlements or join the mainstream of social life which helps the policy makers to formulate reformatory policy. Besides, a close look at the modus-operandi of their crimes is of great relevance to this study as it gives us a clue to prevent future crimes.

Emphasis was also given on the understanding of the nature of their criminal aspects, evaluation of the criminal biography of their parents, grand parents and relationship with criminality vis-à-vis family size, working force, literacy, employment and other factors related to these.

The study of Kapparallatippa covers the whole village, consisting of about 100 house-holds and that of the Sitanagaram which covers about 40 families. There were 409 families of the settlers at the latter village of which only 40 remain today. Besides, there are about 50 families belonging to non-settlers, but they are not within the scope of our present study. Case history methods of collecting information along with interviews were conducted at both these places with the help of interview schedule, which constitute the primary source of the study. The author collected information regarding these tribes from the old people of the village.

Kapparallatippa is only 15 kilometers from Kavali town, situated close to the Grand Truck Road from Calcutta to Madras. Kapparallatippa Settlement was established in the year 1917. This was an agricultural settlement established by the American Baptist Mission at Bitragunta in Nellore district. This was declared to be a part of Kavali Criminal Settlement and was also known as Bawdenpet Settlement or Bitragunta Reformatory Settlement. Kapparallatippa Settlement was fortunate in acquiring large tracts of land. There were 120 houses, besides the Assembly Hall and work-supervisor's houses, on a plot of 102 acres of land. The settlers were allotted land for cultivation.

The Sitanagaram Settlement is situated in Guntur district. The total strength of the Settlement in 1925 was 1,002 and only 69 of them were absconding. The decrease in crime was attributed to the out-of-view members of the Criminal Settlement in Guntur and Nellore. The special feature of Sitanagaram Settlement was that it was Penal Settlement. The Sitanagaram Settlement, which was converted into a free colony after the repeal of the Criminal Tribes Act, was very near to the city of Vijayawada. It was exposed to many employment potentialities for the settlers. The people here belonged to Yerukala tribe.

The people at Kapparallatippa Settlement are Yerukalas and Donga Dasari tribes. The Donga Dasaris were once an integral part of the Yerukalas and later they were considered to be one of the worst criminal tribes in the south because of their mixed character. With the help of the interview schedules, the researcher has made an attempt by taking a deeper insight into the social, economic and administrative problems of the ex-criminals, both at Kapparallatippa and at Sitanagaram Settlement. This programme of reformation through settlement dwellings failed. Absconding was frequent and the missionaries could not control these settlers. The net result was that the Government concentrated more on the prevention of crime than on the reformation of criminals.

The predominant form of social structure of the tribe in both the settlements is patriarchal. The nature of construction of their houses is directly related to their economic condition. No wonder, therefore, that traces of the joint family system can still be seen in their present family size which is quite bulky.

These tribes observe omens and portents and have certain superstitious beliefs. The 'Kulapanchayat' or the Council of elders, which consists of five senior members of the tribe, is competent to decide disputes between their men and wives, feuds between two or more persons, disputes regarding loans, property, land and so on. In spite of their conversion to Christianity, the impact of Hindu religion, its customs and traditions is imbedded. A large number of them, in both the settlements, are aware of an implementing modern family planning methods.

The data in the possession of the researcher establishes the fact that in spite of their grandfather being nomads, the later generation had happily settled down in these settlements. The stigma of criminality is still sticking to them. The British Government in India as well as the present Indian Government came forward to help them to come out of this shell, but their position remains the same even today.

Regarding the continuation of the settlement, there is only one opinion. Already the people of Sitanagaram have come to an understanding that their colony is a 'free colony' which means that no harassment, no ill-treatment, no differentiation between them and the normal citizens is found. At present, they are all cultivators. They felt that the Government should pay more attention to this settlement by providing jobs and improving their physical needs and facilities. They are sentimentally attached to this camp and also are indebted to the land where they were born and brought up.

The ex-settlers are dissuaded from thinking that crime is their life-long avocation. Change is essentially necessary, which is taking place rather slowly. We cannot expect change overnight. We will have to prepare ourselves mentally to absorb them into our fold.

The Kapparallatippa people are very keen to have land pattas conferring ownership rights, irrigation facilities, small-scale industries, and would like to be provided with employment and pucca houses. The Sitanagaram people want liberal subsidies, agricultural and irrigation facilities. Whereas the Kapparallatippa people require the basic needs of life and the people at Sitanagaram want greater welfare measures.

Table 1 shows the opinion about the Police Officers.

Table 1

Opinion about the Police Officers

Opinion	Kapparallatippa	Sitanagaram
Satisfactory	15	30
Good.	0	45
Ill-treatment	28	5
Not satisfactory	41	15
Hatred	16	0
Not bothered	0	5
Total	100	100

75% of the settlers at Sitanagaram are well disposed towards Police Officers, but 85% of the Kapparallatippa settlers are dissatisfied with them. They hate them for their ill-treatment.

At Kapparallatippa, the percentage of people who depend on crime as their profession is more than that at Sitanagaram. This indicates how much reformed the criminals are in the Sitanagaram settlement. Among the fathers of the present residents at Kapparallatippa, 79% reported crime as their profession, which is only 45% in Sitanagaram settlement.

Among the sons at Kapparallatippa, 83% reported crime as their profession, whereas at Sitanagaram 15% of the total persons reported crime as such. This brings the fact that at Sitanagaram not only the total percentage of persons involved in crime is less than at Kapparallatippa but even individuals who participate in crime are less in number.

Comparing the two ex-criminal settlements, it has been proved beyond doubt that the Government has tried to settle these people in agricultural settlements, but it was a failure. The Yerukalas and Donga Dasaries are not a hardworking lot and hence they need some employment which will give them immediate gains.

The differential crime rates and different attitude and opinions are observed among the Yerukala tribes in these two ex-settlements. The following important points of observations have been noted for a comparative analysis.

Firstly Kapparallatippa is an isolated area where the Bitragunta Reformatory Settlement was established. Even the Railway Junction at Bitragunta (an important railway center) is only two kilometers away from this place. The location of the place is adjacent to the Grand Trunk Road giving more scope for wagon-looting. The case of Sitanagaram is different. Though it is a segregated area, it is almost a part (suburb) of Vijayawada City. The District and the Taluk head quarters are very close to this place. The people here visit Vijayawada city twice or thrice a day and this leads to a greater interaction with the urban people.

The land is very fertile in Sitanagaram, whereas Kapparallatippa is unfortunate in having lands which are dependent upon monsoon rains. The irrigation facilities are not sound and the Ramanna Tank needs immediate repair.

Social interaction is greater at Sitanagaram. The ex-criminal tribes belonging to different castes, besides criminals and non-criminals, are living in this village. In Kapparallatippa, there are Katheras and Yerukalas, who are habituated to committing crime. The influence of railways is more a help than a hindrance for criminal operations.

Secondly, social workers have not evinced much interest in Kapparallatippa's affairs. The reputed social worker, Vennelakanti

Raghavaiah of Nellore district, concentrated on Yanadis, the major tribe, while Yerukalas did not attract his attention. So the ex-criminals feel that no body takes any interest in them and hence they are neglected.

Initiative and efforts are more in Sitanagaram village. This is due to political, social, psychological and economic influences, whereas these initiatives and efforts are blunted at Kapparallatippa.

There is always gainful employment at Sitanagaram. When railway bridges were constructed, people carried sand from the river bed to the construction site. Quarrying is providing work to a number of people even now. Rickshaws are given to some villagers, but such opportunities are not available at Kapparallatippa.

Another significant factor is the influence of urbanization and industrialization in Sitanagaram village. There are well established factories, such as power factory, sugar factory, textile mill, and tile factory etc., which offer ample employment opportunities. At Kapparallatippa, there is no industrial climate prevailing.

Thirdly, at Sitanagaram, if and whereas conflict arises between the settlers and the management for a better deal, a negotiated settlement of two points of dispute is attempted. Through this, they attain cultural and organizational eminence.

Social mobility and interaction is more in Sitanagaram village. A number of officials belonging to several departments visit this place frequently. There is ample scope for interaction between the ex-settlers and the people (non-settlers) of Sitanagaram on one hand and ex-settlers and the people of Vijayawada city on the other. So diverse influences made them to understand and grasp things quickly. These opportunities are negligible at Kapparallatippa.

Some settlers from Sitanagaram village participated in the freedom struggle. It came to light during the enquiry that one or two incidents relating to freedom fighting took place here. Participation in politics gave them an opportunity to become politically conscious. They know the techniques and also the validity of petitioning, and they are in a position to fight for rights. All these are absent at Kapparallatippa.

The urban educated and employed persons from Sitanagaram settlement, working away from it, visit their kith and kin in the village and counsel them to be free from crime. They also instill confidence in them. Employed persons are not many at Kapparallatippa.

Although a few Upper Primary Schools are functioning properly in both these villages. There is a Rama Krishna Mission High School only at Sitanagaram village. Many of the children study there. Some are sent to Vijayawada and one or two children are studying at the headquarters institutions at Guntur. At Kapparallatippa, after the upper primary education, very few persons go to the High Schools and even if they go, they cannot afford financially to pursue higher studies. Moreover, the Katheras tribe is not getting all these benefit from the Government and thus are frustrated.

Finally, the leadership is quite different at Kapparallatippa. The innocent, ignorant and the illiterate people at Kapparallatippa are unable to realize their position and are blind followers of these leaders. But people at Sitanagaram are more enlightened. Politically and socially, they are aware of the situation around them and take things in their proper perspective.

Nobody reported crime as a profession at Sitanagaram, although there still exists 10% crime here. Whereas 66% people at Kapparallatippa, both fathers and sons, are criminals. This establishes the fact that still there is crime culture prevailing at Kapparallatippa, whereas it is rapidly vanishing at Sitanagaram.

The attitudinal change, education, awareness, social mobility and other economic facilities kept Sitanagaram people reformed in every sphere of their life. Compared to this, the reformation at Kapparallatippa is very slow indeed.

Inspite of these developmental activities undertaken by the Government, an atmosphere of general discontent prevails in the ex-settlements of Kapparallatippa and Sitanagaram. They are not convinced that the Government is giving as much care and attention on them as they should have. The Government has constructed houses for the ex-settlers at Kapparallatippa in 1986. To provide employment to the young people, educated and uneducated, who are vegetating and whirling away their time, an industry may be started at the instance of the Government in these settlement areas. So that young and energetic persons who are now indulging in pick pocketing, snatching and other criminal acts can very well be kept in profitable engagement.

A radical change is essential in the very socio-economic fabric of the society. Reformatory steps will have to be carried on continuously. The planners, the administrators and the policymakers should treat this an urgent need and try to solve the problems accordingly. They cannot view this problem at par with the Scheduled Tribes. The ex-criminals cannot have emotional affinity with others so long as they are not freed from the 'stigma' and this cannot be wiped out as long as they do not wish to come out of their shells to prove their integrity in society over a long stretch of time.

Constraints of Development of Scheduled Castes in Uttar Pradesh : An Anthropological Overview

Dibakar Basak

In India, after Independence, attempts have been made to formulate policies and provisions for social and economic welfare of all sections of population. Special efforts have also been made to identify programmes for the advancement of 'any socially and educationally backward classes of citizens, or for the Scheduled Castes and Scheduled Tribes', as guided by the Directive Principles of State Policy in Indian Constitution.

The past studies conducted on the problems of Scheduled Castes and their welfare measures have shown that due to dismal performances of various programmes, adequate results of development of this section of population are yet to be achieved. It is, therefore, felt that there is a need to examine these programmes. But, comprehensive scientific studies conducted by outside observers equipped with knowledge of developmental programmes and insights of administrative processes are rare.

The present study would, therefore, be an important contribution in the field of Anthropology, particularly Applied and Development Anthropology.

In the dissertation, experiences on the development of Scheduled Castes in Uttar Pradesh have been portrayed through 7 case studies. In these cases, a lot of field level data as well as secondary information from official records, files, etc., are given about a programme in which it has been formulated and implemented. Attempts have been made to examine important constraints in these programmes for the development of Scheduled Caste population. To understand the issues of development with respect to Scheduled Castes, it is also necessary to know their ethnological profile and their complex and varied socio-economic conditions. These information have, therefore, been incorporated in the dissertation. For conducting the case studies of programmes the researcher has collected materials through : (a) personal observations, (b) personal interviews, (c) official records, and files, and (d) books, journals and other public writings.

The Scheduled Castes of Uttar Pradesh are commonly known as *Anusuchit Jati* or *Harijan*. Earlier they were termed as *Asavarnas* or *Panchamas*. They were relegated to position outside the four pillared structure of the Hindu society and yet remained a part of the system. These castes were placed in the downward scale of the social hierarchy and classified on the bipolarity of purity and pollution. Applications of various principles of the caste system had alienated these sections from the society. The term 'Scheduled Castes' had been for the first time used in the Government of India Act, 1935.

Actually Scheduled Castes do not form a homogeneous group. There are both untouchables and low clean castes people in this category.

To start with, the largest chunk of the Scheduled Caste peasantry in Uttar Pradesh are the poorest people although land plays an important role in their social and economic life. Land holdings among Scheduled Castes are in most cases uneconomic and they are eking out miserable existence from land. Although government lease land have been allotted to the Scheduled Castes but they cannot use these because–(a) land allotted in many areas are not fit for cultivation, (b) physical possession has not been given; and (c) obtaining the initial dose of inputs in the form of animals, implements and seeds has not been possible for them.

In the approach to the welfare of Scheduled Castes, first preference is to be given to the problems of agricultural labourers belonging to the Scheduled Caste communities. These labourers do not get employment throughout the year. Their earnings are very low from wages. The enforcement of minimum wages in agriculture sector has not come about to the appreciable extent so far. The widely rampant practice of bonded labour in the rural areas particularly shows this. The burden of indebtedness among Scheduled Caste agricultural labourers is comparatively higher than the general landless labourers. Besides this occupational group, a large number of Scheduled Caste persons are engaged in their traditional occupations, such as, leather work, fishing, weaving, basket making etc. These occupations are considerded low and contribute to the practice of untouchability. Further, these occupations yield very low returns of their labourers. Due to poor economic condition and high incidence of indebtedness, Scheduled Castes suffer from the worst form of exploitations through the practice of begar (forced labour) as well as debt bondage. Scheduled Castes comprise two-thirds of all bonded labourers in the country. In the post-independence period educational advancement of Scheduled Castes gained national importance, nevertheless the

Government reports indicate that the quantum of incentives provided to Scheduled Castes in improving their participation and retention rates are inadequate. Nearly 80% of the Scheduled Caste population in the country remain illiterate as against 60% of other communities. Their educational backwardness has been observed due to various reasons such as, caste discrimination, poverty, limited exposure to outside world, etc. Alongwith education, one of the basic problems of Schduled Castes is the state of underdevelopment and unemployment. In spite of several programmes, a significant portion of Scheduled Caste population particularly in rural areas are 'not only just poor but almost entirely constitute the poorest of the poor'.

On the social front, untouchability is an important problem of Scheduled Castes people. In rural areas, they are unable to use public places freely. They are not allowed to bring drinking water from the sources meant for all others. They live at the outskirt of the village. Even in towns and cities, mostly they live in segregation. Closely linked with these problems, Scheduled Castes are facing difficulties to get house-sites and houses. The social life of the sweepers and scavengers, flayers and tanners amongst Scheduled Castes are most deplorable. Their problems are, therefore, required to be looked into separately. They are still looked down as a despised and segregated community in the society.

The most important of all the problems of the Scheduled Castes is the incidence of atrocities or crimes perpetrated on this section of population. Reports appearing in newspapers indicate such inhuman actions. The members of this section are humiliated, insulted, man-handled, assulted, burnt alive and tortured and their women folks are raped and murdered. In Uttar Pradesh, as many as 4135 crimes have been recorded during the year 1985 showing an increased trend over the year 1984. These crimes are uniformly spread over in all the districts of the state. Investigations into these cases reveal that these crimes have social and economic causes at the root. Further, a failure on the part of the administration leads to occurrence of such atrocities.

The State of Uttar Pradesh is not only the most populous state in the country but also contains the highest Scheduled Caste population among all the states.As regards the Scheduled Caste population, the state has got the share of 22.39% showing that more than one-fifth of the total Scheduled Caste population of the country live in Uttar Pradesh, followed by West Bengal, Bihar, Tamil Nadu, Andhra Pradesh, Madhya Pradesh, Rajasthan and Karnataka. One characteristic feature of the Scheduled Caste in the state is that they live close to the non-scheduled population. More than two-thirds of the total Scheduled

Caste population are concentrated in the Eastern and Western Zones.

The proportion of urban population among Scheduled Castes is, however, increasing over the years.Distribution pattern of these communities reveal that *Chamars* form an absolute majority in all the districts of western and eastern regions, except Gonda district and Bundelkhand division.

In the western region of the state, two other numerically important Scheduled Caste groups are *Dhobi* and *Khatik*. The eastern region contains groups of *Pasi* and *Dhobi* next to *Chamar*. In the Bundelkhand division, *Kori* and *Dhobi* are found in large numbers with *Chamar*, among the 9 districts of Central division, *Pasi* occupy top position in 5 districts, Sitapur, Unnao, Rae Bareli, Bara Banki and Lucknow and in 4 districts, viz., Kanpur, Fatehpur, Kheri and Hardoi, the *Chamars* are the dominant group among the Scheduled Castes. The caste *Shilpkar* is mainly concentrated in the Hilly region of the State. Like *Chamar* and *Dhobi*, *Balmikis* are scattered all over the state but their largest concentration is in the districts of west plain.

The list of Scheduled Castes of Uttar Pradesh is, however, not fully rational and contained anomalies. As many as 13 tribal communities living in southern portion of the state (Kols, Gonds, *Baigas, Kharwars, Sahariyas, Agarias, Bhuiyans, Korwas, Panikas, Oraons, Patharis, Parahiyas* and *Ghasias* have been included in the list of Scheduled Castes. Further, a large number of communities are listed as unspecified.

Against the above background of nature and size of the problems of the Scheduled Castes, the development programmes of Scheduled Castes are to be examined. While examining these programmes the researcher observed that there are many problem areas in the programmes for the development of Scheduled Castes. Attempts have been made to present these aspects in the dissertation for future courses of actions.

The programmes are as follows :

1. Programmes under special component plan

Many difficulties arose due to lack of definite objectives. The Special Component Plan is very large and not specific and there are nearly 188 schemes/programmes in the plan of Uttar Pradesh. Difficulties arose in every aspect like administrative, organizational and also regarding ensuring cordination during the implementation of the plan.

For proper implementation of the Special Component Plan there should be more communication between officials, fieldstaff and the target groups (Scheduled Caste people). After studying the programmes many important shortcomings have been noticed of which a few are mentioned. The major difficulties noticed in the implementation of Special Component Plan are as follows :

1. The exercise of quantification of funds and physical targets in the state level appeared to be notional and disaggregation of targets was not effectively carried out.
2. At the district level there was no clear picture about the totality of what had been done for Scheduled Castes under the Special Component Plan.
3. The target under the programmes appeared to be very ambitious and could not in fact be achieved. So some measures should be taken for its proper application. They are as follows :
   i) Banks should be involved for the selection of beneficiaries.
   ii) Family oriented programmes should be formulated and implemented according to the profile of the family.
   iii) Scheduled Caste people should be made aware of the benefits of the Special Component Plan.
   iv) More staff should be provided for follow up work.
   v) Back-up services linked with various programmes like marketing, etc., should be provided.
   vi) Departmment should organise training for the proper orientation of the staff.

II Allotment of ceiling surplus land to Scheduled Caste persons

One of the most important measures taken for the land reforms in favour of Scheduled Caste persons of Uttar Pradesh was to allot surplus land under the provisions of the Uttar Pradesh 'Imposition of Ceiling Land Act, 1973.' But after studying the programme following short-comings have been noticed.

1. The ceiling legislation was not implemented in right earnest.
2. In majority of cases surrendered land was in patches and the allottees were given land at different places.
3. Incidents of *Benami* (illegal) transfers of surplus allotted land was noticed etc.

III. Programme of rehabilitation of Scheduled Caste bonded labourers

Considering the importance of eliminating the bonded labour system, the State Government introduced the programme of identification, release and rehabilitation. A study into the programme reveals the following shortcomings :

I) Identification of bonded labourers were found to be slow as officials had got inadequate understanding and confusion about the Bonded Labour Act.

II) The study stressed the need for constitution of the vigilance committees, their functioning and maintenance of statutory registers.

III) The need for intensive studies by the State Government in areas prone to the bonded labour system is felt to locate bonded labourers on a systematic basis.

IV) There is no provision under the existing programme to provide financial help, food, etc., immediately after a person is released.

V) Under the programme, financial assistance of approximately Rs. 4000.00 was provided for a released bonded labourer. The assistance was found to be extremely inadequate.

VI) No norms were followed in respect of providing rehabilitation schemes to the released bonded labourers.

IV. Pre-Matric educational incentives to Scheduled Caste students

The Government of Uttar Pradesh provides incentives both in cash and kind to Scheduled Caste students in order to encourage them for education and also help them to prosecute their studies further. Incentives in cash include pre-matric scholarship, merit scholarship and award scheme. Incentives in kind include mid-day meal, supply of free text books and uniform. The study on the programme reveals many important drawbacks regarding implementing the programmes for the Scheduled Caste people in Uttar Pradesh. These are as follows :

1) Complete information regarding the programme was not available from the records.
2) Coverage is inadequate since a very large number of students who are financially vulnerable do not actually enjoy its benefits.
3) The facilities of mid-day meals, uniforms and text book grants are made available only to a few students.

4) The rates of scholarships are quite inadequate.
5) Supervisors on behalf of the district Harijan and Social Welfare Officers usually disburse the amounts of scholarships to the guardians/parents of the students. This system often created scopes of malpractices. Many students reported that they were not provided with full payments.

V. Reservation for Scheduled Castes in services

The Government establishments, public sector undertakings, statutory and semi-Government bodies, etc., located in Uttar Pradesh are required to make reservation for Scheduled Castes in the services. The policy of Reservation are to be implemented through a number of executive orders/instructions and maintenance of rosters and other relevant records. On examining the implementation of these measures, following important shortcomings were observed, e.g., by rosters were not made properly, adequate steps had not been taken up by the administration to find out candidates, all the officials dealing with the policy of reservation were found to be confused with the orders/ instructions and special recruitment drive for filling up the reserved vacancies are to be arranged from time to time.

VI. Measures for dealing with atrocities against Scheduled Castes

The State Government of Uttar Pradesh have introduced certain precautionary, preventive and punitive measures as well as measures for rehabilitation to check cases of atrocities. But in reality it was very difficult to implement the measure properly for dealing with the programmes.

VII. Programmes of Voluntary Organisations

The development effort by the voluntary organisations has been too meagre in the State of Uttar Pradesh to make a significant impact on the conditions of Scheduled Caste persons.

Discussions on the above programmes reveal a few problem areas. There are still some general aspects to these problems which are required to be attended. These may be identified as below:

1. **Scheduling** The list of Scheduled Castes in Uttar Pradesh as prescribed under Article 341(1) of the constitution are not fully rational and contained anomalies. The specified Article does not seem to specially categorise the most backward among them. Constitutional amendment appears to be necessary for scheduling the weakest among the Scheduled Castes.

2. Strategy of development

a) While dealing with the issue of development of Scheduled Castes, it is essential to consider the philosophy of development as also its methodology and technology. The central problem of the Scheduled Castes in Uttar Pradesh has been their age-long isolation due to the custom of untouchability. Nearly 85% of the total Scheduled Caste population of Uttar Pradesh are illiterate. There is a wide gap between the literacy rates of the Scheduled Castes and the overall population when the figures in respect of rural and urban areas and males and females are compared. Nearly 60% of the Scheduled Caste population of Uttar pradesh are reported to be below the poverty line. Per capita income of about 80% Scheduled Caste population are below the State's per capita income.

The Scheduled Castes of Uttar Pradesh are found to be engaged in various occupations. Isolated and adhoc attempts in development programmes cannot solve the problems of Scheduled Castes. It is necessary to consider an integrated strategy for development. One needs to take three pronged measures viz., protective, promotional and social. The protective measures include protection of existing command over resources, prevention of erosion and consolidation of their position in traditional professions, professionalisation of unclean occupations. The promotional measures involve strengthening of economic base with substantial transfer of resources, carving out further opportunities in all sectors of national economy and skill diversification for vertical and horizontal mobility by intensive educational and training effort. The social measures comprised of intensive social work and effective organisation.

b) The programmes for development should be composite and integrated and must incorporate all necessary linkages right from the Plan formulation stage, with the Scheduled Caste family as the focal point.

3. Legislation

The commission for Scheduled Castes and Scheduled Tribes has noted that the Union Government has no authority to give any direction to the State Government even in cases where the latter could not take effective step either for the protection of the Scheduled Castes or for their social, educational and economic advancement. The commission urged the Union Government to amend the Constitution suitably adding items under the concurrent list in the seventh schedule–(a) Development and welfare of the Scheduled Castes and their social, educational and economic advancement; (b) protection of the Scheduled Castes from social injustice and all forms of exploitation including untouchability; (c) protection of the Scheduled Castes from commission of offences including atrocities against them; (d) public order in offer as it relates to the Scheduled Castes; and (e) reservation for the Scheduled Castes in making of appointments to services and posts in connection with affairs of a State. New legislation is also to be enacted for ensuring strict enforcement of reservation policy with reference to recruitment/promotion to various categories of posts under the Government establishments in the State.

4. Land Reforms

A time bound programme appears obvious to make available ceiling surplus lands to Scheduled Caste landless agricultural labourers and marginal farmers. Steps should be taken to register the names of all share-croppers and other insecure tenants in the land records.

5. Animal Husbandry

The state should adopt a systematic approach through identification of areas and by delivering a total viable package ensuring the provision of infrastructure support of health service, marketing, fodder, feed, etc.

6. Minimum Wages

Minimum wages for agricultural workers should be fully implemented. Both men and women should have equal wages for equal work. The minimum wages should be revised from time to time.

7. Cottage and Village Industries

The Scheduled Caste labourers having artisan background should be enabled to get maximum employment and income from cottage and village industries. A comprehensive programme taking into account all aspects of incentives, training and guidance should be made available to Scheduled Castes.

8. Proverty, Unemployment and Economic Programmes

The removal of poverty has to be taken as one of the major objectives for the development of Scheduled Castes. It is necessary to expand the scope and content of–(a) beneficiary specific programmes, like

Integrated Rural Development Programme; (b) area specific programmes and (c) minimum needs programme, consisting of elementary education for children, adult education, health, rural water supply, link roads, housing, nutrition and electrification.

9. Co-operatives

The poor Scheduled Caste persons can raise their incomes only when they have access to institutional credit and inputs. The rural credit system has to be strengthened.

10. Education

Education is not only a basic input for economic development, but it provides inner strength to community to face new situations in terms of equality. There should be a substantial programmes of financial assistance even at elementary stage.

11. Implementing Machinery

At present, the state Harijan and Social Welfare Department which is mainly responsible for the implementation of development programmes does not possess any worthwhile machinery, specially at the district level for effective supervision, monitoring of information, test checks and inspections. There is a need to evolve an adequate implementing machinery involving functionaries from various departments of the Government.

12. Co-ordination

Lack of co-ordination among the activities of different departments is one of the many factors responsible for ineffective implementation of programmes. The whole problem of administrative co-ordination needs rethinking. The primary function of the administrative head of the State and district should be recognised as development. The district Collector at the district level and the Chief Secretary or Development Commissioner at the state level should review and co-ordinate the programmes. An appropriate institutional framework should be evolved for co-ordination among the Government agencies functioning in the field.

13. People's Participation

Peoples participation at various stages of planning process is limited and nominal. Further, in majority of the programme there has been acceptance without widespread understanding. It is necessary to motivate the people through a massive education programme. While implementing the programme, people should be made aware that it is their own scheme and the Government is simply assisting them.

14. Monitoring, Follow-up and Evaluation

There is absence of proper supervision, follow-up action and above all accountability. Systematic monitoring has, therefore, become absolutely essential. A sub-committee may be created at the village level which would monitor and follow-up the programmes. This sub-committee should make liasion with Block and District authorities.

15. Personal Policy

An effective policy is necessary to implement the programmes. Officers and workers should know their job, understand the problem, develop a line of communication and extend their knowledge and experience. Suitable training programmes may also be organised for the purpose.

16. Data Archives

There is considerable dearth of data to formulate policy and programmes. It is, therefore, necessary to develop a cell where all relevant data relating to Scheduled Castes are tabulated and make the same available in published or cyclostyled form to planners and to researchars and other institutions, engaged in development activities. Information may be required not only for the Scheduled Castes as a whole, but also for particular caste/community separately, so that suitable decisions may be taken from time to time about the scope of operation of the stipulated concessions.

17. Voluntary Organisations

The existing voluntary organisation working with the Scheduled Castes may be strengthened and new organisations may be sponsored to undertake special programmes for the development of Scheduled Castes. Attempts may be made to specify the areas where the participation of voluntary organisations are necessary. Some of such areas which may be identified are (a) carrying out innovative activities under the self-employment programme, (b) supplementing government effort in the selection of beneficiaries and schemes, (c) monitoring the government programmes and giving a reliable feedback to planners and policy makers on the manner of implementation of programmes, (d) ensuring that special legislations intended for Scheduled Castes are properly enforced, (e) training a cadre of grass-root/village workers to help the Scheduled Castes, (f) promoting self-reliance on beneficiaries, and (g) mobilising and organising the poor against exploitation by the intermediaries.

Though based on the case studies on development programmes in the present study, some suggestions are given regarding how to manage the process of development of Scheduled Castes more effectively. These programmes as well as such other projects are still being taken up in the State of Uttar Pradesh. It is necessary to continue action-oriented research on these programmes to find out the solutions of the problems arising out of its implementation.

Section V

Ethnic Interactions and Their Sequel to Socio-Cultural Transformations

Introduction

Rebati Mohan Sarkar

I

The social groups with common cultural traditions centering round likeness in the philosophy of life are commonly known as ethnic groups. Various ethnic groups of such kind inhabit a particular region or locality forming a social conglomerate. In this clustered social situation the individual units are not seen to be dissociated, rather these are linked together and these linkages take the significant role of reciprocal communication of thinking patterns and behavioral activities. Humans interact purposefully, because without interactions it is not possible to satisfy the basic needs. Humans by nature can not live alone–alone they would fail to prepare the grounds in the struggle for existence. In order to be activated more and more in the continuous toil for devising various subsistence strategies as well as to make these effective they, as a matter of course, took special endeavours for group formation. Within the social groups thus formed there are various norms and regulations; the people set themselves in reciprocal relationships. Individuals within the social groups make contacts amongst themselves and thereby interact amongst each other, and in these phenomena there are unity or isolation. Interacting parties may come nearer together or they go farther apart. The trends of association and dissociation characterize the interacting people. Side by side with individual interactions we find the patterns of interaction amongst the ethnic groups. When these groups with specific contents and characters come close to each other with people forming different ethnic groups are to be seen in conflicting atmosphere. It is through the methods of interactions that people learn from each other, they exchange their ideas. Many a time various ethnic groups pick up the cultural traits from neighboring other such groups coming into close contact and through this effort these groups have changed a lot. Sometimes the changes have been so deep-rooted that it becomes difficult to explore their traditional perspective.

Being born and brought up in an explicitly rural setting of the then Bengal, Prof. P. K. Bhowmick could find the picturesque domain of the interaction patterns of the society and culture from close quarters. In course of time he became curious with the multifarious activity-orientations of the variegated ethnic groups constituted by the different castes and tribes. Both the two social phenomenal groups were then working in and around his native village. He not only observed the various behaviour-patterns of the castes but also he felt with deep concern the nature and extent of their working dimensions which in course of time had their reflections in Bhowmick's life-long endeavour to explore that particular human dimension criss-crossed by multi-dimensional ethnic understandings.

Study of the ethnic groups in the background of their change and continuity resulting from the age-old interactions with various human factors has become the specific interest of Prof. Bhowmick from the very inception of his enquiries into the anthropological horizon. His investigations into the nature and extent of the ethnic groups did never focus any light on the concepts and theories of the origin of those groups rather his overall interest was centered round their functional principles. What attracted him very much was the examination of the different socio-cultural factors working in the inner recess of the total social system to make the stratified and unequal perspectives of the ethnic groups oriented society integrated for the interest of existence despite heterogeneous life-philosophy. Frequently the social processes may witness transformations and which are sometimes so deeply rooted to the very foundation of the social setting that abrupt changes set in giving rise to the new thinking patterns and altered social philosophy. The institutions of castes and communities–the traditional ethnic groups in Indian societies–and their holistic behaviour–patterns conditioned by integrated actions and dominant instructions reflect the distinct picture of rural India where the pulse of Indian life situation is to be felt. Prof. Bhowmick's specific approach to feel the pulse of Indian society conditioned by rigid traditions and eventful alterations were out and out based on close set observations of the working of the human social institutions in the rural settings.

Prof. Bhowmick started his research career with the tribal people particularly the Lodhas living in the western part of Midnapur district. It was so-called a criminal tribal group and naturally a problem-ridden community completely detached from the rest of the people. Their criminal propensity was well circulated and the people were all along panicky with the Lodhas. But Prof. Bhowmick dared to take up the specific research work on that community with a pledge to explore the interacting facets of criminality in them and the particular reason of taking up such a peculiar and dreaded profession living in the midst of broader healthy social environs of the region.

After completion of the first phase of his study on the Lodhas he volunteered to take the responsibilities of conducting the welfare activities for bringing healthy atmosphere in the way of life of the Lodhas–declared by the administration as ex-criminal or denotified tribe–under the sponsorship of the central and state governments. At the first instance he selected two villages–one Daharpur near Kharagpur and the other Dholkat near Lalgarh, in Midnapur district–for the economic rehabilitation of the Lodhas through the implementation of a lot of changing situations both in the economic as well as social affairs. He could understand from his broad-based research that until and unless social distance between the Lodhas and the people of other communities was narrowed down, there would be no effective result in bringing those distracted tribal people to the mainstream. While working in connection with the Lodha rehabilitation scheme under the auspices of the Samaj Sevak Sangh,a voluntary organization, started by him with a band of academicians, district administrative personnel and field investigators. Prof. Bhowmick categorically studied the structural and organizational nature of the village Daharpur where Lodhas as well as Munda tribal groups formed a part. He observed that Daharpur was a multi-ethnic village and the different caste groups there follow the traditional hierarchical pattern. The Brahmins are not only enjoying the highest rank but also they received respectful gratitude from the other caste members. The conditions of the Lodhas and the Mundas, living at the outskirts of the village, were different. They were not totally isolated groups but there existed a conspicuous communication gap between the tribal and the Hinduised groups divided into different castes with specific position in the village society.

Prof. Bhowmick by dint of his insight readily realized that the Lodhas were needed to be understood by their co-villagers belonging to the different caste groups as well as by the neighbouring tribe like the Mundas. He was of the opinion that even the abrupt change in the economic perspective would not be able to create the atmosphere of rehabilitation of the Lodhas–there was an urgent requirement for their social adjustment in the village setting. It instigated him to investigate into the social setting of Daharpur village centering round which the Lodha rehabilitation endeavour had been taken up. That very endeavour resulted in the methodical study of the village community. He saw in Daharpur a concerted life led by 10 caste groups with different social and ritualistic position together with 2 tribal communities. He examined the hierarchical patterns of the caste groups–their traditional callings side by side with the present day primary and secondary occupations. Agriculture and allied activities tied up the village people irrespective of caste groups. There was a distinct service and remuneration pattern based on caste professions and it was functionable not only in the economic domain but also in the various socio-ritualistic affairs. There was close set dependence on each other. Life within the village was seen to be governed by various caste-oriented norms, and people in all spheres were under obligation to follow those traditional legislation. Village Daharpur owed its name from the village tutelary deity–the *Daharchandi*. She was adorned annually at the advent of the first transplantation of paddy seedlings. Beside that worship the village had large number of gods and goddesses belonging to the traditional Hinduised as well as folk patterns. In the worship of the Hinduised deities the Brahmin priest of the village used to act as the chief conductor. The other caste groups were engaged in the different performances as per caste tradition and there were arrangements for ritualistic remunerations to the workers concerned. Even the so-called untouchable castes had some essential works to be done in connection with the worship of the village deity. Thus the villagers having different caste categories and diversified social position united unhesitatingly to make the ceremonial occasions successful. In case of the traditional village festival, that was characterized by folk pattern of thinking, there were participation of all the people and without the ritualistic dominance of the Brahmin priest. As for example, the *Gajan* festival of the village presented a different perspective of peoples' participation. There were many instances when caste and community barriers fell; no social bar obstructed the coming of the devotees irrespective of caste and communities to the deities in the temples or shrines. What was more important was that the Mundas and the Lodhas of the village did not find any difficulty to participate actively in that ceremonial performance, rather they were cordially invited as per the norm of the village-level festival. In this domain of study Prof. Bhowmick observed that the religious and ceremonial life of the villagers coincided together to form a concerted group life. On those occasions, individual status, caste demarcation, rivalry and other barriers melted away and a new out look of social collaboration was in operation.

Despite the integrated pattern there were concrete instances of conflict and tension in the village life. Sometimes economic exploitation of dominant and higher castes made the less powerful and lower caste groups agitated and in course of time they developed a fierceful attitude towards the advantageous caste groups, which ultimately resulted in a continuous tense situation. It very often retarded the smooth running of the concerted group life. There were misunderstandings between the caste Hindus and the adivasis, and it was seen from various eventful activities of the village, that it exercised some sort of suspicious and hateful attitudes towards each other. Some developments in the socio-economic affairs, though not very significant, caused a great deal in narrowing down the wide gap between the two groups. It gave Prof. Bhowmick a clue to the fact that the creation of an effective platform for developing a good understanding amongst the different social groups could help in providing the Lodhas a place in the broader social system which they had been lacking due to their criminal propensities. That particular situation ultimately made the village Daharpur a conspicuous social setting for mutual understandings and effective co-operation conditioned by cultural blendings, of course through a long process of reciprocal interactions. In the long run Daharpur was metamorphosed into Bidisa–a new name, a new philosophy of life and a thoroughly changed atmosphere of basic understandings conditioned by criss-crossed facets of human endeavours.

After the publication of the study on Daharpur in *Man In India* in 1963, Prof. Bhowmick became very much interested in exploring the hidden elements in the rural social system working as catalytic agents in changing forces of the age-old thought, and behaviour patterns. In due course Prof Bhowmick has been tempted to look into the conditions of the three other different villages in the region of his interest i.e. in the western border region of Midnapur district. It is to be noted that the criterion for his selection of villages for experimental study is dependent on two factors–one is religious beliefs and the other is the trends of migration. Religion, Prof. Bhowmik believes, is the sentimental issue, which delves deep into the peoples' mind. In the rural communities religion binds the people more closely in comparison to other factors of life. Religion takes active part in group solidarity on one hand and, on the other, it creates the atmosphere of interchanging of thoughts and beliefs when such circumstances arise.

In the next phase of his attempts for observations on the phenomena of socio-cultural interactions amongst the diversified and sometimes with contradictory thinking patterns we find his study on the way of life of a Muslim village, a Christian village and a Tribal Chieftain village. In studying the Muslim village–Kasba–Narayangarh–he has traced the historical perspective in the establishment of the village and the roles of the Muslim rulers in that respect. In this village Muslims live side by side with the Hindus. Despite religious seclusion, there is an intimate and remarkable social linkage between the two groups. In the different social affairs and life-cycle ceremonies invitees come from both the communities i.e., in the ceremonial situations no religious bar is entertained. Social behaviour patterns amongst these two communities have been highly dominated by close-set understandings conditioned by time-long united living on a particular geo-physical setting. There are cases of forging ceremonial relationships between the Hindu and the Muslim individuals, which is no less important, than the real kinship pattern. There are a number of instances of Hindu-Muslim mother and son relationship patterns of ceremonial nature in this village, which signifies the range of social integration of the two communities despite disparity in religious faiths. The servicing caste groups find no hesitation in establishing service relationship with the Muslim families.

Mirpur–a Christian Village–is an example of social isolation. The Portuguese gunners were brought to this locality by the then zaminder because of the protection of his locality from the raids of the Marathas and also from the sea-pirates of Arakan, locally known as 'mag', who used to haunt the place for indiscriminate plundering. Those gunners were given rent-free village to live and that was continuing till date. Still today the inhabitants of Mirpur are all Christians and they trace their descendants from the Portuguese ancestors. The Christian inhabitants of Mirpur are seen to remain isolated from the general people. Though some of them are engaged in the locally oriented agricultural activities, many persons of the village have taken various employments outside the village. Almost all the parents in the present generation are in favour of assigning regional Bengali names to their children. But overall conditions of these christianized people lead almost to a segregated and secluded life. Looking into the life of village Belda inhabited by the tribal Christians together with the non-converted tribal people as well as different caste groups, it would be clear that the village presents a picture of association and accommodation amongst the Hindus and the tribal groups. There is a close-set interaction in the form of economic dealings, service and remuneration patterns and in the organizing of village-level festivals. The servicing Hundu castes have found no hesitation to establish service relationship with the tribal people. But the Christian tribals are conspicuously rigid. They are to follow the Christian code and thus they can not cross the boundary of their religions restriction. They are forbidden to participate in the village level festival. The festivals of the non-Christian tribals are not to be attended though they maintain a hidden linkage with those. The non-Christian tribals do not like to maintain any social connection with the converted tribals even if their tribal basis is the same but the converted tribals find no difficulty in getting the services of the village barber and washer man. The later groups do not hesitate to render these services and this situation is, no doubt, the result of long-term side-by-side living in a particular area. It is to be noted that the converted Christians are very sentimental to attach themselves to the tribal origin at the time of establishing matrimonial relations. In this case Christianity fails to suppress the tribal feelings. From the general behaviour patterns of the inhabitants of four villages having different socio-religious settings, it is observed that there has developed a situation of reshaping the society and forging new relations and at the sometime there are dissensions on the grounds of religion.

But whatever may be the fact religion did never create any hazardous situations in the life of the people with diversified religious faiths living in a close set area. What is more important is that various elements of different religious faiths get intermingled giving a new understanding and a new pattern of joint living. The traditional Brahminic dominance in the Hindu religious domain is not only noteworthy but also it is seen to establish a commanding influence over the modes of behaviour of the people in the graded social system. All types of forces have been compelled, to a great extent, to bow down their heads before that dominating factor of the Brahminical procedures. From his intensive study on the variegated patterns of life and living of the heterogeneous communities having different philosophy and religious orientations, Prof. Bhowmick has been able to present the concrete evidences of socio-religious and behavioural interactions giving rise to a particular condition of the fusion of traits. Man wants security in life and he also wants to keep the life smooth and trouble-free for his family members as a whole. Man prays to the unknown power believing that he is the controller of everything. The prayers are forwarded in the form of worship. These are made for multiple purposes. It may be for the recovery from diseases, getting employment, prosperity and stability in service or business, economic security, protection of the animals in forests, abundant crops, safe delivery of the expectant mothers, success in the examinations and any others. In the traditional temples and shrines there are a large number of deities of different dimensions with which the people irrespective of caste and communities maintain a good relationship for the solution of their day to day problems as well as relief from anxieties. Prof. Bhowmick in his untiring effort to expose the integrating perspective of different belief patterns has put forward his observations on the nature of deities, their modes of worships and the peoples' participation in connection with the four significant temple organizations developed in the border regions of West Midnapur district. The temples are mostly the seats of the gods and goddesses who are processed by rigid Brahminical traditions. There are various restrictions in the modes of worship, which are extensively moulded by purity–pollution concept. But in this particular region, no such Brahminical procedure is seen to be effected deeply into the peoples' mind. These temples are not only visited by the different castes and communities but also the peoples are free in approaching the deities themselves. These temples, according to Prof. Bhowmick, are the dumb witness of different changing patterns of human behavioural activities. In this region amongst the people of different socio-cultural and religion dimensions, interaction of thoughts and ideas have so much been effected that orthodox Brahminism could not raise its head. It is only due to this reason, though there are diversified caste groups here along with the Brahmins, yet the rigidity of social hierarchical pattern could not exert any influence. Amongst the temple priests there are non-Brahmin persons and even the tribal people are seen to officiate in one of such temples of importance. These temple organizations show that the multi-faceted interactions of the people cut across the religious dogma.

In course of his investigations into the nature and extent of the folk festivals and the patterns of all round participation of the people of all statuses of life, Prof. Bhowmick has been able to focus discernible light on the interchange of ideas amongst the diversified groups of people giving rise to the phenomenon of reinforcement of social relations. In all these folk festivals the autochthonous tribal or semi-tribal cultural patterns and conventional customs have been mingled with the lately introduced greater Hindu tradition in this region giving rise to a condition of ritualistic tolerance in stead of conflict thereby developing a trend which is known by the term ritual assimilation. These folk deities exemplified by *Gajan, Karam, Bandna, Tusu* etc., reflect the group mind that includes both the magico-religious and secular social fields of action. The broader perspectives of these festivals work as the fertile fields for interaction of different social and ritualistic understandings. Many a time contradictory ideas and heterogeneous philosophies interact with each other and the process has been continued for the indefinite period. Ultimately the differentiation in thinking patterns is transformed into the trend of assimilation; the avoidance mentality of each other's views has been resulted into the process of assimilation.

With the change of time, a large number of interacting factors amongst the different ethnic groups have been effected which have ultimately enhanced the process of inter-ethnic commingle. After the attainment of independence, massive drives have been taken through various development programmes to inprove the general living conditions of the people. The rigidity of caste norms has been vanished, to a considerable extent, and various governmental support to raise the economic and social status of the down-trodden communities has given these people the scope to come close to the advanced groups of people. This situation has very naturally caused to develop new ideology and new values as well as relief from stagnant life-situation. In course of his study on the changing perspective in the way of life of once inaccessible rural settings, Prof. Bhowmick has pointed out that the changed political situation in the region has provided the lowly and depressed people a better place in the stratified social system. The social atmosphere of the villages has been changed to a considerable extent, and Prof. Bhowmick has noted the instances of inter-caste and inter-tribal marriages in the vicinity of Daharpur–a village where diversified directed changes have set in by the governmental and non-governmental agencies. One Lodha married a Munda widow without any resistance from either community. A boy belonging to *Bargakshatriya* caste married a Lodha girl who read in a school. The societies of the concerned persons did not put any objection. One *Sadgop* boy married a *Kayastha* girl and the marriage was registered. In this way the rural setting as a whole has changed in various ways due to close set ethnic interactions which have been highly effective in consequence of the changed political climate.

During the different periods of history, as Prof. Bhowmick has noted, a number of homogeneous community groups with varied social ideas and philosophies migrated to the region in question. These human communities are exemplified by the *Savars, Kakmaras, Chirmars*, and also the distinct tribal groups like the *Lodhas* and the *Mundas*. The heterogeneous composition of these communities have had to face various social forces in course of their adjustment to the new surroundings; on the basis of which there have flourished multifaceted ethnic interactions through the ages. These interactions have resulted in many significant issues in the mechanism of accommodation and sufferance of the heterogeneous cultural strains. In the perspective of these studies, Prof. Bowmick has observed that in consequence of ethnic interactions a new and effectual reorganization of man's relationship with individual and communities have taken place.

II

Prof. Bhowmick has categorically emphasized that these interacting processes are widespread in the great land mass of India. As a land of peoples with different regions and subcultures, India provides an idea of a symphony in which various tunes and melodies have found a confluence. Cooperation and conflict, consonance and discord, compromise and competition, conservatism and radicalism are the eternal essence of culture. One should, therefore, try to locate, understand and analyse each of the elements in their totality. Prof. Bhowmick could not come out of his own region of study where all his working endeavours were concentrated to examine the process of social interactions, but he had his mind to explore the similar features of ethnic interactions in other regions. He encouraged a conspicuous number of his students to look into that situational context some of whom readily took up that particular pattern of study in preparing their dissertations of Ph. D. Degrees. The specific trends of the studies and their nature of contributions to the issue as raised by Prof. Bhowmick have been systematically analysed on the basis of such works as are available at hand.

Dr. Kalipada Malakar's study on the nature and extent of survival of the Hindu ritualistic traits among the converts highlight the interactional procedures amongst the different religious faiths. It has been seen that even after the embracing of the Islam, the Hindu groups of people continue to maintain some of their former traits of beliefs and practices in their daily mode of life and activities. Similar was the case with the Hindu groups after their conversion to Christianity. They have been christianised after the fulfillment of certain requisite formalities and religious strictures concerned. But in spite of this situation the continuation of the original religious faiths becomes conspicuous in their daily modes of behaviour. The Scheduled Caste groups of 24 Parganas and Midnapur districts despite their conversion to Islam or Christianity have not discarded the original family surnames. The study reveals that these surnames work as the missing link between the converts and the Scheduled Caste Hindus of the region. An enquiry into the nature of the socio-religious festivals observed by the converted Christians brings the fact of their correlation with Hindu festivals in original form. Converted persons to both the Islam and the Christianity are regularly seen to use the Hinduized names which are most often related to the Hindu gods and goddesses. The closeness of the different religious communities as well as interactions of the different types of faiths practically have brought an atmosphere of integration of ideas. In this perspective there has developed no conflicting situation rather a trend of silent accommodation is seen to be reflected. With the changing of time the mentality of the different groups of people is rapidly changing and the old orthodox ideas are in the way of vanishing. It is for this reason social interactions amongst the different religious groups are enhancing which have given rise to a condition of social integration despite religious differences.

Social interactions in all rounded fields of human life are highly discernible in the Sundarban region of West Bengal where diversified ethnic groups have migrated since long time past. In his work on the Sundarban village Dr. Shyamapada Chakraborty has observed the waves of cultural differentiation and assimilation, competition and compromise in the living style of the tribals, Scheduled Castes and caste Hindu groups of people. In the later course when Muslim invasion was effected throughout the then Bengal, the Muslims in course of time, gradually infiltrated into the said region and took firm hold over the old inhabitants. Gradually a close understanding was set-up as there was always a need for united efforts to fight with the adverse eco-environmental conditions on the land mass traversed by the network of rivers and creeks. The tribal groups of people were the original settlers of this jungle-infested region who were brought here by the then British administration to clear the forest for land reclamation to serve the purpose of conducting agricultural activities there. The tribal migrant labourers ultimately became the ryots and they were holding vast fertile land of the region. But with the progress of time Sundarban became the prime attraction of a large number of fortune seekers who gradually settled here and through various cunning ways they snatched away lands from the possession of the simple-minded tribal people. Thus the interactions of the tribal groups of people with the non-tribal groups caused a conspicuous change over the fate of the former groups. From the ryots they became mere daily labourers in their once own land. Whatever may be the fact it is clear that due to the continuous and close set social interactions amongst migratory diversified tribals, caste and community groups a synthesis of cultures has been the result which cuts across the tribe, caste and community lines of thinking. There are concrete instances of close amalgamation of tribal, Hindu and Muslim faiths in the different deities and festivals which are the characteristic features of this unique land mass.

Dr. Kartick Chandra Dalui, in his work on the consequences of social mobility, has tried to put forward the phenomena of social mobility amongst the various occupational groups in Bengal to find out the tendency towards the growth of a national feeling of the people concerned. The Hindu caste groups in Bengal are divided into multifarious occupational groups having particular places in the graded social structure. The author has observed that in course of changing economy in Bengal a large number of sub-castes took agriculture from fishing profession which made the concerned sub-castes to be recognized by the different names and ultimately they were recognized as socially differentiated units. Later on through the process of sanskritization they received separate caste affiliation. When Islam became, to some extent, dominant in the deltaic Bengal many lowly caste groups accepted Islam but in spite of conversion their traditional occupations did not change. The people of Bengal have always been progressive in their behaviour patterns. It is due to this reason the interactions amongst the caste and community groups are seen to be very much effective in this landmass. Inter caste differentiations are not so acute here like other regions of India, rather a spell of socio-cultural integrity is commonly seen which indicates the atmosphere of social adjustment. Trends of modernization have resulted in the growth of various democratic organizations, spread of education amongst the masses as well as the abolitoin of various ill-fated social phenomena which collectively have given rise to the abrupt changing mentality of the people. It has opened up a new and idealistic philosophy of living together despite all sorts of resistance and hazardous phenomena. Here the mobility based mentality has surpassed the rigidity oriented trend of the social system.

Human groups are characterized by various specific traits which govern all spheres of their life and activities. Because of their sentimental linkage with the social mind these are hardly lost from the view of the society, rather these run down from generations to generations, and thereby are identified as traditional features. Human survival strategies are unique of their kind and they, as a matter of course, interact profusely with the ecological settings and environmental perspectives. Therefore, if such a situation arises when the eco-environmental factors are changed, to a great extent, it would affect the nature and extent of socio-cultural trait complexes designing the way of life of the concerned population group. Dr. Amar Nath Paul explains here the changes and persistence of the various socio-cultural and ritualistic traits of the Oraons in three specific eco-environmental zones–chotanagpur, Sundarban and Dooars. In these three distinct ecological perspectives the lifestyles of the Oraons very naturally have faced a lot of changes and those are due to the different patterns of subsistence strategies as developed to make adjustment with the surroundings. But it is to be noted that the interactions with the ecology and environment have, no doubt, opened up a new horizon of life but the basic traditional elements and philosophy of life are found to be continuing.

Dr. Ahsan Ali has forwarded his broad-based observations on the behaviour patterns of the Santals in the background of the changed ecology, economy and political situations in Bangladesh. As per historical records, the Santals from the different regions of central and eastern India especially from Rajmahal Hills migrated to the Barind tract of the then East Bengal, now in Bangladesh. After their settlement here the Santals went through a number of upheavals caused by the nachole Santal movements, abolition of zamindary, introduction of passport system between India and the then East Pakistan, and various communal uprising. Due to these reasons they had a set back. But in consequence of their hard working nature and efficiency in agricultural work, they could make the Barind region prosperous. The Santals here have long been in close association and effective interactions with the non-tribal social system. As regards the performance of the various ceremonies of lifestyle, they maintain their age-old tradition and in this sphere their social isolation is specific. But it is to be noted that they have been in a close process of interactions with the people of the non-tribal communities and due to that situation the tribal culture has been assimilated with the traits of the neighbouring people. Their concept of bonga and its influence has been extended owing to the contact with outsiders. They have started imposing *bonga* concept on the political symbol of the *Awami League*–the boat. Likewise many Hindu gods and goddesses viz., *Kali, Durga, Manasa, Mahadeva* and *Lakshmi* have found place in the bonga pantheon. The Santals converted to Christianity have taken up various traits of Christian belief-patterns into their own religious domain. The effects of Christianity have brought many significant changes in the religious domain where Theistic trends have been intermingled with the Animistic beliefs of the traditional tribal religion.

Dr. Sujit Som has presented his study on the patterns of interactions in the sphere of adaptation to a thoroughly changed surroundings by an uprooted community of the then East Pakistan. It was an attempt of rehabilitation of the Bengali refugees by the Govt. of India at Little Andaman. At the very outset, the uprooted people had to face the eco-environmental condition completely unsuited to them both culturally and biologically, and thus they became totally depressed. But as time went on, they gradually started to feel the reality and through a long process of interactions with the ecological, ethnic, economic, behavioural as well as socio-political setting, the population concerned were able to make themselves adjusted with the alien circumstances. They started establishing their villages of traditional nature where the houses were redesigned and the layout pattern followed their original structural plan of the traditional type so far as the basic social function was concerned. The uncommon environmental effects have made them more and more united socially and psychologically. Therefore, the traditional socio-cultural bonds of the villages and families have tightened their knots of social existence.

Establishment of marriage alliance still does not neglect the norms and regulations of their original patterns. They have introduced all types of traditional worships of the gods and goddesses like *Durga, Kali, Manasa, Bhagabati* and *Saraswati* as well as the religious festival like *Rathajatra*. In these ways the uprooted people have been able to sow the seeds of village cohesiveness. In the agricultural sphere continuous interactions with the land and people have made them successful, to a considerable extent, in growing new as well as traditional crops in the changed habitat. In the development of new technology to suit the specific ecology of the region, their interactions with the aboriginal tribal groups like the Onge and the Nicobarese have been very much effective for successful achievements in the alien land.

In the city atmosphere pavement dwellers have been posing concrete problems throughout the century. Having no permanent hearths and homes they have taken shelter at the pavements which are exclusively meant for the pedestrians. As they have failed to make their both ends meet they have found no other alternative but to migrate to the city where there are certain possibilities of getting chances for earning the living. Dr. Bidyut K. Das, in his study, has pin-pointed the nature and extent of life-situation of these people and their interactions amongst themselves as well as with the city dwellers. The pavement dwellers of the city of Calcutta are the counterparts of the rural poor who belong to the lowest rung of the social ladder and suffer from cumulative inequalities. In course of investigating into their life in the pavements, Dr. Das has observed that at the first stage of their settlement here the social factors like caste, kinship and regional ties play important role, but in due course, their pattern of social interaction vanishes. It is interesting to note that gradually they develop some secondary relations based on the network of contracts and reciprocal give and take in the domain of goods and services. The age-old traditional network of relationship does not hold good here. Interactions with the kin groups are very loose and gradually these fall down. It has been noted that despite living in the same locality, they hardly keep any social contact with their near relatives and even with the brothers and sisters. Their interactions are sometimes found to enhance with the non-kin members. The relation between husband and wife is faded away as well as the parents-children relationship becomes loosened. In the life of the pavement dwellers the traditional patterns of interactions are replaced by interest-oriented interactions. In this setting new social groupings emerge and force to supplement the different crises of life through alternatives. This new type of unstructured social relation develops a new process in the life of the pavement dwellers.

Stratgies for Survival among the Oraons in Diverse Ecological Perspective

Amar Nath Paul

The concept of survival strategy appears for the first time sporadically in the beginning of 1970s and finds place regularly in the social science literatures in the late 1980s. This concept, though opens up a new horizon of research, is still in primordial stage as the scholars with their new logical attempt to explain widely different socio-cultural phenomena under the same epithet (Savishnsky 1978; Jochim 1981; Chambers 1983; Lieten 1989; Van Schendel 1989; Streefland 1989). The present research conceptualizes the 'survival strategy' in terms of two entirely opposed dimensions–subsistence strategies and maintenance strategies. The former refers to those ways by which people assure their physical existence by utilizing natural resources. On the contrary, the second one relates to the ways by which people are able to maintain their identity by retaining age old cultural practices in modified form in spite of changes taking place among them.

II

The present study was carried on among the Dravidian speaking Oraons which are the third largest tribal groups in India. They are considered one of the early settlers of the Indian sub-continent. Scholars have advanced two different views as to locate the origin of these people. One such hypothesis contends that the cradle land of the Oraon was somewhere along Konkan coast in the Deccan long before the Christian era (Dalton 1872). The other hypothesis suggests that the Oraons who were originated from the Dravidian group lived in the Indus valley at least some 3500 years ago since the Dravidian people are believed to be the makers of Indus civilization (Titkey cited in Tirkey 1989). Whichever may be the origin, their migration started long ago and covered a wide range of habitats. The scope of current research is restricted to three different geographical regions–the lataritic Chotanagpur Plateau, the deltaic Sundarbans and the tea producing Dooars of the sub Himalayas. Of all these regions, Chotanagpur happens to be the oldest tract of present day Oraon habitat from where migration took place at varied intervals during British period to other regions.

Today, Chotanagpur represents both geographical and political unit. It is located between 82°20′-87°54′ east longitude and 21°49′-24°48′ north latitudes, covering an area of about 65266.26 sq. km. Administratively, the plateau encompasses a substantial part of the newly created Jharkhand state. It exhibits a tremendous variation in all respects. On the basis of attitudinal differences, the plateau is divided into four physiographic units. It brings about variation in natural vegetation, drainage, climate and so on.

The Sundarbans, lying approximately between 21°30′ - 22°30′ north latitude and between 88°51′ - 91°30′ east longitude, covers an area of 9630 sq. km. in the south east of the state of West Bengal. The entire landscape, which is formed by the deposition of silt, is crisscrossed by numerous tidal rivers and their tributaries. Declared a biosphere, this region is famous for mangrove forest, however, the forest is at present restricted only to the south eastern part of the Sundarbans.

The Dooars, annexed by the British in 1865, corresponds to the present day Jalpaiguri district which is located at the northern part of West Bengal. Geographically, it lies between 26°16′-27°00′ north latitude and between 88°25′- 89°53′ east longitudes, covering an area of about 6227 sq. km. With the exception of the hilly northern fringe, the whole of the Dooars is covered by the alluvial deposits. Well known for its vast forest coverage, the region is also intersected by numerous rivers and hill streams in every directions.

III

In the present research, subsistence strategy as one dominant mode of survival refers to the knowledge of natural resources, employment of tools and technology, and organization of labour in order to extract a living from the world around them. This implies a series of systematically ordered acts which are influenced by local ecology and social environment. The following account briefly describes the subsistence strategies of Oraons inhabiting Chotanagpur, Sundarbans and Dooars.

Chotanagpur

In the olden days, forest played an omnipotent role in the life of the Oraons of Chotanagpur. It was the most basic physical resource where they used to hunt animals, to collect fruits, roots and tubers, and to procure fuel, fodder, building material and so on. With the gradual expansion of human settlement, the forested part at present is greatly reduced and offers very limited scope to the Oraons and other tribal people to depend on this resource. But the Oraons, especially the poorer ones, still collect certain forest produces which are used as substitution for food or traded for earning cash. The most notable forest produces are *sal* leaves, *mahua* flower, *keond* leaves, *sabai* grass etc.

Agriculture is the main stay of the Oraons of Chotanagpur. They are often called a peasant tribe of Bihar (Lall 1960; Mandal 1975). Historically, the traditional right of land belonged to the tribal people of this plateau. But they lost a greater part of their ancestral land to non tribal people when Chotanagpur came under the British rule. With the promulgation of several ostensible measures such as Bihar Tenancy Act of 1885. Chotanagpur Tenancy Act of 1908 and so on, the restoration of tribal land is being effectuated. All the economic rights to land basically fall into two types–ownership right and contractual right with their variants. Owing to plateau region, the land in Chotanagpur is located at different heights. The Oraons classify the cultivable land into two categories according to their relative position. They grow a variety of crops, out of which the most important one are some grains like paddy, millets called *marwa* and *gondli;* a few kinds of pulses namely *urad, arhar, kurthi;* some oil seeds like *sarguja, mustard* and so forth. The agricultural land use pattern reveals that paddy is the most important crop. This is followed in succession by *marwa, urad, sarguja* etc. The ecological condition of the low land favours exclusively the cultivation of paddy while various classes of high land are brought under the cultivation of other crops like *marwa, urad, sarguja* etc. Agriculture is entirely dependent on monsoon rain. Except cowdung and farm refuse as manure, the uses of chemical furtiliser and pesticide are very much limited. All the agricultural activities are done mostly by the family members of both sexes. The additional labour, if any, is met by the reciprocal exchange of labour between families. The practice of hired labour on payment of wage is still not very much popular among them. The surplus agricultural produces are sold at weekly market located in the vicinity of tribal areas. However, they do not get proper price as the middle men collect bulk of local produce at a very low price.

Alongside agriculture, animal husbandry plays a substantive role in the subsistence strategies adopted by the Chotanagpur Oraons. As agriculture is the mainstay in their livelihood, it influences upon the development of livestock rearing which is facilitated by the availability of adequate grazing ground. Cattle, goats, pigs and poultry birds including fowls and ducks are important livestock animals which are domesticated in separate sheds around courtyard within household premises. Cattle, the most important animal, are penned for agriculture and production of milk. Goats are grown mainly for cash. Pigs are reared for cash and are slaughtered on the occasions of religious ceremonies. Poultry birds are kept for cheap source of protein, sacrificial objects and honouring the guests.

Wage labour always occupies an important place in the spectrum of the economic activities among the Chotanagpur Oraons. In particular, the landless and marginal landholders are found to employ themselves as wage earners in agricultural activities. The discrimination of sexes in matters of wage is still continuing as before despite the rule stating equal remuneration. At present, the female labourers earn almost half of the wage of their male counterparts. The Oraons known to be hard working people are recruited for bulk of the labour force in construction works. Due to Govt. of India's reservation policy and gradual improvement of literacy level, many young educated Oraons are employed in both public and private sectors.

Sundarban

The scenario of resource utilisation in the deltaic Sundarban is quite different from the Chotanagpur plateau. The Oraons were brought here as labourers for reclamation of forest land to open up agriculture. They worked as tenants to the landlords till the abolition of Zamindari system, after which they either forcefully took the possession of land or purchased the same at nominal prices. Some Oraons bring under possession temporarily the land from neighbouring people and absentee landlords in the form of lease and mortgage locally called *khaikhalssi* and *ekrat* respectively. For long, agriculture stands as the most basic subsistence strategy of the Sundarban Oraons. The region was previously a mono crop area, *aman* (a kind of crop) being the only crop. The introduction of irrigation has opened up the cultivation of *boro* paddy as a second crop. Compared to *aman* paddy, the cultivation of *boro* paddy is a costly affair which takes into account of the provisions like chemical fertilizer, pesticide, irrigation etc. On the whole, agriculture is characterised by low productivity due to saline soil, brackish water and other environmental hazards such as periodical flood, severe cyclone. In particular, the Oraons and other tribal people own mostly low lying land which is vulnerable to the ingress of estuarine tidal water.

The ecology of Sundarban is an important priority area for the development of brackish water shrimp farming locally called *jalkar* or *gheri* (Pal 1992). It was previously confined to the extensive low lying marshy land. Since the first half of 1980s, the land already put to agriculture is being converted to shrimp farming. The Oraons are of no exception. Under the various socio-economic and political circumstances, the Oraons and other poor people are recently forced to lease out their land mostly to non-tribal people and receive only a paltry sum as lease. A great extent of tribal land has already been leased out to non-tribal who generate substantial profit by practicing shrimp farming there.

Animal husbandry is a subsidiary economic activity among the Sundarban Oraons. They rear animals like cattle, goats, pigs and poultry birds. The motive of keeping these livestock animal does not differ from that in Chotanagpur. The rapid growth of shrimp farming at the expense of agriculture has created acute shortage of grazing ground that in turn reduces the scope of livestock rearing. Even the cultivating Oraons do not always keep them.

The marshy land crisscrossed by numerous streams, rivers, creeks form a unique ecology of fishing in Sundarban. The Oraons with their simple technology are mostly confined to their fishing activity in ponds, ditches, puddles, stagnant water bodies, water channels and so on. It is almost a daily affair. But the best time of fishing is immediately after new and full moon. They catch a variety of fishes, prawn and some other aquatic species by different types of nets depending on the nature of water resources. Except tiger prawn and other fishes of marketable size, they consume others after cooking.

In winter months, the Oraons have practically no scope of earning in their locality. During this lean season, a section of male folk migrates to urban areas and work as daily wage labourers in various construction activities. A few of them are also employed in growing shrimp farming.

Dooars

The ecology of Dooars favours the growth of tea plantation. It was first planted here by the Britishers in 1874 (Burns 1951). Since then, many tea gardens were developed mainly in the northern part of this sub-Himalayan tarrain with the help of imported labour force mainly from the tribals of Chotanagpur. They are often known by the term *modesia* to the local people. The Oraons and other tribal people are successfully adapted to the tea plantation. Employed mostly as wage earners in a sequence of tea garden activities, they are often categorised in various ways–adult men, adult women and children; permanent and temporary workers; garden and factory workers. Tea garden activities involve the participation of both men and women. In general men are assigned to those tasks that require more physical strength and risk of danger. The production of tea depends on the availability of leaves which grow abundantly in the monsoon period. The plucking of leaves is the most dominant and labour intensive activity of all tea garden works. It continues for nine to ten months, being the peak period during rainy season. The wages are paid weekly or fortnightly for eight hours work a day for six days in a week. They have opportunity to earn additional incentive for extra work done beyond the normal working hours. Some other facilities like medical aid, retirement benefits, subsidised food stuff, free fuel are provided to them. However, the tea industry is passing through a precarious condition. As a result, a few tea gardens have already been closed, and some more are on the verge of closure. It has negative impact on the employment of the tea garden workers. At the same time, the scope of other employment is very much restricted to them for their relative isolation in tea gardens.

The tea garden workers including Oraons are sometimes found to be associated with some other activities that are never considered to play significant role in obtaining livelihood. A few young occasionally go to forest in the vicinity of tea garden for collection of edidolus and catching of small animals. They playfully catch fishes in hilly streams or rivers during rainy season mainly for domestic consumption. They often grow some kinds of vegetables on the patch of land adjacent to their respective household. Very few of them possess a limited number of livestock animals which are reared for milking purpose only.

IV

After presenting a detailed account of survival strategies in terms of utilisation of physical resources the present study broadens its contextual meaning by subsuming other important dimension which is equally important and relates to the continuation of custom and traditions associated with birth, marriage, death and religion. All these spheres have undergone a fair amount of change. But there are strong resemblances found in each such sphere among the Oraons inhabiting Chotanagpur, Sundarban and Dooars.

With regard to the child birth, the Oraon women still observe similar kind of restriction and taboo during pregnancy. The customs relating to the bury of placenta after birth in front of door remain almost same. The duration of pollution period upon child birth varies from one region to other, but its attendant customs do not differ much. The age old practice of rice dropping ceremony in naming child is still prevalent among the Chotanagpur Oraon. The traditional practice, though in limited scale, is maintained with little adjustment in other two regions.

Among the Oraons of all regions marriage takes place in full observance of rites. The adoption of local practices as well as the continuation of traditional customs are found to occur simultaneously in their marital rites. On certain occasions, they not only discard a few traditional rites, but also accommodate parallel rites in replacing them. The same rites sometimes assume to take new names in different regions. In spite of regional variation there are many features common to all regions. Marriage is still negotiated by match maker. The various formalities associated with the settlement of marriage do not vary among the constituent areas. While the wedding booth or canopy undergoes some sorts of structural modification, the customs associated with its erection are virtually the same. On the occasion of vermilion exchange, the bride and groom are still required to stand on grinding stone in a traditional way. The customs involving gift-giving ceremony are also deeply rooted in the past. Besides these, many others traits are in close observance of tradition.

The Oraons of widely divergent regions show greater identity in respect of mortuary rites. The burial method of disposing the dead is prevalent among them as a typical Dravidian trait. In Chotanagpur and Dooars, they have a separate burial ground whereas the dead bodies are buried in the backside of household premises in case of Sundarban. During the journey to burial site the custom of throwing the cotton and paddy is practiced by them in all regions. The dead body is always laid in the burial pit in north-south direction. The offering of food to departed soul by the chief mourner takes place for the first three or five days during the pollution period. They still observe customs concerning the calling back of the departed soul by means of burning a thatched shed. Related to this phenomenon is another custom concerning the direction of flame of a burning lamp which is believed to happen due to the entry of soul into room. In all the regions, a doll representing the dead body is burnt. A few cowrie shells which are placed within doll prior to its burning are collected as charred bones and immersed ceremonially in river or any other water source. *Danda Katta* ceremony still appears to be the chief ritual of all funeral obsequies.

With regard to the observances of religious rites, the Oraons of Chotanagpur still follow many of their traditional rituals. As they move from this area to other geographical regions, the numbers of traditional rites are also reduced due to ethno-ecological factors. Despite the disappearance of certain rituals, a number of traditional rites and ceremonies which are of greater importance to them are still found to take place in all the three regions. These religious rituals are considered significant in maintaining the ethnic identity of the Oraons. Maintaining the identity is appropriate in two ways. On the one hand, a ritual taking place in different regions has many common traits. On the other hand, the expression of certain phenomena shows regional differentiation, but their underlying meanings do not change at all. A few common rites deserve to be mentioned in this context. Chotanagpur Oraons celebrate their *Sarhul* festival in an elaborate way at community level whereas it takes place at household level in Sundarbans and Dooars. In particular, *Sarhul* has no independent existence to Dooars' Oraons. It is observed mostly with *Phagu*. But all the Oraons, irrespective of regional variation, offer their first produce at *Sarhul* indicating the beginning of a new year. Traditionally it is connected with the blossoming of *sal* flower as a season's first produce in Chhotonagpur plateau. The same is true for Dooars' Oraons.The non availability of *sal* trees has made the Sundarbans Oraons to take mango and neem as seasons first produce. Chotanagpur Oraons observe different agricultural rites throughout the year. Some of these rites are continued to be practised by the Sundarbans Oraon as the agricultural people. But a great majority of traditional rites connected with agriculture have lost their place among the Dooars Oraons as they do not practise agriculture. It is interesting to note that one agricultural rite called *Nayakhani* in Chotanagpur is common to Sundarban and Dooars. It is connected with the offering of newly harvested paddy. For not being the rice grower the Dooars Oraons observe this agricultural rite in modified manner. They purchase parched rice made from newly harvested paddy and offer these in a ritualistic way. The celebration of *Sohrai* has certain features common to all Oraon habitats. On this occasion, cattle shed is the place where they invoke their ancestral spirits, cook food and eat the same. A red cock is always used as sacrificial object. The ceremonial anointation of cattle marks the chief feature of *Sohrai*. To the Oraons, *Danda Katta* is an important religious rite taking place nearly on all occasions. It assumes various names in different regions, but is performed in similar fashion. The Sundarbans and Dooars Oraons extend this ritual by addition of some other features which seem to be an attempt made by them to re-establish their ethnic identity as having originated from a common stalk in Chotanagpur plateau.

V

In the backdrop of the present research on the survival strategies of the Oraons, two different but opposite trends seem to dominate in conceptualizing the nature of socio-cultural phenomena. Ecology and culture, the two domains are envisaged not as separate entities and are put under a common rubric. The socio-cultural phenomena are subjected simultaneously to these two domains in varying degrees. Ecology is viewed to offer certain possibilities to a group, the members of which make their effort in its exploitation by means of their knowledge about resources and the available technology. Subsistence strategies are the employment of different ways in utilizing the local resources. The variation of resources from one region to other is instrumental for bringing changes within the spectrum of subsistence strategies. Thus these are always linked in an adoptive way to physical resources found in any ecology. In this context, subsistence strategies prove to be dynamic and as such have utilitarian value to the people.

Contrary to these there are the maintenance strategies which seem to play a dual role. Most of the rituals appear to have certain basic traditional socio-cultural phenomena which are in a process of change in a new ethno-ecological context. These changes are due to the deletion or addition of some elements assuming new meaning in the changing perspectives. Alternatively, the rituals associated with various lifestyle also contain features that are not influenced by externalities and continue to make their existence regardless of their regional variation. Here, culture is extraneous to individual and people conform to the essential traits of culture as they belong to a particular social group. The perpetuity of traditional elements forms the basic resistance to change. From this perspective, the socio-cultural phenomena act as inertia allowing a group to a large extent in retaining its traditional identity. To sum up, the issues related to survival strategies have laid the foundation of the operationalization of socio-cultural phenomena by bringing about simultaneously two opposite forces concerning change and continuity.

References

Burns, A. 1951 *History of the British West India.* London : George Allen And Unwin.

Chambers, R. 1983 *Rural Development : Putting the Last First.* Harlow : Longman.

Dalton, E. T. 1872 *Descriptive Ethnology of Bengal.* Calcutta.

Jochim, M. 1981 *Strategies for Survival : Cultural Behaviour In an Ecological Context.* Delhi : Academic Press.

Lall, R. B. 1960 Changing Economy of the Oraon. *Journal of Social Research,* 3 : 82 - 92.

Lieten, G. K. 1989 Industrial Workers in India : Survival at a Higher Level. In : Leiten, G. K., O. Nieuwenhuys and L. Schenk Sandbergen (ed.) *Women, migrants And tribals survival strategies in Asia.* New Delhi : Monohar Publications.

Mandal, B. B. 1975 Arc tribal cultivation in Bihar to be called 'Peasants'? *man in India,* 55 : 255–262.

Pal, A. N. 1992 Development of break fish water shrimp farming And pauperization of tribal people in Sundarban: An interplay of ecology, economy and politics. *Journal of the Indian Anthropological* Society, 27 : 70–77.

Savishinsky, J. S. 1978 Trapping, Survival strategies and environmental Involvement : a case study from the Canadian Sub-Arctic. *Human Ecology,* 6 . 1- 25.

Streefland, P. H. 1989 Modes of survival and survival strategies. In : Lieten, G. K., O. Nieuwenhuys and L. Schenk Sandbergen (ed.) *Women, Migrants and Tribal–Survival Strategies in Asia.* New Delhi : Monohar Publication.

Tirkey, B. 1989 *The Smiling Liraon.* Patna : Navjoti Niketan.

Van Schendel, W. 1989 Self rescue and survival : the rural poor in Bangladesh. In : Lieten, G. K., O. Nieuwenhuys and L. Schenk Sandbergen (ed.). *Women, Migrants and Tribal–Survival Strategies in Asia.* New Delhi : Monohar Publications.

Great Andamanese–A Vanishing Tribe of Andaman and Nicobar Islands

Dilip Kumar Chakraborty

The Andaman Islands are formed of a chain of Islands in the Bay of Bengal. Approximately these are located eight hundred and twenty miles south-east of Calcutta and one hundred and twenty miles from Cape Negris, in Burma. Here the permanently occupied islands are–the Great Andaman and Little Andaman.

Originally, the Great Andaman is the abode of an indigenous group, which we identified as Great Andamanese, who were the first to encounter outsiders broadly from the year 1790 onwards. This has been possible due to the initiative of a number of British Administrators like Blair (1788), Mouat (1863) and others. The initial encounter invited enough troubles and hostility causing a heavy toll of lives of Great Andamanese in particular. Here we should keep in mind that the early inhabitants of Great Andaman used to differ from one another in dialect, style of life, procurement of food and food habits, on one hand, and the conscious effort in maintaining one's distinctive tribal identity on the other. Because, the indigenous group, 'Great Andamanese', originally consisted of ten distinct tribes and had separate territorial affiliation for each of them. Their division is like this–Aka Chariar or Aka Cari, Aka Kora, Aka Tobo or Aka Bo and Aka Yerre or Aka Jeru is under northern group and Aka Juwai, Aka Kol, Aka Bojigyab or Aka Pucikwar, Aka Balwa or Aka Bale, Aka Bea and Aka Bojigugiji.

It is unfortunate that the British Administrators started neglecting the ethnic identity and cultural distinctiveness of the ten tribes and they were lumped together for administrative purposes, as Great Andamanese.

If we look upon the population figure of the Great Andamanese, we find that in 1858, it was a conservative account estimated as 3,500 –whereas in the Census of 1907, they were only 625 (317 men and 308 women) souls. Their decline of population is also noticeable from the

Census of 1931–where the number of pure-breeds includes 74 souls (27 men, 47 women) and the half-breeds represented 16 souls (11 men, 5 women). Likewise, the Census of 1961 recorded the decline of population–where the total number of Great Andamanese represented 19 souls only. However, from my personal contact with the Great Andamanese, I am certain that the census authorities considered it worthwhile to lump the members of pure breed and half-breed together. Again from my fieldwork among the Great Andamanese, during the period between 1973-1977, I found that due to quick depopulation there were only 23 members (14 men, 9 women). From this figure it is evident that following the maldistribution of marriageable mates–the Great Andamanese are indeed in a demographically disadvantageous position, awaiting quick depopulation.

The probable reason might be their addiction towards alcohol and opium, what they mainly learnt from the 'Andaman Home', which the Britishers established to solidify their contacts with the unruly tribal. In absence of any medical facilities, they became easy prey to syphilis and other veneral diseases, which worked against the natural growth of population. Incidentally it may be mentioned the contact with Europeans also created the same situation with the indigenous groups of Melanesian islands (Tangoa, Banks, Torres islands). They are the Europeans only, who introduced several diseases like, measles, dysentery, tuberculosis and various potent veneral diseases, during the period of Penal settlement.

In the face of constant depopulation, the most acute problem they have been facing is the scarcity of marriageable mates. The unmatched sex ratio (14 males and 9 females) cropped up a tremendous crisis to this endogamous group, where most of the women did not get any suitable match in respect of age, as there was no other alternative. The ratio of children to adults is not even encouraging for future growth of population. Under these circumstances they have to give up their customary restriction relating to marriage, except siblings. Moreover, due to the absence of suitable mates, even the formation of a complete family is difficult for the maintenance of a well-knit social organization. The 'local group', which had been in existence earlier, has disappeared due to the sharp decrease in population – that has brought about changes in their economic, social and political life.

At present the Great Andamanese settled in isolation in Strait Island, are nowadays the representative of Jeru group. So they now speak the Jeru dialect in common among themselves. Due to frequent penetration of the non-tribal into their lands, the tribesman slowly dragged off from their original dialect. Many adults of the younger generation, in fact, do not know their original dialects. Such a situation has facilitated the inclusion of some Hindi vocabulary completely alien to them.

Furthermore, the causes of extreme depopulation have totally ceased off their former practice of hunting, fishing and gathering. The different degrees of dependence on sea and forest have absolutely disappeared. The free supply of ration provided by the local administration totally discourages the interest and zeal of their traditional mode of subsistence.

It is revealed from different studies that in course of a prolonged contact with the outside world; a community with less resistance generally adopt some of the socio-cultural aspects of the alien people–whom they are in contact with. In spite of all these infiltration and adoption, they have retained their socio-cultural uniqueness in a very short-cut way. They now emotionally consider themselves as one and the same tribal population just to safeguard their total extinction. They are grateful to the authorities of the Andaman Administration for the implementation of a number of applied welfare measures in their everyday life.

The Santals of Bangladesh

Ahsan Ali

The Santals who constitute one of the largest communities in India and Bangladesh, belong to the Austro-asiatic linguistic group. They have managed to keep their language and traditional system of values as well. According to the Government of Bangladesh Census of 1981, their number is over 202162. In this research work, the researcher has dealt with the Santals of Bangladesh from a historical comparative approach. This is a very brief monographic description of the community reflecting their economic and socio-cultural life.

The Santals–one of the major tribes of India and Bangladesh were massively engaged in the colonial process as they were used as labour force in clearing forest tracts like the Rajmahal Hiills in Bihar. The Santals migrated lastly from Rajmahal Hills and settled in Barind Tract of north-west Bangladesh. They cleared the jungles, terraced the slopes and prepared the land fit for cultivation of winter rice in Barind.

They belong to the Kolarian and the Munda linguistic families, classified under the Austro-asiatic group of languages. Their language, Santali, is one of the oldest dialects of India. Though many of the Santals particularly those living in Bangladesh are bi-lingual, and they are the largest tribe in India and Bangladesh to retain an aboriginal language till today.

The numerical strength of the Santals of Bangladesh was probably at its peak point in Bangladesh towards the end of the British rule in 1947. But their population began to decrease noticeably after the partition of the Bengal in 1947. There are also some other important factors like the nachole Santal (Tebhaga) movement in 1949, abolition of zemindary system in 1950, the introduction of passport system between India and Bangladesh in 1954, communal uprising from 1947, particularly in 1951, 1952, 1957, 1962 and 1965 and some other regional upheavals are responsible for the decrease of Santal population during that period. However, we have no statistical figures of emigrations at different times, nor the total number of the people. According to the latest population Census of 1991, the size of the Santal was 202,162.

Possibly, there are more. Their overall numerical strength in India, according to the 1971 Census survey is 363,3459.

The Santals of Barind· as share croppers came to this profession after the zemindary abolition in 1950 and it continued till the recent past. The Santal as share-croppers gradually turned into day-labourers during this period. After the failure of Nachole movement (Nachole movment was the extension of the historically known 'Tebhaga peasant movement') many of the Santals were killed, arrested and jailed, and their houses were burnt and demolished. This was because the Santal peasants had taken the lead in all the different aspects of the movement. The Santals (including other tribals and Hindus) of Barind became demorilized, and there was a, mass exodus of them , including the Hindus and other tribals. At the present moment, most of the Santals of Barind are landless and they earn their livelihood as wage-earners. They are to accept any kind of manual job, but they prefer to engage themselves as agricultural day–labourers. Now in Barind only 29.09% Santal households practise plough cultivation with a minimal amount of agricultural lands and do not have economically viable land–holdings. The rest 70.97% households are engaged in wage-earning. A full fledged *marjhi* system or village communal system is not to be found now due to the want of membership as the size of village became smaller due to internal and external migration of the Santals. This is the first and the most important step in the disintegration of the communal system which has taken place, because the village communal system (that is an essential part of the Santal communal life) has broken down.

The Santals are painstaking, simple- hearted, efficient agriculturists and excellent hunters. The Santals assert themselves as 'hor' meaning 'man' and differentiate themselves from others who, according to them are 'dikku' or alien. Thus the Santals as an ethnic group have all the time maintained their core culture, in-spite of their conversion into Christianity. The Santals believe in clanship and totemism. Generally in their societies the clans like the Hansda, Murmu, Kisku, Hembrom, Marandi, Soren, Tudu, Pauria, Baske, Besra, Chore and Bedea are very common. All these clans are matrilineal and exogamous in nature and these are associated with some objects–animate or inanimate–like animals and plants and some heavenly bodies. The main function of the clans is to regulate marriage, inheritance, succession and affiliation. Clan membership is acquired either by birth or by marriage. Every clan is divided into a number of sub-clans, called *khut*, which is equivalent to the lineage or *bansha*. The *khut* functions primarily in the worship of *bongas* or deities these deities are also worship during the time of lifecycle ceremonies as well as different festive occasions.

II

The Santal husband and wife are found to be engaged in agriculture viz., to transplant seedlings, to break earth clods and to reap and harvest paddy. Women generally do not sow seeds, as per Santal customs, but work as transplanters. While threshing paddy, both men and women work jointly. Ploughing the field is an exclusive privilege of men, and women are debarred from doing it as a social taboo.

In conjugal life, the Santal woman is self-sacrificing. She will, according to tradition, eat last of all after feeding other members of the family. But the way she exercises her equal rights impresses one so much, so that an observer has been constrained to form an opinion that Santal women work more than their male partners. The equality of status, the women claimed extends even to the drinking cup as well; but a distinction is drawn by her paradoxically enough, when she says : "We drink like men but do not get drunk."

The father is the head of a Santal family and his authority is implicitly accepted by all its members. He, however, does not act arbitrarily. The Santal women are found to be more active in decision –making of the family affairs, because the women are working in the field along with their male counterparts. The women after their work in the evening go to the nearby market to buy their daily necessities of life.

With due regard to the individual differences, it can be said that the relation between a man and his wife is generally good and friendly. Their children are rarely ill-treated. In the event of death of a mother, the child is taken care of by a married woman, who is commonly a paternal relative. If the father of a family dies and the widow is left with minor children to care for, she acts as the family head until the eldest son becomes an adult .

In Santal societies different taboos exist in the midst of social relationship and this taboos like food taboos, sex taboos are very frequently practiced in their day to day life. Through these taboos social restriction among the family members are maintained and side by side joking relations with one another are also practised.

The important milestones in the lifecycle of a man are birth, puberty, marriage and death. Santals consider these events of life cycle associated with the village life. Birth of a child is the blessing of God. This is the Santal concept of birth. Miscarriage is considered to bring ill-luck to the family. At the time of delivery, a midwife, a Santal woman of course in the profession, attends to the pregnant woman with her elderly women relatives. She is locally called *dai* (in Bengali) and she belongs to the Santal community only. In the Santal village in Barind, professional midwife is found. Due to birth of a child, the house and the village become polluted and religiously unclean. To purify the houses and the village, a purification ceremony called *janam chatiar* is held.

The Santal women in Barind generally wear several tattoo marks on wrists, near the end of their forearm and on the chest and also some on their breasts. These marks are usually applied to Santal girls between their eleventh and twelfth year and before their marriage.

It may be mentioned here that cicatrisation of men and tattoo marks on women (*khudni*) in Barind are very much irregularly done, because of the non-availability of the professional *khudni* and an expert of cicatrisation who generally come from Bihar in Barind every year for this.

A Santal marriage is more than an arrangement entered into by two individuals or even two families. It is a matter in which two entire villages are concerned. The prominent role played by the headman and, especially the superintendent of the morals of the youth (*jog manjhi*) in arranging and concluding marriage ceremonies is an indication of the degree to which the entire village community relies on its responsibility in this affair.

Santal marriages are closely associated with religion as is found from their offering of vermilion to *Maran Buru* and a goat to the dead ancestors. Thus, we find that marriage no longer remains a civil contract of getting a life-partner on payment of a price, but it takes the form of a sacrament as well.

The final 'rite de passage' has to do something with the rituals of death which center round the cremation of the dead body. The Santals have their own funeral custom.

When a death takes place in a family, the village headman and the elder folks get together at the house in mourning, then they rub the dead body with oil and turmeric paste. Now, the corpse is taken out of the house in a parkom or *khatia* (a stringed bedstead), placed in the yard and cleaned with cow dung and water. A handful of paddy is spread over the spot and some thrust into the right palm of the deceased and thrown down sometime later. The bier is then carried by four men, followed by a *dahi daka* (a man who places the dead body on the funeral pyre) carrying a winnowing fan containing fire in a bundle of straw, some seeds of cotton, straw picked from the thatch of the deceased, some fried paddy (*khoi*), powder of sun–dried rice mixed with turmeric, cow dung and a small chicken in one hand while in the other, he holds an earthen pot with lid , which will serve as the receptacle of the bones of the dead man after cremation. Now, amidst lamentations, the womenfolk bathe the hands and foot of the deceased .

According to the Barind Santal it is further learnt that the *dahi daka* circles round the funeral assemblage thrice and then places some cotton seeds beneath the four legs of the funeral cot, when the bier is again lifted and the procession slowly moves on towards the cremation ground, but the women of the tribe have no right to proceed further. Instead, they have to go to the bathing-ghat, and have a purificatory ablution and thereafter go to the village lane and light a *dhup* (incense stick).

III

The conditions and incidence of the headman system had come under radical change when the Santals began to settle on the plain land of Bengal, mainly at Barind, after the great Santal rebellion (1855). However, with the passing of the Permanent Settlement Act of 1793, the zemindars became proprietors (in the occidental sense) and landholders. The effect of this new system on the tribal socio-economic structure has created a serious problem, in general, and a change for the worse has been taking place in the Santal political organization in regard to the function of the *manjhi* who is to collect rents and allot lands amongst the Santal tenants, in particular

Among the minor functionaries the *Godet* (he is called as mutha thenga at Barind) is important. His function is to assist the *Manjhi* and he works as a messenger and calls the people to council meetings. When the *bongas* are worshipped, he collects sacrificial fowls for the *Naeke* and the *Jog-Manjhi*. His role, like that of the Hindu barber is in social activities and also in assisting at the sacred functions. He is held to be very impetuous, greedy and clever. He is esteemed by both the *Manjhi* and the *Jog-Manjhi* and also the *Naeke* group. He is given a part of all the sacrifices, and is treated like a sister's son.

IV

Our Barind Santals hold the view that their *bonga* divinities are further divided into household deities, village deities, boundary deities, clan deities and other Santal deities. Further the notion of *bonga* creates new *bonga* by absorbing and assimilating some object or symbols that inspire the Santal community. Thus in Barind an aeroplane is a *bonga*, a political symbol i.e., the symbol of boat of the Awami League is a *bonga* etc. This process of creation of new *bongas* goes on absorbing and merging these symbols until they are Santalized according to the local needs of the Santals. In this way, many Hindu gods and goddesses, such as *Mahadeva* (Siva), *Kali*, *Durga*, *Manasa*, *Laxmi* etc., are all included in the *bonga* pantheon and have their own explanation to them in their own way of life.

On the other hand, due to the influence of the Christianity and a rapid conversion to it in some places of Barind, the Christian prophet (Jesus Christ) has also been included in the list of *bongas*. The sacred ecology or the *bonga* sanctuaries in our Barind villages can be divided into two parts:

a) The inner sacred ecological zones, including all the village households within the villages, the shrines of the village, households and ancestors;

b) the outer sacred ecological zone, including the territory, boundaries, and village outskirts .

In the inner sacred ecological zone, the sanctuaries of the Barind Santals are divided into two types :

1. the village shrine
2. the headman's shrine

The village shrine, as it is found in villages of Barind, is called *Jaherthan* or the place of the goddess *Jaher era*. In our context, a shrine is a natural holy shelter for the objects of cult, where rituals and sacrifices are performed by the village priest, the *Naeke*. *Jaherthan* is located a little way away from the village dwellings inside a bamboo forest.

The sacred ecology in the Santal content refers to that geographical area which surrounds the Santal villages. This area is considered sacred.

V

The Santals do not depend entirely on spiritual methods for solving their problems of illness. They have followed the method of observation and developed a medicine of their own. The *ojha* is not only a spiritual healer, but also a medicine man and he recites incantations and performs sacrifices. These medicines are prepared from plants, herbs and roots used for curing of diseases like fevers, low vitality, madness, small-pox, cholera, leprosy etc. There are also a few persons called *tantrics*, who have a good knowledge of herbs and roots, and administer medicine when called upon to do so. They do not, however, know anything about incantations and sacrifices.

The Santals have a grandeur festival in celebrating the *Sohrae*, their winter harvest home, the biggest annual event of their tribal life. This is a common day of thanks giving to the gods for rain, sun and fair weather who contributed to bumper crop known as *bandhna*, eulogixing in common parlance. This picturesque festival has no specific date in the tribal calendar. It begins on suitable dates for each village. But there is some reservation that the festival must begin before the last day of the Bengali month of *Poush* (mid-January) at least, at Barind. The first day of the festival starts with an initial purification ceremony which is termed as 'um', when the members of the tribe cleanse themselves with a ceremonial ablution. Houses and courtyards are also scrupulously made free from dirt and dust.

The Santals live not only in their human tribal society, but in a greater society consisting of supernatural beings as well. The traditional Santals' greater society comprises 'hor', i.e., man or the Santal; *'Thakur'*, the supreme being; the *bongas;* and non-human monstrous beings as we have already mentioned above. These four orders of beings, especially the first three, are in constant interaction with each other. The behaviors of one can not be understood apart from the others. The supernatural beings are an integral part of Santal social life. That is why it is important to bear in mind the existence of a greater society, and the interaction between the different orders of beings. This traditional greater society has been invaded by the intrusion of alien human elements and culture like Hinduisation, land-lords, money-lenders, centralized political economy, forestless Barind ecology, changing occupation pattern from adhiar to day-labourer of the Santals, and last but not the least, Christianity at Barind. Hence, the old concept of the supernatural world has changed to some extent and the Santals of Barind are in the process of forgetting their original 'Binti' or Santal mythology. The religion of the Santals can be termed as Animism and now, it is an admixture of Hinduism and Animistic beliefs. Again, they are corrupted with Theistic and Animistic beliefs due to effects of Christianity at Barind.

In search of an identity, there is a strong tendency among the Santals at Barind not to accept or embrace any new religion. Almost all the Santals are closely maintaining socio-cultural relations with the low–caste Hindus in this area as a 'Minority community'; yet they are not deeply involved and integrated into Hinduism as such. The

Santals preferred to maintain their own tradition and culture as well as offer respect and regard to Hindu deities when needed. The tilt of adopting a Hindu identity may largely be due to the fact that the assimilation of the Santal culture is taking place in great measure within the overwhelming concentration of their own population in India and in the midst of a predominantly Hindu population. From this study it is revealed that now a days the Santals of Barind prefer the religion of the Hindu or Christian rather than the Muslim.

At present, a sense of consciousness has developed among the Santals in Barind where they are being converted to Christianity in which there are opportunities for betterment of the socio-economic life, in the shape of social security provided by the Christian Missionaries. Conversion to Christianity started long ago during the erstwhile British rule in India. But after the liberation of Bangladesh in 1971, the process of conversion to Christianity has gained momentum due to the divested economic condition of the Santals, as in the East Pakistan period (1947-1970), the main trend of the Santals was to migrate to India due to the communal tension and the torture of the government concerned. Now in Barind, the Santal animist and Santal Christian, are found living in the same village with their *Jaherthan* (sacred grove) and village church respectively. An unalloyed animist Santal village has become rare in Barind.

Biological and Cultural Adaptation : A Case Study of the Refugees Settled in Little Andaman

Sujit Som

Man, in the process of gradual development has distinguished himself as a culture bearing species. He attained his distinct present position through the constant efforts of his unilateral habits of accommodativeness in the sphere of new innovations by way of his capacity to adapt culturally changing environment. A gradual but successfully diversified process of adjustment with the ecosystem, in time and space, resulted in this unique achievement. It is needless to mention that the biological instinct of a man makes it possible for his habit of acquiredness.

The gradual accumulation of all such acquired skills, habits and interactions that favoured man throughout the process has helped to pick up his social nature. This prolonged process indirectly helped man to form collectivities which has boosted up his struggle for existence in an environment set with natural hazards and complex socio-cultural network. Two distinct diversified characters viz., biological instinct and cultural attributes have played vital role in shaping his interaction with the physical environment, natural environment and social environment depending upon acquired skills.

In a living world, culture is a volatile instrument. It encompasses certain structural as well as functional social units like institutions developed out of social relationships, values, beliefs, sentiments, needs etc. In the present work, it was felt essential to explore the extent of culture and ecology, two distinct but interrelated aspects in human life. Thus the meaning of culture and ecology separately and the extent of its relation to social interaction will certainly be an issue not only of social relevance but also for study and general understanding. This is more relevant, as we all know that existence of the society depends on social interactions which is reciprocal and governs one's behaviour as per the expectation of others. Thus the group interaction provides shape to and is shaped by its culture.

Further, culture is characteristically a human product of social interaction. It provides socially acceptable patterns for meeting biological and social needs. Culture is also learned by each person in the course of his development in a particular society, which is necessarily a basic determinant of personality.

It is known to all that a culture is composed of number of individual traits centering around human activities. A trait may be of two types– material trait and non-material trait. The cultural elements pertaining with day to day maintenance produced by man in adapting to and exercising control over their bio-social environment are identified as material traits. The non material aspect is concerned with the religious acts and other types of norms and values as manifested through folkways, rituals and institutional settings.

Further, we know that culture is adaptive as it attributes man to interpose between self and his environment for his security and survival, which can supplement culture as a specific and concrete mechanism employed by a particular animal organism in adjusting to its environment. Due to adaptive nature of culture, the bearer finds it possible to satisfy their both ends whether it is biological or socio-cultural.

II

The issue of refugees is an international phenomenon. This has a direct bearing to the uprooted population either by natural cause or by socio-political tension or ethnic conflicts. Migration has occurred in all phases of human civilization. The dimension and complexity of the process of migration and its underlying socio-cultural, economic, psychological, religious and many other characteristics call for a detailed analysis. In the Asian scene, the problem of uprooting is not uncommon. In the Indian sub continent, the partition of the country had opened up a floodgate of refugees. This necessitated for the government the biggest ever challenge of facing their settlement/resettlement programme. In meeting the challenge of accommodation such a huge number of refugees, the name of the hitherto virgin and largely unsettled islands of Andaman and Nicobar or the Bay Island came first. On the basis of recommendations of different committees concerned with the rehabilitation of refugees in the said island a few families were first inducted in some specified areas of Little Andaman, which is the third biggest island of the Bay Islands. Such resettlement has occurred in three distinct decadal phases in 1949,1969 and 1974. To begin with, it started in the south Andaman as early as in 1949 which was followed by north Andaman, middle Andaman and lately in the Little Andaman and even in certain pockets of Nicobar Island. In the Little Andaman area, the first village, Netajinagar at 8 kms. from Hut bay with 40 families came into existence in 1971 along the sea coast. Ramkrishnapur, the second village on the 22 kms. stretched road in Little Andaman Island, where a segment of Bengali refugees were given settlement/ resettlement. There the inhabitants consisted of 201 families of seven different population groups. The *Namasudras* with 132 families, the *Pondokshatriyas* with 40 families, *Mahishyas* with 9 familes, *Napits* with 2 families and 1 each *Kayastha* and *Jugi* families and a few Brahmin families from six districts. These people came from the then East Pakistan now Bangladesh. Ramkrishnapur is located in the exterior part of the Island. The distance between the sea and the village was considered favourable for agricultural operations. The village has been divided into as many as 6 distinct blocks for the purpose of systematic reclamation of forest land and also for the purpose of allotment of the concerned land to different groups of people.

The psychological orientation of the people inhabiting the new settlements as well as the nature of benefits which the people are enjoying were assessed by way of specific interview in the present work. For the purpose of data collection, along with the use of questionnaire method, participatory observation method and case study method were also adopted. The data thus collected were correlated with census data and a detailed analysis of the picture was made. These were analysed in statistical formats i.e., tables with frequencies so that appropriate sequences are observed and analysed for testing the hypotheses.

Most of the settlers of the village Ramkrishnapur came from different transit camps located in different states of mainland India. In spite of their separate ethnic and regional identities, these people were pooled together under one blanket term of refugee settlers. This was done in order to facilitate the distribution of admissible financial assistance required for their immediate maintenance. But it is interesting to note that some families who did not receive such assistances took their own initiatives and pioneered the process of self-help and provided a leadership to the community for a better settlement.

The village Ramkrishnapur received altogether 201 families of which 129 families i.e., 64.18% are direct from transit camps in mainland while 72 families i.e., 35.82% are from other settlement areas of another island i.e., Neil island in north Andaman. They were given settlement in the village on special arrangement of the local official management. So from the very beginning, population from two distinct streams one having some exposure of island situation and others having no experience at all combined together in developing their settlement in the village. Though a common tendency is very much been observed among the settlers in general to have more land but for reasons known to all of them the settlers had to remain content with standard 5 acres of agricultural land and one-third acres land as homestead land attached to their respective agricultural land. In addition to prescribed cash dole, subsidised ration are also given. Such a type of exercise indirectly acts as a catalyst towards development of dispersed types of village formation around dense evergreen forest. As a result, a sense of traditional village cohesiveness has grown among all the settlers. To begin with , the structural pattern of traditional village settlements like the existence of a landlord, typical village institutions like temple, *harisava, pathsala,* village elders' council, agnetic kins etc., did not exist in such villages initially. The village Ramkrishnapur had seven different population groups of six different districts of origin. *Namasudra* constituted the dominant group and they came from all districts of origin. Though their numerical strength was an advantage in all matters but due to inter district differences arriving at a decision at times was difficult for them as they did not have much of internal solidarity. They constituted 65.68% of the village population and in spite of internal differences, they provided leadership in the allround development of the village. Mention may be made of one member of *Namasudra* group of 5th. Block of the village. He is the only businessman of the village, he takes initiatives in many matters and provides leadership in the village. The village elders' council respects his decision. The lone market is also around his business establishment which at times serves as meeting place of the villagers where intra and even inter settlers issues of differences and general issues of the village are discussed and decision on issues pertaining to the welfare of the village are taken.

The assistance provided to the settlers of Ramkrishnapur is far less than what is required. But villagers attempt their best in overcoming all hazards so that their settlement can get a shape. In doing so, villagers redesign their house sites and also the structural aspects to develop a village of their own tradition. This indirectly helped them in building up village cohesiveness. In this process too, no barrier of caste affiliation or district of origin was considered. This is also a major shift from their traditional village concept. Thereby instead of typical homogenous character of their village, the heterogeneous character prevails all over. The traditional village ties or the concept of *para* has thereby been revived and it serves many a purpose of basic social function next to family.

The basic composition of the village Ramkrishnapur is multi-caste and multi-regional. The average family size of the village is 6 with a sex ratio of 87.89. In the case of each population group it is observed that except the *Brahman* all other caste groups are having more males than females. A tendency of early marriage is a common practice of the village. The rate of literacy, though not encouraged traditionally, but in now setting a tendency towards education as an alternate, has been received by all. Though there are only a few educated persons in the village but that was before their induction to this new setting. The only graduate of the village has been accommodated, suitably in the banking service, which served as a morale booster to all. As a result, acceptance of education by all has been a predominant motivation among the settlers. This is also an indication of accepting the path of creditability as well as sustaining of alternative economic adaptability.

As a result of limitations and non availability of appropriate opportunities as practised traditionally, though girls and boys from the same district of origin are preferred for marriage alliances, taking spouses even from other districts are increasingly taking place. This is a significant shift towards cultural adaptability. Incidence of *Gharjamai* even for intra district marriage is found accepted in the village. In addition, a trend of adpatibility towards marital alliances in the village from other caste groups is also being increasingly found. In the social system disintegration of traditional trilateral inter familial kinship bonds with father's, mother's and wife's parental families are observed by all the caste groups in the village. As a result, a breakthrough in the extended familial norm is found. The simple familial norm is found in common in all the caste groups of the village. The separate family set up has some other fringe benefits available in the prevailing situation. The social system has paved the way for adapting a community system of living. Such an outcome has acted as a catalyst for social realignment to sustain the onslaught of uncommon environmental effect. Incidence of polygynous family to cope up with the prevailing situation though exists in low percentage (2.99%), but it's existence is an indication of social reality and reflects an extent of cultural adaptibility to the new environment.

Occurrence of lowest percentile frequency in complex family types with 1.49% is an indication of certain traditional familial norm still being favoured. The average of family sizes in the village between normal or medium with 5 to 6 members is 39.80% and big with 7 to 8 members is 24.38% followed by small with 3 to 4 members is 21.89% very big with 9 and above is 11.14% and very small with 2 members is 2.49%. So far as religious faith is concerned it is observed that villagers are mostly followers of Lord *Krishna*. Simultaneously they have introduced all types of traditional pujas like *Bhagabati puja* in the first month of *Baisakh* (April –May), *Rathajatra* celebration, symbolic worship of *Manasa puja, Durga puja, Kali puja, Swaraswati puja* and many other community celebrations. These have largely replaced the traditional individual celebration in the village.

The agricultural activities of the settlers round the year indicate that the villagers have adapted certain means to utilize both the high land and low land to the best extent during the rainy and summer seasons. To supplement the loss in agricultural operations, the villagers have adapted growing of vegetables which require minimum involvement of resources with good return. Replacement of cultivation of Jute (a most worthy traditional agricultural product of the settlers) has not taken place. Sugarcane cultivation, though not a traditional means of occupation but had to adapt not as an alternative but to compensate economic loss. The given environment with all its resources combined with the traditional world view and a search for an alternative homeland–all have facilitated the process of psychological adaptation to the given situation.

The fieldwork was carried out in two spells, initially for nearly six months from February 1976 and then in April and May 1986 amongst people in new habitats. These two levels of fieldwork have led to the following conclusions.

1. The population consisting of 201 families from seven caste groups have now constituted a new social world in the ethnic environment of the island. In order to adjust themselves to the new situations, the uprooted migrants have adapted to the new situations and also adopted number of new socio-economic and cultural practices to ensure their survival by exploiting the local natural resources. Adaptation of new techniques by way of renovating and accommodating the old and the new–have all along been observed.
2. The uprooted population adjusted to the new ecological situation to such an extent that the population had to change their traditional social values and the systems so far practised. The age-old traditional concept of caste restrictions got moulded to a great extent. An attempt has been made in the study to highlight the nature and extent of these changes.
3. Interactions with aboriginal tribal groups viz., Onges and the Nicobarese have taken place for sheer economic survival. The adaptation of a new technology in a new setting has led them to totally change their traditional environment and has led to the creation of a cultural landscape.
4. The study will corroborate an understanding of the gamut of new changing socio-religious beliefs, world views and activities under the prevailing circumstances.

From the above study it is apparent that the Bengali refugees within a very short period of time have added a new dimension so far as incorporation of appropriate aptitudes are concerned. They have in the process, also streamlined their traditional systems, values etc. for better living.

Twilight and Dark : Life in a Sundarban Village

Shyamapada Chakraborty

India lives in villages which are basically aggregates of homesteads occupied by people from different castes and communities. Owing to permanent settlement pattern the villagers live in close proximity, developing a face to face relationship though they may be of different caste and community group. Prolonged interaction pattern develops not only intimacy but also some sort of rivalry amongst themselves and these vibrate a village life. Various festivals and familial ceremonies demand mutual interaction and then we find villagers to differ. However, common geographical and environmental settings, historical background, participation in the activities of common interest and festivals, regard for various regional religious beliefs and practices, sharing of commonly imbibed ideas and sentiments bind the people of a village. This will be evident from the various activities of their struggle for existence for a more secured and effective life. This will be evident from their economic socio-political, religious and festive life. Here is a close study of a Sundarban village.

Swarupkati is a Sundarban village situated in Hingalgunj Block of North 24 Parganas district. The Block is under Basirhat sub-division. The village under study has an approximate area of 477 acres of land which was reclaimed and settled around Tillman Henckell's time. The village is bounded in the east by the Sahebkhali river and in the west by village Kothabari, on the river Goureswar. Amberia and Ketarchak are the two villages that lie to the north and south respectively of Swarupkati. The surface road running between Hingalgunj and Lebukhali has bisected the village to the west and east. Two wooden bridges, one at the entry point and the other at the exit point, stand over the canals. The eastern portion of the village is relatively overpopulated with the *Poundras* settling close to the river Sahebkhali. On the western side, mainly the Mundas remain concentrated, though a few of them reside here and there. The *Brahmans*, on the other hand, remain scattered in the eastern block of the village. Sometimes, the *Brahman* families are flanked by two or more *Poundra* families. The *Rishis* (*Muchis, Chamars,* taking Bengali titles) live on a contiguous patch of land in their own huts with hardly any demarcating line. The *Napits* (Barbers) came to the village close on the heels of the *Poundras*. They have settled in a scattered way, though it was a single family even 25 years ago. From the recorded evidence it is found that the Mundas are the autochthones here. They become *ryots* from migrating agricultural labourers. That they built their houses a little away from the treacherous river belts and had once occupied the most fertile land of the village, justify the fact of their being the earliest settlers.

A 1989 survey showed that the total population was 1391 out of which 732 were males and 659 females. The entire population was distributed amongst 283 families. The Scheduled Caste population was male 554, female 498, totaling 1052. Adding the Scheduled Tribe population of 277 that includes 145 male and 132 female, the total strength of SC/ST population stands at 1329. On the other hand caste Hindu population comprising *Brahmans* and *Napits* comes to 62.

Despite its economic backwardness and unenviable geographical location, Swarupkati has a very high degree of literacy amongst its inhabitants. Sixty percent of the total population are either literate or in the primary school where, among other things, they are taught to master the three R's.

In our country, the villages are basically dependent more or less on agriculture, directly or indirectly. With the gradual depletion of familywise land holding, a natural consequence that follows a growing population, the villagers of Swarupkati have resorted to some other callings, not their traditional profession but others on the expediency of the situation and for the prospect of a better income. Many of the villagers have taken profession like fishing, teaching, shop-keeping, self-taught homeopath practicing, vending etc.

In the Sundarban belt, *Poundras* with their Hindu and Buddhist past lived their own life for a long period but Muslim invasions saw the influence of Islam gradually taking a firm grip over the inhabitants in the coastal belt. As a consequence, new deities grew up in a bid to iron out differences between Hinduism and Islam. And there grew in the Sundarbans a culture of the forest. This culture, however, did not follow any uniform line and pattern as such, because of the numerical superiority of the Adivasi with their Hill-culture in the area. As a result a hotchpotch culture rules over the area.

Swarupkati and the village similar to it in the deltaic Sundarbans are undoubtedly separate entities, in as much as these were simply settlement of hired labourers, slowly transforming their character and gaining the status of village. Essentially Swarupkati is an epitome of such on-going process of abstract metamorphosis and its problems are so very common to other villages in the area.

Secondly, the earliest settlers, i.e., the hired labourers of the Englishmen and native zemindars were mostly Mundas, a tribal group from Chhotonagpur region in Bihar. Their exodus from their places of abode was tri-directional with the singular purpose of earning a safe livelihood. Prompted to leave their original hearth and home and inherent right to the forest and its produce, more or less by the oppression of the British masters and their native landlords, some took refuge and employment in the tea-gardens of North Bengal and Assam. Some preferred clearing the jungles of the Sundarbans for a settlement, and the rest got themselves waywardly scattered all over Bengal.

In the Sundarban areas, unfortunately, the land they reclaimed from the forest after a strenuous battle against deadly diseases and wild animals gradually slipped away from their hands. Before the abolition of the zemindary system, the upper caste zemindars snatched away most of the fertile lands from them, sometimes on the fictitious plea of outstanding debts, sometimes by adoption of repressive measures. The zemindars later distributed these lands to the new settlers, mostly *Poundras*, in lieu of handsome 'Salamis' (i.e. advance money). The Mundas, however still recount this in their doleful songs stating the unfortunate grabbing of land by the master marauders. Their dissatisfaction, however never surfaced and they lived peacefully with the other neighbours, at times heaving a sigh of a defeated heart.

Over the years the villagers cutting across caste and community lines and bypassing their separate identity–religious, social and cultural, had opted unknowingly for a synthesis. A blending of culture has grown up. The primeval practices and animistic ritual of the Mundas were welded nicely into the Buddhistic past of the *Poundras* and the Vedic tradition of the *Brahmans*. Though it appears artificial on close scrutiny, this synthetic culture has harmonized the villagers into a single-string musical instrument pouring forth all the seven tunes off a sitar, which reflect in their day-to-day life with the change of the seasons.

The waning forest line and the fast disappearing wild animals have changed the religious fervour of the people to a great extent. Beginning from the primeval worships of *Bara*, a bodyless head image of a jungle god, it has passed through worship of *Dakshin Roy, Kalu Roy, Bonbibi, Gazipir* etc. in the post-independence period and the Hindu gods and goddesses have taken places of pride ultimately.

Moreover, the nature through her tumultuous ravaging whims and caprices has forced the people to foster a unity and cohesion among all the castes and communities in the entire deltaic Sundarbans. Swarupkati has also followed suit. Here, the *Brahmans* are compelled to shed off their age-old pride of superior birth and share the same boat with the so called untouchables, *Rishis* and *Chandals*, for otherwise, they will be forced to fend for themselves, which is neither possible nor practicable. It is in this way that the nature has brought about cohesion and unity amongst all castes and communities.

As a researcher, I venture to suggest, in all humility, the following points for bringing about an all-pervading development of Swarupkati and economic uplift of the people living there : (a) a better communication system should be developed, so as to break the isolation of the people and bring them into the main stream of national developmental upsurge. For this, obviously, we need to develop a well organized river transport service introducing flotillas in place of make-shift jetties, which are both dangerous and costlier to maintain. Inter-village road linkage should be built up. This will help improve economic, social and educational life of the villages. (b) (i) setting up of a high school in the area, either at Swarupkati or at Amberia would ease the problem of the village children, particularly of the girls students. (ii) A college, either at Hingalgunj or at Bhandarkhali or Dulduli would help the students in prosecuting under-graduate studies. Besides, the primary schools are in bad shape, suffering from both lack of space and dearth of teacher–these to be looked into. (iii) Setting up of adult education center and ICDS in the village will not only increase educational standard of the general villagers but also make them more cautious about health hazards and big families. If necessary, voluntary assistance of the educated local youth may be tapped to spread education. With some encouragement, the village youth can bring about comprehensible change in this regard. (c) Though general health of the villagers is more or less satisfactory, one or two health sub-centres may be set-up with the provision for pre and post natal treatment. Existing arrangement must be bettered, so as to accommodate more indoor patient and treat outdoor patient. Health workers and extension workers must be motivated, if not compelled, to pay regular visit to the villagers. It would help the nation at length. (d) Utmost importance should be attached to agriculture of this area. Lack of sweet water, salty clay, more than adequate rainfall and humidity have added to the vagaries of the nature in the area. Agriculture basically in this area remains a single cropping pattern. Improved agriculture with multiple cropping can help improve the lot of the people. Existing protective embankment around the whole island should be strengthened. In suitable areas arrangement for cultivation and pisciculture in the same land simultaneously may be suggested. A reservoir to store rain water can be dug up. This will make double cropping a reality. In some other parts of Sundarbans, exploitation of under ground water has been successful, though to a limited extent. This also can be tried at Swarupkati. (e) The existing two canals originating from the river Ichhamati (Sahebkhali) that cut across the village can be exploited to advantage for pisciculture. Provision of a good seed store in the locality can help the farmers in this area of the island. Inter alia, setting up of a co-operative store can, to a great extent, minimize or even stop exploitation of the common man by the sharks of the trading community. In times of need also it can play a vital role to help the rural poor. (f) With regard to providing some more infrastructural set-ups–a play-ground, a library and a post office can go a long way to assuage the feeling of the otherwise harassed and neglected villagers and improve their living standard. Re-activisation of the moribund local clubs, which are mostly voluntary welfare organisations, can in a way help and benefit the villagers. The Panchayats and the Government setting up of industries that may utilize the available raw materials of the area, particularly cottage industries, can also be considered. However, we should bear in mind that nothing should be done that may disturb the ecological balance of the deltaic area.

It is true that after independence, in the new democratic set-up of the country, the people are in a position to express their views freely and clearly through their elected representatives. For the over-all development of the village whatever little fund is available should be utilized properly. Besides, many more projects and schemes can be envisaged for the improvement of the village. Government money, local enthusiasm and involvement of the people may bring in a sea-change in the lifestyle of the people. Education of the people and the level of literacy should be bettered to enable them to understand the past in the proper perspective and to formulate the future course of action so as to raise their levels of living standard. High expectation and mutual obligations should be strengthened to overcome the difficulties surfaced or unsurfaced, and in this way the village may appear to be a model one in course of time. Socio-economic organizations will have to collaborate with each other in order to project an idea that the village though 'small but is beautiful and complete in all respects.'

Survival of Hindu Rituals among the Converts

Kalipada Malakar

The present study is practically an attempt to determine the extent of survival of Hindu rituals among the converts from the Hindus and to make an objective assessment of how far this survival may help to minimise the communal conflicts and tensions, that affect our national integrity, time and again. This study also widely covers history of conversion from Hinduism to Islam and Christianity, along with many social rituals, including some important religious performances observed by the Hindus, Muslims and Christians, and the converts from the Hindus to the Muslims and Christians. The features of rituals associated with marriage, birth, death and religious performances vary from community to community. Many of these rites and rituals are again attributed to the religious and social ideology of a particular community by their adherents. However, solemnization of marriage according to the *Vedas* and *Upanishadas*, in case of the Hindus, the *Quran* and *Hadis* in case of the Muslims and the *Bible* in case of the Christians, is a matter of great importance, because of its relation to the religious ideas of the three communities. The role of the *Shastric*(scriptural) rites and rituals in traditional patterns of the Hindu, Muslim and Christian marriages centres round the methods of solemnization. The marriage ceremonies of these communities are generally associated with incantations from the *Vedas*, the *Upanishadas*, the *Quran* and *Hadis* and the *Bible*, as the case may be of the communities concerned.

The present survey was conducted among a section of the converted Muslims and Christians to trace the history of their conversion as far as practicable, along with their tendency towards retention of the socio-religious rituals of their pre-conversion society. It has also been analysed how far these converts give their moral support to the observance of such rituals for bringing their community to the level of the Hindus in the social ladder with a view to mitigating thereby the virus of communal ill-feeling.

The prevailing manners and customs, social behaviour and tendencies of the different types of people belonging to different religious faiths like Hinduism, Islam and Christianity, are the real index, by means of which the survival of Hindu rituals among the converts can be assessed. This study as such, deals with these aspects also.

In India, Hinduism manifests itself in many ritual patterns. This country was invaded in 711 A.D. by the Muslims and later on, by some western people who were Christians. Due to circumstantial exigencies and prolonged contact with these groups of people at different places and periods of time, a good number of local people, specially the Hindus, had been either compelled or enchanted to embrace either Islam or Christianity. In many cases, reformatory movements were started from time to time for creation of other smaller sects like those of the Buddhists and the Jains. So in course of this study, it has been revealed how far these segmented religious groups share the traditional patterns of Hindu rituals. In addition to the above, it has also been observed how far this type of common sharing of rituals minimises the prevailing group distances and tensions between the converts and the neighbouring Hindus, thus generating a sense of national solidartity and integrity. This fraternal idea, if further developed, will pick up its own momentum and destory the virus of communal conflicts and develop communal harmony through inter-marriage and common participation in socio-religious rites by the Hindu, Muslim and Christian masses.

For this study the samples have been selected from various sections of the population in some selected villages of the Districts of 24 Parganas and Midnapore in West Bengal, so that a fairly large cross-section of the converts from the Hindu to the Muslim and native Christian may be covered.

At first, distinguished social workers or persons of repute were contacted. Selection of informants had been made in such a manner so that they could supply correct information about the facts of conversion concerning the converted families and the socio-religious rituals observed by them. As a result, delay in collecting relevant data could be avoided. Of course, the author had to reside for days in the localities under study, with the villagers on many occasions, in order to verify physically the particulars regarding socio-religious rituals which were supplied by the informants. Besides, the author as far as practicable, had personally approached the heads of many families, and witnessed their ceremonies relating to marriage, birth, puberty, death and religious performances, etc. and had taken many photographs as documentary evidences.

The chosen rural areas fall under Baruipur, Sonarpur and

Bishnupur Police stations in the district of 24 Parganas and Mahishadal Police station in the district of Midnapore in West Bengal, where a good number of Muslims and native Christians live. Requisite data were made available for the study in those areas. In order to make a comprehensive as well as comparative study with a view to proving how far the religious and social rituals observed by the converts, are in conformity with or deviate from orthodox patterns of the rites and rituals observed by the Hindus, Muslims and Christians. In this dissertation the author has described all the orthodox patterns of rites and rituals relating to religious performances, marriage, birth, childhood, puberty and death prevalent among the Hindus, Muslims and Christians, from some authentic law books of the people belonging to the said faiths.

The history of conversion of the groups of people covered by this study have been collected by the author for compiling a factual history of conversion of the concerned areas. This may be treated as a new addition to the earlier works of various authors. It has been verified by investigation that most of the converts belonged to the Scheduled Castes namely *Teor, Rajbanshi, fishermen* etc. Their family surnames are Das, Mondal, Gharami, Biswas, Naskar, Halder, Sarkar, Mallick, Sardar, Dhali, Baidya, Khan etc., irrespective of whether they are Christians or Muslims. The use of these family surnames has practically revealed a missing-link between the converts and the Scheduled Caste Hindus of the localities, among whom the surnames mentioned are still in vogue. The socio-religious rituals observed by the converted Christians also correlate with many of those observed by the Hindus of the same localities which suggest their Hindu origin. Further, the Hindu names like Gopal, Narayan, Bholanath, Nanda, Kanai, Bhutnath, Gouri, Kalindi, Mukul, Narayani etc. are in use among the converts from the Hindus to the Muslims as well as to the Christians.

A gradual change in various rituals has been revealed here, in the context of time and environment. The present study therefore is intended to build up documents along space and time dimensions. It may also shine as a lesson for communal harmony to those who indulge in communal conflicts, destruction of national property, looting, arson, et,c. which ultimately impair national solidarity and integrity.

The study was conducted in the villages namely Kamlat, Talpukur, Charer Chak, Rammakhaler Chak, Panchghara, Ganeshpur, Naskarpur, and many other villages under the Police stations of Sonarpur, Bishnupur in the district of 24 Parganas. All these villages were thickly inhabited by the converted Christians and Muslims whose forefathers were Hindus. As for example, Ahmed Sahed, a converted Muslim, whose father Ramanath Gharami was previously a Hindu. But later he was converted into Islam and named as Amahat Gharami. In this way different genuine converts were identified and selected for the study.

The author also contacted many aged and elderly converts to know the religious and social rites and rituals practised by their families and also the reason for their conversion.

As a sequel of conquest, the Muslim rulers of Bengal tried conversions–both individual and en masse. Like Buddhism, Islam also had no place for rigid casteism. But the Hindu society was divided into castes–some with a superior status and some with an inferior one and there subsisted ill-feeling and animosity among them. As a result many people with inferior social status took Islam for their survival.

As the low caste people were deprived of many social privileges and had been suffering from social degradation, they welcomed Islam which believes in equality of civil, political and spiritual rights of man and universal brotherhood. It knows no rigidity in casteism and makes no distinction between man and man. In Islam the poor and the rich can dine together and pray to God from the same platform. That was why some Muslim rulers and Kazis succeeded in converting a large number of low-caste people to Islam quite easily. A new Muslim society of converts thus came into existence and gradually they multiplied in number. They followed the Islamic ideals but continued to observe some of their earlier Hindu rituals. In course of time, these rituals were given Islamic patronage and were explained in the background of Islamic tenets. Besides, there was no scope for the converts to be reconverted into the fold of Hinduism, because the Hindus considered the Muslims as *Mlechha*(unclean). Thus continued the process of Islamisation unopposed for a long time. A delve into the socio-religious customs and traditions will convince us that the Hindu rituals have been surviving since long and that their survival is a peculiar phenomenon in Indian society, a society which exists as a unity amidst diversities.

Similar was the situation in the case of converts to Christianity. The British rulers and missionaries were not as much enthusiastic in conversion, as were some Muslim rulers. The incipient conversion was struck amongst the tribals and the low-caste Hindus. They stressed the inequelities of Hindu society and allured these innocent folk into Christianity through offer of jobs, lucrative positions and some recognizable status in the society they lived in. In this way, conversion in Bengal became appreciably large in number. However, though the people embraced Christianity, their attitudes towards the rituals relating to birth marriage, death and so forth did not alter altogether. Often they carried their old Hindu impressions with them. Only they began to explain those rituals in the background of Christian tenets. The converted Christians here still practise many rituals which were originally Hindu in texture and complexion. The survival of Hindu rituals in Indian society which is composed of the Hindus, Muslims (including converted Muslims) and Christians (including converted Christians) in India, is an interesting feature of this society, and these go a long way to explain the unity in the midst of diversities.

Islam like Christianity does not believe in free love which loosens all ties of social relations as free love among the Christians leads many of them to loosing family-tie. Islam unlike Hinduism does not believe in indissoluble binding of man and woman which turns many a home into an actual hell. The Hindus do not believe in free-love but believe in indissoluble binding of man and woman through a marriage. Of course, in modern society many Hindus with modern outlook go in for easy separation of marriage-tie and free-love as well.

Throughout their life-cycles the Hindus, Muslims and Christians observe various socio-religious rites and rituals without which the existence of their social life cannot be imagined even. Rites are magical rather than propitiatory; in other words, the desired objects are attained by ceremonies which are thought to infringe upon the course of nature.

Rites which are instructive in nature are found in every walk of life. These rites are concerned with birth, childhood, puberty, marriage, parentage, death along with some religious performances.

In the Hindu ceremonies folk rites play an important part. Similarly, folk customs, and rites as per beliefs, are performed by the converted Muslim and Christian societies also. The female folk particularly of older generations regardless of caste and creed, are found in every walk of their life form the cradle to the grave, to observe various socio-religious rituals. Of course, the better and educated sections of other countries also cannot help indulging in the observance of some traditional folk rituals and folk practices.

Now-a-days with the spread of education, the system of traditional division of labour that man is to earn money for maintaining his family and woman is to be responsible to look after the domestic affairs of her family, has been lost. At present, many of the educated women working outside for maintenance of their families, are also to look after their domestic affairs. The spread of education amongst women, has given them the chance of doing work with other male partners and free mixing with a large number of male folk has led to an increase in number of inter caste and inter-religious marriages. Besides, with the spread of education many of the old traditional rituals observed during the life-cycle of a man as a social being, have fallen into disuse and the traditional customs are under-valued. Free mixing between marriageable men and women in educational institutions, offices and other common places, has caused many love marriages without any regard to observation of rituals from the law books of the Hindus, Muslims, and Christians. Cases of divorce have increased to a great extent. On the other hand, many old socio-religious superstitions have now become obsolete, as a result rigidity in casteism has been relaxed to a great extent and the people pertaining to Hindu, Muslim and Christian religions after forgetting their barrier, have since long been participating in the socio-religious rites and rituals, fairs and festivals of each religion.

So the present study intends to add something new to sociology or social anthropology. It also shows how people are the object of traditional rituals which they cannot give up even after their acceptance of a new faith. Though some people have very easily adapted new social system, others have not been so and they ultimately retain their traditional rituals. This retention may, in one hand, create confusion in the orthodox idea of a particular religion, yet this on the other hand, destroys the socio-religious narrowness and barrier, and also bridges the gap amongst the different socio-religious ideas, the ultimate goals of which are the same. The idea of retention of old traditions and rituals may help to trace the origin of racial link of many people who will ultimately be the linkage among the conflicting communities.

Performance of rituals jointly by the people of various religions, bring them more close to understand the central theme of their respective religions and prevailing socio-religious beliefs and practices relating to worship of God in various forms during birth, marriage, death, ancestral worship etc., and other religious performances. No doubt, this type of joint performances surely inspire them to love each other's religion, and help them to understand that every religion has taught man to love one another regardless of caste and creed. Besides, it will also let the people of the concerning religions understand that due to this social contact in the changing industrial as well as urban setting, a good number of inter-religious marriages take place although marriage as a whole is deemed to be *Shastric*, religious and spiritual union of two co-religionists. It is a sacrament, indivisible and inviolable binding force for ever between the wedding spouses. In the social set-up complexities of life are disciplined by a good number of religious codes of conduct, sanctions and prohibitions. Of course, many rites are superstitious and developed out of fear for evil spirits or some supernatural elements. There is an existence of *non-shastric* rites. Though many religious rites leading to the spiritual faith are in practice, yet some are on the wane more in the urban and industrialised setting than in the rural folk life.

If the illiterate mass as well as all the literates could understand that they have virtually been following more or less the same socio-religious rituals and come to know the origin of a large number of converted Muslim and Christians, they would surely extend their friendly hands towards destroying the virus of the persisting communal conflicts as well as ill feelings that result in the destruction of national property, solidarity and integrity as well. This will also help the prejudiced, superstitious and orthodox people forget their enmity with the people of the other religious and their joint effort will surely be able to establish communal harmony and universal brotherhood and peace by forgetting the hatred for the people belonging to other religious faiths. This will also help them in isolating the miscreants and opportunists who are virtually believers in no religion but indulge only in massacre, looting, plundering, arson etc. This will let the orthodoxy, superstitious beliefs and practices get loose and will help in creating a common set of practice incorporating the cream of all religious faiths and will ultimately lead to social prosperity and national solidarity as well. If this exotic influence could gather momentum, it will bring about changes in social pattern among the sons of the soil irrespective of caste and creed. As a result the existing caste system will, in course of time, lose its rigidity further. It will strengthen not only inter-caste marriage, but also inter-religious marriage. Communalism will in future be crushed completely and permanently. The primary task to establish a democratic socialism will be to give security of life, property and honour to every citizen irrespective of caste and creed.

Of course, there was a distinct character of this survival of Hindu rituals among the converts; but nowadays due to spread of modern education, as well as rapid urbanization and various employment facilities, the old superstition ridden society has in many respects, been in a process of change. For instance, once the social condition was such that if a Hindu would take meal with a Muslim or Christian, he, some times along with the other members of his family, had to loose his caste status and other associated privileges. Nowadays, even inter marriage between a Hindu and a Muslim or a Christian can hardly make any one an outcaste, specially in the urban social set-up. But up to early 20th century, the orthodox Hindus had observed their own socio-religious rituals and the Muslims and Christians their own. Once the Muslims and the Christians were hardly allowed to participate in the Hindu socio-religious functions. Today customary rigidity under the modern outlook has been relaxed to a great extent in the Hindu and Muslim as well as Christian societies.

At present many orthodox Muslims and Christian along with converts, are found to take active part in some Hindu socio-religious rituals. Likewise, the Hindus also take part in some Muslim and Christian socio-religious functions. Many Muslims are often served meal, being seated in the same row with the Hindus in a Hindu marriage feast. They are also found to participate in the Hindu worship of the Goddesses, like *Durga, Sitala, Manasa, Saraswati* etc.; the Hindu also embrace the Muslims on the day of *Vijaya Dasami* (Immersion day of Durga)–a day for extending love and good wishes to all, irrespective whether they are friend or foe. On the other hand, many Hindus also participate in some Muslim and Christian festivals. This secular outlook in all spheres of life has, today, greatly influenced and moulded the behaviour patterns of individuals also.

Social Attenuation among the Countryside Immigrants : A Study among the Pavement Dwellers of Calcutta

Bidyut Kumar Das

I

Urban population, in general, is always in a state of flux. In 1941, in India the urban population was merely 13.9 percent of the total population, which rose up to 17.3 percent in 1951, 17.9 percent in 1961 and 19.9 percent in 1971. According to the 1971 Census, the total population of West Bengal was 44.3 million, while the urban population was 10.9 million, i.e, 22.76 percent of the whole population figure. In addition to this, there is a sizeable number of 'floating population' who were not included in the census. The growth rate of this 'floating population' is and would have been, of less concern if it did not simultaneously give birth to a number of socio-economic problems arising out of population imbalance which are new and demand immediate and effective solution. This surplus 'floating population' has no standard homes and as such, they are found in clusters at different places of the cities. In Calcutta, Mumbai, Chennai and Delhi, approximately, five million, out of a total 19 million of the 'floating population' live in slum areas (bustis) or makeshift settlements. Calcutta has been a city of immigrants ever since its foundation. Since the 40's, the wave of migration have episodically overwhelmed Calcutta as consequences of disaster or distress. During the Second World War, people flooded into Calcutta because of the Bengal famine of 1943. As a result of the partition of India in 1947 and the 1964 Indo-Pakistan war, a good number of uprooted people stormed into the city to escape political uncertainty and conflict in East Pakistan. In addition to absorbing the refugees from East Pakistan (Bangladesh), Calcutta was also the largest recipient of the inter and intra-state migrants of India.

Calcutta's importance as an economic centre all over India stems from the concentration of industry, financial services and trade activities within the city and in the Calcutta Metropolitan Districts offering all kinds of education and occupational facilities. All these grew out of the concentration of the British trading and, later, industrial activity in Bengal from the days of East India Company. These urban pulls not only centripetally accelerated the ingress of people from different walks of life from different states including the refugees of East Pakistan (Bangladesh), but also to the haves and have-nots of the neighbouring districts. As a result of this continuous flow of the rural poor into urban areas in search of livelihood and their failure to find adequate means to support themselves have originated and increased the growth of roadside dwellers and slum life in the cities. Abrams in his pioneering study of housing problems of the third world city states the overall number of squatters is in no way comparable to that of the cities of India where "in Calcutta for instance, it is estimated that some 60,000 people sleep on the streets."

II

The present study is an exploratory study on rural destitutes who on account of extreme economic hardship and threatening poverty have come as push migrants to urban centres, especially to Calcutta. It aims primarily at getting an insight into the nature and consequence of immigration of these hapless and downtrodden people of our country, from one social boundary to another, and the ultimate result of it. Attempt has been made to examine the ways of life of a section of immigrants in all their major social and economic aspects for a better understanding of the social transformation. These groups of people are overwhelmingly rural migrants. The study of the pattern of social change is concerned with what happens to people steeped in abject poverty and social organization of the village community when they encounter the economic, social and cultural order in the city. Since they live in an interacting system, the multiplicity of reference group induces change in the value system, aspiration and style of life of the poor migrants. Thus the study determines whether and how the extreme living conditions of these immigrants, in an urban occupational environment lead to attenuation of traditional social relations, norms and values and behaviour by the inherent demands of the situation.

III

The study was conducted on a sample Bengali population of 1605 individuals comprising 49.22 percent males and 50.78 percent females, living in 400 households. The social origin of the studied population reveals that there are 26.75 percent refugees from Bangladesh, 68 percent villagers from neighbouring districts while only 5.25 percent individuals from the city proper. The reasons for their migration to the city are many and varied. Frequent draughts and floods, landlessness, poor productivity of soil, lack of irrigation and other modern firming gadgets and extremely acute pressure of man on land, less or no job opportunities for uneducated and unskilled labourers, political disaster and different kind of social and economic difficulties compel the people to leave their ancestral rural homes. These mobile crowds usually throng on convenient 'footpath' (pavement), park side, railway stations, canal sides or any other available open space within the urban conglomeration and identified themselves as *footpath basi* (pavement dwellers). These provide not only short time shelters, but also meet all practical purposes of life from cradle to grave. Domestic life of thousands of such families is spent in the open roadsides in season and out of season throughout the year and even for generation after generation.

These pavement dwellers are the counter parts of the rural poor lying at the bottom rung of social ladder and suffering from cumulative inequalities. The studied population consists of two religious groups, the Hindus (76 percent) and the Muslims (24 percent). The Hindu populations are again subdivided into several castes, which are ranked hierarchically, considering the religious, social, economical and political factors. Although the lower castes comprise a smaller proportion of urban population than the rural population. It is found that the lower castes comprise a disproportionately large percentage of pavement dwellers in the city. Out of 76 percent Hindus under study, 71.25 percent belong to lower or Scheduled Castes, while 28.75 percents belong to middle and upper caste Hindus.

Of the total number of households studied, 32.25 percent of the heads of households were formerly marginal farmers, 17.75 percent sharecroppers, 41.75 percent landless labourers and 8.25 percent artisans and occupational castes. It is significant that out of 71.25 percent lower caste Hindus, 22.75 percent were marginal farmers, 9.50 percent share croppers, 34.75 percent landless labourers and the remaining 4.25 percent artisan and occupational castes.

The difference that lies between the two social categories, the pavement dwellers and the rural poor, is that, since there is very little scope for earning through white-collar jobs for these uneducated and unskilled folks, they sell their labour in the urban market or beg other's mercy for their subsistence. The rural poor, on the other hand, were and are tied to agricultural occupations and are dependent on land and, to some extent, on rural artisan work. The pavement dwellers accept any kind of job that are easily available for their survival. They serve as coolies or porters, casual labourers, handcart pullers, rag-pickers, mason helpers, peddlers and last but not the least beggars;

and the women in some extreme cases indulge in the oldest profession of the world- prostitution. Out of the total of 1605 individuals, there are 69.59 percent earners comprising 35.01 percent males and 34.58 percent females. It is significant that out of the total of 69.59 percent earners, 7.17 percent males and 6.60 percent females are child labours (Who are below 15 years of age) and 7.79 percent males and 7.23 percent females are aged labours (above 58 year of age). Further, almost all the pavement dwellers work in the informal sectors where entry is easy, requiring skill and education is considered extra-qualifications. This can be justified though the occupational status of the population where all the castes (upper, middle and lower) freely accept the job of casual labour or maidservant or begging. Those living in the urban areas are based in an open and large community sectors, whereas those in the villages encapsulated in 'closed' and small communities where their status and position are identified on the basis of caste and the relationships between various castes depending upon ownership, control and use of land as well as on the 'Jajmani' system (patron-client relationship) which specifies inter-related rights and obligations between groups at different caste levels. In short, the relationships of the rural poor with the rest of the social groups of the village community are governed by the 'obligations' that fetter them to the classes or castes on whom they depend for their employment and social recognition.

It is in the urban complex that there are possibilities of crossing the limitations of caste in finding employment on the basis of skill, acquiring education, organizational methods, which fundamentally alter their lifestyle and offer scope for mobility, achievement of social capabilities. It is another situation whether or not they achieve what they aspire to. We refer only to the availability of alternative opportunities, landless labourers or sharecroppers. Their children need not live in a society where there is no escape from ascribed status to which they are born.

But, in reality, the pavement dwellers face a different situation in the city life. They have exceptionally low educational levels, when compared with the rural or urban population, and even lower than slum dwellers. Of the total population, there are only 10.75 percent literates comprising 8.04 percent males and 2.74 percent females. Though poverty is one of the major obstacles standing in the way of sending the children to school, where a child's help in doing domestic chores at home would relieve adult to work outside and earn more, or where the child itself would earn and boost up family income, most of the parents have little or no education and employment aspirations for their wards. Of course, there are some voluntary organizations working among the pavement dwellers and other urban poor (in slums) which, besides other types of services, offer both formal and non-formal education programme, but very little is known about their achievement or failures.

Income, of course, is closely related with the type of employment and it determines one's standard of living. Since the *raison-d-etre* of any human being is food, the type of housing that can be afforded, depends very much on the extent of income that is left over after meeting the most basic requirements of food. Therefore, analyses of the income, expenditure and dwelling pattern of the pavement dwellers have been taken into consideration.

Though there are some uni-member households, majority of the households (about 60 percent) have five or more than five members. The income distribution in relation to family size reveals that 84.50 percent household have income of Rs.200 or below, while only 5.25 percent households earn Rs250 or more per month. The income they earned, at least in terms of cash money may be higher than they earned in the rural areas, but still at present they live at rock-bottom of poverty and there are scant chances of their mobility for higher achievements and development of social capabilities. Of the total population, 22.75 percent households have no fixed shelter, 22.25 percent live in hutments or makeshift shelters while 18.50 percent households have no cooking arrangement but they mainly live on begging cooked food stuffs, and only 12 percent of them cook regularly. Yet, it is a wonder that they do not ever think of returning to their villages. No doubt they lead a very miserable existence on the pavements yet the lure of more earning opportunities, the easy availability of some urban facilities (light, water, medical and public sanitation) and recreation in the urban areas prevent them from going back to their native places. It is important to note that only a small fraction of the pavement dwellers wish to remain on the pavements, while majority of them are willing to shift to other built-in accommodation within the urban conglomeration but are unable to pay the economic rent and alternative employment opportunities that would ensure their better earning.

IV

For their migration and settlement in the city, kinship, caste and regional ties play an important role, but this network exists till the migrants become acclimatized with the pavement way of living and later such affiliations gradually loosen. As a result, some secondary relations, based on the networks of contracts and reciprocal give-and-take in the world of goods and services, enlivens these migrants to continue a miserable life with no future hope and functions as an adaptive mechanism and guide to their behavioral pattern and social identity. Since 95 percent of them are rural migrants, their community, as a whole resembles the village community as they bring with them not only a network of relations but also some corporate institutions, which make up the loss of the total structure of their rural communities. But to these 'have nots', the structural relationships lie on the groupings based on the common interest and association, rather than ethnic, religion or communal basis. Here, the age-old traditional network of relationships are supplemented by the association formed on rationally derived reciprocal interest or friendship groups. They function in their day-to-day life as small credit groups, recreational associates, gossiping and gambling groups or they may be formed at their work places, because of shared occupational interests. Though these ramifications are transitory and generally serve their immediate and short range needs, the whole texture plays an inter-locking network of socialites that help the destitute to sustain their wretched life on the pavement, year after year.

Among the pavement dwellers, the kinship ties are very loosely developed, because they have a very shallow knowledge of kins. In most cases, the knowledge is limited up to the maximum of second ascending generation, because they have never seen or heard of kins in times of their weal and woe. The avoidance of kinsmanship is, to a great extent, responsible for loosening the social pressure in different life-crisis rituals and custom and to estabish a self-centered parochial outlook of the world consisting of only a few primary kins that they identify in their everyday life. Social relations between different kins are measured from their participation in different social rites and ceremonies. In the pavement life, such occasions are seldom observed. Birth or marriage has become a personal affair, where no one is informed or invited. Only some are found to observe a period of pollution and concomitant rites on the death of a very near and dear relative. This sort of loose articulation in kin-relationship is understood through their involvement in different social situations. Of the total number of households, 35 percent have no attachment with their village for several years consecutively, while 15 percent visit their villages by fits and starts. It was also found that those who have fixed shelter and are able to earn their bread regularly have unbroken contact with their rural kins and neighbours. Families with unstable occupations are very low income, or families with low status of occupations, have less contact with their kins and also the number of their effective and intimate kins are few and far between. In the street habitation, which is full of dejection and misery, where emotion and kindness are rarely noticed, the kinship relations become very selective on likes and dislikes, but not on the orders of structural principles. It is found that living in the same locality, many families have no contact with their brother and sister's families, while they have contact with some distant kins or even non-kin members.

V

The life on the pavement has its own dynamism. It may be any crisis, rural or urban, psychological or emotional or social, which acts as the backdrop of pavement dweller's life, but these forces continue to play their part even when life moves on in the pavement. At the beginning of urban life, most of the members of a family maintain their rural traditions, i.e., love, affection and obedience with mutual involvement. But within a short period of stay in such adverse situation such moral obligations gradually fade away when starvation, deprivation etc., confront the individuals and threatens him to death. Clefts are seen in the relations of different members in the family. Individualism develops among the members and, side-by-side, the traditional values gradually slip into oblivion, which results in the disintegration of the original family. Husband and wife relation slackens and that between the parents and children turns away. The cases of extramarital sex relations appear in some cases among them. The sexual morality becomes so loose that formal marriages are not considered as an essential institution to get a child or to form a new family. It is evident from the fact that when one actually lives under the canopy of the open sky, bereft of human emotions like love, sympathy and minimum essentials of human life, one loses all social and moral values. If there is heavy rain in the night, and if one pavement dweller wants a little cover over his head and gets a help from a fellow pavement dweller, he will not bother any more to know the social origin of the latter. Who-ever helps him becomes his friend, much more than his own relatives. In the cold winter nights, if a pavement dweller gets a tattered cloth from his neighbours or share a threadbare blanket, he becomes more than his own kins or relatives. In disease and sickness, in hunger and privation, a new kind of friendship and fellow feeling appears to cement the differences. It is a strange distorted development of social values and ethics, which alternates the life meaningfully. In strange assoçiation , through limitless limitations, new social groupings emerge and forge to supplement the crisis of life through alternatives. It is a process and a new kind of unstructured social solidarity that grows in their lives.

VI

From the above analysiș it is revealed that the poor from rural areas are attracted to the city by its greater glitter of scope for earning from numerous avenues and all for a better life. But their expectations are not wholly fulfilled, for in the city they are engaged in very low income yielding occupations in the informal sectors. As a consequence, whatever may be the degree of difference in their present style of living, the easy availability of some urban facilities and a hope for greater scope of earning avenues prevent them to return to their original homes which are more negative in all spheres and less attractive for any sort of future assurance. Causes regarding the migration of village destitute may be many and varied, but the main cause for which these unfortunate people left their hearth and home was economic. This economic cause, again embraces the village poor in two ways–those who earn but not enough for their subsistence and those who do not earn enough for even a full meal in a day. In latter category who usually fall prey to the lure of a city life for keeping their body and soul together.

The pavement dwellers from a distinct entity and regard themselves or are being treated by the other urban masses as a differentiated community labeling them as *footpath basi,* not in the physical sense of conglomeration of individuals and households with their scrappy belongings, but also by the social and economic reflections punctuated through their way of living and manners and customs. Even the birth on the pavement gives him the status of *footpath basi* in the sense that he/she is being deprived from all joys and happiness of a normal living on earth. The common sentiment based on religion, caste and language slowly disappears and, as such, a new distinctive 'culture/sub culture' gradually develops with extreme economic deprivation and their compromise with the very unsatisfactory conditions of pavement life. In our present political and social system, they will never be able to retrace their steps to their village houses leaving dingy and culturally degenerated pavement shelters, as they feel greater security here. Though they appear to maintain some link both with rural and urban society, but there develops an incipient social world among themselves being expressed on lifestyle and new values, which reflect an imulgum of rural-urban, and the culture of the have-nots. Thus, not only their level of poverty, but of social degradation is involved in the kind of life they lead; their social norms deviated from that of the traditional society and take specific patterns adaptive of the kind of life they live.

Social Mobility in Bengal

Kartik Chandra Dalui

The basic objective of this paper is to contemplate the concept of 'Bengali nationalism' which has been viewed from different angles. At the outset we have examined the anthropological characteristics of the communities and occupational groups in Hindu caste-hierarchy. Then we have analysed the process of Sanskritisation and culture-transformation. Gradually, by critical survey of the historical, socio-economic and political facts, we have explained the nature of social mobility which has a tendency towards the growth of a nationality feeling in Bengal. Ultimately we have, through crucial instances, found 'Bengali Nationalism'..

In this thesis the researcher has tried to show his objectives through the following important aspects.

1. The racial composition of the Bengaleese is the admixer of proto-atustraloid, Aryan and Mongoloid races. The study of the different social groups in Bengal reveals that the Dravidian racial elements are more prominent than other elements. The Aryan race elements are insignificant in the racial composition of the community of Bengal, though Hinduism is a religion of the Indo-Aryans and Bengali language has developed from Sanskrit vocabularies. It is often apparent that the economically advanced and politically privileged strata in the Hindu social system try to establish racial superiority disregarding the age-old evolution of the Bengalee race.

Migrated races of the three broad types viz., black, yellow and white lived respectively in the Decan, the North and the East. With the increase of population in the above surroundings and as a result of socio-economic conflict, migration took place towards deltaic Bengal where they have lost their colour and shape. Among these three types, the Dravidian character is more pronounced than the other two.

2. The racial character of the Bengalis have been differentiated by geographical and socio-economic peculiarities of Bengal. Since the time of the formation of deltaic Bengal and migration of the main-stream of the Dravidian stock along the coast line of the sea and

through the forests of Chhotanagpur, the other two streams namely the contact group of the upper Gangetic plane and the contact group of the North-eastern frontier contributed to the population growth in ancient and medieval Indian history. Under the joint influence of geographical conditions, and consequent socio-economic conditions the immigrants lost their previous racial features and adapted to those conditions of deltaic Bengal. As a result, a separate racial group arose. Among all the cultures contributing to Bengali culture and civilisation, the Aryan one occupied first position in the history of Sanskritisation. During the Hindu period of Indian history, gradually, not quickly but slowly, the Aryan culture had been adopted by the communities of Bengal. Hence, to Bengal, came the Aryan culture, not the Aryan race.

Bengal is surrounded by the hills and the Himalayan ranges on the north, north-east, by sea–the Bay of Bengal on the south; rainfall is heavier in this portion of Indian subcontinent than in northern India.

As a whole, the geographical conditions have differentiated Bengal from the rest of India and this geographical differentiation leads to a racial differentiation. Over and above in ancient and medieval periods, some isolated communities lived in Bengal in geographical isolation.

The upper castes in present Bengal claims them as Aryan as migration took place from the upper Gangetic plane. They brought with them Aryan culture and civilisation as the weapons of social conquest of the people. By introducing Aryan culture and civilisation they established their political power and machinery of economic exploitation maintaining the caste hierarchy in the existing social system.

Through a long process of differentiation in geographical and social isolation, and in natural conditions a type of anthropological group here in Bengal emerged, this group may be termed as a mixed race.

Therefore we come to the conclusion that Bengalees constitute a single homogeneous group formed in a peculiar geographical condition. Natural and social isolation through the process of differentiation have facilitated the process of group formation. All the immigrants have lost their previous racial character, none can establish to-day the purity of the Aryan or Dravidian or any other racial claim.

It has been found that the communities below the rank of clean castes belong to a common stock of origin, that is to say the Dravidian, and their hereditary profession of fishing was the first resource for livelihood in deltaic Bengal. Because, in the beginning of the emergence of Bengal from the sea, there was no other alternative source for living in this place. All the communities particularly the economically backward and politically under-privileged caste still retain their ancestral profession–fishing and have maintained their identity.

In course of the changing economy of Bengal, from fishing to agriculture some of the sub-castes took agriculture and agricultural labour as their profession. As a necessary consequence, subsections came out from units of territorial and endogamous communities for example, from *Kaibartas* the *Mahisyas*, from the *Gops* the *Sadgops*, from the *Telis* the *Tillis*, from the *Karmakar* the *Swarnakar*, from the *Dules* the *Bagdies*, from the *Kaibartas* again the *Pods, Tyors, Jhalos, Malos* etc., came as socially differentiated units. Latter, through the process of Sanskritisation, they became caste units.

During the conversion into Islam in the deltaic Bengal, the different sub-castes particularly the socially unclean sections adopted Islam. But their professional similarity, for instance, fishing and soldiering, and some criminal pursuits like dacoity and robbery are well marked among the economically and culturally backward Muslims and Hindu sub-caste population. This also indicates that they belonged to the similar community having the same racial origin, viz., the Dravidian.

The Brahmins, Kayasthas and Vaidyas as castes to-day can no longer claim Aryanhood. Their cultural, economic and political status index and cephalic index between the higher and lower castes fail to establish the Aryanhood of the high castes.

The nature of soil, climate change, nature of food staff, full play of monsoon, heavy rainfall in summer have all largely contributed to some uniformity of physiological and morphological characteristics. As a result, the original racial features of the Aryans are missing in the evolution of the Bengali race. Even the Dravidian characteristics have also been minimized now.

From the above analysis it is clear that caste groups formed in this region are intimately connected with the geographical and climatic situation. The economy has gradually moved from fishing to agriculture. It has resulted in the growth of various occupations. The *Gops, Sadgops, Tili, Karmakar, Kumbhakar, Malakar, Kansakar, Barujibi, Tambuli, Tanti, Sutradhar* etc., are the different occupational groups that have been created. The process began with the Hinduisation of the communities of Bengal in different epochs.

The recent trend in social mobility in Bengal is against the continuation of caste based hierarchy. Values of caste superiority are not so much accepted by the young generation. As a matter of fact, class based stratification has been replacing the old stratification. The caste system was introduced in unique political and economic situation in Bengal. As economy and politics have taken a new turn so new corresponding stratification is fast coming into existence.

New types of political movement led by Deshbandhu C. R. Das, Netaji Subhas Chandra Bose, Surawardi, Fazlul Haque, Aurobindo Ghosh, religious movement led by Swami Vivekananda, cultural and literacy movement led by Rabindranath Tagore, Sarat Chandra Chattapadhyay and science movement led by Sir J. C. Bose, Acharya P. C. Roy all these served to create a new dynamism and give a new shape to the culture which is the characteristics of the new age.

As a result, a new type of society with a novel cultural orientation is fast emerging. Over and above, the growth of leftist politics and the influence of Marxism have accelerated the process of change from medieval to modern. The spirit of political equality and democratic freedom, humanitarian values, fight against religious orthodoxy and a sense of disengagement from sectional identities–all these have accelerated the process of social mobility.

Under British rule in Bengal, the middle class increased in dimension and depth. The nature of change in landholding pattern, the emergence of salaried professions, business income and the spread of modern education–all these have strengthened the middle class groups in our society.

At present though we see that casteism is on the decline but caste sentiment is still prevailing. Regarding the prevalence of inter caste marriage sentiment, it is found that the upper castes feel a loss of social status while the lower castes feel the raising of status by marriage in an upper caste.

But today as economic and political conditions are fast changing with the introduction of industrialization and with the inception of democratization of political and social institutions in these new social conditions social stratification also is taking a new character.

The special constitutional privileges granted to the Scheduled Caste (formerly unclean caste) have increased the tension between the upper and the lower castes. By these privileges the dominant and more or less economically affluent families among the lower castes have been benefited and they are now almost detached from their own castes and have formed a separate elite group. This is giving rise to a new system of stratification.

Sanskritisation is backed by allegiance to caste based hierarchy characterized by the supremacy of the Brahmins. But present socio-economic factors have been functioning against this traditional pattern of hierarchy. As such Sanskritisation is increasing being replaced by western democratic values which is now considered worth emulating. People are being sharply divided into groups in term of economic and political power. Religious influence as a determinant of human behaviour is on the decline. M. N. Srinivas has analyzed this process as a transition from the Sanskritization model to westernization model.

Due to the introduction of the Panchayati Raj (Local self Government) and parliamentary system of Government in India and due to the influence of educational institutions like the Universities and Colleges, people of the upper strata are gradually becoming conscious of their power. Class-consciousness also makes them polarized in politics. But the illiterate bulk, the destitute millions are still clinging to and guided by a sense of fatalism and mysticism. Institutions like marriage or *Sradha* (funeral) are still prevalent in accordance with the Hindu rituals both among the upper and lower strata of Hindu society. Religious domination is still common among all the castes and sub-castes in the Hindu society.

Sanskritisation as a process is still continuing among them. Castes like *Bagdi, Dom, Sadgop, Tili, Mahishya* etc., had, long before it, been recognised as castes of the Hindu. Gradually some of them raised their position from the untouchables and some are still socially depressed. But the present Indian constitution has abolished untouchability. Anthropological analysis shows that they belong to tribal groups particularly from the Dravidian stock. But through a process of Sanskritisation some of them have been recognised as caste Hindus.

Therefore, Sanskritisation as a process of social mobility is still strong. The nature of Sanskritisation in Bengal has got a very different colour of its own. Religious, social, cultural and philosophical institutions are characterised by local rituals and practices. All these institutions of Bengal have been aryanised but the Aryan institutions have hardly been imposed on them totally.

Even Islamic sects have been influenced by this process. Institutions like *Pir, Satyanarayan* etc., are acting as bridging points between the Hindu sects and Islamic sects.

The gods and goddesses of *Mangal Kabyas* are non-Aryan ones. Female gods like *Annada, Sarada* are the incarnation of Aryan goddesses. But *Dharma* is a non-aryan god *Kali, Chandi, Manasa, Sitala* etc., are non-Aryan goddesses. Culture as depicted in the ballads are sanskritised forms of local culture.

The upper caste of Bengal are professional castes whereas the lower castes are community based. The community based castes like *Kaibarta, Bagdi, Dule,* etc., are more faithful to Vaishnava creed than the upper castes; and the upper castes like *Sadgop, Tili* etc., are also the supporters and upholdres of Vaishnava creed. That is due to the universal appeal of Chaitanyaism.

Sanskritisation has become a more active process in Bengal after Chaitanyadev. The people of the deltaic Bengal accepted Islam not as a means of religious salvation but out of desire of them for economic and political emancipation from the exploitation of Hindu upper castes. The principal motive that dragged the majority of people into Islamic society was social–due to a desire for equality of status and democratic rights, people became prone to accepting Islam. Islam came to Bengal in such a context. This clearly indicates that Islam contributed to social mobility.

The growth of nationalism among the Bengali is the result of a long historical process. Its emergence is due to the geographic, economic, linguistic, cultural and anthropological distinctions of deltaic Bengal. In this sense Bengali nationalism is older than Indian nationalism. When the Indian sub-continent came under the British rule, a feeling of common political consciousness, a fact of common exploitation, a common subjugation and subordination led to the unification of the different social, linguistic, cultural, religious, and economic groups who fought for a common cause. A common master brought the differential elements into a composite whole of Indian nationalism. But the Bengalis as an ethnic group having their own distinct identity, had its emergence long back.

Bengali nationalism has neither been militant nor aggressive, nor has it been any hindrance to the neighbouring nationality. On the other hand it has long been a resistance to and refutation of exploiting machinery of government-alien or indigenous. Bengali nationalism tends to the growth of a culture which teaches the principle of unity of India, the principle of federal functioning of society; it has never tolerated any sort of imposition from within or without.

The Crossbow Complex in Tribal Culture : A Study in Historical Anthropology

Kamalessh Guha

The primitive tribes of India, largely follow their tradition and culture even today. So scholars speculate differently regarding their origin which still remain an important problem of Indian history. Some ethnologists like B. S. Guha, S. S. Sarkar and others firmly believe that these tribals were the autochthons of India while J. H. Hutton, G. A. Grierson and many other ethnologists consider them as archaic surviving exotic people in this country.

To know the reality, the present study has followed a scientific method which includes a model (structural history) and three case-studies (ethnic history). Although these two approaches are quite opposite, yet they are complementary procedures. Therefore, this study has introduced both 'totalistic' and 'particularistic' approaches to cultural history of the primitive tribes of India.

The aim of the present study is to determine the time dimension of Indian aboriginal culture on the basis of its material culture analysis. Therefore, this study has analysed the technological objects (artifacts) in general and the crossbow complex in particular in both space and time dimensions. The analysis is blended with ethnological and historical facts.

As the present study has a historical objective, it has followed the historical method of anthropology to study the historical relationship among the primitive tribes of India. The three parted works are briefly mentioned below.

1) Their material culture includes the agricultural implements and the handicrafts systematically.
2) Their structural history clssified into : (a) Hunter-gatherers of Central and South India and (b) Warriors of North East India based on their dominant interest. The purpose of this classification of tribes is to reconstruct the culture context of their crossbow complex, since these two cultural (or technological) traits have an inner connection in their constructions.
3) The ethnohistory of tribes.

1. The Kadar of Kerela 2) the Ahom of Assam and 3) the Meithei of Manipur. Ethnologically, they belong to three different kinds of ethnic stocks. For example, the Kadars are Negritic-Negroid, the Ahom are Mongoloid and the Meitheis are Caucasoid people in their racial compositions. Moreover, these tribes are culturally different from each other because they follow different kinds of economic activities. The Kadars are food-gatherers and hunters, the Ahoms practise shifting cultivation and the Meitheis are agriculturists.
The Study is based on a material culture analysis. In this work the author has tried to combine the two approaches of Historical Anthropology namely Structural-Fundamentalism and Diffusionism (or Distributionalism), for the reconstruction of the culture history of the primitive tribes of India.

The Distribution of Crossbow Rat Traps in South Asia

Table 1

Type of rat traps	Place of find	People who use the trap	Authors who reported the trap
Spike – arrow type	Singhbhum, Bihar (Central India)	Hos	Sinha*
Spike – arrow type	Mandla, Madhya Pradesh (Central India)	Baigas	Elwin (1939 : 81)
Spike – arrow type	CarNicobar Island	Nicobarese	Chanda (1969 : 11)
Bolt – arrow type	Mymenshing, East Bengal (Bangladesh)	Bengalees	Guha (1966 : 871-872)
Bolt – arrow type	Malabar, Kerala (South India)	Nayadis	Aiyappan (1937 : 28)
Noose type	Malay Peninsula	Semangs	Elwin (1939 : 91)

*** Dr. Surajit Sinha Collected this trap from the Hos of Singhbhum District, Bihar (1940)**

It is used by the Nayadis of South India, the Hos and Baigas of Central India, the Nicobarese, the Malayasians and the Bengalees, who are ethnologically different from each other. The distribution of the crossbow rat trap is not limited to one tribe or one place but extends in many places of Southern Asia surrounding the Bay of Bengal and the Indian ocean. The whole region of the Bay of Bengal and the Indian ocean came under the Portuguese expansionists in the middle ages. Since the Portuguese were experts in making and using the crossbow , it is not unlikely that they also used the same mechanical principle in making the rat trap which they needed for protecting their merchandise from the rats.

The primitive tribes of North-East India are generally described as the warriors of the hills because these people use various kinds of primitive weapons like the spear, shield and crossbow.

The crossbow (or arbalest) was used in war and chase in Europe in the Middle ages. Today, the crossbow is used in different parts of Africa and Asia. It is used by the peoples of West Africa, Madagascar, South India, Nicobar Islands, Assam, Burma, Thailand, Indonesia, China and many other countries of South-east Asia. The diffusion of crossbows in Africa and Asia can be argued in the following ways.

Firstly, the crossbow is not an ordinary bow. It has an additional stock and a trigger mechanism to release the arrow. The trigger mechanism of the crossbow (or arbalist) is an antecedent of the arquebus. Both of them were invented in Western Europe in the Middle ages.

Secondly, there is no historical or archeological evidence that the crossbow was used in Africa and Asia before the advent of the Europeans in these countries for their trade.

Thirdly, there is no environmental influence on the making and using of crossbows. Moreover, the spread of crossbow in Africa and Asia can be explained in terms of the Portuguese colonialist expansion in the Middle ages.

The Kadar, an aboriginal tribe, inhabit the Anaimalai or elephant hills and the great mountain range which extends south-ward up to Travencore. Most of the Kadar settlements are present in the Coimbatore district of Kerala. Many of them are also found near the coastal region of Cochin. In 1971 the total population of the Kadar was 1,120. Ethnologically, the Kadar are different from the Dravidian population of South India because they have 'Negrito-Negroid' physical characters. Culturally, they are animists, food-gatherers, hunters and shifting cultivators. Moreover, they use many kinds of primitive implements like the bows and arrows, digging-sticks etc., for their subsistence and economic activities.

For the reconstruction of the cultural history of the Kadar of Kerala, this study has followed a diffusionist approach to material culture analysis. The purpose of it is to trace the cultural affinity of the Kadars of Kerala with the Bantus of West Africa. It may be recalled that the Portuguese expansionists brought the African slaves on a large scale to India in the Middle ages. The African slaves, on the other hand, had introduced many African customs and traditions in India, which caused great cultural changes in the Indian sub-continent.

The Ahoms called themselves Tai, and it still remains to be explained how they came to be known by their present name. It has been suggested that this may be derived from Shan, or on the Assamese say, *Syam*.... this word, however, is not used by the Assamese when speaking of the Ahoms, but only with reference to the people of *Siam*.

The Ahom, the Shan and the Tai peoples are collectively called the 'Tai race'. They are culturally different from their neighbouring peoples like the Assamese, Burmese, Chinese and Tibatane. Unlike the Assamese, the Ahom practice 'Jhum' or shifting cultivation; they never use the plough for the purpose of their agricultural work. However the traditional Ahom way is disappearing, and the shifting cultivation of these people no longer exist. But the Ahom even today constitute a social group which is distinct from that of the Assamese. It is important to note here that almost all the hill- tribes of South-east Asia (including India) practice shifting cultivation like the African natives. Besides, they also use the medieval European crossbow in their cultures.

The present study reveals that the Siamese people together with the Bantus of West Africa established a 'Siamese-Bantu' dynasty in Assam in the beginning of the sixteenth century A. D. According to the Indian history, the Ahoms fought against the Mughal Empire; but the Indian historians do not know that they established their 'Feulal Systems' or 'Minor dynasties' under the hegemony of the Portuguese in Siam (Thailand). The Ahom (or–A-Ham), being a section of the Bantu tribes of West Africa, continued their traditional shifting cultivation even after making their principality in Assam. On the other hand, the Siamese people were the natives of Siam (Thailand).

The Meithei (or Meitei), whose language–Manipuri–belongs to the Kuki-Chin branch of Tibeto-Burman, are a Hindu people. For the most part, the Meithei resembles physically the Mongoloid peoples of the far north-east of India and of south-east Asia, but there are also Indo-European traits among these people (Hodson 1908:2). The Meithei are the dominant lowland people and the traditional feudal lords of Manipur. Once an independent principality ruled by Meithei rajas, who attained political dominance in the eighteenth century.

As lowlanders, the main occupation of the Meithei is irrigated rice farming. They use a distinctive plough, the discussion of which constitutes an important component of this chapter.

The Meithei are the Hindus of the Vaishnavite division. They are variously considered to be descendants of the ancient Kirat people of the Maharastra age (Chatterji 1950:143) of a Tartar colony from China (Pemberton 1835:36) and related to the surrounding hill peoples (Hodson 1908 : 6 – 7). The author has argued in this paper that Meithei cultural affiliations are in fact with the Rajput from the extreme West of India whose military forays in northeastern India can be traced to the beginning of the seventeenth century.

The primitive tribes of India are conventionally considered to be the user of prehistoric or pre-industrial tools and technology in their culture. But the present study has thrown a new light on the cultural history of these people by analysing the crossbow complex in their culture in the following ways.

1. The Pattern Phenomenon of Crossbow Complex : a New Classification of Indian Tribes

In Anthropology, two kinds of cultural complexes are constructed. One is the Graebnerian Kulturkomplexe or 'culture complex' (German School of Diffusionism) which is taken as tools by ethnologists for the study of the diffusion of cultural traits through migration from one geographical region to another. The other is used by social anthropologists for the study of the integration of culture as a whole, a whole that is more than the sum of its parts. The crossbow complex is an example of the second kind of cultural complex because the crossbow and the crossbow rat trap have an "inner connection" in their construction works.

The crossbow rat trap is a modified version of the crossbow ; the offensive weapon triggered for shooting arrows against their enemies, while the former is automatic for killing rats. In both, bow-stave is transversely fixed on the wooden stock.

Culturally, the crossbow complex has a tripartite system. They are as follows : 1) ideal; 2) modified; and 3) mixed. The geographical distribution of these patterns is given below in a chart.

Table 2
Tribal Implements and Geographical Locations

IMPLEMENTS AND THEIR PATTERNS	TRIBES AND THEIR GEOGRAPHICAL LOCATIONS
Crossbows (Ideal)	Used by the Naga, Ahom, Shan and other warrior tribes of Eastern Asia.
Crossbow Rat Trap (Modified)	Used by the Ho, Baiga, Nayadi and other food gathering-hunting tribes of Central and South India.
Both kinds of Implements (Mixed)	Used by the Nicobarese in Nicobar Island in the Indian Ocean.

Diagram 1

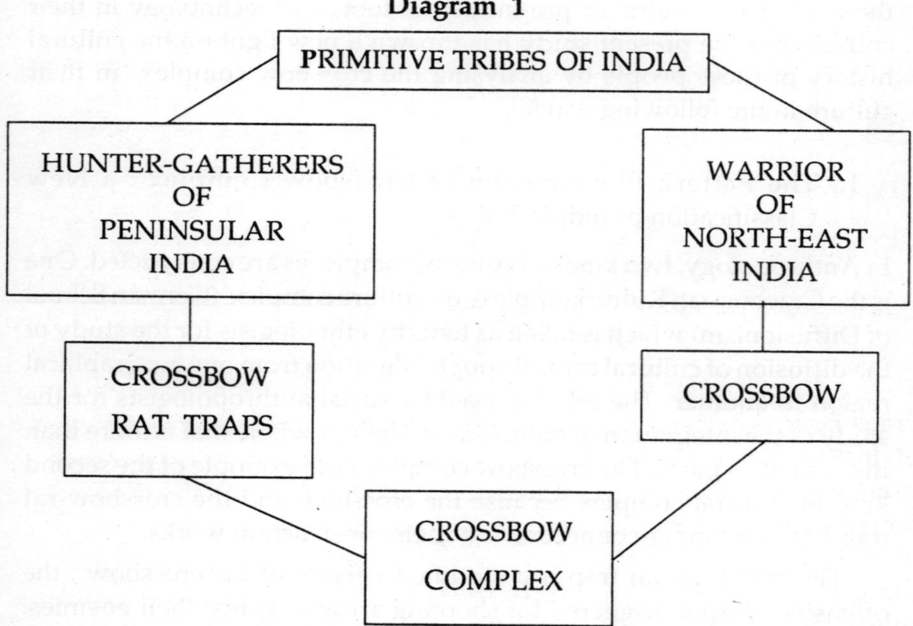

In the above flow chart, the writer has classified the primitive tribes of India into two different cultural types which are found in t.vo separate regions namely. Peninsular India and North-East India. Therefore, they represent two 'unconscious patterns', or 'latent structural forms', or 'configurations' for making the totality of the tribal culture of India. Although the crossbow complex makes a reductionist approach to the study of cultural integration of the primitive tribes of India, yet it gives an 'organismic view' of the tribal culture of India. This structural framework is important to us because it gives a perfection in the reconstruction work.

These primitive tribes live in geographical isolation, yet they have many cultural similarities. A list of essential cultural elements which are common in them are given below.

1. Hunting, fishing and food-gathering
2. Shifting cultivation
3. Personal ornaments made of animal shells, bones and horns
4. Domestic articles made of gourd, wood and bamboo etc.
5. Making of fermented drink
6. Age-grade organization
7. Dormitory institution
8. Cross-cousin marriage
9. Bride-service and bride-price
10. Animistic beliefs (including black magic, sorcery and witchcrafts).
11. Totemism and food-taboos
12. Dwelling patterns (gabbled rectangular or oblong huts, circular huts, tree huts etc.)

2. The Historical Phenomenon of Crossbow Complex : A Dynamic Generalization of Cultural History.

Franz Boas, who believed in historical realism, introduced the concept of 'historical particularism' in anthropology. Therefore, he suggested to analyse the specific or particular artifact or event in time and in space for the reconstruction of cultural history. Following the Boasian concept of historical particularism, this study has analysed the crossbow complex in time and space dimensions for the reconstruction of the cultural history of the primitive tribes of India. Since the crossbow has a technological relationship with the crossbow rat trap, these two instruments or implements are assumed to be historically connected. The determination of an absolute chronology for the crossbow complex of the primitive tribes of India is not difficult to us, if we analyse this particular trait-complex in both time and space. The time-space framework of the crossbow complex is diagrammatically shown below :

Diagram 2

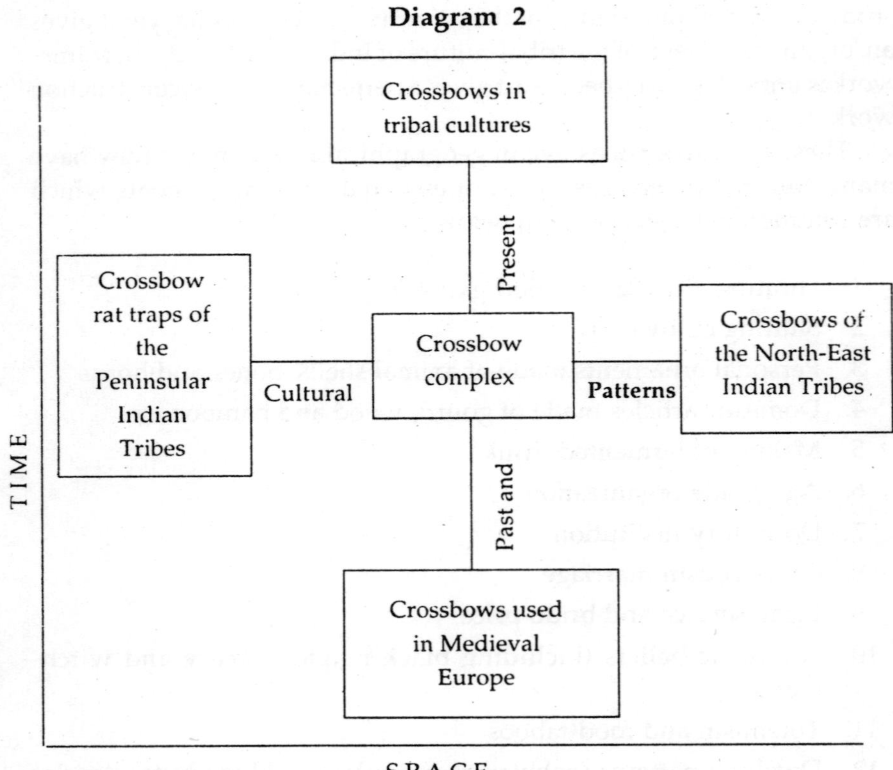

Epistemologically, the crossbow complex acts as a 'bridge' between the present day and the Middle ages because this particular trait-complex has a diachronic aspect. Although the primitive tribes of African and Asian countries use the crossbow complex in their cultures, the crossbow was evolved in Western Europe in the Middle ages. The Portuguese used crossbows against their enemies in the 15th and 16th centuries. Thus in the historical investigation of the primitive tribes of India, the crossbow complex confronts with the Portuguese history in India. To trace the origin of the crossbow complex in Indian tribal culture, we can divide the Portuguese history in India into two 'typical sequences' or phase. At first, the Portuguese collected raw materials from the jungles of the Deccan (or peninsular India) for the expansion of their trade and commerce in South Asia. Later, they started offensive attacks against the Mughals from the eastern-most corner of India after establishing themselves in Pegu (Burma). By following the deductive logic, the writer has taken a middle stand to propose a new hypothesis that the primitive tribes of India being the slaves (food-gatherers) and mercenaries (warriors) of the Portuguese in the Middle ages learnt to use the crossbow complex (including crossbow rat traps and crossbows) not only to protect the merchandise of the Portuguese merchants but also to fight against their enemies. Here the writer has made an attempt to generalise the cultural history of the primitive tribes of India. But this generalisation is of a dynamic nature because the crossbow complex not only makes two 'Sub-systems' or 'configurations' (Food-gatherers and warriors) but also gives their historical background.

It is important to mention here that the barbers of North Africa were called the Moors in the Middle ages. The Portuguese had trade relation with the Moor because the latter practiced slave raids in different parts of Africa. Vesco Da Gama (1498-1524 A. D.), Affonse de Albuquerque (1509-1515 A. D.), Nuno-Da-Cuha (1528 –1538 A.D.), Filippe de Birto e Nicote (1600-1613 A.D.) and Sabastiae Gonzales Tibae (1607–1616 A.D.) were famous slave traders in the sixteenth and seventeenth centuries. Some of them were appointed as Viceroys in India by the Portuguese Government

Furthermore, the writer has followed the Graebnerian cultural complexes to trace the cultural affinities between the primitive tribes (Negrito-Negroid peoples) of India and the African natives. Even today, a number of pan-African elements of social and cultural life like the shifting cultivation, cross-cousin marriage, matrilineal practices, age-grade organization, dormitory institution etc. are present in the tribal culture of India. But many of these pan-African elements of Indian tribal culture are fastly disappearing because the tribal people of India are not only taking the Hindu faiths but also adopting the plough for their agricultural work by the process of 'Sanskritisation' or 'Brahmanization'. So the primitive societies of India are turning into peasant societies day-by-day. Therefore, it is high time to reconstruct the cultural history of the primitive tribes of India with the help of their ethnographic data.

By following the inductive logic, the writer has made three case-studies by the 'method of generalization' of the complex relationship between the tribes (Kadar, Ahom and Meithei) and the Portuguese in medieval India by means of diachronic or ethno-historical studies. It may be recalled that the Portuguese established their Eastern Empire in South Asia in the Middle ages, and they remained in India for more than hundred years. But none has ever thought that the primitive tribes of India are the 'survivals' of the Portuguese colonialist activities in South Asia in the Middle ages. The Portuguese left India for ever; but the tribals, who remained in this country, have preserved their past traditions.

We can construct a design of the anti-Mughal polarization of the Portuguese in Medieval India. In that polarization, the Portuguese made an alliance with the petty chiefs or Zemindars called Raja to fight against the Mughal Empire from different corners of India. It should be remembered here that all the Rajas were not of local origin. Some of them were immigrants from other countries. Unlike the Gonds of Central India, the Ahom and the Meitheis who came from different countries established their principalities in Assam and Manipur respectively in the 16th and 17th centuries.

Finally, it can be suggested that the Portuguese were responsible for the development of different types of tribal culture in India. To stand against the Mughal empire in India, the Portuguese organized the tribal in the following orders : Hunter-Gatherers, Warriors and Feudal lords (Rajas). We cannot see the past events but these tribal orders or cultural types can be probed by means of the political history of medieval India. In brief, we can reconstruct the past history of the primitive tribes of India, if we know the Portuguese history in India.

References

Aiyappan, A. 1937 *Social and Physical Anthropology of the Nayadis of Malabar*. Madras : Government Musueum.

Chanda, S. 1969 Hunting Implements of the car Niebarese and their Affinities with the Mongoloid Races. *The Anthroplogist*, 16 (1-2).

Elwin, V. 1939 *The Baiga*. London : John Murray.

Guha, K. 1966 The Cross-bow Trap of The Hos of Singbhum. *Anthropos, 61*.

Hodson, T. C. 1908 *The Meitheis*. London : David nutt.

Section VI

Rural and Urban Problems and Related Issues

Introduction

Vijoy Sahay

It was Robert Redfield (1950, 1955, and 1956) who first drew the attention of anthropologists to the study of Rural and Urban societies. His study of Peasant Society and Culture (1956) proved to be a trend setter in Anthropology. It gave rise to the concepts of 'folk-urban-continuum great and little tradition', and the 'village studies.' These concepts were abundantly employed by Indian anthropologists in their studies. A number of scholars worked on folk-urban-continuum, and it eventually turned into 'tribe-caste-continuum.' Robert Redfield suggested that the folk and the urban societies should not be studied as existing in two watertight compartments. There was not any contradiction between them; rather they were complementary to each other. They were merely two ends of the same scale. The difference was that due to historical reasons, one exhibited more of folk characteristics at a given time; and the other carried urban characteristics. It was quite possible that in course of time due to interaction and several other factors, any folk society could adopt urban characteristics, and vice versa.

Robert Redfield had applied the folk-urban-continuum in Folk Culture of Yucatan. In the Indian context, it turned into tribe-caste-continuum. Exactly in the same fashion, tribe-caste-continuum suggested that tribes and castes were two ends of the same scale. The former group possessed more characteristics of a tribe, and the latter, that of caste. However, it was interchangeable due to historical reasons. Many of the tribal communities had adopted the characteristics of castes because of their long association and interaction with the caste groups, and vice versa.

Redfield's great and little traditions also became significant concepts in Indian Anthropology. It highlighted that there was preponderance of great traditions in urban societies, whereas little traditions dominated the folk societies. McKim Marriott examined this concept in Kishangarhi, and introduced altogether new concepts in Anthropology, as 'universalization' and 'parochialization.' In the aforesaid concepts he demonstrated how a little tradition, for obvious reasons, assumes the form of a great tradition in course of time, and vice versa.

Earlier, we find that the Anthropologists were primarily interested in the study of the so-called 'exotic', 'savage', 'primitive' or the 'tribal' societies, who lived in comparative social and geographical isolation. Whereas the American Anthropologists were busy in studying the American Indians and in exploring the distant islands of the pacific, the British engaged themselves in the study of the natives of African and Australian communities. As far as the Indian anthropologists are concerned, during the pre-independent era, they were mostly engaged in the study of different tribal communities of Bihar, Orissa, Central Provinces and the Southern States. After the Second World War, the Indian anthropologists began to interact at a larger stage with the American anthropologists. Particularly, after independence, the anthropologists in India preferred to receive training in any of the American Universities than going to the Oxford or to the Cambridge.

During the 1950s and 1960s, the Department of Anthropology at Chicago University emerged as a powerful center of anthropological studies in America. In American Anthropology, it was the era of Robert Redfield, Milton Singer, Julian Steward, and Sol Tax. They dominated the trend of researches in American anthropology. The interaction between American and Indian anthropologists was further strengthened because before the launch of the First Five Year Plan, the government of India invited a number of American anthropologists as consultants. This accelerated the pace of American influence in Indian Anthropology.

As stated earlier, Robert Redfield initiated the study of rural anthropology. In India also the rural and urban societies attracted the attention of anthropologists and sociologists.

Rural and Urban Societies :

There is hardly any precise definition acceptable to all of the rural and the urban societies. Nevertheless, broadly speaking, a rural society is characterized by relative cultural and social homogeneity, thin density of population, informal relations among the members, preponderance of kinship ties and primary groups, subsistence level economy (most often based upon agriculture) and predominance of reciprocal and redistributive exchange. On the contrary, an urban society is characterized by relative social and cultural heterogeneity, thick density of population, formal relationship among the members (where kinship has little importance) and market level economy.

Rural Problems :

The urban and rural problems in India have to be examined in its historical perspective. According to an estimate, even today approximately 80% of the total population of country lives in villages. The rural problems in India have been perennial, though, its magnitude and features have varied from time to time. During the pre-independent era, the rural folk were mostly illiterate, poor, superstitious, lived poorly clothed and had poor health as well. They had little access to the sources of drinking water, particularly due to untouchabilty. They were politically little assertive. And, based upon the concept of purity and pollution, they were strictly hierarchical in terms of caste. As a result, the poor and downtrodden were mercilessly exploited by the higher caste, which generally happened to be the dominant caste owing to their leverage upon land.

After 57 years of independence the situations have not very much changed. The rural folk are still considerably illiterate, poor and superstitious. They still live in very unhygienic condition and inspite of a number of constitutional privileges and safeguards, are denied sources of drinking water as well as entry to the sacred places. The development of communication, spread of education, modernization and political participation have certainly brought some changes. However, there conditions are far from being satisfactory.

One significant change can certainly be observed in rural India; it is the political awareness among them. Several studies suggest that the rural folk in India are politically more aware than the urban folk. The results of the parliamentary and assembly elections of the last five decades are testimony of it.

The problems that the rural people are facing today are manifold. Even in the rural areas the mortality rate has gone down; as a result, the average span of life of an Indian has increased. In comparison to the expansion of population, the production of food grains in the rural areas has not increased. This has given rise to unemployment. Because of illiteracy or inappropriate education the rural youth seldom get appropriate jobs. This is perhaps one good reason that in most parts of rural and tribal India extremist's movement of one type or another has emerged. In most parts of the North-east, the Jharkhand, the Chhattisgrah, the Andhra Pradesh, the Kashmir and the rural Bihar the extremist's movements are continuing unabated.

The rural India was earlier also caste ridden. But in spite of untouchability different castes in a village lived in conformity. But today in place of conformity there exist conflict. It is because of two reasons; first, the constitutional privileges and safeguards are provided to certain sections of population and denied to others. Secondly, the concept of dominant caste has now changed. Because of our democratic structure and the provision of adult franchise, different caste groups have realized the importance of their numerical strength. As a result, in order to gain political and economic mileage, they unitedly cast their vote in favor of their caste candidates. Thus, there exists a contradiction. On the one hand, government enacts laws to obliterate the caste system in India; and on the other, casteism is strengthening because of our democratic structure. It is not only a problem of rural India but that of the whole Indian society.

Urban problem :

The unprecedented rise of population in India has also given unprecedented rise to urban centers in the country. Because of unemployment, the rural youth have been continuously flocking to the urban centers. After independence, the exploitation of natural and mineral resources in the country began at a large scale. It gave rise to new industrial and urban centers. In search of better livelihood, people from the countryside began to flock to the near and distant towns and cities. Millions of people from rural Uttar Pradesh and Bihar are found in metropolitan cities like Delhi, Mumbai and Kolkata. Besides these metropolitan cities, peoples from Uttar Pradesh and Bihar can be found engaged in petty business in different other cities of the southern states.

Such an exodus of rural people to the urban centers has created large-scale urban problems. The biggest slums in the world can be found in Mumbai and Delhi. People in such slums have been living in worst hygienic conditions. There is least to talk about their education. Most of such people have taken to crimes. There has been manifold increase in crime and violence in urban areas. The dowry deaths, the robbery, killings due to property disputes, violence related to premarital and extra marital relationships have become the order of the day in most of the urban centers in India.

It is high time that social scientists in general and anthropologists in particular should come forward to the study of the rural and urban problems and the related issues. Under the dynamic leadership of Late Prof. P. K. Bhowmick a number of researchers studied different facets of rural and urban life including their problems. In the following paragraphs are presented the excerpts and the findings from ten significant researches that were carried out under the leadership of Prof. P. K. Bhowmick.

In first such study, Usha Goela deals with the "Attitude of Working Women towards Others and Vice-versa in West Bengal". The study magnificently relates to various issues associated with the lives of working women as also the problems that they face while in jobs. The author has selected three categories of working women, viz., telephone operators, nurses and doctors. The rationale behind selecting these three categories by the author has been because these women face special difficulties while at work because of shifts in their duties.

The author has divided her work in two parts. In the first part, she has given the account of working women towards their job, income, marriage, husband, children, other family members, health and family planning et cetera. In the second part, she has presented the views of the supervisors of working women. How the working women are looked upon and rated by their supervisor? How do the other members of society in general and family in particular think about the working women?

The data clearly show the number of working women has been increasing. The working women are generally in good health and majority of them have small nuclear families. According to the author, the working women do not favor divorce rather a large number of them desire to live in joint families. Almost all the working women accepted dominance of their husbands. The supervisors are generally satisfied with the performance of such working women. Most supervisors very highly rated the women in their organization. The author finally suggests that there is a need for the development of infrastructure facilities like creches, nurseries, departmental stores, canteens, convenience and family quarters etc., to ensure that women are able to do proper justice to their roles–one at their working place and the other at their homes as housewives.

Subir Bandhopadhyay in his thesis has made a sociological study of the "Cycle-rickshaw Pullers of the Metropolis of Calcutta" (now Kolkata). It is to be noted that most of the rickshaw pullers of the city of Kolkata generally come from the rural areas of the state of Bihar. The author holds the view that although by definition of industrial labor the rickshaw pullers do not belong to the category of recognized workers, they do a very strenuous job of physical labor in the form of self-employment. They also do not belong to the organized sector of employment.

Such rickshaw pullers are mostly unskilled and uneducated

belonging to the rural areas. According to data, there are exceptions where it was found that the individual concern had full school education. However, due to disintegration of rural economy they have been forced by circumstances to take such low class jobs and ekeout their living.

Bela Bhattacharya has made a significant contribution to urban studies in her thesis entitled "Urbanism and Urban Social Structure." It is, in fact, a case study of Krishnanagar, a sleepy town in the state of West Bengal with special reference to the role and attitude of urban women. Krishnanagar is an orthogenetic city. It was a small traditional town developed from a tiny village in the early part of 18th century. According to Bhattacharya, it was a scene of Hindu Brahmanic culture and functionally related with the pilgrimage center of eastern India, Nababwip. From the beginning, the town has been closely connected with the city of Calcutta. The role and attitude of urban women is not as modern as it is in different parts of the country. However, on festive and other cultural gatherings, they could be found very active, whereas their rural counterparts still remained closed behind the doors.

Swaraj Bandhopadhyay has, in his thesis, attempted to diagnose the causes of student unrest in Bengal as related to certain sociological and institutional factors. Badhopadhyay claims to have accomplished it with a multidimensional approach. He has examined the student unrest on the basis of two broad factors, first the institutional characteristics of the colleges under study, and secondly the socio-economic background of the students. The main findings of the thesis of Badhopadhyay are as follows:

First, the enrolment pattern varies from one college to another. It was found that in all colleges, the student population is heterogeneous. The degree colleges have apparently some common features in terms of their structure, such as, student-teacher ratio, admission policy, facilities available to the students et cetra. Such issues were found potent for inducing student's activism. Interestingly the data suggest that in some colleges it was mandatory for every student to become the member of student unions. On the other hand, in some colleges it was a voluntary option for the students to join the union or abstain from it.

Swapan Kumar Sinha, in his thesis, has done a sociological study on 'Child labor in Calcutta'. Besides tracing the history of child labor in Calcutta he has categorized the child labor as: (a) Domestic worker (b) Non-domestic and Non-monetary worker (c) Bonded labor (d) Wage labor. His study reveals that child workers in Calcutta have come from different places like Bihar, Orissa, Uttar Pradesh,

Tamilnadu, Kerala, Andhra Pradesh and Bangladesh. The main cause of abnormal increase of child labor in the city is because of the influx of migrants from the villages to the urban areas in search of employement. As a result of disintegration of village economy and pervading poverty among the working class in the rural areas and at times, the natural calamities also, such as draught, famine, floods et cetra, large-scale migration of people to the urban and industrial centres has been taking place today.

According to Sinha, the most sordid aspect unearthed by this study is the existence of bonded labor. The author has given empirical account of the hours of work that a child labor does, and the meagre amount of salary that he receives from his master. As far as the hours of work are concerned, it ranges from 11-19 hours, and the salary that the child receives per month ranges from Rs. 5-Rs. 65, in addition to daily food (the data was taken in the month of January 1977). In the end, Sinha suggests that mere legislative acts have made little impact either in reducing the extent of child labor or in the improvement of their conditions of work or in the increase of their remuneration.

Milly Day has worked on somewhat unconventional topic of anthropological research. Her topic has been 'Human Resource Development (HRD) With Reference to Public Sector Banks'. Milly has first discussed about the historicity of the very concept of human resource development. She says that until the mid 1960s there was not any such concept in banking services. The recruitment was done on the basis of 'pick and choose', and 'reward and punishment' both of which were of economic nature. After nationalization of the banks in the early 70s the nature of banking services too began to change. Gradually the human elements were recognized in the organization; however its initial results were negative. The employees began to enjoy the newfound freedom and unions were formed and strikes and agitation became the order of the day. However, now the situation has changed, and the condition of bank employees has improved considerably. All this has been possible because of appropriate consideration for human resource development.

Krishna Mittra has collected data from both rural and urban settings. The topic of her thesis has been 'Socio-Psycho-Economic Problems in Hospital Patients in West Bengal'. Her special remark about the problems of people in the urban areas is that the poor get free bed whereas middle class people neither get free bed in hospital nor could they afford the costly treatment in the nursing homes. Her data suggest that in the rural areas availability of medicine, equipments, competent hands, distribution system were totally inadequate. She found that the lack of transport was the biggest problem for patients in rural areas. The administrative control also was lacking there.

Tilak Bagchi in his thesis 'Anthropology of Tribal Food and Food Nutrition-A Comparative Micro Study' has highlighted the ethnographic, demographic, biological, ecological, economic and cultural profiles with reference to food and nutrition of the five tribal communities, viz. the Lodhas, the Mahalis, the Koras, the Santals and the Mundas of Narayangrah block in the district of Midnapur in West Bengal. Bagchi has observed that because of specific ecological factors the region shows sufficiency in food in terms of rice; however, in terms of other classes of food the region lacks. Such lacking of certain item of food creates deficiency in their body. The inhabitants of the region seemed vulnerable to certain communicable deceases. His comments that 'Economic factors precipitate the problem of under nutrition" and that the "cultural factors aggravate intercommunity and intra family variation in food and nutrition" are worth mentioning. Finally Bagchi has proposed an 18-point solution to this rural problem.

Kalachand Saha in his thesis "Attributes of Farming Affecting Fertility and Mortality of Siyalgir of Bengal Orissa Border" has analyzed the fertility data of the population and shows that the Siyalgirs are subjected to a declining fertility trend which may be due to their inbreeding habit and minority position in the social system to dictate socio-cultural affairs. If this continues, the Siyalgirs of Bengal-Orissa border region will be lost. It is very much desirable that at this stage, development planners should come forward to evolve a strategy for preserving the community. The approach should, however, be anthropological to ensure an understanding of socio-cultural realties of the community on the part of both development planners and project administrators.

"Agrarian Unrest in West Bengal with Special Reference to Naxalite Movement" is a meticulous work done by Subhendru Maity. The author has first traced the historical ideology of the movement with reference to Karl Marx, Lennin, Stalin and Mao-tse-tung. Thereafter he presents a vivid account the Naxalbari massacre of 1968 in the Naxalbari police station of Darjeeling district of West Bengal. It is followed by a discussion on the volatile centers of Debra and Gopiballavpur in the West Midnapur district of West Bengal. He has also given account of the tactics of guerilla warfare that the naxalites adopted. In his discussion on the emergence of Naxalite Movement in the country one clearly finds the history and development of left parties and philosophies in India. Maity has also discussed in detail the factors behind the emergence of naxal movements in the country, such as:

a. Concentration of tribal people, who are very ethnocentric.
b. Existence of large tracts of *'benami'* lands, purchased under false titles by *jotdars.*
c. Existence of land covered with dense forest.
d. Frequent clashes between the privileged and the poorer sections of people.

In the end, Maity's remarks are commendable. He asserts that "The ideology of the naxalbari movement was more often imported ideology than one which was related with the condition of the soil. It was not unnatural, then, that the 'sparks' of Debra and Gopiballavpur and similar such 'sparks' in some of the parts of the country, failed to give birth to a big revolutionary fire which was the initial objective of the starting of movement in these areas."

References

Redfield, R. 1950 *The Folk Culture of Yucatan*. Chicago : Chicago University Press.

________ 1955 *The Little Community*. Chicago : Chicago University Press.

________ 1956 *Peasant Society and Culture*. Chicago : Chicago University Press.

Anthropology of Tribal Food and Nutrition : A Comparative Micro Study

Tilak Bagchi

I

In the present work attempts have been made to highlight ethnographic, demographic, biological, ecological, economic and cultural profiles of five tribal communities, in relation to the scenario of food and nutrition. These tribes are the Lodhas, the Mahalis, the Koras, the Santals and the Mundas of Narayangarh Block in the district of Midnapur, West Bengal. The study has been carried out in order to focus on the problems of the said communities and recommend certain ameliorative measures. The profiles of all the different aspects referred to above are interwoven with one another and conjointly provide a holistic picture which would, hopefully, better equip the readers to understand and assess the anthropo-nutritional problems of the tribal communities and also find out, wherever possible, solutions to them.

The five tribal groups under study belong to the so called Australoid racial stock and share the use of Bengali language in common. However, with the exception of the Lodhas, the mother tongue of the remaining four tribal groups belongs to the Mundari category of Austro-Asiatic group of languages. The five tribal groups by and large exhibit certain common ethnic elements because of their prolonged living in close proximity in a geographic region, sharing a common regional culture, emulating the lifestyle of a specific dominant caste as well as following a common mode of adaptation with the surrounding ecology and economy. On the other hand, distinctiveness in the ethno-cultural existence of each of these communities is largely due to its respective heritage and tradition. The tribal groups like the Lodhas, the Mahalis and the Mundas share to a larger extent the cultural norms of the middle ranking caste groups in the vicinity, whom they consider their reference groups, than the Koras and the Santals. Further, the Lodhas, are a denotified community, belong to the category "Primitive Tribal Groups" (PTG); the Mahalis are a basket weaver artisan tribal group; the Koras are traditionally earth workers; the Santals are a settled agricultural dominant tribal group of West

Bengal but not of the region under study and the Mundas are a more Hinduised tribe than the above communities and have interlaced better with the local ecology and economy. The unity and diversity of these tribal communities have made a profound impact on their values, customs, and habits relating to food and nutrition.

II

The demographic profile reveals that in spite of considerable incidence of infant and child mortality, none of the tribal groups under study faces immediately the fear of extinction. Gastro–intestinal disorder including diarrhoea along with inadequate or faulty feeding is a major underlying factor responsible for infant and child mortality. On the other hand, certain demographic parameters, viz., low frequency of large families, relatively limited spread of high dependency ratio, contribute significantly towards better availability of foodstuff. Very high occurrence of remarriage of widows and divorcees also helps to raise the nutritional status of mother and children, who are the nutritionally vulnerable segments of the population. Thus, pre-school children are less commonly reared in broken families. Remarriage of widows and divorcee mothers not only ensures economic support of these women from their newly married respective husbands but also is a source of emotional support for them, which helps better rearing of their children. However, the overwhelming frequency of nuclear families seems to have been detrimental to the nutritional prospect of the pre-school children. In nuclear families during working hours the pre-school children are left alone behind at home or in the custody of their school-age counterparts in the family. It has resulted into a gross neglect of the pre-school children from health, hygiene and nutritional points of view, which in turn has made them vulnerable to virtual starvation, at least, to nutritional impoverishment during the absence of their parents. Seasonal migration by the husband who leaves his wife and children behind and/or resort to polygyny renders the mother and children totally helpless. All this obviously tells upon the nutritional prospect of the latter. Poorer maternal health, lower degree of nutritional status of the mother and her children in particular and the entire family in general become inevitable since married women, particularly the mothers, constitute the pivots of the respective families in terms of food delivery system within the household concerned.

III

The nutritional profile above shows that mild to moderate under-nutrition specially micro-nutritional deficiency is a common feature of the life of the communities under discussion. The variations are both intra and inter tribal as well as seasonal. Deficiency sign of mild form of protein-energy-malnutrition (PEM), retinal and riboflavin deficiency signs are attributable to lower intake of leafy green vegetables and other protective foodstuffs. Lack of bioavailability of iron and improper assimilation of nutrients as a result of diminished metabolic activities and catabolic effect of communicable diseases aggravates under-nutrition. Low intake of fat intensifies Vitamin A morbidities because retinol is a fat-soluble vitamin. Pre-school children are the worst victims of under-nutrition followed by pregnant women, nursing mothers, aged persons and school-age children. Females are more susceptible to malnutrition than their male counterparts. The Lodhas are the worst victims of ravages of malnutrition and are followed by the Mahalis. The Mundas possess better nutritional status than any other tribal group under study. On the other hand low incidence of malnutrition specially macro-nutritional deficiency among the five tribal communities is explicable in terms of nearly adequate or huge consumption of rice.

IV

The area under study is a monocrop region where rice is the staple food. But the production of other varieties of foodstuffs is extremely poor. The tribal folks receive rice and related foodstuffs not only as the main harvested crop but also as a part of their wages. Fish provides a major item of food of animal origin particularly during the later part of rainy season and the period following it. Certain other kinds of aquatic foodstuffs are also available during dry months while leafy green vegetables are available during the late summer and rainy season. Even then, the region does not yield sufficient foodstuffs other than rice to sustain its population. However, the region is neither chronically food deficient nor a nutritionally backward area because of its ecological potentiality to yield sufficient paddy for its population along with marketable surplus of all essential items of food commodities as a result of its positional advantage in the network of communication and transportation system.

Unhygienic environment and sanitation make the region a breeding ground of flies and mosquitoes. It has caused water borne, water associated and vector borne diseases. This fact along with the use of unsafe potable water by the inhabitants of the region has in turn caused secondary under-nutrition owing to synergistic interactions between improper environmental sanitation, unhygienic living conditions, communicable morbidity and under-nutrition.

V

With the exception of the Mahalis, the subsistence economy of the ramaining four tribal communities is mostly pinned to land. They are mainly peasants–either as owner cultivators or Bargadars, i.e., sharecroppers and/or as agricultural labourers. The tribal people do not in many cases consume the entire amount of agricultural products but dispose of part of agricultural product which they produce or receive as a result of share cropping or as wages. A part of it is also disposed of by them in the market for cash, which they require to meet various necessities, repayment of debt and/or payment of a part of the wages of the labourers working on their plots of land. Besides they have a regular involvement in the agricultural activities of the neighbouring non-tribal communities in the form of agricultural labourers and/or sharecroppers. Moreover they maintain an organic solidarity with the non-tribal peasant, artisan and service castes and depend heavily on the wider market economy. Thus at least from the economic point of view the tribal communities under study are the part and parcel of the wider peasant society. The Mahalis, though they work as agricultural labourers during the peak agricultural season, yet eke out their subsistence mainly from making baskets. In this regard, a distinct occupational compartmentalisation has been noted. The Mahalis, produce big baskets which are mainly needed for storing and carrying of betel leaves by the betel leaf growers of coastal Midnapur and Balasore. But they generally do not produce smaller baskets. These smaller baskets are manufactured by the Doms, a Scheduled Caste community. But the Mahalis now face a competition with the Doms and some members of a few other communities, viz., the Santals, the Bagra-Kashtriyas and so on who were traditionally not basket makers but now take to basket making. The latter encroach upon the livelihood of the Mahalis by resorting to making of larger baskets.

It has been observed that the land holding pattern and techno-economic efficiency to exploit resources are the main indicators of prosperity of the communities under discussion as of the rural people of India in general. Constant and regular flow of income from service in organised sectors distort the scenario to a considerable extent in the sense that the people engaged in the said section emerge as the most affluent segment of population in the area under consideration. And both these aspects also deeply influence the economic and nutritional aspects of these tribal communities. The Mundas by virtue of their early settlement in Narayangarh Block as an agricultural community not only exercise control over the greater amount of cultivable land than the other tribal groups but also emerge as prosperous in terms of economy and nutrition. The Koras who are mainly engaged in digging of earth or earth work are reported to have settled in Narayangarh later than the Mundas. The quantum of their land holding and their efficiency to cultivate land fall next to those of the Mundas. The Santals settled in the area under study in comparatively recent years mainly as migrant labourers for the laying of railway track. And, their economic and nutritional profiles are worse than those of the truly agricultural tribal communities, namely the Mundas and the Koras. The stigma of criminality distorted the image of the Lodhas and worked as a strong barrier in the way of their proper assimilation with the wider peasant society in the neighbourhood. Being a traditional hunting-gathering community, the Lodhas continue to cultivate a kind of apathy towards agriculture and also lack of skill in agriculture. Yet, they are now compelled to adapt with agriculture mainly as marginal farmers or agricultural labourers. These factors along with large-scale deforestation render their situation more poverty ridden in comparison with the other communities under observation. Their poverty is reflected in their food intake pattern and other facets of quality of life. As one comes to the Mahalis, one finds that because of the scarcity and high price of bamboos along with the entry of people in this craft as a newly acquired vocation encouraging the entry of the middlemen in this trade. Their craft of basket making has become gradually less profitable. The Mahalis, therefore, fail to raise their economic and nutritional standard.

All the tribal communities under study are either landless or have control over a very small area of cultivable land. Most of them thus may be categorized as landless or marginal farmers. The fragmentation of land (when the tribals have had their own land) and the uneconomic holding of land given to the tribals as part of 'Barga Operation' impede the improvement of economic and nutritional status of the tribal people to a considerable extent. On the contrary, increase in the wages of agricultural labourers and payment of part of the wages in terms of food contribute significantly towards the better availability of foodstuff during the post harvest period and also during the periods of agricultural operation. Thus the annual cycle of living of the tribals mainly alternates between periods of feasts and periods of fasts. The period from December to March is the period of feasts when rice and vegetables are available in abundance. The remaining period is the period of scarcity. However, during the later part of monsoon and post periods fish is available in the region under study.

The economy of the region under study is mainly agro-based. The seasonal unemployment, unwise expenditure mainly in fairs, festivals, life cycle rituals, entertainment of guests, various recreational activities and so on during the period of affluence, little or no habit of savings followed by bondage in debt owing to high rate of interests work for the low level of nutrition of the poor inhabitants of the region. But certain varieties of adaptive mechanism, viz., maximum expenditure on food, specially cereals, widening of food base along with lower economic status (since people become less and less choosy or selective regarding the acceptance of food and other articles as their income decreases) and so on, help the tribal communities, many of whom are poor, to raise their economic and nutritional status to a certain extent.

VI

Food taboos deprive the pregnant and nursing mothers of certain kinds of foodstuffs. The tribals consider pregnancy as a normal phenomenon. Hence, no special measures or food and nutrient supplementation are thought of in relation to the pregnant women and nursing mothers. Rather, food restrictions and prescriptions during pregnancy and the early phase of lactation deprive the mothers and breast-fed babies from getting food and nutrients in adequate amount. Exception may however be noted among a few tribal women specially those belonging to the Mundas and the Koras. They are provided with protective food and nutrient supplementation during pregnancy and early lactation. Direct introduction of adult men's diet as weaning foods, dirty unhygienic milk and or carbohydrate-rich solution as a substitute of breast milk specially when breast milk is not sufficiently available for the infants make the infants and pre-school children susceptible to gastro-intestinal disorders including weaning diarrhoea which in turn has precipitated secondary malnutrition. Rejection of certain vegetables and fruits, which are believed to cause gout and huge consumption of alcoholic beverages as a substitute for other foodstuff also make the aged tribals under-nourished to a notable extent. Customary beliefs, regarding therapeutic diet, indigenous notion of hot and cold food, faulty cooking and feeding imitating the food habits of their reference groups by discarding cheap or abundantly available foodstuff and other sorts of indigenous cultural cognition regarding food adversely affect the nutritional status of the tribal population in general and vulnerable segments of its population in particular. Lack of health and nutritional awareness owing to superstitious prodigalities also serve as catalysts in the process of making the tribal people under-nourished to an extent. One should note, however, the exception as observed in case of a few educated tribals who in the light of their health and nutritional awareness overcome these sorts of unscientific cultural practices to a degree.

VII

In sum, because of specific ecological factors the region shows sufficiency in food in terms of rice but not in terms of other classes of foodstuff. Rather, a degree of deficiency in the latter is noticeable at the level of production. Further, the inhabitants of the region seem vulnerable to certain communicable diseases, which aggravate undernutrition. The economic factors precipitate the problem of undernutrition. The cultural factors aggravate inter-community and intra-family variation in food and nutrients often resulting in adverse conditions of the entire population in general and mother and children in particular.

All these problems are, of course, interwoven with the specific nature of the region and the communities inhabiting it, i.e., the micro setting considered in the present study. At the same time many of them will be found in other similar structural-cultural situations. In many cases, the problems, since they are embedded in total structural complexes and cultural milieu, seem to defy any short cut and tailored solution.

Even, then, a few suggestions in the light of experience gained from the present study may be modestly offered here.

1. Food-in-aid programme should be given prime importance. In such programmes locally available and culturally acceptable foodstuff should be given. For example, porridge prepared from rice, pulse, edible oil and cheap as well as easily available vegetables may be distributed to the vulnerable segment of population, viz., pre-school and school-age children, pregnant and nursing mothers and also to the aged persons as mid-day meal at least during the lean months.
2. System of spot feeding should be introduced in order to stop the sharing of food meant for the vulnerable segment of population by the non-vulnerable or not so vulnerable segments of it in their families.
3. The needy segments of population should be provided supplementation. It is common knowledge that the tribal peoples, particularly those residing in the remote areas situated at a great distance from the Primary or subsidiary Health Centres, find it difficult to collect these items from the social services centres. Hence vitamin and mineral supplementation should be given to the tribal people regularly at their doorsteps.

In case the delivery of these items at the doorsteps of the tribals is not feasible, edible salt distributed to the tribal areas may be fortified with iron, retinol, riboflavin, folic acid and iodine and the same should be distributed to tribal areas at a subsidised rate. Since heavy load of mixed warm infestation has been seen, periodic deworming should be carried out.

4. Community food storage system should be developed to cater to the needs of the people. The system should be attuned to the backdrop provided by the ecology of the region.
5. To make up for the deficiency in kinds of foodstuffs other than rice (in a rice growing area), social forestry may give a greater emphasis to vegetable and fruit bearing trees wherever it is possible. The concerned functionaries in several Government departments should cooperate and conjointly share the task. Like all other developmental activities, in this programme too people's participation and partcipatory management should be encouraged. In this matter the participation by the Panchyats, NGO's and voluntary agencies should also be encouraged. With such co-operative endeavour, soil testing and other technological innovation may be carried not only to explore the feasibility of growing vegetables and fruit bearing plants and trees in areas where other kinds of trees grow and are raised but also in examining the prospect of growing such trees and plants in waste land.
6. In management of forest, the wisdom of tribal people may be utilised. For example, medicinal plants may be planted as per advice of tribal medicine men. The expertise of the Lodhas may be used for collection of honey, Tussar cocoons and so on. Bamboo may be grown in the areas with concentration of the Mahalis. These measures would not only cater to the need of tribal people but also maintain ecological balance by way of increasing natural biodiversity. The Lodhas should be given some alternative forest based livelihood, viz., job in forests, right of collection of minor non-timber forest resources and so on in order to check the indiscriminate felling of trees by them and other forest dwellers.
7. Increased production by domestication of both animals and plants should be done by utilising appropriate technology, available infrastructure and manpower. Such commonly neglected fields such as pisciculture, mushroom cultivation or sal leaf plate making should be adequately emphasised to augment the available supply of food and nutrients and the resource base of the region.

8. The administration must be cautious and vigilant enough to check the process of marginalisation and exploitation of the tribal people engaged in agriculture and other occupations and to protect the land alienation of the region concerned.
9. Immediate steps should be taken to facilitate the formation of and effective functioning of the co-operative societies. The co-operative societies should be provided with adequate infrastructural and financial support to purchase products from the tribals, viz., basket from the Mahalis, honey from the Lodhas, sal leaf plate from the tribal people at a reasonable rate and dispose of the same with a modicum of profit to ensure the viability of the co-operatives and to encourage the tribals, participation in them. They should be adequately equipped and empowered to supply raw materials and also to advance loan at a low rate of interest to the tribals to put an end to or to hold in check the rampant exploitation of the tribal folk by the profiteering middlemen.
10. A food insurance system may be devised and introduced. The tribals may be asked to deposit a certain amount of their harvested crop along with a sum of money depending on their capacity with the co-operative societies or any other societies during the post-harvest period. In exchange of the same during lean periods tribals would be entitled to collect food grains in instalments from the respective societies formed for this purpose.
11. To effect positive improvement in awareness of health, hygiene, food and nutrition, along with the formal education system, non-formal education system also should be adequately utilised. The courses of instruction or for deliberation in both these realms should be framed in view of the local health and hygienic condition, health and environmental sanitary infrastructure, locally available food and nutrients and the potentiality of the region to produce or supply such foodstuff and nutrients and also the cultural practices of the inhabitants.
12. Periodic health camp for tribal mothers may be organised in each tribal area. Health, hygiene and nutritional education should be imparted with the help of audio-visual feedback system and practical demonstration with regard to scientific method of food preparation, preservation, cooking of cheap but nutritious food. Provision may be taken to demonstrate to them the ideal procedure of mushroom cultivation. Cultural programmes viz., Jatra, Cinema and other forms of performing arts help the arousal and dissemination of awareness of health

and nutrition on the one hand and attract tribal mothers on the other.

13. Jobs created under various rural development programmes operated by the Government and NGOs may be operated mainly during agricultural lean periods in order to provide alternative and adequate job opportunities for the tribals. This would stop their seasonal migration to a certain extent.
14. The vulnerable segments of tribal population, viz., widows, deserted women, aged persons and so on may be given some vocational training in the form of tailoring, basket making, mat and fishing net weaving, sal leaf and cup making, paper packet making and so on. The co-operative societies or any other agencies may in this regard help the tribals by providing raw materials and collecting finished goods from their doorsteps.
15. The source of potable water should be made safe for human consumption. In tribal areas under study dug wells are mainly used for drinking water. Hence, steps should be taken to cover the dug wells. For keeping the water of the dug well bacteriologically safe for human consumption, a simple measure may be taken. About 10-20 gms of bleaching powder (since bleaching powder contains roughly 25 percent chlorine) may be mixed with river sand. The said mixture may be kept in a small metallic pitcher, provided with a small hole at its lower bottom. The pitcher should be kept at the lower level of the water of the well by means of rope tied from the ground above. Constant chlorine treatment makes the water bacteriologically safe for human consumption. After a week or so the pitcher may be replaced by another such pitcher.
16. Thetribal people living in non-ITDP areas should also be brought under the public distribution system operating in ITDP areas.
17. Installation of water slit community latrine, bio gas/solar energy plants not only make the tribal habitats free from pollution to a considerable extent but also stops the indiscriminate cutting and felling of trees for fuel purpose.
18. Pesticide should be used regularly at the place of the disposal of refuses as well as various breeding grounds of mosquito for effective vector control.

The above ameliorative measures are, no doubt, suggestions, which seem practicable. These are framed in the light of experience accumulated in the present study. However, further action research in the area of present study or in other areas with an identical structural-cultural setting may help all concerned to combat the alarming consequences of malnutrition in order to achieve freedom from hunger and undernutrition.

Socio-Cultural Attribute of Family Affecting Fertility and Mortality of the Siyalgir in Bengal-Orissa Border Region

Kalachand Saha

The level of fertility and the factors associated with it are important areas of discussion in developing countries which are characterized by tremendous pressure of population and low productivity. In recent years, there has been a good deal of studies on population problems in India also. But the involvement of anthropologists in these studies has not been up to the desired extent. This is somewhat surprising in view of the fact that anthropologists promise to accord a better understanding of all human problems which are rooted in socio-cultural system.

Polgar (1972) has brilliantly analysed the history of anthropological efforts made in the study of population dynamics. He claimed that the first anthropological study on population dynamism dates back to 1891.

In India enquiry relating to fertility and mortality was initiated by the Census of 1911. It gradually gained a momentum through successive decennial census operations. Besides census enumeration, several attempts have been made afterwards to know the different aspects of fertility and mortality. The survey, conducted by the Gokhale Institute of Politics and Economics in six centres in six districts of western India should be mentioned in particular (Dandekar 1959). This study had made an interesting inference, that in recent years the level of fertility in general seems to have remained more or less static. While there are some evidence of certain decline in fertility. This is quite contrary to the findings that are quoted in fertility and mortality studies from different parts of India.

A comprehensive review of available literature on population studies has led the present researcher to concentrate his attention on the socio-cultural problems of the Siyalgirs, a little known ethnic group, living in the border region of West Bengal and Orissa. A preliminary study of their dialect and history of migration indicate that they migrated from the present state of Gujarat. They came and settled finally in their present habitation about some 250 years ago. The fertility behaviour and incidence of mortality among this migrant population reveal some distinctive features that are not usually found with the general population or in any other large size community. Hence the present researcher has selected this small ethnic group of the Siyalgirs for studying their fertility pattern and mortality structure.

The Siyalgirs constitute a small community indeed, being representd by only 1528 souls (male 795; female 733). The area of their present habitat is precisely spread over Jaleswar and Singla P.S. under Sadar sub–division of Balasore district cut across state boundaries and stretched to Danton and Mohanpur P. S. under former Sadar South sub-division of Midnapur district. There are altogether 17 villages where the people are distributed. These villages do not form a contiguous area. Each village is basically an aggregate of homesteads, occupied by many castes and communities.

The general purpose of this dissertation is to delineate an account of fertility and mortality patterns among the members of this ethnic group, which constitute a little known small community of Bengal-Orissa border region. This study, in the first place intends to describe population characteristics and on the background of these characteristics, it is intended to reveal socio-biological facets of fertility performance and mortality pattern, and to evaluate the impact of socio-cultural attributes of family on the level of fertility performances and mortality incidences. Specifically. the objective of this study are :

1. to delineate the fertility and mortality structure of the Siyalgirs with a view to understanding the process of demographic adjustment of a migrant population;
2. to reveal the level of socio-cultural orientation of the family with a view to comprehend the process of socio-cultural adjustment of the migrant population;
3. to assess the impact of socio-cultural orientation of the family on fertility and mortality of the migrant population.

The analysis of the findings of this study has been made to satisfy the above mentioned objectives. To fulfill the first objective, all rates, ratio and indices of birth, fertility and reproduction have been estimated following the current demographic principles and methods. As for the second objective, it has been attempted to measure the incidence of mortality in the family and among the women. Mortality rate, ratio and indices have also been estimated here. To satisfy the third objective, the fertility as well as the mortality is considered as a dependent variable and the socio-cultural characteristics of families of the respondents are regarded as independent variable.

Dependent Variable

The nature of human physiology is such that the fertility of a population can be measured through men as well as women. The present study, however, is made in respect of female population only. This is done for the fact that women are directly concerned with the affairs of reproduction. In measuring fertility it is usual to recall the individual reproductive performance of each woman. This can be done by counting the number of pregnancies on the one hand and by reporting the number of live births on the other. The latter procedure is followed here.

As to the mortality structure, different mortality indices have been worked out to make a clear understanding of mortality background of the population. But for the purpose of studying the impact of socio-cultural attributes of family on mortality incidence, it has been tried here to work out a mortality rate in terms of number of children of a women, who have been died preceding this investigation.

Independent Variable

Both fertility and mortality are biological phenomena; the difference in fertility performance of women may be due to differential biological potential found in these women. Mortality is also regulated by physiological disturbances in most of the cases. But there are reasons to believe that both fertility and mortality in any human society are regulated not only by biological factors but also by the social system. Hence attempts have been made to study the impact of social system on fertility behaviour and incidence of mortality in terms of individuals. But the behaviour of an individual in rural areas get the most expression with reference to socio-cultural orientation of the family in which he or she is affiliated. A family is distinguished by a good number of socio-cultural characteristics. Some of the important characteristics like family income, family education, mass-media exposure of family, social participation of family and value orientation of family are included in this study.

The annual family income which is measured here in rupee value includes, earnings of all individuals member of the family. Such income in total indicates the quantum of annual income of the family.

Education of a family regulates the socio-cultural behaviour of its members to a great extent. But education is a descriptive variable.

Hence, the quantification of this descriptive variable is made in terms of score.

Score ranging from 'zero' has been given to each member of the family depending on their individual level of education. The score thus obtained by all family members, have been added together to get the educational attainment of the family.

The degree of mass media exposure of the family is measured in terms of score obtained by each family members for reading news paper, listening to radio and for going to Cinema. All scores thus obtained by the family members aged 20 years and above, during a complete year, have been added together to get the degree of mass media exposure of the family.

Similarly, the intensity of social participation of a family is measured on the basis of obtained data of the family members aged 20 years and above, depending on the extent of their involvement in different organisation, club, institution etc. Score thus obtained by such family members, have been added together to get the intensity of social participation of the family.

As to the extent of value orientation of family, attention has been focussed on value disposition prescribing traditionalism-modernism. A list of eight value statements has been administered to family members aged 20 years and above. Their responses have been collected on a five point scale–strongly disagree, disagree, neutral, agree and strongly agree. Depending on their reactions, each respondent has been given a score, ranging from 0 to 4. Such scores obtained by their family members, have been added together to get the extent of value orientation of the family.

For the purpose of enumeration, out of a total of 733 female population, 366 unmarried women, 58 widow or divorced women and 14 married women who have not attained menarche at the time of investigation, have been excluded, as all of them were debarred from their fertility performances. Another 14 women married but not enjoying conjugal life, due to long absence of their husbands have also been excluded. One more woman was not interviewed as she lost her husband before the investigation was completed. Thus, the final tabulation of the collected data was made with respect to 280 women.

In the processing of data, the card index method was utilized. A specially designed data card was used to record all the information received on the fertility background of the respondents and incidence of mortality of the children and socio-cultural characteristics of the families of the respondents. The analysis of data was made following the steps of primary tabulations, statistical treatment and final tabulation. As mentioned earlier, the fertility and mortality is considered as dependent variable and the socio-cultural characteristics of the families of the respondents are regarded as independent variables. Each of the independent variables was quantitatively measured and classified under two categories on the basis of median values. Thus each of these independent variables made a dichotomous variable. In order to find out whether there is any annotation of fertility performance or incidence of mortality of children with the socio-cultural characteristics of the families of the respondents, the statistics of students t Test has been employed.

The statistics of arithmatic mean has been calculated to know the generalized level of fertility of the category of women. A similar analysis is made with regard to incidence of mortality. A simple comparison of the two means of the two categories of women may lead to indicate the presence of a difference. Now it may happen that the difference is the result of some chance occurrence. In order to find out whether such a difference is statistically significant or not, the administration of students, t Test has been followed. This way of statistical treatment may help to find out the real difference or similarity in fertility performance as well as incidence of mortality. The occurrence of such a difference or similarity may be resulted from a disparity in age distribution when the estimate is presented against the women. Thus, it becomes necessary to express all fertility performance of each category of women by a statistical measure which is not influenced by the age distribution of that category of women. The statistics employed in this case is the weighted mean which has been developed by Driver (1963) in his study of "Differential Fertility in Central India". In order to know whether the difference in weighted mean fertility or incidence of mortality is statistically significant or not, the calculation of standard deviation and administration of a students t Test have been followed.

An analysis of data on the mobility of the brides reveals that the Siyalgirs have exchanged brides within their own community distributed in 17 villages but showing a preference for a particular village or group of villages. This reflects on their characteristics inbreeding habits which not only limits themselves to exchange their brides within their own community but also within a smaller circle of villages where the Siyalgirs are found to live.

An assessment of data on fertility structure reveals that there are 407 women who have attained menarche, mean menarchal age is 13.11 years. There is also an increasing trend in mean menarchal age particularly among younger women of these 407 women, there are 73 women who have attained menopause at an average age of 40.41 years. The incidence of menopause is earlier among the younger women. Thus, menarche–menopause interval i.e., span of reproductive life is becoming shorter particularly among young Siyalgir women.

The findings further reveal that 280 women of this study have a mean 3.94 conceptions and 3.69 live units.

The net reproduction rate of married Siyalgir women is 0.73619. This indicates that there is a decreasing trend in the population as one thousand Siyalgir women are replaced by only 736 women.

The length of generation of the Siyalgir married women is 29.34 years which shows a close agreement with low fertility. The analysing data reveal that the intensity of pregnancy wastage per thousand of conceptions is 58.88 which is really very high and yields support to the declining fertility trend in the population. The rate of children died per thousand of live births is 204.26 which is very high to affect the rate of natural increase negatively.

The analysis of data on the impact of socio-cultural orientation of family on the fertility of women and mortality of children, indicates that the women who belong to the families, enjoying high incomes higher educational level, high mass-media exposure, high social participation and high value orientation are endowed with relatively higher fertility than the women who belong to families with low income, low education, low mass-media exposure, low social participation and low value orientation. Whereas, the mortality of children as reported to occur among the women who belong to families with higher income, high education, high mass-media exposure, high social participation and high value orientation, is relatively lower than that which occur to women belonging to families with low income, low education, low mass-media exposure, low social participation and low value orientation. Thus, it may now be inferred that the socio-cultural orientation of family have a significant bearing on the fertility behaviour of women and mortality of children among the Siyalgirs.

The analysis of fertility and mortality data shows that the Siyalgirs are subjected to a declining fertility trend which may be due to their inbreeding habit and minority position in the social system to dictate socio-cultural affairs. If the thing continues in such a manner the Siyalgirs of Bengal-Orissa border region may turn into an endangered community. It is very much desirable that at this stage, development planners should come forward to evolve a strategy for preserving the community. The approach, should however, must be anthropological to ensure an understanding of the socio-cultural realities of the community on the part of both development planners and Project administrators.

This dissertation has tried to develop a method for the study of fertility and mortality behaviour of the population in a small community. The general outline of this study is so designed that it can give a fair treatment to all academic and applied aspects of population statistics with reference to a particular field situation. On the academic side, the method followed and the materials presented in the study are to help the population anthropologists and sociologists in predicting the future fertility trend and to develop some methodological refinements; and on the applied side, the nature and contents of this study are expected to render some practical help to policy makers, planners, administrators and welfare workers in getting facts from actual field situation and in understanding the figures in the background of some tangible terms of references.

References

Dandekar, K. 1959 *Demographic Survey of Six Rural Communities.* Poona: Gokhale Institute of Politics and Economics.

Driver, E. D. 1963 *Differential Fertility in Central India.* Princeton : Princeton University Press.

Polgar, S. 1972 Population History and Population Policies from an Anthropological Perspective. Current Anthropology, 13.

Attitude of Working Women Towards Others and Vice-Versa in West Bengal in Contemporary Times (Year 1975)

Usha Goela

In these days women are working at par with men in various fields. The Indian women working outside their homes who have recently achieved freedom and privilege through Constitution and social tolerance, have achieved a new role to their existing roles of housewives and mothers. This new role is not only having its impact on their way of thinking and behaviour but is also bringing a change in their outlook towards their family and children and various other issues related to their lives. This in turn is affecting their likes and dislikes, relationship within the family and with the society at large. Thus a change in the attitude of working women is bringing a change in the society and this changed society in its turn becomes instrumental in changing the life pattern of the working women.

In the traditional setting, women's role in terms of her duties and responsibilities was clearly defined and there was no conflict in fulfilling these roles. But the newly emerged status as 'working women', has further added more duties and responsibilities which creates conflict, contradiction and dilemma in their present ways of life. The working women have to manage the house, bring up and educate their children, act as loving partner of their husbands and act as obedient daughter and daughter-in-law to their parents and in-laws, like all other non-working women. This ultimately raised the question as to what extent the working women feel about their dual role. Do they feel happy and satisfied psychologically and emotionally? Do they think that they are able to bring justice in performing their dual roles simultaneously?

A working woman is making her contribution to the society with all her sincerity and hard working. What "others" feel about her is another aspect of the same problem. Do they feel that women are contributing to the happiness of the family and maintaining the standard of living and building the nation strong or what do they feel otherwise?

These are some of the burning issues which needed close

examination. Hence the present study has been taken up on the topic *Attitude of Working Women towards others and Vice-Versa in West Bengal in Contemporary Times*.

The present study is a humble attempt to find out the attitude of middle class educated women who have taken up some gainful employment outside their homes and also to study the attitude of society towards these working women.

In the first part of the study the researcher has tried to find out the attitude of the working women towards "others". In this connection different issues which are closely related to the working women's life, thinking and behaviour have been taken into consideration. These are: how has the job affected their attitude towards marriage and their relations with their husbands, children and family members? How does the working women view the freedom given to them? What are their personal interests and how far are they involved in recreational, cultural and other activities? How have their works influenced their attitude towards family planning and what views do they hold about some of the current problems faced by the society? How do they spend their income and how do they compare themselves with their sisters, the non-working women?

The second part of the topic the *attitude of "others" towards working women* deals with what the members of the society feel about working women. How do they view about the 'working women'? What opinion do they hold about their efficiency and capability? What do they think about women's dual role at home and at working place? The term "others" here relates to the members of the society in general.

Only three categories of working women have been selected for the study. These comprise of Telephone Operators, Nurses and Doctors. In all 300 women, 100 in each category, have been studied. To study the second part of the topic i.e., *attitude of "others" towards working women*, only the office supervisors of the working women have been taken into consideration.

In the present study, the questionnaire method supplemented by interview and case studies has been used. Two sets of questionnaire were prepared to cover the two different parts of the study i.e., one for the working women and the other one for "others" viz., their supervisors. The data were collected from Telephone Bhawan and from Hospitals in Calcutta.

Collected data were analysed separately for all the three categories of women. Since each group of women had different education, training and job requirements, three main variables viz., age, education and marital Status were used in tabulating and analysing the data.

Besides these three variables, other variables relevant to the particular case were also considered. Certain particular cases have also been studied in detail and case studies prepared for these.

Attitude of working women towards others

Here the researcher categorises the working women into two distinctive parts belonging to two different strata. A large majority of women working as telephone operators and nurses usually do accept their works mainly for economic reasons i.e. to support family income. But on the other hand majority of the female doctors accept their profession not only to become self independent worker but also to develop their skilled knowledge for themselves as well as for a noble purpose.

A large majority of women working as telephone operators and nurses usually work for economic reasons i.e. to support their families and to supplement their family income. Most of the women doctors work to make use of their high education, for liking the profession and to become economically independent. Some of them work "to help others".

More than half of the sample of working women is married. The percentage of mutually settled marriage was highest among doctors (59.00%) while among telephone operators and nurses it was 32.00% and 37.50% respectively. An overwhelming majority of working women support inter-caste marriage. They do not consider caste, class and dowry as barriers and try to minimize the gap of social inequalities. However, they still prefer traditional types of marriage rather than Registration marriage.

Though most of the unmarried women are desirous of getting married, yet quite a few of them decide not to get married. These women want to lead an independent and free life and consider that marriage is not necessary for living a happy life. Majority of married women do not support divorce since they hold that divorce brings unhappy consequence to the wives and children both. Divorce, they think, should be resorted to in the extremely difficult situations when all other efforts to save the marriage have failed.

Working women face various problems in their working places. Besides the problems of coming from long distances, round the clock shift duties, lack of transport and canteen facilities, women also feel that they are paid low salaries as against their job and workload. In case of female doctors the problem is quite different in nature. The female doctors in their day to day experiences are not getting equal status with their male colleagues at their work places. They feel discouraged and disappointed when they face men's prejudice against them.

Despite the fact that these women face various problems at home and at work place, they have good relations with their bosses and colleagues and desire to continue their job until their retirement. A significant number of women prefer for part time jobs firstly because they think that their long absence from home caused the suffering of their family members and secondly they like to avoid the hazards of shift duties causing strains and affecting their health.

The working women also show their positive attitudes sharing their income with their family members. Most of them feel that they are happier than non working women for several reasons. They consider themselves as the economic asset contributing to the family income. They enjoy their work and success in their careers which brings lots of happiness to them

Majority of the married women express that their husbands extend co-operation to them and also share some household duties. The women feel that though their working and earning have raised their status in their family and they are consulted in the family matters yet many of them frankly admit that whenever any difference of opinion arises on any issue they have to support the decision of their husband and accept the subjugated status.

These women also prefer small families. 40.00% of them have one child, 20.00% have two children, 13.00% have three or more children. They want to maintain improved standard of living and high quality of child care. A few women report that the working women have very little or no time for effective communication with their children, giving them good training and satisfying their psychological and emotional needs. Women also prefer to live in joint families as they get family support and security for their children when they are out of house.

It is observed that majority of working women have good health. Only 16.60% experience ill effects of the job due to long journeys, shift duties and irregular schedule of food and sleep.

The working women opine that society should change their outlook towards them and give them necessary co-operation and recognition by which they can make their environment happier. For this they require better infrastructure facilities like departmental stores, canteens, easy conveyance for travelling and improved family quarters and crèche for children etc for them.

Attitude of "others" towards working women

In the second part of the study, views of their supervisors have been incorporated so as to examine how the working women are looked upon and rated by them and what views they held as "others" i.e., members of the society on various issues dealing with women and their work.

Majority of the supervisors of working women feel that women share work in all the fields and rate them at par with men as regards regularity and punctuality in attendance. They hold the views that only some women are willing to come early or stay beyond duty hours, if the job demands so. They consider this matter only due to their family commitments. This reason also prohibits them against doing overtime job. 64.24% respondents from supervisors show that the reason of long absenteeism of women is due to family affairs.

According to observation of the supervisors, women show their unwillingness to stay beyond office house though they are not less capable than men in their job. They consider that women can be entrusted with responsible work, for they are at par with men. None of the supervisors consider women less in honesty, rather 58.30% consider them more honest than men. Supervisors opinion was equally divided (50.00%) when they said that married women work as hard as unmarried women.

Regarding leave, 70.00% supervisors judge that married women take more leave. Majority of the supervisors of doctors consider that married female doctors, working under them, are as active and hard working as unmarried female doctors and also take the same amount of leave. According to the opinion of the supervisors, highly qualified and highly paid women have higher degree of career commitment apart from their marital status.

The study of the *attitudes of working women towards others and vice-versa* helps one to understand the outlook and behaviour of working women towards various issues examined in the study. It also gives an understanding of what other members of the society feel about them and view their working. The study provides to suggest the changes that are occurring in beliefs, ideas and thinking of working women and also in the society.

This study also suggests some measures which may be looked into and taken into consideration by the government and society to achieve the ultimate goal of bringing harmony and peace in the society and build a strong nation. It further suggests to give necessary attention in planning of job facilities for women and provide necessary infrastructure facilities so as to ensure that women are able to do justice towards their family and by performing their dual roles in a better way.

Urbanism and Urban Social Structure

(A Case Study of a Town of West Bengal with Special Reference to Role and Attitude of Urban Women)

Bela Bhattacharya

The study analyses the social structure of Krishnanagar, a middle class town of West Bengal. Special emphasis has been focused on the 'family' which is considered to be most resistant to change. However, the urban families have been facing impact of rapidly changing conditions accompanied by India's growing industrialization as well as western influence. The urban people are also being exposed to the new technique of mass communications, such as newspaper, magazine, radio and television etc., and other urban facilities. These are of particular importance in a study of social change in an 'orthogenetic city'. The choice fell on the town, Krishnanagar, for the following reasons.

1. The town is a traditional one and had been developed from a village in the early part of 18th century.
2. It was the seat of Hindu-Brahmanic culture and functionally related with the pilgrimage centre of eastern India, Nabadwip.
3. Since the beginning, the town has been closely connected with the 'Primate city', Calcutta.
4. The location is on the border of West Bengal and Bangladesh (formerly East Pakistan) and since independence there has been a continuous flow of migration from Bangladesh. More than 50 percent of the total populations are migrants.
5. The town is not only at the middle point of two distinct cultural sub-regions which are divided by the Ganga but also a commercial as well as district administrative headquarters. Hence the town is an important center from cultural and socio-political consideration.

The sample families were selected by examining the records available in the Municipal office. To start with, from the 156 blocks as given in the Municipal office, sample study areas were identified. At the time of identification, a rough idea of the nature of population was also gathered. On checking them (by going to the spots for check-up of the town) population was stratified into two categories–old settlers (residents) and new settlers (migrants). These lists were prepared for the different blocks separately. Eight blocks of each type were selected by adopting the technique of random sampling. Then all the houses for the two categories were numbered. The size of the selected samples was 600 families of which 264 were residents and 336 migrants. The total population of the sample families were 3620 individuals. The subtle factors which bind the population together in groups are extremely hard to break down into measurable units. So the best clues have been obtained by verbal statements and also by participant observation method. In the field, schedule and questionnaires were used to collect required information.

Krishnanagar (23°24'N and 88 °31E) is classified into category II town (below 100.000 but above 50,000) by Census of India 1971, and from demographic and socio-cultural points of view, Krishnanagar cannot be considered as a class I city. The sex-ratio characterizes this town as a residential one; the occupation and livelihood pattern suggest its non industrial nature and this town can be classified as a service town. The industrial activity is largely in the form of small-scale, household industries of which taps and dyes, hosiery, porcelain, and clay models are important commodities manufactured for export. Foodstuff, medicines and clothes are important commodities for import. The town is a suburban trading center and an administrative headquarter of Nadia district.

The natural units of the town are Para (neighborhoods) which are named according to the jatis who were the original inhabitants of the respective locality e.g. *Kayet* para, *Revi* para, *Choudhury* para, *Ghosh* para, *Kumar* para, *Bagdi* para, *Chasi* para, *Malo* para and so on. Therefore, original social structure of Krishnanagar can be readily apprehended from the list of the paras. This *jati* para is characteristic of the old settlement of the town. The new settlement is mostly populated by the migrants and most of the localities of the new settlement are named as colonies. Besides, the town can be functionally classified into three sectors.

1) Old localities surrounding the Rajbari–Krishnanagar proper.
2) Centre of trade, commerce, court and Government offices–Goori, a settlement of latter days.
3) Newly settled colonies at the periphery of the town.

Distribution of population in different religious groups shows that the Hindus constitute more than 90 percent. Then comes the Muslim population which is little more than 5 percent ; the Christians constitute more than 3 percent and the combind strength of the Buddhists, Jains and Sikhs is very low (0.4 percent). The caste wise classification of the Hindus reveals about 91 percent general caste, 8.9 percent scheduled caste and 0.3 percent scheduled tribes. Among the Hindus, the percentage distribution shows that the upper and middle castes constitute 37.3 percent and 47.2 percent respectively. The low castes constitute 10.6 percent. The Vaishnabs constitute 4.9 percent. The Brahmin caste is numerically dominant having about 21 percent population. The sex-ratio is about 1130 per 1000 female. The children (0-14 years) constitute more than 33 percent and little more than 56 percent belong to the working force (15-54 years). The old persons constitute 10.1 percent. The sex-ratio in different age groups does not show any significant difference except children where preponderance of male is 2.5 percent than that of female. So far as their marital status is concerned, 58.6 percent are never married, 34.3 percent married and 7.1 percent widowed. Married males and females comprise 17.1 percent and 17.2 percent respectively. Percentage of widow (6.1 percent) is more than widower (1.0 percent). Obviously never married male (35 percent) is more than female (23.2 percent). The literacy rate is 76.7 percent. There is discrepancy between literacy rate of male and female. Literacy rate above 7 years to 34 years is about cent percent.

The economic condition of the urban dwellers is not satisfactory. Only thirty percent are earners. The percentage is higher among the Christians (40 percent); then comes the low caste population (38 percent). But only 28 percent of the upper castes are in gainful employment. Among the Muslims, the percentage varies between 29 and 30. The age for individuals varies from community to community. Among the upper/middle caste families, it is usually not before the age of 20 or 22 years that a boy seeks a gainful occupation. Among the low castes, Muslim and Christian the age of the job seeker is often not more than fifteen years.

The pattern of occupation is now changing. Only 18 percent adhere to the caste bound occupation. The upper and middle caste people are now taking up inferior occupations e.g. hawker, vendor, peon, servant, skilled and unskilled labourer and likewise. Upward mobility can be traced among the low castes and other traditionally lower class people.

The downward mobility for the upper and middle castes and upward mobility of the low castes and other communities alter the traditional social stratification and a new system of stratification has been emerging. The most striking fact about occupation is that above 4 percent of the total population are female earners. Adoption of gainful occupation by the females, especially, among the upper and middle castes and classes, is very important and can be taken as an indicator of social change.

The female population who are engaged in gainful occupation constitute 8 percent of the total female population. The percentage of the earning females is the highest among the Christians (18%) and then come the low castes (14%). It is the lowest in the Muslims (4%). Among the upper and middle castes corresponding figures varies between 7 percent and 8 percent. Women belonging to upper and middle castes are mainly engaged in the superior jobs like maidservant, biri binding etc. A few of middle caste women run small shops.

The distribution of family size reveals that 1-2 member size constitutes 11.6 percent, 3-5 member size category comprises 36.7 percent, 6-10 member size category constitutes 42.7 percent, more than 10 member only 9 percent. It is difficult to classify family type into two types–nuclear and extended–because there is a great variety in nuclear and extended families. Therefore, 3 types classification–nuclear, nuclear with dependent member and extended family–has been adopted. And accordingly there are 58 percent nuclear families, 22 percent extended family and the rest are nuclear with dependents. Extended family is higher among the upper castes–28 percent and low castes–24 percent. The middle castes and the Muslims have only 17 percent for each.

It is interesting to note that the family composition of the middle castes and upper castes on the one hand and the Muslims on the other hand are different in one respect at least as the number of children is more in Muslims and dependent kins are rare in their family but among the upper and middle castes the dependent kins are more and found in many cases. When family types are seen among the residents and migrants, it is found that the incidence of extended family is higher among the residents and conversely nuclear family is higher among the migrants. Some low caste families prefer joint family. In fact, higher incidence of extended family in lower castes is directly related to their social status. The extended family is found to be favoured by the largest percentage (80 percent) of the female population in an opinion survey. A strange paradox was, however, noticed in the investigation taken up that the extended family was favoured by those who do live in a nuclear family. On the other hand, those who live in the extended family evinced an attitude of lukewarmness and cavalier.

Among the dwellers of Krishnanagar the relations between males and females are traditionally prescribed by rules of caste and religion. In this paper some observation has been made on male-female relations focusing on four issues which may be taken as indices of modernity: the free-mixing of males and females, self-choice of one's marriage partners, inter-caste marriage and divorce have been delineated. For this 125 females of different castes and communities, excluding Muslims, were interviewed. Their attitudes towards each of the four indices of modernization are discussed below.

Traditionally, in our country, free-mixing of males and females has been frowned upon. Of late, however, there is some relenting in this matter. Increasingly women are participating alongside men in social, political and economic activities. Support for secluding women is gradually becoming a thing of the past. And co-educational schools from the primary to the post-graduate level provide increased opportunity for free-mixing. Against this background, it is worth considering the attitudes of women in a provincial town like Krishnanagar towards the free-mixing of males and females.

As used here, free-mixing means friendship between males and females; it should not necessarily be taken to sexual intimacy. In the assessment of this attitude, it has been found that a number of factors, such as the caste of the males and females, their respective class status, and also their educational backgrounds are important. The free-mixing of males and females having parity in all these respects is less resented than when a gross disparity of caste, class endogamy is noticeable and which is still one of the dominant mores of our society. Free-mixing within the circle of caste-class endogamy, therefore, meets with less disapproval from peers and parents. About one-half of the 125 women said they were in favour of free-mixing. There was little difference in this attitude between native residents and migrants. However, if we look at the breakdown by caste, we see that two-thirds of the upper caste women said they were in favour of free mixing, while three-fourths of the lower caste women and even more of the Vaishnaba women were not. On the other hand, none of the Christians said they were against free-mixing.

Regarding class based interaction almost three-fourths of the upper middle class women favoured free-mixing, while 100% of the lower class women did not. The data on free-mixing were taken on the basis of four points.

1. Friendship between males and females
2. Visits to each other's homes
3. Going to the cinema or other places together
4. Establishment of intimate relations, with or without intentions of marriage

Though almost half of the 125 women said that they favour free-mixing, but in actuality only 14 had male friends. Of these, 10 were between 18 and 25 years old, 3 were between 26 and 30, and the other was in the 31-35 year. As Krishnanagar is a district town, naturally going to cinema or making intimacy with their boy friends is also a rare incident. 10 out of the 14 women go to the cinema or other places of enjoyment with their male friends. But generally, unmarried couples avoid cinemas, theatrical performances, or other public places in the locality. According to them, Krishnanagar is so small a town that it is very difficult to move together without being seen or noticed by elders or local people; and they are afraid of being talked about. The precincts of the local Roman Catholic Church offer a much desired shelter to burgeoning lovers. However, courting couples also take opportunities to get out of Krishnanagar and go to Calcutta or nearby Ranaghat or Santipur.

Being intimate is also to be found among the respondents. It is interesting to note that of the 14 women with boyfriends, only 3 have established intimate relations, with or without the intention of marriage. The other 11 interviewees said they were not in favour of such intimacy.

To sum up, it can be said that a limited shift is taking place towards more free-mixing between males and females. Though the number of cases is still quite negligible, free-mixing is present in the town of Krishnanagar.

Attitudes on the Self-Choice of Marriage Partners

In Krishnanagar, a large number of females are still prepared to bow to the wishes of their parents or other elders in the selection of their life partners. The largest proportion of women who were for self-choice belonged to the upper middle class; all the lower class women said they were against it. The least educated women were the most against the self-choice of mates. Over half of the 18-25 year-old girls said they were against choosing their own partners, whereas a larger percentage of the women between the ages of 26 and 40 expressed favour on this issue.

There seems to have been a hesitant change in outlook among the females in Krishnanagar regarding the self-choice of partners. Out of 125 respondents, only 7 of them actually had married according to their own choice. Four of these women belong to the upper middle class, 2 to the lower middle class, and 1 to the lower class. Five of them are from upper castes, I from a middle caste, and 1 from a low caste.

Attitudes on Inter-caste Marriage

Strict adherence to caste endogamy is a feature of most Hindu marriages. Despite many efforts to change this custom, with legal attempts going back over 1000 years, "the moral force of caste is still so great, and Hindus are still so caste-minded, that it is questionable whether legislation will break it" (Kapadia 1966: 119). Inter-caste marriages are now-a-days a much discussed subject. Fifty-eight percent of the women expressed their favourable attitude towards inter-caste marriage. And among East Bengal migrants to Krishnanagar only half of the migrants showed their negative attitude towards it, whereas nearly three-fourths of the native residents expressed negative opinions of this practice. By caste, the upper castes split about fifty-fifty for and against; the middle castes were about one-fifth for and about three-fifths against, with the rest expressing indifference.

It is true that with the advent of technological development, some major changes in the caste system have taken place. One of these changes is greater freedom in the choice of occupation. Also, under pressure of necessity, eating in canteens and hotels, or taking food and drink while travelling, is mitigating caste distinctions and leading to increased social intercourse among the members of different castes. But such changes in parts of the caste system must not be over-emphasized, for they have not produced any overall effect on the system as a whole. Change due to conviction must not be confused with change due to the pressure of circumstance.

This study suggests that caste loyalties are still very strong, even among educated people. But factors that tend to accelerate the tempo of inter-caste marriage are present: co-educational colleges and mixed employment settings, for example.

Attitudes on Divorce

In India, instances of divorce are still very rare. Of the female respondents only 24% favoured divorce if the husband was found to be unfaithful; 69% were against this, while 7% were indifferent to the question. The percentage of East Bengal migrants in favour of divorce is almost twice than that of Krishnanagar natives. Most women gave expression to immense dislike of the very idea of divorce, the lower class being particularly sharp in their comments. The moderate views of the economically upper middle class women reflect a change in their outlook.

Attitude to divorce varies from caste to caste. Illicit relations by either spouse is a major ground for divorce among the lower castes; among the middle and upper castes domestic disharmony is the more frequent ground for divorce. The percentage in favour of divorce is about the same (29% to 30%) for upper and middle castes and

Vaishnabas. Most of the Christians, being Roman Catholics, were against divorce.

The majority of respondents who are in favour of divorce think it may take place as they do not love each other, or they have failed to adjust to one another, or the incompatibility between them is such that compromise is impossible, or because one of them is of loose character.

The striking fact in the Krishnanagar investigations is that practically no divorce has yet taken place. There are only two cases of separation among the lower classes. This does not mean that everyone enjoys a happy married life, but rather that are prepared to make great adjustment to stay together. Though instances of divorce are still very rare in this traditional town, the differences of opinion among the women is significant, as it reflects a change in views towards marital relationships.

Foot Notes

1. Total population of Krishnanagar Municipality is 139070 having a sex ratio of 1028 per thousand female. The literacy rate is 86.47. The literacy rates for male and female population are 90.85 percent and 82.48 per cent respectively. Therefore there is discrepancy of about 7.8 percentage points between literacy rates of male and female.
   Work participation rate is 32.93 and the rate among the male is 54.00% and for female 11.25%.These informants were selected through a process of multi-stage stratified sampling. The Krishnanagar populations were first stratified into native residents and East Bengal migrants. Then each of these categories were stratified according to age differences. The 125 women interviewed were selected randomly, from this stratified pool (Census 2001).
2. As used here, class and caste are not identical, though it is found that high caste status is generally correlated with high class status. The several classes are here defined with respect to monthly income: lower class–Rs.100 to 250; lower middle class–Rs.251 to 500; middle class–Rs.501 to 750; upper middle class –Rs.751 upwards. The category of upper class is omitted because no Krishnanagar family in the sample earned more than Rs.2500.
   Regarding the different levels of education, illiteracy is defined as not knowing how to read or write even one's own name. Primary school is a four-year program for the youngest children and others who have never learned the alphabet. Persons who have attended at least two years of school are included in this category. Junior level standard requires completing primary school plus two additional years of schooling. The school passed level requires completing primary school plus 6 additional years of schooling or else passing the school leaving examination conducted by the State Board of Education. An intermediate level education requires attending college for two years, while a graduate education requires completing the college programme successfully.

References

Census of India 2001 Series–20, West Bengal, Kolkata.

Kapadia, K. M. 1968 *Marriage and Family in India*. Bombay: Oxford University Press.

Child Labour in Calcutta–A Sociological Study

Swapan Kumar Sinha

Child labour in Calcutta has been in existence since the days of Job Charnok, the founder of Calcutta. The Royal participation in the shipping of Hooghly in the later part of 17th Century changed the composition of city's population. It is reported from the Gazetteer of Calcutta, August 1831, that two girls who escaped from the home of one Syed Hussain in Calcutta, complained to the police that they were bought and employed as slaves. Among the child labour, generally two broad classifications can be made–one is self-employed and other one is wage earner. Garry Rodgers and Guy Standing of ILO categorized child labours as (a) domestic worker, (b) non-domestic and non-monetary work, (c) bonded labour and (d) wage labour.

Most of the self-employed workers live with their family and come to the city at the very dawn and return at dusk or late evening. However, among the wage earners the major number of children work in hotels, restaurants, tea stalls and sweet shops. These establishments can be sharply divided into two categories one is the posh-establishment for the higher income groups and the other for the lower income group.

In pursuance of the objective of the research programme, it was decided to cover a sizeable stretch of urban areas for the systematic collection of data from the working children mainly through personal interviews and participant observation. These working children represent a fraction of total labour force.

Working children engaged in hotels and restaurants, sweetshops and tea stalls in the city were selected for this study. It is worthnoting that there is no female worker in these sample establishments. Not more than 2 children have been selected from one establishment. In selecting these establishments, two points were kept in mind–

(1) Densely located establishment areas, and

(2) Establishments scattered at every corner of the city.

Hotels and restaurants, tea-stalls and sweetshops located on 87 streets, roads and in some other areas were selected for this study.

The total number of working children covered by this survey is

800. After making a list of all working children, one case was selected after interval of every four, i.e. out of 800 child workers, every fifth case was taken from the list. The procedure has been followed to make it a representative one.

In studying the working children in the city of Calcutta, observational technique and questionnaire have been followed. The researcher also tried to collect case histories of individual child labour and relate the same with the findings otherwise generated. Data collection was started from Ist January, 1977 and ended in the month of January, 1980. The child being immature, it is difficult to get answers promptly from them. Even they could not follow the questions always. Moreover, fear and anxiety compelled them to remain silent or to give wrong answers in many cases. Much has had to be elicited therefore through observation. While asking the question, the mode of delivery, movement, and the total behavioural pattern of the child were observed. The researcher always tried to eschew the preconceived notion which may misrepresent the findings. Observation was made almost round the clock. To unfold the behavioural pattern and way of living, sudden visits at different times in different seasonal conditions were made. Even during the period of rainy season, the researcher observed the working children in the midst of heavy shower and water-logging for on the spot study. Participant observation technique was also applied. The researcher as a customer visited their establishments to make closer, correct and scientific observation. In times of participant observation, one thing always was kept in mind, that the child worker should not, by any means, identify the researcher.

A questionnaire cum schedule was made to get the desired information from the respondents. To get proper answers, the respondents were interrogated and observed.

The study has been divided into four phases. The first phase is related with child labour, as a labour unit. The next phase is the study of rural life of India and nature of migratory character. The third phase is pertaining to employment and its impact. The fourth phase was a mixed experience of the researcher about the politicians and national leaders who pretend sympathy for the working class.

The following are the main findings.

The present study has revealed that child workers in Calcutta have come from different places of West Bengal, Bihar, Orissa, Uttar Pradesh, Tamil Nadu, Kerala, Madhya Pradesh, Andhra Pradesh and Bangladesh.

The main cause for abnormal increase of child labour is the flow of migrants from the villages to the urban areas in search of employment, as a result of disintegration of village economy and pervading poverty among the landless and working classes there. Besides, there are other causes like food, natural calamities and drought, which affect large section, at times. Most of the migrant children have come from the families of landless and marginal farmers. Such migration clearly shows the inequality in the distribution of land. Driven by acute poverty, most (91.25%) of them left their villages and become floating children of the city. Domestic quarrel (2.5%), urge for self-dependence (0.63%), and abandoned child (3.12%) have also caused such migration. These causes have also emerged from poverty. Communal riots (2.5%) and political unrest have also added up their number. Most of the migrants are 'linked migrants'. Thus a 'rural and urban chain' is formed, as they keep regular contact with their villages. Continuity of migration is also noticed, as they bring new children later.

Most of the children, are, however, found to be employed in the unorganized sector. The highest concentration is 5-7 workers in an establishment. Next is 2-3 workers in an establishment. One worker establishments constitute only 5% of the total, and lowest category is 26-30 workers per establishment.

Among the working children, 0.63% earn Rs. 5/-per month, 3.12% Rs. 6.00-10 per month, 13.75% Rs. 11.00-15.00, 23.75% Rs. 16.00-20.00, 24.37% Rs. 21.00-30.00, 11.25% Rs. 31.00-50, and 1.87% Rs. 51.00-75.00 per month. Along with monthly income, they are provided with food. It was also found that .63% children earn Rs. 75.00-100.00 per month without food. It is to be noted that 20.63% children are unpaid. They work without any cash remuneration. Besides monthly income, they have other subsidiary income, though their percentage is very small. Out of 11.88 per cent of this group, 8.75% children get bonus (in cash). It is noteworthy that they earn this little extra amount by working for a few hours more beyond the scheduled duty.

There is no fixed working hour for such children. Majority of the children work untiringly for 11-15 hours a day, to satiate the customers. Generally work starts at dawn and finishes at 11p.m to 12 midnight. They have to remain confined for a very long time in an unhealthy environment. The border line between slavery and long hours of exploitative labour in their case is very thin, as they have to work up to 19 to 20 hours a day to serve their families. 5.62% children work only 8 hours a day, 3.75% work 9 to 10 hours a day, 67.5% 11 to 15 hours a day, 20.63% 16 to 18 hours a day, and 2.5% 19 to 20 hours a day. These long hours of confinement in dark unhealthy places can only be compared with slavery.

The extent of exploitation does not rest there. Half-day leave in a week is allowed to 1.25% children, 15% children get 1-day leave in a week, 5.62% children enjoy 2 days leave in a week. 0.63% children are allowed to enjoy when occasion demands. The rest period is also affected, having generally no good or healthy place to retire, and by doing domestic chores of the employer and at times in personal bickering. It shows that 38.13% children get no rest. ½ hour rest in a day enjoyed by 4.37% children, 7.5% children enjoy 1 hour rest. 3.13% children get rest for one hour and half 42.5% get 2 hours rest, and 4.37% children get 3 hours daily. But in fact they do not get rest. They have to take bath and meal and do their routine morning duties during the rest time.

The standard of literacy among the child labour is very low. The percentage of illiterate children in West Bengal is 28.75% but the proportion of illiteracy among the working children is very high the percentage being 60.62%.

The most sordid aspect unearthed by this study is the existence of so called 'bonded labour' practised in different fashions. Here bonded child workers cannot become free until the debt incurred by their fathers is fully repaid by their labour. Two cases of such bonded child workers were found during the survey.

It is high time that a start should be made to eliminate all forms of child labour in every sphere, to save a greater part of humanity from utter ruin. The Government of India has begun taking steps in this respect and has adopted quite a number of preventive and ameliorative legislative measures. But as our study shows, legislative acts have had very little impact either in reducing the extent of child labour or in the improvement of their conditions of work or in the increase of their remuneration.

Calcutta Cycle-Rickshaw Pullers : A Sociological Study

Subir Bandyopadhyay

To find the extent and nature of occupational changes and mobility in the context of industrialization, replacing the caste-bound occupations, and to understand the new working conditions, the cycle-rickshaw pullers of the fringe areas of Calcutta have been probed and presented in detail as a case study. Although the cycle-rickshaw pullers do not belong to the schedule of recognised workers, or belong to the organised sector of employment, all the same, they do a very strenuous job of physical labour in the form of self-employment. They are mostly unskilled and uneducated and come mostly from rural areas. Their emotional level, as such, are comparatively low with a few exceptions, where it was found that the individual concerned has had full school education. Some of them belonged to the average middle class rural family, having agricultural lands or a particular type of traditional profession. But due to the disintegration of the rural economy at present for various causes, they have been forced by circumstances to take such a menial job, to eke out their existence and to support their families.

II

The survey was undertaken with the help of a structured questionnaire. The number of respondents was 400. The interview was conducted directly contacting the respondents. The schedule was divided into six heads. Each division was designed in a way as it will give a clear idea of the respondents' view on individual and social issues. The divisions were made to elicit the following data:

1. Personal
2. Financial information
3. Behavioural details
4. Socio-economic background
5. Concept of family planning
6. Other details.

Some questions were supplemented with other related enquiries for a better understanding of the respondents' replies and for collecting correct information as far as possible. In giving personal information, the respondents were asked questions about their present and past dwelling places. They had to reply some other queries like (a) Educational Qualification (b) Caste whether S.C. or S.T. (c) Religion (d) Marital Stalus whether married or not (e) Mother tongue. Apart from these the cycle-rickshaw pullers were also asked about their father's and grand father's and father-in-law's occupation, the duration of cycle-rickshaw plying and/or whether they were previously employed in other jobs.

The survey was conducted in the fringe areas of Calcutta. The division was made as East, West, North and South sectors. In each sector, a number of rickshaw stands were sampled on the basis of density of population, importance of the spot with regard to business and occupational centres and their geo-physical location. In all, 15 such selected spots were surveyed. Among the rickshaw pliers of every stand a reasonable number was selected for interview. The areas selected for survey had importance from different aspects. The demographic importance has been taken into consideration. The survey sites were selected on the basis of their economic importance also. The spots of South and North Calcutta have attained greater importance from the demographic and socio-economic point of view. The areas surrounding these survey-spots are inhabited by a large number of migrants from Bangladesh. As a result their economic and social status are different from those of other neighbours.

III

a. History of cycle-rickshaw as a vehicle

To know about the evolution of the cycle-rickshaw, we have to trace the past history of its invention which was done abroad. The man who made the first ridable bicycle was Kirpatrick Macmillan. But Macmillan's crude steed of wood with turning treadles, rods and cranks on the back hum was forgotten before he had established itself as a machine for personal use. The term rickshaw has been derived from Jin Ricksha, a Japanese term. It is a small, covered, two-wheeled vehicle, usually carrying one passenger and pulled by a man. It was used in Japan since 1870.

The three-wheeled cycle-rickshaw has a mechanism identical with the ordinary bicycle. The rider sitting on a flexible leather saddle steers it by the handle bars attached with the forks, turns a driving sprocket attached to two cranks by pedals, transmitting motion to the back wheels. Propelling motion is transmitted from pedalling sprocket to a second sprocket fixed on the rear wheel by means of an endley chain running over both sprocket of the cycle-rickshaw. It is a developed form of monocycle and bicycle and is found in almost all the towns and villages of India now. Even with a minor difference in mechanism, they are found in other countries like Indo-China, China, Hongkong and France. The cycle-rickshaw can run 6 to 10 miles per hour.

b. Socio-economic background

The overall information on cycle-rickshaw collected by the field survey and other sources reveal that this vehicle is found in almost all cities and suburbs of all the states in India. Cycle-rickshaws are now found to ply in almost all districts of West Bengal too. It is an astonishing fact that in Siliguri over 30,000 (at present it is more than that) cycle-rickshaws ply daily on the streets of the town. It has been found from field study that unlike Calcutta, the cycle-rickshaw is a very important vehicle in all suburban town. In the capital city, there are about 30,000 hand rickshaw pliers. Of them only 20% are owners of their vehicle.

This field survey was conducted in different zones of Calcutta metropolitan area like Jadavpur Station, Tollygunj Club, Russa Road and Garia Bus Stand at the extreme south. In the north zone, the selecetd spots were–Baranagar, Dunlop Bridge, DumDum Railway Station. In the Eastern side Kasba, Tiljala, Ballygunge Station were surveyed. Apart from these places, Roy Bahadur Road of Behala was also covered. At each such site, an approximate number of average respondents were interviewed.

The cycle-rickshaw pliers under study are found to have migrated from different districts of West Bengal. All these areas are village-oriented. Apart from these, there are some refugees from Bangladesh. A good number of village youths have also come from the fringe areas of Calcutta and work as cycle-rickshaw pliers to earn their livelihood.

Case of Migration

The study reveals the details of the places and districts from where the respondents have migrated into the urban areas of Calcutta to earn their livelihood. They did not however at first join this poor and socially downgraded occupation. But after a prolonged effort to secure other conventional and better paid jobs failed, they adopted this form of low-stature self-employment. Statistics reveal that out of the total number of respondents, majority are Bengalis belonging to West Bengal or Bangladesh. 24% respondents have come from different districts of West Bengal. 23% have migrated from Bangladesh. These migrants have come in different phases till 1964. In respect of other states, the migrant have come mostly from Bihar, Uttar Pradesh (U.P.) and Tripura. Among them, majority have come from Bihar. Out of 400 respondents 22% have influxed from Bihar and 3-5% form U.P. In case of West Bengal the migrants are mainly from 24 Parganas (South), Midnapore and Howrah. Some are the original residents of Calcutta. The distribution of district wise percentage in case of West Bengal are:

(i) 24 Parganas–62%, (ii) Midnapore–9%, (iii) Howrah–4%, (iv) Kolkata–17%. Likewise from Bangladesh the percentage are : (i) Dhaka–11%, (ii) Barisal–6.25% and (iii) Faridpur–1%. The percentage of cycle-rickshaw pullers from Bihar are: (i) Muzzafarpur–9.75%, (ii) Samastipur–3%, (iii) Munger–2.75% and (iv) Darbhanga–2.25%.

Parents' Occupational Status

The socio-economic background of the Rickshaw pliers will be more evident from their parental occupational status. It has been revealed that the father of 54 (13.5%) respondents were engaged in business. 26 (6.5%) of them worked as labourers, 76 (19%) were service-holders and168 (42%) had agricultural occupations. This is one of the important findings as it shows that 42% respondents' fathers had agricultural background. On the analysis of the findings it can be said that many of them had a good social background and status even up to their father's generation. Now coming to the previous occupations of the respondents the position is revealed as follows:

Table 1
Occupation of the Respondents

Age group	No occupation	Business	Labourer	Service	Others
15 – 20	26	2	13	7	16
21 – 30	81	7	51	19	27
31 – 40	28	7	33	13	17
41 – 50	17	1	11	3	7
51 – 55	2	-	-	3	1
Above 55	2	1	2	2	
Total(400)	156	18	110	47	69
Percentage	39%	4.5%	27.5%	11.75%	17.25%

Educational Background

Data have also been collected on the educational background of the respondents. The following Table 2 will reveal the picture.

Table 2

Education of the respondents

Age group	Educational standard (coded)	Number
15-20	3	6
	4	8
	5	-
Total		14
21-30	3	12
	4	43
	5	5
	6	6
Total		66
31-40	3	14
	4	19
	5	6
	6	1
Total		40
41-50	3	1
	4	8
	5	1
	6	-
Total		10
51-55	3	-
	4	1
	5	1
	6	1
Total		3
Above 55	3	-
	4	2
	5	1
	6	-
Total		3

The educational background of the respondents in different age groups in the total aggregate shows that at primary levels the number of respondents is higher than those who are Secondary or Higher Secondary passed. The total number of respondents comprising all the age groups who are between primary to upper and secondary level is 136.

Codes used : 3 = Passed primary level
4 = Between Class V to Class VIII
5 = Above Class VIII to Secondary passed level
6 = Upper than Secondary level or Higher Secondary passed and higher (higher means College education).

Caste Affiliation

Caste identification presupposes various ascribed factors of a particular caste. It is associated with socio-economic activities and the status of a man. At the first stage, caste is an ascribed position but their position or status then enables a man to achieve various status positions and have access to various facilities in our society. The overall caste-hierarchy of the cycle-rickshaw pliers under study is not linked to a low position only. Some among them have had quite higher social status in the villages.

Table 3

Caste Affiliation

Caste	Number	Percentage
A. Brahmin	9	2.25%
B. Baidya	2	0.5%
C. Kayastha	72	18%
D. Scheduled Caste	119	29.75%
E. Scheduled Tribe	4	1%
F. Muslim	13	3.25%
G. Others	181	45.25%
Total	400	100%

c. Cultural Profile

The cycle-rickshaw pliers have a special mode of gestures and conversation, peculiar to their profession. In most of the cases their behaviour is usually rough and aggressive. But not all of them are cast in the same model. It was observed that those who had received a bit of education and had comparatively higher family background and culture, behave differently and politely. It has been found that the aggressive attitude prevalent among them is the outcome of the negative attitude of the society to this profession even though society gets a vital service from them.

This inferiority complex is the result of the general dealing of the people with them. The passengers call them 'rickshaw-walla' and their mode of conversation with them is not polite. It is one of disdain and contempt as if they are not human being. It has been gathered from the respondents that the passengers treat them only as petty carriers, unlike the drivers of other vehicles. The behavioural standards that the passengers maintain with the drivers of other vehicles like Mini Bus, State Bus or even their conductors are far more polite than with them. The behavioural standards maintained with men of other vehicles have developed through some presumptive psycho-social value considerations. The modes of calling, talking and courtesy tounged in such dialogues are associated with conventional value consideration of such jobs. The social status and educational attainments of the occupation are factors by which the existing status concept of a profession is determined. This psycho-social process and status determination is linked with every occupation. This has been the sociological process behind the arrogant attitude of the passengers towards the cycle-rickshaw pliers. Among the cycle-rickshaw pliers it was also found that they very often use 'slang words' in their usual conversation. Some of the code words are 'Pakhi', 'Charai', 'Biliti'. Many of them often drink 'cholai' a special type of country liquor. It has become a part of their habit. The 'rickshaw-wallas' have developed an antagonistic attitude towards the general society and behave in a rough and rude manner, using at times their own slangs. They do it when any dispute arises in payment of an agreed fare, or a passenger wants to go a further distance than what was settled. Often they refuse to take any passenger according to their mood.

Rituals and Traditions

The cultural life covers a wide area of the total life-span of an individual. Maintenance of family traditions like–worships, *bratas* and other rituals form the core of the cultural life of the people. The survey was made to assert how far the respondents were able to continue their familial tradition after having adopted the occupation of cycle-rickshaw plying. It was found that they stick to their traditions as far as possible, but cannot observe these in detail due to the lack of means and because of the new environmental and professional changes. They go at times to their villages and maintain contact with their kith and kin for being apprised in time both about such rituals and festivals and other family needs. There are others however, who do not keep such links with their families and the latter too, do not do so.

d. Social consciousness and other issues

Though the cycle-rickshaw pliers differ from the common people on many respects, it has been found during the survey that they do certain works, behave and perform certain social duties according to the conventional code. Their mode of living is a bit different from the common norms. But many of them are found to live with their families and perform their domestic duties and discharge their responsibilities to their relatives as found in the case of other families.

Ownership of the vehicle and Trade Union activities

The sources of finance for purchasing the vehicle, political consciousness and involvement of the cycle-rickshaw pliers in Trade Union activities constituted other areas of enquiry. The findings can be shown in the following Table.

Table 4

Ownership of the Rickshaw and Level of Income of the respondents

(N=100)

Below Rs. per Month.	Owns	Does not	Whether member of Trade Union Yes	No
150/-	—	1	1	—
150 - 199/-	1	5	3	3
200 - 249/-	2	13	11	4
250 - 299/-	4	8	10	2
300 - 349/-	9	31	34	6
350 - 399/-	3	9	8	4
400 - 500/-	2	11	10	3
Above 500/-	-	1	—	1
Total	21	79	77	23
Percentage	21%	79%	77%	23%

The above Table 4 shows that among the 100 (Sampled out of 400) rickshaw pliers only 21 are owners of their rickshaws (i.e., 21%). it is further found that of these 21 owners, 45% are in the income group of Rs. 300–349; 4 or 20%belong to the income group of Rs. 250–299; 3 or 15% in the income group of Rs. 350–399 and 2 or 10% are in the income group of Rs. 200–249.

Attitude to Saving

It has been found that most of the cycle-rickshaw pliers do not try to save from their monthly income. It has been estimated that they can (if they so wish) save some amount of their monthly income, but they do not do it. The psychology necessary for development of the saving habit is linked with other allied cultural and social sense of every group of individual. It is the case with the cycle-rickshaw pliers also. The overall absence of this saving psychology is a typical feature of their occupational group.

The saving attitude among different caste groups (out of sample 100) can be stated as such. Out of 4 Brahmins, none saves anything monthly. Among the Kayasthas and other castes out of the 64 respondents 17 or a little more than 26% save monthly. Among the Scheduled Caste respondents numbering 28, only 4 or 14% have the habit to save. The fact can be deduced from the reality that the Kayastha and other caste respondents have a tendency of saving more than the other groups. The Brahmin and the Muslim rickshaw pliers save nothing. The respondents belonging to Scheduled Caste group also save a very small amount monthly.

Respondents' impression on the usefulness of Trade Union

1. Most of them (out of 100 samples) 77 stated that trade union is an effective instrument to solve any dispute regarding 'fare' with passengers. The disputes arising out of street accidents between two rickshaws or other vehicles, regarding payment of compensation or effecting repairs, are settled amicably.
2. Some respondents have expressed their opinion on trade union differently. They opined that union does a good service by strictly maintaining the rule of adhering to one's turn in the line at the rickshaw stand.
3. Sometimes troubles crop up due to violation of traffic rules, smuggling of liquors or carrying of contrabands. In such cases, their vehicles are seized by the police and they are confined to the local police station for further interrogation. In such cases, to prevent harassment the union leaders get them released with

the vehicle with whom they generally have good terms and political link up.

4. Respondents also view and take their 'union' as an instrument of "welfare action". The union helps to solve their family problem i.e., quarrels, disputes in the family. The union also offers loan for marriage, house-building, festivals and other contingencies. This really helps to generate a sense of unity and a sense of group identity among the cycle-rickshaw pliers. The union also provides leadership to observe 'strike' for fulfilling their pending occupational demands etc.

Types of Rickshaw pliers and their job preferences

Taken 100 as a sample out of 400 a focussed information was also collected on their job preferences. Out of these 100, 64 opted for service in factories of organised or unorganized sectors, 21 liked to take employment in 'office'. Some young rickshaw pliers preferred to take or start any kind of business where they can be self employed.

Conclusion

Whatever may be the existing image of cycle-rickshaw pliers in our society, it is an undeniable fact that they are part of the socio-cultural whole and thus their awareness and social participation should be encouraged. The Governmental authority should play a positive role in financing the purchase of a rickshaw. In this way profit making through ownership can be eliminated. The Govt. of West Bengal has a permanent department with funds for promoting small scale business and village industries. The Government can help them to purchase cycle-rickshaw on easy installment through this department. Cycle-rickshaw pullers can be provided a better housing facility from KMDA or similar organisation. It has been also found that cycle-rickshaw pullers are prone to suffer from diseases like T.B., Hydrosil, problems of chest and arms and veneral complaints. Their children suffer from malnutrition, rickets and night blindness. The E.S.I. or other voluntary associations can make arrangement for at least licensed cycle-rickshaw pliers.

The position now is that the cycle-rickshaw pliers are gradually becoming socially conscious about different social issues. The lumpen tendency (as so long propagated) is not the final word about their character. On many occasions it has been found that the rickshaw-pliers protest against their colleagues for misdeeds and dishonesty. From the angle of Developmental Anthropology it is necessary that more effort should be made by voluntary organisations to help the rickshaw-pliers in all possible ways to upgrade or better their lot of life.

Socio-Pscyho-Economic Problems of Hospital Patients in West Bengal (1965-75)

Krishna Mitra

The present study is concerned with the problems of Hospital Patients in West Bengal in the sixties and seventies. The basic purpose of her study was to identify a few urban and rural areas and make case studies at Hospital, Nursing Homes, Medical Research Centres, Primary Health Centres in rural and urban agglomerations, slums and some other populated areas.

The case study format was applied for studying all the selected cases and there social, psychological, economic backgrounds and related problems were intensively analysed.

She had special remark of the problems of poor who in the urban areas could avail free bed treatments but the real crunch of problems in urban areas was the middle class people who neither could avail costly treatments nor had the facility of free beds.

In rural areas she observed that health workers and doctors in rural practice were helpful for the masses but for acute problems there was neither any provision nor opportunities. Particularly, the availability of medicines, equipments, competent hands, distribution system are totally inadequate. She found transport problem of the patients was the biggest problem and also lack of administrative control over health workers and also doctors.

Her case study schedules were statistically analyzed to bring out ready direction which all had pointer towards application of all recognized systems of medicines and treatments like Allopathic, Homeopathy, Herbal, Unani, Dentistry at appropriate level and areas.

The real pointer though was towards the inadequacy of the state health system, awareness of the rural people of the availability of such help was the second pointer. There was a demand from the entire health system not only to expand and discipline but to add all out multi-disciplinary awareness programme too and at the same time take the help of social workers, spread all over to bring system that work at those levels. She also pointed out the basic needs of data bank throughout the state for the proper implementation of health system to assess in advance the seasonal or epidemic needs of precautions. Hospital patients that could evolve better socio-psycho-economic system in West Bengal and that should have a continuous research and development programmes which would lead to much advanced speculations and precaution which would surely reduce the problems. In the realm of economic development, it was discussed that dependence on state subsidiary could be smoothly eased out to develop among the patients a sense of responsibility and for that matter suggested health insurance policies in an wide range spread out all over.

Agrarian Unrest in West Bengal with Special Reference to Naxalite Movement

Subhrendu Maity

Organized mainly by the leftist political parties, there had been a number of widespread agrarian unrests in West Bengal as well as in some other states of India during the last three decades. The main aim of the movement was to force the Government to fulfil its commitment mainly to effect equitable redistribution of land among the landless peasantry, who had been deprived variously by the landholding classes and who were in extreme poverty and misery ever since the introduction of the land tenure system of 'Permanent Settlement' in 1793 in Bengal and later in other states of India by the British. As such, they became extremely restive and had resorted at times to armed conflicts with the land holding classes for acquisition of adequate agricultural land for their survival. The permanent settlement system was mainly introduced by the British for the facility of collection of land revenue through intermediaries called 'Zaminders' vesting with them large estates, as was done in the feudal system. Naturally, the peasants were reduced into mere tillers and serfs and had no title or right on the land they cultivated. Under such condition they suffered from perpetual misery.

So the rural sector, especially the agrarian belt, is sizzling with unrest. Sometimes this unrest get manifested in violent forms at different places. In West Bengal there have been a series of such major agrarian unrest and clashes. The Naxalite Movement of 1967–71 was one such form of violent protest and it took almost a revolutionary shape. This movement compelled both the Central and the State Government to introduce certain basic land reform measures to pacify the agitated peasantry.

II

The problem dealt with in this dissertation is entitled *Agrarian Unrest in West Bengal with special reference to Naxalite Movement.* The depth and magnitude of this movement have induced the present author to study the manifold causes and aspect of this agrarian tension in West

Bengal. The author selected two volatile centres, Debra and Gopiballavpur in the district of Midnapur (west) in West Bengal, which harboured and supported the famous Naxalite Movement, as it would offer a wider perspective, being an epicenter of the revolutionary Naxalite Movement that aimed to effect land reforms by 'armed conflict'.

The movement originated in the Naxalbari Police station in the district of Darjeeling. Shortly after the uprising of Naxalbari in the year 1968, Debra and Gopiballavpur, the two almost unknown villages in the district of Midnapur, became the strongholds of this movement, and thus became famous all over the country for resorting to 'Guerilla warfare' tactics for forcing land reforms. This movement gradually spreaded to many other places of West Bengal, as well as, to different parts of India. Earning the name, 'Naxalite Movement' this movement mobilized the peasants, as well as the rural proletariat and channelised their craving for land by grabbing political power through armed struggles.

The agrarian relations in the district of Midnapur have undergone several basic economic and political changes in recent years due to the mighty impact of this movement. It has also been a scene of intense political conflict between the land holding groups and the landless peasantry in recent times. The district, particularly its southern border region, constitutes an important centre for the study of the traditional pattern of social stratification and response to the changes in economic and political structures, from time to time. The conflict between these stratified classes mainly centres round economic issues, but in its form and expression, it is a political conflict.

The significance of the Naxalite Movement was that it was the first 'Maoist' type of movement in this country. Charu Mazumder, the main propagator of this movement, involved the principles of Mao-Tse-Tung every now and then, and directed the party cadres to conduct it strictly on the lines of the great Chinese leader. He also referred to Marx, Lenin and Stalin to justify this armed struggle by the peasantry. There were basic differences of opinion between the Naxalite, the CPI (ML) and the other communists as well as several leftist parties in regard to resorting to armed struggle for land reforms. Their open advocacy of armed struggle was not supported by other parties. They had adopted the stand of total boycott of elections and rejected the path of Parliamentary systems. On the other hand, they depended on annihilation of 'class enemies'. As a result, this party was isolated from the mainstream and was looked down upon as a 'terrorist extremist group'.

The movement of Naxalbari as it was developed in Debra-Gopiballavpur and later in the district of Birbhum represented three stages of actions and their dimensions in West Bengal. In Naxalbari, the idea was given shape by way of a 'model armed struggle' in the year 1967. In Debra-Gopiballavpur the guerilla warfare was launched with fire-arms and the 'guerrillas' claimed themselves as a Liberation Army in 1971 at the last phase of this movement.

After the Naxalbari uprising, the movements of Debra and Gopiballavpur included forms of armed conflicts of the peasants for seizure of lands from the Jotedars and other rich land-owing classes who owned large tracts of surplus land. This movement took the shape of a bitter 'class struggle' and created a keen 'class consciousnesses' among them. The form they adopted was essentially a guerrilla tactic, which was given a lot of emphasis by Charu Mazumder in 1968. This according to him, was a part of the operational technique for launching a 'real revolution'. " Like fish in water" the CPI(ML) leaders joined hands with the peasants assuring that this would enable them to secure land for everybody. They so intimately befriended and allied with them, that the local people particularly a section of the scheduled castes and tribes, loved and took them as their real friends and offered them all sorts of protection so that they could conduct guerilla activities in these areas for annihilation of the 'class enemies'. After the formation of the CPI (ML), for integrating and politicizing the leadership with the poor and landless peasant masses, a good number of students of Calcutta Colleges and Universities with 'brilliant' academic career joined the party to lead the movement. Though they had started initially with a misty idea of the Naxalbari pattern of uprising and launched the armed struggles for seizure of crops, but at that time they had no specific programme beyond the propagation of the politics for seizure of power through armed struggle and shouting slogans and holding public demonstrations.

Agrarian Unrest may some times be fomented by different ecological situations, economic stress and historical circumstances. The most important contributory factors that triggered off the revolutionary situation were :

a) concentration of the tribal people, who have a strong in-group sentiment; i.e., ethnocentrism;
b) existence of large tracts of 'benami' lands purchased under false titles by the Jotdars and wealthy classes;
c) existence of land covered with dense forests;
d) frequent clashes between the privileged and the poorer sections and the like.

Besides, the leadership motivated the poor and the neglected peasants for some immediate gain, by promising to allot them all the seized lands, which was another potent contributory cause that had sparked off the armed struggle in Debra and Gopiballavpur.

The guerrilla peasants decided that they would forfeit the properties of 'class enemies'. The 'class enemies' did not constitute a homogenous group and as such different forms of 'punishment' were meant for the following categories. The seizure of land would take the following forms :

i) all properties of exploiting Jotdars ;
ii) half of the property of all Jotdars ;
iii) all properties of police informers ;
iv) half of the property of small brokers;
v) not to forcibly capture the properties of rich peasants, middle peasants and sympathetic Jotdars ;
vi) not to search for real 'vested' lands for the time being;
vii) protect the properties of friendly classes from the police, as well as hooliganism of Jotdars by armed guerilla units; and
viii) snatched firearms will be used if necessary, at the time of operation to protect the guerilla fighters.

IV

It has been found that the history of Indian Communist movement during the period 1967–71 was one of 'fragmentation and disorientation' of the party both in West Bengal and other parts of India where it was extended in the later phases. It had been imbued and propelled, to a large extent, by the ideological inspirations of the Chinese peasant movement. Though this movement was initiated from Naxalbari for securing right of land for the landless peasants, it ultimately deviated from that aim, by giving the call for the seizure of the administrative control of state power through armed struggle, and also degenerated into rank murderous activities by killing of many innocent people, heedless of the consequences that it might create, both for the party and the society at large.

The armed agrarian revolution in West Bengal as well as in India, to effect land reforms by forcibly grabbling the land of Jotdars by singling them out as 'class enemies' failed for various reasons as noted below.

i) An armed revolution needs long preparation and a very strong and well-knit organisation, adequate suppliance of arms and ammunitions and long skillful training in the use of arms.

ii) The weapons procured and used in this movement were more or less rustic and incompatible and inadequate for an armed revolution, specially against the army and police of a modern state. Naturally all their attempts resulted into utter misadventure without a proper cause to boost and because of the lack of public support.

iii) Due to extreme poverty and to satisfy their immediate needs a section of the peasantry deviated from the main aim of the movement and indulged in loot and forcible harvesting of paddy not only of the big Jotdars and money lenders, but also of other small farmers who had hardly 2–4 bighas of land and were themselves poverty stricken.

iv) By nature Indian people are averse to bloodshed and murder irrespective of its cause. They consider bloodshed and murder as crime. Naturally, bloodshed and indiscriminate murders which were committed by the Naxalites during this movement alienated a large section of the people who in the hope of getting land, supported the movement some way or other at the initial stage.

Besides, the Naxalites leaders adopted the course of 'guerilla warfare' through armed struggle in India on the Chinese pattern. But this technique was somewhat incompatible in the Indian context. The revolution in China was conducted in the thirties and forties in dissimilar conditions than those which were prevailing in India in the seventies. The Chinese Government and administration were decentralised then, with a weak Government at the centre, which was also weakened by the prolonged war with the Japanese during that period. But in India, the Government was very strong and intensely centralised and its administrative machinery was highly effective as compared with the corresponding Chinese Government. The ruling class of China was politically isolated from the common masses for which the revolutionaries won the active support from a large section of the people against the Japanese by their daring struggle. But in India, the people were not ready for an armed struggle and the ruling class had much influence and hold on the common masses. Besides, the Indian Army was very powerful and well equipped just like the army of any other developed country of the West. As a result, it was not possible for the Naxalite Guerillas who were insignificant in number and did not have more than a few pieces of guns and rifles, to organise any attack against the army or the police for seizure of the state power by force. With their traditional weapons, they created troubles in isolated pockets in the village side and fled when counter attacked by the police or the army units.

The impact of Naxalism amongst the common masses became very weak as the movement was started without any proper ideology for the masses. On the other hand, people observed that Naxalites meant a 'terrorist party' who were more interested in murder, dacoity and gun snatching in the villages. In the urban areas, their activities comprised of the murder of some political leaders and educationists; creating disturbances in educational centres; beheading of statues of national leaders; hurling of bombs in educational institutions including examination center and cinema halls. It was also noticed that the big merchants and the other exploiters/usurers lived without fear by giving these persons whatever they demanded.

The Naxalites in Debra and Gopiballavpur could not organise the common masses for 'class struggle' nor could they consolidate 'class consciousness' which were the main aims of the Naxalites. They mostly depended on the tribal and scheduled caste people for launching the movement, who were unaware of the ideals and aims of the revolution. Later on when most of the upper caste people joined this party, most of the rural poor who had initially joined the movement, became disillusioned. They assisted the Government in suppressing the movement, which had lost its direction by indulging in free loot, arson, murder and killing.

Thus the Naxalbari movement, which was undoubtedly initiated with great ideological fervor, however, failed to change the exploitative socio-economic structure of the country. Their tactics did not ultimately conform to the revolutionary message of Mao-Tse-Tung. Mao-Tse-Tung said that the revolutionary movement has to be modified according to the actual conditions of each country, effecting a "synthesis of the universal truth of Marxism-Leninism". The ideology of the naxalbari movement was more of an imported ideology than one which was related with the condition of the soil. It was not unnatural, then, that the 'sparks' of Debra and Gopiballavpur, and similar such 'sparks' in some other parts of the country, failed to give birth to a big revolutionary fire which was the initial objective of the starting of movement in these areas.

A Diagnostic Study of Student Unrest in West Bengal as Related to Certain Sociological and Institutional Factors : A Multi-Dimensional Approach

Swaraj Bandyopadhyay

The study primarily concerns the significant issue of students' behaviour and the academic administration. It is envisaged that students' unrestful behaviour has so far been subjected to research by different researchers from different angles. Evidently such factors like students' socio-economic background, their future aspirations, motivations, etc. have got priority over any possible role played by the institution itself, for example, in terms of its various structural and organizational characteristics like admission policy, classroom environment, teaching standard, examination system, financial condition, location, etc. which, as a matter of fact, may 'trigger' the activists', actions.

In the study, emphasis has been laid on two broad factors, which presumably have been taken into account simultaneously while evaluating the problem of students' unrestful behaviour in this State.

First, the institutional characteristics of the colleges i.e., mainly focusing on the structural and organizational characteristics of the colleges studied and their probable bearing, if any, on the students' behaviour in a particular organizational set up; and secondly, the students' socio-economic background traits, and their possible role in the process of students' activities and their changing behaviour.

Do the structural characteristics and organization patterns of the degree colleges have anything to do with students' different activities? What type of structures are more susceptible to students' unrestful behaviour? What could be the perceptible alternatives to that? Some of these crucial issues the study attempted to examine. There is no denial that the problem has different facets but its consequences on the structure and organization pattern and vice-versa probably could not be denied too. Having stated this, it does not necessarily mean that the study did not take into account the impact of the interface forces (mainly political) which very effectively works on almost every broader system of the society in general, and the education system being an open system, in particular.

II

In sum, an attempt has been made to diagnose the combined effect/ impact of a host of organizational and interface factors along with the students' socio-economic background characteristics on the emergence of the process of students' unrest in the degree colleges of the State.

A suitable number of colleges situated in Calcutta, 24-Paraganas, and Howrah, constitute the sample of the present study.

All the colleges are essentially degree colleges offering one or more courses in Science, Humanities and Commerce. In terms of type of management they fall in four categories viz, Government, Sponsored, Non-Government, Private and Missionary Colleges. Though most of the sample colleges are male colleges but still a few co-education colleges had also been included in the sample of the study.

Two questionnaires were designed. One was distributed among the Heads of the Institution, or the person next to him and few senior Professors. This was followed by interviews of those who filled in this questionnaire.

Average number of respondents from each college was 3 for this category and they all have/had experience with their respective institutions for about 10 years on an average. The latter feature of the respondents made the study more worthwhile with their enriched and experienced information.

The second questionnaire was distributed among the students of randomly selected colleges.

III

Two clear points emerged from the analysis of the students' characteristics data.

First, enrolment patterns vary among the types of colleges; and secondly, the sample colleges have heterogeneous student population in terms of their socio-economic characteristics and other background traits. It was also evident that students' composition is directly related to these institutional characteristics, which either control or induce students' activism.

The degree colleges in the State apparently have some common characteristics in terms of their different structural features. A micro view however, reveals that they distinctly differ among themselves in terms of teacher-student ratio, facilities available to the students, admission policy, students composition, etc. It has also been found that some of the above stated issues are relevant/potent enough for inducing students' activism in an institutional set-up.

The study further revealed a few interesting features regarding overall characteristics of the broad types of colleges i.e., Government, Sponsored, Private and Missionary. They differ distinctly from each other in terms of admission policy, students' economic condition, and teacher-student ratio; whereas it has been found that in terms of frequencies of examinations conducted in a college in an academic year, there does not exist any marked difference among them. With regard to the nature of membership in the students' union of the colleges, it is observed that there are about 45% colleges in the sample where it is "obligatory" for students to become a member of the students' union of the college. Thus, it appears that in those colleges even general students do not have any "choice" whether or not to become a member of the union.

IV

The study essentially attempted to highlight whether or not institutional characteristics contribute in anyway in the process of students' activism in the degree colleges in the State. It has been revealed that though apparently much difference does not exist in the structural characteristics of the sample colleges, there are distinct differences in the areas like admission policy, teacher-student ratio, space, facilities, among the broad types of colleges. Occurrence of students' unrest in the degree colleges has been found to be contingent among others, to a great extent, on these institutional characteristics.

Moreover, the study substantiates further by exploring information regarding the general issues involving unfavourable situations in these colleges. Majority of the degree colleges in the State have been found to suffer from inadequate infra-structural facilities, which in turn is attributed to the cause of students' activism. This, as has been revealed by the study, definitely holds true for the sample colleges.

Human Resources Development (HRD) with Reference to Training in Public Sectors Banks (1969-1987)

Milly Dey

The concept of human resource development was not at all known before the early sixties in the commercial banks. Even the personnel management concepts were hardly understood by the banks. The connotation of the words like 'industrial relations', 'staff welfare', 'staff motivation', 'classroom training', 'performance appraisal', 'manpower planning' were all unheard of. In those days, banks handled staff functions through the staff departments. The main functions of staff departments were recruitment, transfer, promotion and punishment. Even the recruitment policies followed by banks in the past had hardly any scientific basis. In several cases, minimum qualifications were not insisted upon and even non-matriculates were recruited for clerical posts. There was no proper evaluation of capacity and very often relationship and recommendations played a big role in selecting the employees. The lack of proper training facilities further aggravated the situation and the banks found themselves manned by a large number of the employees who had very little interest in the type of work they are required to carry out and also had no identity with the goals and the objectives of the organizations. Those working in staff departments had no special skill, training or aptitude in this area. The posting in staff departments, however, carried a lot of prestige on account of the power and authority enjoyed by the officials working there and the favours they could bestow on others.

Soon after the independence, the government had shown much concern for labour welfare. A number of new labour legislations aimed at securing benefits for the labour were enacted and the old labour laws were amended to make them more labour oriented. There was improvement in working and service conditions but there was no matching improvement in personnel skills. As a result, discipline became the casualty. The new found freedom could not be channelized properly. The managing staff was not trained to motivate the staff and to win them over with proper style of functioning. As such, the functioning of the commercial banks was adversely affected. The government tried to bring order by setting up tribunals to settle down the disputes. The award of the tribunals had the effect of bringing about some sort of standardization in service conditions of the bank employees. This alone was, however, not enough. There was need for improving discipline, efficiency, productivity and sense of involvement with the banks. It was not possible to bring about these improvements through change in service conditions only. The managers were not formally trained in the techniques of personnel management/human resource management.

In the early sixties, the new concepts of personnel management were being experimented in India by some of the enlightened managements based on the successful experiments carried out by the companies in Europe and USA after the Second World War to overcome the problem of stagnation and declining profits. Multinational companies having their network in India also introduced Personnel Management techniques after successful implementation of the same in their home countries.

To equip the existing as well as to develop the new staff for manning the new branches, it became necessary to arrange for external and internal training. So projects for opening training centers and training colleges were taken up. Gradually, the concept of zonal recruitment, all India recruitment, and objective tests was developed.

After nationalization of fourteen banks, many public sector banks employed specialists to manage these departments. In the early seventies, the management institutions in the country had started producing a good number of specialists in the area of personnel management and industrial relations. Many of those young graduates found their way in the public sector banks. After the personnel administration and the industrial relations were professionalized in public sector banks, the concept of HRD got the attention of the management of the public sector banks in the mid-seventies.

The concept of HRD gradually dawned upon the management of the public sector banks who started perceiving and conceiving that the human resources was not only the most important resource but was also the most expensive and most delicate resource which required a very gentle handling. Formal HRD activities commenced simultaneously in the seven associate banks of State Bank of India of Baroda at the end of 1976.

Gradually, the management of all the banks perceived that the effective utilization of human resources be it in the macro or micro levels, need to be achieved at any cost. They feel that the old idea of treating the human resource as factor of production should be given up, as only the motivated and conscious human element inspired with the quality of work life can make any enterprise economically viable. Therefore the management of the banks consider that the human resources need to be treated as high field investment as effective optimum utilization of the same which alone generate higher productivity and profitability in the public sector banks.

In this perspective, it shows to the management of the banks that HRD is not reduced to a concrete mechanical system rather a total organizational effort is to be made to improve the effectiveness of the human element within the organization. Before the introduction of HRD as a system, the management felt it necessary to create a HRD climate and the HRD activities should be assigned to a senior manager.

There is however, a widespread feeling among the people that HRD is merely a "fashionable term" and basic thrust of HRD is not felt at the operational level in the public sector banks.

The public sector banks are at present handling multi dimensional functional areas touching many facets of society with an extremely huge and complex work-force. Considering the magnitude of human resources, there is an imperative need to develop and train the human resources to gear up for a better customer service.

It is imperative for a service sector like banking that a fairly well structured Human Resources Development policy and its implementation with a decentralized approach is to be installed at different levels so that HRD moves near to the problem areas. HRD in the context of banking is not only acquisition of new knowledge and skills but also acquiring capabilities to manage both internal and external environment, attaining self-confidence and motivation so as to improve the customer service in order to meet rising expectation of the customers.

The prime challenge for the top management, personnel and HRD functionaries today is to mould the beliefs and values of their employers in favour of the HRD policy and systems. For this, the top management commitment to HRD is utmost necessary but moulding the required attitudinal orientation is a continuous effort.

In view of the utmost importance and utility of HRD in a service sector, the researcher felt inclined to study in depth the multidimensional activities of HRD and multifaceted training system prevalent in the public sector banks. The researcher also intended to make comments on the point on what should be the desired level of

HRD and training system in the public sector banks, the service sector possessing one of the huge manpower.

The year 1969 was the starting point of this research work. Although the incidents of the preceding year i.e., the history of the banks culminating in the year 1969 with the bank nationalization, has been taken into consideration, but emphasis has been laid from the year 1969 as the commercial banks became public sector banks through the process of nationalization at that period.

For this study the main objectives of the researcher were as follows:

1. to make exhaustive study as to whether the philosophy of HRD has been accepted by the public sector banks and what is the present HRD system and practices in these banks;
2. to highlight the other major sub-systems of HRD in order to critically evaluate whether those sub-systems of HRD have been utilizing effectively as supplementary and complementary elements of training in public sector banks;
3. to make an in depth study on the procedure of identification of training need, adoption of various training methodologies vis-à-vis the use of Audio-Visual Aids, and the method of evaluation of the training;
4. to examine critically how training as sub-system has been exploring for the development/upgradation of various skills of the employees in Public Sector banks so as to attain organizational effectiveness;
5. to identify whether the executives at different cadres in public sector banks perceive any gap in their knowledge, skill and attitudinal level;
6. to make effective and meaningful suggestions for improvement of the total HRD system in general and training as sub-system in particular.

Keeping the aforesaid objectives in view, the researcher made every effort to cover all twenty eight public sector banks from all the regions in India to get an all India representation in the study. Out of these numbers, six public sector banks and three corporate training colleges and three training centers from eastern region, one public sector bank each from western and northern region and one corporate office of public sector banks from the south in addition to one corporate training college from the south were chosen at the macro level. The Public Sector Banks are treated as samples for the purpose of study. And the samples are selected in such a way so that maximum information for analysis of the data is feasible.

The researcher has mainly concentrated on the eastern region but a few other selective public sector banks of other regions have also been taken. After the selection of the regions, the researcher concentrated on the issue of selection of public sector banks from the selected regions. As such, keeping in view the selected regions, United Bank of India, United Commercial Bank, Allahabad Bank, State Bank of India, Bank of India, Bank of Maharastra, Canara Bank, Punjub & Sindh Bank were selected for the study. Ultimately, the following offices were identified for the purpose of in-depth study.

Eastern Region

i. Corporate Office of United Bank of India
ii. Corporate Training College of United Bank of India
iii. Corporate Office of United Commercial Bank (UCO)
iv. Corporate Training College of UCO
v. Corporate Office of Allahabad Bank
vi. Corporate Training College of Allahabad bank
vii. Zonal Office of State Bank of India (Kolkata)
viii. Staff Training Centre of State Bank of India, Kolkata
ix. Branch Office of Bank of India, Kolkata
x. Staff Training Centre of Bank of India, Kolkata
xi. Regional Office of Canara Bank, Kolkata
xii. Staff Training Centre of Canara Bank, Kolkata

Western Region

Corporate Office of State Bank of India, Bombay

Northern Region

Corporate Office of Punjub & Sindh Bank, New Delhi

Southern Region

i. Corporate Office of State Bank of Andhra, Hydrabad
ii. Corporate Training College of State Bank of India, Hydrabad

Data have been collected by the researcher using the following methodology. Questionnaires have been prepared before hand in three forms viz.

a) Short questionnaires for the Officers belonging to scale I to III
b) Long questionnaires for the Officers belonging to scale IV to VI
c) Detailed and in-depth questionnaires for the Principal/Chief instructor of the training college/Head of HRD or training section have been administered.

These three forms of questionnaires were posted by mail to all over India. In short, the research items included the following :

1. Distributing and collecting the questionnaires personally from the Corporate Office as well as the Zonal Office in Eastern Region in particular from West Bengal and outside West Bengal.
2. Where the Officers were reluctant to fill in the questionnaires on their own, the researcher in such events had to take their views on each question of the structured questionnaires through interview.

The value and importance given to the human resources in the public sector banks could not be imagined in the past, still it must be said that the HRD departments in most of the public sector banks under study operate merely as show pieces. There is no worth-while contribution of these departments and whatever is done by them is merely an image projection exercise. HRD functionaries in the major public sector banks have no sincerity in their approach and have no real concern for the development of the employees. This is one of the reasons for not achieving any substantial result in solving complications in human relations or the problems pertaining to industrial relations, despite the extended set up of department in all public sector banks. Secondly, the top management never took initiative to ensure that the right people with the right approach are asked to manage the function. There can be specialists from outside and there can be officers from within. In fact, it is a blending of the two which can bring out the best result. The growth of HRD and its successful implementation will only be possible if the top management of the public sector banks provide full support to HRD programmes not merely by endorsing the programmes but by joining actively in the developmental endeavour. Only then the benefits of HRD system in the public sector banks will be achieved to its full extent.

It is the law of competition and survival of the fittest that plays a vital role in the competitive environment. The choice is either to prove and prevail or to become feeble and weak. Therefore, a bank offering better customer service will go a long way not only in surviving in the competitive market but also in strengthening and establishing itself in the industry. For improving customer survice there is an urgent need to evolve a philosophy of discipline and uniformity of approach in enforcing it. This should be followed by educating the employees about the concept of discipline and the need to adhere to the norms. The officers/executives need to be exposed to the enforcement of discipline in both the positive and negative styles through an adequate training.

One of the greatest challenges which the public sector banks are facing at present, is the requirement of motivating the workforce. The traditional patterns of motivation which were largely founded on the economic rewards and authority, have failed to deliver the goods on a long term basis. Thc complex milieu of labour welfare approach, growth of unions, rising standards of living, better educational backgrounds and awareness have raised the expectation level of the employees. There is scope of infusing positive motivation among the employees. In this sphere, the role of training and development as sub-system of HRD is immensely important. To meet the challenges ahead and to cope with the transition in technological era, it is highly necessary that the employees of the public sector banks need to develop specialised skill, functional knowledge and attitudes conducive for organisationals effectiveness.

If the public sector banks would like to play a dynamic and active role, it is necessary that their manpower must be trained in a new way. The public sector banks have established training institutions called training colleges or centres in all over India.

Keeping the facts in the foregoing paragraphs, the researcher is of the opinion that the management of the public sector banks under study are not seriously keen to implement training, as a sub-system of HRD as modus operandi to change the attitude or behaviour pattern of the employees of the public sector banks. Training is imparted only as a matter of routine job and not to accelerate the on-the-job skill or functional knowledge. Without identifying the training need, selection of the employees are being done on the basis of unsystematic 'pick and choose method' leading to wastage of man-power and the cost involved, the consequence of which brings organisational ineffectiveness. In such haphazard method of conducting training courses, it is impossible to develop human relation skill either in the form of inter-personal competence or resolving industrial relation problem on human footing or resolving conflict between various cadres in the public sector banks. Moreover, it has been established from the interview of the executives of the public sector banks that some typical types of functional training programme or cross-functional behaviour science/skill development programme/computer operational programmes are earmarked for the officers or non-officers year after year. This sort of training programme is identical with the earlier training programmes and is going on year after year. This only creates monotony or boredom among the employees. In such repeatative training course, without identifying training need on systematic basis, one can hardly assess the depth of learning of the employees. The employees nominated to such training courses also do not apply their minds to enhance their levels of knowledge or acquire any new skill which they can implement in their working situations. Thus, the basic objectives of conducting the training courses are lost in the process. The training period becomes a paid holiday for the participants nominated to attend internal/external training courses. For this lapses, not only lack of training need identification is accountable but also lack of co-ordination between the training institution with the personnel department are responsible along with the apathetic attitude of the top management.

Training programme designed and developed by the public sector banks should be active, need-based and relevant. An effective training programme is one which enlists active participation. Research in training techniques conducted in India and aborad has emphasized upon the fact that to be effective, training has to lay emphasis on learning rather than teaching, doing rather than listening and discussion rather than dictation.

Statistics relating to training in banks reveal that in the last eight to ten years, the number of employees trained during each year has covered one-fifth of the total staff. That means, the employees have had to wait for even five years to get their turn for training. This has to be viewed against the fact that the recent years have seen the emergence of new concept and new areas such as lead bank scheme and credit planning, IRDP, performance budgeting , growing incidence of sick units, merchant banking and sophisticated foreign exchange operation–all these need effective handling which in turn necessitated adequate training and exposure. The relevance of training also stems from the fact that communication channels within the public sector banks are hard pressed to cope with growing requirements.

Part III

Appendices

Appendix I

বর্তমান বঙ্গসমাজে যাদুবিদ্যা ও লোকায়ত বিশ্বাসের ধারা

শোভা রানী চক্রবর্তী

সাম্প্রতিকালে নানাভাবে বর্তমান সমাজের নানা দিক নিয়ে মনন, অনুশীলন বা পর্যালোচনা শুরু হয়েছে, এর মাধ্যমে আমরা সমাজের অনেক বিস্মৃত অধ্যায়ের নজির পাই—যা বর্তমানের মানুষের মনে ও তার দৈনন্দিন কর্মধারায় ব্যাপ্ত হয়ে রয়েছে। পরিবেশ-পরিমণ্ডলের বন্দী মানুষ কেবল বাঁচার তাগিদে নয়, এক অনাবিল সুখ শান্তির জন্য নানা বিরুদ্ধ পরিবেশের মুখোমুখি দাঁড়িয়ে তাকে আয়ত্ত করার চেষ্টা করেছে। কালক্রমে মানুষ প্রকৃতিকে জয় করতে সমর্থ হয়েছে, বাড়িয়েছে নিজ স্বাচ্ছন্দ্য ও নিরাপত্তা। অপরদিকে অতীত সমাজ জীবনের অনুশাসন (Institution) বা ধীর পরিবর্তিত (Transformed) রীতিনীতির ক্ষীণ মূর্ছনা দূরাগত সঙ্গীতের মতো অস্পষ্ট হয়ে গেলেও অতীত স্মৃতি বিজড়িত রীতিনীতি বা বিশ্বাসের পর্যালোচনা করে নিঃসন্দেহে চলমান সমাজের একদিকে আলোকপাত করতে চেষ্টা করেছে।

ইতিহাসে থাকে সন, তারিখ ও ঘটনার পুঙ্খানুপুঙ্খ প্রকাশ। কিন্তু সমাজের ও জনগণের যে সামাজিক ইতিহাস তাকে সন- তারিখের মধ্যে আবদ্ধ করা কঠিন। কারণ এর পরিবর্তন হয় দীর্ঘদিন ধরে এবং জনগণের সচেতন মনের অলক্ষ্যে। তবে তার উপর যে সন-তারিখের বা ঐতিহাসিক ঘটনারাজির প্রভাব পড়ে না এমন নয়। তবুও একথা অনস্বীকার্য যে সামাজিক ইতিহাস জনগণের দৈনন্দিন কর্মপদ্ধতির এক বিস্তৃত বিবরণ বা ঘটনাপুঞ্জের অকৃত্রিম সমাবেশ, যার সবগুলির এক মিশ্র অভিব্যক্তিই হল সমাজ ও সংস্কৃতির এক বেগবতী দ্যোতনা।

প্রবহমান যুগের সঙ্গে তাল রেখে সমাজও এগিয়ে চলেছে। বিভিন্ন অবস্থার পরিপ্রেক্ষিতে দৈনন্দিন জীবন যাত্রার নবরূপায়ণে ব্যক্তি সম্পর্কের যে হেরফের হয়েছে, তাতে সমাজের মানচিত্রের নানা বৈচিত্র্য প্রতিভাত হয়। ব্যক্তিজীবনের প্রভাব যেমন অন্যকে প্রভাবান্বিত করে, তেমনি সমাজজীবনে তার প্রতিক্রিয়াকে অস্বীকার করা যায় না।

লোক অর্থে স্বাভাবিকভাবে জনসমষ্টি বোঝালেও বিশেষ অর্থে এমন মানুষের গোষ্ঠীকে বোঝায় যাদের উপর বিদগ্ধ বা পরিশীলিত মানুষের প্রভাব পড়েনি। এ লোক প্রকৃতি পরিবেশের বন্দিদশা থেকে সম্পর্ক মুক্ত হতে পারেনি এবং পারেনি বলেই তাদের ব্যক্তি জীবনের সমস্যার মুখোমুখি দাঁড়িয়ে জীবন সংগ্রামের প্রতিটি মুহূর্ত্ত অত্যন্ত সতর্ক থেকে দিনচর্যার বিভিন্ন আচরণে যে বিশ্বাস প্রতিফলিত হয়েছে বা আচার অনুষ্ঠানের যেসব রূপ নিয়েছে সেগুলিই লোকায়ত বিশ্বাসের বা দিনচর্যার বিভিন্ন দিকমাত্র।

মানবসমাজের শৈশব থেকে বর্তমান যুগ পর্যন্ত এক নিরন্তর সংগ্রামের মহড়া চলছে প্রকৃতির

সঙ্গে মানুষের। কখনও সেই সংগ্রাম স্বীয় জীবনরক্ষার জন্য, কখনও বা ব্যষ্টি বা সমষ্টির অধিকার ও আক্রমণের উন্মাদনায় মুখর। প্রগৈতিহাসিক যুগে , মানুষের আদিম বংশধরদের নানা দুশ্চিন্তায় সন্ত্রস্ত থাকতে হতো। কেননা সেদিনের পৃথিবী ও তার পরিবেশে ছিল সম্পূর্ণ অন্যরকম ও অজ্ঞাত। একদিকে মুর্হুমুহু ভূকম্প, জলপ্লাবন, তুষার বন্যা, আবার অন্যদিকে বিরাটাকৃতির ম্যামথ, সিংহ, ব্যাঘ্র, সর্প প্রভৃতির মতো হিংস্রজন্তুর দাপাদাপি তখনকার মানুষের জীবনযাত্রায় বিরাট বিঘ্ন সৃষ্টি করেছিল। আবার খাদ্যবস্তুর অপর্যাপ্ততা, ব্যবহারিক দ্রব্যসম্ভারের দীনতা ও অপ্রাচুর্য তাদের অর্থনৈতিক পরিবেশকে অনিশ্চয়তায় ঘিরে রেখেছিল। সেই সঙ্গে রোগব্যাধি, মহামারীর নৃশংসতার অভাব ছিল না। এ ভীতি ও শঙ্কা, ঝড়, ঝঞ্ঝা, বৃষ্টি ও তুষারপাত, দিবারাত্রি, ঋতুভেদ, জন্ম ও মৃত্যু, নিদ্রা ও স্বপ্নের বিকার সেদিনের অজ্ঞ মানুষের মনের মণিকোঠায় নানা বিশ্বাসের, নানা শক্তি কল্পনার এক ইঙ্গিত দিয়েছিল। সে অজ্ঞতা, অসামর্থ্য ও বিশ্বাস পরিকল্পনার দৃঢ়তা এসব অত্যাশ্চর্য অঘটনের কারণ খুঁজে পাবার চেষ্টায় তাকে রূপক দৈবশক্তি বা অশরীরী অতিপ্রাকৃত শক্তির কল্পনায় নিবিষ্ট করেছিল। আদিম শিকারজীবীদের উপকরণ বা সম্পদ সৃষ্টির মাদকতায় মানুষের সংস্কৃতির অভাবনীয় পরিবর্তন ঘটল, পরিবর্তন হল তার পরিবেশ পরিমণ্ডলের। প্রকৃতি- নির্ভর মানুষ ধীরে ধীরে প্রকৃতির উপর শাসন শুরু করল অগ্নির প্রজ্বলনে, কৃষি বা শিল্পের সূচনায়। তার সেই প্রাচীন অসংলগ্ন সমাজজীবনের গতিপথ গেল পাল্টে। তার রীতিনীতি, কর্মানুসরণের নানা দিক প্রয়োজনীয় হয়ে উঠল। তখনকার বিস্ময়াবিষ্ট মানুষ আবার নতুন ভাবে ব্যাখ্যা করার চেষ্টা পেল, চলল তার বিশ্লেষণের পালা। সাধারণ ভাবে বিচার করলে দেখা যাবে মানুষ তার অনিশ্চয়তাকে, বিফলতাকে অথবা জীবনেব সংগ্রামের প্রতিটি মুহূর্তকে ভাবী জয়-পরাজয়ের আশঙ্কায় এক বিশ্বাসের মধ্যে টেনে নিয়ে ক্রিয়াকাণ্ড ও আচরণের মাধ্যমে পূর্ণ সার্থকতা বা অখণ্ড শান্তি বা নিরাপত্তার যে পন্থা গ্রহণ করল, তাই হল আদিম মানুষের ধর্মবিশ্বাসের গোড়ার কথা। সেদিনও মানুষ বুঝেছিল জীবন ক্ষণস্থায়ী, শক্তি সীমাবদ্ধ। তাই জীবনের বহু কামনাও অপূর্ণ থেকে যায়। স্বামী- স্ত্রীর অকৃত্রিম ভালবাসা, বিবাহ বন্ধনের কঠোর সামাজিকতা বিচ্ছেদের করুণসুরে মূর্ত হয়ে উঠে, নিশ্চিত কৃতকার্যতা বিফলতার বন্যায় প্লাবিত হয়। তবুও মানুষ সব হারানোর দুর্ভাবনায় অবসরে তার মৃত্যুজয়ী কল্পনাকে মনের মধ্যে চিরজাগরূক রাখার প্রবল চেষ্টা পায়। এ পাওয়া না পাওয়া, শঙ্কা বিপদকে এক অশরীরী শক্তির প্রকাশ বলে সেই শক্তির কাছে আত্মসমর্পণ করে। তার সঙ্গে রয়েছে এ সকল প্রকাশিত অপ্রকাশিত অলৌকিক ক্ষমতার বিভিন্ন বিকাশ,—দেবশক্তি-প্রেতশক্তির আনাগোনা। জীবন সংগ্রামের নানা অধ্যায়ের এ এক অভিনব অভিযোজন, সংস্কৃতির নিত্য পরিবর্তনের বিকাশের এ ইঙ্গিত বা মূর্ছনা।

এ ধর্ম বিশ্বাসের মূলে রয়েছে যেকোনো ঘটনাকে ব্যাখ্যা করার চেষ্টা। আদিম মানুষ প্রতিটি কার্যের বা ঘটনার এক সূত্র খুঁজে নিয়েছে, তার কারণ যে ব্যাখ্যায় যখন কার্যকারণ সংযোগ ঠিকমতো সাধিত করা যায়নি তখনই তাকে বিভিন্ন শক্তির খেলা বলে ধরে নিয়ে ইন্দ্রজাল বা মায়া কৌশল দিয়ে তাকে বশ করার চেষ্টা পেয়েছে। যেমন আন্দামান দ্বীপপুঞ্জের অধিবাসীদের বিশ্বাস, ঝড়ঝঞ্ঝার, দেবতা হল 'বিলিকু'। তিনি কোন কারণে ক্ষিপ্ত হলেই তার বহিঃপ্রকাশ ঘটে ঝড়ঝঞ্ঝার মাধ্যমে। ওঝা ঐ দেবতাকে বশীভূত করার জন্য তীর ধনুক নিয়ে ভয় দেখায়। আবার যেখানে শক্তি প্রয়োগের ব্যর্থতা প্রকটিত হয়ে উঠে, সেখানে ঐ কাল্পনিক অতিপ্রাকৃত অশরীরী শক্তিকে পূজা, স্তুতি, প্রার্থনা, অর্চনা, উপহার, বলিদান দ্বারা, কখনও আত্মশ্লাঘার মাধ্যমে ঐ শক্তির কাছে নতিস্বীকার দ্বারা, মানুষ

অভীষ্ট পূরণ করার চেষ্টা পেয়েছে। ধর্মাচারণের মাধ্যমে এভাবে জীবন সংগ্রামের ব্যর্থতাকে প্রতিহত করার এক সুকৌশল অভিব্যক্তি নিহিত হয়ে রয়েছে। বলা বাহুল্য এ ধর্মবিশ্বাস বা ইন্দ্রজালের পশ্চাতে রয়েছে একান্ত বিশ্বাস আর আচরণ।

ইন্দ্রজাল একধরনের মায়াবী কৌশল যাতে নানা ঘটনার এক প্রত্যক্ষ সম্পর্ক বিদ্যামান, যার জন্যে কোনো কৌশলের বা ফলপ্রদ বিদ্যার অথবা অবাস্তব শক্তি কল্পনার প্রয়োজন হয়। দেবতাকে এবং অপদেবতাকে বশে রাখার জন্য আদিম মানুষ যাদুক্রিয়ার অনুষ্ঠান করত। যাদুর উপর ছিল তার অটুট বিশ্বাস। যাদুশক্তি এক রহস্যময়ী শক্তি। সে মনে করত যাদুর দ্বারা যা-খুশি করা যায়। বৃষ্টি নামানো, ঝড় ঝঞ্ঝা রোধ করা , প্রচুর ফসল উৎপাদন করা , অনিষ্টকারী অপদেবতাদের বিতাড়ন, শত্রুনিধন, এমনি যা কিছু তার জীবনের প্রয়োজনে আসে, সবই যাদুবলে—আদিম মানুষ বিশ্বাস করত এবং এ বিশ্বাসে বিশ্বাসী হয়ে সে নানারকম মন্ত্র সহযোগে, উপাদান সহযোগে ক্রিয়াকাণ্ড করত।

ইংলণ্ডের কোনো কোনো অঞ্চলের মহিলারা নাকি প্রেমাস্পদ হতে বঞ্চিতা হলে সেইসব ব্যক্তিদের কিছুটা চুলের গোছা গরম জলে ফুটিয়ে নেয়। যখন ফুটন্ত জলে ঐ চুলগুলো নড়বে তখন সেই প্রেমাস্পদ অধীর যন্ত্রণায় কষ্ট পাবে। পশ্চিম বাংলায় ঐ ধরনের যাদুর অভাব নাই। কঠিন দীর্ঘমেয়াদী রোগভোগে যখন রোগীকে ভাল করার আর কোনো পথ থাকে না, তখন একজন বিশেষ ঐন্দ্রজালিক রোগীকে কোন তে-মাথানি রাস্তার মোড়ে গভীর রাত্রে নানা অনুষ্ঠানের মাধ্যমে স্নান করায়। স্নানের শেষে তার ব্যবহৃত কাপড় ঐ জায়গায় ফেলে দেওয়া হয় যা অন্য ব্যক্তি স্পর্শ করলে তার দেহে ঐ ব্যাধির অনুপ্রবেশ ঘটবে এবং পূর্বোক্ত রোগী ভালো হয়ে উঠবে। উপজাতি সমাজে কোনো ব্যক্তির ব্যবহৃত দ্রব্যসম্ভার অতিসাবধানে রাখা হয়। বিশেষ ভাবে নব জাতকের সঙ্গে যে নাভি প্রভৃতি অংশ পরিত্যক্ত হয় সেগুলি কোনো কোনো উপজাতি সদর বাড়ির চৌকাঠের কাছে অথবা রান্না ঘরের মেঝেতে প্রক্ষিপ্ত করে দেয়।

অতিপ্রাকৃত শক্তিকে মানুষ ভয় করে। তাই বিশেষ বিশেষ ব্যাপারে বিধিনিষেধ মেনে চলে। অনেকের বিশ্বাস এসব বিধিনিষেধ মানার ফলে অনেক নিশ্চিত বিপদের আশঙ্কাকে এড়ানো যেতে পারে। আন্দামানের আদিবাসীরা কোনোদিন মৌমাছির চাক পোড়ায় না। তাদের ধারণা মৌচাক পোড়াল ঝঞ্ঝার 'বিলিকু' ক্রুদ্ধ হবেন, আবার ইনি রুষ্ট হলে নানা প্রকার প্রলয় ঘটাতে পারেন। আমাদের দেশে শাণ্ডিল্য গোত্রীয় লোকেরা শালমাছ খায় না। অবশ্য অন্য কূল বা গোত্রর লোকেরা অনায়াসে ঐ শালমাছ খেতে পারে। প্রত্যেক 'কুল' (class) এর লোকেরা এক একটা বিশেষ বস্তুকে কুল-দেবতা বা 'টোটেম'(Totem) বলে মনে করে।

এইভাবে সমাজে নিরুপদ্রবে বাঁচার তাগিদে নানা অনুশাসন বা ধর্ম বিশ্বাসের উদ্ভব হয়। আবার সেগুলিকে ঠিকভাবে সমাজদেহে ছড়িয়ে দেবার জন্য বিশেষজ্ঞের আবির্ভাব ঘটে। যারা নানাভাবে বা নানা আখ্যায় আমাদের কাছে পরিচিত। এই আদিম শঙ্কা, সমাজে বিশেষ করে পরিশীলিত সমাজের দোরগোড়ায় কেমন ভাবে ঠাঁই পেয়েছে, সে সবের এক মূল্যায়নের প্রতিষ্ঠা এ নিবন্ধে প্রতিবর্ণিত হয়েছে।

আর্য সংস্কৃতির মানুষের সাথে মুখোমুখি সংগ্রামে আদিম বাসিন্দাদের অনেক গোষ্ঠী সম্পূর্ণ বিলুপ্ত হয়ে গেছে। যারা অপেক্ষাকৃত দূরে সরে গিয়ে বাঁচতে চাইল, তাদের জীবন যাত্রাও বহিরাগত আর্যগোষ্ঠীকে প্রভাবান্বিত করেছে। সুতরাং ইতিহাসের প্রতিটি অধ্যায়ে যেখানে আদিম মানুষের

সঙ্গেঁ বহিরাগত মানুষের সংঘাত ঘটেছে অথবা ভাবের আদান প্রদান হয়েছে তার মধ্যে এই সকল প্রাক আর্যগোষ্ঠীগুলির অনুশাসনের নানা দিক নানা ভাবে মূর্ত হয়ে রয়েছে। সুতরাং সমাজ ও সংস্কৃতির ক্রমবিবর্তনের খতিয়ানে আদিবাসী সংস্কৃতির এক সার্থক মূল্যায়ন করা যায়।

সেইজন্য অথর্ববেদে , মহাভারতে, তন্ত্রশাস্ত্রে, কৌটিলেরর অর্থশাস্ত্রের মধ্যে এর বহু প্রমাণ পাওয়া যায়। আজও বিংশ শতাব্দীর বিজ্ঞান প্রশস্তির যুগে সূক্ষ্ম বিজ্ঞান বিশ্লেষণের পাশাপাশি এ বিশ্বাস কাজ করে চলেছে। আদিবাসী ও পরিশীলিত সমাজের মধ্যে আজও এ বিশ্বাস দৃঢ়ভাবে কাজ করে চলেছে, তাদের জীবনের ছন্দকে প্রভাবিত করেছে।

ভারতবর্ষের প্রায় সমস্ত আদিবাসী বা উপজাতিই কম বেশি কৃষ্ণ যাদু (Black Magic) বা ক্ষতিকারক যাদুর চর্চা করে। যদিও সকলেই জানে এর প্রয়োগ অ-সামাজিক, তথাপি সকলে এর মোহমুক্ত হতে পারে না। নিজ স্বার্থসিদ্ধির জন্য গুণিনরা অন্যের ক্ষতি করে এবং তারা মনে করে যে অন্যের ক্ষতি করার স্বাভাবিক ক্ষমতা তাদের আছে। লোকের ধারণা মন্ত্রশক্তিতে কোনো অশরীরী আত্মাকে বশীভূত করে তারই ক্ষমতাকে যাদুকর কাজে লাগায়। কিন্ত যারা দৈব বলে বলীয়ান অর্থাৎ যারা দৈবশক্তি প্রাপ্ত হয়ে মানুষের কল্যাণ করে তারা নানা রকম ক্রিয়াকাণ্ডের দ্বারা রোগীকে বা ক্ষতিগ্রস্ত লোকেদের সমস্ত দুর্দশা দূর করার চেষ্টা করে।

অবশ্য মানুষ যখন কোনো কাজের সূক্ষ বিশ্লেষণ করতে পারে না তখনই কৃষ্ণ যাদুর কথা তার মনে হয়। যেমন হঠাৎ কোনো একটি লোক মারা গেল, একটা সুন্দর সতেজ গাছ শুকিয়ে গেল বা গরুর দুধ শুকিয়ে গেল তখন সাধারণ মানুষের ধারণা হল কোনো যাদুকরই এ কাজ করেছে। তখন তারা কোনো একজন অপেক্ষাকৃত শক্তিশালী যাদুকরের কাছে এই প্রতিকার প্রার্থনা করে। কারণ কোনো সাধারণ লোকের পক্ষে এর প্রতিকার করা সম্ভব নয়। তিনিই শক্তিশালী যাদুকর যিনি বহু সমস্যার সমাধান করেন।

Appendix II

Principal Works of P. K. Bhowmick

List of Articles

Year	*Name of paper*	*Published in Journals/Books (ed)*
1954	Lodha Marriage Custom	Man in India. Vo. 34, No. 2
1954	Further notes of Lodha Marriage	Man in India. Vol. 34, No. 4
1955	Savaras of Midnapur	Vanyajati. Vol. 3, No. 2
1955	Social and Religious Officials of Lodha Caste	Man in India. Vol. 35, No. 2
1955	Lodhas of Midnapur	Vanyajati. Vol. 3, No. 4
1955	Treatment of Diseases among the Lodhas of West Bengal	Man in India. Vol. 35, No4
1956	A cattle Caressing Festival	Folklore. Vol. 1, No. 2
1956	Physical Affinities of the Lodhas of Midnapur	Man in India. Vol. 36, No. 2
1956	The Lodhas of Midnapur	Sunday, Hindusthan Standard
1957	Lodhas and their Folk Songs	Vanyajati. Vol. 5, No. 1
1957	The Bandana Festival of Midnapur	Man in India. Vol. 37, No 1
1957	Further Bandana Songs	Man in India. Vol. 2, No 1
1957	Karam Parab in West Bengal	Indian Folklore, Vo. 2, No. 1
1957	Castes Occupation and Status (Jointly with B. Bhattacharjee)	Man in India. Vol. 37, No. 1
1957	Annual Festivals of the Lodhas of West Bengal	Man in India. Vol. 37, No. 3
1957	Rural Rehabilitation	Man in India. Vol. 37, No. 3
1957	Religious Ideas of the Lodhas of West Bengal	Vanyajati. Vol. 5, No. 4
1957	Recreational life of the Lodhas	Vanyajati. Vol. 6, No. 1
1957	Bandana Songs	Indian Folklore. Vol. 2, No. 1
1958	Tusu Festival of Midnapore	Indian Folklore. Vo. 3, No. 3
1959	The Kakmara–A Nomadic community in West Bengal	Man in India. Vol. 39, No 4
1960	Four Temples of Midnapore	Man in India. Vol. 40, No 2
1960	Lodha Villages and Demographic Aspects	Vanyajati. Vol. 8, No. 2
1960	A note on the Lodhas of Midnapur	Socio-Economic Research Bulletin. Vol. 1, No. 1

Year	*Name of paper*	*Published in Journals/Books (ed)*
1960	Economic Life of the Lodhas	The Eastern Anthropologist. Vol. 13, No. 3
1960	Some Social Movements in Midhanpore	Man in India. Vol. 40, No 4
1961	Artificial Relationship in Midnapore	Man in India. Vol. 41, No 2
1961	Crime and Criminals among the Lodhas of West Bengal	Vanyajati. Vol. 9, No. 4 1961
1961	A short note on the Gajans of Midnapore	Man in India. Vol. 41, No 2
1961	Criminal Propensity and The Lodhas	Amrita Bazar Patrika. Puja Annual.
1962	Chirmars of Midnapore	Man in India. Vol. 42, No 2
1962	Folk Festival in West Bengal	Illustrated Weekly. July 29, Sunday. Vol. LXXXIII.
1962	Rain and the primitive Man	Folklore. Vol. 3, No. 10
1963	Caste and Service in a Bengal village	Man in India. Vol. 43, No 4
1963	Some problems of the Lodhas. A Denotified community of West Bengal	Bulletin of the Cultural Research Institute. Vol. 2, No. 2
1963	Kakmatas, Our little known Nomadic Neighbours	Hindustan Standard. November 24
1964	Further Collections on Tusu Songs	Folklore. Vol. V, No. 3
1964	Gajans–a Regional Festival	Folklore. Vol. V, No. 9
1965	Some aspects of Folk Festival	Folklore. Vol. VI, No. 2
1965	Fields Research and Social Anthropology	Folklore. Vol. VI, No. 11
1965	Mundas and their ways of living in West Bengal	Adibasi. No.1
1965	Welfare Measures and Basic Resistances to their Implications	Journal of Social Research. Vol. VIII, No. 2
1965	Kasba Narayangarh, A Muslim village	Man in India. Vol. 45
1966	An integrated plan for the Development of the Lodhas and other Tribals of Midnapur, West Bengal.	Vanyajati. Vol. XIV, No. 2
1966	Lodha and other Tribes of Midnapore	Vanyajati. Vol. XIV, No. 2
1966	Mirpur–A Christian village	Man in India. Vol. 46, No. 3
1967	Ways to Educate the Tribals	Adibasi. Vol. IX, No. 1

Year	Name of paper	Published in Journals/Books (ed)
1967	Living Conditions and Social Disabilities of the Sweepers at Tamluk in Mjidnapore of west Bengal	Report of the Commissioner, for Scheduled Castes and Scheduled Tribes.
1967	Panoramic of the Dhansola Rehabilitation Scheme	Village Survey Monograph, Census Publications, Government of West Bengal, Calcutta.
1968	Economy and Society of the Primitive People in India	Cultural Forum. Special Education Number.
1968	Occupational changes in two villages of Bengal	Man in India. Vol. 48, No. 1
1968	Development scheme as Factors of Social and Economic changes: a case study of the Lodha rehabilitation center at Daharpar	Journal of Social Research. Vol. XI, No. 1
1968	Four Midnapore villages	District Hand Books, Midnapore, Census of India. 1961
1969	Caste and Changing Occupation: Study of Belpahari Market	Human Events. Vol. 3, No. 2
1969	Changing Societies in Frontier Tracts of Bengal	Bulletin of the Ramakrishna Mission Institute of Culture. Vol. XX, No. 9
1969	Women in Nursery Women in Indian Folklore; (ed.)	Rhymes of Border–Bengal.
1970	Welfare Programmes and Administration for Development and Integration	Tribe. Vol. VII, No. 1
1970	Castes and Conflict in a Bengal Village	Bulletin of the Socio-Economic Research Institute. Vol. 4, No. 1 & 2
1971	Primitive Packaging	Journal of Packaging and Allied Industries of Paper and Print. Vol. 2, No. 2
1974	Some Aspects of Functioning of Secret Societies	Folklore. Vol. XVI, No. 2
1975	A Social Sub-System in Frontier Region in India	Bulletin of the Cultural Research Institute. Vol. II, No. 1 & 2
1975	Essential Primary Consideration for Rehabilitation Scheme.	Vanyajai. Vol. XXIII, No. 4
1975	Retribalization Community in Search of a New Identity	Man and Life. Vol. No. 1, 2 & I

Year	*Name of paper*	*Published in Journals/Books (ed)*
1976	Tribal Folk in our Welfare State	ERA. Vol. 1, No. 7
1976	Emerging Problems of the Scheduled Castes in West Bengal	Man and Life. Vol. IX, No. 3 & 4
1976	Problem of Denotified Tribe : A Case Study of the Interaction of Govt. and Diverse Ethnic Groups in Fringe Bengal	Man and Life. Vol. II, No. 3 & 4
1977	Concept of Disease, Gods and Goddesses	Journal of Social research. Vol. 20, No. 2
1977	Folk Festivals in the Border Regions of West Bengal	Bharat Prativa. Vol. 1, No. 2
1977	Cultural continuity in Socio Economic changes: A study in Religious Complex in Rurbun Setting	Journal of Socio-Economic Study. Vol. II
1977	Developmental Approach to the Problems of Adivasis: Denotified (Ex-Criminal) Tribe of West Bengal	Journal of Social Research. Vol. XX, No. 1
1977	Education of Under Privileged: A suggestion	Man and Life. Vol. 3, No. 1 & 2
1978	Approach to Tribal Welfare	The Bulletin of the Department of Anthropology, Dibrugarh University. Vol. 7 & 8
1978	A Political Anthropological View of the West Bengal State Polls in 1977 (with R.K. Gupta)	Man and Life. Vol. 4, No. 1–4
1981	Impact of Industrialisation on the Tribes: A Background Situation in West Bengal	Man and Life. Vol. 7, No. 3 & 4
1981	Rehabilitation of a Denotified Community: The Excriminal Tribe of West Bengal	Journal of Royal Anthropological Institute. Great Britain and Ireland. Vol 1, No 44
1982	Ethno-Cultural Contacts, Conflicts and Co-operation in the Ramayana : A Sociological Overview.	Journal of Social and Economic Studies. Vol. X Pt.. I & II
1982	Varnajati and Indianization of Indigenous Ethnic Groups in the Mahabharata	Man and Life. Vol. 8, No 1 & @. Reprinted in Uttarayan, Deradun souvenir.
1983	The Lodha 'A Denotified Community of West Bengal	Man in India. Vol. 63, No. 8

Year	*Name of paper*	*Published in Journals/Books (ed)*
1984	Human Adaptation to Extreme Climate	Samranika. Annual Publication, Vol. 2
1984	Development Anthropology	The Eastern Anthropologist. Vol. 37, No. 4
1984	Nature of Exploitation in the Tribal Situation: an overview	Adibasi. Vol. XXIV, No. 3 & 4
1984	Strategy of Development for Primary Groups. A Case Study of the Lodhas of West Bengal	Development Strategies of Primitive Tribal Group (ed.)
1985	Social Organisation of the Chenchus. A Gathering Hunting Tribe of Andhra Pradesh.	The Journal of the Asiatic Society. Vol. XXVII, No. 3
1985	Tribal Situation in West Bengal	Indian Anthropologist. Vol. 15, No. 1
1985	Education for Tribal Women: A Suggestion.	Tribal Women and Development (ed.)
1986	University of Calcutta and L.K. Anantakrishna Iyre, 1920–1933	Man in India. Vol. 66, No. 4
1986	Indebtedness,Land Alenation and Restoration of Land. Some Aspects of Economic Life: A Case Study in Border Bengal	Alienation of Tribal Land and Indebtedness (ed.)
1986	Tribal Migrants in the Himalayan Region: A Case Study of the Munda Festival in Plantation.	Ecology, Economy and Religion of Himalays (ed.)
1987	Voluntary Effect in Tribal Development: The Bidisha Experiment.	Journal of Social and Economic Studies. Vol 4 No 2
1987	Development and Anthropology Rebuilding Rural and Tribal India	Anthropology, Development and Nation Building (ed.)
1987	Continuity and Change in an Indian Village	Tradition and Development (ed.)

List of Books

1963	*Lodhas of West Bengal. A Socio-Economic Study.* Calcutta : ISRAA.
1969	*Occupational Mobility and Caste Structure in Bengal.* Calcutta : Indian Publications.
1976	*Socio-Cultural Profile of Frontier Bengal.* Calcutta : Punthi Pustak.
1978	*Occultism in Fringe Bengal.* Calcutta : Subarnarekha.
1980	*Some Aspects of Indian Anthropology.* Calcutta : Subarnarekha.
1989	*The Chenchus of the Forests and Plateaux : A Hunting-Gathering Tribe in Transition.* Calcutta : ISRAA.
1990	*Applied-Action-Development Anthropology.* Calcutta : ISRAA.
1994	*Primitive Tribal Groups in Eastern India.* New Delhi : Gyan Publishing House.
2000	*Tribal Literacy in West Bengal.* Calcutta : R. N. Bhattacharya.
2001	*Rethinking Tribal Culture in India.* Calcutta : R. N. Bhattacharya
2002	*Caste in Bengal Border.* Calcutta : R. N. Bhattacharya.
2002	*Customary Law of Austric Speaking Tribes.* Delhi : Kalpaz Publications.

Note : All these articles have been collected from Prof. Bhowmick's original list of publications. Only a few of the articles have been omitted due to incompleteness. The list of the references is kept unchanged. Except these articles he has written more than ten books and near about 100 popular articles in Bengali which have been published in different journals, government bulletins, little magazines and newspapers. The Bengali Books and Articles are not given in the list.

Appendix III

Scholars whose synopses were not available

Name	*Year of the Award*	*Title of the Thesis*
ChittaRanjan Malos	1973	Where the Two Communities Meet– A Study of Hindu-Muslim Interaction
Swapan Kumar Bhattacharyya	1975	Modern Farm Practices and Their Impact on the Farmers in a Block of West Bengal
Ujjal Kanti Roy	1978	Economic Infra-Structure of the Scheduled Tribes of West Bengal and Possibilities of Development An Applied Anthropological Approach
S.N. Chakrabarty	1980	Urban Unrest in West Bengal
Madhusudhan Chattopadhyay	1981	From Migratory Ethnic Agricultural Labours to Settled Cultivators
Jawharlal Dutta	1994	Change and Continuity Surdarban Tribes in Transition: A Micro Study

Appendix IV

Glossary of the Terms : Castes and Tribes

Scheduled Castes

Agaria — A community of Madhya Pradesh. It's name is derived from aag (fire), appropriately associated with the furnace used for smelting iron ore. They also call themselves Lohar (loha meaning iron) and are referred to as Patharia in Rewa, and Kelha Agaria in Chhattisgarh. Risley also identified them as cultivators with sub tribes like Paharia Agaria, Asur-Agaria, Lohar-Agaria etc. They speak in Chattisgarhi,an Indo-Aryan language and use the Devanagari script.

Agharia — Agharia, a trading and cultivating caste of Bihar and upper India who are probably closely related to Agarwals.

Ahir/Goala/Gauli/Jadav

A cowherd caste of Bihar and upper India. They are also identified as a sub-caste of Goalas. They belong to the milk-man caste. This Ahir group is predominant in Bihar. They are employed by different communities to watch their cattle in the pastures.

Ahom — The Ahoms were originally a Tai speaking people. Their original homeland is believed to be in Thailand. They are a Mongoloid group. In course of their migration they crossed Burma and entered Assam through the Patkai ranges. They are listed as OBC by the State Government. They are a landowning community and are well-conversed in the matter of business and trade.

Bagdi — Same as Barga Kshatriya.

Baiga — The Baigas are notified as a scheduled caste in Uttar Pradesh. Baiga is a synonym for Bhuiyar. The Bhuiyar accept food and water from the Ahir, Nai, Manjhi and

Chero communities. Patron-client relation or the jajmani system exists with the Brahman, Nai and Dhobi. Cultivation and agricultural labouring are their present and traditional occupations. In Madhya Pradesh, they act as village priests and medicine men, distributed in the forest hill tracts of the Mandla and Balaghar districts.

Bagal A caste of herdsmen and cattle-breeders. At present, the majority of this caste group work as agricultural labourers. They are widely distributed along western Midnapore. They are identified as a relatively little known community.

Bauri A caste of non-Aryan descent. They follow the profession of cultivators, earth workers and palanquin bearers. They belong to the scheduled caste community.

Baniyas In Andhra Pradesh, the Kapus, Sondhis and Sowcars are known as Baniyas. They are the small merchants and businessmen of the locality.

Barga Kshatriya

A cultivating and menial caste of West Bengal. Now they are identified as scheduled caste. In caste hierarchy, their position is low.

Barujibi/Tamali

The Barujibis are the clean caste in Bengal. A large section of them live in Midnapur district. Generally, they are the betel dealers and betel producers. Other caste groups take water and food from their hands.

Bhuinya/Bhuiya

They are distributed in the districts of Keonjhar, Sundargarh, Mayurbhanj and Sambalpur of Orissa. They practise hunting, shifting cultivation and settled agriculture. Oriya is their mother tongue. Wells and water sources are shared with other communities but not the burial ground. Among the Dravidian races of West Bengal and Chhota Nagpur a large endogamous group is found who call themselves Bhuiya and believe this to be their original designation.

Brahman/Brahmin
A priestly caste possessing the highest rank in the social ladder. They occupy a very high position. Now the Brahmans have accepted many new professions, besides their scholarly pursuits.

Chamar They belong to the untouchable group and do leather works and unclean jobs. They are found extensively in northern Indian States.

Chandal An untouchable scheduled caste group found in many parts of our country. They are identified as low caste. Even in our *puranas* their names were referred to.

Chirmar A hunting community of the western part of Midnapur. They are the killers of birds.

Dhemur They are the low caste people engaging themselves with the business of fishing. Their socio-economic status is low.

Dhimal They are the caste like ethnic group living in Nepal. They are not SC or ST as in Nepal such types of groupings are not in practise. They are patrilocal community.They practice agriculture and are usually share croppers and agricultural labourers.

Dhoba In West Bengal, they are known as Dhopa, Dhobi or Rajak. Their traditional occupation is washing of clothes. Many of them have taken to agricultural labour as a subsidiary occupation. As one of the servicing castes, they serve others as washermen and at the same time avail themselves of the services of other castes. They perform many ritual functions during the time of birth, death and marriage.

Dom A low caste people who work as scavengers, drummers, etc. They are found extensively in Bengal, Orissa and upper India. They are commonly known as Chandals.

Dule/Dulia A scheduled caste, an untouchable group of West Bengal. They are also the sub-caste of Bagdis in Bengal. They are fishermen, Palanquin-bearers and general labourers.

Ganda They are the weaving caste of Chhattisgarh as like the Tanti of Bengal.

Ghasia They are the same group as the Mahara. The community earlier was palanquin bearers. Now their profession is day-labouring.

Gop A Milk-maid community often they sell milk. Sometimes they are also known as the Cattle-herding community. They constitute a clean caste. The Brhamins take water from their hands.

Hadi They are the untouchables associated with low ranking occupation belonging to the lowest rung of the social ladder. They are also the bone-gatherers.

Jhalo A scheduled caste of West Bengal. They are not untouchable but their position is low in the caste hierarchy.

Kadar A non-Aryan caste of cultivators, fishermen, day-labourers in Bhagalpur and the Santal Parganas, probably a degraded offshoot of Bhuiya tribe.

Kachari They are the aborigines or earliest known inhabitants of the Brahmaputra valley. The Kacharis are closely allied to the Koch. The Kachari language belongs to the Tibeto-Burman family of languages. Out of them the Chutia, Moran, Koch or Rajbangshi have originated. They have become Hinduised and do not identify themselves with the Kachari. The Kachari are now represented by the Mech in western Assam, the Bodo in central Assam, the Dimasa and the Hojai in north Cachar Hills. Borokachari and Sonowall Kachari are also the branches of kachari tribes.

Kahara They are all low caste people engaging themselves with the business of fishing. Their socio-economic status is low.

Kaibarta/Kaivarta

A cultivating clean caste of Bengal. A section of the Kaibartas is identified as Haliya Kaibarta who resort to agriculture. They are often known as Mahisyas. The other group is known as Jalia Kaibarta who are identified as fishermen (SC).

Kakmara A nomadic community of the southern part of Midnapur district. The literal meaning of Kakmara is the crow-killer. Even now they eat the flesh of the crow.

Kanwar They adopt the same profession as the Panikas. They are the weaving caste of Chhattisgarh.

Karmakar A clean caste of Bengal. They belong to Nava-sakha group, i.e., highcaste. In Bengal, a synonym for Kamar, in Hazaribagh a title of Kahars. They are the metal-working caste of Bengal. In Midnapur, there are eight classes of Kamar viz., Lohar-Kamars, Kansaris, Swarn-Kamars or Goldsmith etc.

Karwa A section of chamars in Bihar.

Kayastha A writer-caste or scibes of eastern and upper India. They claim to belong to the high caste and their position is just below the Brahmins.

Kewat They are low caste people, engaging themselves with the business of fishing. Their socio-economic status is low.

Koch The Koch claim themselves to be Kshtriyas in the Varna system. The share wells and water sources, the crematorium and schools with other community members. They are the Hindus. They belong to the land holding community. Their traditional and present occupations are horticulture and settled cultivation.

Koshtas They are the weaving caste of Chhattisgarh as like the Tanti of Bengal.

Kumar/Kumhar/ Kumbhakar

The potter castes of Bengal, Bihar and Orissa. The Kumar is an artisan caste group of Assam. The name Kumar is the corrupt form of Kumbhakar which has been derived from two root words–'Kumbha' means earthen pot and 'kar' means market. They are the Sudras. But they are one of the clean castes of Bengal. They make various utensils with clay. Except the Brahman and Kaysatha, all the neighbouring communities accept cooked and uncooked food from them.

Kurmi A very large cultivating caste of upper India, Bihar, Chhota Nagpur and Orissa.

Majhi The traditional occupation of the Majhi is fishing, substantiated by daily wage labour and cultivation. They are Hindus and worship their family village and regional deities.

Mahara A community of low caste in Chhattisgarh. They were earlier the palanquin bearers.

Mahishya A cultivating and land-holding caste of Bengal, Orissa and Bangladesh. Previously they were also known as Halia Kaivartas as they practise plough-cultivation. They are the high caste.

Malakar A caste employed making garlands and providing flowers for the service of Hindu temples. They are the florists, an artisan class of Bengal who belong to Nava-shaka group. They make different types of ornaments with flowers, decorate temples and do floral works.In Bengal the caste is included among the Nava-Sakha and its members trace their descent from the garland maker.

Malo Same as Jhalo, a scheduled caste of West Bengal.

Manipuri/Meitei

Meiteis are one of the major sub-groups of the Manipuria in the state of Assam. Among the Meiteis there are two caste groups – Brahman and Kshatriya.

Mehtar/Mahettar

They are the untouchable caste of Chhattisgarh as well as Bengal, Bihar and Orissa. They are traditionally engaged as sweepers and scavengers. They are also known as Hari, Lalbegi, Bhangi. In Andhra Pradesh they are known as Valmiki. They are also known as Chamar or Dewar.

Namasudra A synonym for Chandal. An exterior caste of cultivators and boatmen in Bengal. But now they work as agricultural labourers or daily labourers. They are the scheduled caste of Bengal.

Napit/Nai A Barber caste of Bengal. The caste is clearly a functional group. In Hindu society their role is important. All social and religions ceremonies like birth, marriage and death are not possible without their involvement. But in caste hierarchy their position is low.

Nat They are a community of professional dancers, singers and acrobats of Rajasthan. Three synonyms for this tribe viz., Bazigar, Sapra, Gulgulia, are prevalent in different societies.

Nayadi The Nayadis are one of the scheduled castes of Kerala and Tamil Nadu. The word Nayadi means hunter and they are in fact skilful hunters. Some of the primitive Dravidian traits they possess. They are the aborigines and autochthones of Kerala. They follow Hinduism. Their traditional as well as present-day occupation is begging. The are considered as low caste group. They are not permitted to enter temples and streets used by upper castes even to this day.

Panika Their occupation is carpentry and they are the scheduled caste community of Chhattisgarh. They are all weaving caste like the Tanti of Bengal.

Pasi They are the scheduled caste population of Bihar, West Bengal and Uttar Pradesh. Their traditional and present occupation is toddy-tapping. They share water sources with other tribal communities. Many of them have taken cultivation instead of their traditional calling.

Paundra/Paudra Kshatriya/Pod
A caste of lower Bengal. Their occupations are fishing, cultivating, trading etc. Their position is low in caste hierarchy. They generally belong to the scheduled caste of Bengal.

Rajbanshi They are the scheduled caste community of Bengal. But they are familier as fisherman community. Traditionally they are agriculturists. A few of them depend on inland river fishing. They are also a cultivating and landowning community of North Bengal. They are also known as Desi or Bahey and Rajbansi kshatriya.

Rajbanshi (Koch)
The name is derived from the word 'Rajaghariah' or

	'Rajbongsa' meaning king's family or royal family. They are the direct descendants of the Koch Rajas. They are identified as Koch or Mech.
Rauts	They are the clean caste of Chhattisgarh known as Ahir/Goala/Gauli etc. They are the cattle-herders group. Agriculture is also practised by them in the present-dey society. Socially their position is not low.
Rishi	An untouchable scheduled caste group. They are like the Muchis, Chamars etc., and are associated with lowly occupation.
Tai	The Tais are the Mongoloid group. Originally they belong to the Tai Royal office. They had a principality of their own in Hukong Valley.
Tambuli	They are also referred to as Tamuli or Tamil. In West Bengal, they are concentrated in Burdwan and Hooghly districts. Though the Tambuli are a landowning community, majority of them depend on business. The Tambuli is a Jal-chal group. Brahmans accept only pucca food from them.
Tanti	The Tanti is a weaver community inhabiting in Orissa, West Bengal and Bihar. They constitute the weaver caste of Bengal and Bihar, probably a functional group, developed under the pressure of the natural demand for woven cloth.
Teli	An oil pressing community belonging to Nava-Sakha (nine castes) - a high caste group of Bengal. In Bengal, the higher sub-castes of Telis, who have abandoned the oil trade and become bankers, money-lenders, cloth-dealers and shop-keepers. A Brahmin takes water from their hands.
Teor/Tyor	A sub-caste of Bagdis and Kaibartas in Bengal. They are scheduled caste and serve as fishermen and boatmen. Now they have engaged themselves in different agricultural works.
Thakur	They belong to the agricultural community. They till lands. In Chhattisgarh, these people are found in large numbers.

Tili An oil selling community. Their social status is the same as Teli.

Sadgop A land-holding agricultural community of Bengal, who claim to be equal to the Vaisyas and superior to goala or milkmen.

Shilpakar Shilpakars belong to the untouchable Dom category. Their community name is derived from their traditional profession of carrying palanquin.

Sutradhar Sutradhar is one of traditional communities of the Barpeta district of Assam. The word Sutradhar is a combination of two words–Sut and Dhar. Sut means tune and Dhar means link up. So the meaning of the word 'Sutradhar' is linking up the tune (Satriya & music). They are lower than the Brahman but higher than the Dhoba, Napit and other low castes.

Swarnakar A high caste group that belongs to Nava-sakha. The prepare various types of ornaments from gold, silver etc. They are known as Goldsmith. In Bengal, they are known as a section of Kamar.

Vaidya They constitute an upper caste group in social hierarchy. Sometimes they are known as medicine men in rural society.

Vaishnaba A religious sect which worships Lord Vishnu as the greatest god. They are converted both from caste Hindu and scheduled caste communities.

Valmiki/Balmiki

They belong to an untouchable group in different parts of India. Their position is low in caste hierarchy. They are associated with ritually low types of works. They are a scheduled tribe in Andhra Pradesh. In Uttar Pradesh they constitute scheduled caste, but not so in Andaman.

Kols,Gonds, Baigas, Kharwars, Sahariyas, Agarias, Bhuiyans, Korwas, Panikar, Oraons, Patharis, Parahiyas and Ghasis :

These 13 tribal communities living in southern portion of Uttar Pradesh have been included in the list of Scheduled Castes. Previously these ethnic groups were considered as scheduled tribe. But now, after the efforts made by the Government for their uplift and betterment of social life, they are being regarded as Scheduled Tribe.

Scheduled Tribes

Bhoksa A Himalayan community that inhabits the Tarai areas of Dehradun, Nainital, Bijnor, and Pauri (Garhwal districts of U.P.). They are known as Mehra in Dehradun district.The traditional occupation of them is agriculture and animal husbandry. Previously they practised shifting hill cultivation. They are the scheduled tribe of India.

Chenchu They are a hunting-gathering tribe of Andhra Pradesh. The Chenchus speak dialect of Telegu. The Chenchus have been classified as proto-Australoids.

Dimasa The Dimasas are one of the Kachari tribes of Assam. Agriculture and shifting-hill cultivation is practised by them. Boro Kachari, Sonowall Kachari etc., are the branches of Kachari tribes in Assam.

Garo They concentrate in the Garo hills of Meghalaya. They are matrilineal. They practise shifting (Jhum) cultivation. The general trend of north-eastern Mongoloid group is found among them. They mainly reside in Nagaland, Assam, Tripura, Mizoram etc. The Garo of Assam call themselves a 'chik' (hillman) like the Garo of the Garo Hills. They are mainly settled farmers. They speak a dialect of the Garo language which is known as Awe. The Garos of Assam do not have any hierarchical stratification.

Godaba A scheduled tribe of Andhra Pradesh. They were previously engaged in food-gathering economy. Many sub-divisions are found among them. They are like the Parengi, Kapu, Bonda, Gutub, Kathera etc.

Gond They are found in the Uttar Kannad district of Karnataka and are different from the Gond community of Central India. The Gonds possess land and are engaged in cultivation. They follow Hindu way of life. Numerically the most dominant tribe of India, their homeland extends from the Satpura range down to the Godavari, from Uttar Pradesh (Gonda district) and north Bihar to Andhra Pradesh and from Maharashtra to Orissa. Mainly they practise agriculture, but now they are engaged in various economic activities.

Great Andamanese

The Great Andamanese form one of the four Negrito tribes of the Andaman Islands. They are scheduled tribes. They speak the Jeru dialect among themselves, and Hindi with outsiders.

Ho They are concentrated in the Kolhan area of the Singhbhum district of Bihar, Orissa, West Bengal and Madhya Pradesh. They maintain economic relations with local artisans. They belong to agricultural communities.

Kharwar A Dravidian cultivating and land-holding tribe of Chottanagpur and Southern Bihar.

Kolam They are the scheduled tribes of Adilabad district of Andhra Pradesh. The Kolam speaks in Kolami, a Dravidian language, among themselves. They are mostly cultivators or wage labourers.

Konda Reddy They are distributed in the east and west Godavari districts and Khamman district of Andhra Pradesh. They belong to the Dravidian family of languages. They practise cultivation. Previously they were shifting cultivators but now they are agricultural labourers.

Kora A scheduled tribe of West Bengal. Generally they are found to live in West Bengal, Bankura, Midanpur, Purulia etc. Cultivation and day-labouring are their occupations.

Korwa Settled cultivation and hunting and gathering are their present and traditional occupations. The word (Korwa) is derived from the Dravidian word. They live in the states of Madhya Pradesh, Bihar, Orissa and West Bengal.

Koya They are the scheduled tribes of Andhra Pradesh. They go for hunting, gathering and also do agricultural work.

Lepcha They are the Mongoloid group concentrated in Dzongu district of Sikkim and the Darjeeling district of West Bengal. Traditionally, they were hunters food gatherers and pastoralists. Now-a-days, they are primarily a community of land-owning cultivators.

Lodha A scheduled tribe of West Bengal. Once they were known as criminal tribe, but now they constitute a denotified community. They are also caterogirsed as PTG due to their primitive hunting-gathering economy. Now they are opting for agriculture related work.

Mahali A scheduled tribe of West Bengal. Basket-making is their traditional occupation.

Munda A Dravidian tribe of Chhotanagpur. But now they are also one of the major scheduled tribes of Bengal. Cultivation is their main economy.

Naga They are one of the dominant communities of Nagaland. They conform to the Mongoloid pattern. They primarily depend on the indigenous method of wet terrace cultivation. They also hunt, engage in gathering, fishing, shifting cultivation and animal husbandry.

Sema Naga The Semas are a major Naga tribe. The Angamis call them Semi and they call themselves Sumi. They are a nomadic group. In the field of art and handicraft they show their excellence. Weaving is their traditional occupation which is exclusively managed by their women-folk.

Nicobarese A scheduled tribe in Car-Nicobar Island. Nicobarese is the generic name for all indigenous people of the Nicobar Islands. Most of them understand Car Nicobarese. The Car-Nicobarese have adopted a variant form of the Latin script for their language. The traditional food of the Nicobarese include pandanus, yam, banna, coconut and wild fruits. It is an "Austro-Asiatic" sub-family language, according to Peter W. Schmidt who has grouped it together with the Munda language and the Mon-khmer languages"

Onge The Onges are one of the four 'scheduled' Negrito tribal groups of the Andaman Islands. The Onge speak their own language, which has no script. They have now become horticulturists with the intervention of the Government. Before that they led a nomadic life. They are also encouraged to collect forest produce like honey and resin and make traditional cane baskets.

Oraon A Dravidian speaking tribe of Chhotanagpur. But now they are settled in different parts of Bengal accepting various types of occupation. In Jalpaiguri they work in tea gardens. In Sundarbans they are engaged as agricultural labour. In Calcutta they work as Dhangar.

Rabha A Scheduled Tribe of West Bengal. They are Mongoloid in origin and cultivation is their main profession.

Santal A large Dravidian tribe of Bengal, Bihar and Orissa. Agriculture is their main occupation. They constitute the schedled tribe of West Bengal.

Savara A generic term of a tribe. In West Bengal the Lodha, Siyalgir, Shikaris, Chirmar, in Orissa the Hill kharia, Pania Bhanga, are known as Savara. In Andhra Pradesh the Gadabas identify themselves as Savaras. Some of these groups are identified either Schedule Caste or Schedule Tribe in different areas. Savara is also a sanke charming community of Midnapur district of West Bengal. They are not Schedule Caste or Schedule Tribe. They belong to little known community seeking for the status of Schedule Caste or Schedule Tribe.

Siyalgir They are claiming to be the scheduled tribe like the Savar of West Bengal. Earlier they were known as hunters and used to kill Jackals (siyal) and eat their flesh.

Tharu They are one of the primitive tribes of the Uttar Pradesh. They are scheduled. They used to hunt and gather food but presently they depend on settled cultivation.

Yerukalas Once they were identified as criminal tribes of Andhra Pradesh. Now they are listed as an ex-criminal tribe of the same area. Earliers many of them acted as dacoits, burglars and thieves of there area. They mainly live in the districts of Guntur, Kurnool, Cuddaph and Anantapur.

Subject Index

D

E

F

G

H

I

J

K

L

M

N

O

P

Q

R

S

T

U

V

W

Z